The Armies of
Ancient Persia:
The Sassanians

The Armies of Ancient Persia: The Sassanians

Kaveh Farrokh

Pen & Sword
MILITARY

First published in Great Britain in 2017
and reprinted in 2017 by
Pen & Sword MILITARY
An imprint of
Pen & Sword Books Ltd
47 Church Street
Barnsley, South Yorkshire
S70 2AS

A CIP catalogue record for this book is available from the British Library

Typeset by Concept, Huddersfield, West Yorkshire, HD4 5Jl
Printed and bound in Padstow, Cornwall by TJ International Ltd

Pen & Sword Books Limited incorporates the imprints of Atlas, Archaeology,
Aviation, Discovery, Family History, Fiction, History, Maritime, Military, Military
Classics, Politics, Select, Transport, True Crime, Air World, Frontline Publishing, Leo
Cooper, Remember When, Seaforth Publishing, The Praetorian Press, Wharncliffe
Local History, Wharncliffe Transport, Wharncliffe True Crime and White Owl.

For a complete list of Pen & Sword titles please contact
PEN & SWORD BOOKS LIMITED
47 Church Street, Barnsley, South Yorkshire, S70 2AS, England
E-mail: enquiries@pen-and-sword.co.ok
Website: www.pen-and-sword.co.uk

To My Late Brother and Closest Friend, Henry

Acknowledgements

My special thanks to Steven Weingarter and Phil Sidnell for their extreme patience, support and encouragement for completing this project.

Contents

List of Plates viii

List of Figures and Tables x

Introduction xi

Historical Timeline of the Sassanian Empire xxiv

  1. Martial Ardour, Origins and Missions of the Spah 1

  2. Organization: Military Titles and Recruitment 8

  3. Military Reforms of the Sixth Century CE 23

  4. Military Training, Polo, the Hunt, and Military Music 38

  5. Archery 56

  6. The Savaran 72

  7. Infantry, Auxiliary Contingents and Naval Forces 120

  8. Preparations for War 141

  9. Tactics and Strategies along the Roman and Caucasian Frontiers 149

10. Logistics and Support 183

11. Post-Battle Scenarios and War Diplomacy 187

12. The Spah in Central Asia: Warfare, Military Developments and Tactics 194

13. Military Architecture 224

14. Siege Operations 243

15. Sassanian Military Culture 273

16. Military Weaknesses of the Spah 297

17. The Fall of the Spah and the Empire 315

18. Post-Sassanian Resistance and Rebellion against the Caliphate 332

19. Legacy 344

Maps 357

Notes 368

References 415

Index 435

List of Plates

1. Ardashir I receives the diadem of *Farr* from Ahuramazda at Nagshe Rustam.
2. Triumph of Shapur I at Nagshe Rustam.
3. Close up of Shapur I at the triumphal scene at Nagshe Rustam.
4. Panel featuring two equestrian joust-battle scenes of Bahram II at Nagshe Rustam.
5. Bahram II surrounded by an audience of nobles and knights at Nagshe Rustam.
6. Narses receiving the *Farr* diadem from Warrior Goddess Anahita at Nagshe Rustam.
7. Enemy knocked off his horse by lance impact of Hormuzd II.
8. Close-up of Hormuzd II and rear regalia of his horse at Nagshe Rustam.
9. The Zoroaster cube at Nagshe Rustam.
10. Shapur III slays a leopard with his sword.
11. A dismounted Bahram Gur slays a boar with his sword, fourth century CE.
12. Bahram Gur hunting with his famed skills in archery.
13. Shapur II hunting lions with the Parthian shot.
14. Pur-e Vahman engaged in the Parthian shot against a pursuing lion.
15. The enthroned 'Khosrow I Anoushirawan' clasping his sword.
16. Close-up view of the sword clasped by the enthroned Khosrow I.
17. Late or post-Sassanian *brahmag e artesharih* discovered in the Caucasus.
18. King Pirouz in a hunting area.
19. Unidentified Sassanian king hunting ibex and gazelles.
20. Recreation of an *aswar* cavalryman from the third century, western Iran.
21. Recreation of a Sasanian 'tanurigh' cavalry warrior, sixth to early seventh century CE.
22. Recreation of a Spahbed from the late sixth or early seventh century.
23. A Spahbed riding with his *redag* from the late sixth or early seventh century.
24. Sogdian armoured cavalry from Central Asia, seventh to eighth century.
25. Sassanian royalty hunting, using a courtly finger release.
26. Recreation of a Sassanian sword, dagger and pearl studded royal belt, late sixth to early seventh century CE.
27. A sword presentation *shapsheraz* ceremony of a nobleman presenting a sword to a King, with an armoured warrior in attendance.

28. Dismounted Sassanian Savaran knight with sword with Kushan or East-Iranian type blade.

29. Dismounted Savaran knight engaged in archery as at the Battle of Anglon.

30. Detail of suspended *tirdan*.

31 Savaran officer with lance.

32. Savaran officer engaged in horse archery.

33. Close up of riveted Sassanian helmet with mail.

34. Late Sassanian sword with gold sheeting shown from front and rear.

35. Detail of late Sassanian sword.

36. Sassanian fingercaps.

37. Shapur III and Shapur II posing with scabbard-slide broadswords at Tagh-e Bostan.

38. Relief at Tagh-e Bostan depicting the investiture of Shapur II or Ardashir II.

39. Investiture scene above the late Sassanian armored knight at the vault at Tagh-e Bostan.

40. Tagh-e Bostan Royal Hunt at the right side of the grand Iwan.

41. The late Sassanian knight at the great vault or Iwan at Taghe Bostan.

List of Figures and Tables

Figures
1. The Firuzabad joust relief 82
2. Scabbard-slide swords 86
3. Bargostvan horse armour 88
4. Early Sassanian bridles 97
5. Equestrian tack 98
6. Late Sassanian belts 102
7. Sword mounts 103
8. Late Sassanian swords 104
9. Sassanian stirrups 107
10. Central Asian frontier warriors 202

Tables
1. Examples of Middle Persian Sassanian Archery Terminology 69
2. Partial Lexicon of Middle Persian Sassanian Military Terminology . . . 90
3. Late Savaran Equipment as Cited by Dinawari, Bal'ami and Tabari . . . 108
4. Four parallels between *Kitab ol Ayin* and *Strategikon* 167
5. Sassanian Siege Warfare Equipment as Reported by Arabian Sources with (Mainly) Arabic Terminology 253
6. Sassanian Terms in Reference to *Brahmag e Artesharih* 283
7. Comparisons Between the *Kitab ol Ayin* and *Nihayat al S'ul* 353

Introduction

The military legacy of the Sassanians has certainly been significant, from the beginnings of their dynasty when its founder Ardashir I Babakan (r. 224–240 CE) overthrew the Parthians in the battle of Firuzabad (224 CE). Lukonin has noted that the Sassanian state was essentially military in character, eager from the outset to (1) score victories over the Romans and to (2) demonstrate Sassanian military superiority over the de-centralized and recently overthrown Parthians.[1] Apparently the early Sassanians viewed their military successes against the Romans of greater domestic and economic value than their victories in Central Asia, but this most likely changed as the empire faced increasingly dangerous armies from Central Asia. Nevertheless, as noted by Howard-Johnston, the Sassanians proved to be the military equal of the Romans, a fact the latter pragmatically accepted after their defeats in the third century CE.[2]

This introduction is intended for the reader to be broadly familiarized with the historiography of Sassanian militaria, key archaeological sites, metal works and other artifacts, etc. depicting Sassanian militaria (weapons, horsemen, etc.). Mention must be made of some important divergences between a number of Western military historians and their Iranian counterparts with respect to a number of domains pertaining to Sassanian historiography, a topic discussed further below. The chapter then concludes with an overview of the Islamic-era Iranian epic, the *Shahname*.

Works on Sassanian Militaria: An Overview

One of the most constructive developments in Iranian studies has been in the study of Sassanian military history, especially with respect to Sassanian-Roman, Sassanian-Central Asian and Sassanian-Arab military relations. Classical sources such as Ammianus Marcellinus, Procopius and the *Strategikon* remain seminal in studies of Sassanian militaria, but these traditional sources can now be complimented with yet more sources. Much credit must be attributed to Western scholars such as Greatrex, Dodgeon, Lieu, Charles, etc. who examined many hitherto unknown (or ignored) Classical sources such as Cedrenus and Theophanes as well as Armenian sources (e.g. Sebeos). Readers are referred to Dodgeon and Lieu's *The Roman Eastern Frontier and the Persian Wars (AD 226–363)* for an excellent resource for an exhaustive range of Classical references with respect to the earlier Sassanian centuries, Greatrex's *Rome and Persia at War: 502–532* for an excellent study of the sources pertaining to Kavad I's wars and Greatrex and Lieu's *The Roman Eastern Frontier and the Persian Wars Part II (AD 363–630)* of the wars from the time of Shapur II to Khosrow II and the period after the Heraclius-Khosrow II wars. Provision of an entire list of Western works in

Sassanian militaria is provided in the references section, however works of other western scholars in this domain include Schindel, Bivar, Cosentino, Coulston, Dignas, Winter, Foss, Howard-Johnston and Whitby.

Of equal significance are the works of East European scholars such as the late Inostrancev, especially in his examinations of post-Pahlavi sources and studies on Sassanian cavalry. Insotrancev's works (esp. 1926) are possibly one the earliest works by European scholarship on Pahlavi to Arabic translations of Sassanian militaria. A new generation of exemplary East European scholars include Mielczarek, Cernenko, Kurbanov, Michalak, Olbrycht, Kolesnikoff, Nikonorov, Pigulevskaya, Raspopova and Brzezinski, who have contributed mightily to the domains of Scytho-Sarmatian, Medo-Achaemenid and Partho-Sassanian militaria.

These (Western and East European) works are especially adaptive as these help complement the works of Iranian military historiography on the Sassanians. Iranian military historians have been producing texts on the subject of the Sassanian military since the 1930s with numerous works in more recent times. Examples include Matofi's Persian language two-volume compendium on the military history of Iran since the Indo-European arrivals onto the Iranian plateau and other works by Manouchehr M. Khorasani tabulating weapons development in Iran since the Bronze Age as well as a lexicon of Iranian military terminology. Iranian scholars have also worked to rehabilitate hitherto ignored Arabian works containing Pahlavi (Middle or Sassanian Persian) to Arabic translations of Sassanian military literature (i.e. *Ayin ol Akhbar*). In this respect, the multi-volume works of Mohammadi-Malayeri have been significant. Mention must be made of the works of the late Shapour Shahbazi, whose numerous works on the Sassanian military include the excellent discussion of the subject in the *Encyclopedia Iranica* as well as numerous other papers and publications. There are a number of excellent Iranian military historians who write almost exclusively in Persian such as Jalali, Mashkoor, Farzin, Pazoki, Pirnia, Sami, Saket, Yahaghi, and Moghtader. The author endeavors to introduce these Persian-language works to Western and European scholarship on the subject; Iranian scholars' (Persian and English written) works consistently account for the works of Western scholarship and Classical sources in their publications. As noted already, the works of European scholarship are critical in any examination of Sassanian military history.

Thanks to works of Iranian military historians and Western scholars, much information from 'eastern' sources or more specifically, (pre-Islamic) Iranian as well as Islamic-era sources can also be examined. This assists us in shedding a wider and more detailed perspective on the Sassanian military. Nevertheless, the task of accessing such sources is a challenging task. As noted by Farzin: 'Unfortunately our awareness of the mechanism and workings of governance and information regarding the nature of the different Divans [Books/Archives] of this era [Sassanian] is slight – the knowledge we have of these is derived from the early centuries of the Islamic-era.'[3] Inostrancev has provided a comprehensive analysis of these sources, greatly assisting scholars in the categorization of the available sources.[4] According to Inostrancev, the *Ayin-Nameh* or the *Ketab ol Rosoom* is the most seminal document outlining Sassanian governance and military affairs;

while no direct copies of these have survived, the information in these texts can be extracted from early Islamic-era texts.[5] Post-Islamic scholar al-Masoudi (896–956 CE) writes in the *Al-Tanbih wa al-Ashraf* that the *Ayin-Nameh* was a large tome of a few thousand pages which was available to the mobads and other higher officials.[6] Nevertheless, the *Ayin-Nameh* is by no means completely lost. Thanks in large part to the efforts of Ibn Qutaybah Dinawari (828–885 CE)[7] portions of the *Ayin-Nameh* were preserved in his *Uyun al-Akhbar*, a development which is of great assistance to scholars interested in the Sassanian military. Specifically Dinawari's *Uyun al-Akhbar* has preserved important knowledge of the Sassanian military with respect to military assembly, tactics, training and instruction, traps and ambuscades, reconnaissance, characteristics of successful military commanders, the capture of enemy strongholds and castles[8] and other military affairs discussed more fully in the upcoming chapters of this text. As noted by Inostrancev, this document is 'a Sassanian military treatise and gives us an idea of the rules and tradition of the military art among the Persians'.[9] Mention must also be made of the *Sirat-e Anuhsiravan*. Readers are also invited to consult Rubin's overview of such sources in his article on the reforms of Khosrow I Anoushirvan.[10]

Excellent sources displaying valuable information for the study of Sassanian military culture are rock reliefs and Sassanian metal works (many examples available at the Hermitage Museum at St. Petersberg and other Western museums). Below is a brief overview of important archaeological sites, metal works and museums pertaining to Sassanian militaria.

Archaeological Sites: Rock Reliefs

There are seven sites in Iran of significance to Sassanian military history, especially with respect to visual representations of events (victories, ceremonies, etc.), personnel (king, magi, shahanshah, etc), weapons and armour.

Firuzabad. Located in Fars province, this major relief depicts the battle between Sassanian rebels led by Ardashir I and the Parthians at Firuzabad; this is of major significance as it displays the state of Parthian and Sassanian armour in the early third century as well as other information on military equipment and combat such as lance combat and wrestling (details discussed in Chapters 6 and 15).

Nagshe Rustam. Located in Fars province, the Kuh-e Rahmat section of the Nagshe Rustam site displays the following six Sassanian monarchs:

Ardashir I (r. 224–242 CE): engaged in the *farr* or *xwarrah* (divine glory) ceremony in which the king on horseback receives a diadem (representing the Farr) from Ahura-mazda, the supreme Zoroastrian god, who is also on horseback.

Shapur I (r. 242–272 CE): the most well-known of the Nagshe Rustam panels which displays the victories of Shapur I over Emperor Valerian and another figure, possibly Philip the Arab or the Helleno-Roman general Cyriades.

Bahram II (r. 276–293 CE) [relief 1]: the first of two major reliefs dedicated to the king. The first is more 'ceremonial' and notable for the presence of members of the nobility and possibly the grand magus Kartir. Of military interest is the king appearing with what appears to a large broadsword [relief 2]: this displays the king in lance combat in two panels (details discussed in Chapter 6).

Narseh (Narses) (r. 293–303 CE): ceremonial or investiture scene of the king beside a female entity bestowing the Farr in the form of a diadem, most likely Anahita who is also the Iranian goddess of war (Chapter 15). Recent scholarship, however, has proposed that the figure is that of the king's queen, Shapurdukhtat.

Hormuzd II (r. 303–309 CE): this panel shows the king unseating an enemy in a lance duel.

Collectively the Nagshe Rustam panels provide detailed information on the savaran knights with respect to mail, *bazu-band* (circular-shaped laminated armour or 'bands' fitted together for the arms), *bargostvan* (horse armour) lances, quivers, sheathed swords, various other details of military equipment as well as *neshan tamga*-type symbols.

Bishapur. This site provides more detailed representations of the victories of Shapur I seen trampling the dead figure of Emperor Gordian III, clasping the right hand of Emperor Valerian and faced with the kneeling figure of Emperor Philip the Arab. The Shapur I panels also provide an excellent display of nobles, savaran and infantry.[11] Overall, the Shapur I displays show the types of swords and quivers deployed at the time, as well as (*brahmag e artesharih* 'warrior costumes', see Chapter 15) and horse regalia. The Bishapur site also provides a display for Shapur II (r. 309–379 CE) who sits on a throne with feet pointed outwards and holding a broadsword. There are also displays of nobles and magi at the Shapur II panels. Other triumphal scenes at Bishapur are a Roman delegation (which includes senators) surrendering to Shapur I, Emperor Valerian's chariot captured by the Sassanian spah (army) and defeated foes bringing tribute to Shapur II.

Taghe Bostan. This site is located about 5km to the northeast of Kermanshah in western Iran. This site bears critical information on the spah and military customs in the later Sassanian era. Located across a body of water is a grand *iwan* vault which has an arch carved out of rock richly decorated with a diadem. There are two panels at the entrance; these face each other to the left and right sides of that entrance. The right and left sides of the grand iwan display the royal hunt (Chapter 15). In the interior of Taghe Bostan's iwan vault stands a grotto of a late Sassanian knight on horseback, often identified as Khosrow II and his steed Sabdiz. Clearly visible in remarkable detail are the knight's helmet which has two 'eyes' and a veil-like mail mesh covering the face. Other important military information on the knight are the late Sassanian *bargostvan* (horse armor), tirdan (quiver), partly intact lance with many details on late Sassanian mail. The upper register of the vault at Taghe Bostan (located on the back wall) displays the investiture of Khosrow II. The site will be further discussed in Chapters 4, 6 and 15.

Other Sassanian sites. There are other sites of interest to Sassanian military historiography:

Nagshe Rajab: showing the mounted figure of Shapur I; standing behind the king are four warriors with broadswords.

Sar Mashad: relief on the mountain side showing Bahram II defending his queen against an attacking lion.

Tang-e-Sarvak: features four panels, notably that of the reclining king attended by three warriors who stand with what appear to be javelins and spears. The site has inscriptions in Sassanian Pahlavi, Parthian Pahlavi and Greek. The Haji Abad site is of interest with its depiction of Shapur and Sassanian archery.

Museums Housing Sassanian Items

There are numerous museums that house valuable Sassnians items, notably military equipment, regalia and (in the case of the Hermitage), a long kaftan of the type typically worn by Sassanian warriors. Readers of this text would find the items housed at the following museums of interest: the Hermitage (St. Petersburg, Russia), the British Museum (London, England), National Museum of Iran, Reza Abbasi Museum (Tehran, Iran), the Metropolitan Museum of Art (New York, US), Bibliotheque Nationale (Paris, France), the Louvre (Paris, France), the Kabul Museum (Kabul, Afghanistan), Cabinet des Medailles (Paris, France), Museum fur Islamische Kunst (Berlin, Germany), the Baghdad Museum (Baghdad, Iraq), the Cincinnati Art Museum (Cincinnati, US), The Walters Art Gallery (Baltimore, US), the Romisch-Germanisches Zentral Museum (Mainz, Germany), and the Royal Museums of Art and History-Iranian Collection (Brussels, Belgium).

Sassanian Metal Works

Numbers of the above museums (especially Hermitage and the British Museum) house numerous Sassanian plates or metal works. These provide very valuable information on Sassanian military equipment and fighting styles. These plates fall into five broad categories. The first category shows the rider wielding the sword, the second shows the 'forward' archery shot, the third the 'backwards' Parthian shot, the fourth shows spear combat on foot with the fifth representing late or early post-Sassanian equestrian militaria. Many of these plates (where the figure is mounted on horseback) also provide detailed information on equestrian attire.

Sword combat on horseback. The first category of sword combat on horseback is seen with the figure of Shapur I hunting deer (British Museum, London. Inv.BM.124091). This clearly depicts early Sassanian swords, tirdan (quiver), riding style, and the fencing style 'Sassanian grip' (known as 'Italian grip' in the West). The same type of sword grip is illustrated in another plate at the British Museum (Inv.BM.124092) showing an unidentified Sassanian king on horseback cutting through the back of the neck of a lion that is attacking the rider's horse. A third depiction of the Sassanian sword grip is seen with Bahram V Gur using this technique to hunt boars (Hermitage Museum, St. Petersburg. Inv.S-24). Another depiction of the Sassanian grip by a warrior on foot, (Hermitage Museum, St. Petersburg, Inv.S-42) is that of Shapur III killing a leopard.

Horse archery. The second category of mounted archery is seen in the plate of King Pirouz or Kavad I hunting ibex (The Metropolitan Museum of Art, New York. Inv.34.33). This plate shows the tirdan, a (partly visible) Sassanian bow being drawn and a (partly visible) sword, equestrian furniture and horseback riding style. There is also another metal plate (more rather a drinking bowl), showing either King Pirouz or Kavad, engaged in the hunting of ibex and boars (Private Collection of the late Roman Ghirshman, 1962). This also shows the tirdan, with partly visible Sassanian bow and sword, along with equestrian furniture and riding style. There is also a plate depicting the mounted figure of what may be Khosrow II engaged in hunting with the Sassanian bow (dated sixth–seventh Centuries CE; Bibliotheque Nationale de Paris). This plate also provides details on a partly visible sword as well as equestrian attire. An interesting variation of the mounted monarch theme is that of Bahram V Gur (accompanied by the diminutive figure of Azadeh) riding a camel while engaged in the hunting of game (dated seventh century CE, Hermitage, St. Petersburg, Inv.S-252). Bahram is seen with a tirdan, firing missiles with a Sassanian bow; notable is the plate's depiction of Sassanian missiles. Perhaps the most unusual depiction of Sassanian archery on horseback is that of the metal plate at the National Museum of Iran showing an unidentified king shooting while riding his horse backwards. There is also at least one depiction of Sassanian archery on foot, namely the figure of Pirouz shooting missiles at rams during the hunt (Hermitage Museum, St. Petersburg, Inv.S-216).

Horse archery: Parthian shot. For the third category of the Parthian shot, there are at least three distinct plates available. One of these is housed at the Hermitage Museum in Saint-Petersburg (Inv.S-253) which displays the hunting of lions by Shapur II. This plate depicts the king engaged in the Parthian shot, with clear displays of the Sassanian bow, archery style, sword and equestrian attire. Another plate showing the Parthian shot is that of an unidentified Sassanian king hunting ibex and gazelles (Hermitage Museum, St. Petersburg. Inv. S-297). This fully displays a Sassanian sword and bow as it is drawn. The third depiction of the Parthian shot with the post-Sassanian Pur-e Vahman plate is discussed further below.

Lance and spear combat. The fourth category of plate, with javelin and spear, is best represented by at least two plates. The first, housed at Berlin's Museum for Islamische Kunst (Inv.I.4925) is that of an unidentified Sassanian king about to hurl a short javelin as he is engaged in the hunt against boars, lions and bears. The second is that of an unidentified Sassanian king on foot, hunting boars with a spear (Private collection of Leon levy and Shelby White, New York).

Late or Post-Sassanian militaria. The final category of plate is that of Pur-e Vahman engaged in the Parthian shot (Hermitage Museum, St. Petersburg,

Inv.S-247). What makes this plate unique is its display of late and early Islamic-era Iranian equestrian military equipment. Note that all of the previous plates (including that of Khosrow II) show the 'traditional' early Sassanian straight and broad-style swords and riders without stirrups. The Pur-e Vahman plate shows the rider with stirrups and a lappet suspension sword (as opposed to the traditional broadsword-scabbard suspension sword). The partly visible tirdan also appears to be different in shape than the more 'tubular' shaped quivers examined in the previous plates. Other plates housed at the Hermitage (e.g. the Kulygash artifact) will be discussed in Chapters 4, 6 and 7.

Western and Iranian Scholarship: Divergences
It is also important to note a number of divergences that exist between Iranian military historiographers and a number (although by no means all) Western military historians with respect to Sassanian military history. There are two major domains where certain Western historians diverge from their Iranian counterparts, notably with respect to the Achaemenid legacy in the Sassanian military and the legacy of the Sassanian military on non-Iranian armies during the pre- and Islamic-eras.

The Sassanians and the Achaemenid Legacy
The position of traditional Iranian military historiography (notably that of Shahbazi[12] and Jalali[13]) is that the Sassanian dynasty sought to revive the martial traditions and empire of the ancient Achaemenids. The traditional source of evidence for this viewpoint has often been sought in the Classical sources. According to Herodian,[14] Ardashir I, who had toppled the Parthians in 224 CE, had demanded from Emperor Alexander Severus (r. 222–235 CE) that Rome turn over to the new Iranian state all those territories that had been a part of the former Achaemenid Empire (550–330 BCE). Ammianus Marcellinus notes that the theme of an Iranian ancestral right to the legacy of the ancient Achaemenids occurred once more in the time of Shapur II (r. 309–379) in the context of his correspondence with Emperor Constantius II (r. 337–361 CE).[15] The following statement, for example, by Cassius Dio with respect to Ardashir I is of interest: 'He [Ardashir I] accordingly became a source of fear to us; for he was encamped with a large army so as to threaten not only Mesopotamia but also Syria, and he boasted that he would win back everything that the ancient Persians had once held, as far as the Grecian Sea, claiming that all this was his rightful inheritance from his forefathers. The danger lies not in the fact that he seems to be of any particular consequence in himself, but rather in the fact that our armies are in such a state that some of the troops are actually joining him and others are refusing to defend themselves.'[16]

Dio's statement is of interest in three ways. First, it affirms the Classical sources claiming that the Sassanians wanted to revive the Achaemenid legacy. Second, it reveals Roman concerns over Sassanian military capabilities. Third, Dio has admitted of unspecified numbers of Roman forces joining the Sassanian spah (army). There was in fact an elite cavalry unit known as the *jan-separan* or *jyanavspar* which may have been, according to Nafisi[17] and Pirnia,[18] partly staffed by Greco-Roman troops who had deserted the Romano-Byzantines to join the Sassanian spah (army) (see further discussion of this topic in Chapter 6).

A number of Western historians have pointed out that the attribution of an Achaemenid legacy to the Sassanians by the Romans may have been motivated by contemporary propaganda. Greatrex has noted that the notion of the Sassanians attempting to re-instate their Achaemenid legacy is disputed,[19] with Potter[20] and Blockley[21] rejecting notions of Sassanian knowledge of the Achaemenids. Nöldeke [22] followed by Mommsen[23] are perhaps the first Western historians of the late nineteenth century to have questioned the idea of Sassanian cognizance of the Achaemenids and their legacy.

Yarshater is perhaps the first Iranologist to question the view that the Sassanians attempted to revive the more ancient Achaemenid institutions.[24] Daryaee for example has noted that 'it is clear that there is no explicit mention of the Achaemenids in the Sassanian material';[25] however, as seen further below, Daryaee also does not categorically rule out Sassanian cognizance of the Achaemenids, especially as knowledge of the latter was known to the Jews resident in Iran. Daryaee concludes that 'By the late Sassanian period a "Zoroastrianization of memory" had been created in Persia … The Achaemenids were compressed and synchronized with the Kayanid kings in the new history … the Sasanians, who had risen from the same province as the Achaemenids, chose to connect themselves to the Kayanids who were the rulers of Eran, and let the Romans keep the history of the Achaemenid kings.'[26] The term 'Kay' (for Kayanid) is associated with the figure of Wishtasp in the Parthian work, *(a)yadeger-e zareran*; with the term *xwarrah* (divine glory) also becoming associated with the Kayanids in the *Avesta* texts. Thus Daryaee concludes that the 'sacred historiography' began with the *Avesta*, with the Sassanians becoming the descendants of the Kayanids.[27] Shahbazi has asserted that the early Sassanians knew of the Achaemenids with the shift to Kayanid mythology having taken place later during the Sassanian dynasty,[28] an assessment with which Daryaee concurs.[29]

Charles concludes that the Sassanian military had no essential connection to the Achaemenids,[30] arguing that the Classical sources were projecting propaganda by identifying the Parthians and Sassanians as the heirs of the Achaemenid military tradition. Charles further avers that the Classical sources are wrong by stating that the Sassanian elite unit of 'Immortals' is a conscious attempt at reviving the Achaemenid tradition of 'Immortals'. He essentially proposes that the Sassanian designation of Immortals (*Javidan, Zhayedan*, etc.) on an elite cavalry unit has no historical connection to the Achaemenid infantry unit of that designation. Charles' proposal has yet to find acceptance among mainstream Persian-language military historians such as Imam-Shoushtari, Jalali and Matofi.

Potter has noted that the attribution of Achaemenid motives upon the Sassanians was essentially a Western or Roman projection upon the Iranian Empire they faced at the time.[31] The main projection in this context is the Western or Roman view of the Sassanians as the 'new Achaemenids' at war with the Romans, much as the Achaemenids had been against the Hellenic world since Marathon.

Thereby the contemporary Sassanians are seen as harboring the same territorial ambitions as the Achaemenids of old. The views of Potter, etc. cannot be so easily dismissed as the Greco-Alexandrian martial legacy was very strong in Rome. This was spectacularly evident in 2 BCE with the re-enactment of the battle of Salamis (September 480 CE) by Emperor Augustus (27 BCE–14 CE)[32] in which 'Athenians' fought the 'Persians' in a grand naval battle at the Naumachia in Rome;[33] this was a massive spectacle for which an artificial lake was constructed for the battle to be re-enacted by several thousand men.[34] It is interesting that Augustus, who was a contemporary of the Parthian Empire (c. 250–224 CE), had just sent off a military expedition against the Parthian king Farhad (Phraates) V (r. 2 BCE–4 CE). The 'Salamis show' was Augustus' way of linking Rome with ancient Greece and the Parthians with the 'Persian enemy'.

It is very possible that Roman 'Achaemenizing' of the Sassanians was meant to propagandize the vision of the long-standing hostile 'Persian other' who perpetually stood in military opposition against the Greco-Roman world. Nevertheless, the perspectives of researchers such as Potter and Charles have yet to be supported by the entirety of Western scholars. Fowden for example, has not ruled out the notion of an Achaemenid military legacy upon the Sassanian military.[35]

Iranian military historians disagree with the thesis that the Sassanians lacked cognizance of Achaemenid military traditions. Farzin, for example, argues for a direct linkage between Sassanian military units such as the jan-separan or jyanavspar (Chapter 6) and the Achaemenid military based on his analyses of Classical sources and the *Shahname*.[36] The Iranian military history tradition also argues that the reason the Sassanians endeavored to create a powerful military machine was to enable them to realize their dreams of a revived Persian Empire.[37] In support of Jalali's stance of Sassanian cognizance of the Achaemenid military heritage is Whitby's citation of Ardashir I having killed off the ninety descendants of the kings established 550 years previously by Alexander.[38] Ardashir's actions may suggest that he was cognizant of the Greco-Alexandrian occupation of Iran in past centuries. This is consistent with the aforementioned assessment of Shahbazi that the early Sassanians knew of the Achaemenids.

Frye and Brown have argued that tales and legends of the Achaemenid past would probably have been retained in some form,[39] even if precise information of the past had faltered. The existence of monuments in particular could not simply be ignored by the Sassanians.[40] This leads to the question of why the Sassanians would carve their rock reliefs at Nagshe Rustam, which hosts the Achaemenid tombs of Darius the Great, Xerxes I, Artaxerxes I, and Darius II.[41]

Post-Islamic epic literature discussed later in this chapter certainly makes clear that the post-Sassanian Iranians knew of Alexander or *Iskandar*, knowledge which must have derived from Iran's pre-Islamic past. Sarkhosh-Curtis notes of Islamic-era Persian epics such as 'Firdowsi's description of Alexander in his *Shahname* of the early eleventh century and Nizami Ganjavi's *Iskandarname* of the twelfth century'.[42] Amanat[43] and Rose[44] also note of pre-Islamic Iranian sources (e.g. *Dinkard*) describing Alexander (known as the 'Great' in the West) as the

'Accursed'. On the other hand, the argument may be made that the sources were 'distorted' or perhaps altered later. Frye and Brown, who disagree with the latter thesis, argue that legends and stories from the Achaemenid past had not simply disappeared by the time of the Sassanians. Daryaee offers an intriguing explanation by noting that Jews of Persia were cognizant of the legacy of the Achaemenids at the time of the Sassanians, especially through the Bible and the Talmud, and they most likely transmitted knowledge to the Sassanians of Iran's glorious (Achaemenid) past.[45]

Another question is one of ruins, especially Persepolis. These did continue to exist, but is it possible that somehow the significance of these ruins was completely forgotten? In this respect, Whitby emphasizes the point that Achaemenid monuments were still standing at the time of the Sassanians which 'would have prompted the creation of appropriate explanations'.[46] There are also four interesting scratched figures at Persepolis known as the 'Persepolis Graffiti' which portray costumes typical of late Parthian and early Sassanian nobility.[47] The question that can be posed here is *why were these inscribed at Persepolis?* Did the artists who created the images simply draw all of them at Persepolis out of sheer coincidence? This is highly unlikely. A more pertinent question is whether those artists were attempting to associate their contemporaries with some other 'forgotten' glory or *farr* (Iranic: divine glory).

A Islamic-era example of the Iranian recollection of Iran's pre-Islamic imperial heritage was first published 150 years ago. These are the writings in Dutch by Willem Floor which were compiled of Safavid Iran. Floor's works, which were translated to Persian by Sefat-Gol in 2003, reported that numbers of inhabitants of the city of Shiraz claimed that their city had been originally founded by Cyrus the Great (r. 559–530 CE), the founder of the Achaemenid Empire.[48] There are also indications that the kings of the Safavid dynasty themselves were at least partly cognizant of Iran's pre-Islamic heritage. A hint of this can be seen in a European artistic portrayal of the Safavid dynasty's King Shah Abbas (r. 1587–1629 CE), whose copper engraving by Medieval artist Dominicus Custos has the Latin inscriptions *Schach Abas Persarum Rex* (Shah Abbas the Great monarch of Persia) and *Mnemona Cyrus* (the Memory of Cyrus the Great). Matini (1992) has discussed the pre-Islamic elements of Iran in the Safavid dynasty. Such reports may question in part the notion of Iranians' having forgotten their ancient pre-Islamic past. If the inhabitants of Shiraz in Fars were able to recall the memory and identity of Cyrus 2,300 years after the founding of the Achaemenids, this then raises the possibility that the Sassanians, having risen 500 years after the Achaemenids in Fars, may have also had at least a partial recollection of the Achaemenid legacy.

A more recent example of this can be found in the early Qajar era where Fathali Shah (r. 1794–1834 CE) commissioned his own rock reliefs at Taghe Bostan (above the left panel of the royal hunt at the entrance to the vault), apparently hoping to triumph over imperial Russian armies invading Iranian territories in the Caucasus in the early 1800s. It is clear that the Qajars knew of the Sassanians and their exploits, despite their lack of knowledge of the specifics of history and archaeology known by present-day scholarship. Fathali Shah and his contemporaries had not read any Western books on the significance of Taghe Bostan or other ancient Iranian sites at the time, as Western scholarship of pre-Islamic Iran had not yet matured to its present-day level. The first comprehensive book in English on the subject by Rawlinson was not published until 1888; even this was not available in Persian at the time. Put simply, the fact that the Qajars did not know of the specifics of the Sassanians may not necessarily imply that they were ignorant of their military legacy. It is also notable that a rare *farman* (Royal edict) declaring the issue of a *neshan* (medallion of merit) during the later Qajar era in 1920 displayed symbols of Persepolis, despite the fact that (1) Persepolis itself had yet to be fully and professionally excavated by the University of Chicago in the 1930s (Ernst Herzfeld and Erich Schmidt of the Oriental Institute of the University of Chicago led the excavations) and (2) Achaemenid studies were still in their early stages of development and would not fully enter the mainstream nationalist discourse of Iran until the advent of the Pahlavi dynasty (1925–1979).

Potter is correct in noting that Shapur I (r. 240/42–270/72 CE) left no recorded inscriptions specifically stating that he identified himself with Darius the Great and his grandiose territorial ambitions.[49] However this particular omission does not necessarily prove of Shapur I's ignorance of the Achaemenid legacy. It is possible to surmise that Shapur I may have never intended to recreate a vast new Iranian Empire (à la the Achaemenids). Shapur I had witnessed the campaigns of his father Ardashir I, and may have realized that though the spah was more than capable of defeating invading armies, it was not capable of conquering the Roman Empire. Even after the military reforms of the sixth century CE, the spah continued to face chronic shortages of professional military manpower, notably armoured knights. As a result, Shapur I may have instead remained content at having 'merely' defeated three Roman emperors. Towards the end of the dynasty Khosrow II did indeed attempt to recreate the territorial boundaries of the Achaemenids as they had reached at their maximum extent during the reigns of Darius the Great and his son Xerxes.

Partho-Sassanian Militaria: The Legacy

A new generation of Western military historians such as Cosentino and Olbrycht now acknowledge the importance of the Iranian legacy in the Western military tradition. This is in contrast to the more circumspect view of Richard Keegan, who states that 'True, the Persians ... had fielded squadrons of armored horsemen and even armored horses at an earlier date [than the western Europeans] ... to ascribe the origin of heavy cavalry warfare to them is risky.'[50] This viewpoint has been questioned in modern Western scholarship as a result of a re-examination of the primary classical sources as well as by Iranian military historiography (esp. Babaie, Matofi and Jalali). Western scholars of note who diverge from Keegan's thesis include Nickel, Herrmann, Boss and most recently Consentino. This topic will be further discussed in the final chapter of this text.

Misconceptions in Terminology

It is necessary to address misconceptions regarding Sassanian military terminology that have been popularized in Western popular and academic literature by David Nicolle's text on the subject. One of these is the claim by Nicolle that military leaders of Sassanian infantry (*paighan*) formations were led by *paighan-salah*, which is categorically incorrect as *salah* is an Arabic term meaning 'weapon'. *Salah* is totally unrelated to Middle or Modern Persian (or any Iranian language); as noted by Tafazzoli, the correct term for leader of the infantry is *paigan-salar*;[51] with *salar* being the Sassanian-Pahlavi term for 'military leader'. Nicolle's misconception may be derived from his excellent knowledge of Arabic and Arab militaria, which may explain his confusion between Arabic (i.e. *salah*) and Persian (i.e. *salar*). Nevertheless, Nicolle's text on the Sassanian military (especially its sections on the role of Arab warriors) is recommended reading. Also recommended is Peter Wilcox's first popular Western text dedicated to an overview of the domain of Partho-Sassanian armies.

Another view that may be questioned is the notion of 'Persian conservatism'[52] with respect to the willingness to adopt new military technologies. First, Iranian military historians such as Jalali challenge this notion by noting that the Sassanians often sought ways of adapting to new techniques of warfare, especially in the recruitment of auxiliary units from the Caucasus, Central Asia, etc.[53] Second, highly significant changes were introduced into the weaponry of the spah due to military contacts with Central Asia, especially with respect to sword suspension and archery equipment. In the case of swords, these completely changed as they were no longer of the strict 'broadsword' type. A new 'pistol grip' was introduced to replace the handle of the traditional broadsword that was withdrawn from battlefield service (Chapter 6) and relegated to ceremonial duties (Chapter 15). The two-handed sword was also withdrawn and is not seen in the armies of the spah following the introduction of new equipment.

The *Shahname* Epic of Firdowsi

Firdowsi's Persian-language epic, which was written in the post-Sassanian Islamic-era (composed c. 977–1010 CE), is a classic work of poetry blending the myths and historical memories of ancient Iran. More specifically, this work outlines its version of the history of the Persian Empire from the beginning of time until the downfall of Persia. The *Shahname* is actually based for the main part on a work of prose of the same title by Firdowsi in Tus, Khorasan. That same (original) *Shahname* prose is primarily based on the Middle Persian (Sassanian Pahlavi) *Xvatay-namak*, which means *Book of Kings* just as *Shahname* does in New Persian (Parsiye Now). The *Xvatay-namak*, believed to have been composed in the later Sassanian period, outlines the history of Persia from its mythical origins to late Sassanian times, with an emphasis on its military heroes and kings, notably Khosrow II (r. 590–628 CE). Zaehner notes that the content of the *Xvatay-namak* is reflective of information of the later Sassanian period but lacking information of the earlier period of the dynasty (third–fourth centuries CE).[54] Firdowsi's *Shahname*, however, is also believed to have drawn upon other critical Middle

Persian sources, notably the *Karnamag-e Ardaxsir-e Papakan*, which pertains to the history of Ardashir I Babakan, the founder of the Sassanian dynasty. Safa for example, has noted of the strong parallels between the Middle Persian *Karnamag-e Ardaxsir-e Papakan*, and Firdowsi's *Shahname* with respect to historical accounts, terminology and phrases.[55] The *Shahname* is also influenced by the north Iranian, notably Soghdian, literature of Central Asia. Iranian literary researchers have conducted valuable research into the north Iranian domains of Iranian mythical figures, notably Ansari's extensive survey of the tales of the *Shahname*'s epic hero, Rustam, that have been written in Soghdian.[56]

From a military history viewpoint, the *Shahname* provides vivid descriptions of battles, duels and usage of weapons. Farzin has noted of the importance of the *Shahname* with respect to the pre-Islamic military history of Iran, especially with respect to the martial traditions of the Sassanians, notably battle tactics, organization, duels, military culture and banners.[57] Citing Nöldeke, Inostrancev observes that the armour of warriors described in the *Shahname* is closer to those of the Sassanian era than those of the tenth–eleventh centuries CE.[58] Two important articles published in the *Katsujinken* journal by Khorasani et al. have clearly outlined the importance of the *Shahname* as a key reference in the study of pre-Islamic Iran's military history, especially with respect to the tactics, weapons and techniques of Iranian warriors. Iranian military historiography (e.g. Matofi, Jalali) often cites the *Shahname*, especially with respect to Sassanian military history. There are several excellent western translations of the *Shahname*, the most recent of these being Dick Davis' three-volume translation which was nominated as the 'Book of the Year' by the *Washington Post* in 2006.

Firdowsi was himself a descendant of the Dehkan clans[59] which were the backbone of the Sassanian cavalry from the sixth century CE. It was in 976 CE that Bailami, the minister of Mansur Samani of the Samanid dynasty (819–999 CE), appointed Daqiqi (chief poet of the Samanid court) to translate the *Shahname* into New Persian.[60] According to Axworthy, Firdowsi 'continued and completed' the project that Daqiqi had begun, which resulted in the New Persian *Shahname*.[61] This was completed after three decades, resulting in a massive tome of 30,000 rhyming couplets.

Iranian military culture as whole, meaning not just Iran proper but the larger milieu of the now lost Scythians and Sarmatians-Alans, was especially tied to the 'knightly' chivalrous tradition and duels, a concept which can be broadly described as the *pahlavan* tradition (Chapter 15) which the *Shahname* extols. The pahlavan tradition survived the fall of Sassanian Persia to Islam in 651 CE to re-emerge with the Safavid military tradition of Iran in 1501–1736 CE. The founder of the Safavid dynasty Shah Ismail I (r. 1502–1524 CE), strongly identified his kinship with the Persian mythological and historical figures of the *Shahname* (i.e. Fereydoun, Khosrow, Jamshid and Zal)[62] and commissioned a special copy of this for his son and successor Tahmasp I (r. 1524–1576).[63]

Historical Timeline of the Sassanian Empire

Wars of Ardashir I Babakan (r. 224–242 CE)

Battle of Firuzabad (224 CE): Ardashir I Babakan defeats Parthian dynasty and establishes the Sassanian dynasty (224–651 CE).

Ardashir I and his son Prince Shapur attack and eject Roman forces from Mesopotamia (229 CE); rejection of Emperor Alexander Severus' (r. 222–235 CE) letter for spah to withdraw; Ardashir I captures Cappadocia.

Alexander Severus counterattacks (231 CE) on three axes: northern thrust into Cappadocia, Armenia, northern Media and Atropatene, southernmost thrust into Mesopotamia across Tigris-Euphrates rivers possibly towards Khuzestan in southwest Iran; central thrust toward Ctesiphon; Romans achieve success with northern thrust, southern thrust does not reach Khuzestan; Legio IV Scythica moves from Dura Europos against Ardashir I but is defeated.

Battle of Ctesiphon (233 CE): Emperor Alexander Severus (r. 222–235 CE) defeated at the decisive Battle of Ctesiphon (233 CE); Roman attempt to destroy Ardashir I and the spah fails; Alexander Severus reports outcome of campaign as a major military success to the Roman senate.

Battles of Shapur I (r. 240–270 CE)

Shapur I captures Nisibis and Carrhae, thrusts into Syria (c. 241–242 CE); Shapur I conducts military campaign against Gilan in northern Persia and the Kushans (in Central Asia); Gordian III deploys to Antioch, recaptures Nisibis and Carrhae (242 CE), defeats spah at Rhesaina (242 or 243 CE); Gordian III advances towards Ctesiphon but faces determined resistance by spah.

Battle of Misiche (244 CE): Gordian III defeated and killed in the vicinity of modern-day Anbar in Iraq, Misiche renamed 'Peroz Shapur' (lit. 'Victorious Shapur').

Battle of Barbalissos (c. 253 CE): Emperor Philip the Arab attacks Sassanian empire; Roman army of 60,000 destroyed by spah at Barbalissos.

Battle of Edessa-Carrhae (c. 260 CE): defeat of Roman army of 70,000; Emperor Valerian, the Praetorian prefect, senators, high ranking officials as well as large numbers of prisoners captured.

Inconclusive battles with Odenathus (260–261 CE); spah unable to subdue the armies of Palmyra; spah pushed out of Antioch, Nisibis, Edessa and Carrhae; Sassanians repel Odenathus outside of Ctesiphon.

Hormizd I to Bahram III (270–293 CE)

No major Roman invasions/wars between Rome and Sassanian Empire during reigns of Hormizd I (r. 270–271 CE) and Bahram I (r. 271–274 CE).

Roman Emperor Carus (r. 282–283 CE) advances to Ctesiphon but is reported as having 'died from lightning' during reign of Bahram II (r. 274–293 CE); Emperor Diocletian (r. 284–285 CE, 285–305 CE as co-emperor) installs Arsacid prince Tiridates (Tirdad) upon Armenian throne (c. 288).

Brief reign of Bahram III (r. 293 CE); no major battles with Rome.

Wars of Narseh (Narses) (r. 293–302 CE)

Narses invades western Armenia and Roman-held Syria (295 CE).

Emperor Diocletian dispatches Galerius to repel the Sassanians; spah defeats Galerius at ar-Raqqah (Callinicum and Carrhae region) (295 CE).

Galerius counterattacks (298) and defeats Sassanians in Armenia and at Battle of Satala; many Sassanian nobles and members of Narses' family captured.

Reign of Hormizd II (r. 302–309 CE); Hormizd II's oldest son Adur-Narseh is successor but he is assassinated in that same year (r. 309 CE); Zoroastrian magi and nobles blind another one of Hormizd II's sons after the latter's death and imprison another (Hormizd) who later escapes to Rome (323 CE).

Wars of Shapur II (r. 309–379 CE)

Infant Shapur II born as king (309 CE); administration of empire by advisors until Shapur II reaches maturity.

Arab invaders occupy southern Mesopotamia, Khuzistan and much of Iran's Persian Gulf coastline.

Shapur II counterattacks: spah lands in Bahrain; combined Arab forces of Abdul Qays, Taqlib and Bakr bin Wael defeated; Arab invaders expelled from southern Iran and Mesopotamia; Sassanians conclude campaign by driving into Arabian interior, reaching al-Najd.

Shapur II commissions construction of 'War-e Tazigan' (Wall of the Arabs) in Hira region in southwest of empire for protection against future Arab raids.

Shapur II besieges Nisibis thrice (337 or 338 CE, 346, 350 CE) but city avoids capture by Sassanians.

Shapur II forced to suspend operations on Roman frontier to battle Kidaro-Chionite invasion from Central Asia (350 CE).

Siege operations (359–360 CE): capture of Amida, Busa, Rema, Singara and Bezabde (360 CE); failure of Emperor Constantius II (r. 324–361 CE; co-emperor 337–350) to re-capture Bezabde (360 CE), retreats to Antioch.

Emperor Julian (r. 362–363 CE) invades Sassanian Empire in 363 CE; spah defeated in front of Ctesiphon which avoids capture by Roman forces; Julian thrusts deeper into Persia, prevails at Battle of Maranga but spah including elite savaran cavalry remain intact; Julian killed during a savaran raid against the Roman columns.

Jovian (r. 363–364 CE) succeeds Julian and negotiates peace terms with Shapur II; Rome cedes Nisibis and fifteen other fortresses, much of Roman Mesopotamia, Armenia and Georgia.

Ardashir II to Yazdegird I (379–420 CE)

Reigns of Ardashir II (r. 379–383 CE) and Shapur III (r. 383–388 CE); no battles with Rome; treaty between Rome and Sassanians partitioning Armenia (384 CE).

Brief reign of Bahram IV (r. 388–399 CE) followed by Yazdegird I (r. 399–420 CE) who is briefly succeeded in 420 CE by Shapur IV (r. 420 CE) and then Khosrow 'The Usurper'; no military conflicts with Rome.

Wars of Bahram V Gur (r. 420–438 CE) and Yazdegird II (r. 438–457 CE).

Ascension of Bahram V Gur (420–438 CE).

War with Romano-Byzantines (421 CE): Romano-Byzantine General Ardaburius attacks into Armenia, defeats Sassanian forces and lays siege to Nisibis; Bahram Gur advances towards Ardaburius, who then withdraws from Nisibis; Theodosiopolis besieged by Bahram Gur; Grand Vizier Mehr-Narseh leads successful attacks by Sassanians over the Romano-Byzantines; war ends with peace treaty (422 CE) between Bahram Gur and Emperor Theodosius II (r. co-emperor 402–408; 408–450 CE).

Large-scale Hephthalite Hun invasion from Central Asia (420 CE); Bahram Gur inflicts major defeat upon Hephthalite forces (421 CE).

Armenia annexed by Bahram in accordance with requests of Armenian nobles (428 CE).

Ascension of Yazdegird II (r. 438–457 CE)

Outbreak of war between Sassanians and Romano-Byzantines (438 CE); spah defeats Romano-Byzantine forces; Theodosius II sues for peace.

Kidarite Huns attack northeast of empire from Central Asia (early 440s CE). Sassanians engage in major war with Kidarites (c. 443–450).

Yazdegird II issues edict calling on Armenians to abjure Christianity in favor of Zoroastrianism; Armenians rebel, resulting in Battle of Avaryr in 451 CE.

Sassanians defend against renewed attacks of Kidarite Huns (c. 457 CE).

Wars of Pirouz I (r. 459–484 CE)

Ascension of Hormizd III (r. 457–459 CE); Prince Pirouz I defeats his brother Hormizd III and secures Sassanian throne with Hephthalite military assistance (459 CE).

Spah engages in battles against Kidarite Huns (from early 460s CE); Pirouz I sends embassy to Emperor Leo (457–474 CE) declaring his victory over Kidarites in 466 CE; but successful conclusion of spah campaigns achieved later (with Hephthalite support since 466) in 468 CE.

Hephthalites replace Kidarites as primary Central Asian military power; city of Balkh in Central Asia captured by Hepthalites (c. early 470s CE), resulting in war with Sassanian Empire.

Pirouz I's first Hephthalite campaign (474–475 CE): Pirouz and his army are trapped by Hephthalites forces, Emperor Zeno (474–491 CE) provides massive gold payment to Hephthalites to allow Pirouz and his forces to return from Central Asia; Bactria and Tocharistan occupied by Hephthalites.

Pirouz I's second Hephthalite campaign (476–477 CE): King Kushnavaz of Hephthalites defeats Sassanians and captures Pirouz I, who is forced to pay a large ransom for his release; Taleghan and Merv fall under Hephthalite control.

Pirouz I's third Hephthalite campaign (484 CE): Pirouz I is killed and his army annihilated when Kushnavaz's forces lure the Sassanians into a massive ditch with traps; much of Khorasan and modern Afghanistan captured by Hephthalites.

Balash (brother of Pirouz I) ascends throne (484–488 CE); peace treaty with Hephthalites, who force Ctesiphon to pay heavy annual indemnities; peace treaty with Armenians affirming their Christian faith with Armenia remaining under Sassanian administration.

Wars of Kavad I

Kavad I (son of Pirouz I) (r. 488–496; 498–531 CE) rebels against Balash, ascends throne in 488 CE; ejected from power in 496 CE in favor of his brother Jamasp/Zamasp (r. 496–498 CE) who is placed on throne; Kavad returns in 498 CE, recaptures throne with Hephthalite assistance.

Emperor Anastasius (r. 491–518 CE) refuses Kavad I's appeal for subsidies to pay the Hephthalites, resulting in outbreak of war.

Kavad I's First Romano-Byzantine War: Sassanians capture Theodosiopolis (502 CE) and Amida (early 503 CE); defeat of Romano-Byzantine counteroffensive to retake Amida; Sassanians fail to capture Edessa; armistice follows in aftermath of Khazar invasions of Caucasus in 505 CE.

Kavad I's battles in Caucasus (505–c. 515 CE); defeats invasion of Armenia and South Caucasus by Khazars; construction of Darband Wall in Caucasus initiated; Romano-Byzantines agree to pay subsidies for Sassanian defences in Caucasus.

Breakdown of negotiations between Kavad I and Emperor Justin I (r. 518–527 CE); Iberian king of Caucasus defects to Romano-Byzantines (524–525 CE), leading to outbreak of war.

Kavad I's Second Romano-Byzantine War: battles fought in Caucasus and north Mesopotamia between Sassanian and Romano-Byzantine forces (526–527 CE); Lakhmid Arab ally of Sassanians, Al-Mundhir, attacks into southern Mesopotamia; ascension of Romano-Byzantine Emperor Justinian (r. 527–565 CE).

Battle of Thannuris (528 CE): defeat of Romano-Byzantine General Belisarius; Sassanian victory notable for spah's use of prepared traps.

Battle of Dara (530 CE): Belisarius defeats General Firouz; Sassanian forces suffer heavy casualties, elite savaran unit of Immortals decimated but spah remains intact.

Battle of Callinicum (531 CE): General Azarethes leads spah and Lakhmid Arab allies to victory over Romano-Byzantine forces and their Hunnic and Arab-Ghassanid foes; Belisarius escapes; Azarethes dismissed by Kavad I for heavy losses at Callinicum, Belisarius also dismissed for his performance in the battle by Emperor Justinian.

Kavad I renews invasion of Romano-Byzantine territory (531 CE): Sassanians besiege Martyropolis; death of Kavad I and approach of Romano-Byzantine forces obliges Sassanians to lift siege and return to Sassanian territory.

Wars of Khosrow I (r. 531-579 CE)

Ascension of Khosrow I; military reforms (initiated possibly during reign of Kavad I), notably expansion of elite savaran cavalry corps by recruitment of lesser Dehkan nobility, formation of four regional (spahbod) commands.

Pax Perpetuum (Eternal Peace) concluded (532 CE) to settle territorial disputes between Sassanian and Romano-Byzantine Empires.

Ostrogoth king Witiges sends embassy to Khosrow I (538 or 539 CE) to warn Sassanians of impending Romano-Byzantine strike against Sassanian Empire.

Khosrow I attacks Romano-Byzantine Mesopotamia and Syria, Sassanians capture and sack Antioch (540 CE), fail to capture Dara; Khosrow I pressures Romano-Byzantine cities for ransoms as he heads back to Sassanian territory; General Belisarius summoned to lead Romano-Byzantine armies against Khosrow I.

Khosrow I arrives at Lazica in Caucasus at request of local king (541 CE), siege and capture of Romano-Byzantine garrisoned Petra; Belisarius strikes into Mesopotamia but fails to capture Nisibis.

Romano-Byzantine forces defeated in Armenia by General Nabed (542 CE); Khosrow I returns to Sassanian territory.

Sassanians besiege Edessa (543 CE), but payments and negotiation by city's leaders persuade Khosrow I to abandon siege,

Romano-Byzantine forces fail to capture Petra (547 CE), but succeed in their second attempt (551); several more battles in Lazica until c. 556–557 CE.

Khosrow I in alliance with Gok Turks crush the Hephthalites (557–558 CE); Turks annex Hephthalite territories to the North of Oxus River, Sassanians to the south of the river.

Peace treaty concluded between the Romano-Byzantine and Sassanian Empires (561 CE).

Khosrow I dispatches Sassanian force led by Vahriz to assist Yemenite Arabs in expelling Abbysinian invaders (575 CE); Abyssinian(s) counterattack but Vahriz's forces are ultimately successful by late 590s CE.

Emperor Justin II (r. 565–574 CE) rejects 561 CE peace treaty, attacks Sassanian Empire with unsuccessful siege of Nisibis (572 CE); Sassanians counterattack and capture Dara (573 CE) and sack several Romano-Byzantine cities; Justin sues for peace, Dara remains in Sassanian hands.

Emperor Tiberius II Constantine (r. 574–582 CE) maintains period of truce with Sassanians; Khosrow I attacks Romano-Byzantine territory (576); Romano-Byzantine armies counterattack into Atropatene.

Sassanians defeat Romano-Byzantine forces in Sassanian Armenia (577); Khosrow I attacks Romano-Byzantine Mesopotamia (578); Romano-Byzantine general Maurice counterattacks into Arzanene and Sassanian Mesopotamia, forcing spah to abandon its advance in order to defend Sassanian territory.

Peace negotiations attempted but discontinued after death of Khosrow I (579 CE).

Wars of Hormizd IV, Career of Bahram Chobin and Ascension of Khosrow II

Ascension of Hormizd IV (r. 579–590 CE).

Maurice launches powerful attack into Sassanian territory in (580 CE) with another major offensive towards Ctesiphon (581 CE) but is forced to withdraw after Sassanians launch major offensive into Romano-Byzantine Mesopotamia.

Major invasion of Romano-Byzantine territory by Sassanians halted (June 582 CE); Tiberius II dies (August 582 CE), Maurice becomes Emperor (r. 582–602 CE).

Battles between Sassanians and Romano-Byzantines continue (584–589 CE); Khazars attack in Caucasus, Arab raid in southwest, and major threats from Central Asia.

Invasion of northeast by Turkish Khagan along with Hephthalite and Kushan auxiliaries (588 CE), fall of Balkh; General Bahram Chobin of Mehranid House defeats Turco-Hephthalite invasion, restoring Sassanian hegemony in the northeast.

Bahram Chobin conducts successful campaign against invading Khazars in Caucasus (c.589 CE).

Bahram Chobin initially successful against Romano-Byzantine forces but defeated by General Romanus along the Araxes River (c. 589 CE).

Relations deteriorate between Bahram Chobin and Hormizd IV; troops sent by Hormizd IV to arrest Bahram join him instead; Bahram's forces march towards Ctesiphon, Hormizd IV killed in palace coup in favor of his son, Khosrow II (590 CE).

Khosrow II flees as Bahram captures Ctesiphon and assumes leadership of Sassanian Empire (590).

Khosrow II seeks sanctuary with Maurice in Constantinople; agrees to cede much strategic territory and fortresses along western Sassanian frontiers and the Caucasus in exchange for Romano-Byzantine assistance to regain throne.

Khosrow II advances with Romano-Byzantine allies to defeat Bahram at Ganzak and then capture Ctesiphon with support of majority of Sassanian leadership (591 CE).

Wars of Khosrow II

Assassination of Emperor Maurice (r. 582–602 CE) by Phocas.

Dara falls to Sassanians (603) after 9-month siege.

General Jhuan-Veh defeated in Armenia by Romano-Byzantine forces (Spring 604); Jhuan-Veh replaced by General Datoyan who defeats an Armeno-Byzantine force near Gerik then withdraws into Atropatene.

General Senitam Khosrow (c. 605–606 CE) and his army deploy out of Atropatene into Armenia; Romano-Byzantine forces led by Theodosius Khorkhoruni defeated at Anglon, with Theodosius captured later in another Sassanian attack. Senitam Khosrow thrusts into Anatolia to inflict major defeat on Romano-Byzantine forces west of Theodosiopolis resulting in the capture of several Romano-Byzantine fortresses.

General Ashdad Yazdayar defeats a Romano-Byzantine force at Basean and pursues its remnants to Satala, captures Theodosiopolis; Romano-Byzantines pushed to western fringes of Armenia.

Sassanians capture several important Romano-Byzantine frontier fortresses (604–610 CE); northern Mesopotamia cleared of Romano-Byzantine forces after fall of Cephas, Amida, Tur Abdin and Mardin; southern Mesopotamia cleared of Romano-Byzantine forces after fall of Callinicum, Edessa, Resaina and Zenobia.

Emperor Heraclius (r. 610–641 CE) seizes Romano-Byzantine throne, makes unsuccessful peace overtures to Khosrow II.

Battle of Dhu Qar (610 CE): Arab tribes of the anti-Sassanian Bani Sheiban alliance defeat Sassanians in southwest of empire.

General Shahen defeats new Romano-Byzantine force near Theodosiopolis; all Caucasus cleared of Romano-Byzantine forces by 611 CE; Shahen invades Anatolia, captures Caesarea in Cappadocia followed by the fall of Melitene.

Capture of Emesa, Apamea and Antioch (613 CE) by General Shahrbaraz; Heraclius' counterattack defeated at Emesa; combined armies of Heraclius, Theodore and Nicetas defeated by Shahrbaraz in Syria, followed by Heraclius' defeat at Cilician Gates; Shahen links up from north with Shahrbaraz.

Capture of Jerusalem (614 CE) by General Shahrbaraz after 18–20-day siege.

Shahen thrusts into Anatolian mainland (614–615 CE); Mediterranean coast reached, Chalcedon falls to Sassanians; Heraclius attempts peace negotiations with Shahen; Constantinople senate send three ambassadors to negotiate peace with Ctesiphon; ambassadors executed by Khosrow II; General Philipicus drives towards eastern Anatolia; Shahen abandons Chalcedon to pursue Philipicus; Shahen defeats Philipicus and returns to Chalcedon.

Sassanians capture Sardis (616 CE); fleet constructed and launched against Constantia (Salamis) (617 CE).

Shahrbaraz invades Egypt (618 CE), captures Alexandria (619 CE) and completes conquest of Egypt (621 CE).

Fall of island of Rhodos (Rhodes) to Sassanians (622 CE).

Heraclius advances into Armenia and defeats a Sassanian force led by an Arab general (622); Shahrbaraz marches into Armenia and is defeated by Heraclius who returns west to confront Avar invasion from the Balkans.

Heraclius returns to attack Armenia (624 CE), wheels south into Nakhchivan; Shahrbaraz heading westwards turns toward Armenia to confront Heraclius who gathers allies among Caucasian kingdoms and Khazar Turks in north Caucasus.

Sassanian armies of Shahrbaraz, Shahen and Shahraplakan march against Heraclius' forces in Caucasus (625 CE); Spah defeats Heraclius then advances toward Constantinople to join forces with Avars and their Slavic allies; Heraclius heads west to defend Constantinople; another Romano-Byzantine force sent to Lazica along Black Sea.

Theodore (Heraclius' brother) engages Shahen and defeats him (626 or 627 CE).

Shahrbaraz's siege of Constantinople (626 CE) with Avar and Slav allies unsuccessful; Shahrbaraz meets Heraclius, agrees to withdraw his forces from Constantinople and suspend operations for the duration of the war.

Heraclius counterattacks (626 CE), lands a major force with the Romano-Byzantine fleet at Black Sea coast (Circassia region) to link up with Khazar allies; Khazars attack and sack Albania;

Heraclius and Khazars link up in Georgia; Romano-Byzantines and Khazars invade Armenia where they are joined by large numbers of local warriors.

Heraclius and allies invade Atropatene (Iranian Azerbaijan) and advance into Iraqi Kurdistan; major Sassanian force led by General Razutis destroyed at Battle of Nineveh; Heracles sacks palace of Dastegerd and approaches Ctesiphon.

Palace coup deposes Khosrow II (23–24 February 628 CE); former king's half-Byzantine son, Shiroe, ascends throne as Kavad II, kills many of Sassanian nobility; signs formal peace treaty with Heraclius, formally ending war between Romano-Byzantine and Sassanian Empires; Heraclius returns to Constantinople in triumph.

Kavad II dies (6 September 628 CE); his infant child Ardashir III placed on throne.

General Shahrbaraz captures Ctesiphon and puts Ardashir III to death (27 April 629 CE); sends remaining savaran forces to defeat new Khazar invasion in Armenia.

Shahrbaraz assassinated and Princess Borandokht ascends throne (17 June 629 CE).

Borandokht succeeded by Shapur-e Shahrvaraz or Shapur V (16 June 630 CE).

Shapur-e Shahrvaraz or Shapur V deposed in favor of Princess Azarmidokht (630–631 CE).

Second reign of Borandokht (631–632 CE).

Ascension of Yazdegird III (r. 632–651 CE).

Arabo-Islamic invasion of Sassanian Persia

First Arab attacks into Sassanian empire (633–634): Mosni bin Haresa occupies Hira; Arab victory over a combined force of Sassanians and Christian Arabs in the Battle of Ullais (634).

Sassanians counterattack: General Rustam Farrokhzad expels Arabo-Muslims from Hira; General Mehran expels other Arab raiders from Sassanian territory; Arab General Muthanna succeeds in uniting large numbers of Christian Arabs into the Muslim cause.

Battle of the Bridges (634): first determined Arab invasion of the Sassanian Empire defeated by General Bahram.

Battle of Qadissiya (637) resulting in great Arab victory, General Rustam Farrokhzad killed: Yazdegird flees Ctesiphon; Arab forces besiege and capture Ctesiphon (638).

Battle of Jalula (637): Arabs defeat Sassanian forces led by General Mehran; southern Iran and Persis invaded by the Arabs; fall of Ahvaz in Khuzestan; Bahrain island used by Arabs to land along southern Iranian coastline.

Battle of Nihavand (651): Arabs defeat last stand by Sassanians in vicinity of modern Malayer; Yazdegird III and remnants of Sassanian military flee to the northeast; Arabs invade west and northwest Iran; Rayy (near modern Tehran) falls to Arabs; Arabs reach southeast and engage in major battles to capture Sistan (Saka-istan) (651–652 CE).

Yazdegird III and followers escape to Merv; Yazdegird III assassinated for his purse by a miller (651 CE); Prince Pirouz III and remaining Sassanian entourage escape to Tang China.

Nobleman of Karen clan organizes a new army from Baghdis, Kuhistan and Herat which is destroyed by the Arabs (652 CE).

Pirouz III plans to build a new military force with Chinese assistance to liberate Iran in early 660s CE but plans never materialize.

Resistance against the Caliphates

Revolts in occupied Media region suppressed in 650s CE; several revolts in occupied Fars region break out (mid-late 650s CE); all suppressed by Caliphate forces.

Resistance in Central Asia suppressed by Caliphate (early 700s–740s CE).

Anti-Caliphate rebellion in Khorasan led by Sindbad (775 CE) supported by northern Iranian regions; Caliphate suppresses rebellion but northern Iran remains defiant.

Anti-Caliphate rebellion in Transoxiana in Central Asia led by Muqanna (776 CE), capture of Bukhara; Turks join Iranians in Samarqand to inflict defeats on Caliphate forces (777 CE); caliphate strikes back and crushes Muqanna (780 CE).

Anti-Caliphate rebellion in Central Asia led by Rafi bin Laith (806 CE) crushed by Caliphate (810 CE).

Anti-Caliphate resistance (650s–late 700s CE) in northern Persia; Arabs find region difficult to subdue.

Rebellion of Babak Khorramdin in Azerbaijan against the Caliphate (816–837 CE) with aim of restoring the 'Khosrovian' (Sassanian) rule; Caliphate's General Afshin leads caliphate's final campaigns against Babak from 835 CE; Babak's Bazz castle captured by Caliphate (August 837 CE); Babak executed in Samara (January 838 CE).

Chapter 1

Martial Ardour, Origins and Missions of the Spah

The *shahanshah* (king of kings) was the supreme leader of the Sassanian *spah* (military, or armed forces). Under the shahanshah served an efficient hierarchical bureaucratic machine that was composed of military, civilians and religious officials. Greatrex cites the importance of the noble clans (traditionally seven in number) whose power could at times rival that of the shahanshah.[1] Greatrex further avers that the Sassanian political-military apparatus ran most efficiently when a strong king was at the helm.[2]

This chapter will briefly sketch the factors that led to the rise of the spah as one of the military superpowers of its day. Iranian military tradition identifies four general factors as having been essential in the formation of the spah. Jalali categorizes these as historical, political, economic and socio-cultural (the latter overlapping with geographical and religious factors as well).[3] Before this discussion a brief overview is provided concerning the martial ardour of the warriors of the spah.

Roman Sources: The Martial Ardour of the Spah

The Sassanian spah was a formidable military machine during the Sassanian Empire's 427-year existence (224–651 CE). Sassanian martial ardour was no less fervent than that of the Romans, and the soldiers of both empires drew upon the military talents of each other. Thanks in large part to the efforts of Western scholarship and Iranian military historians much information has been uncovered regarding the formidable nature of the spah and its warriors. The resilience of the Sassanian military machine has been attested by the soldier-historian Ammianus Marcellinus, who served in the Roman armies that fought against the spah in the fourth century CE. As noted by Marcellinus: 'In military system and discipline, by continual exercises in the business of the camp ... they [Sassanians] have become formidable even to the greatest armies ... so brave is it [the spah] and so skilful in all warlike exercises, that it would be invincible were it not continually weakened by civil and by foreign wars.'[4]

The *Expositio totius mundi et Gentium* corroborates Ammianus by describing the (Sassanian) Persians as 'brave in wars'.[5] The martial ardour of the *savaran* elite cavalry was especially respected by Roman troops. Libanius wrote a detailed description of the savaran from Roman eyes in 365 CE, just two years after the defeat of Emperor Julian's invasion of the Sassanian Empire:

> [A] cloud of dust rising in the distance, such as would be made by [Sassanian] cavalry... made them turn to flee ... when a squadron, and that only a small

one, showed itself, they prayed earth to swallow them up, preferring to suffer any fate than look a Persian in the face ... the word 'Persian' put a stop to their [Roman troops] being troublesome, and everyone used to say 'Here comes a Persian soldier!' and they forthwith turned red in the face and jumped away ... the Persian terror, growing in the course of long years had become so fixed in them that somebody said they even would have trembled at the Persians in a picture.[6]

Marcellinus also elucidates the military challenge posed by the spah when he comments that 'many of our [Roman] armies having often been entirely destroyed by them'.[7] These observations are notable as Rome was the military superpower of its day and was master of the Mediterranean and its lands as well as much of Western Europe. Contemporary Western military historians such as Howard-Johnston acknowledge the spah's formidable nature by noting that 'the Sassanian empire was, from the first, the military equal of the Roman empire, and second that, after a delay for mental adjustment, its parity was recognised and accepted by the Romans.'[8]

Historical Factors

As discussed in the introduction, a select number of Western historians and non-military Iranologists now diverge from Iranian military historians with respect to historical factors and the spah. As noted in the introduction, the position of traditional Iranian military historiography (i.e. Shahbazi,[9] Jalali,[10] etc.) is that the Sassanian dynasty sought to revive the martial traditions and empire of the ancient Achaemenids. The traditional source of evidence for this viewpoint has often been sought in the classical sources. Western-based Iranian historians however, now argue that the Sassanians had no military memory of the Achaemenids. As noted in the introduction, Charles concurs with this view, arguing that the classical sources were simply propagandizing by identifying the Parthians and Sassanians as the heirs of the Achaemenid military tradition.

Iranian military history tradition also argues that the reason the Sassanians endeavoured to create a powerful military machine was to enable them to realize their dreams of a revived Persian empire.[11] Readers are referred to the introduction chapter for further discussion of this topic.

Domestic Political Factors

The spah also played an important role in the empire's domestic politics, namely to preserve and protect the Sassanian monarchy. This was a complex political issue lasting to the final days of the dynasty, as potential rivals to the throne could arise anywhere from the western Iranian highlands to the interior of Iran and the east (notably Khorasan and Saka-istan).[12] Specifically this region comprised an 'inner arc' of the provinces of Pars (the Sassanian homeland), Maha (Media), and Parthia, which surround the largely uninhabited and arid Iranian interior. The 'highland' region was composed of the northwestern and northeastern marches of the empire. The northwestern marches consisted of Aturpatekan (ancient Media

Atropatene, corresponding to Azerbaijan province in Iran's northwest) as well as Albania (modern-day Republic of Azerbaijan) and Armenia in the Caucasus. The northeastern marches were essentially those regions facing the Central Asian region, roughly modern-day Khorasan (in Iran), with the major military base at Merv in modern-day Turkmenistan. The highlands and the inner arc were generally settled by aristocratic military family groups under the leadership of the *vuzurgan* (modern Persian *buzurgan*; great clans/families/grand dignitaries). The Sassanian dynasty had had the support of these vuzurgan in its ascension to power, both in the overthrow of the Parthian dynasty and the defeat of Roman thrusts into the Iranian realms.

Despite having supported the Sassanians against the Parthian dynasty, the formidable vuzurgan of the predominantly Parthian clans retained the military potential of rebelling against the Sassanian throne. Put simply, the Parthian vuzurgan could challenge the political supremacy of the Sassanians by military means, as these provided the spah with its best-trained and equipped elite savaran cavalry. The Parthian clans certainly contributed to the collective defence of the 'Eiran-Shahr' (Sassanian Empire) and were fully involved in the military expansion of the realm; nevertheless, they exercised a great deal of autonomy from Ctesiphon, a legacy of the decentralized policies of the former Parthian dynasty. Bavzani has noted in this regard that the Sassanians differed in at least two ways from their Parthian and Achaemenid predecessors in that they 'had a powerful central government and declared an official state religion'.[13]

Professor Pourshariati has noted the potential political rivalry between the Parthian and Sassanian aristocratic houses of Iran and argues that this rivalry, which had existed since the early days of the Sassanian dynasty, contributed to the undermining of the spah on the eve of the Arabo-Islamic invasions in 637–651 CE. There is evidence that Parthian political animosity toward the Sassanians also existed in the cultural sphere. The Institute of Oriental Studies of the Russian Academy of Sciences, for example, has examined a Parthian-Pahlavi inscription of two Parthian youths who mock the founder of the Sassanian dynasty, Ardashir I Babakan, by saying that he rides a donkey instead of a horse.[14] Parthian resentment at being overthrown was perceived as a military threat by the Sassanians, who viewed a powerful spah as essential for protecting against possible rebellions and attempted coups d'etat.[15]

A final point, while beyond the scope of this text, pertains to the ethnic origins of the Sassanian dynasty. The Sassanians are often referred to as a 'Persian' dynasty, which is strictly true if we consider their geographical origins in Persis. But it is quite possible that the Sassanians were of wider Iranian origin. Tabari mentions a letter written by the Parthian king Ardavan V in which he referred to Ardashir I as a Kurd 'who was brought up in the tents of the Kurds'.[16] According to Zarrinkub, Ardashir was a 'Kurd ... raised by the Shaban'.[17] These highland connections may partly explain why Ardashir was able to recruit excellent Mede and Kurdish fighters into the spah. This may have been one of those military factors which proved significant in repelling the Roman invasion of the newly established Sassanian Empire in 233 CE.

Foreign Policy: Territorial Expansion, Defence of the Eiran-Shahr, or Both?

The Sassanians were determined to defend those lands they identified as belonging to Iran, including those territories located outside of modern Iran proper. At the same time, such policies led to expansionist ambitions, which led to the spah's determined efforts towards improving their defensive as well as offensive capabilities. This meant that the technology of warfare played a crucial role in the spah's (and, indeed, the Sassanian Empire's) history. As noted by Masia, Sassanian imperial ambitions resulted in constant military contacts and technological exchanges with Rome, Armenia and various other polities of the Caucasus and Central Asia.[18]

Like the Parthians before them, the Sassanians made Ctesiphon (in Mesopotamia) their capital and fought to extend their sway into Albania (modern Republic of Azerbaijan), Iberia (modern Republic of Georgia), Armenia and eastern Anatolia (i.e. the Cappadocia-Pontus regions). Their expansionist efforts often brought them into conflict with the Romans (and, later, the Byzantines), who coveted those same lands. The Sassanians were also active on their northeastern (i.e. Central Asian) frontiers. After the subjugation of the Kushans in the Ardashir I-Shapur I era (mid-third century CE), the spah's strategy for Central Asia consisted mainly of repelling nomadic incursions by Chionite, Hephtalite-Hun, and Turkic invaders. The spah was to achieve spectacular expansion into Central Asia following the campaigns of Bahram Chobin (588 CE) and Smbat Bagrationi (607–617 CE). In summary, the Sassanians had no choice but to ensure that the spah was as efficient and powerful as possible to: (1) repel Roman attempts to conquer Sassanian territory; (2) attempt expansion into Roman-held territories; and (3) defend the Central Asian frontier and expand further into that region whenever strategic-military circumstances were favourable for doing so. This would also help explain the aggressive military posture that was to be adopted by the spah well up to the last days of the dynasty.[19]

As the Sassanian dynasty solidified its rule and established its military power, the spah was obliged to factor in the defence of strategic fortress-cities and land routes against its Romano-Byzantine and Central Asian rivals. Two major metropolitan centres that became critical strategic assets were Nisibis (on the modern-day Turkish-Syrian border) and Merv (in present-day Turkmenistan). Separated by a distance of approximately 1,800km, these cities were critical to the defence of the realm: Merv was a bulwark against invasion from Central Asia and Nisibis anchored the defence of the empire's western marches against the Romano-Byzantines.

Economic Factors

The spah was critical to the economic welfare of the empire. A strong military machine would help deter attacks by aggressive foes such as the Romano-Byzantines, Khazars, Central Asian nomads and the Arabs. A successful invasion of imperial territory would devastate agriculture, and disrupt trade and industry.

The capture and/or destruction of cities meant that conquered Iranian populations could be killed off, displaced or enslaved. These outcomes could also wreak havoc on the Sassanian economy. While the empire, like Rome, certainly had its share of diplomats, it was ultimately the Sassanian military that ensured the security and well-being of its economy and people.

The Iranian economic situation was dire in the early third century when the Sassanians seized the throne. The preceding Parthian dynasty had suffered a series of serious defeats by Roman armies with Ctesiphon having been sacked three times, in 116, 165 and 198 CE by Emperor Trajan (r. 98–117 CE), General Gaius Avidius Cassius (briefly emperor in 175) and Emperor Septemius Severus (r. 193–211) respectively. These defeats had inflicted severe economic blows upon the Parthian realm. In 198, for example, the forces of Septemius Severus had emptied much of Ctesiphon's treasury, hauling its contents off to Rome and thereby inflicting a crushing blow to the Iranian economy. Put simply, Iranian (Parthian) military weaknesses had resulted in battlefield defeats against the Romans, leading to negative consequences for the economy.

The Sassanians realized the importance of a strong spah for protecting their growing economic prosperity,[20] especially by the time of Khosrow I Anushirvan (r. 531–579 CE). As noted by Lukonin, 'the large clans, the Shahs of the cities as well as large segments of the nobles, required a powerful government that was capable of dominating Mesopotamia, the heart of Eiran-Shahr, thereby revitalizing the economic life of the entire nation.'[21] The spah was responsible for defending a vast economic zone resting upon territories that were endowed with rich soil, agricultural fertility, and abundant water supplies sustaining dense concentrations of highly (economically, intellectually and technically) talented populations. These regions which faced the Romano-Byzantines as well as the Arabs to the southwest were the Sassanian provinces of Khuzestan (ancient Elamysis), Mayshan (near the Persian Gulf outlet of the Tigris and Euphrates rivers), Ashuristan (situated roughly between Tigris and Euphrates rivers), Garmakan (south of Zab river), Hedayab (or Adiabene between the Greater and Lesser Zab rivers), and Arbayastan (or Mesopotamia on the upper Euphrates region). The spah's military role in defending this vital region against foreign aggression was critical to the empire's foreign trade and economic stability.

There were other critical trade routes apart from those in Mesopotamia and the western provinces that required the spah's protection. The Silk Route meandering through Central Asia was also of critical importance to Ctesiphon. Khosrow I had endeavoured to dominate the Silk Route, which was also coveted by the Gok Turks of Central Asia. It was this economic rivalry that led to the decisive confrontations between the spah and the Gok Turks in Central Asia. As noted by Tashkari, '[T]he critical importance of the Silk Route obliged the Sassanians to engage in hostile relations against the nomadic tribes of Central Asia.'[22] The Sassanian and Roman empires competed in the Silk Road trade, especially in its western terminus in the Near East. Mashkoor has noted that Sassano-Roman military confrontations were attributable in part to each party's ambition to dominate the Silk Road trade.[23] The spah's wars in Lazica against the Romano-

Byzantines in the Caucasus in 541–561 CE were also fought in part for economic reasons; Khosrow I was endeavouring to secure access to the Iberian (modern Georgia) coastline's lucrative Black Sea trade. The importance of the spah for the Sassanian economy is perhaps best summarized by Tajbakhsh: '[T]he expansion of farming and the thriving of the economy is directly related to the security afforded and power wielded by the central government with this security being created under the shield of a powerful military.'[24] The empire's construction of long walls along the Causcasian and Central Asian frontiers, for example, was undertaken not only to defend against invaders but to also protect economic assets, especially important trade routes, metropolitan centres and agricultural zones. A robust economy was also vital to the state's ability to maintain a powerful standing army.

Socio-Cultural Factors

Jalali has cited three social factors as having been critical in the formation of the spah.[25] The first of these was Iran's multi-varied population featuring a diverse range of languages and religions. The spah's role was to enforce Ctesiphon's centralized system of government and ensure that Iran's diverse regions and provinces would remain united. The Sassanians refrained from the type of loose autonomy system that had existed under Parthian rule.

The second socio-cultural role of the spah cited by Jalali entailed the enforcement of a legally consistent system of law and order across all the empire's provinces. The spah's role was critical in allowing the Sassanian judicial system to function for the empire's citizenry throughout the realm.[26] This was part of the Sassanian Empire's attempts at centralization; under the previous Parthians, legal systems and courts had been characterized by regional diversity.[27]

The third role of the spah was to preserve the culture of Iran against foreign invaders, or as Bayani states: '[T]he role of the Sepahiyan [military personnel] was to act as a gigantic shield for Western Asian civilization by defending her against the barbarian tribes.'[28] Interestingly, the Romans and succeeding Romano-Byzantines were not seen as 'barbarians' but instead as more of a civilizational equal of the Iranian realms, a sentiment immortalized by the message of King Narseh (r. 293–302 CE) to Galerius: 'The whole human race knows that the Roman and Persian kingdoms resemble two great luminaries, and that, like a man's two eyes, they ought mutually to adorn and illustrate each other, and not in the extremity of their wrath to seek rather each other's destruction.'[29]

A fundamental role of the Sassanian knight was to protect the culture and civilization of Persia against destruction at the hands of barbarian invaders (Chapter 15). The king was also the military defender of the faith. King Narseh, for example, identified himself as 'the righteous defender of the Iranian gods, the traditions of the ancestors and the rights of the Iranian [Persian and Parthian] aristocrats'.[30] Later Sassanian kings are seen extending their role as military defender towards not just the Aryan pantheon but also that of the Christian church, as exemplified by King Hormuzd IV (r. 579–590 CE).

McDonough has also noted the Sassanian monarchy's sense of defending the Aryan settlers and culture of the realm;[31] the term 'Aryan' corresponding to speakers of the Iranian branch of the Indo-European linguistic family, mainly Parthian and Sassanian Pahlavi (Middle Persian) and other Iranic vernaculars.[32] The Aryan identity was to be extended to the Armenians who already had strong ties to the Iranic world (notably their admixture with the Parthian nobility) in cultural-linguistic terms and (especially) in the military domain (Chapters 6 and 19).[33] Nevertheless, the Sassanian Empire was characterized by a very high level of non-Aryan ethnic, linguistic and religious diversity and sought to synthesize its (Aryan and non-Aryan) subjects into the Eiran-Shahr. Hence many of the cultural and intellectual accomplishments of the empire's non-Aryan subjects were to be supported by the state and were therefore entitled to military protection against outside (military) aggression. Thus, for example, the Sassanians extended their protection to the Jewish sages of the fifth century CE who compiled the so-called Babylonian Talmud and to Neo-Platonic scholars expelled by Justinian I from the Academy of Athens, Nestorian and anti-Chalcedonian Christian leaders and even Christian intellectuals who were advisors to the top levels of Sassanian leadership.[34] This facet of Sassanian rule may explain why the spah continued to attract the highly professional Christian Armenian *naxarar* knights well into the last days of the dynasty (Chapter 12).

Chapter 2

Organization: Military Titles and Recruitment

The *Letter of Tansar* makes clear that there were two main divisions in the Sassanian army (or spah) by stating that 'the military, that is to say … the fighting men, of whom there are two groups, cavalry and foot-soldiers. Within them are differences of rank and function.'[1] The *Dinkard* corroborates the *Letter of Tansar* by noting that 'in the estate of warriors there are two groups: the cavalry and the infantry, and other military functions'.[2] Promotion in the Sassanian spah was based on military experience and merit, an observation corroborated by the Islamic-era *Al-Siyasat al-Ammiyyah*, which states that 'another good rule is the one according to which nobody should be promoted to a superior rank before going through inferior ranks. In this respect the Persians have abundantly been praised.'[3]

This chapter provides an overview of the key military commands of the spah. Important titles, such as the *eiran-ambaraghbad*, are discussed in Chapter 10. The other chapters of this text will focus on the various branches of the spah (cavalry, infantry, elephant corps, etc.) and on tactics, ceremonies, training, the prosecution of war, military architecture and siege warfare.

Organization: Overview of Pahlavi Terms for 'Army' and other Military Terms

The Sassanian military machine is most often identified as *spah* in the Pahlavi texts (*sepah* in modern Persian). The Old Persian and Avestan term is *spada*, however the term *kara* was also used to designate the Achaemenid military. The root term *kara-* was to persist after the fall of the Achaemenids and survive into the Pahlavi lexicon of the Sassanian military. This became *kara-wan*, which is 'military column' or 'troops on the march' in Parthian (more specifically Manichean) Pahlavi. However by Sassanian times the military meaning of *karawan* had given way to the non-military meaning of what is popularly known as the 'caravan' in which a group of people travel together.[4]

While *spah* is used in this text to designate the Sassanian military machine, there were actually a number of other terms that also signified 'army', 'military power' or 'armed forces'. One such term was *zor*; in modern Persian *zoor* translates roughly as 'power' or 'strength'.[5] Other terms of this type were *lashkar* (which in modern Persian designates a regular military division) and even *asp ud mard* ('horse and man') which appears to have referred to an army. The term *lashkar* was to also enter the Armenian military lexicon as 'army' by the fifth century CE. There was even a designation for the armies of adversaries, which were identified as *hen*, which was a derivation of the Avestan *haena*. Interestingly, *hen* was to also enter the Armenian military lexicon bearing not just the meaning 'army of the enemy, but also 'pirate' and 'thief'. There are also numerous terms in the Pahlavi military lexicon for 'battle' and/or 'war' such as *ardig, karezar, jang, pad-razm, nibard, zambag* and *paykar*.[6]

Organization of Spah Military Units

The spah based its organizational model upon the *vasht-drafsh-gund* system of its Parthian predecessor. The *vasht*[7] designated a small detachment of troops commanded by the *vasht-salar*.[8] The *drafsh* (lit. banner) was a larger unit of possibly up to 1,000 troops.[9] Each drafsh featured its own unique heraldry and banners, these varying in accordance with its clan of origin.[10]

The *gund* was the divisional designation for the Sassanian military with a possible size of 12,000 troops.[11] The term *gund* appears to have originally meant 'regiment' or 'legion', but in Pahlavi texts it can also mean 'army'.[12] In command of the gund was the *gund-salar*.[13] The same term has also entered the Armenian military lexicon.[14] It is possible that the Parthian gund of General Surena in the Battle of Carrhae in 53 BCE numbered 10,000 troops. The gund-salar command is attested to well into late Sassanian times during the reign of Khosrow II (591–628 CE)[15] with elite gund detachments, such as the 4,000-man Gund Shahanshah regiment of General Rustam Farrokhzad being present at the Battle of Qadissiyah (Chapter 6) in 637 CE.[16]

Interestingly, the gund-salar title survived for some time after the fall of the Sassanian Empire in 651 CE. Tabari writes about a certain Mahuya, the *marzban* (see below) of Merv who came to visit Imam Ali (660–661 CE), the Ummayd caliph at the time, to reconfirm a treaty that had already been arranged by Mahuya and an Arab general named Ibn Amir.[17] The imam then wrote an official letter to the *dehkans* (Chapter 19) and savaran(Chapter 6) in which he referred to the *jundsallarin*,[18] which is the Arabicized plural version of the term gund-salar.

The hazar designation. *Hazar* (thousand) is a Sassanian military term. The ancient Achaemenids employed the decimal system for organizing their military but this does not prove that the Sassanians did so as well. While no direct evidence of a Sassanian decimal organization system has been uncovered, Nöldeke has suggested that such a system did exist based upon the Sassanian title of *hazarmard* (lit. 'thousand-man').[19] Another similar expression is that of the *hazarpet* (commander of 1,000). The Pahlavi term *-pet* is derived from Avestan *paiti*, which is *bad* in modern Persian. Pourdavood defines these terms (*paiti, pet*) variously as 'commander', 'greater', 'chief' and even 'endowed with god-like qualities'.[20] The hazarmard or hazarpet would often be selected from among the best *sarhang* (colonel) of a particular gund; this title was considered to be a great honour within the spah, as it signalled the warrior's military merit and prowess in battle. It would not be uncommon for several hazarmards or hazarpets to be serving in the spah while on military campaign.[21] The term *pet* also entered the Armenian military lexicon.

It is noteworthy that the ancient Achaemenids did have the military term *hazarpati* or *hazarpatish* to designate the commander of 1,000 troops who could also be the court's master of ceremonies.[22] It is possible that the hazar system had a direct parallel in the Parthian military as well. Lucian's report in the second century CE, for example, mentions the distinct *draconis* battle standard under which 1,000 warriors (presumably knights?) would have fought.[23] Lucian's report is consistent with the report of 1,000 knights having been present at the Battle of Carrhae in 53 BCE, which suggests that the Parthians organized their forces into distinct units of 1,000 warriors (either horse archers or armoured knights).[24]

The importance of the *hazar* designation can be seen in the early days of the Sassanians with inscriptions of Shapur I identifying a certain Babak/Pabag as the *hazaruft* (chiliarch).[25] The term evidently had acquired a 'higher' meaning in the earlier Sassanian era, which is to say that it meant more than just a commander of 1,000 men. Mehr-Narseh, a high-level minister of Yazdegird I (r. 399–420 CE), for example, was known as the hazarpet of Iran (Eire-an) and An-Iran (An-Eirean).[26] The *hazar* designation then appears to have been 'downgraded' back to the designation of commander of 1,000 by the latter days of the Sassanian dynasty. One example is a certain Gusdanaspes who commanded 1,000 men in the army of General Shahrbaraz in the early seventh century CE. This also suggests a decimal system for the spah (or at least for elite cavalry units). Dinawari, among other Islamic writers, appears to corroborate the hazar designation when he describes Khosrow II seeking refuge with Emperor Maurice (r. 582–602 CE) against Bahram Chobin, who had seized the throne of the Sassanian Empire in 590 CE.[27] Dinawari notes how Maurice agrees to Khosrow II's request and provides him with a force which included 'ten of the Hazarmard'.[28] So important was the *hazar* title that it actually superseded that of the *aswaran-sardar* or *framandar savaran* ('commander of the savaran'; see below).[29]

Numerical status of the spah. Estimates of the numerical strength of the professional core of the Sassanian spah vary considerably depending on primary sources consulted. Alexander Severus asserted in his 'victory speech' to the Roman senate on 25 September 233 CE, that his forces had killed '120,000 of their [Sassanian] cavalry'.[30] It seems likely, however, that this figure is a gross exaggeration, especially as it is cited in the *Historia Augusta*, the credibility of which has been called into doubt by Western scholars.[31] As well, Iran's smaller population base in comparison to Rome's militated against Iran being able to field such large numbers of professional cavalry. This is consistent with Tabari's report that the spah had, at maximum, between 60,000 and 70,000 professional troops (savaran and Dailamite infantry) in 578 CE (250 years after Severus' speech).[32]

Upper Military Levels of the Spah
Pigulevskaya has ranked the three most important military titles of the spah in the following order: *argbad* (most important), followed by *arteshtaran-salar* and *spahbod*.[33] The functions of these commands are discussed in more detail below.

Note that the role of other top commanders responsible for the spah's logistics and support system (*eiran-ambaraghbad, akhorbad* and *stor-bizishk*), legal system (*zendanigh* and *spah-dadvar*) as well as ceremonial and prestige titles (e.g. *shap-sheraz, yalan-bad,* etc.) are addressed in Chapters 10, 11 and 15.

Argbad. Noldeke has defined *argbad* as the commander of a region;[34] other scholars contend that it means 'supreme tax collector'.[35] In Pahlavi however, the term *argbad* is literally translated as the commander or keeper of a castle or fortress (*arg*) or 'citadel chief'.[36] The noun *arg* has endured into modern or New Persian and applied to locales such as the *Arg-e-Bam* (castle of Bam), which was built in 500 BC and ravaged by an earthquake in December 2003.

In a sense Noldeke's definition is at least partly correct, as the argbad was not only the commander of a castle but also the territory around it. Hence, all other troops outside of that fortress but within the territorial boundaries of the fortress' jurisdiction were under the command of the argbad. Thus, the argbad possessed formidable military authority. The first Sassanian military leader with the argbad designation was Ardashir I Babakan, the founder of the dynasty.[37] More specifically, Ardashir's father Babak, with the support of the Bazarganian clan, had succeeded in securing for him the coveted military command of argbad for the Darabgird fortress.[38] The regal origins of the term help explain why it became the most prestigious military title within the spah.[39] Western scholarship notes the importance of this office by the fact that the argbad 'appears several times as the authorized representative of the king'.[40] There were other high notables besides the argbad, one of these being the *bedakhsh*, which has been translated as a 'viceroy' or 'grand vizier'.[41]

An office similar to but lower in stature than the argbad was the *dizbed* (commander of the fortress). The Shapur inscription at the Kaabe Zartosht, for example, makes mention of a courtier of Shapur I named Tir-Mehr who was the dizbed of a locality named Shahrgerd, located near modern-day Kirkuk[42] in Iraqi Kurdistan.

Arteshtaran-salar. The Middle Persian (Pahlavi) military designation *arteshtar* (modern Persian: *arteshdar*) generally translates as 'miles' or 'soldier/combatant'.[43] The origin of the term is of interest in that it is of old Iranic Avestan origin: *rathaesta* (lit. war champion/hero, warrior)[44] which points to a common Indo-European origin with Sanskrit's (linguistically close to Avestan) *rathendha* 'charioteer'.[45] There appears to be an equivalent in Old (Achaemenid) Persian as seen in the term *ratesda* which appears in the Persepolis Tablets.[46] *Rathaesta* is also the designation of the second class of proto-Iranian (Aryan) society, the warrior elites (following from the first who are the magi or priests).[47] The prestige of the term endured into the Sassanian era, when the Middle Persian term had become *arteshtar*.[48] However, Sundermann has argued that the term itself did not have a practical application in Sassanian society; it was only the office of the arteshtaran-salar (lit. commander of warriors) which was of prime practical (military) importance.[49] Specifically, the arteshtaran-salar was more important that the *eiran-spahbod* (see below) but below that of the *argbad*.[50]

Bearers of the arteshtaran-salar title hailed from the empire's top families; one notable example being Kardu, who was the son of the empire's *vuzurg-framandar* (grand vizier) Mehr-Narseh in the fifth century CE.[51]

The term *salar* (commander) also requires some examination. This can broadly be translated as 'officer'; however it is often used in the second part of the spah's compound military titles. Salar however could also designate non-military commands such as the *andemankaran-salar* (master of ceremonies), the *vastryoshan-salar* (master/director-general of taxes/taxation), the *dehsalar* (master/head of the village), or the *khvan-salar* (master of the royal cuisine/kitchen).[52] Interestingly, Foss has determined that the term entered the Greek lexicon as *sellarious* during the Sassanian conquest and occupation of Byzantine Egypt during the 620s CE.[53] Another military title that requires mention is the *ham-harz* (adjutant),[54] which was possibly the equivalent of modern day non-commissioned officer. The term is of Parthian origin and has entered the Armenian military lexicon as *ham-a-harz*.

As noted by Shahbazi, 'with the revival of Kiyani Pahlavan names in the Sassanian era, a commander-in-chief position with full powers known as the arteshtaran-salar was created in accordance with the terminologies of the Avesta [Zoroastrian religious text]'.[55] As a result the arteshtaran-salar was to transform into a ceremonial and religious post bereft of true military function.[56] The office of the arteshtaran-salar continues to appear in the spah during the reign of Kavad (r. 488–496 and 498–531 CE), with a certain Siyavash who held this title during Kavad's time.[57] Finally, Tafazzoli has noted that the arteshtaran-salar is the same designation as the *spahbodan-spahbod* (general of generals).[58] The latter has also noted that the office of the arteshtaran-salar was not eliminated as a result of the reforms of Khosrow I Anushiravan (r. 531–579 CE), but was simply stripped of some of its functions.[59]

Eiran-spahbod. The office of the eiran-spahbod was similar to the arteshtaran-salar without the ceremonial-religious aspects characteristic of the latter. Although this office was unique to the Sassanian spah, the root of the term is found in older Iranic languages. In Old Persian (of the Achaemenid era), for example, there is a term known as *spadhapati* followed by Middle Persian (Pahlavi) *spahbod* for which an Armenian variation, *sparapet*, is also found. Spahbod is the Iranic equivalent of 'general' or 'army chief', making this person a high military official.[60] The eiran-spahbod[61] was the commander in chief of all troops of the spah. As head of all national security affairs, the eiran-spahbod was responsible for the efficient distribution of the armed forces throughout Iran to ensure the maximization of the empire's foreign defence requirements as well as internal security.[62]

Given the critical importance of this office, it was the king who selected his best and most trusted military commander for the eiran-spahbod post.[63] The prestige of the eiran-spahbod was highlighted by the fact that his arrival into a fortress, barracks or any other military establishment would be announced with various drums and *zornay* musical instruments.[64] The eiran-spahbod could also be the minister of war; however, when the king took command of the spah in time of war, the eiran-spahbod would act as the military chief of staff.[65] The king also authorized the eiran-spahbod to negotiate peace terms with adversaries upon the conclusion of battles and/or wars.[66] The eiran-spahbod also commanded all provincial and district forces and assigned armies to the provincial and district commanders. As well, he was entitled to partake in meetings between the top minsters of state, especially in the formation of the war council (Chapter 8) prior to the outbreak of hostilities.[67] The office appears to have reached the apogee of its prestige during the reign of Yazdegird II (r. 438–457) when the eiran-spahbod was ranked as the highest (military and civilian) official of the realm.[68] As a result, the eiran-spahbod was entitled to a large share of captured enemy supplies and booty in case of victory.[69]

The *Buzurgan* and the *Azadan*

The best-quality cavalry and top-level commanders typically hailed from the upper classes. These were known as the *vuzurgan* or (New Persian) *buzurgan*, which would literally translate as 'grandees, magnates'.[70] Lukonin cites these as 'heads of the noble clans, semi-independent rulers of small provinces, and … persons in state service'.[71] The most distinguished of the buzurgan were of course the members of the Sassanian royal house, with the other most prominent clans being the Karen, Suren, Guiw, Mehran, Spandiyadh and Aspah-bad. These were all of Parthian origin with the Aspah-bad, Suren and Karen adding the suffix '-Pahlav' to their clan names (i.e. Suren-Pahlav), evidently to highlight their Arsacid heritage. When the Sassanians first seized the throne of Iran in the 220s CE, the buzurgan joined them, thereby adding their provinces to the emerging Sassanian realms. Examples include the Karen (rulers of much of Media), Mehran (rulers of Rayy, near modern Tehran), Spandiyadh (rulers of Nahavand near Kurdistan) and Suren (rulers of Saka-istan in southeast Iran) who joined their realms to Persis in the new Iranian confederation of the Sassanians. Mention is also made in earlier Sassanian sources of the noble clans of Persis, most notably the Farrekhans, with other noble clans of Parthian origin being the Varaz and Andigan in the court of Ardashir I.[72]

The military role of the buzurgan or upper nobles was highly significant. One example is that of the *suren*, who traced their distinguished military tradition to a Parthian military leader of the title who destroyed the invading Roman forces of Marcus Lucinius Crassus at Carrhae in 53 BCE. Another suren played a major role in the operations that defeated another Roman invasion of Iran in 363 CE (Chapter 9). Another example of the buzurgan origins of the spah's top level commanders is Bahram Chobin of the Mehran clan, who was instrumental in defeating a massive Turco-Hephthalite invasion in 588 CE (Chapter 12).

District and Regional Commands

As noted previously, the spah was often faced with military threats of invasion from the northeast, north, the southwest and the west. The spah's military solutions for these threats was to (1) build a series of defence walls and fortifications along these frontiers (Chapter 13); (2) settle warlike tribes in close proximity to the borders; and (3) assign regional commands such as the *marzban* and *paygospan* offices. For internal security duties for towns and villages throughout the realm, the spah entrusted the *tirbad* commands to supervise them.

Marzban. The *marzban* is defined by Mahamedi as 'one who protects the land frontier' or 'margrave'.[73] The term is literally translated as 'guardian/warden' (*ban*) of the borders/marches (*marz*). This leads to the conclusion that the marzban was responsible for the empire's frontier defence, an interpretation that is consistent with the descriptions of this post of a prime Islamic-era source, Yaghoubi.[74] The marzban was also responsible for a number of other military functions. When war became imminent, the marzban was responsible for the mobilization of military forces within his jurisdiction and for deploying these to join the main body of the spah. With the outbreak of war, the marzban would act as one of the spah's military commanders subordinate to his region's respective spahbod.[75] In peacetime, the marzban remained responsible for the supervision of those troops in his area of jurisdiction but could also be delegated to bureaucratic duties as determined by the state.[76]

Interestingly, there appear to have also been a number of 'lesser marzbans' with their own unique titles. Examples include the *shahab* in Azerbaijan,[77] the *kanarang*[78] in the Khorasan region facing Central Asia, as well as the *bedaksh* in Georgia and Armenia.[79]

Paygospan. The functions of the paygospan have proven challenging to decipher given the variance of source citations and interpretations in the secondary sources. What is fairly certain is that the paygospan was a prestigious title bestowed by the king himself. In general, it would appear that the paygospan was initially responsible for running the state's affairs in their respective regions.[80] Confusion with the term may have to do with the fact that the paygospan worked alongside the spahbod in their respective regions, leading to varying interpretation of the paygospan office. Wiesehofer, for example, contends that the paygospan was the military commander of a province.[81] This is not altogether different from Yaghoubi, who interprets the paygospan as 'the one who drives enemies away from the homelands'.[82] By the end of the Sassanian era the paygospan office appears to have undergone changes in its function, sometimes even resembling that of the marzban, as in the case of the marzban of Isfahan being referred to as paygospan.[83]

The changes were most apparent at the conclusion of the reforms of the sixth century CE (Chapter 3), which according to Adontz resulted in:

> the separation of military and civilian power, the padhghospan serving as the instrument of civilian authority, and the spahbadh of the military ... The offices of padhghospan and spahbadh may in effect be compared to those of prefectus praetorio and magister militum in the Roman Empire ... Such a similarity between the divisions of the Roman and Persian Empires can hardly be fortuitous; there is evidently some connection.[84]

Adontz's observation may suggest that the Sassanian high command had possibly been studying the Roman system of military and civilian administration and factored these into their military reforms. Rome and Sassanian Persia certainly 'borrowed' military ideas from each other; for example, the Iranian savaran cavalry influenced the formation of the Roman *clibanarius* (Chapter 19) and the spah adopted Roman siege technology (Chapter 13).

Tirbad. The term *tir* is the Iranic word for 'arrow' or 'missile', and as the term *tirbad* suggests, this is the designation for the leader of a contingent of archers. Nevertheless, *tirbad* was also a regional command term, albeit at a much lower military rank that all those mentioned in this chapter (except perhaps the paighan-salar, discussed in Chapter 7). Tirbad units were often assigned to the empire's villages to act as government security forces. The combat role of tirbad units will be more fully discussed in Chapter 5.

The *Aswaran-Sardar* or *Framandar savaran*

The *aswaran-sardar* (commander of the cavalry)[85] was one of the most highly prestigious and coveted titles in the spah. The meaning of the term *aswar* (cavalry),[86] however, was to change (or broaden) in its military functions during the Sassanian dynasty. By the latter Sassanian era, aswaran had come to also mean 'officers of the army'.[87] The term *savaran* is thus used in this text to specifically designate the elite cavalry units from the dynasty's earliest days to its end.

As the spah's elite cavalry units hailed from the empire's upper clans, the commander of the cavalry corps was inevitably nominated from these same elite clans.[88] Known also as the *framandar savaran*,[89] the aswaran-sardar was so highly respected for his military acumen that he could sometimes be assigned to the office of regional spahbod. This helps explain why commanders of the savaran corps were often placed in command of other non-cavalry units of the spah.[90] The role of the spah cavalry (tactics, various elite units such as the *javidan* (*zhayedan*), *pushtighban*, etc.) will be discussed further in Chapter 6.

Other Military and Non-Military Officials Accompanying the Spah

When war was imminent, the Sassanian spah would convene a council of war (Chapter 8) which also included numbers of non-military leaders of the empire, notably the *eiran-dabirbod* and the *mobadan mobad*, as well as other military offices such as the *dezhban*.

Dezhban. Another key military post in the spah was the *dezhban*. Broadly speaking *dezhban* means 'guardian'; however the precise meaning of the term in Middle Persian (Pahlavi) is more complex. In the Sassanian era, military officials were designated to supervise the efficiency and conduct of the spah's various divisions. Firdowsi's *Shahname* reports the existence of this office as far back as the reign of Ardashir I.[91] The primary role of the dezhban officers when accompanying each gund division in times of war was to oversee the efficiency of the troops and military camps[92] (Chapter 11). The dezhban was also responsible for ensuring that the troops would not mistreat non-combatant civilians. Hormuzd IV, for example, is reputed to have given specific instructions for his troops to avoid harming farmers and disrupting their works.[93] If a soldier was found guilty of having committed crimes against civilians, the dezhban was entrusted with meting out punishment for such offences.[94] The role of the dezhbans with respect to desertions will be further explained in Chapter 11.

Eiran-dabirbod. Among the important officials who accompanied the gunds of the spah during campaigns were the *dabirs*. The term *dabir* is roughly the equivalent of scribe, recorder, writer, etc. In practice the dabir was much more than a scribe, being more of a high-ranking advisor who was also a scribe. Middle Persian and Parthian writings in the Dura Europos synagogue, for example, cite several dabirs being present among the distinguished visitors to the locale.[95]

According to Islamic-era historian Al-Jahshiyari, the dabir would be assigned by the king to the spah during its campaigns and given a chief advisory position among the field military commanders.[96] The dabir's level of importance was such that a gund would halt and deploy under his advisement.[97] Interestingly, critical statements by the chief military commander in the field (especially important news, proclamations, notifications and warnings) would be recorded by the dabir, which would then make the command 'official'.[98] The dabir was also entrusted with recording the details and outcomes of battles. This was of course of prime importance as records of recent and past battles would form an archive of critical military information. More specifically, archives of past battles recorded by the dabirs would allow the spah and the war council in particular to objectively assess past military performance against their adversaries (Romano-Byzantines, Central Asian warriors, etc.), which would facilitate more objective battle planning in anticipation of the next war.

Candidates for the office of dabir attended an academy known as the *dabirestan* and were selected as dabirs on the basis of objective examinations conducted by their principal instructors.[99] Academy graduates would be designated either 'scribe of the army' or 'secretary of the army' (*gund-dabir* or *spah-dabir*). These titles are attested to as far back as the time of Yazdegird I (r. 399–420 CE)[100] and continued into late Sassanian times when, for example, a certain dabir known as Farrokh was ordered by Khosrow I to supervise the payment of pension funds to the children of slain warriors.[101] Dabirestan graduates with lower examination scores and aptitude, however, were assigned to the *kardar* (high official) offices.

Dabirs were accorded a number of important privileges on par with the upper nobles, knights and priesthood, one of these being exemption from taxes.[102] Dabirs could also be assigned the task of governing important metropolitan centres, one such case being a governor of the empire's capital Ctesiphon being addressed as a *dabirbod* during the reign of Khosrow I.[103] Khosrow I even appointed a dabir named Behrawan to the post of military chancery as the equivalent of the modern-day minister of defence or minister of war.[104] In short, men of learning were held in very high esteem by the Sassanian spah.

An example of the dabir's recordings can be seen in the late Sassanian era in the context of general Bahram Chobin's rebellion against the Sassanian dynasty at Ctesiphon. Bahram Chobin, who rebelled against Khosrow II's father Hormuzd IV, had marched towards Ctesiphon through Rayy, being joined by many savaran veterans in western Iran.[105] In response, the nobles of Ctesiphon conducted a coup d'état by slaying Hormuzd and placing his son Khosrow II 'Parviz' on the throne.[106] Following the failure of Khosrow's attempts to negotiate with Bahram, Khosrow and his army attempted to confront the general in the vicinity of Holwan. But no actual battle took place as the bulk of Khosrow II's forces simply defected to Bahram. Islamic-era historian Dinawari cites a certain Yazdak, Khosrow II's dabir, who is said to have recorded that 'the army of Khosrow Parviz all defected and joined Bahram ... none stayed with Khosrow Parviz except his uncles Bindoe and Bestam, Hormuzgorabzin, Nakharjan, and Shapur the son of Abrkan'.[107]

The mobadan mobad. The Zoroastrian magi were well integrated into the political and military machinery of the Sassanian Empire.[108] Leading all of the empire's *mobad* (head/chief priest) religious personnel was the *mobadan mobad*. The importance of the mobad within the military leadership is attested to in the symbolic presence of the Zoroastrian deity Ahura-Mazda in the investiture ceremonies of Ardashir I (r. 226–241 CE) at Naghshe Rustam, Shapur I (r. 241–272 CE) at Nagshe Rajab and Khosrow II (r. 590–628 CE) at Taghe Bostan. The military-theology link is highlighted by the Ahura-Mazda figures at Nagshe Rustam and Nagshe Rajab being depicted as savaran knights. Interestingly, there is also a depiction of the Iranian goddess of fertility Anahita at the investiture of King Narseh in the late third or early fourth century CE.[109] Representations of the mobad can be seen in locales such as the fourth bas-relief at Nagshe Rajab[110] and at Nagshe Rustam. In the latter locale there is a depiction of what is most likely Mobad Kartir (standing with two other courtiers) to the right of Bahram II (r. 276–293 CE).[111] Kartir, who was the mobad for Shapur I (r. 241–272 CE) and his successors Hormuzd I (272–273 CE), Bahram I (273–276 CE) and Bahram II,[112] achieved increasingly important titles during his long career, one of these being the *hamshahr mobad od dadvar* (head/chief priest and adjudicator/judge of the realm/empire).[113] By the fourth century CE, the rising importance of the mobad function led it to be placed below that of the office of *hazarbod*.[114]

Abbas and Imam-Shushtari cite the practice of assigning mobads as 'spiritual' supervisors for the savaran: 'Ardashir I would assign a Mobad ... to every unit of 1,000 savaran ... this Mobad was to observe the merit of the savaran and was aware of their boldness and bravery and to bring these to the attention of the king'.[115]

The above description places the mobad in a capacity that was more than just a spiritual advisor or chaplain for the savaran unit. The mobad was in a sense 'ranking' the martial ardour of the troops on the battlefield. This required the mobads to accompany savaran units to the battlefield in order to directly observe their combat performance. It is also possible that the mobads could have chosen to take part in combat, especially if this helped stiffen morale against determined enemies such as the Romano-Byzantines.

Mobads are shown in Sassanian reliefs depicting the triumphant Sassanian kings. One of these is a mobad believed to be Kartir in the relief of Shapur I at

Nagshe Rajab; another mobad figure (also possibly Kartir) appears in Shapur I's military triumph scene at Bishapur. These depictions highlight the importance of the mobads within the spah: it is notable that in both of these reliefs, the mobad figure stands in the presence of the king and his savaran knights with their broadswords.

Recruitment of Auxiliary Units

As noted previously, the spah's core of elite cavalry derived from the nobility and (after Khosrow's reforms) the *dehkans* (landed gentry) of the 'lesser nobility'. The empire also expended prodigious efforts towards recruiting the best possible fighters into the spah, both from within the realm and outside its frontiers. Warriors from within the Iranian cultural and/or historical realm or Eirean hailed from the empire's various provinces. Warriors recruited from *Un-Eirean* (or *An-Eirean*) hailed from regions not considered to be part of the cultural and historical realm. The bulk of these recruits acted as cavalry support for the spah (Chapter 7), with northern Iranian warriors being especially prized as excellent close-quarters infantry fighters. Note that by the end of Khosrow I's reign, the spah had established military colonies along the Central Asian and Caucasus frontiers, and along the strong defensive walls in those regions[116] (discussed more fully in Chapter 13).

Benefits of recruiting auxiliaries. There were two benefits for the spah in recruiting auxiliary units for the regular armies: (1) increased martial prowess, and (2) acquiring warriors who may otherwise have joined enemy armies (especially those of Rome).[117] The first of these entailed the injection of 'fresh blood' into the veins of the spah, or more specifically bringing in warriors with new modes of fighting, equipment and martial ardour. This was in turn advantageous to the spah in two distinct ways. First, the spah's leadership would be able to examine new and different weapons systems and modes of warfare. Second, the recruitment of brave and resilient warriors would help elevate the martial ardour of the 'regular' armed forces, especially on the battlefield. Auxiliary troops could also become more motivated as battlefield fighters, especially when promised rewards of titles and estates by the Sassanian leadership. Another benefit of recruiting formidable martial peoples was in being able to channel their martial energies to the benefit of the empire. In this regard, the *Siyasat-Nameh* of Nizam ol-Molk noted the following:[118] '[A]ll of these seek to outdo one another, and since these have been the rule of the warrior peoples, they all endeavour hard and seek a good name. Therefore when their hand goes to the weapon, they shall take no step back until they have shattered the enemy army.'

The second benefit of recruitment for the spah, acquisition of warriors who might otherwise join the enemy, was definitely strategic. In addition, the acquisition of these troops helped alleviate the empire's chronic shortage of quality military manpower. The more of these the empire could recruit on behalf of the spah, the less likely they were to augment the numbers of dangerous military rivals such as the Romano-Byzantines. Such sentiments were duly expressed by

Khosrow Anoushirvan with respect to numbers of Khazar Turkic warriors who were seeking to gain military service with the spah. According to the *Raftarnameye Anoushirvan*:[119]

> [I]n the 37th year of my reign as monarch, four groups of the Khazar Turks each of whom had their own king ... requested us to allow each of them with their retinues to fall under our service and for them to undertake any task we demand of them, and to not take to heart [forgive?] all that happened prior to my reign ... I [Khosrow Anoushrivan] saw this benefit in accepting them: one, their resilience and insistence, second, I feared arousing their animosity and thus turning them to the Caesar [Romano-Byzantine Emperors] or other kings.

The above report makes clear that Khosrow I realized the danger of alienating those Khazars who had petitioned to enter service as auxiliaries for the spah. It is thus ironic that Khosrow II failed in his diplomacy to gain the military allegiance of the Khazar Turks, who indeed forged an alliance with Emperor Heraclius, with disastrous results for the Sassanian Empire (Chapter 16).

One liability, especially with recruits from non-Iranian regions, was that they were unfamiliar with the spah's system of methodical military organization. These types of warriors fought in the traditional fluid and rapid cavalry tactics, which hailed from the steppe cavalry traditions of Central Asia and Eastern Europe. These skills were of course greatly valued by the Sassanians, who sought to preserve them within the battle order of the spah. The spah's solution for doing so was to often designate the most capable warriors of such units as official military delegates and liaisons. While it is not clear if such officers were allowed to take part in military councils before the onset of wars (Chapter 8), their military performance is highly indicative of the successful battlefield coordination that was achieved between them and the regular spah units. Below is a brief over-view of the general categories of recruitment (Arab auxiliary forces are discussed in full in Chapter 7).

Guidelines for recruiting and retaining auxiliaries. The *Sirat Anoushirvan*[120] provides six general guidelines for successful recruitment of non-Iranian auxiliary warriors. The first is for the shahanshah to do his utmost to cultivate the friend-ship of the warrior group. It was understood that recruits won over by friendship would fight harder for the empire than those who were forced to fight by the spah. Second, as noted previously, the Sassanians offered each group military service within the spah, both alongside regular spah units as well as in fortresses as garrison troops (Chapter 13). Third, the Sassanians ensured that each unit of the auxiliary forces would be assigned a regular *sardar* (officer) of the spah. This sardar would address the aforestated issues of supervision and coordination with the spah.

The fourth guideline involved the transfer of rewards and payments and was viewed with special regard. This was because a system had to be implemented to ensure that all rewards and payments bestowed by the shahanshah for the auxiliary recruits would be promptly delivered. For the system to function, the spah would rely on its complement of dabirs and other high officials to ensure that all payments arrived on time from the shahanshah to their designated persons. The fifth guideline concerned the construction of roads and places of settlement. Expenditure of funds was very much a part of the spah's economic tactic to 'win the hearts and minds' of the auxiliary forces and their families who had been allowed to settle in the empire. The ultimate aim was to win the recruit over by making him feel that he was a citizen of the empire.

Perhaps the most interesting method of recruitment and retention was by efforts towards cultural assimilation.[121] Non-Iranian recruits would be exposed to Iranian culture in an attempt to 'Iranicize' these warriors. This would presumably enhance the recruits' loyalty to the Sassanian state over time, especially after the passage of a few generations. Imperial Russian invaders of the Caucasus in the early nineteenth century viewed Persian language and culture as a military threat as these often served as a rallying point for Caucasian peoples to resist the Russian invasions (see Chapter 15, 'Military Culture').

Northern Persia. The spah recruited three of the major warrior peoples of northern Persia into its ranks. The first were the tough Dailamite fighters who proved especially valuable to the empire as combat infantry, filling a very important military niche for the spah (Chapter 7).[122] The Dailamites also helped stabilize Sassanian authority in northern Iran, a task which the previous Parthian dynasty had failed to accomplish. A second group was the Gils of modern day Gilan. The third major north Iranian warrior people recruited into the ranks of the spah hailed from modern-day Gorgan, who were mainly used as light cavalry.[123] The Dailamites and Gils were already fighting in the ranks of Shapur I's military, with elements of these being present even earlier during the campaigns of Ardashir I.

The Caucasus. The Romans and the Sassanians had agreed to a partition of Armenia in 387 CE. This division placed much of the Armenian heartland in addition to Albania (modern Republic of Azerbaijan), Iberia and Lazica (mainly modern-day Georgia), inside the Sassanian domain. The Armenian monarchy did not survive past the fifth century CE, with a Sassanian marzban often being installed as governor in the region until the fall of the empire in 637–651 CE. The Iranian Transcaucasus region was mainly governed by numbers of local princes loyal to the shahanshah, many of whom had actually converted to the Zoroastrian religion.[124]

It is true that the 'Aryan fundamentalist' edicts of Yazdegird II against the spread of Christianity resulted in a major Armenian rebellion and the Battle of Avaryr in 451 CE, but succeeding Sassanian kings acknowledged the Christian faith of the Armenians and Caucasians in general. What bound the Armenians and other regions of Perso-Caucasia was the common pre-Islamic Iranic civilization[125] which also bound them to the martial arena of the Iranic world.[126] Albanian cavalry in particular was highly prized in the spah and its commanders were beholden to the marzban of Azerbaijan (below the Araxes river in northwest

Iran).[127] Albanian cavalry supported the savaran cavalry as early as the reign of Ardashir I.[128] They also fought in the armies of Shapur II at Amida in 359 CE (Chapter 14), and under the command of the drafsh-e kaviani during the Battle of Qadissiyah in 637 CE (Chapter 17). Moses of Dasxuranxi's *History of the Albanians* expostulated upon the heroic exploits of the *sparapet* (Sassanian: spahbod) of Albania at Qadissiyah.[129] The loyalty of the Albanian region to the Iranian cultural realm remained strong even after the Russian conquests of 1828, with Russian officials complaining to St. Petersburg that 'almost all of the residents of Baku are secret spies for the Persian'.[130]

Other Caucasian fighters who proved exceptional as warriors were the Armenian knights, especially those led by Smbat Bagratuni. The latter and his warriors were inducted into the ranks of the savaran through the granting of prestige titles in the Sassanian court.[131] The role of the Armenian knights will be discussed in greater detail in Chapter 6.

There were other Caucasian fighters whose capabilities were highly valued. The empire, for example, made efforts towards recruiting warrior peoples such as the Iranic Alans (who served in the armies of Shapur II),[132] Svants and Sabirs (who fought alongside Kavad),[133] the aforementioned Khazars and the Sunitae.[134]

Central Asia. A very important region for recruitment of excellent cavalry auxiliaries was Central Asia. Recruits typically included the Iranian Kushans, and the other Hsiang-Nou-related peoples such as Turkic, Chionites, and Hephthalite warriors.[135] The armies of Ardashir I had contingents of Kushans and even some Chionites.[136] The latter became especially prominent after the successful conclusion of Shapur II's campaigns in Central Asia in 349–350 CE. Shapur II recruited their king Gumbrates and his warriors for the campaign against the Romans, especially for the siege of Amida in 359 CE[137] (Chapter 14). Chionites were to appear later in the armies of Yazdegird II during his campaigns in the early 440s CE.[138] Hephthalite contingents were also present in the armies of Kavad, proving instrumental in enabling him to re-capture the throne from his brother Jamasp in 498 CE (he ruled for only two years, 496–498 CE). As a major crossroads between Persia, China and India, Central Asia was an important region for developments in military technology. This process played a contributing role in the incorporation of Central Asian military innovations in equestrian equipment, cavalry tactics, suspension technologies for swords, quivers, etc.

Iranian plateau, eastern and western Iran. The warriors of the Iranian plateau had been recruited into Iranian armies since the times of the Achaemenids. Khosrow I worked to ensure that these formidable warrior peoples who were often nomadic or inhabited the Iranian mountains engaged in regular military service.[139] In Sassanian times, the leading clans of these warrior tribes were expected to dispatch gifts (or symbols of tribute) to Ctesiphon on the occasion of the *Nowruz* (Iranian New Year) and the *Mehregan* (celebration of Mithra). When war was imminent, the leaders of these tribes were expected to dispatch cavalry and infantry forces; the clan leaders themselves or delegates from the clan could at times be leading these forces into battle.[140] One notable clan was the Parizi of the modern-day Kerman region whom Khosrow recruited into the spah; Khosrow dispatched numbers of these to serve in other provinces of the empire.[141]

Daryaee has noted of a prominent group of nomads identified by the Middle Persian term 'Kurd'.[142] As explained by Daryaee, this term may have been used for the Kurdish people who were predominantly nomadic; in Middle Persian the term designated nomads in the larger context. They were effective warriors, especially as slingers and javelin men and it would appear that they, like the northern Iranians, were employed in the Sassanian spah.[143]

Modern-day Seistan and Baluchistan in the Iranian southeast were also important recruiting areas for the spah. They were home to the ancient Iranic Saka who had moved with other Iranian peoples onto the Iranian plateau during the great Indo-European migrations in the early second millennium BCE. The Sakas had seen military service in the armies of the Achaemenids and a group of these, the Parthians, were instrumental in restoring Iranian independence by ending the rule of the Seleucids. Not surprisingly the Sakas were among the earliest contingents to join the spah, notably during the campaigns of Ardashir I.[144] The Sakas of Seistan were especially valued by the Sassanians. Their prowess as cavalrymen also earned the respect of Ammianus Marcellinus, who characterized the Seistani contingents of Shapur II at Amida in 359 CE as 'the fiercest warriors of all'.[145] Khosrow I Anoushirvan was especially keen to recruit the Saka, with Reza estimating up to twelve large contingents of these having been formed during the reign of Khosrow I.[146]

The martial ardor of the indigenous tribes of the Iranian plateau endured into the Islamic era. These tribes were recruited by the founder of the Safavid Dynasty, Shah Ismail I (r. 1501–1524 CE) as part of his quest to restore Iran's independence in the early sixteenth century CE. Nader Shah (r. 1736–1747) also recruited the indigenous tribes of the Iranian plateau. He recruited some to serve as cavalry but also trained many others to serve as close-quarters combat infantry and musketeers who were instrumental in inflicting several defeats on Ottoman Empire forces. During his conquests one group of descendants of these ancient Indo-European warriors of the Iranian plateau were the Tangestanis, who would become known for their martial ardour in the nineteenth and the twentieth centuries CE in battles against invading British Empire forces.

Chapter 3

Military Reforms of the Sixth Century CE

The Sassanian Empire instituted a number of critical military reforms which bore results by the mid-late sixth century CE. These reforms were essentially a determined series of improvements undertaken over the course of decades and aimed at enhancing the spah's military effectiveness. The impact of these reforms may be classified in five general categories. The first was in the rationalization of the empire's defence by the implementation of a system of four regional commands. This system of four spahbods was intended to enhance the spah's effectiveness in combating simultaneous attacks on several fronts. In essence, this was the empire's answer to the danger of combined attacks by the Romano-Byzantines, Khazars, Arabs, and Central Asian nomads along the western, northern (Caucasian), south/southwestern and Central Asian fronts. The second set of reforms was in the regularization of rigorous military inspections. Third was the construction of new defence walls and fortifications as well as improvements to existing structures along critical frontier regions, a topic discussed in Chapter 13). Fourth was the formation of a new class of cavalry elites known as the *dehkans*. The latter were more beholden to the state than their azadan 'upper counterparts' whose power, prestige and elite status posed potential challenges to Sassanian political authority. The fifth possible impact of the reforms was in the appearance of the highly effective Dailamite infantry, which strengthened the spah's battlefield effectiveness.

Background to the Military Reforms: Kavad and the Mazdakite Rebellion
The origins of the military reforms have often been attributed to the reign of Khosrow I Anushiravan[1] (r. 531–579 CE), but in practice the origins of these reforms had a number of sources. The first appears to have been the military defeats in the wars with the Hephthalites in the 480s CE (Chapter 12), which required drastic changes in military equipment (see below). The second may have had their origins during the reign of Khosrow I's father, Kavad (r. 488–496, 498–531 CE) who had sought to curb the power and influence of the upper nobility. Daryaee provides a concise overview of the role of Kavad in using the prophet Mazdak and his rebellion to achieve this goal.[2] Rubin contends that the Mazdakite rebellion was (simplistically put) a 'communist' type movement seeking absolute egalitarianism regardless of class or rank. According to Rubin the Mazdalite movement 'had been orchestrated ... by the king himself, in order to achieve precisely the purpose of overthrowing the nobility'.[3] Kavad's actions caused a bitter reaction among the upper nobles and priests who deposed him in 496 CE, and imprisoned him in the so-called Prison of Oblivion and placed his brother Jamasp/Zamasp on the throne. With the assistance of his sister, Kavad

fled the prison and sought refuge with the Hephthalites in 498 CE. The Hephthalites agreed to support him with troops to regain his throne.[4] Kavad and his 30,000-man Hephthalite force faced little difficulty in recapturing the throne and deposing Jamasp/Zamasp.[5] The fact that Kavad and the small Hephthalite force achieved success with relative ease may be due to either (or both) of the following causes: the desperate state of the Sassanian spah, which at this time was unable to organize a powerful military opposition; and the fact that many in the spah may not have supported the upper noble-priestly elites who had deposed Kavad in favour of Jamasp/Zamasp.

The ascension of the anti-Mazdakite Khosrow I resulted in the murder of Mazdak and the brutal suppression of his followers.[6] Interestingly, Pigulevskaya is of the opinion that the nobles greatly enhanced their estates and wealth in the immediate aftermath of the suppression of the Mazdakite rebellion.[7] What is generally agreed upon is that like his father and predecessor, Kavad, Khosrow I also sought to curb the power and influence of the upper nobles. Darayee notes that he did not restore the power and influence of the upper nobles and shifted his support toward the 'lesser nobility' known as the *dehkans* . Khosrow implemented a series of significant military reforms which were probably begun in Kavad's time. As will be discussed below, the upper nobles, who could not be wholly politically controlled by the king, had held a virtual monopoly over their provision of high quality savaran cavalry.

The Four Regional Spahbods
One of these reforms was the abolishment of the office of the eiran-spahbod in favour of four generals of spahbods.[8] Each of these was a regional commander for the empire's north, south, west and east respectively.[9] The Pahlavi scriptures identify these specifically as *abaxtar-spahbod* (spahbod/general of the north), *nemruz-spahbod* (spahbod/general of the south), *xwarasan-spahbod* (spahbod/general of the east) and *xwararan-spahbod* (spahbod/general of the west).[10] The xwarasan-spahbod and xwararan-spahbod were the most important as these faced the nomads of Central Asia and the Romano-Byzantines in Mesopotamia respectively.[11] The nemruz-spahbod was responsible for the Persian Gulf region and especially for defending against Arab raiders who could land by vessels on the empire's Persian Gulf islands and along the southern Iranian coastline. The Arabs of course could and did attempt raids from northern Arabia into the empire's southern Mesopotamian regions.

The abaxtar-spahbod was responsible for guarding the empire's Caucasian frontiers against nomadic raiders emanating from the south Russian regions. The abaxtar-spahbod was also called *spahbod-adurbaygan* after Iran's Adurbaygan region in the northwest (modern Azerbaijan province in Iran).[12] This spahbod in particular was a very important office, as it covered all ingress routes into northwest Iran, hence being one of the 'gates' into the Iranian interior. Quoting early Islamic-era geographers, Markwart cites the following: 'Djarbi or the countries of the North form the fourth part of the Persian Empire under the rule of a spahbadh who is known under the name of Adarbayjan-spahbadh, this quarter includes in itself Armenia, Adarbayjan, Rey [near modern Tehran] . . . Alania and others.'[13]

This indicates that the spahbod was responsible for the defence of a wide region which included not only the contemporary province of Azerbaijan in Iran today but also Armenia, much of the Caucasus and even areas up to the vicinity of modern-day Tehran. Azerbaijan has remained a strategic pivot since ancient times as well as the Islamic era. The military significance of Iran's Azerbaijan province was that of a 'double-shield' guarding the vital Caucasian passes from attacks launched by dangerous nomadic intruders and defending against attacks into Iran's northwest from the east Anatolian and northwest Mesopotamian regions. The term *spahsalar* (military equivalent of the spahbod), for example, could also be used to designate the commander of the Adurbaygan-Caucasus front as seen in Khosrow I's designation of a spahsalar for this critical post.[14]

Interestingly, the *Bundahishn* text which provides the specific spahbod designations also mentions a certain *spahbodan-spahbod* or 'general of generals'.[15] The citation of this title by the *Bundahishn* would suggest that this office supervised and coordinated the four regional spahbods, especially when the empire would be caught in a multi-front war obliging the spah to fight on separate fronts simultaneously. This scenario did occur during the long war with Byzantium in 603–628 CE during which the empire faced a major Arab raid at Dhu Qar in 610 CE along the empire's southwestern marches as well as a dangerous Turco-Hephthalite invasion from Central Asia in 619 CE. The *Shahname* also cites the 'quatro-spahbod' system during the time of Khosrow II with some interesting details: mention is made of a 'Farrokh-abad' (evidently in reference to Farrokhan Shahrbaraz) who was dispatched with 12,000 savaran to *Marz-e Rum* (the borders of Rome or Romano-Byzantium),[16] with 12,000 savaran knights sent to the Caucasus to confront the Alans, and another 12,000 savaran knights sent to Khorasan to *Marz-e Heptal ta Marz-e Chin* (the Hephthalite border and the border of China).[17]

Khosrow I's division of the empire into four major military zones greatly increased the military efficiency of the spah. Prior to these reforms, the Sassanian Empire was beginning to resemble the Achaemenid realm of old with its large number of satrapies. Each of these required its own bureaucracy and regional command, which were both costly and inefficient. Khosrow solved this problem by having all of these merged into four large regional military commands.

However, the power distribution system of the new regional command system was more sophisticated than just having spahbods in place. First, each spahbod also had a marzban commander subordinated to his office.[18] In addition, the king also assigned a viceroy-type office known as the *paygospan* to each of the four regions. The empire's limited military resources across the realm were now more efficiently managed as a result of Khosrow I's elimination of the eiran-spahbod office.

A 'mystical' or mobad connection for the reforms? Adontz highlights an intriguing connection between the four-spahbod system and ancient Iranian cosmology.

As noted by Adontz, in this system: 'heavenly sphere was also divided among four spahbods: the star Tistar watched over the East, Sataves, over the West, Vanand, over the South, and Haptoring, over the North ... There is no doubt in this case that these cosmological concepts of the Persians were a direct reflection of the administrative divisions of Persia, of its division into four commands.'[19]

While the domain of Iranian mythology and cosmology is outside the scope of this text, it is significant that the Sassanian military command was very much cognizant of its 'connection' to Iranian cosmology, mythology, etc. This may suggest that the mobads had perhaps also played a role in the military reforms of the sixth century CE.

Kavad: instigator of reform? The spah, like its Parthian predecessor, had always faced the prospect of fighting a two- (or multi-)front war which imposed financial burdens on the empire. Yazdegird II, for example, had faced a serious Armenian revolt in the Caucasus in reaction to his attempts to replace their Christian faith with Zoroastrianism while facing the prospect of a serious Kidarite threat from Central Asia. Even after the defeat of the Armenian revolt in 451 CE, the Kidarite threat remained serious, well into 457 CE when Yazdegird II passed away.[20] The Christian Albanian neighbours of the Armenians had even opened the gates of the Derbent Pass to allow the Huns to stream forth from the northern Caucasus to harass the empire's northern marches. As noted previously, it was precisely these types of dangers of multiple attacks by different enemies from different fronts that necessitated a new military rationale for the empire's defence. The question, however, is whether these reforms began with Khosrow I or whether these had an earlier origin during the reign of Kavad. Rubin attributes the origins of the reforms to Kavad, a long drawn-out process which was finally bearing tangible results by the 560s CE.[21] Schindel concurs that it was Kavad, and not his son Khosrow I, who first successfully implemented the spah's prose-cution of a multi-front war by fighting against the Romano-Byzantines and also expelling the Hephthalites from Khorasan by the early 500s CE.[22]

The Empire's Finest Hour? Four-Spahbod System Preserves the Empire (572–595 CE)

The four-spahbod system was to be put to the test during the latter days of Khosrow I's reign. After the Sassanians' successful military alliance with the Turks against the Hephthalites, relations with the Turks (Chapter 12) had cooled considerably due to disputes over the Silk Route trade. The breaking point was the Turkish demand for free access to Iranian markets, which was economically untenable for the empire. Sizabul or Ishtemi Khan, the khagan of the Western Turkish Khanate, dispatched an embassy to Justin II (r. 565–578 CE) in 568 CE to propose a Turkish-Byzantine military alliance against the Sassanians. Justin II dispatched Zemarchus, the commander in chief of Romano-Byzantine forces in the Middle East, to accompany the Turkish embassy back to the khagan. Zemarchus returned to the Byzantine Empire with another Turkish embassy by 571 CE. The Zemarchus mission ensured that the Byzantine Empire and the

Turks would coordinate their military actions in a massive pincer movement to crush the Sassanian Empire and divide its assets and territories.

Howard-Johnston has summarized the plans of Justin II for the destruction of the Sassanian Empire.[23] Justin II's meticulous military plans also involved what may be termed as 'Byzantine diplomacy'. Negotiations had been underway in 569–570 CE to instigate a massive anti-Sassanian uprising in Perso-Armenia in 572 CE. Sassanian military responses to the rebellion would then provide Justin II the pretext he needed to intervene in the Caucasus by the spring of 573 CE. The grand pincer blow would then unfold as such: the Romano-Byzantines would launch massive attacks along the Sassanian Empire's western Mesopotamian front while the Turks launched powerful offensives from the empire's northeast. Thus the Sassanians would experience the nightmare scenario of a war on three fronts: the Caucasus, the west and Central Asia.

Perhaps what is most interesting about this phase of Sassanian military history is the paucity of sources regarding Turkish military operations from Central Asia against Iran's northeast. There is little information from the sources as to the specific regions where the Turks would have attacked, the size of their forces and the nature of their weapons and tactics. Even Tabari, for example, fails to provide any references to these events. This has led to conflicting interpretations as to what actually happened along the northeast front in 572–573 CE. Greatrex and Lieu suggest that no operations of note took place. Howard-Johnston suggests that the operations must have taken place, for had they not, the Romano-Byzantine sources would have recorded their indignation at having been betrayed by the Turks.[24] Reza has suggested that Ishtemi Khan did launch a fierce attack but became bogged down in the wall defence lines the Sassanians had built against potential Central Asian invaders (Chapter 13).[25] If this is accurate, then this would suggest that the war council had already anticipated the size, timing and direction of the Turkish attacks, thus placing enough troops within the formidable defence walls to hold and even repel the Turkish assaults. Howard-Johnston pinpoints the loci of the Iranian defence against the Turks being located at Merv and Nishabur.[26] These important cities were in effect fortresses serving two military functions: (a) defending the approaches towards the northern part of the Iranian plateau, and (b) serving as the vanguard system of the great walls of Tammisha and Gorgan, built over time to defend Iran against attacks from Central Asia (Chapter 13).

It is not clear how far the spah would have counterattacked, but judging from subsequent events the northeast sector of the four-spahbod system had succeeded in preserving the frontiers. Reza notes that Khosrow I and Ishtemi Khan agreed to cease hostilities, allowing the spah to then shift the bulk of its forces from the northeast towards the dangerous western theatre.[27] This would have presumably occurred from 573 CE, when the cessation of hostilities had been made permanent by a peace treaty, giving the war council the peace of mind to thin out its forces in the east for the western showdown. Reza's analysis is interesting as it runs contrary to that of Howard-Johnston. The latter in fact suggests the opposite, by stating the plan of the war council was to launch 'a swift offensive blow ...

to be struck against the main Roman army in northern Mesopotamia, taking it from the rear in an unexpected direction; with the Romans temporarily disabled, forces could be redeployed to the east in the hope of forcing the Turks to abandon the war or to face the full weight of Sassanian armed might.'[28]

In summary, Reza suggests that the Sassanians may have had a 'Turks first' policy in which the spah would first hold and defeat the Turks along the Central Asian frontier to then shift the bulk of their forces westward towards the invading Romano-Byzantines. Howard-Johnston's suggestion is that the Sassanians had a 'Byzantines first' strategy to then shift their forces eastwards against the Turks.

Reza (1995) and Howard-Johnston (2010) are in overall agreement regarding the spah's general military strategy: the spah was perhaps the world's first military machine to devise a Schlieffen Plan solution to a multi-front crisis. The Schlieffen Plan was the Imperial German Army's plan in 1914 to decisively defeat France in a swift campaign and then concentrate its forces in the east to confront the Russians. Despite being chronologically separated by over 1,200 years, both Imperial Germany and the Sassanian Empire had to rely on a sophisticated system of logistics, communications and land routes to ensure the swift shuttle of their respective armies between east and west (or west to east).

Before addressing the question of how the Romano-Byzantine threat was dealt with in the west, questions may be posed as to how the empire dealt with the rebellion in Perso-Armenia. What is certain is that the leader of the Armenian rebels, Vardan Mamikonian, had achieved considerable success and, thanks to Byzantine military support, was able to capture Dvin by 572–573 CE. The situation became especially desperate by 575 CE as Romano-Byzantine raiding parties thrust deep into Albania (modern Republic of Azerbaijan). This was a very serious threat in its own right, as it could lead to Romano-Byzantine intervention south of the Araxes River into Atropatene (Azerbaijan province in Iran) and northern Iran. The loss of the Caucasus could also lead to another potential disaster. In such a scenario, the restive Khazars in the northern Caucasus could contemplate their own ideas of military action against the empire. Confronted by these dire prospects, the war council managed to apply just enough military force to prevent a complete collapse of the northern sector of the four-spahbod system. As early as late 572 CE, local Sassanian forces proved just sufficient to contain the Caucasian crisis. Another important development was that other local Christian populations did not rise in pro-Roman revolts, a fact of great military significance for the Sassanians. So, even as the Romans did take full advantage of the fall of Dvin, this success did not translate to anti-Sassanian military support from the Iberians (in modern Georgia), Albanians or other Christianized tribes of the Caucasus. In this way, the Roman-inspired and supported rebellion in Perso-Armenia could be sufficiently contained until the crises in the east and west had been resolved.

The aging Khosrow I and the war council devised a highly effective plan to defeat Justin II's offensives. At this juncture, the primary goal of the Romano-Byzantine campaign was to capture the formidable fortress-city of Nisibis. Control of this strategic locale would allow Justin's armies to thrust south into the

Mesopotamian heartland. Khosrow I decided to deploy his armies towards the south of Justin's armies. He marched up the Euphrates and reached Circesium. From there, a large raiding party was dispatched up the Khabur River, but the main blow was Khosrow's drive towards Nisibis. This move proved a brilliant success, catching Romano-Byzantine forces besieging Nisibis by surprise. A fierce battle ensued with the spah inflicting heavy losses and emerging victorious.[29] Justin's forces had been scattered, resulting in the lifting of the siege of Nisibis. The Romano-Byzantine forces now retreated in haste to the safety of the west: they withdrew past Dara towards Mardin. Much of this disaster had been due to the failure of Justin's Arab Ghassanid allies in providing intelligence and reconnaissance of the spah's deployment and location. Khosrow I lost no time in exploiting his successes before the Romano-Byzantines could recover. The siege engines abandoned by his opponents at Nisibis were now pressed into service with the spah, which had deployed to Dara, which fell to Khosrow I in 573 CE after a six-month siege (Chapter 14).

According to Howard-Johnston's 'Byzantines first' thesis, the successes in the west allowed the war council to shift troops towards Turkish threats in the east.[30] In this endeavour, Howard-Johnston proposes that the spah also thinned out the troops on its already hard-pressed Caucasian front. This would then explain the aforementioned successes of the Romano-Byzantines in being able to thrust into Albania in 575 CE. Howard-Johnston avers that it is not clear if the Sassanian contingents arriving in the northeast remained purely on the defensive or whether these counterattacked into Turkish-held territories, especially Soghdia. He suggests that final peace arrived through negotiations. Recall Reza's mention of a negotiated peace between Khosrow I and the Turks, but he reported these as having taken place in 572–573 CE. Also, as a proponent of the 'Turks first' thesis, Reza suggests that the spah not only defended its northeastern frontiers with success (which Howard-Johnston does not object to) but also proposes that Khosrow I's forces launched deep attacks as far as Kabul and cleared the Turks out of Tocharistan but failed to capture Soghdia.[31] Military successes are attributed to superior training, tactics and armaments of the elite savaran in particular, which by that time (presumably with the onset of the military reforms) was markedly superior to its Turkish counterparts.[32] It was the veterans of these operations who, according to Reza, were then transferred west to combat the legions of Justin II. The military ascendancy of the spah over the Turks and their Hephthalite allies was certainly demonstrated later in 588 CE and 619 CE (Chapter 12).

Two elements are clear at this stage. First, Turkish-Byzantine relations had deteriorated by 576 CE, a clear indication that Justin II's attempts at a multi-front offensive against the Sassanian Empire had failed. By this time, there appears to have been no military threats by the Turks. Second, whether there had been a 'Byzantines first' or 'Turks first' strategy in the Sassanian version of the Schlieffen Plan, it is certain that by late 575 CE or early 576 CE, the war council was able to finally focus on Perso-Armenia in the Caucasus. This signalled the onset of the final operations of what may be termed as Justin II's War.

Khosrow I again took command of the spah in the upcoming operations. Assembling his forces in Atropatene, Khosrow I marched into Bagrewand and from there thrust north towards Theodosiopolis where he halted at its environs. The march was then resumed into Cappadocia aiming towards the fortress-city of Caesarea, but Romano-Byzantine military action barred the ingress of Khosrow I's forces through the mountains. The Sassanians then attacked the fortress-city of Sebasteia, which was captured and sacked. This success proved short lived. When Khosrow I deployed southwards towards Melitene, the Romano-Byzantines successfully counterattacked, capturing much of the royal baggage train, and then inflicted further losses on Khosrow I's armies as they crossed the Euphrates back into the Sassanian territory. The spah and Khosrow I had clearly failed in their first attempt to eject the Romano-Byzantines from Perso-Armenia. The restoration of Sassanian authority would not take place until after the passing of Khosrow in 579 CE, a task delegated to the marzban of Atropatene, who apparently engaged in counterinsurgency operations as well as combat with local Roman forces. In essence, even though Khosrow I had not been able to eject the Romano-Byzantines from the Sassanian-Caucasian domains, the four-spahbod or 'quatro' system allowed the Sassanians to finally prevail.

The critical western theatre remained stable. The Romano-Byzantines then launched a massive attack into southern Mesopotamia in 581 CE but the spah counterattacked in the Edessa region. A war of attrition was initiated lasting from 582–587 CE, in which the Romano-Byzantines failed to prevail. Despite some modest successes in 586 CE, Romano-Byzantine losses were heavy, leading to protests, mutiny and a slowing down of operations, especially in 588, which allowed the spah to dispatch a modest contingent of elite savaran cavalry to defeat a massive Turkish-led invasion in 588 CE.

Meanwhile, the strategic nightmare had the potential to worsen by becoming a four-front war. The war council placed a high priority on the security of the Persian Gulf, as indicated by the long campaign of the Vahriz contingent in Yemen, which lasted c. 570s–595 CE (Chapter 8). The Arabs outside of Yemen, especially those along northwest Arabia facing the Romano-Byzantines and Sassanians, could certainly take advantage of the spah's military preoccupations to launch their own raids from the southwest. As noted already, the pro-Roman Ghassanids had already been assigned the task of supporting Justin II's military thrusts in the western theatre. If Justin II could succeed in mobilising other Arabs against the Sassanian Empire, he could then create more military distractions for the spah and force it to further disperse its military resources. This potential disaster was successfully averted, not by military means, but by diplomacy. Whatever the Roman efforts may have been to win over the Lakhmids, it is certain that the latter never joined Justin II. Instead, it was Khosrow I who now had the option of deploying his forces along the northern Arabian marches to then strike into Romano-Byzantine territory. Therefore, if Justin II decided to strike more to the south of the Sassanian empire, Khosrow I could potentially outflank such thrusts, by wheeling through northern Arabia.

It is perhaps no exaggeration to state that had the four-spahbod system failed during these critical military crises, the empire may well have fallen in late 570s or early 580s CE.

Aftermath of success: Khosrow I's warning to posterity. One of the most interesting yet little-noticed aspects of Khosrow Anoushirvan's four-spahbod system is illustrated in a speech attributed to him in the *Sirat Anushirvan*, presumably in the latter years of his rule:[33]

> From the day I assumed reign over you [citizens of the empire], suspending the sword on the neck [Baldric hanging?], I placed myself as target for swords and lances ... all this for the defence of you ... and for the welfare of your nation. At times at the farthest borders of the east, sometimes at the furthest western border, once in the south and once towards the north ... your enemies were broken and defeated and are now annihilated from their large numbers of dead.

This speech is in reference to Khosrow's campaigns against the Romano-Byzantines (especially siege warfare), northeast (Central Asian frontier), south (especially Yemen and Persian Gulf region) and the northern Caucasian frontier. Nevertheless, despite the successes of the four-spahbod system in protecting the empire against the Romano-Byzantines, their Ethiopian clients in Yemen, the Turco-Hephthalites in Central Asia and Khazars in the Caucasus, Khosrow also warns his citizens and the spah against complacency and underestimation of the empire's enemies:[34]

> Enemies have remained for you ... those who have survived ... to this second enemy [future threats?] ... rise to battle against them and defeat them, it is at that time when your victory, power, pride, beneficence, blessings, ascendancy ... serenity, peace and health become complete. If you shirk from this task and show lack of resolve and the enemy achieves dominance over you, then *all your past victories over the enemies in the east, west, north and south will no longer be victories for you.* [emphasis added] Thus endeavour to destroy these remaining enemies as you did your enemies in the past.

Khosrow is clearly warning the spah and the empire's populace that, irrespective of the empire's military successes, threats are never completely eliminated. Instead, the shahanshah advocates a state of constant combat readiness. The warning is also an acknowledgement or appreciation of the military potential of all enemies (east, west, north and south) and their capacity to threaten the empire in the (near and distant) future. The Hephthalites, for example, had been defeated by Bahram Gur (r. 420–438 CE) in 421 CE but militarily recovered 63 years later to kill King Pirouz and defeat the spah in 484 CE (Chapter 12).

Military Inspections and Reviews
One of the most critical military reforms implemented during the reign of Khosrow I was in the 'army office' which would approximate the modern day

equivalent of the ministry of war. Identified as *diwan al-jund* by Dinawari[35] in Arabic, or the *divan spah*,[36] this was essentially an 'army office' which was under the supervision of a *dabir* (see Chapter 11) whose functions in this capacity are further discussed below. As noted by the *Tarikh-e Gozide* text, this office 'had been organized [by the Sassanians] with the affairs of [military] reviews having been given a great deal of importance'.[37] Nevertheless military reviews were not a new feature introduced by Khosrow I, as these had existed in the earlier years of the spah. The *Farsnameh* makes reference to a military assembly and a 'weapons bearer' at the time of Shapur I:[38] '[T]he next day they stood in the arena, and the Shah separated/selected 1,000 famous men all of whom were of the Spahbods, Sar-Hangan, and Sar-Lashkaran and told them "select from among you a man to be weapons-bearer, on condition that he be manly".'

This 'weapons bearer' appears to have acted much as a dabir at the time of Khosrow I. The military review was reformed, allowing the spah to assess its potential readiness for battle; this included a compendium of personnel, which was kept in the tomes of the divan spah.[39] These records provided detailed information enabling the spah to regularly calibrate its military potential, which translated to increased effectiveness on the battlefield.

In Khosrow's time, the office of the divan spah was held by a dabir named Pabag or Babak whose post was of considerable importance in the spah and the empire in general.[40] The dabir's functions in this office were threefold:[41] (1) inspection of spah troops every four months; (2) improvement of military equipment in all spah units; and (3) supervision of military instructors in areas such as archery, cavalry warfare, etc.

There was also a highly rigorous system of military reviews which was essentially an extension of the dabir's inspection system. These military reviews, which could last up to forty days, are described by Dinawari's *Akhbar al Tawwal* as follows:[42]

> All ranks of the military are to be present with their weapons and equipment ... also [who are to be present] are the instructors of the cavalry and firing [of missiles/archery] ... sitting atop a platform bedecked with expensive carpets was Babak in front of whom would pass [march past] him all the military personnel ... the king himself [Khosrow Anoushirvan] would pass [march past] Babak with his clothing [uniform?] and weapons ... military equipment consisted of ... armour, breastplate, helmet ... two bazuband [armour for arms], two greaves, shield, lance, and a Gorz [mace] that is tied to the waist ... quiver with thirty arrows, two bows.

The dabir was responsible for ensuring that each warrior's equipment and clothing [uniform?] were in the best condition possible. This was part of Khosrow I's overall effort to ensure that the spah would be in a constant state of battle readiness, prepared to deploy in short order against invaders from the north, east, west or south.

Dinawari's report also makes clear that nobody in the spah, including the king himself, was above the dabir's criteria of military excellence. Babak reportedly 'failed' Khosrow I during a military inspection as the king lacked two bowstrings (*zeh e yadaki*) among his array of equipment that included mail, *bargostvan* armour for his horse, helmet, neck-guard, hand-guards, greaves, lance, shield, mace suspended by the belt, axe, bow case carrying two bows, etc.[43] Khosrow then 'corrected' this by riding away from the review to then attach two bowstrings to his 'back' (presumably the back of his helmet); the king then presented himself for a second time to Babak who then 'passed' the king by 'declaring his name out loud to then record his name in the Divan registry'.[44] Babak is then reputed to have asked Khosrow I for clemency for having been so harsh during the review. The king responded by stating, 'He who is harsh with us in accordance with the application of the law and royal weapons, then we are humbled before him as his conduct is like the bitter medicine one must ingest for one's welfare.'[45]

The state records of the divan were integral to the system of *rozyaneh* (wages, payments) during the military review process. Troops would stand at the ready in a formal military assembly to then be summoned one by one by the dabir, who after closely inspecting the warrior's attire and weapons would then dispense his rozyaneh.[46] The amount of rozyaneh to be dispensed to that warrior was already recorded next to his name in the tomes of the divan. The rozyaneh could also be bestowed by the dabir by giving the warrior a special seal known as the *golgosp*, which bore a monetary value (somewhat like a high value 'token'). After the review and assembly, the warrior would take his golgosp to an official known as the *bondar* (treasurer) who would then provide him the rozyaneh in accordance with the value of the golgosp. Khosrow also formalized the process of granting property to warriors so that they could support themselves until they reached enemy territory.[47]

The *Shahname* has made references to the importance of the military review in the spah. The king is described as sitting on a royal elephant witnessing the march-past of warriors from Bardeej and Ardabil:[48] *Be-ayand va az pish oo begzarand* [They came and passed by him/next to him] / *Mard o Mobad o Marzban beshmorand* [Man and Mobad and Marzban they counted].

The *Shahname* notes that among the warriors participating in the review are 100,000 *separ-dar va joshan-daran sadd-hezar* (spear-bearers and those wearing/possessing *joshan* armour) followed by the savaran units.

The tradition of the formal military review was to endure long after the demise of the Sassanian Empire into the time of the Mongol conquests. Mongol troops were routinely inspected to ensure that their equipment was in the best condition before embarking on their campaigns.[49]

'Surprise' military inspections. There was also a system of 'surprise' inspections, when the shahanshah would arrive at the head of a large force to inspect military forces in the empire's different regions. This was an effective system as it ensured that no advance information would be provided for these 'surprise visits' by the shahanshah, who would initiate a rigorous inspection regimen upon his arrival. This system ensured that garrisons throughout the empire remained in a constant state of military readiness.[50]

Different types of military reviews. In practice there were seven distinct reviews by late Sassanian times:[51] (1) peacetime military reviews of the strict military type discussed above; (2) military reviews for troops and warriors expecting payment by the state; (3) reviews taken upon the arrival of an important official or general to a city or garrison; (4) reviews of foreign troops wishing to enter service with the Sassanian spah (in such cases troops were carefully inspected to evaluate their military discipline and eligibility); (5) important national celebrations such as Nowruz (Iranian New Year) and Mehregan (festival of Mithra); (6) reviews for welcoming foreign dignitaries; and (7) reviews for military preparation before the outbreak of war (Chapter 8).

A New Cavalry Elite: The Dehkans

The Sassanian nobility were not a singular monolithic unit, but could be generally broken down into two classes, the greater and the lesser nobility. The greater nobility was a smaller group composed of elites who were essentially landed gentry (much like the later European nobles) who had great estates and massive wealth inherited and accumulated across the generations. It was typically from these families that the spah's primary source of elite knights was recruited. Many members of these families also inherited their military titles across the generations.[52] There appears to have been a registry of professional cavalry hailing from the upper nobility. This registry is seen in the Sassanian law book known as the *Matigan e Hazar Datastan* which has a section entitled *Asabar Nipek* (List of Knights/Cavalry) which also describes specified allotments of land for the purpose of 'fully equipping' the knight.[53] These same upper nobles appear to have had a list of dependants who were 'free members of a community' who were apparently armed at the expense of the upper noble to then form a personal core of professional warriors which also acted as the magnate's bodyguard.[54]

This system of state recruitment from the upper nobles posed two general liabilities for the spah. First, these upper nobles wielded considerable political and economic power, which challenged Ctesiphon's endeavours towards increasing centralization of the state. Despite the Sassanian administration's efforts to move away from the looser system of government of the former Parthians, Ctesiphon was not a strict 'capital' as Constantinople was. The majority of the nobles did not reside in Ctesiphon, in contrast to Constantinople where the majority of Romano-Byzantine nobles were located. This meant that, as many nobles resided outside of the capital, enforcement of royal edicts could pose problems if the nobles chose to resist them.[55] In military terms, these upper nobles who were much like the later European feudal lords were generally not dependent on Ctesiphon for their wealth or maintenance of their military retinue and knights. This posed a constant danger in that the feudal lord(s) could easily shift their loyalties from Ctesiphon, which could pose the mortal danger of the political disintegration of the Sassanian state.[56] In this context, the knights who were linked to the feudal lord in their immediate vicinity would look to him for leadership rather than becoming beholden to the shahanshah in Ctesiphon.[57] This type of situation could become accentuated if the political integrity of the state became endangered as a result of Sassanian political infighting or dangerous invasions that directly menaced the integrity of the leadership in Ctesiphon.

While the relationship between the nobles and the monarchy was relatively stable, dissension among the nobility could have critical military consequences for the spah. The *Letter of Tansar*, a contemporary document believed to have reflected the troubles particular to the earlier part of Khosrow I's reign,[58] has a section in which Aristotle advises Alexander on how to manage the conquered Iranian realms by appointing local Iranian nobles as administrators:[59] '[T]here will appear among them so much disunity and variance ... so much opposition and rivalry about power ... they will have no desire to seek vengeance upon you [Alexander], and being preoccupied with one another will not be free to think upon the past [Alexander's conquest of Achaemenid Iran]'.

Whitby notes that the author of the letter put this 'accurate but highly sensitive advice in the mouth of a foreigner' (Aristotle to Alexander).[60] In this context, the letter was meant to demonstrate the importance of having the nobles counterbalance each other's power. While these upper noble families could and did provide the Sassanian Empire with its finest elite knights, another pool of troops was needed to both augment and counterbalance the existing cadre of upper noble knights.

The first problem of the spah was also related to the second: numbers of available high-quality and well-trained warrior knights. A chief weakness of the spah was its limited manpower base (Chapter 16), meaning that the spah's professional core of warriors (especially savaran) would have great difficulties replacing high battle losses, especially after prolonged military conflicts. This was a critical problem as the empire faced threats along its western as well as eastern frontiers, and in the northern Caucasian theatre and the south and southwest. The empire could not afford heavy losses of professional personnel within a short time period as this would lead to a dangerous military vacuum which potential enemies could exploit.

Khosrow's solution to these problems (lack of control over the upper nobles and paucity of numbers) was to promote the lesser nobles known as the dehkans into the ranks of the savaran. (The role and military functions of the dehkans will be further elaborated in Chapter 6.) As noted by Rubin, the refurbishment of the military as a result of the reforms had the following impact: 'Instead of an army of retainers, bought to the field by powerful feudal lords over whom the king had little control, there was now an army directly recruited and remunerated by the king.'[61] In the overall sense, the creation of the dehkan corps through Khosrow's reforms may have also been an endeavour to create a more evenly armed and armoured force of savaran. However, despite this innovation and the continuing recruitment of auxiliary forces, the spah's manpower problems were never fully solved (Chapter 16).

The formalization of the dehkan cavalry corps also resulted in the state assuming responsibility for the standardization of armaments. This was a significant step towards creating a more professional and standard armoured cavalry force. Prior to this the quality of equipment (armour, swords, etc.) of each individual knight could vary according to the person's noble rank and especially wealth. It is possible that given the expense of the necessary equipment, the state had been content in the past to have the wealthy nobles pay the costs of their own armaments, and thus save money for the state's coffers.[62]

In practice the reforms resulted in a hybrid of the old system and the new such that at wartime the upper nobles would rally around the national banner called the *Drafsh Kaviani* in defence of the realm, alongside the newly formed professional corps of dehkans who were paid by the state. The spah in turn would also be supported by foreign auxiliary units during its campaigns (Chapter 7).

The critical importance of funds for the creation and maintenance of a powerful military machine was duly appreciated by Khosrow I. The following quote ascribed by al-Masoudi to Khosrow I reads: 'Kingship is based on the army, and the army on financial resources, financial resources are based on the land tax [*kharaj*], and the land tax is based on the cultivation of the land [*imara*].'[63]

The dehkans, who were highly loyal to the state military and political apparatus, were also part of the larger context of fiscal reforms who could act as Ctesiphon's provincial tax collectors and administrators. Ultimate control of the taxes rested upon the *dabirbod* corps, which acted as the land tax secretary of the state.[64]

Dailamite Infantry

Another contingent of warriors to become increasingly integrated into the spah was the tough Dailamite infantry from the Dailam highlands in northern Persia (see Chapter 7). Dailamite troops significantly enhanced the spah's military performance, especially for combat in non-cavalry terrain such as mountainous and forested regions. The importance of infantry had been appreciated since the days of Ardashir I (Chapter 7) and continued as an integral element of the spah up to the reforms. Eventually the Dailamites dominated the domain of infantry warfare in the spah, especially from the time of Khosrow I.

It would appear that Khosrow and the military leadership recognized the fighting capabilities of these northern Iranian infantrymen, which the spah desperately needed to counter the superbly trained and skilful Romano-Byzantine professional infantry. As will be seen in Chapter 7, the Dailamites were apparently highly respected by their adversaries.

Other Military Reforms

One of Khosrow's most important military reforms was the build-up of the empire's Maginot-type defence works and fortresses, a topic discussed in a separate chapter. Complementing these developments were Khosrow's efforts to repair the empire's road system. The objective of the latter was to facilitate the rapid deployment of the spah along north-south and east-west axes to (1) reinforce military fortifications threatened by invasion; (2) dispatch forces to areas already overrun by invading forces; or (3) assemble along border areas in preparation for strikes into enemy territory. An efficient road and transport system was critical for these purposes.

Khosrow's reforms concerning the introduction of new military and equestrian equipment may have already begun during the reign of Kavad. The spah had suffered a number of serious military defeats against the Hephthalites in the mid-late fifth century CE, which led to the adoption of new military equipment. One example was the phasing out of the broadsword scabbard slide in favour of the Central Asian lappet suspension system (Chapter 6). It is also possible that the later Sassanians had adopted stirrups (Chapter 6).

Chapter 4

Military Training, Polo, the Hunt, and Military Music

Sassanian military training began at an early age and encompassed a wide domain. This included not just weapons and martial arts training but also the game of polo, the hunt and intellectual pursuits, notably chess. The spah had professional military instructors and references to Sassanian training are found in the Classical sources. Martial music also played a prominent role in not just the Sassanian military, but also in the armies of the Parthians and Achaemenids.

Sassanian Military Training: An Overview

Shaabani has summarized the importance of military training for the Sassanian military machine in observing that the constant struggles against formidable opponents necessitated the formation of a professional warrior class which was dependent upon an established tradition of rigorous training in physical fitness, martial arts and the use of weapons.[1]

Formal military training was given high priority in the spah, resulting in highly professional cavalry troops and (by late Sassanian times) skilled Dailamite infantry. Jalali has summarized the training of professional Sassanian troops as being composed of two general phases.[2] The first was the induction to military training from an early age. Sassanian warriors in general are believed to have trained from the age of five to twenty-four years of age.[3] Strabo notes that the martial subjects taught to the Iranians between those ages were archery, equestrian skills and the throwing of spears.[4] Training was actually more extensive, especially with respect to martial arts (see *zoorkhaneh* below). Military training would be entrusted to professional veterans of past wars (see *andarzbad aspwaregan* below). Once youths had reached a high level of military proficiency through training, they would enter the second phase, which was their assignment to spah military units. This topic is discussed below under *nawreseda-jawanan*.

The outcome of Sassanian military training is perhaps best characterized by Ammianus Marcellinus, a Greek soldier in the Roman army, who described the Sassanian Persians as 'splendid warriors'.[5] Libanius reports that the Sassanian spah was a highly professional force which placed a heavy emphasis on military training: 'They equipped their own forces and bought their preparation to perfection in every form, cavalry, men at arms, archers and slingers. They trained to a consummate degree what methods had been their practice from the beginning ... the length of their preparation and the period of training'.[6]

Libanius further avers that the Sassanians endeavoured to improve the training of their professional troops to 'add to their existing methods'.[7] The knights of the savaran professional core in particular are noted by Ammianus as having undergone 'hard service ... military training and discipline, through constant exercise in warfare and military maneuvers'.[8] There is also an interesting reference to the Battle of Singara (343 or 344 CE) in which Sassanian troops arriving in the battle theatre are described by Libanius as having 'practised their training on the march'.[9]

Libanius' descriptions would indicate that hard training was not confined to the elite savaran cavalry but also to other services such as slingers, archers and armoured infantry. The Sassanians, like the Romans (later Romano-Byzantines), were cognizant of the necessity of learning from their battle experiences and recording these into manuals, not unlike the *Strategikon* attributed to Emperor Maurice (r. 582–602 CE). Sassanian military experiences and knowledge are described in Chapter 8 of the *Dinkard*, with a number of other sources such as the *Ayin-Nameh* (Chapter 19). Pigulevskaya notes that the Sassanians heavily emphasized military training in sword fighting, lance combat, archery and equestrian warfare.[10]

The Andarzbad Aspwaregan

Officers bearing the *andarzbad aspwaregan* designation were highly prestigious and essential military personnel within the Sassanian spah. These were professional military men and veterans responsible for ensuring that all savaran units received the best possible military training to maximize their battlefield effectiveness. The spah designated andarzbads to various barracks to train savaran knights in (1) the use of weaponry; (2) horseback riding; and (3) battlefield military techniques.[11] The *Letter of Tansar to Goshnasp*, for example, makes reference to cavalry instructors being assigned to various cities and villages throughout the empire 'to keep warriors in towns and countryside practised in the usage of arms and related arts'.[12]

These andarzbads were rigorously inspected, especially following the reforms of the sixth century CE (Chapter 3). Dinawari's Akhbar ol Tawwal reports:

> Every four months when troops were obliged to engage in the [military] review and to present their weaponry [or weapons inventory] ... the instructors of the spah were examined/evaluated on the basis of their instruction abilities with respect to cavalry and archery, with respect to whether these instructors had excelled in their instruction or if they had declined in their instruction abilities.[13]

This passage makes clear the level of importance accorded to high-quality military training by the spah. The intensity of training provided by the andarzbad aspwaregan combined with the pahlavan martial ethos (Chapter 15) resulted in the forging of a formidable battlefield force. One of the main objectives of this vigorous training was to produce pahlavan knights who were cool, collected and composed on the battlefield. Amminaus Marcellinus provides an interesting clue with respect to the discipline of the savaran knights during Julian's invasion of the Sassanian Empire in 363 CE: 'Part of them [the savaran] who were prepared to fight with pikes *stood immovable*, so that you might have fancied they were *held in their places by fastenings of brass*' (emphasis added).[14]

The notion of standing motionless, yet prepared to spring into action at the first signal by one's commander, is an ancient Iranian tradition. An ancient Kurdish legend in northwest Iran from the Sardasht area, for example, notes of how a small band of Mede warriors would stand motionless with their weapons, ready to spring into action at their *sardar*'s command, just as their more numerous Assyrian enemies were assembling to attack them. Composure and self-control before battle was also a powerful signal to the enemy of one's high level of military professionalism and discipline.

Even as the signal was given to attack, this action was not to be launched in a wild and hasty fashion. Instead, the savaran knights were to attack in a methodical, calm and collected manner, which was again the result of their intensive training. This behaviour of the savaran knights during the attack is described in the *Strategikon* (late Sassanian era) as follows: 'They then join battle with calmness and determination, marching step by step in even and dense formations ... For the Persians do not attack in a disorderly fashion ... but cautiously and in good order.'[15]

This description reveals a military force that was as professional as its Romano-Byzantine counterparts, who also laid a very heavy emphasis on a high level of training and self-discipline for their troops.

Education of the Knights: Frahang and Chatrang

Education of the knights was not strictly confined to military training. Sassanian military culture deeply emphasized *frahang* (modern Persian: *farhang*) whose Greek cognate is *paideia*, which broadly denotes 'culture'. As noted by Daryaee, the Sassanians had a series of *frahangestan* (lit. 'education schools/academies') which taught a curriculum of physical education and intellectual courses.[16] Daryaee further avers that 'attendance at the Frahangestan demanded that a well-rounded person had to show prowess both in physical and mental training'.[17] The physical courses were typical of overall military training, notably jousting and horsemanship, polo, the hunt and other related (martial) skills. Intellectual courses emphasized literacy of manuscripts (writing from dictation, bookkeeping, etc.), memorization of holy statements, writing and calligraphy, and the arts (music, songs, dances, and poetry).

Another important topic taught at the frahangestan was board games. These were *new-ardaxshir* (backgammon), *catrang/chatrang* (chess) and *hashtpay* (board similar to that of the chessboard; this had sixty-four squares with eight rows of eight squares). Discussion of the origins of these games is beyond the scope of this text, but suffice it to say that the subject is disputed, even among Iranian historians. Darayee, for example, contends that both chess and backgammon have Indian origins,[18] with Yektai disputing the Indian roots of chess by attributing an Iranian origin.[19] Nevertheless, it is notable that the earliest surviving chess pieces are from Sassanian Persia, dated to the late sixth or early seventh centuries CE. Of interest here are the board games and their relevance to the military training of the knight; in particular, chess appears to have been most closely associated with the military arts and the cultivation of intelligence. A passage in the *Wizarishn-e Chatrang ud Nishishn-e New Ardaxshir* describes an Indian king (Dewisharm) who sent his minister (Taxritos) with thirty-two emerald chess pieces and a letter to the Sassanian king, Khosrow I. The letter challenged Khosrow to solve the logic of the game. Khosrow's minister, Wuzurg-Mehr (modern Persian: Buzurg-Mehr) reputedly solved (or unlocked) the rationale of the game by drawing parallels between military functions and the chess pieces:[20] 'King like the two overlords, the rook [on] the left and right flank, the minister like the commander of the warriors, the elephant like the commander of the bodyguards, and the horse like the commander of the cavalry, the foot-soldier like the same pawn that is at the front of the battlefield.'

The passage then goes on to describe how Wuzurg-Mehr defeated Taxiros three times at the game. While the historicity and authenticity of this incident can be questioned, the story makes a clear parallel between chess, intelligence and the military domain. Modern research has confirmed that consistent involvement in chess results in a series of cognitive benefits such as increased IQ (including mathematical and reading skills) as well as problem solving and critical thinking skills within an array of complex situations.[21]

Graduation from Formal Military Training: The Nawreseda-Jawanan

As noted in Chapter 3, military inspections became much more thorough after the reforms of the sixth century CE. Inspections could last up to forty days, with the king himself subject to critical review. The *Shahname* frequently states that the savaran knights had to be highly trained in riding and the use of weapons. The sons of the nobles were ordered by the king to undergo rigorous military training from an early age.

The *Shahname* has detailed this process,[22] noting that the initial stage of professional instruction would take place on the nobleman's estate. Training included horseback riding, archery, the use of maces (*gurz*) and lance fighting.[23] Once the boy had 'acquired strength and achieved perfection in every pursuit' he would be sent to the royal training grounds of Ctesiphon. The young warrior, known as the *nawreseda-jawan* (lit. 'newly arrived youth'), would record his name in the king's military registry, the *Divan*. The boy was then assigned living quarters in the military training school of Ctesiphon. The instructors of the royal academy were veterans of past wars, who passed their valuable knowledge to the next generation of the savaran. Previous training in horsemanship, archery, *shamsher-wazig* (lit. 'sword-play'), mace and lance fighting were perfected (see also *zoorkhaneh*, below). At this juncture the *jawan* would have completed his training, but would not yet be a professional warrior.[24]

As noted previously by Jalali, the completion of training of the nawreseda-jawan would be followed by his assignment into the ranks of the savaran with his name now registered in the imperial *Divan* tomes. The entire ceremony was probably overseen by the andarzbad-aspwaragan. The nawreseda-jawan was now allowed to fight under one of the drafsh (banners) of Persia with the warrior armed and paid directly by the state. Nevertheless, the actual training was not yet complete. To become a true permanent member of the elite savaran, new recruits such as the nawreseda-jawan had to demonstrate their bravery and resilience in the anvil of battle. As noted by Firdowsi, the nawreseda-jawan would enter war along with the pahlavans,[25] indicating that the new warrior had yet to prove himself as a pahlavan knight. Only when the recruit had successfully proven his mettle on the battlefield would he be formally awarded a *basu-band* (a ceremonial armband, not to be confused with the ring armour for arms, also known as *basu-band*) and the *kamar-band* (decorated belt).

Training for Horses and Men: Polo

Chaugan-wazig, or polo, was one of the most important sports used for the training of the savaran knights.[26] This game cultivated the rider's sense of horsemanship in concert with his adept handling of the *chaugan* (Persian: polo stick or mallet) and ball. It also significantly enhanced the rider's equestrian skills along with his hand/eye coordination.

The *Ayin-Nameh* contains very specific instructions on how the game must be played, especially with respect to training hand-eye coordination. The excerpts below from the *Ayin-Nameh* provide specific instructions concerning the use of the polo stick (control, coordination, focus, and power), treatment and guidance of the horse, safety of other players, respect of the playing field's boundaries, and control of one's negative emotions during the polo game:

> [H]it the ball with swift stroke, twirling the hand in the proximity of the ear and lowering the Sauljan [a type of polo-stick] to the level of the lower part of the chest ... the stroke should be directed sideways, carefully, with attention, with precision and only the point [of the Sauljan must] be used and the course of the ball towards the goal [must] be protected. Further, the ball [must] be driven from its place ... hit it [the ball] under the belly-band of the horse from the side of the upper part of the chest, with a moderate strength, and try and reach the goal and win; and one must not try, when hitting the ball, to help with the whip, and [one must] not hit the ground with the Sauljan, and, when using it, not break it on account of the lack of skill, and not hurt the legs of the horse, and [one must] be careful not to hurt whomsoever might be racing [with one] across the maydan [the stadium's playing field], and to direct well the horse in his swift course, and be careful not to fall and not to be hit, and not allow any place to anger, abuse, irritation, dispute ... one should not run against and knock off those sitting on its [the stadium or maydan] walls.[27]

One salient feature of this passage is the reference to swiftness with respect to the stroke of the polo stick and the riding of the steed. The element of swiftness in action and reaction appears to have been integral to the Sassanian warrior's training, not only in polo but in all aspects of martial training. Roman respect for the quickness of Sassanian warriors is addressed by Libanius, who wrote to Modestus (in the context of Rome's wars with Shapur II) that 'you act well in imitating ...

the Persians in your swiftness'.[28] Swiftness is also a feature of Persian archery, as attested to by Romano-Byzantine sources (Chapter 5).

The game of polo was not simply about the men who rode the horses, but also about the level of training the horses had achieved. Libanius makes this clear by stating that 'these men had to ride a horse that obeyed their voice instead of the bridle'.[29] Without this level of training for his horse, the rider would have great difficulty in directing his chaugan with precision, control and speed. In a sense, the game of polo cultivated a close connection between rider and horse that would prove critical on the battlefield. The rider's ability to adeptly handle and deploy his array of weaponry on the battlefield was highly contingent on his horse's level of training. Indeed, that level of training could mean the difference between life and death for the rider in a combat situation.

Polo was a highly prestigious sport practised by Ardashir I, the founder of the Sassanian dynasty, and is cited as one of the most important activities in the Middle Persian *Romance of Ardashir*. The game of polo was as important to Sassanian Persia as chariot races were to the Romano-Byzantines. The Arabian caliphs adopted the Sassanian game of polo, with the Arabs then transferring this game to the Europeans. In the West the Persian legacy of polo is manifested in the word *chaugan*, which has Western phonological cognates such as *chekan* (Russian), *choca* (Spanish-Portuguese), *chicane* (French), or *schaggun* (German).

The Hunt: Training for War

Another important venue for military training was the royal hunt, which could involve the use of sword, lance and archery against beasts, either on horseback or dismounted. Hanaway describes three major aspects of the hunt in the Persian cultural milieu:[30] the linkage between hunting and warfare, an arena for physical action, and the display of ruthlessness.

Equivalence of the hunt and warfare and the hunter-warrior. The hunting 'arena' was analogous to the battlefield: the hunter was the equivalent of the warrior with his prey being his battlefield adversary. As noted by Hanaway:

> Hunting and war ... resembled each other strongly in practice ... [they] required bravery, strength and skill ... dangerous activities involving risk to both the hunter and the warrior. In both, the prey, human or animal, was pursued, eventually to be caught and killed. The techniques were similar and the weapons were the same, and in each case large numbers of men and horses were involved.[31]

The linkage between warfare and hunting is made very explicit in the Islamic-era Persian literature, notably by Farrokhi, who addressed Massoud of Ghazna (r. 1031–1041 CE) in the following fashion:

> Since hunting to some extent resembles war, out of passion for battle when you are resting from war your thoughts turn to hunting ...[32] Sometimes your sword raises dust from the enemy's head; sometimes your arrow takes vengeance on a lion's breast ... On hunting day it matters not to you if it be a fox or a lion: in

battle it matters not to you if they be foot soldiers or horsemen[33] ... On the day of battle you take every king, on hunting day you take every lion.[34]

In a sense the hunt was the Sassano-Persianate world's approximation of the modern-day 'live fire' exercise meant to simulate (or re-create), as much as possible, the dangerous circumstances a soldier would encounter on the battlefield. Once again, this is indicated in Islamic-era Persian literature, as when Saad-Salman (c. 1121) notes: 'You are victorious, a king, a Khosrow, a Lord ... a city-conquering general and a lion-hunting king[35] ... You are a King-hunter and when there are no kings left, of necessity you hunt [the] lion.'[36]

Similarly, Moezzi enjoins warriors to 'be a lion and all your enemies be prey'.[37] The (pre-Islamic) archetype of the hunter-warrior survived the fall of the Sassanians to be preserved in the characters of Rustam (in the *Shahname*) and Garshasp (in the *Garshaspname*).[38]

Physical action: display of bravery, skill and stamina. The Sassanians recognized that skills, bravery and physical stamina required in the hunt are equally important on the battlefield. The weapons used on the battlefield, notably spears, swords, and archery are also used against beasts. Skill is of course paramount but of equal importance, especially in the Turco-Iranian (pre-Islamic and Islamic-era) military tradition, are the associated qualities of bravery and physical endurance. The hunt is both test and training for the hunter, as he must fuse his combat skills, courage and stamina just as he would as a knight fighting against formidable Romano-Byzantines or Turkic-Hun warriors.

Ruthlessness: hunt or be hunted. This quality of the hunt as display and training is critical as it involves the concept of 'kill or be killed'; or, as Hanaway wrote, as 'hunt or be hunted'.[39] The hunter is deliberately placed in dangerous situations where he could be fatally attacked by boars or lions, or be trampled to death by wild onagers, and it is at this critical moment when his choice of weapons will determine his survival. Likewise when fighting against opposing warriors, the knight's choice of weaponry is critical depending on battlefield circumstances and especially with respect to perceived combat strengths and weaknesses of his enemy. Hesitation, even for a moment, could spell the difference between life and death when fighting against wild beasts or enemy warriors. In contrast, ruthlessness of action conveyed the warrior's lack of remorse, doubt and hesitation in killing off his opponent. This aspect of his military training served to not only enhance his fighting skills and increase his physical strength, but also to further develop the 'non-physical' attributes of bravery, valour, resoluteness and composure in the face of blood and death.[40]

Sassanian representations of the hunt. There are at least two primary sources for the display of hunting motifs, these being the panels at the entrance to the vault or *iwan* of Taghe Bostan as well as Sassanian metalwork. The right side of the grand iwan at Taghe Bostan shows the deer hunt taking place within an enclosure or garden-type compound. In one scene, Khosrow II is shown with a bow and lappet suspension sword; a page holds an umbrella over the king's head. Other nobles can be seen engaged in the hunt, with musicians in the background blaring what appear to be long wind instruments (horns?). One figure in particular is seen with his back to the viewer, shooting an arrow downwards at fleeing game.

The left side of the grand iwan shows a boar hunt, again within a giant enclosure or 'paradise'. One scene shows Khosrow II (with front or chest area towards viewer) drawing his bow while standing in a boat with a number of musicians. The target of Khosrow II's archery is a boar which is first leaping towards him and is then shown as killed. Of special interest is a rare Sassanian depiction of elephants, which were highly regarded by the Sassanian nobility (Chapter 7). These are on the left side of the panel: there are eleven elephants forcing a mass of boars to flee before them. On the right side of the panel are at least three elephants transporting recently slain boars. Sassanian metalwork representations of the hunt are discussed below.

A description of the Persian hunt: the Garshasp-Name. There are numerous descriptions of the hunt in Islamic-era Persian literature, notably in the *Shah-name*.[41] The *Garshasp-Name* of Asadi-Tusi in particular provides a vivid description of the Persian hunt. Composed around 1072 CE, the themes provide insight into the hunt in both the pre-Islamic and Islamic eras. Note that this poem is derived from pre-Islamic themes: Garshasp, the hero of the poem, is father to Nariman and great-grandfather to Saam, whom Firdowsi identifies with the (Old Iranian Avestan) *Kereshaspa*. Asadi-Tusi describes Garshasp's engagement in the Persian hunt as follows:

> The dust raised by the horses darkened the sun, and the necks of the onagers were in the lassos of the heroes ... the ground was like onyx under the stags' hooves, and the soft sand and hard mountain slopes were red with blood ... From every hilltop a lookout would shout, and the heroes would raise as much dust as fleeing demons. Garshasp ran on foot and laid an ambush for stags, and when they came near, he leaped from his place, seized their antlers and threw them down. He grasped two sets of antlers, and in a passion dashed one against the other. He struck them so hard that their bodies became weak, then he broke their heads and necks.[42]

Asadi-Tusi has provided a number of distinguishing features in the above passage. The first is how the hero Garshasp was willing to dismount from his horse to entrap and kill his prey. The hunt therefore is not simply confined to action on horseback but also on foot. This is vividly depicted, for example, in metal plates which show a (unidentified) Sassanian king hunting boars on foot with his spear;[43] Shapur III (383–388 CE) slaying a leopard on foot with a sword;[44] and Pirouz (r. 459–484 CE) hunting ibex on foot with his bow.[45] There is also a depiction of Bahram II (r. 274–293 CE) at Sar Mashad where he is shown killing lions as he stands on foot to defend his queen. While this is not an actual 'hunting' context, the Sar Mashad representation and the metal works indicate that the Sassanian knight was expected to be proficient in the use of his array of weaponry (spears, swords, archery, etc.), whether on foot or horseback, both as hunter and as battlefield warrior. The second point (at least with respect to weaponry) is the use of lassoes to ensnare the necks of the prey from horseback, much as the lasso had been used by late Sassanian knights as cited by Tabari (Chapter 6) and even as far back as Achaemenid (or pre-Achaemenid) times by Sagarthians. The third aspect is the ability of the hunter to engage and kill his prey without weapons, literally with his bare hands. Seizing the antlers of stags to then throw them onto the ground, not to mention Garshasp's smashing of the heads of the stags to slay them, are feats that require tremendous physical strength, agility and overall fitness. The warrior in turn was expected to be proficient in hand-to-hand combat during battle, especially wrestling and physical strength (see discussion below). Closely intertwined with the concept of physical strength and combat skill (empty-handed and with weaponry) is the ability to singlehandedly fight against multiple opponents. This is seen in the descriptions of warrior-hunter heroes in the *Shahname*, notably Bizhan, who slays numerous boars during the hunt, and Rustam, who remains to fight on the battlefield despite being faced with overwhelming numbers of the enemy.

Also notable is the mention of lookouts signalling the location of potential prey to the hunters. This is somewhat similar to the spah's system of vanguards. These moved ahead of the main military force to occupy strategic positions for the gathering of valuable intelligence to then communicate the location, strength and dispositions of the enemy to the main spah force.[46]

The zoorkhaneh, varzesh-e-bastani and traditional Iranian martial arts: a Partho-Sassanian legacy? One of the most important qualities expected of Sassanian warriors was raw physical strength. The *Shahname* emphasizes this quality for warriors by equating truthfulness with physical strength and character flaws and mendaciousness with physical weakness.[47] The *zoorkhaneh* (lit. house of power) and its *varzesh-e bastani* (lit. exercises/sports from ancient/pre-Islamic times) provides a fascinating window into Iran's traditional strength and martial arts training. The zoorkhaneh is the traditional Iranian martial arts school which has for centuries been an important medium for training Iranian warriors. The roots of this can be traced to the pre-Islamic Zoroastrian tradition. Beizai-Kashani has noted that the exercise equipment of the varzesh-e bastani was essentially derived from traditional Iranian weaponry going back to ancient times.[48] Khorasani has provided an exhaustive overview of the zoorkhaneh,[49] with Abbasi's text having provided a comprehensive overview of the history of wrestling since ancient times in all regions of Iran.[50]

The trainee of the zoorkhaneh was and remains the pahlavan. The Pahlavi (Middle Persian) term *pahlavan* hails back to Partho-Sassanian times (250 BCE–651 CE) which generally describes a warrior endowed with courage, generosity, conviction, fairness and mercy in battle. These are combined with a profound sense of obedience and camaraderie concomitant with a high level of frahang (culture and moral conduct), as well as a duty to protect the weak and helpless, and to treat non-combatants with generosity.[51] Interestingly, Chardin, writing during the Islamic Safavid era of Iran (1501–1736 CE), notes that the wrestlers of the zoorkhaneh are known as *pehelvon* (pahlavan) which he describes as meaning 'gallant' and 'brave'.[52]

Meel, sang and other ancient Persian weights. The *meel* is a mace-like wooden exercise tool used for building physical strength and stamina. The zoorkhaneh routine requires that the pahlavan wield one meel per hand, and to be able to move, swing and gyrate these in a series of coordinated and specified movements. Each meel weighs between 25lb and 60lb and can stand up to 4½ft tall. An 'average' pahlavan can easily lift 60lb meels per hand. Heavier meels for more advanced zoorkhaneh pahlavan athletes can weigh in at 110lb each. Meel workouts are coordinated by the drumming and songs of the *morshed* (lit. spiritual/ wisdom guide).

There is also the equivalent of the Western 'bench press' in the traditional zoorkhaneh. Known as the *sang* (lit. stone/rock), this was originally based on the *separ* (shield). Contemporary versions of the sang are built of wooden planks, in contrast to the past when actual stone was used. The sang is equipped with handles allowing the pahlavan to engage in bench press-type exercises. The zoorkhaneh bench press is considerably more difficult that its modern Western counterpart as the pahlavan must engage in a variety of different types of lifts. For example, the pahlavan must push the sang up from different angles, in contrast to the Western athlete who only pushes the bench press upwards. Suffice it to say that the sang exercise is highly demanding, which in combination with other zoorkhaneh workouts builds up a high level of physical strength.

There were other types of ancient 'weights' used by the pahlavans for martial training. One of these is seen in a rare photograph of the late pahlavan Reza Zanjani who performed curls with one type of traditional Iranian weights.[53] This type of weight has a bar for fixing weights on each end; however, the weights themselves are not disc-shaped in the modern sense of contemporary weights. Instead, they are globular in shape. These are approximately 20cm in diameter and made of metal. There are four such globular weights attached to each end of the bar (total of eight globes). Abbasi notes that 'in addition to his talents in wrestling, [Reza Zanjani] was one of those pahlavans who performed incredible feats of strength to his last days'.[54] Abbasi's observation is verified when considering the combined weight of the four globular weights. According to the Technicon Engineering table, each standard steel ball of 20cm diameter (high carbon, chrome alloy or stainless steel) weighs in at approximately 72lb.[55] Therefore the total amount of weights being curled by Reza Zanjani would have been approximately 288–290lb. The notion of physical strength and the pahlavan are integral in the zoorkhaneh. The pahlavans of the spah were no different; the *Shahname* is replete with references to the primacy of the legendary warrior-hero Rustam's physical strength. While specific training regimens and exercise equipment dated to the Sassanian era have yet to be identified, the zoorkhaneh legacy of ancient Iran would strongly suggest that the savaran knights and Dailamite warriors were heavily trained to develop physical strength. Recall for example the aforementioned discussion on the Sassanian hunt where warriors were expected to fight dangerous beasts at close quarters with or without weapons. The adept handling of close-quarters combat weapons (i.e., swords, lances, etc.) had to be combined with physical strength when confronting dangerous beasts (i.e., wild boars, bears, etc.) or when locked in close-quarters combat against the formidable troops of the Romano-Byzantine tradition or the Turkic-Hun warriors of Central Asia. Heliodorus has noted in the *Aethiopica* that the Sassanian warrior selected for the elite savaran was 'chosen for his bodily strength'.[56] This would strongly suggest that the spah valued physical strength in its warriors and emphasized this in its training regimens. More on the importance of physical strength will be discussed shortly below under the topic of wrestling.

Takhteh shena. These are ancient Persia's version of the contemporary western push-up exercises. The pahlavan places his hands on a wooden plank (1m length, 10cm width). There are five types of *takhteh shena* push-ups: (1) push-ups with legs close to each other; (2) push-ups by turning to the right and left side; (3) push-ups with fast movements; (4) single push-ups; and (5) push-ups with open arms and legs. Takhteh shena push-ups are often done in groups. Note that each takhteh shena movement is synchronized with the drumming and songs of the morshed.

Kabade. This is a 'bow' of iron or steel with an iron-chain string. It is possible that the *kabade* was derived from archery equipment in Iran's pre-Islamic era, however this thesis does require research to substantiate. One kabade measures at around 150cm in length and weighs approximately 45lb. One kabade exercise involves holding the device over the head to then swing it from left to right. This exercise results in a profound increase in stamina, especially with respect to the pahlavan's cardiovascular and muscular systems. This would have increased the warrior's battlefield endurance, especially with respect to repeated handling of close-quarters weapons or archery equipment. When faced with formidable opponents such as the Romano-Byzantines or Turco-Huns, Sassanian warriors would be required to wield and deploy their weaponry for long periods of time. If the warrior lacked cardiovascular and muscular endurance, his performance and efficacy in the use of these weapons would be imperilled. While no direct evidence exists that the kabade was used in Sassanian times, it is possible that variations or earlier versions of the kabade was used by Sassanian military instructors in training warriors.

Pa zadan. The *pa zadan* routines involve a series of exercises performed with a variety of traditional athletic tools meant to increase speed and reaction time. Exercises include a series of stepping workouts and avoidance training. These train the pahlavan to avoid the blows of opponents in face-to-face combat.

Charkh. The *charkh* is an exercise in which the pahlavan steps into the middle of the training arena to then engage in spinning. The spinning, which is coordinated with the drumming of the morshed, is first done slowly and then increased, becoming steadily faster. This particular exercise was one of those intended to train the pahlavan to combat against superior numbers of the enemy. This tactic was apparently used by Iranian warriors during the Safavid era, when they often had to fight against much larger numbers of Ottoman troops. In such a scenario, the pahlavan would hold his sword or dagger with an outstretched hand to then 'spin and slash' his way out through the enemy. While the charkh is an ancient Iranian combat technique, no actual (Sassanian) depictions of this have been identified. Given the fact that the Sassanian spah (like the later, Islamic armies of Iran) was often faced with situations where its warriors had to fight against superior numbers of troops, it may be safe to assume that Sassanian military training would have taken this factor into account by developing suitable exercises.

Koshti. Mohammad-Jahani has noted that wrestling in Iran dates back to ancient times and is rooted in the Zoroastrian religion.[57] The Zoroastrians had a sacred belt known as the *kustik* (Sassanian Pahlavi) with the term *koshti* meaning 'wrestling' in modern Persian. It is important to note that traditional Iranian martial arts were not confined strictly to wrestling. The Dailamites of northern Persia, whose skills in close-quarters combat were acknowledged by Agathias[58] combined a variety of combat methods. Wrestling is in fact an ancient tradition in northern Iran (in practice throughout Iran), but the northern Iranian variety was different in that it resembled the modern day mixed martial arts of the UFC variety where combatants deploy a variety of techniques during combat, namely, wrestling, kicking, punching, etc. The 'mixed' form of wrestling from ancient northern Iran endures to this day in Iran's northern Gilan province where the locals exercise this combat form of combining wrestling with punching.[59]

The *Shahname* cites the importance of wrestling (and its 'mixed' nature) in settling the outcome of combat between champions. Note the following verses from the *Shahname*:[60] *Cho Shiran be Koshti bar Avikhtand* [like lions they started to wrestle] / *Ze Tanha Khoy va Khon hami Rikhtand* [with their bodies and shed each other's blood].

The reference to *khon hami rikhtand* [shedding of blood/each other's blood] during the koshti would suggest that this type of ancient wrestling involved other forms of mixed martial arts, like the ancient Dailamite techniques discussed earlier. Sims, Marshak and Grube have noted that the notion of combat between champions is in fact indicative of a larger martial culture extending from the Baltic region to Russia, Iran and the Turco-Mongolian steppes of Central Asia.[61] These researchers have also alluded to the fact of how such heroes would clash three times, using different weapons in each encounter. If the weapons failed to produce victory, the combatants would resort to wrestling and it was in this arena where sheer physical strength would decide the outcome of the duel. Note the strong parallels between the Sims, Marshak and Grube study and the above-mentioned verses of the *Shahname* with respect to the primacy of wrestling and physical strength in combat.

The use of sound to project explosive shouts against the enemy during hand-to-hand combat was also prominent among Sassanian warriors,[62] this being intended to frighten and/or demoralize their opponents. This is not unlike the projection of the *kiai* (battle shouts) made by later Samurai warriors of the

Japanese martial tradition. The use of sound, especially martial music, is further discussed below.

Shamsher-wazig. One particular form of *shamsher-wazig* (fencing and sword combat) is the so-called Italian grip, which is first seen in Sassanian metal plates. Specifically this is depicted in a metal plate of Shapur I, who wields his sword by wrapping his forefinger around his sword's quillons as he slays a deer during the hunt.[63] This Sassanian method was essentially a new and efficient method of the 'thrust-and-swing' technique of fencing. The 'thrust' aspect was especially improved by this grip as shown in the plate of Shapur I, as this moves the centre of gravity much closer to the tip of the sword. The result was a more powerful thrust as the warrior lunged forward. The grip also allowed for a more powerful sword strike. This Sassanian style of sword grip was not known to the Roman-European arena and was to be adopted by the Arabs who then transmitted this to Spain and hence to Europe where it became known as the 'Italian grip'.

One interesting exercise dating from ancient times which was apparently revived during the Safavid era pertained to *shamsher-wazig*. In this exercise, heavy weights would be attached to each arm and shoulder when fencing.[64] Instructors gave specific exercises for sword movements, including left-right, up-down and backward slashing actions. The objective of these exercises was to increase the pahlavan's endurance and physical strength in combination with his fencing skills.

Stick combat. Stick fighting was an ancient sport and was clearly seen among troops of the caliphates. This martial art form is still practised by the Lurs and Bakhtiaris of western Iran.[65] The pahlavans of Safavid times reportedly wielded sticks (wrapped in wire) that weighed up to 20lb.[66]

Ancient Iranian legacy in the Safavid era. It is possible that a number of training exercises and treatises on warfare from the Sassanian era had been revived by the Safavids for the pahlavan warriors of that era.[67] These military training methods which were based on ancient Iranian martial traditions yielded success for the Safavid military against the Ottoman Turks in the early 1600s CE. One such example occurred at Yerevan where the occupying Ottoman garrison which had held out for months against a Safavid besieging force was quickly overwhelmed and forced to surrender after fierce close-quarters hand-to-hand combat in June 1604.[68] While Ottomans were certainly among the world's best troops at the time in the use of firearms, the Iranian troops they faced at Yerevan were, according to Vecchietti, 'expert in fighting with sword, lance and bow, and ... were greatly superior to the Turks in this'.[69]

Martial Music
Music has been integral to the martial traditions of Iran, in both the pre-Islamic and Islamic eras. Nevertheless, the significance of martial music in the armies of pre-Islamic Iran and other West Asian militaries has generally received little

attention by Western scholarship. As noted by Nikonorov, music in the pre-Islamic Iranian and Central Asian military traditions served three major purposes:[70] (1) as battlefield signals for manoeuvres such as attacks, defence and other important actions; (2) for inspiring martial ardour and combat resilience within the warriors; and (3) to cultivate dread and foster demoralization among enemy troops.

The *Shahname*, which is essentially an epic compendium of the pre-Islamic martial traditions of Iran, makes reference to specific musical instruments, as discussed below. The mythical hero Houshang is described as the inventor of the *qodum* (kettledrum), Jamshid as the progenitor of the *zornay* (oboe); trumpets and horns are attributed to Manouchehr and Afrasiyab.

The Achaemenids. Writing in the Islamic era, Ibn Zayla reported that the ancient Persian kings used 'noisy instruments' during their battles.[71] Sekunda has discussed an Achaemenid bronze figurine once housed in Rome's Pollak Collection which depicts an Achaemenid trooper blowing a horn.[72] Xenophon reported that young military trainees would awaken every morning to the sound of bronze instruments.[73] Alexander is believed to have adopted Achaemenid or 'Oriental' drums to accompany the military melodies of his trumpets.[74] He also added more 'noise' to his martial instruments by his incorporation of what has been described as a 'huge organ' which (if the sources are to be believed) was audible for a range of approximately 100km![75]

The Parthians: battlefield percussion. Strabo, writing around the early 60s BCE during the time of the Parthians, noted that the youth of Iran were not only taught music but were trained to be called to arms by the sound of brass instruments.[76] The Parthian battlefield musical instrument par excellence was the drum, as reported in the battle of Carrhae (53 BCE) by Plutarch.[77] Justin noted that the Parthians gave their battlefield signals with the 'tympanum' and not with trumpets.[78] The mainly infantry-based Roman armies faced by the Parthians are reported as having entered into battle with the sound of wind instruments.[79] Herodian certainly mentions the drum as being among the repertoire of Parthian instruments.[80]

Plutarch has provided an exceptionally detailed account of the battle of Carrhae, with a very informative description of Parthian percussion instruments, especially the (battlefield) drum. This is described as hollow and 'pot-like' in shape, covered by a (skin) membrane with a series of bells hung around it.[81] Specifically the bodies of these drums, known as *naqareh* in Persian, were made of clay and covered with membranes through the method of crossing thongs.[82] These drums were usually struck by sticks and appear to have varied in size from large to small, although specific dimensions have yet to be determined and await further research and study. In general larger drums were carried by pack animals, most likely camels. It is generally accepted that the Parthian kettledrums were of the single or paired type with the latter carried by pack animals.[83] The armies of the Islamic era often used camels or even elephants to transport percussion instruments to the battlefield.[84] General Surena's drummers at Carrhae were most likely a combination of horsemen carrying kettledrums of the 'pointed helmet' type (see below) as well as camels carrying the larger 'pot-type' drums.[85] The use of camels for carrying pot-type drums is reported by the thirteenth century Italian traveller Marco Polo, who noted that Mongol warriors entered battle when given the signal by their *nakar* or nagara drummers.[86]

Another type of drum in Central Asia among the Uzbek and Turkic peoples featured a body construction of the metallic 'pointed helmet' type covered with an animal-skin membrane. This could be played with hands, a whip or two sticks. These could be carried on foot or fastened with leather straps to the saddle. It is known that early (pre-Islamic) Turkic tribes did use drumming much like the Parthians and the Sassanians (Chapter 12). These survived the Classical era to be used by the Turks, Uzbeks and Ottomans in the later Islamic era. The nineteenth century Hungarian scholar and traveller, Arminius Vamberry, for example, noted that the forces of the Emir of Bukhara entering the city of Samarqand were accompanied by horsemen beating these types of kettledrums with sticks; these were suspended by straps to the saddle.[87] Ottoman armies and their Tatar allies who often sought to invade Iran during the Safavid period used kettledrums of the same type. Interestingly, Ottoman-Tatar usage of these kettledrums was to be adopted by the armies of medieval Europe (especially the Hungarians and Poles).[88]

Martial music as battlefield weapon: Carrhae (53 BCE). Parthian battle doctrine was essentially of the all-cavalry type in which heavily armed and armoured lancers closely cooperated with horse archers. Parthian kettledrums were used to coordinate the actions and strikes of the lancers and horse archers, but there was also a key psychological aspect to Parthian battlefield percussion. Struck by special sticks, Parthian drums emitted a terrible sound, something akin to a mixture of thunder and beastly howls. The sound range of these drums is believed to have radiated for several kilometers.[89] These terrible sounds combined with their intense volume were certainly intended to strike fear in the enemy ranks. Inexperienced enemy troops unaccustomed to such sounds were certainly vulnerable to this form of psychological warfare. The Parthians had trained their horses to remain calm when these drums were struck,[90] while in contrast enemy horses unaccustomed to Parthian battlefield percussion were in danger of losing their nerve.

At Carrhae, Surena was clearly using a number of other psychological techniques alongside his drumming during his confrontation with the Roman forces of Marcus Lucinius Crassus. First, Surena was careful to pull back the bulk of his primary force behind an advancing force to mislead the Romans as to the real size of the Parthian army. Second, as the clash of arms became imminent, Surena executed yet another ingenious scheme he had devised to shock his Roman opponents. The Parthian lancers had been instructed to cover themselves with hides in order to conceal their formidable armour. Then as the battle drew near with Parthian drums thundering louder and louder, Surena gave the signal to his knights to drop their covers. This had a dramatic impact as the Romans all of a sudden witnessed their 'humble-looking opponents' literally being transformed into heavily armoured knights shining with Marginian steel. After crushing the attacking force led by Publius Crassus (Marcus Lucinius' son), the Parthians attacked the primary Roman forces once again, accompanied by the sound of drums as well as battle cries and hymns.[91]

The Sassanians: expansion of battlefield instruments? Military music was an integral part of the Sassanian spah. Farmer notes that the three primary military instruments of the Sassanians were percussion-drums, pipes and trumpets.[92] The display of trumpets in a military context is depicted on a post-Sassanian Soghdian silver dish housed in the Hermitage Museum depicting trumpeters in a fortress.[93] The battle would begin in earnest with the sounding of trumpets and drums that would normally be the signal for the savaran knights to commence their attack.[94] The attack of the savaran knights[95] would be supported by the archers[95] who directed their missile salvos against the enemy (Chapter 5 and 6). The spah's military music was a signal system with different notes and sounds designating specific battlefield commands (i.e., savaran knights to advance, archers to fire, etc.). The second role of martial music was psychological in that it was meant to bolster the fighting spirit, resilience and morale of the troops during battle.[96]

The use of drums and percussion to direct battlefield movements was continued from the Parthian era by the Sassanians. The Sassanians had inherited much of the military tradition of the Parthians, with many of the most prominent Parthian clans continuing to provide the spah with its finest cavalry (Chapter 6). While no specific studies have explored the transition of military music from the Parthian into the Sassanian eras, it would be safe to assume that much of this (especially percussion) was passed on to the spah after 224 CE. The military status of Parthian martial drummers is not known, but it may be assumed that they formed a distinct, specialized body or corps within the Parthian military.[97] What is clear is that music played an important role in the Sassanian state. Ardashir I (r. 241–272) elevated the status of musicians in his court, with Bahram Gur (r. 420–438) further elevating their status during his reign. It may be possible that musicians formed a distinct corps within the spah, however this thesis requires further research to substantiate.

There are two other key questions with respect to martial music and the spah. The first is whether battlefield musicians were strictly 'musicians' or whether they could double up as warriors? If these indeed did double-up, then they evidently carried smaller (i.e. kettledrum-type) instruments to then be able to quickly switch to hand-held weapons or archery as battlefield circumstances dictated. The second question is whether these warrior-musicians were infantry or cavalry? A hint as to the answer may found in the Ottoman armies of the 1500s CE, where Turkish cavalrymen would beat their small kettledrums and then draw their deadly sabres just before they got near enough to their enemies to engage in face-to-face combat.

The Sassanians most likely expanded the repertoire of percussion rhythms to accommodate their own innovations in battlefield tactics. Note that Sassanian tactics became more sophisticated than those of their Parthian predecessors, who maintained what was essentially an all-cavalry force until their overthrow in 224 CE. As noted by Nikonorov, the Sassanians used the kettledrum for battlefield coordination, which prompted the Romano-Byzantines to also adopt the kettledrum for similar military purposes.[98] The use of the kettledrum by the Byzantines is reported as late as the tenth century CE in Leo Diaconus' *History*, where the author notes this instrument being used to direct cavalry manoeuvres during battles.[99] The Sassanians also made use of the kettledrum as a psychological weapon. Agathias, for example, noted how Sassanian besieging forces at the Phasis fortress in the 550s CE used military drumming and battle cries to undermine the morale of the besieged.[100]

The most comprehensive view of instruments in a martial context is seen at the aforementioned panels at the entrance to the vault or iwan at Taghe Bostan. Musicians occupy a very important status at the hunt, alongside figures of hunters engaged in archery. Khosrow II (r. 590–628 CE) accorded a very high rank to the 'royal' musicians as indicated in his convocation of both governors as well as musicians during an opening ceremony on an embankment of the Tigris River.[101] Each of the two royal boats has a musician (harpist) seated next to the king. Each boat has yet another boat following it carrying a band of (half a dozen) more harpists. There is also a (fifth) boat ferrying a band of men who appear to be singing and clapping (to keep time) in unison. A very interesting depiction is that of women singers again clapping together (to keep time) with another row of harpists along with other musicians playing mouth-organs, tambourines and oboes. Finally there is the figure of the king mounted on his horse flanked by a servant holding an umbrella for the monarch; in this venue there are trumpeters, drummers and other figures who appear to be singers. It is clear that these musicians were not simply making 'white noise' or providing mere entertainment in the modern-day sense; their music was helping to create a 'martial atmosphere' for the hunt. Likewise, music played an important role on the battlefield. This is seen in the earlier armies of India where Strabo reports musicians and musical instruments being present in the military forces of Chandragupta Maurya of the late fourth to early third centuries BCE.[102] Like the Parthians and the Sassanians, the ancient Indians also used percussion for signalling and directing the movement of troops on the battlefield.[103]

The *Shahname* provides explicit descriptions of instruments prominent in the martial music of pre-Islamic (notably Sassanian) Iran.[104] Wind instruments include horn/trumpet-type instruments such as the *buq*, *karanay*, *shaypoor*, and *ruyeen-ney* (brazen pipe); as well as the *ney* (reed). As in Parthian times percussion-drum type instruments also feature prominently, notably the *koos* (kettledrum), *tabira* (drum), *sinj* (cymbal), *zang* (sonnette) and *daray hindi* (Indian bell). Ibn Zayla also cites bells hung from elephants which the Sassanians deployed on the battlefield (Chapter 7).[105]

The *Shahname* makes references to Shapur I having 'paraded his drums, banners and troops'[106] prior to his showdown with Emperor Valerian at Barbalissos. Another key reference to military instruments in the *Shahname* is to the fateful battle between the spah led by king Pirouz and the Hephthalites led by Kush-navaz who emerged victorious (484 CE):[107]

Bar amad ze har do sepah boogh va koos
Hava shod ze gard e sepah anboos
Chenan tir-baran shod az har do rooy
Ke chon ab-e khoon andar amad be jooy

Interestingly both the Sassanian and Hephthalite armies employed trumpets and drums/percussion [*har do sepah boogh va koos*], which resulted in the antagonists unleashing massive volleys of archery [*chenan tir-baran shod az har do rooy*], that inflicted terrible casualties or the spilling of 'streams of blood' [*khoon andar amad be jooy*].

There are other examples besides those in the *Shahname* describing the koos and tabira in martial situations. Gorgani's *Vis o Ramin* (written in circa 1050s CE), for example, mentions these instruments.[108] Of special interest is the mention of a battle drum identified as a *tombag* in the Middle Persian or Sassanian Pahlavi *Ayadgar e Zareran*, which appears to have been based on a Parthian battle epic. The modern Persian *donbak* has a goblet-type shape played in a rather sophisti-cated fashion requiring considerable dexterity with the fingers; however, it is not clear how the drumming was done in a Sassanian battlefield context. A version of the Sassanian-era tombag has survived in modern-day Tajikestan where it known by the locals as the *tablak*.

A note on other instruments. The flute also apparently played a critical role in the martial traditions of Iran, although more research is required in this area. Ibn Khordadbeh, for example, attributes the invention of the flute to the Kurds. This is interesting, as Shah Ismail (r. 1501–1524), the founder of the Safavid dynasty who hailed from a partly Kurdish ancestry,[109] sounded his 'mystical' flute to signal the retreat of his remaining warriors after the disastrous outcome of the Battle of Chaldiran against the formidable Ottoman armies in 1514.[110]

Chapter 5

Archery

Archery has played a seminal if not primary role in the military history of Iran since the earliest Indo-European arrivals onto the Iranian plateau. The prestige and high status of archery has been noted by some of the earliest works of Iranian mythology. One example is the ancient *Avesta*, which honours the mythical archer Erekhsha, whose arrow shot spanned incredible distances. A passage in the *Tir-Yasht* describes how 'the mental arrow [speed immeasurable and only mentally conceived] ... was of Erekhsha, the swift Iranian archer, the swiftest archer among all Iranians'.[1] Perfection in archery was also considered a triumph of the intellect, as indicated by the *Menog-e Xrad (Minoo Kherad)* which states 'the spirit of complete mindfulness a bow, and the spirit of liberality an arrow'.[2] Suffice it to say that archery in ancient Iran was not just a functional military arm, but a martial tradition closely intertwined with a unique mythological and intellectual tradition.

Tabari reports of three famous archers from the Sassanian era: Bahram Chobin, Sukhra and Arash. Firdowsi's *Shahname* cites Saam as ancient Iran's greatest mace-warrior with Arash as Iran's greatest archer.[3] Archery was considered almost sacred among the officers of the spah. General Vahriz, for example, shot an arrow towards the location where he was to be put to rest upon his passing.[4] Persian archery has been praised by a multitude of Classical sources, including Herodotus,[5] Strabo,[6] Procopius[7] and Ammianus Marcellinus, who remarked that archery was an art 'in which ... that nation [Persia] has always been most skilful from the cradle'.[8]

Archery Training

Mastery of the bow is achieved with continuous and consistent practice over a long period of time. Training in archery is also very hard work, as the objective is to be able to draw the bow with full strength, yet retain control when shooting the missile.[9] Citing Bartholomae's works on ancient Persian archery, Modi reports, 'The more you draw your bow with all your possible strength, the more distant the arrow will go. So, put forth all possible energy in your work and the result will be proportionately good.'[10] Put simply, archery skill was not singularly defined by how fast the archer shot his arrows, but also by the strength of his draw, which was critical to the missile's propulsion (especially velocity and penetration power).

The primary objective of archery training was to ensure that the bowman's hands remained consistent and steady throughout the entire process of drawing his bow and releasing the missile. Matofi notes that the novice would first train on a smaller bow known as the *lozum*, which was incapable of propelling arrows with the speed and power of regular military bows.[11] Extrapolating from Islamic-era manuals, it would appear that Sassanian training bows of increasing sizes and weights were given to young trainees as they progressed with their training and acquired greater skill.[12] The conclusion of training meant that the Sassanian archer was capable of drawing his bow and releasing his missile with full manual control with no unsteadiness in the hands. The Sassanian archer drew his bow with skill, power and smoothness of motion, a task which required decades of training. As noted in Chapter 4, military training in a variety of domains, especially archery, would extend from the ages of five to twenty-four years.[13] Even as the warrior acquired mastery in the use of the bow, he would continue to hone his skills in peacetime, a practice broadly known as *tir-wazig* (arrow play).[14]

Sassanian proficiency in archery was the result of intense training that was based upon elaborate theoretical foundations recorded in texts.[15] The emphasis on horse archery is seen from the early days of the Sassanian spah. Training in archery was highly praised, as seen in the Pahlavi *Romance of Ardashir*, which mentions a hero who had received the best *frahang* (education required to become a knight, see Chapter 4) and who devoted much of his time to archery training at the court of the shahanshah.[16] The early savaran knights of Ardashir I (r. 224–242), facing the invading forces of Roman Emperor Alexander Severus (r. 222–235), are described by Herodian as thus: 'use the bow and the horse in war ... reared with these from childhood ... [they] never lay aside their quivers or dismount from their horses'.[17]

An interesting form of horse archery training is seen with respect to Islamic-era Safavid methods involving the Parthian shot. In this training method the rider was to engage in the Parthian shot by aiming his missile towards a cup placed on top of a 120ft-tall pillar. The objective was to accurately strike the target while riding at a full gallop.

A very detailed description of Sassanian archery training is provided in the *Ayin-nameh*:

> [I]t is a good thing when teaching shooting with arrows, that the pupil should hold the bow, clasping the same with the upper part of his left hand and the arrow clasping the same with upper part of his right hand and [that] the wrists [of his hands he should press] to his chest, and that he should look towards the place where [stands] the teacher of archery. And it is advisable to raise the bow, bending a little its horn, and to grasp it firmly with three fingers, and to bend the forefinger on the string, and to hold in the twenty-three, as if in the sixty-three, and to clench firmly the three, and to turn the chin towards the left shoulder, and to lift the head, and to lower the neck, and to stoop with the bow, and straighten the spine, and to lower the upper part of the arm, and to bend the bow rising [in the saddle], and to stretch the string to the [level of the] ear, and to raise the eyes, to inspect attentively the place [of the opposition] of the head of the arrow, not to move one's teeth, not to turn one's eyes, not to rock the body.[18]

It is clear that the Sassanians were not only heir to a longstanding archery tradition dating back to the Parthians, Achaemenids, Medes and early Indo-European arrivals, they had also formalized and refined these into sophisticated methods of training. A key question with the above citation is in regard to the terms 'twenty-three' and 'sixty-three': it is not clear what is meant here. According to Inostransev,[19] the right hand in the Sassanian Persian convention served to express units and decades; the middle, fourth and little finger stood for units with the forefinger and thumb for decades. In order to 'express' the figure three, the bowman would firmly press together his little finger, fourth and middle fingers. The left hand served to express hundreds and thousands. The 'expression' of the three is in apparent reference to the Sassanian draw with the emphasis of using the little finger in this draw. Another note of interest is that the term *shast* means both 'sixty' and 'thumb' in Persian. Apparently the instructions are in reference to how the thumb is to be placed within the fingers drawing the bowstring. According to Inostransev, the term 'twenty' is very much like 'sixty' and is simply another variation of how the thumb is placed within the drawing fingers. What may be surmised is that the position of the three fingers is consistent with the position of the thumb in relation to these varying numbers (twenty-three versus sixty-three). What is clear is that the Sassanians were cognizant of various methods of drawing the bow, a topic further discussed later in this chapter.

Sassanian Archery Equipment

Archery equipment comprised of the bow (*kaman*), arrows (*tir/tigr*), incendiary arrows, finger guards, bow case (*kamandan*) and quiver (*tirdan*).

Kaman (bow). The basic bow consists of two components, the body and string. The back is the surface furthest from the string with the belly being the inner surface. The curve above the grip, the area where the archer holds the bow, usually at the bow's centre, is often cited as the upper limb, with the area below the grip as the lower limb.[20] Paterson has noted that the Persian bow was con-structed in the following fashion.[21] The *kaman-saz* (bow maker) began construc-tion with a wooden core which would have the requisite quality of absorbing glue effectively. Different combinations of wood (i.e. cornus, maple, mulberry, etc.) were often built into the bow's core to maximize its strength and flexibility. The core consisted of five parts: grip, two *dustar* and two *siyah*. The latter were the bow's strong, thick and unbending ends. The thin and flexible dustars were the parts of the bow which would be bent when it was being drawn. The parts were then glued together. Bows were usually carried by the right hand with missiles shot with the left hand. Nevertheless, left-handed and ambidextrous archers were highly prized for tactical reasons (Chapter 9).

Construction of the Sassanian bow was meant to achieve a balance of strength, under the forces of tension-stress and compression, as to enable the transfer of potential energy to the bow to then release (or propel) this as the (kinetic energy) of the missile. The bow would have to be designed in such a fashion so that the forces of compression and stretch would not result in distortion of the bow, otherwise this would negatively compromise the smooth transmission of poten-tial to kinetic energy required for the efficient launch of the missile. The

Sassanian composite bow, and indeed all such weapons (especially the Turkic-Hun-Avar bow), was ideally suited for warfare as it could be kept strung for long periods of time without the loss of power (especially in comparison to the more primitive wooden bows). The composite bow could be kept braced for the length of the spah's campaign and even ready for deployment in case there was a surprise attack by the enemy. The importance of archery to the savaran is indicated by Tabari, who noted that savaran knights carried two spare bowstrings for their composite bows as part of their standard equipment.[22] The Iranian term for bowstring is *zeh*, which technically means 'cord of an arrow'.[23] Tafazolli traces the origins of this term to the *Draxt-i-Asurig* dated to Parthian times, in which it is stated that the zeh was constructed of goat sinew.[24]

Coulston's comprehensive paper on Roman archery equipment[25] provides the thesis that the Romans adopted the Avar-Hun-Turkic bow as a result of military contacts on their Danubian frontier. It is possible that the Sassanians adopted the Avar-Hun-Turkic bow after the major military reforms of the sixth century CE. Prior to those reforms, 'pre-Hun' Sassanian and Roman bows featured long and slender ears. Khorasani notes that after the reforms Sassanian bows become more 'Hun-like', featuring shorter ears, longer limbs (in proportion) with possibly wider limbs.[26] The adoption of such equipment is not unlikely as the spah did adopt the lappet suspension system and possibly stirrups (Chapter 6).

Following his analysis of the *Adab al Harb va Shojaie*, Matofi suggests that the Sassanians built different types of bows depending on military requirements, available raw materials and geographical regions.[27] Khorasani has summarized these as *sandare* (resin), *nashab* (a type of Iranian tree used for making bows), *zarang* (an Iranian mountain tree with very strong wood, often used for making arrows), *sheiz* (ebony), *gazb* (any straight branch used for making arrows), *bashjir* (a type of Iranian tree, often used for arrow construction) and *shang-sheryan*.[28] Matofi then explains that the horns of certain beasts were cut and glued with a substance known as *sirishm* ('glue' derived from sinew) to the bow's belly.[29] The back of the bow was then tightly covered with *pey* (sinew) followed by the covering of the bow with the bark of an Iranian poplar tree (*khadang*).[30] After painting the bow, the weapon was preserved with *roghan-kaman* (oil for bow), which Karpowicz describes as being a mixture of resins and oil melted together.[31]

Finger guards. Finger guards significantly decreased the pressure upon the bowman's fingers when drawing the heavier compound bow. Evidence of the early use of such devices in the ancient Near East can be seen in the seventh century BCE Zinjirli, Syria. Overlaet has provided a comprehensive overview of three late Sassanian finger guards built of bronze, metal and gold.[32] Discovered in northern Iran, the dimensions of the finger guards have the following ranges: bronze (length 7.2cm, width 2.9cm); silver (length 7.8cm, width 2.9–3.2cm) and gold (length 7.0cm, width 3.3–2.6cm). It is clear that these finger guards had an oblique cut/opening allowing the archer to bend his fingers. Each of these finger guards has two loops or 'eyelets' attached at their bottom. These allowed small chains to be fitted through to then be crossed on the back of the archer's bow-string hand. This was necessary to prevent the finger guards from just dropping off the hand. The depiction of such a finger guard-and-chain system is seen on a Sassanian silver plaque from Sari (Mazandaran province in northern Iran) housed in the National Museum of Iran. A Sassanian king is drawing a bowstring with chains (or strings) seen at the back of his hand. There is a circular ring on the back of the hand where the chains (or strings) are attached. One of the chains (or strings) then disappears from view between an outstretched index and middle finger. The other chain (or string) disappears between the third or ring finger and little finger. There are then two chains or strings that go from that ring to each end of the wrist; evidently these connect in some fashion (through another ring?) at the back.

Arrows (tir/tigr). The typical Sassanian arrow (*tir* or *tigr*) measured 80–85cm. They were typically constructed by cutting a joint in a reed for the nock. The shaft of that reed was constructed of wood and fletched with three vanes. The *Mehr-Yasht* makes mention of a variety of arrow heads including 'vulture-feathered', 'horn-handled', 'iron-bladed', 'gold-notched', 'falcon-winged', 'yellow-pointed', 'gold-pointed', and 'lead-poisoned'.[33] Tafazzolli's studies of ancient texts also reveal 'eagle-feathered' and 'three-feathered'[34] arrows. Most likely each of these served a distinct battlefield function, but more research is required to exactly ascertain the function of each type of missile. Sassanian arrowheads appeared to have generally been of the tanged type (at least according to the finds at Dura-Europos) but many socketed types have also been discovered. Libanius also reports of dart-type weapons[35] (possibly 9–40cm in length) employed by Sassa-nian infantry, and it is possible that variations were available to the savaran.

Another note that must be made with respect to missiles has to do with specific battlefield roles. The common assumption is that the arrow was to kill the opponent, but missile fire could achieve the disabling of the opponent without necessarily killing him immediately during battle. For example, when faced with a heavily armoured opponent, the Sassanian archer could direct his fire towards the more vulnerable (or less well-protected/armoured) parts of his opponent's physique. The missile could be fired towards the opponent's hands, arms (lower or upper) or legs (upper or lower) not just to injure his opponent but to 'lock' the stricken part with other parts of his body. As an example, one may observe a metal plaque of Bahram Gur (r. 420–438 CE) hunting game while riding a camel.[36] One stricken animal appears to have two hooves locked together by an arrow with a U-shaped head. On the battlefield, a skilful archer was possibly able to do the same with an enemy combatant by 'locking' his arms or legs together with a single missile. Thereby if such a 'Bahram Gur' technique was used on the battle-field, it would have allowed the infantry archer to have a means of firing against a Romano-Byzantine infantryman who was closing in on him. Note that the pene-trative power of his missile would be multiplied in proportion to the lessening of the distance between him and his opponent.

It was possible to fire arrows in such a way to disable or kill two opponents simultaneously – again, a task contingent upon the archer's skill. Yet another narrative of Bahram Gur pertains to his boyhood when he was hunting with an Arab king named Manzar. Coming upon a lion about to slay a wild ass, Bahram fired a single arrow which killed both animals.[37] In combat situations the Sassanian archer (foot or mounted) was possibly capable of targeting two men simultaneously. In such a scenario an arrow could be shot to penetrate the head of an enemy infantryman and that of his comrade behind him. The archer might also endeavour to 'lock' the limbs of two separate opponents.

Incendiary arrows. A deadly tactic with Sassanian archery was the use of incendiary missiles. Put simply, missiles were not always required to be directly aimed at personnel, especially during sieges. Incendiary arrows could be directed into the interior of the enemy city or fortress towards storage areas for food, fuel, etc. Houses with wooden or straw roofs could be quickly set ablaze and thus spread havoc among the defenders. At the very least, a successful incendiary assault would diminish and even distract the defenders from the task of defending their city or fortress against their Sassanian besiegers.

Miller, McEwan and Bergman report on a series of studies with incendiary arrows.[38] They note that a simple bow could fire an incendiary arrow to set ablaze the roof of a two-story building from a distance of 30m at 40m. An incendiary arrow with a naphtha-soaked ball at its tip was most effective when shot from a composite at less than half-draw; if this were done at full-draw, the fire would be extinguished. Miller, McEwan and Bergman do note that defences against incendiary archery had certainly been built in the Near East as far back as pre-Achaemenid times, especially in the construction of a 'double line of defensive walls separated by sloping dead ground'.[39] These of course could be overcome with siege technology, an art of war well mastered by the Sassanians, who were highly effective in the construction of mounds and archery ramps in siege towers (Chapter 14).

Kamandan (bow case) and tirdan (quiver). One of the features that distinguished earlier Parthian archery from its later Sassanian counterpart was in the way the two armies carried their archery equipment. The earlier Parthians deployed the typical combined (quiver and bow) *gorytos* case, with the Sassanians deploying the separate kamandan and tirdan. It would appear that in practice the gorytos had given way to the separate tirdan and kamandan among the later Parthians as well, since both Parthian king Artabanus V and his vizier Darbandan are seen with the tirdan in the Firuzabad joust scenes (see Chapter 6). The total number of arrows carried in the tirdan of the Sassanian warrior was thirty, a tradition that can be traced back to the ancient Avesta.[40]

With the adoption of Central Asian technology by later Sassanian times, the tirdan and kamandan were now suspended by the lappet suspension system usually used for swords. The lappet system involved the use of straps suspended from the belt and fastened to the item (sword scabbard, quiver, etc.); this allowed the warrior to adjust the tilt or angle of suspension of his equipment rather than having that item always hang perpendicular to the ground. The Sassanian lappet system for archery equipment involved a single belt with separate lappets for the kamandan and the tirdan. The Taghe Bostan knight has his tirdan slung to his right side, much like the earlier savaran knights (swords suspended at left side). Nevertheless, there appears to have been other ways of carrying the bow, at least among the cavalry. The stag hunt scene at Taghe Bostan for example, shows the king's bow slung around his shoulders.

The Panjagan: Drawing Method or Arbalist?

In reference to the *Ayin-Nameh* Inostransev reports of a weapon that is capable of 'shooting by "fivers" i.e. five arrows at a time'.[41] Cited as the *panjagan* ('five device'), it is not possible to ascertain whether the weapon (or launching device) was for the simultaneous shooting of five arrows. The term is attested to in Arabo-Muslim sources, notably Tabari,[42] Jahiz,[43] and Maqdasi.[44] According to the latter, 'the Panzagan (Panjagan) is shooting five arrows'.[45] Tabari's similar description defines the panjagan as 'five arrows that are shot by single drawing'.[46] Tafazolli's research on Middle Persian military terminology leads him to define the panjagan as 'fivers, a kind of arbalist'.[47] Perhaps this was some type of cross-bow weapon, as the same Ayin-name cited by Inostransev does describe what may be a crossbow-type device for the launching of naphtha and incendiary projectiles which may be missiles or clay 'grenades'.

The panjagan raises questions as to why such a weapon was built and deployed. Was this yet another attempt by the Sassanians to 'shoot faster' or was there another tactical reason? This weapon may have served certain specific functions, such as focusing a high rate of fire against specific targets, possibly enemy armoured knights. In such a scenario the (possible) crossbow device would have had to be able to propel its missiles with sufficient power to penetrate the enemy's armour. It is not clear how the panjagan was reloaded. Perhaps there were pre-arranged (five arrow) clusters to help quicken the reload process after the first five missiles had been fired. This then raises the question of how long would it have taken for the knight to reload the device with a fresh batch of five arrows. When engaged in the reload process, the knight would have been vulnerable to enemy action (i.e. counter-missile fire, closing in by lance, etc.). If rapid reload was not possible, then the panjagan may have been a 'fire and forget' system, meant perhaps to give an initial edge in offensive power prior to the opening of the lance charge.

Another possibility is that the panjagan was devised as a portable 'mini' missile barrage system to fire into enemy lines prior to the lance thrust, thereby making this a weapon that was coordinated with the archer corps.

The Nawak Dart-Firing System

The *nawak* was essentially an archery system for the launching of darts. In essence, this is what Nicolle describes as an 'arrow-guide held against the bow to form a temporary crossbow'.[48] Nicolle further avers that the missiles were not arrows but shorter darts, varying from 10–40cm in length. These apparently had greater ranges than standard Sassanian arrows, were virtually undetectable in flight and capable of effective penetrations, especially at shorter ranges. Their more compact size allowed mounted or foot archers to carry larger numbers of these into battle. Another advantage was that enemy troops could not fire the nawak projectile back into Sassanian lines.

The nawak was certainly useful against enemy infantry, especially of the dangerous Romano-Byzantine type which would be closing into the Sassanian lines. The weapon, like the panjagan, was apparently also intended to penetrate the armour of mounted warriors of the Central Asian and Romano-Byzantine type, especially at closer ranges. The nawak, however, was to fail spectacularly against the Arabs at the Battle of Qadissiyah (Chapter 17).

The Sassanian Draw

Recalling the previous discussion of the *Ayin-Nameh* and its archery training instructions, it is clear that the Sassanians were very specific in how their bows were to be drawn. Sassanian metal works in general depict the Sassanian method of drawing the bow as wrapping the middle and third (or ring) finger around the bowstring. The main limitation with the metal works however, is their two-dimensional nature. These only provide us with a partial view of how the Sassanians drew their bows. Specifically, these visual limitations prevent us from seeing the full implementation of the *Ayin-Nameh*'s terms 'twenty-three' and 'sixty-three' (especially Insotransev's explanations). Nevertheless the metal works' display of the index finger provides critical information on Sassanian archery.

The metal works often display the index finger as 'pointed' (or stretching out along) in the forward position parallel to the arrow. The pointed index finger served a practical function by securing the arrow against the bow through lateral pressure. This action secured the arrow from falling off the bow as the horse archer was engaged in rapid and forceful movements. The 'pinkie' or little finger is either parallel to the index finger or pointing at an angle downwards. This can be seen clearly in the depiction of the horseman in the hunting scene panel at Taghe Bostan where he draws the bow in precisely this fashion. It is possible that the thumb was placed next to the index finger on the inside of the bow. In this case, the nock of the arrow would be held between the (extended) index finger and the thumb. As a result this type of draw would have needed two finger guards. The thumb certainly played a critical role in the draw, as reported in the *Ayin-Nameh*.

It is possible, though by no means proven, that the Sassanian draw may have earlier Iranic-Scythian connections. There is a depiction on an Attic black figure amphora (d. 510–500 BCE) of a Scythian using this type of Sassanian draw, but this illustration clearly shows the thumb not being used (it is seen above the hand) which is inconsistent with the Ayin-Nameh report.

Other methods of the draw. There appear to have been variations of the Sassanian draw during the tenure of the spah in 224–651 CE. Overlaet reports of one Islamic-era description of a Sassanian-type draw in which the little finger is wrapped in conjunction with the middle and ring fingers around the bowstring.

This implicates three finger-guards in this type of draw.[49] Interestingly, Patterson and Bivar, as well as Faris and Elmer, have reported of a Slavic method of drawing which is based on this 'three-finger' method with the thumb clearly not used. Finger guards were definitely used, much like those cited earlier in the Overlaet study.

Mention must be made of the Mediterranean draw in which (1) the nock of the arrow was placed between the index and middle fingers; (2) with these being used to pull the bowstring; and (3) the index and middle fingers could be joined by the ring finger. The Sassanians may have learned of and possibly used this method as a result of their military encounters with the Romano-Byzantines. Finally there is the distinct 'Mongolian' draw in which the thumb is locked around the bowstring which is blocked by the index finger. This type of draw was being practised much earlier by the Huns and Hephthalites, who may have introduced it to the Roman and Sassanian militaries respectively. There is a very clear depiction of the Mongolian draw on a silver plate being deployed by an early Islamic-era (c. early eighth century CE) mounted Sassanian-type nobleman from Merv (in Central Asia) identified as Pur-e Vahman. Matofi also notes that the *Shahname* is laden with descriptions of Sassanian methods of drawing the bow.[50]

Infantry Archers

Infantry archers had been an integral part of the armies of Iran since the Indo-Europeans arrived onto the Iranian plateau. As in Medo-Achaemenid times, infantry archers were a highly valued military asset of the Sassanian spah. The Romans also had a healthy respect for Sassanian infantry archers, who were possibly among the best-trained archers of the Classical era. These were used both in sieges and set-piece battles.[51] Left-handed archers were especially valued as these could (1) hold the bow with their left hand while bending the bowstring with their right hand as well as being able to (2) hold the bow with their right hand to then bend the bowstring with their left hand.[52]

Each infantry missile contingent was led by a tir-bad commander. The tir-bad organized his unit in such a way as to maximize its effectiveness. This was often done by organizing the unit into teams capable of relieving each other during battle; one unit would fire while the other would rest and reequip with missiles to then take over when their comrades' arrows were exhausted. As noted by Zakeri, Sassanian infantry archers would advance forward in close ranks to bombard the enemy with massive missile volleys.[53] The foot archer had a buckler hanging from his shoulder which was intended to protect his head and neck.[54]

Hekmat notes that these units often placed their large shields in front of them to form a 'wall' when in a static position, and then proceed to direct their fire against enemy formations with a high degree of effectiveness.[55] These shields would typically be of the palisades type when fighting from a defensive position[56] or in sieges. Towers would be constructed with ramps for the archers to fire into enemy fortifications and cities (Chapter 14). There was also an elite unit of archers which was responsible for defending the royal throne and Drafsh-e Kaviani to the death.

The composite bow allowed for the smooth implementation of the spah's doctrine of firing from safe distance against the enemy. Foot archers were to provide a furious, voluminous, and deadly barrage of missiles against the enemy to 'soften' them up for the savaran's lance thrusts. The barrage of the foot archers was an essential part of the savaran's primary offensive strategy as they could direct their fire against those enemy sectors targeted for the savaran's assaults. The archers would also be entrusted with the suppression of the enemy's own archery corps. The primary aim was simple: to so weaken the enemy ranks that they would break under the savaran's assaults. In this endeavour, the Sassanian arrow storm was also a psychological weapon meant to demoralize the enemy.

Foot archers were also critical in defending the field army from enemy attacks or counterattacks during battle. Archers were also highly effective in helping repel or weaken enemy infantry assaults. This was especially important when facing the very tough and well-trained Roman (and later Romano-Byzantine) infantry, who often got the upper hand against their Sassanian counterparts in close-quarters combat. In such a scenario the contest would be between the ability of Roman infantry to close the gap as soon as possible with the Sassanian formations before the latter's foot archers could exact too high a toll. Sassanian foot archers were also of great utility in helping block attacks by Romano-Byzantine lance-bearing cavalry. If the enemy succeeded in reaching their front lines, the foot archers would be able to fire backwards while fleeing in the 'Parthian shot' style. It must also be noted that the Sassanians deployed archers atop elephants (Chapter 7). This tactic provided an excellent elevated platform for archers who could fire more efficiently against enemy infantry, cavalry and even defending troops in sieges.

Sassanian Horse Archery

The Sassanians relied upon two types of cavalry for their archery, the regular professional savaran corps as well as the light cavalry, the latter often being auxiliary forces recruited from the interior of Iran as well as Central Asia and the Caucasus. The savaran were associated with archery from the earliest days of the dynasty and evolved towards a more 'composite' force by the sixth and seventh centuries CE, being equally adept with lance, close-quarters combat and archery (Chapter 6). Sassanian savaran composite knights were adept at firing their missiles from either the left or right sides at full gallop, and to direct their missiles against their enemies in pursuit and even in retreat (see Parthian shot, below).[57]

Light cavalry auxiliaries could use their archery for various functions in support of the regular savaran such as harassment, screening and skirmishing of the enemy infantry. Auxiliary cavalry were also effective in scattering enemy light cavalry as their archery could injure their opponents' unprotected horses, making them unmanageable and resulting in the breakdown of the cohesion of the enemy's formations.[58]

Volume of missile delivery. The ability of pre-Islamic Iranian armies to launch missiles from horseback reached its apogee with the Sassanian spah. Sassanian archery was famous for its ability to deliver large numbers of missiles within a short time frame, this being duly noted in Classical sources, notably Procopius in reference to the Battle of Dara in 530 CE[59] (Chapter 9). The question that may be raised is: how many missiles could be delivered by Iranian horse archery within a specified amount of time? Heath was the first to address this question with respect to Parthian horse archery, who reportedly fired an average of eight to ten shots per minute.[60] The application of these numbers may be seen at the battle of Carrhae where the 11,000 Parthian warriors of General Surena destroyed the Roman forces of Marcus Lucinius Crassus leading a force of 30,000–40,000 Roman troops in 53 BCE. Of Surena's 11,000 troops, 10,000 were horse archers who proved decisive to the Iranian victory at Carrhae. In the course of twenty minutes a Parthian archer could then fire between 160–200 missiles. Applying Heath's system for Carrhae, one may calculate 200 missiles (fired per horse archer in twenty minutes) multiplied by 10,000 (Surena's horse archers at Carrhae) to arrive at a total range of 1.6–2 million missiles fired against Roman troops. While Heath's numbers are certainly impressive in theory, these very high rates of fire may be questioned as seen shortly below in the discussion of Sassanian archery.

To address the question of amount of missile delivery over a period of time, one must first take into consideration the capacity of the tirdan (quiver; see below) which was thirty arrows, with later Sassanian knights carrying an extra tirdan in battle. If the horse archer/knight was able to unleash five missiles within five seconds, then he could empty a single Kamandan (of thirty arrows) within thirty seconds. According to Miller, McEwan and Bergman, the average rate of fire for pre-Islamic (non-Sassanian) West Asian/Near Eastern foot archer was thirty arrows shot within three minutes.[61] These statistics would indicate that Sassanian archery had become a highly efficient arm of the Sassanian spah.

If the Savaran knight used his second (or reserve) tirdan, then he could unleash sixty missiles within one minute. This would be calculated at sixty (missiles/minute) multiplied by 10,000 knights of an elite unit (e.g. *jhayedan/javidan*) resulting in an astounding total of 600,000 missiles fired per minute. These statistics appear consistent with Classical reports of Persian archery being able to achieve a high rate of fire over a short period of time.[62] Nevertheless, the Classical reports and calculations in this chapter (i.e. 600,000 missiles/minute) must be taken within the context of the archers' physical exhaustion. In practice, even the most fit and adept archer is forced to rest after shooting sixty missiles (i.e. emptying two quivers) in rapid succession. Archery simulations by expert archers have consistently demonstrated that the musculature of the arms and chest area become heavily taxed after the rapid firing of sixty missiles. Therefore, while Sassanian archers could certainly fire very rapidly within the first one to two minutes, it is doubtful that this high rate of fire could be maintained without interruption on the battlefield.

Missile distance and velocity. Houtum-Schindler defined the distance of a Persian bowshot as being one *amaj* (an Islamic-era unit approximating an eighth of a mile, or 220 yards)[63] or 150 meters. Studies by the Royal Ordinance Small Arms Division in Enfield, United Kingdom, have calculated the average velocity of the reed-shaft missile fired from a composite bow as ranging between forty-five to fifty meters per second.[64] Note that the conclusions of this study are not wholly applicable to Turco-Iranian archery as the composite bows reconstructed by the British military were confined to the more primitive angular composite bows of ancient Egypt. Therefore to arrive at a more accurate index of arrow velocity with respect to Turco-Iranian archery, new studies are required that replicate the (composite) bow construction and accompanying firing methods. Nevertheless, using the index reported by the Royal Ordinance Small Arms Division, an average arrow travelling 150 meters would take approximately 3–3.3 seconds to reach its target.

Missile distance, arrowheads and penetration. As noted previously, Sassanian missiles were characterized by different types of arrowheads in accordance with different battlefield functions. In general, heavier arrows with powerful (penetrative) arrowheads for penetrating the armour of opponents were fired at shorter distances with lighter arrows fired over longer ranges for purposes of harassment, massed barrages, etc.[65] It is likely that battle planning by the military leadership also involved decisions as to what types of arrows were to be used by their archers; this would undoubtedly be a function of the battle situation (battlefield or sieges, etc.) and types of opponents faced (light or heavy infantry, armoured heavy cavalry, light cavalry, etc.).

Karasulas' study of effective (penetration) range concludes that deadly penetrations were possible even at ranges of 175 meters, assuming that the bows were of the Central Asian or Sassanian type.[66] To achieve higher accuracy, the archer would have to fire at much closer ranges, which Karasulas suggests would be in the fifty to sixty meter range. At these closer ranges, penetration would be far deadlier and fatal to the opponent, even if he were armoured. Thereby missiles fired over the range of sixty meters were intended for the massed barrage or 'katyusha' effect, i.e. to deliver a massive number of missiles without necessarily intending to strike specific targets.

Nevertheless the discussions of arrowhead-type and battlefield function, and mass of missile delivery must be taken within the context of Newtonian physics: momentum = mass × velocity. Velocity is indeed important as it entails distance travelled (by the missile) over a period of time. Hence, penetration is also a function of the speed in which the missile (mass) is being delivered, a concept generally true of all types of arrowheads. As per the effectiveness of the sheer mass of fire or the aforementioned 'katyusha' effect, this can in turn be challenged by the effectiveness of armour used by the opponents at the receiving end of the archers. At the siege of Rhodes in 1522 for example, Turkish archers were shooting (with composite bows) at European knights clad in heavy plate armour at point-blank range. Despite this, the knights kept fighting. Observers report that the knights resembled 'porcupines' meaning that the Turkish arrows had hit their targets and even lodged into the European armour but failed to penetrate these to effectively injure their opponents. As a result, the knights were generally unwounded and able to continue the battle. The Rhodes example is illustrative of the thousand-years arms race between the penetrative effectiveness of kinetic weapons (archery) versus armour resilience.

The Parthian shot. The Sassanians certainly inherited the 'Parthian shot' from their Parthian predecessors. Put simply, the Parthian shot is the action of shooting backwards while riding away from the enemy. However, the Parthian shot was not Parthian in origin and can be traced to much earlier times. One of the earliest depictions of the Parthian shot can be seen in Assyrian artwork depicting Mede horsemen turning backwards in their saddles to shoot their missiles as they ride away.[67] The North Iranian Saka Paradraya (Scythians) are also depicted as employing the Parthian shot,[68] which would indicate that this combat form most likely originated in the Saka-Scythian steppes.

Nevertheless it was among the Parthians and the later Sassanians where the Parthian shot became integral to the regular battle tactics of Iranian armies. This was especially effective if an Iranian force had been either defeated and forced to withdraw or was simply feigning flight to draw the enemy in pursuit. The ability of the Sassanians to turn a rout into a victory while being pursued was greatly feared by the Romano-Byzantines. Procopius notes of Belisarius in the aftermath of his victory over the Sassanians at Dara in 530 CE (Chapter 9) when his forces engaged in pursuit: '[T]he pursuit was not continued by the Romans over a great distance. For Belisarius and Hermogenes refused absolutely to let them go farther, fearing lest the Persians through some necessity should turn about and rout them while pursuing recklessly.'[69]

In such a scenario the Romano-Byzantines could be engaged in pursuit of the Sassanians who could all of a sudden shoot backwards with the Parthian shot. The pursuers would be mauled by the missiles, especially as they rushed forward. This would have caused dislocation in their ranks, allowing the 'fleeing' savaran to then wheel about to strike their pursuers at their flanks, front or rear, in the Central Asian horse archer method. Such a scenario could entail encirclement by the cavalry as they fired their missiles into the enemy. In addition, the savaran could choose to deploy close-quarters combat weapons (swords, axes, maces) or engage in lance attacks.[70] It is noteworthy that the *Strategikon* claims that the Sassanians were not capable of turning against their pursuers when engaged in retreat.[71] It is not clear why the *Strategikon* and Procopius provide divergent reports regarding the Sassanian ability to turn about when pursued. What is clear is that the Parthian shot was a combat form practised by the spah well into late Sassanian times. This is attested to by the post-Sassanian figure of Pur-e Vahman who is seen engaged in the Parthian shot on a metalwork plate.[72]

Sassanian Archery in Battle

Archery was critical to the spah's battle doctrine in four ways: (1) support of savaran lance thrusts; (2) defence against enemy (infantry and/or cavalry) assaults;

Table 1. Examples of Middle Persian Sassanian Archery Terminology.
(source: Tafazolli, 1993)

arrow	*tigr/tir*
arrow play	*tir-wazig*
bow (note: *sanwar* and *dron* may also denote 'crossbow')	*kamam* (modern Persian *kaman*); *sanwar*, *dron*
bowstring	*zih*
quiver	*kantir* or *kantigr* (modern Persian *tirdan*)
crossbow	*sanwar*

(3) siege operations for the taking of cities; and (4) counter-siege operations in the defence of cities and fortresses against enemy besiegers.

Critical to Sassanian archery was its role as a type of heavy missile barrage on the battlefield. As noted previously, Sassanian archers were able to deliver a very heavy rate of fire over a short period of time, a capability seen approximately fourteen centuries later with the katyusha rockets or 'Stalin organs' deployed by the Soviets against German forces during World War II. The formidable and destructive power of Sassanian archery was duly appreciated by the Romano-Byzantines whose *Strategikon* recommended:

> In battle launch the charges and attacks when close to the reach of the bows, even and in dense order, and swiftly, lest through a delay in getting to hand-to-hand combat, the enemies [Sassanian archers], sending a continuous shower of arrows, get to afflict our soldiers [Romano-Byzantines] and horses with even more missiles.[73]

The advice of the *Strategikon* was consistent with previous Roman tactics which attempted to close in on enemy infantry archers to then force them into close-quarters combat. Sassanian horse archery was certainly more challenging to charge towards, as these could just as easily give way and engage in Parthian shot tactics. Below are descriptions of three battles in which Sassanian archery played a prominent role.

Siege of Amida (359 CE). Shapur II placed the Roman-held city of Amida under siege in 359 CE (details of entire siege in Chapter 14). One of the spah's remarkable operations during Amida's siege was the dispatch of a 'commando' style mission of crack archers. A team of 'seventy Persian archers of the royal battalion, men of eminent skill and courage'[74] succeeded in infiltrating the third tower of one of Amida's towers at night with the guidance of a deserter. Arriving undetected, the 'archer commandos' kept a low profile throughout the evening. They sprang into action in the morning, when after the raising of a scarlet (or reddish) flag, they began to fire furiously into the city's interior 'with prodigious skill'.[75] This strike was coordinated with a massive attack by the besieging force encircling Amida. The raid certainly came as a shock to the Romans, but the royal archers, though resolute and skilful, were doomed. Their supplies of arrows were eventually exhausted, allowing the Romans to overwhelm them with either archers or infantry. Amida was captured, with the distinguishing feature of archery having played a key role throughout the siege. Central to Sassanian archery during the siege of Amida was their ability to sustain a 'shower of missiles from the archers …'.[76]

Battle of Callinicum (531 CE). The details of the battle of Callinicum fought between Sassanian general Azarethes and Romano-Byzantine general Belisarius are outlined in Chapter 9. Our discussion here pertains to that phase of the battle where the savaran had broken into Belisarius' right flank and were threatening to destroy his entire force. At a critical juncture where the savaran were charging into Belisarius' remaining forces, Romano-Byzantine and Sassanian archers engaged in the exchange of missile fire. Procopius provides the following description of that archery exchange:

> [T]heir [the Sassanians'] missiles were incomparably more frequent, since the Persians are almost all bowmen and they learn to make their shots much more rapidly than any other men, still the bows which sent the arrows were weak and not very tightly strung … The Roman bowmen are always slower indeed, but inasmuch as their bows are extremely stiff and very tightly strung …'.[77]

According to Karasulas,[78] the high poundage Turco-Avar-Hun inspired Romano-Byzantine bow was most likely at its highest level of effectiveness when fired by foot archers on the defensive. This was due to the stability of their platform. The savaran who were now charging towards the remaining Romano-Byzantine forces found themselves facing deadly volleys of missiles. When the savaran engaged in their own archery, their (mounted) platform provided less stability than their foot-based counterparts. Thereby, according to Karasulas, the issue was platform stability, and not necessarily the 'weakness' of the Persian bows as Procopius and the *Strategikon*[79] have suggested. While Sassanian cavalry could certainly fire on the move, this mobility would have prevented their own powerful bows from being used as effectively. Perhaps if stirrups had been available to them the savaran would have been able to deliver their missiles with greater penetration power. This situational liability may perhaps explain in part Procopius' report that Byzantine archery was more powerful during this battle. The savaran were certainly able to fire back and, as Procopius avers, they did so with greater speed. The question of the power of Sassanian bows (and archery in general) is certainly demonstrated in the Battle of Anglon just eleven years later.

Battle of Anglon (542 CE). A major showdown occurred at Anglon, Armenia, in 542 CE between Sassanian forces led by Nabed (Nabades) and 30,000 Romano-Byzantine troops.[80] Byzantine forces had proceeded to attack the 4,000-man Sassanian force at Anglon, unaware that the Sassanian sardar (commander) Nabed had prepared a dangerous ambush for them.[81] Procopius has provided a vivid overview of the ensuing battle:[82]

> [A]ll of a sudden the men who were in ambush [Sassanian spah] … came out from the cabins along the narrow alleys … great confusion fell upon the

Roman army, and Nabedes let out the whole Persian force upon his opponents. And the Persians, shooting into great masses of the enemy in the narrow alleys, killed a large number without difficulty ... Romans did not withstand the enemy and all of them fled as fast as they could ... especially all the generals ... kept fleeing still faster ... had not the courage to array themselves against the Persians if they overtook them ... this proved a disaster for the Romans ... so great as to exceed anything that had ever befallen them previously ... great numbers of them perished and still more fell into the hands of the enemy. And their weapons and draught animals which were taken by the enemy amounted to such an imposing number that Persia seemed as a result of this affair to have become richer.

Procopius' description makes clear that it was Sassanian archery that had played a critical role in inflicting the defeat upon the Romano-Byzantine forces at Anglon. Nabed's ambush was effective as it had drawn the Romano-Byzantines into the narrow streets of Anglon, allowing Sassanian archers to fire at relatively close range, thus maximizing the penetrating abilities of their missiles. The close proximity allowed the missiles to penetrate the armour of their enemies. In addition, their ability to achieve high rates of fire meant that the trapped Romano-Byzantines were being subjected to deadly volleys of missiles, again at relatively close range. This would explain the subsequent rapid retreat of the surviving Romano-Byzantine troops from Anglon and their abandonment of weapons in haste. Anglon was a clear case where the spah prevailed exclusively through archery.

Chapter 6

The Savaran: Weaponry, Equestrian Equipment, Development and Prestige Units

The territorial extent of the Sassanian Empire posed great challenges for the spah. The vast distances between the western (Romano-Byzantine), northern (Caucasian passes), southern and Central Asian frontiers borders necessitated the formation of a powerful strike force capable of rapid deployment within the empire's boundaries. Jalali notes that the savaran elite armoured knights were the spah's tactical answer to the Sassanian empire's requirements for defending its large landmass with its limited military resources.[1] In a sense they were the spah's elite and primary battlefield instrument. Their performance often influenced the course and outcome of battles, especially in military encounters against the Romano-Byzantines or the warrior nomads of Central Asia. The savaran became the spah's military backbone for the defence of the realms of Eiran-Shahr or the Sassanian Empire. As further noted by Jalali:[1]

> The Savar-e Nezam Sangin Aslahe were equipped with a variety of offensive weapons. With regards to weapons these were the best equipped in the [Sassanian] army... one of the reasons for the advance of Iranian armaments in ancient times was due to numerous battles and wars with enemies ... the element of war was a major factor in military innovations ... and tactics.

After a brief review of the term 'savaran', this chapter will first discuss the predecessors of the savaran followed by the development of the savaran, which can be divided into three phases: the early phase (224–late 200s/early 300s CE); transitional phase (early 300s–490s CE); and the final phase (c. 490s/early 500s–651 CE). The chapter also examines elite units of the savaran as well as allied prestige units such as the Armenian naxarar knights and the Lakhmid Arabs.

Like the Parthians before them, the Sassanian savaran were equipped with a variety of offensive and defensive equipment. Also discussed are military developments of Sassanian weaponry, which (broadly speaking) underwent parallel changes as the Sassanian military (mainly the cavalry) went through three general stages. The first stage began with the defeat of the Parthian dynasty at Firuzabad in 224 CE to Sassanian defeats in Armenia (296 CE) by Maximianus Galerius.[2] The second or middle stage can be roughly traced to the arrival of Shapur II (r. 309–379 CE) whose reign witnessed a series of military developments resulting in the appearance of new varieties of weapons, armour and helmets. This period came to an end with the defeats and death of King Pirouz (r. 459–484 CE) against the Hephthalite Huns in 484 CE. The final or late stage may be traced to the Kavad (r. 488–496, 498–530 CE) and Khosrow I (r. 530–579 CE) eras during which Sassanian weaponry underwent a series of changes, including distinct signs of Turkic-Hun influences from Central Asia. These types of weapons were to be produced until at least the 637–651 CE era during which Iran was to fall to the invading Arabs. Sassanian tactical developments will be examined in Chapters 9 and 12. Archery will be discussed in this chapter, with the main topic already discussed in further detail in a separate chapter. Shields are also addressed in this chapter with further examination of shields being made in Chapters 7 and 14.

An Overview of Terminology

There are a number of designations for the term *savaran*. The Islamic-era *Taj* by Al-Jahiz defines these with the Arabicized *aswaran*.[3] The actual Pahlavi term is *asobar* or *asbar* (plural: *asbaran*) with the term *asb* meaning horse. As noted by Jalali, 'asbaran' does not mean cavalryman in the ordinary sense but is specifically referring to the elite knights, much like the designation 'chevalier' in French.[4] These elites were recruited from the most militarily capable members of the upper nobility. The latter's wealth allowed them to acquire the highest-quality weaponry which the Sassanian military industry was able to produce.[5] The upper elites who formed the core of the savaran were then joined by the 'lesser' Dehkan nobility after the reforms of Khosrow I in the sixth century CE (see below and Chapter 3).

Clibanarius and cataphractus. At this juncture a distinction must be made between the terms *clibanarius* and *cataphractus*. In general, the latter is defined as the armoured knight who rides an unarmoured horse, with the clibanarius being the armoured knight who rides a horse which is also armoured. The clibanarius is usually in reference to the Persian style heavy cavalry (armour for man and horse) in Roman sources.[6] As noted by Roztovzeff the, term 'clibanarii' 'was adopted by the official language and the writers of the later Roman Empire ... to distinguish the "Cataphractii" of the Roman auxiliary forces from the real "Clibanarii" of the Persian and later Roman army ... the Cataphractii wearing no helmets and using horses not protected by armour as a rule.'[7]

Speidel does not agree with this clear-cut distinction between the clibanarius and cataphractus.[8] Astutely referring to the Claudiopolis (Bithynia) inscriptions, Speidel notes of the existence of a particular unit that bears both designations. Speidel hypothesizes that the cataphractus was in reference to any unusually armoured cavalry with the clibanarius (in accordance with the Notitia Dignitatum) being of the 'Mesopotamian' type. Essentially, Speidel has questioned the simple horse armoured vs. horse unarmoured distinction. Coulston had speculated that the term clibanarius referred to cavalry armed with bow and lance with some armour for their horses, with the cataphractus being 'not of the Oriental type' who were armoured riders, some of these possibly with horses that were armoured, and bearing the 'Western combination' of lance and shield.[9]

Grivpan and tanurig. Grotowski and Brzezinski[10] as well as Frye[11] have noted that the Greek terms *klibanion* and *klibanarios* as well as the Latin term clibanarius was most likely borrowed from the Pahlavi Persian term *grivpan*.[12] This term is interesting as it literally means neck (*griv*) guard (*pan/ban*) or *gardaan-ban* in modern Persian. Bivar hypothesizes that *griv* also denotes the broader term of 'life 'and 'self' in other languages, hence *grivpan* may have also meant 'life preserver' (in Parthian and Sassanian Pahlavi) which would have then been linguistically applied to the lamellar armour of the Partho-Sassanian knights.[13]

Zakeri suggests that the term clibanarius (in the sense of heavily armed horseman) is in effect a synonym of the Pahlavi term *tanurig*.[14] Mehreen (Shustari) and Jalali define tanurig as 'the heavily armed/armoured savaran of Iran'.[15] Linguistically, tanurig is connected to Pahlavi *tanur* which itself is related to Aramaic-Syriac *tannur* (bread oven). The term tanur is interesting as it may be in reference to the hot weathers of the empire's western frontiers towards Rome where temperatures must have become unbearably hot for the warrior fitted with such close-fitting and heavy armour. Hence the term tanurig is apparently a reference to 'oven men'! Rundgren however offers the explanation that the (Aramiac) tanur was assimilated with the Pahlavi term *tanvar* (body protection)[16] which is a cogent (linguistic) argument. Technically speaking it is not possible to know whether Sassanian warriors referred to their armour as grivpan, tanur, or tanvar.

Predecessors of the savaran: Chorasmian, Achaemenid and Parthian Heavy Cavalry

The Sassanian savaran were in a sense the descendants of the Parthian armoured knights. The Parthian armoured corps was itself a descendant of cavalry developments in Achaemenid Persia and Central Asia.

Central Asia, Chorasmia and the Scythians. It was in circa 500s BCE Chorasmia in Central Asia that the first prototypes of the armoured lancers appeared. These had been the tactical answer of the settled Chorasmian-Massagatean population against mounted raiders who often rapidly raided the settled agrarian zones adjacent to the Chorasmian oases. The tactical answer to the deadly raids of these fast and nimble steppe cavalry was the development of mounted lancers. Close examination of the available evidence suggests that the early Chorasmian 'knights' were not all yet equipped with suits of armour for man and horse. This can be clearly seen on a terracotta flask that was excavated from a tomb at Koi-Krylgan-Kala along the banks of the Oxus River in Central Asia. This has been dated to around the early third or late fourth century CE. As noted by Sekunda, this flask features a depiction of a Chorasmian 'knight' without armour (for rider or horse) but which is also 'the earliest representation of the long two-handed cataphract lance, known as a Kontos.'[17] This Chorasmian lancer was also lightly equipped, as the Koi-Krylgan-Kala terracotta figure only shows a short dagger fitted inside his belt. The first steps however had been made towards the development of 'knights' as subsequent developments soon revealed.

While the long lance was a primary weapon against the horse archer, Michalak has noted that these early Chorasmian 'knights' soon adopted scale armour. This was in contrast to their lightly armoured opponents whose primary mode of battle was horse archery.[18] Chorasmian lancers wore scale or plate armour tunics of the type seen in northern Iranian peoples, with examples of these evident among the Saka Paradraya (European Scythians). The armament of the Chorasmian two-handed lancers was soon augmented with swords, with the adoption of helmets further enhancing battlefield survivability.

The military developments of Chorasmia, which were soon followed by developments in Achaemenid Persia, also spread to other Iranian-speaking peoples across the steppes, reaching the Saka Paradraya (European Scythians).[19] A series of archaeological expeditions at Staikin Verkh in the forests of northern Ukraine have revealed valuable information on the types of armour and armaments used by the Saka Paradraya. One of these finds was heavy armour composed of metallic plates sewn onto a leather base. This was in fact an 'armoured suit' composed of a vest that afforded excellent protection for the entire torso and arms along with 'trousers' providing similar protection for the legs. The Saka Paradraya armoured cavalry were armed with a comprehensive array of weaponry such as swords, lances, battle axes, and archery equipment with protection afforded by shields. The Saka Paradraya appeared to have differed somewhat from the rest of their Iranian-speaking cousins further east in Central Asia or in Persia with respect to helmets. A local innovation by the Saka Paradraya as found near the Novoroznovka region was the application of metal scales onto leather caps, not unlike the armour 'suits' just described.

The first true knights of the Achaemenid spada. Early Iranian cavalry at the time of Cyrus the Great (r. 559–530 BCE) wore one-piece helmets of bronze or iron, and were most likely armed like their infantry with either thrusting spears or javelins. Military and cultural contacts with Central Asia led the Achaemenids to adopt northern and eastern Iranian cavalry technology (i.e. harness) and armour by the end of the fifth century BCE.[20] Perhaps the most significant encounters were the battles of Cyrus the Great against the Massagetae, who defeated and killed him in 530 BCE. The Massagetae wore scale armour, a feature which was soon adopted by the Achaemenid cavalry. These types of armour were most likely in Achaemenid units by the time of Darius the Great (r. 522–486 BCE) who had subdued the Massagetae and Central Asia by the 510s BCE.

The east Iranian and Saka cavalry from Central Asia in Achaemenid service are described with defensive equipment such as helmets, suits of scale armour, and cuirasses, as well as being heavily equipped with close-quarters combat weapons.[21] By the time of Xerxes' invasion of Greece, Achaemenid cavalry used the *kopis* slashing sword, archery and javelins in battle.[22] The Achaemenids, like their fellow Iranians from Central Asia, were aware of scale armour, but thanks to Chorasmian-Saka influence, Achaemenid cavalry discarded their javelins and regular spears in favour of the two-handed lance,[23] resulting in the birth of the first true Persian 'knights'. These were elites recruited from the 'Aryan' *azata* (upper nobility). Nevertheless, it is far from clear as to when exactly the lance was adopted, as Herodotus' descriptions of Achaemenid cavalry in Greece describe these with javelins only. But, and as noted by Head, the painted sarcophagus of Klazomenai (500–475 BCE) does show a cavalryman deploying a long thrusting spear.[24] The figure has been identified as a Scythian, but his headgear is actually of the rounded Achaemenid-Persian type and he also uses a kopis slashing sword not characteristic of Scythian swords. Head also notes of a later list of the Babylonian colonist Gadal-Iama's equipment showing two heavy spears.[25] The Saka contingents of Xerxes during his invasion of Greece are of interest: the Saka Haumaverga of Central Asia, for example, were most likely armed with archery equipment, long and short swords and axes.[26] While most of the Saka cavalry in Xerxes' time were lightly armoured 'horse archer' types, there were smaller numbers of armoured mounted troops.

What is clear is that Achaemenid cavalry continued to develop and evolve after the failure of the campaigns against Greece. By the time of Artaxerxes II at the battle of Cunaxa in 401 BCE, Achaemenid heavy cavalry are described in the following fashion, with 'flashes of bronze ... spearpoints ... cavalry with white armour'.[27] Xenophon's *Anabasis* describes the 600 cavalry of Cyrus the Younger (d. 401 BCE) as follows:[28] 'armed with cuirasses and thigh-pieces ... all wore helmets except for Cyrus ... all their horses had armour for the forehead and breast; and the cavalry also carried Greek sabres.'

Xenophon also describes in the *Cyropedia* the guards of Cyrus the Great; these were evidently an allusion to the contemporary guards of Cyrus the Younger who were equipped with bronze armour and helmets with side-pieces of horse-armour which also 'doubled up' as protection for the riders' thighs.[29] The thigh pieces cited by Xenophon and the 'double duty' horse side armour served as a type of 'ran-ban' (thigh protector), an interesting innovation meant to provide protection against blade weapons, spears, javelins, etc. This served to enhance the overall armoured protection of the Achaemenid cavalry, especially when fighting against enemy infantry. Scale armour continued to be used after the Achaemenids well into the Parthian era, but the concept of the ran-ban was abandoned in favour of the Scythian scale-armour trousers of the style seen at Staikin Verkh, Ukraine. The beginnings of the Iranian-style Bargostvan horse armour are also seen in the above description. This was to be further developed by the Parthians and the Sassanians. Nevertheless, javelins were still in use by the Achaemenid cavalry in 401 BCE. Xenophon also thought highly of the cornel-wood construction of Persian javelins, which proved decisive in their victory over Greek cavalry at the battle of Daskylion in 396 BCE.

The spada (Achaemenid army) become the Classical world's first imperial army to develop formal units of heavy cavalry. Nevertheless, the bulk of the Achaemenid cavalry remained unarmoured even up to the time of Alexander's invasion.[30] Armoured cavalry appeared to be more of an 'elite' force which the Achaemenids proved unable to expand to larger numbers. One reason for this may have been the time and expense required to equip the entire cavalry force with the equipment necessary for heavy cavalry. While Achaemenid armoured cavalry did fail against the invasion forces of Alexander, the doctrines of the future Parthian and savaran cavalry elites were already in the process of development during the Achaemenid era. This was the doctrine of heavy missile fire unleashed by archers in support of armoured cavalry charges, a technique which was to reach its apogee during the Sassanian era (Chapters 5, 9 and 12).

Alexander and the Seleucids. Despite their formidable striking power, Achaemenid heavy cavalry proved incapable of countering the combined arms doctrine of Alexander, which adroitly combined heavy infantry, cavalry and the Macedonian phalanx. Interestingly, javelins are reported in use by the Achaemenid cavalry as late as the battle of the Granicus River (May 334 BCE), which proved less effective than the longer spears of Alexander's Companion Cavalry, which Arrian explains as having been crucial to the Hellenic victory.[31] In the aftermath of the Achaemenid defeat at the ensuing Battle of Issus (1 October 333 BC), the spada constructed longer lances[32] that were distributed, along with longer swords, to numbers of Achaemenid cavalry.[33] The horses of the Achaemenid cavalry at Issus had been protected by armour plates.

Nevertheless, Alexander did see the utility of Iranian heavy cavalry and did deploy these in his forces during his invasions of Iran and India. Badian, for example, has noted that 'Bactrians, Soghdians and Arachosians ... served under Alexander before the Indian expedition ... Bactrians and Soghdians ... serving the new King [Alexander] gained entrance to the Companions. Others [Iranian cavalry] followed as they came to be drafted into service.'[34] It would appear that the mass of the Iranian recruits came after the battle of Gaugamela (331 BCE), especially when large numbers of these arrived in Alexander's camp during his repose in Hyrkania and Parthia in 330 BCE. Of interest at Gaugamela were the 2,000 Central Asian Saka cavalry who according to Arrian were armoured, as were their horses. The same however may have been true of the Bactrians as well as the Armenians and Cappadocians who were also present at the battle.[35] Olbrycht's recent analysis of the role of Iranian units in Alexander's army has led him to conclude that:[36]

> the first Iranian units enlisted in Alexander's army were the cavalry detachments formed in Media; one of them, consisting of Iranian aristocrats, was sent to Arachosia in the autumn of 330 ... Recruitment of Iranians for Alexander's army reached large proportions when the king established the hippakontistai division in 330. Three years later, during the war in India, Iranians made up the most sizable ethnic component of Alexander's invasion force.

The Iranian cavalry referred to by Olbrycht are of the late Achaemenid heavy armoured type. Alexander evidently valued their military potential, a sentiment echoed earlier by Xenophon. Alexander's successors in Iran, the Seleucids, are believed to have deployed heavy armoured cavalry of the Iranian type by the second century BCE, and possibly earlier in the third century BCE.[37] Units of light cavalry were raised as well, one example being Alexander's recruitment of mounted javeliners, most likely from northern Persia or its environs. In the wars of Alexander's successors, Antigonos at Paraitakene did deploy 1,000 Parthian and Mede light cavalry in 317 BCE.[38]

It is possible that Antiochus III (r. 223–127 BCE) may have taken a keen interest in armoured cavalry during his campaigns against the Parthians after 200 BCE. There are three reports of Seleucid armoured cavalry as reported by Polybius: the first of these being present at Angion in 192 BCE during the pre-senting of the Syrian envoy at that locale, the second report is of two years later when 6,000 armoured cavalry of Antiochus III took part in the Battle of Magnesia in 190 BCE, with the third occasion in which 1,500 armoured horsemen of Antiochus IV (r. 175–164 BCE) participated in a military parade in Daphne in 155 BCE.[39]

The Parthians (247 BCE–224 CE). The Parthians were deploying cavalry of the armoured type as early as the third century CE.[40] These knights wore helmets of the one-piece type, not unlike the twentieth-century CE US-pattern M1 helmets. The primary offensive weapon of the Parthian knight was the lance.[41] Knights were also equipped with swords and appear to have carried quivers in the later Parthian era (220s CE), at least as seen in the Firuzabad reliefs discussed further below. The question of quivers is interesting and, according to Cassius Dio, Parthian knights carried no shields.[42] Both Sallust[43] and Justin[44] emphasized how armour covered the entire rider and horse. There are some indications of earlier Hellenic influence on earlier Parthian cavalry, at least as seen in the representa-tions of the cuirass in some of the Parthian arts, but this never became popular mainly due to its restrictions on movement.[45]

The proportion of armoured lancers to horse archers at Carrhae in 53 BCE was evidently ten to one, with the overall numbers of lancers being slowly augmented over the ensuing centuries until the early 220s CE.[46] When engaged in battle against Roman forces, the role of Parthian armoured lancers was to attack and pin down the enemy infantry. Parthian horse archers would support the armoured lancers by discharging their deadly volleys of missiles into the opposing infantry, while also attempting to outflank the enemy.[47] Parthian horse archery was essen-tially based on tactics of skirmishing, harassment and feigned retreat,[48] and unlike the knights, horse archers were ill equipped for close-quarters combat as they were both lightly armed and armoured.

This was essentially the lance-missile combination designed to destroy the opposing Roman-type infantry forces. The archers would overwhelm the enemy with their missiles in the endeavour to place them in a state of disarray, disorganiz-ation and demoralization, making the enemy infantry exposed and vulnerable to the armoured lancers. As the integrity and cohesion of the enemy forces dimin-ished, they would be more vulnerable to the strikes of the armoured lancers. The feigned retreat by the horse archers would be a dangerous 'bait' for both enemy infantry and cavalry. Determined charges by the enemy infantry outside of their static lines would avail little as the horse archers would either opt to continue galloping away, or all of a sudden turn back to resume the firing of their missiles. The charging enemy infantry would now be trapped in place, exposed to archery, with no options for further advance or retreat back into the safety of their lines. Charges by the enemy cavalry would be met in a similar fashion but the real danger would be the famous 'Parthian Shot' (Chapter 5). In this scenario the 'retreating' horse archers would all of a sudden turn backwards in their saddles to shoot their missiles while their steeds were still galloping forward. The missiles would make a devastating impact on the ranks of the pursuing enemy cavalry.

Representations of Parthian cavalry are relatively few and mostly dated to the later Parthian era (first to third century CE). As noted by Herrmann, representations of Parthian cavalry can be seen at the poorly preserved sites of Behiston (known as the Gotarzes relief, first century CE); Sarpol-e Zahab (first century CE); the Elamite inscription at Tang-e Sarvak (early third century CE); as well as the graffiti of Dura-Europos (early third century CE).[49] Other representations of Parthian horsemen can be seen in the sculptures at Hung-e Kamalvand, for example. Interestingly all of these sites are located in the southwest regions of Iran. The shortage of sites is also paralleled with the shortage of available artefacts.

The lance-missile combination was certainly effective at Carrhae where the Parthian cavalry (armoured knights and horse archers) of General Surena defeated a Roman force three to four times their size. It was at the Battle of Carrhae where the Parthian knights made their combat debut as organized units of cavalry.[50] While the Roman implementation of countermeasures such as the recruitment of auxiliary horse archers did help preserve the Roman position in the Near East, Rome in turn was prevented by the Parthian military from conquering Iran.

The First Stage: The Early Savaran (224–late 200s/300s CE)

The Battle of Firuzabad in 224 CE was where the early savaran made their successful combat debut by overthrowing the Parthian dynasty. As noted previously, the Parthians clearly segregated their lightly armed and armoured horse archers from their lance-wielding knights, with Sassanian knights having also deployed archery equipment. The early Sassanian cavalry did resemble their Parthian predecessors in that heavily armoured knights were supported by 'sagittari' type horse archers. While Parthian and Sassanian knights appeared similar, it would be erroneous to assume that the two corps were strictly identical. There were in fact critical differences between the corps with respect to swords, armour and archery, and the latter's possible implications on horse archery warfare. From what can be surmised, the Parthians had no infantry at Firuzabad,[51] so they appear to have been operating on their classic all-cavalry doctrine.

An overview of the arsht (lance) and nezak. Wilcox describes the Parthian *kontos* (lance) as being twelve feet long, bearing a 'sword-like' blade as well as a spike at the other end of its shaft.[52] Khorasani's studies on five excavated Parthian lance heads housed at the National Museum of Iran[53] has revealed the following information:[54] (1) the lance heads were built of iron and of the socket type, meaning that they were (literally) socketed on the lance shaft; and (2) the length of the lance heads varied from a range of 23.2cm to 37.5cm.

According to Wilcox the Parthian lance was used in two ways: (1) one handed: over the arm and downward to stab the opponent; and (2) two-handed: lance carried with two hands (as in bayonet combat) in a level 'face to face' fashion.[55] The first method (one-handed) was suitable against non-cavalry targets such as infantry or dismounted enemy cavalrymen. The efficacy of this method was definitely proportional to the knight's stability, especially as stirrups had not yet been invented during the Parthian era. The knight's stability also affected the efficacy and power of the two-handed lance charge. But as the discussion below will illustrate, Parthian and Sassanian saddle technology provided Iranian knights with sufficient stability to allow for the effective delivery of their lance charges.

Early Sassanian lances known as the *arsht* were apparently not too different from their Parthian counterparts. Interestingly the term *nezak* (spear) also appears during the Sassanian period, perhaps to distinguish this from the arsht. The semantics of the Persian term 'ak' roughly conveys 'smaller than' or 'lesser than', such as the term Mazda (the supreme Zoroastrian entity) versus the (prophet) Mazd-ak, whose name roughly denotes 'lesser angel'. This leads to the speculation that the Sassanian Pahlavi term nezak (modern Persian: *neyze*) was a 'smaller' or shorter version of the arsht, which may have been the primary weapon of a Sassanian infantry contingent known as the *neyze-daran* (Chapter 5).

The two-handed 'bayonet'-type wielding of the arsht appears consistently in Sassanian reliefs. Of special interest is the depiction (though partial due to damage) of the one-handed downward 'stab' by the figure of the Sassanian knight (possibly Khosrow II) in the late Sassanian era. By this time improvements in Sassanian saddle technology as well as the possible (though by no means certain) introduction of stirrups would have facilitated the efficacy of the one-handed (as well as the two-handed) method.

The lance charge: force and angle of delivery. The primary battlefield function of the savaran knights was the lance charge, a role which was to remain to the last days of the dynasty. The lance was held by two hands, in a horizontal orientation at the waist level and carried along the right side of the horse's neck.[56] As the knight gained momentum during his charge into enemy lines, he would grasp the shaft of his lance firmly to avoid his hand from sliding on the shaft upon impact. The knight would also hunch slightly forward and brace his legs tightly to brace for the impact against his target. Note that although stirrups had not yet been invented, contemporary saddle technology allowed the rider to maintain his stability (see below).

There are two critical questions to be asked: (1) how much force is necessary to unhorse an opponent (as is seen at the Firuzabad joust discussed below); and (2) the most effective angle in ensuring the maximum effectiveness (power and penetration) of the lance thrust. There are currently a number of popular venues where medieval jousting is being re-enacted with a series of informal studies that are addressing these questions. These however rely on the medieval style of jousting where the lance is couched under the armpit, which is wholly different from the Iranian (Sarmatian, Parthian and Sassanian) style of lance charge in the Classical era. Nevertheless, irrespective of style of lance handling (two-handed or armpit-couched) the issues of force and angle of impact is critical. The question of force of impact must be addressed by the science of physics, specifically with this equation: mass (combined of knight and horse) × velocity = force of impact. In layman's terms, being hit by the lance charge is the equivalent of being hit by a small-to-average size automobile. This also speaks highly to the composure, training and sheer courage of the Roman infantryman who would stand his ground in the face of the knight and his lance that were about to ride down upon him in combat.

Angle of impact refers to two distinct domains: the up-down versus left-right angles. An interesting paper by Berg and Lampe addresses the question of angles of impact during the lance impact. Berg and Lampe define the up-down angle as [Φ] or the vertical plane and the left-right angle as [Θ] or the horizontal plane. What is the optimum horizontal angle [Θ] for the lance to strike the opponent horseman? More specifically, if the lance of the Sassanian knight is held parallel to the right side of the horse's body, then at what angle would his lance achieve the 'best hit' against another opponent horseman? That would depend on what side of the opponent horseman's body the lancer is targeting. If the knight is aiming for his opponent's right side (the area from top of right shoulder to middle of right side of torso), the angle would most likely range roughly between 0–45 degrees, which we will designate as [Θ_a]. If the knight aims to hit the opponent's left side, then the angle of impact would be greater than 45 degrees, a statistic which we will designate as [Θ_b]. Berg and Lampe note that the optimum angle of impact of the lance is where it 'strikes nearer to the center of the … torso, the lance head will be less likely to be deflected and the blow will be much more solid'.[57] This would be best achieved by aiming towards the opponent's stomach.

The up-down angle [Φ] or the vertical plane of impact has much to do with the type of opponent being faced: infantryman or cavalryman. When charging against an opponent horseman, the optimal impact would be (as with the angle between Θ_a–Θ_b) the one that strikes at the centre of the opponent's stomach area. This could be achieved by simply keeping the lance parallel to the ground; this would be contingent upon the two-handed method described earlier. If the rider holds the lance in the medieval 'armpit couched' position, he would then have to depress his weapon to between 0–45 degrees to be able to deliver his blow to the opponent's stomach area.

Critical to the successful strike was the construction of the lance itself. The lance would be mobile during impact therefore it would be subjected to high levels of compressive stress. A lance of weak construction or one with a weak area could break upon impact, especially during contact with an armoured opponent of similar mass. It is not clear what type of woods and materials were used in the construction of shafts of the savaran's lances, but it is clear that these were built to withstand high levels of stress upon impact.

Another question which may be raised is whether there had been a doctrine for (or experimentation with) the tactic of having the horse move forward with its hooves lifted much as a show horse would do when he or she jumps over an obstacle. Was it possible that as the lancers were about to impact the enemy front line, they could have engaged in this 'horse jump forward' technique? The momentum of the impact of the hooves at the enemy's shield would have been great, especially given the momentum already built up by the charge. In a sense the lancer would be 'lunging' or 'jumping' forward just before the moment of impact to magnify the impact of his charge into the enemy.

Lance battle at Firuzabad. It is possible that the lance-duel and *mard o mard* (man to man) depictions at Firuzabad were close to the portrayal of actual battle scenes. Lance duels were part of the pre-Islamic Iranian martial tradition that encompassed the wider Iranic arena, notably the Sarmatians of the East European steppes. The battle in such a scenario would have most likely involved a combination of horse archery, lance and close-quarters combat. The decisive factor appears to have been lance charges, as the armoured knights could not be defeated by contemporary archery. The reason according to Bivar was because 'armour had established its superiority over the missile'[58] by this time, which protected knights from being picked off at long range by archery (see 'armour' and 'super-heavy knights' further below).

The Firuzabad joust panel portrays three distinct duels from left to right. At left can be seen an unknown Sassanian knight wrestling a Parthian opponent. The centre panel depicts Crown Prince Shapur unhorsing the Parthian grand vizier Darbandan with the final and right panel which shows Ardashir I unhorsing his opponent, Parthian king Artabanus V.[59]

Lance duels at Nagshe Rustam. Another important arena displaying the lance duel of the earlier Sassanian knights is of course at Nagshe Rustam, where four of the panels represent this type of combat. The older of these reliefs is a double panel where one is situated on top of the other. These represent King Bahram II (r. 276–296 CE) in lance combat. The top panel portrays a lance duel between

Figure 1. The Firuzabad joust relief: (*right*) Ardashir I lances his opponent, Parthian king Ardavan V, whose horse topples backwards; (*middle*) prince Shapur lances his adversary, possibly Parthian vizier Darbandan; and (*left*) unidentified Sassanian warrior and Parthian wrestling on horseback, with Sassanian having the upper hand by having trapped his opponent in a headlock. (Drawing by Farrokh based on original by Erik Smekens of Ghent University)

Bahram II and an unidentified enemy, who may be a Roman cavalryman as the figure bears a partial similarity to a Roman cavalryman depicted in the 'Sarcophagus of Helena' in the Vatican. Bivar has suggested that the Roman figure is that of Roman Emperor Marcus Aurelius Carus (r. 282–283 CE) who according to the Liber de Caesaribus was '... consumed by a thunderbolt ...'[60] near Ctesiphon. It is possible that the 'bolt of lightning' which killed Carus in July or August 283 during his offensive in Iran was due to Sassanian military action, which may have been depicted in the top panel of Bahram II's lance duel at Nagshe Rustam. An indication of this may have been provided by Armenian historian Moses Khorenatsi who identifies Carus but cites his Sassanian opponent as 'Artashir'. According to Khorenatsi, Carus was victorious in his first battle against the spah, which was then reinforced with contingents from Tajikestan. The spah then 'gave battle a second time to the Roman army on both sides of the Euphrates. In the battle Carus was killed at Rinon. Similarly Carinus [Carus' son as attested to by Khorenatsi] ... was slaughtered with his army; those who survived turned in flight.'[61]

Nevertheless, another possibility to consider is that the panel at Nagshe Rustam may also be 'symbolic' in that it is Bahram's way of claiming credit for the death of Carus, which may have occurred through other types of military action (i.e. archery) or even the more remote possibly of assassination by some of his own ambitious officers.

The lower panel of the double panel representing Bahram II may be in reference to the king's battle against an unknown Sassanian prince or his victory over his rebellious brother Hormuzd Kushanshah. Bahram II's main achievement during his reign was his ability to confront the invasion of Carus from the west and to defeat the ambitions of his brother Hormuzd Kushanshah. This leads to the third lance combat panel at Nagshe Rustam where a Sassanian king (possibly Bahram II) battles a Roman opponent (typified with an angular type visor) whose lance has been broken during combat.[62] The fourth panel depicting lance combat is that of Hormuzd II (r. 302–309). Although the identity of his opponent is not certain, it may represent the figure of a viceroy named Babak.[63] Apart from the symbolism of the depictions, all four Nagshe Rustam panels have one important element in common with the Firuzabad panels: the primacy of lance combat due to the effectiveness of armour against missiles.

Armour. One of the most salient features at Firuzabad is how both sets of protagonists (Parthians and Sassanians) are heavily armoured. This similarity in heavy armour is more apparent than real as there are critical differences in the type of armour utilized by the Parthians and Sassanians as seen as Firuzabad. Examination of the lance joust scene at Firuzabad would indicate that the Parthians used armour of the lamellar type with the Sassanians (the unknown knight, prince Shapur and Ardashir I) all appear with shirts of mail.[64] The mail shirts of all three figures extend to the thighs above the knees. There are also vests worn over these mail shirts (the torso of the unknown knight is mostly covered as he is wrestling his Parthian opponent) with Ardashir I also having a sort of medallion clasped over his vest with four straps.

The origins of mail are difficult to pinpoint exactly, but there has been a find of a mail in a fifth century BCE Scythian tomb near modern-day Kiev at Zharovka. It is also possible that mail originated among the Celts who then passed this technology to the Romans,[65] who were using mail by the third century BCE, although its use was limited to their wealthier elites. This was mainly due to the fact that mail was a difficult and expensive system to produce. The manufacture of mail entailed the processes of wire-drawing and the fastening of links (presumably with rivets like medieval mail). These were expensive and labour intensive to produce, but by the second century BCE Roman depictions of mail were becoming more common. By the third century CE, mail was being produced by the Sassanians in Persis. There have also been finds of mail at Dura-Europos (dated c. 256 CE). Evidently the early Sassanian knights placed a high priority on the mass production of mail, as this was highly useful for covering gaps and joints, and its lighter weight provided greater mobility and was also 'cooler' to wear in the hot climates of typical Near Eastern battlefields.

But was mail the main reason why the Sassanians prevailed over the Parthians at Firuzabad? Mail could not by itself provide sufficient protection against missiles. As a result, the Sassanians combined mail with other types of armours, notably vambrace systems and breastplates. Bivar[66] and Shahbazi[67] have suggested that a major factor in the savaran's victory over their Parthian counterparts at Firuzabad was due to this more advanced system of 'combined' armour that utilized both 'traditional' types of armour (i.e. lamellar) in concert with mail. At the very least, this armour 'combination' system allowed for greater flexibility of movement and resistivity against missiles, which could prove decisive on the battlefield.

What is also of interest is the lack of shields as seen by the depictions at Firuzabad, much like the Sarmatians of Tacitus. A number of reasons may be surmised for this. First, the lack of shields among the early Sassanian knights may suggest that they were most likely well protected against contemporary archery. Put simply, their 'combination armour' may have been powerful enough to safely repel most missiles, although more studies may be required to investigate this assertion.

Helmets. The Sassanian military which inherited the helmet construction technologies of their Parthian predecessors, were to also introduce a number of changes and innovations that continued to the seventh century CE. One of the earliest known Sassanian helmets is that of the fallen Sassanian soldier at Dura-Europos. This was constructed of two pieces, a left and a right side attached together with two iron bands with riveting technology. Known usually as the 'ridge helmet' by western historians, this stood around 25–26cm. This type of helmet also appeared among Roman forces in the third century CE after their military encounters with early Sassanian forces.[68] The ridge-helmet also had mail hanging from its sides; the Sassanians would continue to incorporate mail into their helmets into the latter days of the dynasty (as noted below). The Dura-Europos helmet did belong to a Sassanian infantryman, however this type of helmet, or variations of thereof, were also probably deployed by the Sassanian cavalry.

Despite the Dura-Europos findings, depictions provided at the rock relief sites of Naghshe-Rustam, Bishapur or Firuzabad fail to clearly reveal the employment of the Spangenhelm (riveted construction type) in the early days of the dynasty (especially early third century CE). Nevertheless it is fairly certain that the early Sassanians were cognizant of the construction methods of four-lobed Spangenhelm helmets. This is indicated by the find of a fourth century terracotta displaying a Sassanian knight wearing a four-lobed Spangenhelm helmet. The availability of this technology allowed the Sassanians to equip many of their forces (cavalry and infantry) with a standardized and robust helmet.

The visual depictions at Naghshe-Rustam, Bishapur and Firuzabad are in the Achaemenid 'profile' style, meaning that troops and images are shown two-dimensionally from the side.[69] This means that helmets can only be seen from a side view, such that helmets of the Dura-Europos type can appear as simple one-piece conical helmets, when in fact the image could just as easily be representing a ridge helmet of the riveted type. At this juncture it may be possible to surmise that the helmets seen at the three sites may be a mix of ceremonial and military (possibly riveted) helmets, especially those at Bishapur where a trooper is seen with a symbolic tall headgear piece adorned with a beak and large eyes, typical of the Iranic mythological-bird. All three sites provide depictions of early Sassanian swords and tir-dan (arrow-cases). It is also possible that the early Sassanians employed helmets of the one-piece type somewhat similar to Second World War 'US M1' helmets seen among Parthian knights, and that at least some of the helmets depicted at the three sites are of the one-piece type.

Blade weapons. Sword development went through two general phases, an early-middle phase ranging from the early Sassanian era (early 220s CE) to the late fifth century CE (after the death of king Pirouz in 484 CE). Early Sassanian swords were reminiscent of their Parthian predecessors which had numerous parallels with (northern Iranian) Sarmatian characteristics (e.g. globular pommels). The early Sassanian sword would be slung in the traditional scabbard slide which would be suspended from the belt at the right or left side. The suspension of the scabbard was made possible by a metallic arch-shaped brace. This had short and flat plates at each end which were fastened (possibly riveted) to the scabbard. The weapon would stand vertical in relation to the ground when the cavalryman was at rest. The sword would be suspended in such a way as to maximally facilitate access to the hilt. Interestingly, the depiction of Shapur I at Nagshe Rustam shows the monarch pressing his hand on the hilt of his sword (in scabbard), thereby pushing it 45 degrees to the right. This 'tilting' action may have served a ceremonial or symbolic function; however more research is required to assess this hypothesis. Nevertheless the 'tilting' function certainly served a practical purpose

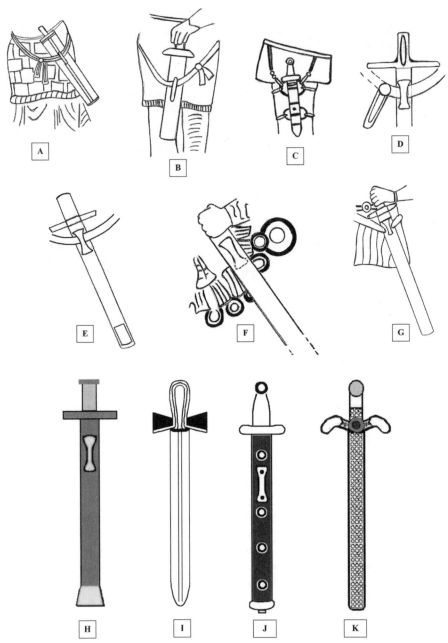

Figure 2. Scabbard-Slide Swords: (A, B) Kushan swords from Gandaharan stone reliefs; (C) Parthian and Sarmatian 'thigh' dagger; (D, E) Bishapur third century CE; (F) Shapur I at Nagsh-e-Rustam third century CE; (G, H) Bishapur third century CE; (I) Sassanian, circa fourth to sixth centuries CE, scabbard for (J) based partly on finds made in Tcherdyne (Perm); and (K) Khosrow II at upper vault at Tagh-e-Bostan, seventh century CE. (Drawings by Kaveh Farrokh, 2004)

among early Sassanian infantry; the latter was obliged to 'tilt' his weapon upward when marching to prevent the scabbard from dragging on the ground.

Similar in appearance to the Western European 'broadsword', the early-middle Sassanian sword was built with a long and broad blade, wide (sword) guards and broad pommel. In these respects the Sassanian sword was not much different from its Parthian predecessors. The Parthian (and early Sassanian) sword had much in common with the (post-Yueh-Chi) Kushan types which were prevalent in second century CE Central Asia and modern-day Afghanistan. The attribution of a Kushan origin for the broadsword which then entered Parthian Persia is possible. The partial statue of the Kushan king Kanishka the Great (r. 78–127 CE), for example, depicts him standing with what appears to be a European-type broadsword. The predecessors of the Kushans, the Yueh-Chi who arrived into Afghanistan, were themselves a northern Iranian people whose military technologies were analogous to their western (north) Iranian Sarmatian cousins who were dominant to the north of Caucasus, modern day Ukraine and segments of Eastern Europe. Partho-Sassanian cultural and economic contacts with the Sarmatians through the Caucasus[70] and the Kushan legacy to the east would have allowed for the exchange of military technologies which in turn bore a distinct influence on the swords of the early savaran.

Sassanian swords, however, were not mere copies of Parthian and Kushano-Sarmatian styles. Examples of variation among Sassanian swords are found, notably Han Chinese-style sword guards which were generally smaller than typically broad Parthian and early Sassanian sword guards. There was also a unique 'Persis' style pommel featuring spherical 'bulbs' or even ends that would radiate towards the outside. This type of pommel can in fact be seen in the sites of Bishapur and Naqshe-Rajab. Slimmer than its Parthian predecessor, the Sassanian sword was also longer, having been extended to a length of approximately 1–1.11m; the width of the blade having ranged between 5–8.5cm. The scabbard-slide sword continues to be displayed until at least the late fourth century with Ardashir II (r. 379–383 CE) and his predecessor Shapur II (309–379 CE).

Daggers are also displayed in Sassanian reliefs, a feature seen prominently in the depictions of earlier Akenakes daggers of Medo-Persian troops at Persepolis, the ceremonial capital of the ancient Achaemenids. Notable in early Sassanian arts is the dagger strapped to the thigh of the knight, a feature seen among the northern Iranian Sarmatians. These would have been prominent in the Caucasus and parts of Eastern Europe during the early years of the Sassanian dynasty.

Equestrian equipment. A key point to be addressed is how the lancer ensured the full integrity of the impact of his weapon without the benefit of stirrups. Rider stability was essential to allow him to deliver maximum impact and penetration possible without being unseated at the moment of impact. Before the Parthian era, namely the earlier Achaemenid and even Assyrian eras, saddle blankets were the main 'seat' of cavalry, from which they were able to discharge missiles, retain their stability when hurling javelins or even attempt to thrust with the contemporary lighter lances of the period. Nevertheless, the utility of the saddle blanket for affording rider stability was limited, especially when attempting to charge with heavier lances against robust targets such as phalanxed infantry or opposing cavalry. Once again, Saka/Scythian or steppe technology was to lead the way in technological change. A fourth century BCE vase from the Saka Paradraya or European Scythian area of Chertomlyk shows a rider with a saddle blanket rolled forward to allow for a better 'brace' when impacting against targets during the lance charge. More advanced technology is seen at Pazyryk in what is perhaps one of the first brace saddles or more appropriately four-horn saddles. It was during the Parthian period when these four-horn saddles were fully developed, an innovation which allowed the rider to strike stronger targets with heavier and sturdier lances. Perhaps the earliest known representation of the four-horn saddle is seen at Sar-e Pol-e Zahab; this is of course a partial representation but the front horn is clearly visible. The four-horn saddle was essentially a saddle with four 'horns'; two at the front and two at the back. The issue, of course, was (and as previously mentioned) being able to deliver the heavy lance strike at a high level of momentum without becoming unseated from one's steed. As noted before, momentum was greatly increased due to an increase in mass (especially with respect to the amount of armour for rider and the Bargostvan horse armour) which necessitated the need for a new type of saddle. The four-horn saddle was able to 'brace' the rider firmly in place despite his increased momentum, a function that the Achaemenid saddle blanket was wholly unsuited for.

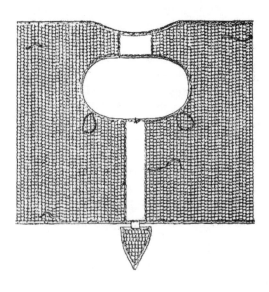
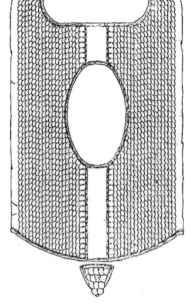

Figure 3. Drawings of Bargostvan horse armour of scale over leather base, discovered at Tower 19, Dura Europus.
(Farrokh, 2013, based on original drawings by Brown, 1936)

Perhaps the best representation of early Sassanian 'non-saddle' equestrian equipment is seen at the panel depicting the investiture of Ardashir I by the supreme Zoroastrian god, Ahura-Mazda at Nagshe Rustam. This representation clearly shows elaborate bridles of the early Sassanian savaran with respect to the noseband, cheek strap, throat lash, brow band and headpiece, plus another strap that runs from the centre-front of the steed's head.[71] The cheek-strap and nose-band of Ardashir I's steed are decorated with applied decorated plaques bearing symmetric crenelated shapes with Ahura-Mazda's steed items decorated with circular plaques. The bits of these early savaran steeds are constructed in parts (cheek-bit, noseband and noseband muzzle).

Sassanian horses of the savaran were also armoured. Findings at Dura-Europos provide an excellent overview of late Parthian and early Sassanian horse armour or *bargostvan*. This covered the torso of the horse with armour constructed of metallic scales with an oval opening for the area where the knight would be seated. The Dura-Europos findings also revealed armour for the horse's neck and head as well as greaves.

Possible drawbacks of lance combat. There were a number of problematic aspects to lance combat. First, how would the lancer recover his weapon if this had been dropped during combat? This would be difficult if not impractical under combat circumstances. Second, what would happen if the lance broke during combat? Third, how would the lancer be able to deploy his archery equipment or close-quarters combat weapons? Would the lance then simply be disposed of by dropping it, to then deploy one's bow and missiles or to draw the sword etc.? Coulston has noted that attaching the long contus lance to the side of the horse was highly impractical.[72] It is clear that more research (especially re-creations along the lines being done in the West with respect to medieval jousting) is required to investigate this domain.

The archery question. While the specific details of archery equipment and combat have already been explored in Chapter 5, the role of archery in the early savaran requires discussion. The figures of Ardashir I, his son Prince Shapur and an unknown Sassanian knight in the Firuzabad panel are either engaged in lance combat or wrestling, but these figures do display the tirdan. In similar fashion, the figures of Darbandan and Artabanus at Firuzabad are also displayed with the tirdan suspended to their sides. Nevertheless, the deciding factor remains the same: the devastating impact of the lance. This however does not mean that archery became irrelevant or even less relevant; in fact the archery of the early savaran proved to be a decisive factor in their victory over Roman forces near Ctesiphon in 233 CE (Chapter 9).

If Sassanian 'horse archers' were armoured then these could engage in more effective horse archery as their armour may have afforded them better protection against enemy missiles in comparison to their lightly armoured counterparts. Armoured horse archers were in fact nothing new in the time of Ardashir I. There is in fact a clear depiction of a Parthian armoured horse archer (*shivatir-e zrehbaran*

Table 2. Partial Lexicon of Middle Persian Sassanian Military Terminology.

Offensive Weapons

zay, zay-abzar; zen-abzar, sneh/sneih	weapon (general terms)
abdast	gauntlet
tabar	hatchet, axe; battle-axe (*tabarzin* which is also hatchet)
warz/wazr	club, mace; mace play (*warz-wazig*)
awestarag	blade
dar, tex	any blade weapon
shamsher, safser	sword, sword play/fencing (*shamsher-wazig*)
dasnag	short dagger
celan	dagger, knife (*kard*, which also means dagger)
kamar	sword-belt, belt (*kamar-band*)
niyam	sheath
fras	javelin
astr	javelin, missile weapon
nezag	lance, spear
kamand	lasso
pilak-xan (modern Persian *falakhan/falaxan*)	sling
asp-son; astar (whip); *astar-e-asp* or *asp-astar* (horse whip); these can also be weapons	horse whip

Defensive Equipment

helmet	*khwod; sarwar, targ*
hauberk, neck guard	*griv-ban/griw-ban*
armour	*gurdih, pos/posh; zreh*; note: *zreh* can also mean 'mail coat'
shield	*spar, magind*, shield-play (*spar-wazig*)
thigh guard	*ran-ban*
finger guard	*angust-ban* (built of goat-skin)
tunic (armoured?)	*pedan*

in Middle Persian) at Dura-Europos.[73] Sassanian armoured horse archers would have held a number of tactical battlefield advantages against the Romans. First, the armoured horse archer could have felt safer than his unarmoured counterpart to discharge his archery at closer distances towards stationary enemies such as Roman infantry troops. The discharge of the missile at closer distances would allow for greater velocity and kinetic energy, thus achieving greater damage (or penetration) upon impact. However, even shots from closer ranges had their limitations, as the mass of the arrow remains constant and negligible. This is why well-built and resilient armour remained so effective against archery, even in dangerously closer ranges. Conversely, the arrow that travels a longer distance would lose a greater proportion of its kinetic energy as a result of atmospheric resistance or friction.

It is possible that Ardashir's victory at Ctesiphon in 233 CE (Chapter 9) may have been partly indebted to the role of the Sassanian armoured horse archers and missile-firing 'regular' savaran. The effective range of arrows shot from bows of compound construction would have been around 229–230 meters with 91–122 meters being especially effective at penetrating armour.[74] Perhaps the savaran had been able to venture closer than the effective 91–122 meter range to deliver missiles which resulted in strikes of greater power and penetration. The state of early Sassanian 'combination' armour at this time would have provided a high level of protection, however, by venturing too close to Roman lines (i.e. 40–50 meters); these savaran would have been dangerously exposed to deadly countermeasures such as javelins. Perhaps part of the reason why the Sassanians are reported as having suffered great casualties at Ctesiphon in 233 CE may have been due to their pressing archery attacks at closer ranges.

The Transitional Era (early 300s–490s CE): Experimentation with Super-Heavy savaran

The second stage in the development of the savaran was a doctrinal shift to super-heavy cavalry in which there was an increase in the armour of the knights. Ammianus Marcellinus and Heliodorus are two sources that provide a vivid description of such knights by the time of Shapur II and his wars against Rome, namely the battles against Constantius II (r. 317–340; co-emperor 337–340) to the invasion of Sassanian Persia by Julian the Apostate (r. 363).

The super-heavy savaran. The *Aethiopica* of Heliodorus provides a very detailed description of the heavy 'super' armoured knights of Shapur II as they would have appeared in the early 350s CE:

> For in fact it is this brigade of Persians [super-heavy knights] which is always the most formidable in action; placed in the front line of battle, it serves as an unbreakable bulwark ... Their fighting equipment is furnished in this way: a picked man chosen for his bodily strength, is capped with a helmet ... His right hand is armed with a pike of greater length than the spear, while his left is at liberty to hold the reins. He has a sabre slung at his side, and his corselet extends, not merely over the breast, but also over the rest of the body ... the rider bestrides him [his horse], not vaulting of himself into the saddle, but lifted up by others because of his weight.[75]

Libanius provides a number of interesting observations with respect to the 'armour upgrades' of these types of knights in the time of Shapur II: '[D]arts, sabres, spears, swords and every warlike implement were forged in a wealth of material ... these men had to ride a horse which obeyed their voice instead of a bridle, and they carried a lance which needed both hands.'[76]

The Libanius and Heliodorus descriptions make clear that these new type of knights were not only chargers who were tasked with breaking into (or through) enemy lines with their lances or pikes, but were also expected to engage in close-quarters combat as indicated by their formidable inventory of close-quarters combat weapons.

Armour. Ammianus Marcellinus' description of the super-heavy savaran and their formidable armour during Julian's 363 CE invasion of the Sassanian empire states: 'All the troops were clothed in steel, in such a way that their bodies were covered with strong plates, so that the hard joints of the armour fitted every limb of their bodies.'[77]

The increase in armour served three battlefield purposes. First, the rise in armour protection was meant to maintain the knights' immunity against battle-field missiles. In a sense this function was nothing new when compared to the early savaran, with the difference that these knights were apparently meant to have even greater immunity. The second advantage of increased armour lay in the efficacy of the decisive lance charge, which would now be delivered with greater momentum. In theory at least, this increased weight would increase the knight's chances of breaking through enemy lines. Like Heliodorus, Libanius highlights the spah's *Durchbruch* doctrine of creating a super-heavy force of savaran immune from enemy weapons:

> [H]e [Shapur II] contrived to make his cavalry invulnerable ... he did not limit their armour to helmet, breastplate and greaves in the ancient manner nor even to place bronze plates before the brow and breast of the horse, but the result was that the man was covered in chain mail from his head to the end of his feet, and the horse from its crown to the tip of his hooves, but a space was left open only for the eyes to see what was happening and for breathing holes to avoid asphyxiation ... the name 'Bronze men' was more appropriate for these ... they entrusted their body to the protection of iron mail ... the unbreakable nature of their armour.[78]

It is clear that the increase in armour also included mail which was now extended, according to Libanius, to cover the knight from the tip of his head to his feet. The 'combination armour' system of the earlier savaran was now made much more comprehensive. Interestingly, Tafazzoli cites a Pahlavi quote, *Zenagen Ishted pad chafar handam*, which translates as 'he is with armour on his four limbs',[79] but this may be in reference to the late or even earlier Sassanian eras.

The third reason for the 'armour upgrades' was for combat against Roman infantry. The Heliodorus and Libanius descriptions make clear that the spah was intending to field a force of super-heavy knights that were also immune, as much as possible, against all forms of blade weapons. Limb protection for arms and legs was paramount in combat against the tough, superbly resilient and well-trained Roman infantry, who would stand their ground and fight the heavy Sassanian knights at close-quarters. Heliodorus has provided a very detailed description of the armour of the super-heavy savaran and how it was constructed:

> [P]lates of bronze and of iron are forged into a square shape measuring a span each way, and are fitted one to another at the edges on each side, so that the plate above overlaps the next one to it, all forming a continuous surface, and they are held together by means of hooks and loops under the flaps. Thus is produced a kind of scaly tunic which sits close to the body without causing discomfort, and clings all round each limb with its individual casing and allows unhindered movement to each by its contraction and extension. It has sleeves, and descends from neck to knee, with an opening only for the thighs ... as is required for mounting a horse's back. Such a corselet is proof against any missiles, and is a sure defence against all wounds. The greaves reach from above the flat of the foot to the knee, and are joined onto the corselet.[80]

Helmet. The Spangenhelm helmet continued its evolution during the reign of Shapur II. By the time of Julian the Apostate's invasion of Persia in 363 CE, Sassanian Spangenhelms were constructed of four to six metal lobes fitted together by metallic bands and frame; the pieces were fastened together by rivets. On average the Sassanian Spangenhelm was about 20cm wide and approximately 22–24cm in height. Interestingly, north Iranian *bashlyk* conical themes are commonly found in Sassanian Spangenhelms, especially with those found in Mesopotamia and Iran. Decorative themes were often emphasized as seen in the overlays of gold and silver sheets around 0.1–0.2mm thick. The sheets were often impressed with Iranic mythological bird designs such as the varanga and *simurgh* designs.

Heliodorus notes of the mounting of metallic face masks on Sassanian helmets, which is consistent with the Sassanian philosophy of developing 'heavy knights' during the fourth century (especially during Julian's invasion). Heliodorus describes the helmet of the 'heavy knights' as having been 'compacted and forged in one piece and skilfully fashioned like a mask into the exact shape of a man's face; this protects him entirely from the top of the head to the neck, except where eye-holes allow him to see through it'.[81]

Note how Heliodorus' description complements that of Ammianus Marcellinus, who observed the following regarding the helmets of the super-heavy knights: '[O]n their heads were effigies of human faces so accurately fitted, that their whole persons being covered with metal, the only place where any missiles which fell upon them could stick, was either where there were minute openings to allow of the sight of the eyes penetrating, or where holes for breathing were left at the extremities of the nostrils.'[82]

Both Heliodorus and Ammianus note that face masks were fitted onto the helmets of these knights, but what is less clear in these descriptions is the manner in which these helmets were actually constructed. Were these one-piece US-style M1 helmets as seen among the Parthian knights, which were then possibly riveted with face masks? Or were these of the two-piece type seen in earlier Sassanian armies, or of the multi-plate riveted Spangenhelm type? Whatever the possible mode of construction of such helmets, one point is clear: these were designed to be as robust as possible on the battlefield by protecting the rider's head and neck from destruction.

Lance combat. The lance continued to be the Iranian knight's primary 'first strike' weapon and, as such, was a major influence in the development of the spah's tactical doctrine. The essential mechanics of lance combat remained in the same style as seen in the Firuzabad reliefs as well as Sarmatian depictions (esp. at Kerch), where the knight charges at his opponents wielding his weapon in the two-handed manner. Nevertheless it is incorrect to assume that the savaran were not trained to fight with lances and spears when dismounted. There are two depictions of the savaran fighting dismounted with spears and lance-type weapons from the fourth century CE to later Sassanian times. One of these shows a (unidentified) Sassanian king hunting with his spear.[83] Another plaque (silver and gilt) housed at the Hermitage shows two dismounted eastern Iranian (Khorasan-Soghdian type) knights of the later Sassanian era (sixth century CE, found at Kulagysh) wearing full armour (mail and laminated) as well as Spangenhelm type helmets, fighting each other. The figure to the right is confronting his opponent to the left with his lance held slightly upright and in the two-handed bayonet fighting style. His opponent (to the right) is shooting an arrow at him. The battle of two knights using bow and lance is typical of mounted troops, but this plaque shows them engaged in the same combat on foot.

Swords. The works of Armenian historian G.A. Tiratsian describes Sassanian knights of the mid fifth century CE as having carried three types of blade weapons. In Armenian these are described as *tour*, *sousser* and *nran*. The tour is the Armenian definition of the Sassanian short sword. This may have been a descendant of the *Akenakes* type short sword[84] used by Medo-Persian and Saka troops of the Achaemenid armies[85] as well as by the Iranian-speaking Saka Paradraya or Scythians of the ancient Ukraine.[86] The Sassanian tour was attached to a *goti* (belt) on the warrior's right side. The tour was also used by the Palmyrans of the third century CE and the later Iranian-speaking Soghdians of Central Asia in the late and post-Sassanian eras (seventh–eighth centuries CE).

The sousser is the Sassanian long sword often seen depicted in Sassanian metalworks and rock reliefs. This was slung on the warrior's belt to his left side. Suspension was by the scabbard slide method. What is of key interest at this juncture is the possibility of a 'transition' occurring with sword suspension at this time. Examination of the swords of Shapur II and Shapur III at Taghe Bostan reveals that instead of scabbard slides, the kings' sword suspension systems to be an adaptation of the rosette form to the double locket-device.[87] According to Masia, this is an indication that the scabbard slide was no longer used and possibly have even become obsolete by this time.[88]

The third type of weapon, the nran, is the Iranian-type dagger attached to the warrior's thigh. This type of dagger was in fact in use by the wider Iranian-speaking realm, especially by the Sarmatians, who used such weapons as late as

300 CE as they entered service in the Roman armies.[89] This was often 'hidden' by the folds of the pants, especially with earlier Sassanian dress.

A note on the two-handed sword. Mention must be made of the Sassanian two-handed sword. An example of this was uncovered by an Iranian archaeological team in 1961 and is now housed at Tehran's National Museum of Iran.[90] This is the only Iranian (Sassanian) two-handed sword that has thus far been excavated. Despite reports of two-handed (Parthian and Sassanian) swords in statues, stone reliefs and metalworks, none of them bear any resemblance to the two-handed sword in the National Museum of Iran.[91] The dimensions of the Sassanian two-handed sword are as follows:[92] (1) total length of the sword is 116.5cm (total length of the blade with its reinforcement on the forte measures 86cm with the blade itself at 85cm length); (2) length of the handle is 31cm, with two discs placed at a distance from each other on that handle (distance between the discs is 21.5cm). The blade of the weapon is slightly curved, which raises questions as to whether this was the original design or whether this was simply deformed over time (the blade has been heavily eroded).

This two-handed sword raises several questions. The first, partly addressed in Chapter 4 with respect to training, pertains to the requisite strength, stamina and agility of the warrior required for handling such a weapon. The second question concerns the essential nature of sword combat. The sheer size of this weapon renders its employment problematic, hence a matter of conjecture at this juncture. The design of this weapon would make it impractical for European Heidelberg-style fencing. It is possible to assume that this two-handed weapon was most likely handled in the later West European fashion of the 'Knights Templar'-type sword, but this assumption requires rigorous research before any definitive conclusions may be drawn. In any case, it must have been a formidable weapon in close-quarters combat, especially when wielded by well-trained and physically resilient Sassanian knights. The question can also be raised as to which elite knights – e.g., the 'super-heavy' types or even the 'Mirmillos' armoured gladiator-type infantry alluded to by Ammianus (Chapter 7) – employed two-handed swords.

Archery. Although the topic of archery has already been discussed in Chapter 5, Bivar has suggested that archery may have declined amongst the heavily armoured savaran during this stage of development.[93] This would at first appear to be true, at least among the super-heavy savaran reported by Heliodorus: they have swords, pikes, etc., but no archery equipment. So now we have a return to the 'Parthian binary cavalry' by the 350s CE in which there was a strict division between 'pure knights', meaning devoid of archery, versus a separate corps of 'regular' savaran of the earlier type. The latter certainly wielded archery equipment, with a possibility that a portion of these were 'seconded' into a separate corps of Parthian-style armoured knights *shiva-tir*. The Sassanian shiva-tir was not truly Parthian, as (noted earlier) their armour would have most likely included mail.

Bivar's astute observation notwithstanding, it is not likely that archery declined as a whole in the spah as this arm was integral to the Iranian (and wider Iranian-speaking) military tradition. The use of archery as missile support for attacking savaran forces and for repelling enemy attacks remained integral to the spah's doctrine to the last days of the dynasty. The super-heavy savaran were apparently an experimental phase which would be abandoned by the sixth century or perhaps by the end of the fifth century.

Equestrian equipment. Ghirshman's discoveries provide an excellent overview of some of the types of equestrian equipment used by the savaran of the fourth century CE. The discovery consisted of two sets of cheek-bits along with accompanying noseband/muzzles. The bits were straight mouth pieces connected to curving pieces; these were composed of iron.[94] Note that there was no ring attaching the cheek-piece to the bridle.[95] The cheek-bit and noseband/muzzle technology was in fact in use before the advent of the Sassanians, but these had been 'deleted' during the time of Shapur I by having been replaced by lighter and simpler versions. Evidently this new technology did not remain long, as the 'older technology' of the noseband/muzzle cheek-bit combination was re-introduced during the period of the mid-late fourth century CE.[96] As a result the savaran corps confronting Julian's invasion of Persia in 363 CE were using this more 'traditional' technology. It is clear that the spah had decided that this very same technology was more efficient than its 'simpler' counterparts used in the time of Shapur I.

Super-heavy knights in battle. Jalali notes that despite their heavy armour, the super-heavy knights were not impeded by their fittings.[97] The super-heavy knight's armour and helmet was crafted and fitted with such skill that no impedance or discomfort would be caused by the knight's bodily and especially limb movements. As further adduced by Jalali, these knights were able to charge with a high degree of confidence into enemy lines, confident of the ability of their armour to repel missiles and even javelins and light spears. As noted previously, the momentum of the super-heavy knights was certainly more formidable with their additional armour, which would result in a greater impact. Nevertheless, it is not yet possible to quantify the super-heavy knights' exact amount of impact, at least as per Newton's second law (force = mass × acceleration). However, the aforementioned study on Medieval jousting by Berg and Lampe is a good reference source which refers to computer simulations being developed at the Worcester Polytechnic Institute for the study of the kinetics of the joust.

Once these knights had impacted the enemy front lines, they would (at least in theory) cause dislocation within the enemy ranks. This would provide for a number of options. The first option was the 'Parthian' one in which the knights would withdraw after their lance thrust, to allow for mounted archery to take its toll. Then, after the conclusion of the missile attacks of the mounted archers, the super-heavy knights could resume their attack into the now more weakened ranks. This cycle of lance charges-mounted archery could be repeated a number

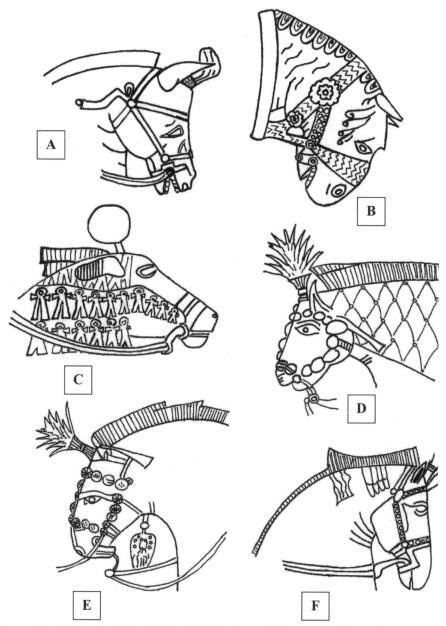

Figure 4. Early Sassanian bridles: (A) Snaffle bridle, Shapur I, third century CE (see Herrmann, 1980); (B) Illustration of Savar bridle based on gilded silver Sassanian metalwork (fourth century CE) at Louvre (MAO132) (see photo by Macquitty, 1971); (C) Horse bridle of Ardashir I at Firuzabad, early third century CE (see Herrmann, 1989); (D, E) Horse bridle from Persepolis graffiti, late second to early third centuries CE (Persepolis in situ, Harem section); and (F) Horse bridle of Ardashir I at Darabgerd, early third century CE (see Herrmann, 1989).

(Drawings by Kaveh Farrokh based on originals by Herrmann)

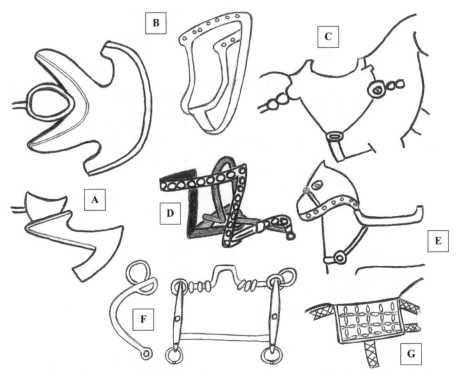

Figure 5. Equestrian tack: (A) Saddle (see Ghirschman, 1973); (B) Noseband/muzzle found at Susa (see Ghirshman, 1977); (C) Sassanian horse at Bishapur, possibly belonging to Shapur I, early third century CE (original photo by Khademi, 2003); (D) Noseband and bit (Metropolitan Museum of Art); (E) Terracotta figurine from Masjed-e-Suleiman (see Ghirshman, 1973); (F) Iron bit from Northern Persia (Daylaman) (see also Herrmann, 1989); and (G) Saddle cloth (Cleveland Museum of Art). (Drawings by Kaveh Farrokh, based on originals by Herrmann)

of times to ensure a breakthrough. The 'regular' savaran, who would presumably be similar in armour and weaponry to the earlier savaran, would have had the option of being 'mounted armoured archers', but these could also 'double up' on the battlefield for close-quarters combat (i.e. the aforementioned 'Italian grip').

The aforementioned descriptions provided by Armenian and Classical sources make clear that the super-heavy knights were equipped for close-quarters combat. Thanks to their 'impenetrable' armour, these super-heavy knights would (at least in theory) be able to stand up in close-quarters combat against combat infantry and light cavalry. In practice, the Romans proved consistently able to repel the Sassanians in close-quarters combat, with even the super-heavy knights being vulnerable when locked in close-quarters combat against Roman infantry.

Weaknesses of the super-heavy knights. Despite their formidable armour and weaponry, the super-heavy savaran were beset by a number of serious weaknesses. As noted in previous writings by the author, there are marked parallels between the spah's thesis of 'the more armour the better' with that of the German war planners during the Second World War. Healy has summarized the German tactical (mis)conceptions succinctly by noting that 'Model's [*Generalfeldmarschall* Walter Model, one of the top commanders at Kursk] assumption was that the sheer weight of the German armoured fist must in the end break through, and in the fallacy of that assumption lay the key to the Red Army's victory on this battlefield.'[98] The German army's notion of the 'sheer weight of the ... armoured fist' bears parallels with the spah's doctrine of the all-out armoured lancers breaking through enemy lines with the 'sheer weight' of their assault. Nevertheless, the spah discovered, as did the Wehrmacht at Kursk, that the fallacy of 'the more armour the better' is not necessarily true on the battlefield.

The 'upgrades' in armour came at a heavy price. While true that Heliodorus noted how the armour of these heavier knights was 'proof against any missiles' this and other associated advantages could be negated if the knights became bogged down and forced into prolonged close-quarters combat with the Roman infantry. This is because the heavier armour significantly limited the ability of the knights to fight over longer periods of time. This may partly explain Ammianus Marcellinus' observation during Julian's invasion of Persia in 363 CE that Sassanian warriors lacked the capacity for long-term endurance in close-quarters combat.[99] Ammianus' observation on the heavy knights may be explained by their quick (or premature) exhaustion as a result of excessive weight. This was because the super-heavy savaran had been 'perfected' for one primary task: propelling the all-powerful lance assault against enemy lines.

The ever-inventive Roman infantry found an unorthodox if not highly dangerous tactic for coping with the attacks of the super-heavy savaran during Julian's invasion of Persia in 363 CE. The legionaries would stand firm as the super-heavy knights approached their lines to then quickly dive underneath the horses in an attempt to stab the animal from underneath; these tactics were reminiscent of the doomed Gaul warriors who attempted the same tactics against Parthian armoured knights during the Battle of Carrhae in 53 BCE. This Roman tactic was partly aided by the limitations in the knights' field of vision imposed by the metallic face-masks of their helmets. The openings provided for the eyes on these masks limited the visual perspective of the knight, resulting in dangerous blind spots. These would become a serious battlefield liability as the super-heavy knights neared Roman infantry formations. Interestingly, these same types of blind spots had allowed Soviet combat infantry to approach some of the German Elefant tank destroyers at Kursk to place explosive charges on them virtually undetected.

Massive armour could also be overcome with advances in missile technology, a factor which may have contributed to the defeats of the super-heavy savaran against the Hephthalites in Central Asia in the 480s CE (Chapter 12). Put simply, as armour increases in power and sophistication, so too can the missile technologies designed to penetrate these. The same missile-versus-armour dynamic has held true to the present day with respect to kinetic weapons and propelled missiles against the armour of modern-day tanks.

The 'Composite' Savaran (c. 490s/early 500s–628 CE)

The last and final stage of the evolution of the savaran was characterized by two important developments. The first development was the induction of the dehkan corps to augment the ranks of the savaran, a process which was a direct outcome of the reforms attributed to Khosrow I. The super-heavy cavalry concept had been clearly abandoned by the early sixth century CE (or earlier, by the late 400s CE), especially in the reduction of armour for both warrior and horse. The second development witnessed the abandonment of the super-heavy cavalry concept in favour of the 'composite' warrior proficient in both archery and lance combat. There were also very important changes to military equipment, notably with respect to swords, archery equipment, armour and equestrian equipment. Many of these changes most likely had their origins in the battles and defeats against the Hephthalites in the 480s CE.[100]

The dehkans. As noted by Reza, the state of the cavalry after the implementation of the sixth century reforms was the creation of two general classes of savaran: the azadan (upper nobility) and the lesser gentry of dehkans.[101] The rise of the *dehkans* helped augment the numbers of professional armoured cavalry for the spah, which had been traditionally provided by the upper elites. The dehkans were also meant, at least in part, to politically counterbalance the mighty influence of the same cavalry elites of the 'upper nobles' they were intended to support in battle. The dehkans were provided with financial support by the state to facilitate the costs of their arms and armour.[102] This new force of savaran was now able to field a truly single force with other distinct (or dedicated) archer cavalry units phased out in favour of the 'composite' cavalryman.

The composite cavalryman. The composite knight was different from his super-heavy predecessor by virtue of his use of the bow and shield. The bow which had previously been the preserve of horse archers and light auxiliary cavalry was now integral to the main corps of the savaran. The new savaran were indeed 'composite' as these now united the functions of the horse archer as well as close-quarter combat into one single corps. These were in a sense a more 'universal' force as they were capable of fighting against the nimble mounted steppe warriors on their own terms as mounted archers or as lance chargers against Romano-Byzantine armies along the empire's western frontiers.

Tabari has provided an exhaustive description of the late Sassanian composite knight's equipment, which are as follows: a helmet with two spare bowstrings behind it (not clear exactly how this was done), breastplate, mail shirt extending below the knees, arm and thigh guards, greaves, lance, lasso, sword, mace (attached to girdle), axe, a bow case carrying two bows, a quiver containing thirty arrows and a shield.

Perhaps the most comprehensive representation of the late Sassanian or composite cavalryman is at Taghe Bostan in western Iran near Kermanshah. Identified as Khosrow II, this has an enclosed type helmet with a mesh of mail hanging from its frontal rim, covering the face. The rider can see through the helmet through two openings shaped like eyes. To the right of the knight is a quiver (with a slight horn-tubular shape) filled with arrows. The lance rests on his right hand in the 'upper arm method' but it may also be resting on the shoulder. In contrast to earlier depictions at Firuzabad and Nagshe Rustam, there is now a small shield attached to the knight's forearm. Like the earlier savaran knights there is a mail shirt, with the Taghe Bostan version now reaching to the knees (note that the mail at Firuzabad extends to above the knees). It is certainly possible that the warrior is wearing additional armour under his mail, possibly a breastplate and/or lamellar.

Swords. The period following the Hephthalite wars (480s CE) led to various changes in sword construction as well as the adoption of various Turkic-Hun technologies, notably with respect to sword suspension. These changes were in fact part of a larger shift in military technologies that were being introduced by nomadic peoples such as the Avars, Turkic peoples, various Hunnic peoples, etc., who were now ranging across Central Asia as well as Eastern Europe. Swords were now suspended by a new unique method in which scabbards were attached to the warrior's belt by means of two adjustable straps. Each of these straps ran through a loop at the rear of P-shaped mounts fastened to the scabbard. The P-shape-and-strap system allowed the cavalryman to adjust the angle of suspension of his sword. This resulted in two significant improvements. First, unlike the earlier scabbard-slide swords which simply hung down vertically, the P-mount adjustment allowed the cavalryman to suspend his sword more efficiently. Access to the sword was thus facilitated in comparison to earlier scabbard slides. As noted previously, the older scabbard slide obliged the rider to 'tilt' the scabbarded sword by its hilt by one hand just to facilitate the extraction of that sword from its scabbard by his other hand. The new P-mount system changed that. The sword could be permanently tilted by means of the straps such that drawing the sword involved a single action (drawing the weapon) as opposed to two actions (tilting the scabbard and drawing the weapon). In addition to reducing the number of actions for drawing the sword, the P-mount resulted in yet another factor that improved battlefield performance in general. As noted previously, the early Sassanian infantryman would have been obliged to tilt his sword by pressing his hand on the hilt just to avoid dragging his weapon on the ground as he marched. Now, like his cavalry comrades, a new generation of Sassanian infantrymen would be able to march into battle without the tilt problem. The adoption of such P-mount swords was duly seen among the Dailamite infantry (Chapter 7), who were now able to calibrate the tilt of their swords by simply adjusting the length of the two straps.

In addition to Sassanian P-mount swords currently housed in Western venues (i.e. British Museum, Musee de Louvre) there are two such swords available in the National Museum of Iran. One of these weapons revealed the following dimensions: sword length (with handle and excluding scabbard) of 106.5cm with a weight of 1,350 grams.[103] Interestingly the weight of this weapon is identical

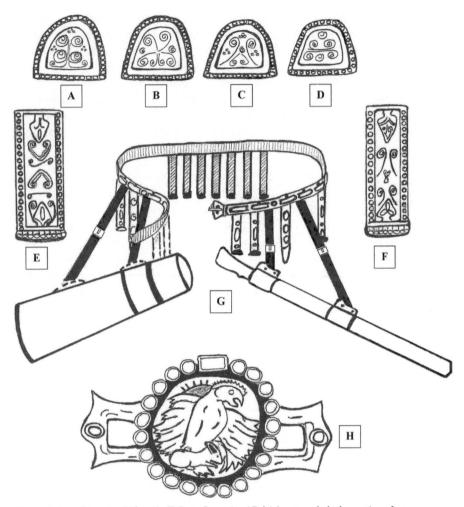

Figure 6. Late Sassanian Belts: (A–F) Late Sassanian 'Celtic' pattern belt decorations from Northern Persia; (G) Turkic-Avar lappet style suspension for swords and quivers; and (H) Gold belt buckle found in Nihavand. (Drawings by Kaveh Farrokh, 2004)

to the late Sassanian P-mount sword housed at the Musee de Louvre in Paris (1,350 grams).[104]

There were in fact a variety of mounts that are not even 'P' shaped. Balint's examination of Sassanian military relations with the steppe peoples in the later Sassanian era has examined these in detail by highlighting the different designs of such mounts which included D, 'ear-shaped', rectangular combined with D, etc., designs.[105]

These changes in sword suspension may be seen at Taghe Bostan. Here, specifically at the right panel depicting the stag hunt on the ingress into the vault can be seen a mounted figure engaged in archery during the hunt. Unique in this

Figure 7. Sword mounts: (A, B) Avar; (C) East Iranian/Soghdian; (D–I) Hunnic or Turkic; and (J) Late Sassanian to early post-Sassanian Dailamite (see also Masia, 2000 and Balint, 1978). (Drawings by Kaveh Farrokh, 2004, based on originals by Balint)

depiction is a sword and sheath suspended in the tilted or 45-degree manner. This is consistent with the P-mount type suspension. Yet, in that same panel can be seen the figure of the king (Khosrow II) resting his hand on his sword which is then tilted, indicative that he may possibly be carrying the traditional and out-dated ceremonial scabbard-slide weapon. Another possibility is that king is simply resting his hand on what is already a P-mount sword, but the former possibility (ceremonial sword) cannot be ruled out as the upper panel inside the vault does show Khosrow II standing with a ceremonial broadsword (Chapter 15).

Archery equipment. Archery had in fact re-asserted its importance among the knights over the battlefield, due to important developments in composite bow and equestrian technology by the sixth century CE. Procopius notes that the cavalry of this time were not just armoured riders but also expert archers capable of firing effectively from their right or left sides and delivering missiles of such force that these could punch through shields and armour, much as the Parthian horse archers had been able to achieve against the Roman forces they had faced at Carrhae in 53 BCE.[106] Further details pertaining to mounted archery have already been discussed in Chapter 5.

Armour. One of the most important implications of the development of the composite cavalryman was in the reduction of armour for both warrior and horse. This was clearly an indication that the spah was sacrificing armour in favour of

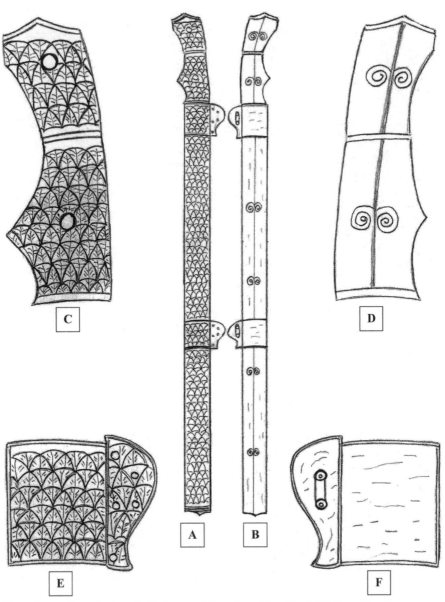

Figure 8. Late Sassanian swords: Entire sword from front (A) and back (B); Sword handle at front (C) and back (D); and Sword mount at front (E) and back (F). (Drawings by Kaveh Farrokh, 2004)

flexibility of movement and reduction of battlefield fatigue. In one sense this was partly a return to the early savaran knights of Ardashir I who had achieved an effective balance between protection and striking power. This again leads to interesting parallels between Sassanian cavalry warfare and modern tank warfare. The most effective tanks are often those judged as having achieved the optimum balance between three domains critical for battlefield survival: protection (or armour), mobility and firepower. Examples of such vehicles in armoured warfare include the Soviet T-34, Pzkw V Panther, the M1 Abrams and the Challenger.

The evolution of armour from the days of the early savaran to the late Sassanian era may be characterized as the gradual replacement of scale by lamellar armour forms[107] concomitant with the continual use and development of mail. While no complete and/or intact samples of early and late Sassanian mail have been found to allow us to exactly outline the evolution of Sassanian mail, it is fairly certain that the Sassanians had mastered the technique of fashioning mail corselets composed of metallic rings that were both stronger and more durable than before.[108]

Helmets. Late Sassanian helmets show distinct changes with respect to shape and overall design. The helmet of Khosrow II (r. 590–698) at Taghe Bostan in Kermanshah Western Iran is now spherical in shape instead of the (Bashlyk) conical type. The usage of facial protection is also different in that in place of an iron mask there is now a ridge atop the ocular areas with distinct arch-like openings or eye slits decorated with 'eyebrows'. Mail covers the rest of the face, and there is also mail extending to the shoulders. The helmet also shows evidence of imperial decorative motifs. A globular object (possibly metallic) sits atop the helmet with ribbons in tow. There is also a gem-like object placed in the centre of the helmet's forehead with two rows of pearls extending from it.[109]

Shields. The small shield at Taghe Bostan may have 'doubled up' to act as protection in close quarter combat situations as well as being used to deflect missiles. Coulston has suggested that this small shield functioned to protect the face and neck, 'acting more as a sode and ailettes than as shields proper'.[110] It is thus possible that these shields were used in conjunction with swords and maces during close-quarters combat.[111]

Gurz (mace). The primacy and importance of the gurz in the Iranian martial tradition is testified for Khorasani's *Lexicon of Arms and Armour from Iran* from Iran which cites a total of fifty-five different types of gurz (actual weapons and citations in Iranian mythology and epic literature).[112] Khorasani's earlier text, *Arms and Armour from Iran*, provides a detailed history of the gurz in Iran since the eighth century BCE.[113] Findings dated to the Bronze Age at Marlik have revealed at least two examples with 'hammer heads' that appear to have been used as sledge hammers.[114] The Bronze Age maces from Iran had hollow interiors to allow for wooden shafts to be inserted. The abundance of such finds makes clear that close-quarters combat was integral to the military training and combat doctrine of the knights. Put simply, the gurz was integral to the Sassanian knight's ability to shatter the enemy's armour (see below).

The gurz is an ancient Iranian weapon and can be traced to ancient Iranian mythology, notably as the primary weapon of the *izadan* (benevolent spiritual deities) of the *Avesta* holy text.[115] In the *Shahname* epic, the hero Fereydoun strikes the decisive blow against the evil Zahak's helmet, shattering it.[116] Koby-linsky defines the gurz as maces of varying types, notably those bearing an egg shaped or spherical shape (circumference 7–15cm) mounted on a wooden or metallic handle ranging 60–70cm in length,[117] although these could also be in the range of 40–55cm as well. The same *Shahname* notes the following regarding the primacy of the gurz during the Sassanian era by alluding to Khosrow I Anoushirvan I: *Agar Khosrow Ayad be Iranzamin* [If Khosrow were to arrive into the Iranian realm] / *Nabinad bejoz Gorz o Shamshir e Kin* [He would see nothing expect maces and sharp shamshir swords].

In reference to the *Shahname*, Allan and Gilmour have noted the importance of the gurz to Iranian cavalry.[118] The construction of the gurz (according to the *Shahname*) was of solid steel (handle and head) to achieve maximum weight for the achievement of devastating shattering power. By the Islamic era, the size and weight of a warrior's mace in the Persianate world was correlated with his prestige,[119] a military tradition which may have roots in the pre-Islamic Sassanian era. Harper describes the ox-headed mace as the gurz par excellence for use by kings, champions as well all other warriors of the armies of Iran.[120] There is also the depiction of ox-headed maces in the Sassanian context.[121] The first (in the British Museum) is that of a warrior in Sassanian attire, about to strike a demon figure devouring a human form. The second is the Sassanian painting at Kuh-e Khwaja in Seistan (south-east Iran) showing a seated figure with a mace raised, being approached by several supernatural entities (one of these bearing three heads). Interestingly, Zoroastrian magi or priests who bear the symbolic ox-headed mace in various ceremonies refer to this as 'the mace of Fereydoun' or 'the mace of Mithra', whose weapon in this context appears to be integral to his role in the defence of justice.[122] The *Shahname* also mentions a warrior 'bearing a gurz in his grasp'.[123] The gurz certainly survived into the Islamic era. One example is seen in the case of the guards of Ziyad Ibn Abihi, who were of the former savaran carrying spears and maces.[124]

Tabarzin (axes). The battle-axe is an ancient weapon of the Iranian plateau; many have been found in Luristan.[125] The battle-axe was employed extensively by the Medo-Persian troops of the Achaemenid Empire , especially during the Greco-Persian wars and Alexander's invasion of Iran.[126] Pour-Davood reports that the term 'axe' is termed *chakosh* in the *Avesta* holy text.[127] This chakosh weapon of the *Avesta* is essentially an axe that is flung at the enemy. The term *chakosh* has undergone a semantic shift over the centuries, as it means 'hammer' in modern or New Persian.[128] There are in general two terms that designate the battle-axe since Sassanian times, the *tabarzin* and the (Islamic era) term *tabar*. The *Dehkhoda Lexicon* provides two meanings for the 'tabar': the first is that of a 'normal' axe that is used for chopping wood, and the second is that of a battle-axe.[129] Al-Sarraf disagrees with the popular (Iranian) notion that the tabarzin represents a smaller battle-axe versus a larger version axe or tabar. Instead, Al-Sarraff identifies tabarzin as the genuine term for battle-axe dated to the Sassanian era and lasting to the twelfth century CE.[130] Al-Sarraff then suggests that the term 'tabar' as 'axe' came into use from the late eleventh or early twelfth centuries CE. According to Al-Sarraff, the Sassanian tabarzin was characterized as having a long shaft upon which was mounted a 'massive, broad blade'.[131] Examination of the Parthian axe-head housed at Tehran's National Museum of Iran showed that the height of the bulged area of the Parthian shaft-head where the actual shaft is inserted is 4.5cm, with the axe-head being 13.5cm in length.[132]

Matofi has noted that the tabarzin could be the alternative to the gurz.[133] This statement is of course consistent with that of Tabari who noted that the warrior had to choose between using the tabarzin or the gurz as carrying both would be too cumbersome.[134] The tabarzin certainly endured as a primary weapon of importance among Iranian warriors after the fall of Sassanian Persia to the Arabo-Muslim armies in 636–651 CE. This was especially the case in Khorasan and those Persian Khorasani troops who were in the service of the Caliph al-Ma'moun. These Khorasanis reputedly took great pride in their usage of the tabarzin.[135]

Equestrian equipment and the question of stirrups. A key question here is: did the late Sassanian composite knights have stirrups? The issue of stirrups has been strongly debated, but Michalak and Herrman have proposed that the later savaran used stirrups. Michalak notes that despite the partial damage to the feet of the knight at Taghe Bostan, 'the firm settling in saddle and the position of the legs, which are moved slightly forward and not hanging loosely down'[136] would suggest that the rider was using stirrups. Herrman notes that the lack of support behind the Taghe Bostan knight's saddle is indicative of him using stirrups. It is not clear how the reins are held at the Taghe Bostan vault as the aforementioned small shield on the knight's left forearm is hiding the reins he is holding. The issue of where stirrups may have been invented will be addressed in Chapter 12, but it is possible that this technology had reached the western fringes of Central Asia from northern China by the late 400s CE, especially in the case of the Hephthalites. The question as to how early this technology became available to the spah remains debatable, but the discovery of a pair of iron stirrups in the Marlik region dated to the late sixth to early seventh centuries CE[137] makes clear that these were in use by the time of Khosrow II or possibly earlier.

Figure 9. Sketches of the Sassanian stirrups discovered at Marlik, presently housed at the Römisches Germanisches Museum in Mainz, Germany. (Drawings by Kaveh Farrokh)

Table 3. Late Savaran Equipment as Cited by Dinawari, Bal'ami and Tabari.

	Dinawari, *Akhbar ol Tawwal* (ed. de Guirgass, 1888, p. 74)	Bal'ami, *Tarikhe Bal'ami* (as cited by Tafazzoli, 1993, p. 194)	Tabari, *Tarikh al-Rusul wa al-Molook* (ed. De Goeje, 1879–1901, vol. 1, p. 964)
sword	*na*	*shamsher*	*saif*
mace	*gurz* (suspended at belt)	*amud-e ahanin* (mace of iron)	*gurz* (suspended at belt)
club	*amud* (precise difference with *gurz* unknown)	*na*	*amud* (precise difference with *gurz* unknown)
battle axe	*tabarzin*	*tabarz/e/n* (hung from pommel of saddle)	*tabarzin*
lance and/or spear	*rumh*	*neyze*	*rumh*
belt	*mintaqa*	*kamar*	*mintaqa*
quiver	no distinct *tirdan* mentioned but notes of 30 arrows	*tirdan* (containing 30 arrows & attached to right side of saddle cantle)	no distinct *tirdan* mentioned but notes of 30 arrows
bowcase	*qaba* (contains 2 bows or as per Tafazolli (1993, p. 194) crossbows with bowstrings)	*kamandan* (attached to left side of saddle cantle)	*qaba* (contains 2 bows or as per Tafazolli (1993, p. 194) crossbows with bowstrings)
two bowstrings hung separately behind helmet	*watarain*	*watarain*	*watarain*
shield	*turs*	*separ*	*turs*
helmet	*miqfar*; Dinawari also mentions *baiza* (difference with *miqfar* unclear)	*khud/khod*	*miqfar*
chain for helmet	*na*	*selsele-aviz*; mail chain hung from behind helmet to protect neck	*na*
mail tunic	*dir*	*zereh*	*dir*
mail and plate-armour tunic; unclear if sources refer to Islamic-era *jowshan* (Kobylinsky, 2000, p. 68) or pre-Islamic *jowshan* (Pahlavi) (Khorasani, 2010, p. 193)	*Gawshan*	*Jowshan*; Bal'ami also notes that *Jowshan* was worn over the Zereh.	*Gawshan*
greaves and brassards	*saqain*	*na*	*saqain*
horse armour	*tiqhfaf*	*bargostvan*	*tiqhfaf*

Note: Only Firdowsi makes mention of the *kamand* (lasso) (ed. & tr. Osmanov, 1960–1971, vol. 7, p. 63)

The introduction of this newer type of saddle and stirrups resulted in significant improvements in the military performance of the composite knight. This new technology gave the knight a more secure and stable platform with which to deploy his archery equipment, lance and close-quarters weapons with much greater proficiency.[138] It would appear that the cheek-bit and noseband/muzzle remained in use. Herrmann suggests this was used in the late Sassanian era and points to the depiction of this technology in a sixth century CE rock-drawing of a horse at the Thalpan Bridge along the Karakorum highway as well as the seventh century CE Soghdian wall paintings at Panjikent (near Samarqand).[139]

The late Sassanian bargostvan underwent significant changes. In contrast to the bargostvan of the earlier savaran, the display seen at Taghe Bostan only provides partial protection for the horse. Specifically, the amount of shielding is limited to the horse's head, neck and frontal (chest) area only. The bargostvan at the Taghe Bostan vault appears to be constructed of metallic lamellar in contrast to the knight whose outfit is mail.

Mention must be made of the *Shahname* in reference to combat horses and equestrian equipment. The *Shahname* distinguishes between three types of horses, the standard *asb* (word for horse in New Persian), the *rakhsh* (horse of red and white colour) and the *tagavar* (rapid and noble steed).[140] It is interesting that a clear semantic distinction is made between the asb and tagavar, suggesting that these may have served distinct military functions, with the latter perhaps being more suitable for horse archery and/or lighter cavalry. The role of rakhsh is less clear but it is the horse of the epic hero Rustam, and may have been of the type employed by the armoured cavalry elites. The *Shahname*'s description of equestrian equipment (New Persian) is of interest as well.[141] There are at least two types of saddles, the *zin* (standard saddle) and the *zin-e khadang* (saddle constructed of birch). The *fetrak* were saddle straps used to secure baggage on the saddle. There are also two types of harnesses, the *setam* (standard harness) and the *zarrin setam* which is a more 'noble' type of harness applied with a gold inlay. Other terms include the *enan* (rein/bridle), *naal* (horseshoe), and the *taziyane* (riding whip).

Standard tactic or a late Sassanian development? Belnitsky[142] and Reza[143] report of an interesting 'post-breakthrough' tactic utilized by the savaran of Bahram Chobin in their battles against the Turco-Hephthalites in 588 CE. In essence, this occurred after 4,000 of Bahram's savaran had broken through enemy lines. The savaran, no longer acting as an 'armoured fist', could not simply fan out to mop up as Turco-Hephthalite resistance remained fierce. The savaran are then described as having operated at a distance of twenty meters from each other as they continued to lunge into the Turco-Hephthalite lines. This would have allowed each knight to engage in close-quarters combat with swords, maces or axes. It is possible that this was a late Sassanian tactical development but it is equally likely that this was developed in earlier Sassanian times. There are no reports of such tactics cited by Western or Classical sources.

Weapons and Close-quarters Combat

This section discusses the savaran's usage of weaponry in face-to-face individual combat. One of the notable features of the aforementioned discussion on lance combat at Firuzabad is the fact that no swords are being drawn in combat. The explanation for this is not just in the attempt by the illustrators to depict a 'symbolic joust'. The reasons were also pragmatic: swords by themselves cannot shatter or penetrate heavy armour in close-quarters combat. In such situations the knight must resort to the gurz (mace) and axe to shatter his opponent's armour. Fighting face-to-face is seen from the beginnings of the Sassanian debut, as again displayed in Firuzabad where the unknown Sassanian knight wrestles his counterpart on horseback. Nevertheless swords are by no means useless in close-quarters combat for the following three reasons. First, swords were effective against 'softer' leather armour as seen in Central Asian opponents, although it must be noted that the latter had varieties of highly resilient excellent (non-leather) metallic armour as well (Chapter 12). These would of course be even more devastating against lightly armoured or unarmoured cavalry who would be caught by the savaran in close-quarters combat (i.e. the later pro-Roman Ghassanid Arabs). Second, swords could be highly effective in Cossack-style pursuits of fleeing enemy infantry, be they unarmoured or armoured. In the latter case the Sassanian knight could engage in downward left-right or right-left slashing motion with his blade to sever the fleeing infantryman's neck. The third reason why swords were effective lay in Sassanian techniques and training for wielding swords. As discussed in Chapter 4, the so-called Italian grip, first seen among the Sassanians, provided a more powerful thrust at the sword tip as well as more effective 'slash' or swing.

Sami has emphasized the importance of the *kamand* (lasso) among the late savaran.[144] The kamand was in fact nothing new in the inventory of the savaran and indeed of Iranian cavalry since Achaemenid times and possibly even earlier. The Sagarthians, an ancient Persian tribe, did fight with lasso on horseback[145] as did many of the Iranian Saka cavalry from Central Asia. The lasso was a useful weapon as it could ensnare an enemy cavalryman's hand as he attacked by sword, or could also be used to tangle the enemy's neck to then pull him onto the ground. Jalali has questioned the value of the kamand among the savaran, arguing that it was not practical as a battlefield weapon;[146] nevertheless the honoured status of the lasso is cited by Tabari who described Bazanush [Emperor Valerian] as 'a proud knight of illuminated spirit and much valued by the Caesars, a lasso-thrower great in fame and lofty of dignity'.[147] The lasso was certainly employed on the battlefield. According to Josephus Flavius' *Jewish Wars*, the Armenian king Tirdad narrowly avoided capture after having being caught by the lasso of an Alan warrior in 72 or 73 CE.[148] The battlefield lasso was also apparently utilized by the Sassanians as a unit of measurement. The *Shahname* hero Kay-Khosrow is said to have built a dome with high vaults, ten kamand (lasso) lengths across after his capture of the fortress of Dezh-e Bahman in Azarbaijan.[149]

***Statistical analysis of the* Shahname.** In a detailed analysis of the *Shahname*, Khorasani, Shafeian and Singh have collated data with respect to the frequency of weapons usage against opponents in hand to hand combat.[150] This data on (types of) weaponry usage is compared to the areas of the opponent's body targeted in face-to-face combat. The following weapons are used with respect to frequency (numbers (n) cited in parenthesis) in close-quarters combat: lance ($n = 33$), bow/archery ($n = 27$), sword ($n = 25$), mace ($n = 21$), lasso ($n = 10$), and dagger ($n = 9$). Note that with respect to the lance, the researchers were not just tabulating the standard weapon used by the knight but also spears, javelins and tridents. The body areas most targeted with respect to frequency (numbers (n) cited in parenthesis) are: the waist ($n = 28$), head ($n = 27$), neck ($n = 19$), the adversary's steed ($n = 18$), flanks ($n = 10$), chest ($n = 9$), shoulders ($n = 5$), back ($n = 4$), arms ($n = 2$), and buttocks ($n = 1$).

The lance is very interesting as it is the weapon most frequently deployed; not surprisingly as this is consistent with savaran-doctrine of launching their primary strike by closing in with the lance. The area most targeted by the lance is the waist/gut area ($n = 18$) which is 55 per cent of all thirty-three strikes. Interestingly the chest was not frequently targeted by the lance ($n = 2$). While the opponent is armoured, the bone structure of the opponent's rib cage may also provide some additional difficulty for effective lance penetration as opposed to the softer belly.

Following the lance, archery is also a primary weapon, which is consistent with the spah's doctrine of destroying as many of the enemy at a distance (Chapters 5 and 9). Interestingly, the most targeted area is the opponent's horse ($n = 10$) which would be consistent with cavalry warfare, especially in Central Asia. The other most favoured archery target was the opponent's head ($n = 6$). Success in this action would be most practical as it would entail the instant dispatch of the enemy.

The data provides interesting information regarding close-quarters combat in which the sword is the most favoured weapon ($n = 25$) followed by the mace ($n = 21$), lasso ($n = 10$) and dagger ($n = 9$). Therefore, the sword is the weapon of choice in face-to-face combat. In such encounters the most targeted area is the opponent's head ($n = 10$) followed by the neck ($n = 5$). As in the archery case, successful blows to the opponent's head would secure more rapid success, while damage inflicted on the opponent's limbs would not necessarily eliminate him from combat. This would also explain why the head is also the most frequent target of mace strikes ($n = 11$). Interestingly the area most targeted by the warrior with his dagger was the opponent's neck ($n = 6$) which, if successful, could result in the rapid termination of the enemy. Another weapon targeting the enemy's neck was the lasso ($n = 6$). This would allow the knight to pull his enemy off his horse to then dispose of him with sword, mace, etc. Another motive for using the lasso may have been to capture key enemy commanders.[151]

Prestige Units of the Savaran

As noted previously, the Pahlavi linguistic nomenclature of the *Asbaran* designated them as cavalry 'elites'. Within these cavalry elites were also select prestige or 'higher elites' distinguished by their exceptional martial abilities on the battlefield, designated roles (i.e. royal guard units) as well as in their quality of arms and armour. Farzin has suggested that such units often served as elite guards for the shahanshah, a military tradition which he attributes to pre-Sassanian times, back to the time of the Achaemenids.[152] Farzin discusses an Achaemenid era panel which displays a guard, dressed in Mede attire, armed with a spear, bow and short sword, and standing to the rear of the king. To the rear of this guard stand two guards, identified as the Achaemenid-era 'Immortals' who hold spears whose butts are adorned with a globular or 'apple'-like attachment.[153]

By the Sassanian era, a Pahlavi term for the guards of the shahanshah was the *ham-harzan* (singular: *ham-harz*), also found in Armenian. The term is derived from Parthian Pahlavi *hm-hrz*, which is suggestive that such elite 'royal' guards were in service during the Parthian era. Examining the *Karnamg-e Ardashir*, Mashkoor[154] and Hedayat[155] variously define the hmhrz as 'spear-bearer', 'guardian', and 'guard with spear'.

Javidan or zhayedan. The Immortals known as the Javidan or zhayedan were probably one of (if not the most) prestigious of all elite units within the savaran of the Sassanian spah. Their commander was known as the *var-thragh niyagan khodai*.[156] The Javidan were on the whole better trained and better equipped with higher quality armour and weapons than the rest of the savaran forces,[157] making them in a sense, the 'elite of the elite savaran'. These Immortals certainly shared the same title as their ancient Achaemenid counterparts, but differed in one critical aspect, mode of combat. The Achaemenid Immortals were primarily an infantry force while the Sassanian Javidan or Zhayedan fought as cavalry.

The origins of the Javidan are attributed to the founder of the Sassanian dynasty, Ardashir I 'Babakan' (r. 224–242) who formed these as the Darbar [royal court] guard.[158] The *Shahname* appears to have made a reference to the Javidan during one of Ardashir's battles with Kurdish warriors; these are described as *savaran-e shamshir-zan-e dah-hezar* ('the 10,000 sword wielding/sword fighting savaran'). The *Shahname*'s report of 10,000 troops is exactly the same number of troops reported in the ancient Achaemenid unit of the same name.

It would appear that recruitment for the Javidan came from those troops who had displayed the highest possible valor and fighting skill on the battlefield. They were thus responsible for setting the best example of martial conduct for the entire savaran corps. The Javidan would fight even when the odds had turned against them on the battlefield. One example of this occurred during the Battle of Dara in 530 CE in which the Javidan, despite being caught in a hopeless situation, opted to fight to the last man rather than surrender.

Pushtighban or pushtiban. Another prestige imperial guard unit is known as the *pushtighban* (Pahlavi: life guardians) or (New Persian) *pushtiban*. In modern Persian the term pushtiban essentially refers to one's dependable and supportable friend or ally, especially in challenging and confrontational situations. Nyberg has also suggested that the Pahlavi term *pusht-aspan* (note phonological parallels between -aspan and -iban) is another term for the savaran.[159]

Recruitment for the pushtighban hailed from the upper nobility. An officer of this unit was according to Foss, the pushtighban-salar[160] with unit commander (according to Farzin) known as the pushtighban-sardar[161] who was one of the highly honoured intimates of the entourage of the shahanshah.[162] Another term that has sometimes been used in reference to the commander of the pushtighban was *hazarbod* (commander of 1,000) discussed in Chapter 2. This would imply that this was a small elite unit of just 1,000 warriors, which has led to suggestions that this was a royal unit responsible for the security of the shahanshah and the house of Sassan.[163] The pushtighban acted as the royal escort for the shahanshah and his entourage along both their left and right flanks. This would suggest that this unit may have been present in any battle which the shahanshah had chosen to attend.

Being directly responsible for the person of the shahanshah, the pushtighban, much like their comrades in the Javidan, were very well trained, staffed by warriors of the highest calibre, and equipped with the highest quality swords, helmets, lances and shields produced by the spah.[164] It is possible that the 'Royal Escort' cited by Ammianus Marcellinus as having accompanied Shapur II during his attacks towards the gates of Amida in 359 CE was the pushtighban.[165] It is also possible that Heliodorus' aforementioned 'brigade of Persians' of superheavy savaran may have been the pushtighban. Tabari makes an interesting reference to elite knights, possibly the pushtighban, during Shapur II's campaigns against the Arabs who had overrun, raided and pillaged much of the empire's southwest, advanced along the empire's Persian Gulf coast and even overrun Persis:[166] '[H]e [Shapur II] selected 1,000 riders from the bravest and most warlike warriors, ordered them to advance at his command ... and attacked the Arabs who regarded Pars [Persis] as their own private territory ... he wrought appalling havoc amongst them, took them into harsh captivity and chased away any who were left.'[167]

Tabari's description may also suggest that Shapur II had not strictly recruited from a single elite corps (i.e. pushtighban) but may have selected his best knights from the spah's entire array of elite contingents. The relatively small number of 1,000 knights apparently proved more than sufficient in not only ejecting the Arab invaders from the empire but also in making deep inroads into Arabia itself, approaching the city of Medina.[168] The Arabs, who had hitherto faced little opposition from the spah, now realized that their infantry and cavalry lacked the armour, close-quarters weaponry and archery necessary to confront the spah's heavily armed and armoured cavalry elites. The Arabs would avenge these defeats in the seventh century CE (Chapter 17).

Jan-separan or jyanavspar. One of the most interesting elite units of the savaran was known as the *jan-separan* (lit. 'those who depart from their lives' or 'those who sacrifice their lives.'), from the original Pahlavi *jyanavspar*.[169] The origins of these terms in the Sassanian spah may be traced to the *Karnamg-e-Ardashir* and the *Menog-e Xrad*. The latter text for example has a verse stating, 'seek to endeavour and be Jan-separ'.[170] In the *Karnamg-e-Ardashir* there are specific references with respect to Ardashir I Babakan and the savaran: 'The savaran of Ardashir made great efforts and fought hard battle/battled [in the] Jan-separan [manner] ... Ardashir sent person[s] and spah and 400 men who were Honarmand and Jan-separ ... Barzak and Barzator ... in the tradition of the Jan-Separan.'[171] Note that the term *honarmand* is derived from *honar*, which translates as 'martial valour' in Pahlavi and not as 'artistically talented' as it does in modern Persian.

The origins of the jan-separan unit in the spah appears to have come from those savaran who were especially brave, audacious and skilful in battle, with the distinguishing feature of being willing to risk death for the welfare of their comrades on the battlefield. It was this willingness to 'court death' that earned them the title of jan-separan as well as *jan ou bespar* and *jan bespar*.[172] This may explain why these units were often placed at the forefront of attacks alongside other crack elite savaran. The *Shahname* mentions the term *janvespar* as late as the time of Khosrow II,[173] which suggests that this unit remained in service to the last days of the dynasty in the seventh century CE.

One of the most interesting questions pertaining to the jan-separan is in regard to the ethnic composition of the unit. At first glance, the unit appears to have western Iranian origins, especially Kurdish as the term jan-separan is virtually identical in meaning to Perso-Kurdish *pishmarg/peshmarg*, which also means 'one who is close to/courts death' or 'one who sacrifices his/her life'. Nevertheless, it would appear that there also were non-Iranian recruits within the jan-separan, as one of the famous leaders of the unit known as Jalinus bears a name which is Hellenic rather than Iranian.[174] This raises the possibility that the jan-separan may have included deserters from the Romano-Byzantine armies, mercenaries as well as other (non-Iranian?) volunteers.[175] What is clear is that this unit fought with distinction and was honoured as one of the most prestigious of the savaran. Farzin notes that the leader of the jan-separan was a bodyguard of the shahanshah, accompanying him in all occasions of state and war, and was even allowed to sit on a designated 'lesser throne' in the Sassanian court.[176]

The gund shahanshah. An interesting elite unit that appears by the later sixth century CE is the *gund shahanshah* (lit. army division/unit of the King of Kings). This unit especially distinguished itself under the command of Bahram Chobin during his battles against the Romano-Byzantines prior to his victories against the Turco-Hephthalites in Central Asia in 588–589 CE. While little information is available on the specific tactics and equipment of this particular unit, it is highly probable that the gund shahanshah would have been equipped with the best equipment (offensive and defensive weaponry), armour, helmets typical of the composite late savaran type. Like the previously mentioned royal and prestige units, the warriors of the gund shahanshah would have been selected from the best battle-hardened veterans of the savaran. These most likely had their own distinct 'royal' *brahmag e artesharih* (costume of warriors) although the details of these cannot be ascertained with certainty.

Naxarars: the Armenian Knights

The geographical term Perso-Armenia corresponded to those regions east of the upper Euphrates as well as those regions of Armenia which were under Sassanian rule. This region came under Sassanian political influence after the Romano-Sassanian treaty of 390 CE and subsequently incorporated into the Sassanian Empire from 428 CE, being then administered by a marzban. The citizens of the region, especially the warriors and nobility, had been heavily Iranicized as a result of previous rule by Parthian princes between the years 63–390 CE. This resulted in a heavy Iranian influence upon Armenian armoured cavalry warfare such that Armenian and Sassanian knights closely resembled each other in equipment and fighting methods.[177] Nevertheless, it is incorrect to conclude that the Armenian and Iranian military traditions were identical. Ayvazyan notes of a distinct Armenian military tradition with respect to infantry, slingers, swordsmen, shield-bearers, mountain warriors and many other types of warriors.[178] Ayvazyan also avers that the Armenian *sparapets* (equivalent to Persian spahbod) maintained a highly professional school, doctrine and martial tradition of warfare which was passed on across the generations of Armenian warriors.[179]

The Armenian knights known as the *naxarars* were considered to be the most important of all allied units of the spah.[180] It is true that the conversion to Christianity had resulted in anti-Sassanian rebellions, notably the famous Battle of Avarir in 459 CE; however a number of Armenians did serve in the spah with high distinction. As noted by Daryaee, 'the few "evil" Naxarars mentioned in the Armenian historical narratives who supported the Sassanians were those who in fact chose to keep their ancient Armenian tradition at the expense of the new-comers ... adoption of Christianity ... divided Armenian society for some time to come.'[181]

The term 'naxarar' is believed to be a Persian loan-word[182] and was essentially a baron or lord who ruled his hereditary feudal-style lands and estates.[183] It was these feudal lords and their retinues who formed the core of the naxarar knights.[184] The pro-Iranian Armenian knights of Armenia (which also had a strong pro Romano-Byzantine faction) were provided considerable autonomy by Ctesiphon. The main proviso was for them to acknowledge the shahanshah and to provide their knights in support of the spah in times of war.[185] Armenian knights, for example, were present in the armies of Kavad in his campaign against the Romano-Byzantines in 502 CE.[186]

The naxarars were especially professional as armoured knights, fighting in exemplary fashion with the lance and in close-quarter cavalry warfare. Iranian military historiography describes the Armenian naxarar nobles as being exemplary in the martial tradition of cavalry warfare, possessing high quality armour (for knights and horses) and weapons, and being constantly engaged in intensive cavalry exercises and all forms of weapons training during peacetime.[187] The naxarars were especially versatile with their weapons, being equally formidable with these whether they fought as cavalry, infantry or in mountain warfare.[188] Armenian knights were especially formidable in close-quarters combat, priding themselves on their ability to split the helmeted head of an opponent with a sword all the way through the neck and shoulders.[189]

When called to service to Ctesiphon, each naxarar had his own banner around which his private army and retinues would rally before they joined the spah. The shahanshah and the spah conferred the highest honours on the naxarars who rallied around the drafsh-e kaviani at times of war. When Armenian knights neared the gates of Ctesiphon, the shahanshah would send a high ranking emissary to formalize their welcome to the capital. The emissary would inquire on behalf of the king as to the state of affairs in Armenia, a question that would be repeated three times. Once assured that the Armenian knights were happy with the state of their homeland, the shahanshah would then himself appear and honour them by personally inspecting their military review.[190]

The spah greatly respected the Armenian knights, as these were often able to hold their own in combat against vastly larger numbers of troops. One prime example of this is Armenian General Smbat Bagratuni, who led his knights in 619 CE into Central Asia to inflict crushing defeats on numerically superior Turco-Hephthalite forces that were threatening the northeast marches of the Sassanian Empire (Chapter 12). Armenian naxarars distinguished themselves repeatedly when fighting alongside their comrades-in-arms, the savaran. Sebeos has reported that, concerning the leading nobles of the naxarars who joined the banner of the spah: 'These are the princes of the Armenian nobles who [joined] him [Bagratuni] with each one's own contingent and banner. Varazshapuh Artsuni, Sargis Tayets'i, Artavazd and Vstam and Hmayeak Apahuni; Manuel, Lord of Apahunik; Viram, Lord of the Golt'nik'; Sargis Dimak'sean; Sargis Trpatuni; and others of the nobles.'[191]

The naxarars and Bagratuni helped the spah achieve some of the most dramatic Sassanian victories against the Turco-Hephthalites and were awarded high honours in recognition of their service (Chapter 15). Naxarar knights were reported as fighting alongside the savaran right up to the final days of the Sassanian Empire, when they battled against Arabo-Islamic forces at the Battle of Qadissiyah in 637 CE. The long casualty lists of Armenian knights killed and wounded at Qadissiyah is clearly indicative of how hard they had fought in that fatal battle.[192] The role of the 'Numerus Felicum Persoarmeniorum' unit in Roman service will be discussed in Chapter 19.

The Lakhmids

The Lakhmids were among the most valuable of the empire's Arab auxiliary troops (indeed of auxiliary troops in general). As noted by Greatrex, 'the Lakhmids ... emerged as the privileged ally of the Persians'.[193] Hailing originally from Yemen, the Lakhmids were Christian Arabs who by the 260s CE had established their capital in Hira (modern Iraq). Like the Sassanians, the Lakhmids had a well-organized army along with a mercenary elite guard based at their capital at Hira featuring a brick-walled compound and a two-storey fortress.[194] The Lakhmids proved especially capable in confronting the pro-Roman Ghassanids and even their Roman-Byzantine allies, as was the case with the Lakhimid ruler al-Mundhir in the 520s CE.[195]

The Lakhmids were equipped much like the savaran and proved to be highly capable, resourceful and resilient warriors. The Lakhmids played a critical role in the ascension of Bahram V Gur (r. 420–) to the Sassanian throne. Bahram had been raised and educated since his childhood in the court of Al-Na'uman, the

Lakhmid vassal king of Hira. He thus had the full military support of the Lakhmid Arabs of Hira.[196] Na'uman's support materialized in the provision of a large number of Lakhmid Arab cavalry who were equipped and trained like the savaran. These provided a formidable military escort for Bahram on his advance to Ctesiphon. The arrival of these forces along with the support of Mehr-Narseh and the acquiescence of the nobility after negotiations allowed Bahram to secure the Sassanian throne at Ctesiphon.[197] Lakhmid warriors were most likely equipped with Sassanian-type armour and even mail, long swords, narrow-blade spears, horse armour (bargostvan) and helmets of riveted construction. The most effective unit of the Lakhmids were the Wada'i, which comprised 1,000 savaran dispatched by the shahanshah on a rotational basis to support the Lakhmid kings.[198] Combining the renowned toughness of the desert Bedouin warrior with the military creed of the savaran, the Lakhmids proved themselves to be excellent knights, as demonstrated in their support of Azarethes during the Battle of Callinicum in 531 CE (Chapter 9).

Iranian Knights of the East: Savaran-e Khorasan

One of the significant long-term effects of the sixth century CE reforms was the creation of a distinct class of dehkans in eastern Iran and Soghdia (especially the city of Samarqand). According to Reza, these became known locally as the *akhshid* and the *afshin*.[199] What is of special interest is that each of these 'eastern Dehkan' nobles employed a specialized bodyguard unit known as the Chakeran (singular: Chaker) who are also cited in Chinese sources as 'Chou-ki'.[200] The Chakeran were paid directly by their Dehkan overlords, obligating them to accompany the dehkans to battle.[201] These 'eastern dehkans' and their Chakeran clients were generally equipped and attired like their western savaran comrades, yet they also exhibited a distinct military tradition unique to their regions.

The metal plate of the dismounted knights of the Khorasan and Soghdian type discovered at Kulagysh are highly significant as these portray Sassanian military fashions from the empire's eastern realms in the later periods (sixth-seventh centuries CE and after). These are armed in the full panoply of the late Sassanian composite knights described earlier: tabarzin (battle-axe), gurz (mace), swords, lances and archery equipment. Their swords are, judging from their empty scabbards, suspended with the P-mount lappet system (their mounts are actually more 'D' shaped). The Soghdian temple located between Panjikent and Samarqand features paintings of Soghdian knights with swords that are attached very high, with the hilt of the sword situated at shoulder-level of the archer.[202] The daggers are suspended from the belt in the horizontal orientation. In another Soghdian temple, there is evidence of a baldric hanging of a sword of one knight and the dagger of another. It is also notable that in Soghdia there are depictions of the 'traditional' scabbard slide sword (suspended vertically) as well as the lappet-suspension swords, just as in Taghe Bostan. This highlights the link in military culture between the eastern and western Iranian knights, both of whom pay homage to the 'traditional' broadsword. It is also of interest that a local narrow version of sword, which was most likely used for fencing, is also seen among the Soghdians by the late or post-Sassanian era.

The Khorasani knights also differ from their 'western' composite counterparts in one very important aspect: the way they wear their armour. These knights wear 'coats' of armour which are of the lamellar type; at Taghe Bostan, the knight inside the vault is seen with mail. Nevertheless they do also wear mail, but this is worn underneath the lamellar armour. The lamellar suit only has short sleeves with the lower parts of the arms covered by mail (suggesting that mail is worn underneath the lamellar suit). Technically these are most likely not 'sleeves'; possibly, they are shoulder guards meant to protect the outside part of the arms (the mail would at least partly cover the armpits). The warriors also have mail hand guards covered by some sort of protection (hardened leather or metallic armour). The legs are clearly protected by armour of the lamellar type seen by the knights at Firuzabad in 224 CE. It is possible that east Iranian leather capes were reinforced with square metallic plates, laminas, lamellas, or even rings of mail.[203] A wall painting at Panjikent also depicts knights wearing what appears to be a silk cape over their armoured tunics to provide some protection against the heat of the sun; this was also a fashion prevalent among the savaran of the empire's western regions.

A curious feature concerning the Kulagysh find are the two duelling warriors' helmets. These have three pointed spires with the middle one having a globe on its top. These helmets do not appear functional, and are possibly (like the 'ceremonial' sword of Khosrow II at the Taghe Bostan vault) meant for some symbolic purpose; or, they may designate some sort of rank. A wall painting at Panjikent also depicts a knight wearing a helmet featuring a face guard of mail, which is strikingly similar to the late armoured knight at Taghe Bostan.

An interesting fragment of a mural at Samarqand dated to the seventh century CE depicts knights with conical helmets featuring high side plates intended to protect the shoulders from axe, mace, and sword strikes sliding down the helmet. Like their other savaran comrades in eastern and western Iran, these particular knights wear mail protecting their necks and arms. Their legs appear to be protected by armour but it is not clear of what type. Equipment consists of axes, short swords, maces, small shields, lances, as well as bows and arrows. Curiously, there is no depiction of quivers or bow cases in the Samarqand mural. Other Soghdian depictions display warriors with significant shoulder protection, which is a wide cape of armour (not clear if this is constructed of mail or scales).

Yet another detailed representation of the late and post-Sassanian cavalry of the Khorasan and Central Asian type is the Pur-e Vahman metalwork dated to the seventh or early eighth centuries CE.[204] The rider is engaged in the Parthian shot with his bow of the Turco-Iranian or late Sassanian type. The bow is drawn in the Mongolian manner but the index finger for 'pointing' at the direction of the arrow is also used. The sword is slung at the left side and suspended in the lappet system with the tirdan (quiver) slung to his right (presumably by means of the lappet system). The rider is definitely using stirrups. The rider (presumably

Pur-e Vahman himself) does not appear to be wearing armour, which is consistent with the milieu of the hunt. Like the Pur-e-Vahman depiction, Soghdian depictions from the seventh century CE show knights riding with stirrups.

The term *savaran-e Khorasan* (savaran of Khorasan) remained highly prestigious in the Iranian cultural milieu even as cavalry technology changed, and with units formed and disbanded along the arrival and departure of numerous dynasties over the centuries. One of the most notable savaran units bearing the prestigious Khorasan title was the savaran-e Sepah-e Khorasan (the savaran from the army of Khorasan) of Nader Shah Afshar (r. 1736–1747).[205]

Chapter 7

Infantry, Auxiliary Contingents and Naval Forces

The Sassanian spah was notably different from its Parthian predecessor in that it was not simply an all-cavalry force. Cavalry of course retained its elite status and continued to develop until the later Sassanian era, but these were not the only elements in the battle order of the spah. There were in fact important auxiliary units, especially infantry, slingers and the elephant corps. There are also references to a camel corps and even chariots, although the latter would have been long obsolete as a battlefield weapon. The spah also recruited light cavalry auxiliaries to support the savaran. Arab Lakhmid cavalry, equipped and trained much like the savaran, also gained an important role, especially by the early fifth century CE. Women also served in the Sassanian military, a topic which is also briefly addressed in this chapter. Another interesting domain is the Sassanian navy in the Persian Gulf and its role since the founding of the dynasty in the early third century CE.

Sassanian Infantry

As in the previous Achaemenid and Parthian dynasties, infantry units were ranked as second in status to the savaran cavalry. Nevertheless, Kolesnikoff has noted that infantry troops formed a significant portion of the Sassanian spah.[1] Extrapolating from the available sources, Jalali identifies three distinct units of infantry:[2] *paighan* heavy infantry (i.e. heavily armoured and armed), light infantry and infantry archers discussed previously in Chapter 5. To these must also be added the Dailamites, who were to rise in military importance from the sixth century, as well as the *neyze-daran* and the peasant infantry. While most Western scholarship has acknowledged the importance and efficacy of the Dailamites, assessments of Sassanian infantry are generally negative. This perspective has been challenged by Howard-Johnston, who cautions that 'the contemptuous dismissal of the Persian infantryman as an ill-equipped, unpaid, rural serf (Ammianus Marcellinus, XXXIII, VI, 83) should be trusted no more than the grossly exaggerated eastward outreach of Sassanian power which is said to embrace China (Ammianus Marcellinus, XXXIII, VI, 14)'.[3] This section endeavours to distinguish between the different types of infantry and suggest that Western assessments may have at least partly to do with the poor combat performance of the peasant levies or infantry.

Paighan: heavy infantry. The commander of an infantry detachment was the *paighan-salar*.[4] However, the term *paigh* or *payg* (foot soldier)[5] requires more research as it is not clear if the description refers to lightly armed peasant levies pressed into service or more professional infantry. This may partly explain why there appears to be some confusion in the distinction between the poorly trained and armed peasant light infantry, paighan and the neyze-daran. Penrose, for example, identifies the peasant infantry as the paighan, but does acknowledge the existence of a separate force of 'regular combat infantry'.[6] As noted by Jalali, the duties of the paighan-salar's infantry during peacetime were internal security activities for the empire, not unlike modern day policing.[7] While such forces were most likely drawn from the peasant population, they appear to have been distinct from those strictly peasant levies pressed into service for siege works, baggage handling, etc. (see below). Paighan units in every province would be placed under the command of local regional commanders for deployment as security forces or 'gendarmes' in urban centres to help maintain law and order.[8] The paighan-salar could also be placed as the head of prisons as seen in reports of such an officer in command of the prison at Dastegerd in late Sassanian times.[9] For such duties and responsibilities, the paighan must have had at least some rudimentary military training and equipment for combat. This was a task for which the strictly peasant infantry were, according to Roman accounts (see Procopius below) wholly unsuited. Daryaee defines the paighan as having been armed with spear and shield,[10] while Jalali defines such spear and shield-equipped troops as a subdivision within the paighan.[11] Both Jalali[12] and Sami[13] concur that the paighan were the spah's standard heavy infantry, especially until the rise of the highly effective Dailamite infantry of northern Iran appearing from the time of Khosrow I in the sixth century CE.[14] Interestingly, the 'professional' infantry aspect of the term *paighan* has entered the Armenian lexicon as *payik*.[15] There are indications that professional heavy infantry troops were registered on state rolls and paid in cash like the cavalry elite.[16]

Sami has noted that paighan formations were usually deployed to the rear of the savaran.[17] According to Jalali, the role of the paighan was to provide combat support for the savaran corps as well as protection for the light infantry and foot archers.[18] In practice, foot archers would first be placed ahead of the paighan to fire their missiles. Once their missiles were exhausted, the foot archers would retire to the rear of the paighan.[19] The light 'peasant' infantry performed as logistics, support and siege work personnel; and, since they had very low combat skills (see below), they relied on the paighan and savaran for their battlefield survival.

What is certainly clear is that well-armed paighan armoured infantry were in service with the spah from the early days of the dynasty, especially during the campaigns of Shapur I against the Roman Near East in the mid-third century CE.[20] It is possible to reconstruct these paighan thanks to the findings of a Franco-American excavation team that discovered the remains of a fallen Sassanian soldier in Tower 19 at Dura-Europos that had been subject to mining operations by the spah.[21] The paighan wore a 'T-shirt' style short-sleeved mail garment reaching to his hips. He was armed with a rectangular shield of wickerwork construction and wore a two-piece riveted 'ridge' helmet (see Chapter 6). According to Zoka,[22] Hekmat[23] and Jalali[24] the paighan were typically armed with swords, daggers and other hand-to-hand weapons such as maces. This equipment would suggest that the paighan were expected to engage in close-quarters hand-to-hand combat against their Roman counterparts, especially in siege scenarios. Nevertheless, Roman infantry would often gain the upper hand in close-quarters combat against the paighan. Lee has correctly noted that despite the Roman edge in infantry, the Sassanians were able to compensate for this weakness with their highly effective cavalry forces (the savaran) and efficient siege warfare.[25] Interestingly, Ziapour reports that the paighan wore leg protection (like the cavalry) in the form of lamellar type armour (made of hardened leather or metals) worn over leather trousers.[26] While certainly possible, this assertion has yet to be corroborated by archaeological finds.

Ammianus Marcellinus provides an interesting description of Sassanian heavy infantry (or 'gladiators') at the time of Julian's invasion of Iran in 363 CE. According to Ammianus: 'Their infantry are armed like Mirmillos [a type of armoured gladiator] and are as obedient as grooms.'[27] This observation from the fourth century CE is indicative of two things. First, it is clear that these Sassanian infantry are well armed and armoured. But the same description also raises more questions, especially in the use of the term *mirmillos*. Why would Ammianus refer to this term as opposed to just 'heavy infantry'? Perhaps he was applying the term mistakenly, but this cannot be substantiated. Another possibility is that the Sassanians may have attempted to develop a heavier version of their regular Dura-Europos-type combat infantry, like the super-heavy savaran discussed in Chapter 6. If that is the case, these troops would have had formidable armour, possibly of the 'combination' type of mail (possibly worn over lamellar), and met-allic ring armour for the arms as well as greaves to give them a more 'mirmillos' type appearance. At the very least these troops were equipped with armour in the Dura-Europos style and carried long straight swords, but whether these resem-bled those of the savaran in 363 CE with respect to dimensions such as length, etc. cannot be fully ascertained. What is clear, however, is that these Sassanian infantry were engaged, overcome and defeated by their Roman counterparts as Julian drew close to Ctesiphon in 363 CE.

The second point made by Ammianus with respect to the 'mirmillos' is that they were 'as obedient as grooms'. This suggests that these were highly disci-plined and trained, consistent with Sassanian training regimens in general (Chapter 4). In any case, this particular topic certainly requires further study to help shed light onto developments in Sassanian heavy infantry at this time.

The paighan were also employed alongside battle elephants. In the fourth century, the paighan, for example, are reported as advancing alongside battle elephants (as occurred during Shapur II's siege of Nisibis in 350 CE; see Chapter 14). In contrast to the prestige of the *framandar savaran* however, the paighan-salar was not as highly regarded within the spah military, as the infantry corps was considered inferior in status to the cavalry.[28] Nevertheless, this asser-tion does require further investigation, at least with regard to the Dailamites of the later Sassanian era[29] (see below).

Dailamites. In contrast to peasant recruits, the Dailamites were among the best professional infantry fielded by the spah, being especially adept in close-quarters combat.[30] These could and did engage the formidably trained and resilient Romano-Byzantine infantry. Dailamite warriors were especially adept in the use of a variety of close-quarters combat weapons such as swords and daggers,[31] and two-pronged javelins (known in Persian as *zhupin*) used for 'thrusting and hurling'[32] in close-quarters combat.[33] The Dailamites actually excelled far more in their face-to-face combat skills in comparison to their archery.[34] As noted by Matofi, the Dailamites were especially renowned for their skills in the use of the tabarzin (battle-axe) and shield in close-quarters combat.[35] The tabarzin was especially effective in helping shatter the enemy's armour.

Overlaet's exhaustive report on findings made in northern Iran demonstrates that the Dailamites were armed with the same type of late-Sassanian swords,[36] Spangenhelm helmets[37] and archer's fingercaps[38] as their savaran comrades in the spah. It is also significant that these finds also include strap mountings, gold ornaments, belt decorations, etc. that were worn by members of the nobility and the elite savaran knights.[39] Note that the Dailamites were using the same type of lappet-suspension system swords utilized by the savaran which, unlike the earlier (prelappet) scabbard-slide broadswords, would not drag on the ground when the infantryman was on the march (Chapter 6). The use of such equipment and regalia would suggest that the Dailamites may have had a relatively high status within the spah.

Mobbayen has provided an overview of the origins and characteristics of the spah's Dailamite warriors.[40] These hailed from northern Persia, living mainly in the mountainous regions with their ethnic cousins, the Gels, mainly inhabiting the Caspian Sea coast of northern Iran. Mention has been made of a certain Barvan or Parvan as the primary township of the Dailamites in Islamic times (c. 816 CE), however the exact location of that locale remains uncertain.[41] A prominent clan cited in early pre-Islamic times is the *Jastan*.[42] The tough climate of forested northern Persia has been home to generations of warriors who not only served the Sassanians, but also defeated several attempts by the Caliphate to absorb the region after the fall of the Sassanian dynasty (Chapter 18). The Dailamites were to become especially prominent during the wars of Khosrow I, especially in the Persian Gulf-Yemen theatre (see section on naval forces later this chapter) and in Lazica (in modern Georgia of the Caucasus, see Chapter 14). They were to also engage in the Battle of Qadissiyah against the Arabs in 637 CE (Chapter 17).

The neyze-daran. There was also a subdivision within the *paighan*, identified by Jalali as the *neyze-daran* (foot spearmen).[43] They appear to have been specialized in spear combat and, like all paighan units, were placed in front of the foot archers. It is not clear how the neyze-daran would have confronted attacking Roman troops. If it is assumed that these were armed and armoured like the heavy infantry, then these could presumably engage in close-quarters combat. It is not clear how their spears would be employed, meaning whether these would be used for thrusting or simply hurled at the enemy. If the neyze-daran were lightly armed and lacked armour, then these may have engaged in the 'hurl-and-run' tactic, especially in scenarios where Roman infantry would have been rushing towards them. There have been suggestions that the neyze-daran would at times be able to stand up to Roman infantrymen in close-quarter combat situations.[44] Mention must also be made of javeliners recruited from the Mede highlands of Iran[45] who would employ thongs for both hurling and spinning their javelins in flight which would increase their accuracy and power of penetration.[46] These could prove especially effective as auxiliary forces in blunting enemy infantry or cavalry attacks either in support of the neyze-daran or even the savaran.

Light peasant infantry. Hailing from the lowest ranks of Sassanian society, the light infantry were recruited from the peasant population. Treated virtually as serfs, they were typically unpaid by the state during their term of service.[47] Lacking in military training, Sassanian light infantry were poorly armoured and armed, often only having a short dagger for defence.[48] The light infantry, who often worked as servants for the savaran cavalry, were also utilized in siege operations for manual labour and associated tasks such as the construction of mounds, various military earthworks and the digging of trenches. In this respect these personnel were especially valuable for long, drawn-out siege operations in locales such as Amida or Nisibis. The capture of Dara in 573 CE by Khosrow I (r. 531–579), for example, was greatly assisted by the efforts of 120,000 light infantry who were essentially labourers for Sassanian military engineers building large mounds (for more on siege operations, see Chapter 14).

It would appear that the 'infantry' so derided by Procopius are these peasant infantry in contrast to the professional types such as the aforementioned Daila-mites or paighan types. Note Procopius' description of the Sassanian infantry contemporary to the reign of Kavad during the battle of Dara (530 CE):

> [F]or their whole infantry is nothing more than a crowd of pitiable peasants who come into battle for no other purpose than to dig through walls and to despoil the slain and in general to serve the soldiers. For this reason they have no weapons at all with which they might trouble their opponents, and they only hold before themselves those enormous shields in order that they may not possibly be hit by the enemy.[49]

Such types of 'infantry' were a part of General Firouz's Sassanian forces and indeed performed poorly as they dropped their shields and abandoned the field in haste. They simply had no chance of survival in close-quarter combat against the professionally trained Romano-Byzantine infantry. This would certainly explain why the Romano-Byzantines took such a heavy toll of these troops.

Sassanian infantry: a new view? Not surprisingly, Roman descriptions of Sassa-nian infantry troops are logically, if not overwhelmingly negative. The question, however, is the calibration of Procopius' designation of 'infantry'. His description makes very clear that these were peasant levies pressed into service as infantry. But Procopius' descriptions are at variance with the earlier Sassanian *paighan* warriors seen at Dura-Europos (early third century CE) or the Sassanian 'gladiators' seen at the time of Julian's invasion of Persia (363 CE) who wore armour, helmets and swords. Procopius' own description makes clear that the infantry he was describing 'have no weapons at all with which they might trouble their opponent'. Overemphasis upon this reference may lead to linear conclusions with respect to Sassanian infantry in general. Western scholarship has in fact acknowledged the need to revise traditional Western views of Sassanian infantry. Penrose, for example, has noted that negative Roman opinions of Sassanian infantry (as a mass of poorly equipped and incapable serfs) was based on their confusion between peasant-type troopers versus regular Sassanian infantry.[50] Ward concurs by stating that 'although at various times during the dynasty the Sassanian infantry was reported to have been no more than a levy of peasants with little tactical value, for most of this period they appear to have been a disciplined and skilled force'.[51]

Close-quarter combat was in fact highly esteemed in the ancient military tradition of Iran, as seen for example in the *Shahname* which describes Bahram Gur as having killed two lions with his tabarzin on foot.[52] Nevertheless, as noted by Sidnell, when it came to face-to-face combat against the formidable and superbly trained Roman foot soldiers, the spah placed its primary focus upon the savaran to defeat them.[53]

The Camel Corps

While information on Sassanian camel corps is scant at best, some units of these appear to have existed, at least in the mid-sixth century CE. Russian researchers have cited a rebel named Anoushzad supported by the 'Imperial Camel Corps'[54] who rebelled against Khosrow I (r. 531–579 CE). More research is required to examine the primary sources for this citation as well as the size, composition and armaments of such corps. Interestingly, camels are not mentioned as a primary battlefield weapon by Classical or Arabo-Islamic sources. Perhaps the Parthian experience of employing camel cataphracts by Ardavan (Artabanus) V in the three-day battle against the Roman forces of Macrinus at Nisibis in 217 CE dissuaded the Sassanian spah from organizing such corps into their regular battle order. At Nisibis, the Romans successfully deployed caltrops to disrupt the attacks of the Parthian camel cataphract corps; the caltrops injured the soft spongy feet of the camels, thus dangerously disabling them on the battlefield. Despite this shortcoming, camel cataphracts could be especially effective, given the warrior's elevated position on the beast, as well as being an excellent platform for archery.

There are two prominent displays of camels in Sassanian arts. The first is Bahram Gur engaged in archery during the hunt as he rides a camel (Hermitage, St. Petersburg, Inv. S-252). The second is seen in the right side of the grand *iwan* which depicts the royal hunt of Khosrow II (Chapter 4). In this display (on the upper left side of the panel) can be seen five camels carrying off deer already killed by the royal hunting party. Apart from the aforementioned Anoushzad case, the camel corps do not appear to have a primary unit in the spah. Perhaps there were ceremonial units or support units (logistics, etc.) but there is little mention of these being used alongside the savaran, battle elephants, infantry, etc., in battle-field situations.

Chariots: Ceremonial or Military role?

Following his defeat at Ctesiphon in 233 by the savaran led by Ardashir I (Chapter 6), Emperor Alexander Severus (r. 222–235 CE) delivered a bombastic victory speech to the Roman senate (25 September 233 CE), which among his many claims, was the alleged destruction of '1,800 scythed chariots' of the Sassa-nian spah.[55] Iranian military historians often refer to the presence of the *arabeh* (chariot) in Sassanian armies,[56] which may be partly based on a literal inter-pretation of the Alexander Severus speech of 233. It is very unlikely that the spah would have been using Achaemenid-era type scythed chariots over 500 years after their complete failure against the invasion forces of Alexander. Western military historians are in general agreement that scythed chariots were not a major element in the battle order of the spah and had no (military) role to play in any of the major battles between the Sassanian empire and the Romano-Byzantines.

It is possible that some type of chariot was retained (or resurrected) for cere-monial battlefield purposes. Mashkoor notes that following a major battle between the spah led by General Razutis and the Romano-Byzantines in 12 September 627 CE,[57] the Sassanians were defeated following the death of Razutis, which resulted in the capture of twenty-seven Sassanian *drafsh* (banners, see Chapter 16) and a number of *arabehaye jangi* (war chariots). Perhaps these were ceremonial in nature as the utility of such vehicles would be dubious at best on the battlefields of the time. Perhaps this ceremonial aspect may have been a throwback to a more proto Indo-European tradition;[58] the Irish sagas for example make references to the *Carpat* (Old Irish: chariot).[59]

Arab Contingents of the Spah

Arab contingents were of critical importance to the spah. In practice, the martial abilities of the Arabs were important to both the Sassanians and the Romano-Byzantines. The Arabs were also situated along trade routes, cities and regions that were of vital importance to both the Romano-Byzantines and Sassanian Empires. Arab auxiliary forces played a vital role for the Sassanians in three major ways.[60] First, they were able to protect trade routes, especially those near to or traversing the Arabian Peninsula against Arab raiders. Second, they played a vital role in shielding the cities and villages of southern Iraq (again) against Arab warriors who would launch forays from Arabia towards the southwest. Third, Arab auxiliaries played a vital role in preventing Arabs from entering southern Iran to raid the coastal trading ports of the empire's Persian Gulf coastline.[61]

While the Arabs had not been trained in regular military doctrines or siege warfare, the Sassanians (as well as their Romano-Byzantine rivals) found two military uses for their Arab recruits.[62] First, the Arabs were masters of the desert and often acted as heralds and guides for Sassanian armies during their campaigns along or across the empire's southwestern marches. Their mastery of the desert also allowed them to track down political opponents, regular criminals and deserters from the spah. Second, Arab auxiliaries were excellent as light cavalry. The Arabs were able to launch very rapid cavalry raids and pull back just as rapidly before the enemy was able to coordinate an effective response.[63] Often during such raids the Arabs would secure plunder before making good their escape.[64] The spah found this Arab ability of special utility against Roman forces, especially when they would be methodically organizing themselves before the onset of a major battle. Arab warriors recruited for auxiliary roles were presided over by sheikhs and tribal leaders who would cooperate directly with the spah.[65]

Light Cavalry Auxiliaries

The Sassanians also employed Turkic contingents in the role of light cavalry.[66] Depending on battle circumstances these contingents (both Turkic and Arab) provided flank security for Sassanian armies; struck at the enemy's flanks simultaneous to the main attack by savaran heavy cavalry at the centre of the battle line; and, in the event of a breakthrough by the savaran knights, exploited deep into the enemy's rear.[67] In general, they operated much like the Parthian horse archers of old, being equipped with light armour only and employing bows as their primary weapon.

As noted previously in Chapter 2, there were numerous auxiliary cavalry forces recruited by the spah, including Khazars from the Caucasus, Albanians, and Hephthalites from Central Asia. Iranian light cavalry were also recruited, especially from Gilan in the north, Saka-istanis from southeast Iran and Kushans from Central Asia.[68]

Slingers

Matofi has noted that slings are one of the oldest battlefield weapons of Iranian armies since antiquity.[69] The *pilaxan* (sling)[70] was as simple as it was effective. Round pellets or stones were placed inside a fur, or a leather belt attached at the two ends by a rope.[71] The pouch or bag was then spun over the head a few times, then one of the ropes was let go to allow for the release of the stones or pellets over a distance.

Slingers were recruited by the Achaemenids[72] and were certainly reported in Sassanian times by Roman sources such as Libanius in reference to the battle of Singara (343 or 344 CE).[73] The Sassanians continued to recruit slingers[74] from the Mede highlands of Iran.[75] These were especially effective as pellets propelled by slings were very difficult to detect due to their high velocity, which contributed to their deadly impact. Slingshots were used to shoot pellets that were often difficult to evade and could kill or injure a whole array of enemy troops, even those with armour and helmets. An attack by armoured cavalry could be disrupted by experienced slingers.[76] This was due to the stones or pellets acquiring power and momentum through the rotating movements of the sling.[77] Slingers often supported archers during sieges, as reported at Amida where the constant barrages of the archers and slingers reputedly 'never ceased for a moment'.[78] This suggests that slingers combined and coordinated with massed archery could have possibly been highly effective in blunting enemy infantry and cavalry assaults. The sling was also a much cheaper weapon than the bow and did not require as much physical strength to operate during battle. Despite this, the sling was a very difficult weapon to operate and required much training to ensure battlefield effectiveness.[79]

Interestingly the Pahlavi term 'pilaxan' has entered the military lexicons of Georgia and Armenia but not specifically as 'sling'. In Armenian *pilikon, pilikwan, piliwan* means 'a large crossbow or arbalest', while in Georgian *pilakvani* or *pilagani* denotes 'catapult'.[80] The sling possibly also acquired a high status by late Sassanian times among the elite savaran. For example, the post-Sassanian *ayyaran* (persons associated with the warrior class from the ninth through to the twelfth centuries) regarded the sling as one of their favourite weapons.[81]

Women in the Sassanian Spah

Women have appeared in the armies of ancient Iran. A summary of a report made by the Reuters News Agency in 3 December 2004, entitled 'Bones Suggest Women Went to War in Ancient Iran' noted that DNA tests made on a 2,000-year-old skeleton of a sword-wielding warrior in northwest Iran have shown that the bones belonged to a woman.[82] The time length of 2,000 years would place the warrior-woman in the Parthian era. Alireza Hojabri-Nobari (head of the archaeology team) reported the following in an article appearing in the Persian-language newspaper *Hambastegi* newspaper in Tabriz: 'Despite earlier comments that the warrior was a man because of the metal sword, DNA tests showed the skeleton inside the tomb belonged to a female warrior.' Hojabri-Nobari further emphasized that the tomb which included warrior weapons was just one of 109 unearthed in northwest Iran thus far, with DNA tests scheduled for the other entombed skeletons. The article in *Hambastegi* further mentioned other ancient tombs belonging to Iranian women warriors that have also been excavated near the Caspian Sea in northern Iran.

Tombs attesting to the existence of Iranian-speaking women warriors have also been excavated in Eastern Europe. Cernenko, for example, has noted of the tomb of a Scythian female warrior contemporary to the Achaemenid era of Iran at Ordzhonikidze which had a javelin, spear, gorytos containing a bow and arrows, and a 'pocket' in the gorytos containing a knife.[83] Brzezinski and Mielczarek have noted of the presence of female 'Amazon' warriors among the proto-Sarmatians in the fifth century BCE carrying short swords, archery equipment and spears.[84] Pokorny has noted that the etymology of 'Amazon' is derived from old Iranian *maz* (combat) resulting in the North Iranic folkname *ha-mazan*, meaning 'warrior'.[85] This is certainly disputed as seen in the arguments of Mayrhofer.[86] Sekunda has noted of Greek vase art depicting 'Amazon' women warriors in the 450s BCE typically dressed in the Persian manner (short tunic, trousers elaborately patterned, pointed hat with cheek flaps, long neck guard) and carrying Achaemenid-style shields.[87]

Women did continue to appear in Sassanian armies. As noted by Ward 'Sassanian armies also included substantial numbers of women'[88] with Dodgeon and Lieu highlighting the fact that 'the presence of substantial numbers of women in Persian expeditionary forces is often noted by Roman authors'.[89] Zonaras specifies their military role in the third century CE by noting that 'in the Persian [Sassanian] army ... there are said to have been found women also, dressed and armed like men'.[90] Women were also hired as merchants to act as sutlers for the Sassanian army during its campaigns.[91] Women were recruited for combat roles at critical times, one example being at Singara (343 or 344 CE), of which Libanius reports that 'the Persians enlisted the help of their women'.[92] This strongly suggests that Iranian women, like the menfolk, were trained in the arts of war and capable of wielding weapons when called to duty by the spah.

The *Shahname* emphasizes the role of warrior women such as Gordafarid who, in a combative encounter with Sohrab, (son of warrior-hero Rustam) is described as 'turning in her saddle, drew a sharp blade from her waist, struck at his lance, and parted it in two'. There are numerous names in Iranian folklore of anti-Arab resistance fighters including Apranik (daughter of General Piran who fell at Qadissiyah in 637 CE), who fought in 632–640 CE; Negan, who led an anti-Arab resistance movement and died in combat in 638 CE; and the Parthian-descended Azadeh Dailam (the so-called Free One of Dailam), who led the military resistance in northern Iran against the expansion of the Arab-Caliphate in the 750s CE (the Dailamite warriors of northern Persia continued to resist the Arabs long after the fall of the Sassanian empire in 650 CE; see Chapter 18). Mention in this regard must be made of Banu, wife of Babak Kharramdin who fought against the Caliphate for decades before his castle of Bazz in Azerbaijan was captured and sacked by the Caliphate's Turkish troops in 838 CE.

Pil-savaran: The Elephant Corps

Hekmat has ascertained that the Sassanian elephant corps essentially fulfilled the same role in the spah that chariots had during the Achaemenid era.[93] In practice the Sassanian elephant corps were entrusted with a number of duties. First, while the function of the elephant as a primary 'Durchbruch' (breakthrough) weapon is not altogether accurate, these animals were highly valued by the spah and did partake in a number of battles[94] (see discussion later this chapter). The elephants often played the role of support and stood to the rear, providing a psychological boost for the various arms on the battlefield, especially infantry.[95] The elephant could also be used as a psychological weapon to frighten enemies unaccustomed to such beasts.[96] In this endeavour, the spah did employ battle elephants to target inexperienced Roman troops and Arabian warriors in attempts to influence the course of battles.[97] Interestingly, Sassanian elephants were also used in siege operations[98] as a type of 'living mobile tower' in the spah's inventory of siege engines for the taking of cities[99] (Chapter 14). The elephant corps was also utilized for the transportation of men and supplies.[100]

The Achaemenid question. The early Achaemenids did not utilize battle elephants, at least as attested by Classical sources in reference to Cyrus the Great and Darius the Great. Classical sources also make no mention of elephant units in the army of Xerxes during his invasion of Greece in 480 BC. Some Iranian historians have argued that Achaemenid expansion into western India as well as southern Egypt towards Ethiopia must have had (at least in part) the assistance of battle elephants.[101] The Achaemenids were certainly in contact with India and would have had access to elephants. Classical sources however, fail to verify the existence of elephant corps during the early-to-middle part of the Achaemenid dynasty.

The first mention of elephants in Achaemenid service comes from Arrian (3.8.6) who cites fifteen of them in the army of Darius III (r. 336–333 BCE) at the Battle of Gaugamela (331 BCE). The elephants were employed by Darius' Indian allies. Charles, citing mainstream Western scholarship, notes that Arrian's account suggests that the elephants were not employed in the battle.[102] Arrian does verify that Alexander captured Darius' elephants along with his baggage train after the battle.[103] Achaemenid elephants are also reported by Quintus Curtius Rufus, who noted that Alexander received a gift of twelve elephants from the satrap of Susa as Hellenic invasion forces were nearing the city.[104] Mainstream Iranian historiography takes a different view from Classical sources and mainstream Western scholarship. The *Iranshahr* text, for example, claims[105] (1) a total of 500 elephants in the entire Achaemenid military machine of Darius III, with at least 50 of these being present at Gaugamela; and that (2) Achaemenid elephants were a source of great anxiety among Alexander's forces.

Origins of Sassanian elephant corps. The key question is: when did the Sassanians introduce the elephant into military service? Ardashir I's Parthian predecessors, who had ruled Iran for nearly 500 years, are not believed to have used elephants, possibly having regarded these as unreliable battlefield weapons. The Parthians (like the Sassanians) relied primarily on cavalry forces but did introduce camel cataphracts towards the end of their dynasty.

The *Historia Augusta* does claim that Ardashir I had 700 elephants of which Alexander Severus allegedly killed 200 and captured 300 (18 of these were allegedly sent to Rome). Charles, however, notes that the thesis of Ardashir having had elephants is largely based on the *Historia Augusta*'s highly exaggerated and unreliable claims of Emperor Alexander Severus' alleged 'victory' over the Sassanians.[106] Scullard was of the opinion that Ardashir I's son and successor, Shapur I, deployed elephants against Roman armies.[107] Shapur is cited by the *Historia Augusta* as having been halted at Resaina by Gordian III,[108] who is then described as having dispatched to Rome at least twelve elephants.[109] Tabari also gives an interesting reference, stating 'Shapur, the man of the armies, rode out against them with elephants covered with blankets and with heroic fighters.'[110] This reference would suggest that such elephants were not protected by armour but the reference to 'heroic fighters' is less clear as it does not specify if these are armoured knights or strictly archers.

Nevertheless, and as noted in the introduction of this book, the *Historia Augusta* is generally no longer regarded as a reliable source for the study of Sassanian military affairs in the third century CE. The unreliability of the *Historia*

Augusta leads Charles to 'refrain from using this material as proof that elephants were used by the Persians in the first half of the third century CE'.[111] Interestingly, neither the *Chronica*[112] nor other sources[113] mention any Sassanian elephants being encountered in battle by Galerius, who had been tasked with fighting the Sassanians by Emperor Diocletian (r. 284–305 CE)[114] in 297 CE. The Armenian historian Moses Khorenatsi, however, notes a contemporary of Diocletian, the Armenian king Tirdad, as having battled the Sassanians and 'scattered the ranks of elephants'.[115]

While certainly true that the *Historia Augusta* is unreliable (as Charles avers), the notion that Ardashir had no elephants at all cannot be so singularly dismissed. According to Azari,[116] 'after his conquests of Khorasan, Khwarezm, Central Asia and Turan, Ardashir I entered northwest India and conquered the Punjab. As Ardashir advanced further he was given gifts of jewels, gold, and a large number of elephants by Junah [a local king].' Perhaps early Sassanian armies in the third century possessed elephants with the proviso that (1) these were not available in the numbers claimed by the *Historia Augusta*, and (2) elephants may not have been deployed against Rome as claimed by the *Historia Augusta*. Support for the latter assumptions is found in Herodian (6.5.1–6.6.6) and Zonaras (12.15), neither of which mention Sassanian elephants being used in battle against Alexander Severus. Nevertheless, more research is required regarding the use of war elephants by the Sassanians in the third century as the Classical sources alone fail to settle the issue. The Islamic-era historian al-Tabari (citing the poet Amr bin Ilah), for example, writes of the fall of Hatra (cited as al-Hadr) to Shapur, which occurred in 240 CE, by stating that 'Sabur [Shapur I] ... attacked them [the Hatrenes] with war elephants.'[117] Interestingly, the *Shahname* reports that Ardashir I not only deployed battle elephants but that he placed these in the front line,[118] which contradicts other reports of how these elephants were deployed by the spah, as discussed in the remainder of this chapter.

Shapur II's battle elephants. It is clear that Shapur II (r. 309–379 CE) not only possessed elephants but also deployed these in battle against the Romans. The *Orationes* of Libanius asserts that Shapur II 'had acquired a stock of elephants, not just for display but to meet the needs of the future.'[119] Shapur II put his battle elephants to use in his siege of Nisibis in c. 337 CE, the year in which Emperor Constantine the Great (r. 306–337 CE) died. As noted by Theodoret, 'Shapur used as many elephants that he could muster' to prosecute the siege of Nisibis.[120] Interestingly, as claimed by Theodoret, Nisibis' defenders resorted to sending swarms of gnats to attack the trunks of the Sassanian elephants![121] The new Roman emperor, Constantius II (r. 324–361 CE; co-Augustus 337–350 CE) arrived at a settlement with Shapur II, which led to a temporary cessation of hostilities. Shapur and his battle elephants returned to resume the siege of Nisibis for the second time in 346 CE.

Elephants were again used by Shapur II in yet another siege of Nisibis in 350 CE. In reference to the latter event, Julian's encomium of his cousin Constantius II declares of Sassanian battle elephants that they 'came from India and carried iron towers full of archers'.[122] The elephant's high platform afforded Sassanian archers a key advantage in the delivery of precise and damaging archery. The sources also note that these elephants, acting in concert with the savaran knights, were deployed against Nisibis' formidable walls.[123] These describe the elephants moving in concert with armoured infantry or 'hoplites' who were then used to press on the attack after the savaran had been repelled with heavy losses.[124] Interestingly, Roman sources also report of Sassanian elephants being armoured,[125] yet these also were repelled by Nisibis' missiles (for more on the sieges of Nisibis, see Chapter 14).

Sassanian battle elephants are described by Amminaus Marcellinus, a Greco-Roman warrior-historian who also partook in the battles against Shapur II. Marcellinus describes Shapur II's 359 CE siege of Amida (modern-day Diyarbakr, Turkey) as thus: 'With them [Sassanian army], making a lofty show, slowly marched the lines of elephants, frightful with their wrinkled bodies and loaded with armed men, a hideous spectacle, dreadful beyond every form of horror, as I have often declared.'[126] Shapur II captured Amida but losses to his elephants were heavy (see Chapter 14). Despite their frightening appearance, the elephants at Amida were successfully repelled by Roman forces utilizing burning torches. As noted by Azari, the siege of Amida resulted in heavy losses for the Sassanian army, with the elephants proving ineffectual during the siege.[127]

Julian's invasion of Sassanian Persia in 363 also witnessed the deployment of Sassanian battle elephants. The first battle in which Julian's forces encountered the beasts was at Coche. Sassanian tactics are of interest as the heavily armoured savaran are placed at the front, followed by lightly-armoured infantry behind them with the elephants situated behind the infantry. Perhaps the elephants served a sort of 'reserve' option in case the savaran and infantry failed against the Romans. If this were the function, then these certainly failed as Julian is described as having defeated the Sassanians, who had no recourse but to flee to the safety of the walls of Ctesiphon.[128] Shapur II's elephants did little to hold the Sassanian lines against Julian's advance, which resulted in very heavy Sassanian casualties.[129] One theory is that the elephants may have possibly served as the Sassanian army's baggage train.[130] In later battles Ammianus does describe *'gleaming elephants'*,[131] most likely referring to the gleaming armour of the beasts. These however are not generally described as forming direct frontal attacks against Roman forces during set-piece battles. As Julian advanced deeper into Sassanian territory the Sassanian spah abandoned set-piece battles in favour of rapid lightning strikes against the advancing Roman forces. It was during one of these attacks when the savaran struck at the rear of Julian's column.[132] As Julian rushed to intervene against the attacking Sassanians to the rear, the centre of the Roman lines came under attack by the savaran supported by elephants.[133] The Romans succeeded in driving off the elephants at first but when Julian was critically struck by a spear the elephants returned to the theatre.[134] Following Julian's death, Jovian, who was elected as the new emperor, assumed command. Apparently emboldened by the withdrawal of Roman forces from Iranian territory, the Sassanians launched a frontal attack against Roman forces followed by the thrusts of the savaran.[135]

What is interesting in the Jovian engagement is the application of the elephant-savaran doctrine of attacks. In this scenario, the elephants attack first, being apparently employed as a shock arm to cause dislocation and disarray among enemy forces. The savaran would then follow up with the intent of breaking through the Roman ranks. The main focus of these attacks was directed against Roman infantry rather than cavalry. This doctrine, however, appears to have been only applied during rapid-strike attacks rather than regular set-piece battles in 363.

Elephant warfare from Yazdegird II to Khosrow II. Elephants certainly remained within the Sassanian battle order after the long reign of Shapur II. The late Major-General Gholam-Hussein Moghtader notes of the Sassanian elephant corps that 'the numbers of elephants during ... the Sassanian era ranged from 200–700 ... the Iranians were so impressed with the elephant that these would also be deployed in battles in mountainous regions obliging them in these situations to build/pave suitable roads ... elephants were also used to besiege cities.'[136] Moghtader's reference to elephants in mountain warfare refers to Sassanian military operations in the Caucasus. Referring to the works of the Armenian epic histories written in the late fifth century, the late Said Nafisi noted that 'the elephants imported from India formed a reserve force in the [Sassanian] army with this animal causing fear in the Roman army ... tall towers were built and placed upon the elephants; these [towers] would then be occupied by armed troops ... these [towers] were also decorated with many banners ... these elephants with towers would be placed to the rear of the main force to act as its guardian.'[137] Nafisi is referring to the role of the elephant corps acting as a kind of reserve force and probably to also help bolster morale among frontline troops (cavalry, infantry and archers). The main issue with the epic histories, however, is that it is not possible to chronologically ascertain specific events/battles as cited by the document.

Yazdegird II (r. 438–457 CE) certainly deployed battle elephants against anti-Zoroastrian Armenian forces at the Battle of Avaryr or Vartanantz (451 CE). A medieval Armenian painting of the battle depicts Sassanian battle elephants being ridden by archers and infantry. These are situated to the left of the painting. According to Armenian art historian, Vrek Nersessian,[138] these troops represent the Sassanian Javidian or 'Immortals' (Chapter 6). The elephants are shown advancing very closely together with no gaps between them, as if these formed a sort of mobile wall. Also notable in the painting is the illustration of the 'seat' of the Sassanian troops atop the elephants. The seat is not shown with any walled protection (or indeed any protection), which would imply that the Sassanian troops atop the elephants are vulnerable to Armenian missiles. The Sassanian troops (archers and infantry) are shown wearing helmets and armoured suits stretching just below the knees. The elephant-borne archers are also shown firing a volley of missiles against the Armenian knights. While it is not clear to what extent these elephants were in the battle, the Armenian portrayal implies that either (1) they played an important role, or that (2) their portrayal was meant to distinguish the Armenian 'cavalry only' naxarar knights versus their savaran counterparts, whose elite units were riding elephants.

Martial feats involving elephants cite the legendary Iranian king Bahram Gur (420–438 CE), who is known for several of his daring exploits. One of Bahram's feats involves the slaying of a dangerous rampaging elephant in India. Tabari describes Bahram as having first shot an arrow between the eyes of the beast, then, after forcing it down by pulling its trunk, finished off the animal by severing its head with a sword.[139]

A major military encounter involving elephants in Central Asia against the Hephthalites in 484 CE ended in disaster and the death of Sassanian King Pirouz (r. 459–484 CE). The number of elephants in that debacle is variously estimated at 50[140] to 500 beasts.[141] The Hephthalite leader, Kushnavaz, led the Sassanian army into a huge camouflaged ditch set with deadly traps (Chapter 12), resulting in the destruction of the bulk of the savaran, infantry and battle elephants.[142]

On rare occasions, elephants are sometimes seen among the Sassanian's non-Roman enemies. One example is the case of the Sassanian expeditionary force in Yemen, which had been dispatched there by Khosrow I Anushirvan (531–579). The leader of the Sassanian force, Vahriz, confronted the Abbysinian occupier of Yemen, Masrooq bin Abraha, who is described as having sat on an elephant.[143] Khosrow I deployed battle elephants during his battles against the Byzantines, especially during the siege of Edessa in 543 CE.[144] He also dispatched battle elephants into the Caucasus during his battles with the Byzantines for control of Lazica in 551 CE.[145]

The late Sassanian armies of Khosrow II (r. 591–628) also utilized battle elephants as he thrust towards Dara in late 603, which fell to him after a nine-month siege in 604. In the second of three battles for Dara after the siege, Byzantine sources report of Khosrow having 'put together a fort with his elephants'.[146] Perhaps this was in reference to Sassanian elephants moving very closely together (as at Avaryr in 451), these then resembling a moving fort of armoured elephants featuring turrets with archers. When the tide of war turned in Byzantium's favour by 627 CE with the forces of Emperor Heraclius thrusting into Sassanian Mesopotamia, elephants were deployed as part of the Sassanian defence.[147]

Elephants during the Arabo-Islamic invasions (637–651 CE). Arabo-Islamic sources provide extensive reference to Sassanian battle elephants, especially in the context of the Arabo-Islamic invasion of Iran in 637–651 CE. One of the first major battles fought between the Arabs and the spah was the Battle of the Bridges. The Arabs led by Abu Ubeidah Taghti had crossed the Euphrates. Facing the Arabs was General Bahram, who deployed a force of armoured savaran knights and battle elephants. According to Masoudi, 'the Arabs witnessed weaponized elephants and had never seen any phenomenon such as this … they all fled and most of them died by the sword and even more by drowning in the Euphrates'.[148]

Bahram's elephants appear to have acted as 'super-panzers' that also doubled as missile platforms for Sassanian archers. Taghti's Arabs soon gave way to the combined savaran-elephant thrusts. It would appear that Bahram had reacted quickly against Abu Ubeidah by not allowing his Arabs time to properly organize after landing on the eastern (Sassanian-held) side of the Euphrates. Rapid charges by the lance-armed savaran accompanied by war elephants (whose archers discharged volleys of missiles) had undermined the cohesion of Taghti's forces. Taghti himself was killed fighting a Sassanian battle elephant. According to the *Futuh ol Boldan*, Taghti had gotten close to the elephant and struck with his sword at its trunk and foot; the elephant then crushed Taghti by trampling him under its feet.[149] The death of Taghti proved too much for the Arabs. Proving unable to resist the savaran-elephant assaults, they were now forced to flee back to the western side of the Euphrates River. Arab losses are described as 1,000 killed, 3,000 drowned (during the retreat across the Euphrates), and 2,000 deserters, leaving just 3,000 men to retreat.[150]

The four-day battle of Qadissiyah, which essentially sealed the fate of Sassanian and pre-Islamic Persia, witnessed a significant deployment of battle elephants by the spah. Tabari reports that the Sassanian general Rustam Farrokhzad deployed a total of thirty battle elephants during the battle.[151] Masoudi's descriptions of Rustam's elephants state that 'these were placed at the front … upon each elephant was seated 20 of their warriors with armour and horned helmets … around each elephant stood infantry, cavalry, and warriors'.[152] This description conveys the impression of a 'strike group' not unlike the US Navy's Second World War carrier-based strike groups in the Pacific theatre, in which aircraft carriers would be escorted by battleships, cruisers, etc. Rustam's battle elephants were now protected by infantry and savaran. Interestingly, the infantry (most likely Dailamites) were entrusted with close-quarter combat duties, in case Arab troops attempted to close in on the elephants. Warriors aboard the elephants would be tasked with discharging their missiles at the Arabs from their elevated platform. Perhaps most significant is how (as per Massoudi's description), the elephants were 'placed at the front', indicating a major doctrinal shift from the Sassanian spah's doctrine of elephant warfare from the time of Shapur II. As noted previously, elephants would be placed to the rear of the main army, with these being used in combination with the savaran in rapid hit-and-withdraw strike packages. Rustam was now wielding his battle elephants as part of his primary strike forces against the Muslim Arabs. Nevertheless, not all thirty elephants were part of the strike package, as Masoudi cites only seventeen of the animals being employed in this fashion.[153]

The Arabs led by Saad Bin Ebi Waqqas, however, had absorbed the lessons of their defeat at the battle of the bridges. At first, the presence of the elephants did cause consternation among the Arab cavalry. Ibn Khaldun writes that 'the sight of the mountain-sized elephants caused the Arab horses to flee, forcing the Arabs to dismount their horses to fight.'[154] Numbers of these Arab troops closed in to engage and overcome the escorting infantry of the elephants. This then allowed them to get close to the elephants and tear their girths. As the elephants collapsed, the Arabs quickly killed the archers and warriors who sat atop the creatures. The Arabs devised other ingenious ways to disable Rustam's elephants. One of Waqqas' commanders, Ghagha bin Amr, who had arrived from Syria by the third day of the battle, thrust his spear into the eye of a white elephant, a tactic which was quickly adopted by the other Arab warriors on the battlefield. In practice, bin Amr was most likely accompanied by ex-Byzantine spearmen who knew of this tactic due to Byzantium's past wars with the Sassanians. Yet another tactic against the elephants was offered by anti-Zoroastrian deserters of Rustam's spah. These informed Waqqas' Arabs of tactics for striking at the elephants' trunks.[155] These tactics proved immensely effective as numbers of the stricken elephants panicked and ran amuck within the Sassanian ranks.[156] In response to this disaster, Ibn Khaldun further records that 'the Iranians were now determined to withdraw their elephants from the battlefield.'[157] According to one legend, Rustam was killed by an elephant which fell over him in the fourth and final day of the battle.[158] There are in fact several varying accounts of Rustam's death at Qadissiyah. Another account claims that an elephant (or mule) laden with sacks of treasure fell on the unfortunate Rustam, severely injuring his arm, which allowed an Arab warrior to kill him.[159]

Elephants as symbols of regal splendour: the case of Khosrow II. Khosrow II is well known for his love of elephants. Masoudi writes that 1,000 elephants were housed in the royal stables,[160] while the author of the *Zein ol Akhbar* claims that the king kept 1,200 of the animals.[161] So fond was Khosrow II of his elephants that he is reputed to have lamented that 'if only the elephant were not Indian but Iranian instead'.[162] The regal aspect of the Sassanian elephant is perhaps best immortalized at Tagh-e Bostan in western Iran where a panel depicts the royal hunt. Clearly visible in the panel are elephants that accompany the royal hunt retinue, with the beasts carrying boars recently killed during the hunt. Interestingly, the elephants also seem to combine with the trumpeters and knights in driving the herd of boars ahead of them.

The splendour of late Sassanian battle elephants was evidently appreciated by Khosrow II's opponent and ultimate nemesis, Emperor Heraclius (r. 610–641 CE). According to the *Chronicle of Seert*, Heraclius may have dreamt of Khosrow II as a warrior riding an elephant![163]

Strengths and weaknesses. The most potent asset of the battle elephant is perhaps psychological: its size, strength and appearance could certainly inspire dread among troops and cavalry unaccustomed to elephant warfare. The elephant's thick hide provides a great amount of protection against most types of conventional archery and blade weapons. The elephant's height certainly afforded Sassanian archers an excellent platform to shoot missiles onto their battlefield adversaries. But the raised position could also be an Achilles heel, as the archers and soldiers atop the elephant were themselves highly visible as targets of opportunity and vulnerable to missiles.

The elephant is also a formidable beast to control in battle. When sensing mortal danger, it has the potential to run amuck against its own armies. Exactly such a scenario is reported at the third siege of Nisibis in 350 CE. During this operation the Sassanians mounted a determined attack with their elephants against the walls of the city. The elephants then ran into soft, muddy earth as a result of the siege operations. Many of the beasts then sank into the soft terrain, which spread panic among the other surviving beasts. Instead of pressing on with the attack, these Sassanian elephants turned around to run amuck within the Sassanian ranks, crushing large numbers of troops in the process.[164] Interestingly, nearly fourteen centuries later, Indian battle elephants of Moghul Mohammad Shah were to about-face and crush their own troops in response to the stratagems of the Iranian warlord, Nader Shah (r. 1735–1747) during the battle of Karnal.[165]

The Sassanians certainly learned quickly from their elephant disaster at Nisibis. They later (especially during Julian's 363 CE invasion) took the precautionary measure of placing a mahout armed with a handle fastened to his right hand. The knife would be deployed to slay the elephant by severing its vertebrae in case the beast went out of control.[166]

Another weakness of Sassanian battle elephants was the spah's lack of effective tactics for countering determined and experienced enemy infantry that managed to get close to the beasts. While escorting Dailamite infantry and savaran were certainly formidable, elephants were highly vulnerable if the protecting troops were overcome. As noted previously, the Arabs devised three stratagems to eliminate the Sassanian elephant threat on the battlefield: (1) launching spears into the exposed eyes of the beasts; (2) attacking their vulnerable underbellies; and (3) severing the straps of the cabs ferrying Sassanian troops, resulting in the latter spilling to the ground.

A final note of trivia in this discussion is the use of the Persian term *fil* (from Middle Persian: *pil*, elephant) for the position of bishop in *shatranj*, the Persian term for chess. Interestingly, the same is true in Indian chess where the term *fil* is also used for Bishop.

Sassanian Naval Capabilities: An Overview

By the onset of Sassanian rule in the early third century CE, Iranian maritime technology had resulted in the construction of vessels capable of transporting larger amounts of cargo over greater travel distances. Ardashir I was keen to establish military control over the Persian Gulf to dominate that region's trade routes.[167] This is corroborated by Islamic-era historians such as Thalabi, Hamza of Isfahan and Tabari, who record that Ardashir founded at least eight port cities. Note that these included ports established in the major waterways of Sassanian-ruled Mesopotamia and Khuzestan. The identified riverside ports include Bahman Ardashir (Forat of Maisan), Astarabadh Ardashir (former Charax), and Wahasht Ardashir, with ports on the Persian Gulf itself including locales such as Rev Ardashir (on the Bushehr Peninsula) and Kujeran Ardashir (probably opposite Kish), and Batn Ardashir (along the Arabian coast of the Persian Gulf opposite Bahrain island). The *Karnamye Ardashir e Babakan* provides a detailed account of the military campaign which Ardashir I fought to secure Kujaran. This success allowed the Sassanian military to effect naval landings in Bahrain as well as opposite Bahrain along the Arabian coast to subjugate the local tribes ensconced there.[168] Ardashir I is then reported as having recruited Arab seafarers as advisors for building the Sassanian navy.[169] Sassanian ships were known as *kashtig* (modern Persian: *kashti*) with the leader of the navy known as the *navbad*.

The empire's main venue for seaborne commerce was the Persian Gulf and from there into the Indian Ocean and (by late Sassanian times) beyond into the Pacific Ocean and to China. Overseas trade was a major source of revenue for the empire, especially from the reign of Khosrow I. It resulted in the founding of a number of coastal cities along the Persian Gulf coast, from the modern-day Shaat al Arab/Arvand Rud waterway ingress in the west to the shores of modern-day Pakistan to the east. As hypothesized by Curatola and Scarcia, 'these were fortified way stations along the coast controlled by the Persians'.[170] The domain of studies pertaining to Sassanian coastal defences, however, is in progress at the time of writing. Nevertheless excavations thus far have provided great insight. Researchers generally agree that Sassanian coastal structures were intended to both accommodate commercial shipping and to also defend against seaborne attacks and attempted landings by hostile forces.

The vast majority of seaborne threats against the Sassanian Persian Gulf coastline were posed by Arab seaborne raiders emanating from the southern shores of the Persian Gulf in Arabia. The Arabs posed critical challenges to Iran's military position in the Persian Gulf region and the south during the early years of Shapur II's reign (310–379 CE). Driven by economic poverty and famine, Arab tribes from Hajar and Bahrain streamed across the Persian Gulf to attack and plunder the entire southern Iranian coastline from Khuzestan to the port city of Rev Ardashir. According to the Bundahishn, 'in the reign of Shapur son of Hormuzd, the Arabs came and seized the banks of the River Karun (Ulay) and remained there for many years pillaging and attacking'.[171] Southern coastal regions such as Rev Ardashir, for example, were plundered by Arab raiders who had arrived from the southern regions of the Persian Gulf.[172] These attacks were viewed with special alarm by the spah, which assembled, under Shapur II's leadership, a striking force at Gur. This army then boarded ships at ports along the Persian coastline that landed first on Bahrain, Ghateef and Yamama to then campaign along the northern Arabian coastline. The campaign in Bahrain was especially bitter, with Shapur II and the spah having to engage in close-quarter combat.[173] After clearing the Arabs in Bahrain, Ghateef and Yamama, Shapur II struck deep into the Arabian hinterland, reaching all the way into Yathrib (later named Medina). The spah was overwhelmingly successful in defeating the Arabs, who at the height of their success had even occupied territory in Iran's southwest.[174] As a result of Shapur II's military campaign, the Persian Gulf once again became safe for Sassanian maritime commerce, with Charax having been superseded by Astarabadh. Sassanian maritime ascendancy is affirmed by Ammianus Marcellinus who reported that 'there are numerous towns and villages on every coast and frequent sailings of ships'.[175] It is possible that the military port base at Siraf was built during Shapur II's reign, in order to guard against future landings by Arab raiders (see Chapter 13).

By the time of Khosrow I Iranian naval technology had continued to advance, with notable innovations such as a redesigned rig and a system of five to seven sails. Sassanian vessels could now transport up to 700 passengers/troops and crew along with 'a thousand metric tons of cargo'.[176] The Sassanian navy is reported as having been capable of monitoring the security of Iranian maritime commerce in the Persian Gulf as well as protecting Iran's southern Persian Gulf coastline against seaborne raids.[177] Sassanian maritime capabilities were to prove vital in confronting a serious military threat during the reign of Khosrow I. The pro-Byzantine Abbysinian occupation of Arabia Felix (near modern Yemen) in 531 CE jeopardized Iranian hegemony in the Persian Gulf and even exposed Iran's southern Persian Gulf coastline to naval attacks. The Sassanians could now be faced with a two-front war in which Byzantium could coordinate its land-based assaults into western and northwest Iran/Caucasus region with the naval land-ings of their Abbysinian allies along the southern Iranian coastline. Khosrow I responded by agreeing to support Yemenite anti-Abbysinian rebels led by Sayf Bin Dhu Yazan.[178] A Sassanian fleet was launched from Iran's southern ports to transport an expedition force led by Vahriz that landed near Aden (for further details, see Chapter 8). Khosrow I also had plans to secure the fortress of Petra along the Black Sea coast (in modern-day Georgia) to use as a Sassanian naval base on the Black Sea[179] (for more on Petra see Chapter 14).

As noted by Sami, military ascendancy by the spah and the navy in the Persian Gulf had by the early 600s (1) allowed for a significant expansion in Sassanian maritime commerce far beyond the Persian Gulf; and (2) barred the Romans from dominating the Persian Gulf militarily, politically or economically.[180] The Sassanians certainly displayed their naval capabilities during the long wars between Khosrow II and the Romano-Byzantines. As their armies reached the Mediterranean shores of modern-day Turkey, they built a fleet to attack the Aegean theatre. The Sassanian fleet attacked Constantia (Salamis) in 617 CE and then launched a naval attack against Rhodos (Rhodes) to capture this in 622 CE. The discovery of a hoard of Sassanian coins dated to 623 CE suggests that Samos may also have fallen to a Sassanian naval assault.[181] Had Khosrow I been able to retain Petra and build a Black Sea fleet, the Romano-Byzantines would most likely have faced greater opposition to their naval landings in the Caucasus during Heraclius' counteroffensives in 622–627 CE. The very long coastline of Armenia and northern Anatolia along the Black Sea allowed Heraclius to coordinate his naval landings in such a way as to allow him to outflank the Sassanian spah. When Heraclius launched his fleet from Constantinople towards the Black Sea's Caucasian coastline there was no Sassanian navy in place to challenge this force. This allowed Heraclius to land his forces against no opposition in the region of modern day Circassia. Heraclius then linked up with the Khazars in 626 CE to attack the Sassanian region of Albania (modern-day Republic of Azerbaijan) in the Caucasus.

Towards the end of the Sassanian dynasty, however, the Arabs were to take advantage of Sassanian military weaknesses in the aftermath of the Khosrow II-Heraclius wars to invade Iran. Just as the Arabs were pushing into Sassanian Iran, Arab troops arrived by vessels to land along Iran's southern Persian Gulf coast-line to then push into the interior of the realm. The Arab ability to mount seaborne raids into Iran's Persian Gulf coastline surfaced as late as the eighteenth and nineteenth century during the reigns of Iran's Zand (1750–1794) and Qajar dynasties (1794–1925).[182] Historically, Arab raids in the pre-Islamic and Islamic eras were made possible in those times when Iran lacked a navy and well-fortified ports and coastal bases.

The legacy of the Sassanian navy has remained in the Persian Gulf region to this day as attested by the use of Pahlavi (Middle Persian) naval terminology amongst the Arabs.[183] Some of these original Pahlavi terms are *balanj* (cabin), *bandar* and *bar* (port); *daftar* (sailing instructions), *dunij* (boat of a ship), *didban* (lookout boy), *rah-nameh* (nautical instructions) and *nav-khoda* (captain).[184]

Chapter 8

Preparations for War

This chapter examines the processes of war planning and preparation by the spah. Critical to this process was the role of the war council. The spah also implemented rigorous evaluation processes upon its warriors and commanders to assess their fitness and readiness for battle. War planning often took geographical factors into account with vanguards and reconnaissance also playing a critical role. Of special interest is the importance allotted to intelligence gathering, information warfare and propaganda. Finally, the spah also engaged in a number of interesting rituals prior to the onset of battles.

The War Council: Decision Making and Consequences

When war was imminent, the king would engage in an official conference or 'war council' with the highest ranking members of the military and civilian leadership to discuss military strategy and policies. As noted by Hekmat, the king and the war council considered three general factors to determine whether the spah was to be mobilized for war: (1) the relative military strengths and capabilities of the spah vis-à-vis its adversaries (i.e. Romano-Byzantines, Hephthalites, etc.); and (2) the potential impact of war upon the empire's populace, economy, etc.[1] The spah would then act in accordance with the decisions of the war council, with the king entitled to 'veto' the council's decision as to whether the empire should go to war.[2]

The war council would often be composed of the *eiran-spahbod, vuzurg-framandar* (prime minster), *eiran-dabirbod, strvoshbod, hebarbodan-hebarbodh*, and even sometimes the *stabodh* (master of ceremonies).[3] As noted in Chapter 3, the office of the eiran-spahbod had been abolished by the reforms of Khosrow I, who replaced it with four regional spahbods responsible for defending the empire's Caucasian, Mesopotamian, Persian Gulf and Central Asian fronts respectively. As a result, the spah's war councils from Khosrow I's reign to the end of the dynasty no longer featured an eiran-spahbod but only those spahbods whose regions were militarily involved.

It is remarkable how similar the spah was to its Romano-Byzantine counterparts by placing its primary emphasis on careful planning and professional military leadership. This is corroborated by Maurice, who observed of the Sassanian military that 'for the most part they prefer to achieve their results by planning and generalship; they stress an orderly approach rather than a brave and impulsive one'.[4] There may be at least three reasons why the spah placed such a heavy emphasis upon planning and professional leadership. First was the reality of the empire's limited military resources, especially professional manpower, which meant that the spah had to seriously consider ways of minimizing casualties, especially among its professional core of savaran elite cavalry (Chapter 6). The second consideration, rationalized during the reign of Khosrow I, concerned the dangers of fighting wars on multiple fronts simultaneously. The spah was constantly faced with the danger of having to fight on several fronts, necessitating maximum efficiency in the use of limited military resources. Planning in such scenarios had to take several other factors (besides battle tactics) into account, especially logistics and speed of deployment (e.g. how quickly x-amount of troops could be deployed to the Central Asian front and how rapidly more troops could be deployed to the western, Roman frontier). Third was the attainment of battlefield experience against the Western world's most formidable military machine: the Romano-Byzantine army. The Sassanians were certainly aware of the professionalism and competent leadership of their adversaries, who were undoubtedly meticulous and thorough in their battle plans. In cognizance of Romano-Byzantine military innovations and tactics, the spah's commanders would most likely have realized that they also had to refine and improve their war planning.

The Darigbedum. Warriors and commanders who especially distinguished themselves in battle were bestowed with the title of the shahanshah's select *Darigbedum* of the Royal Household.[5] Bahram Chobin (Chapter 12) was the recipient of such a title due to his battlefield exploits as a military commander against the Romano-Byzantines in Armenia, Mesopotamia and especially at Dara[6] during the reign of Khosrow I. Bahram was allowed to partake in the important meetings of the war council; it was during such a council in 588 CE when Bahram was selected as commander to confront the Turco-Hephthalite invasion from Central Asia (Chapter 12).

Military Consequences of War Council Decision-Making

Two cases concerning the war council and Khosrow I (r. 531–579) are of interest as in one case he rejected the council's decision to avoid war with the Hephthalites (see Chapter 12) with another case in which the king decided to support the council's recommendations for military intervention in the Persian Gulf areas as outlined below.

The Yemenite War (early c. 525–598 CE): Khosrow follows advice of the war council. The Yemenite Arabs had risen in revolt against the pro-Byzantine Abyssinian invaders who had invaded Yemen by crossing the Red Sea from northwest Africa.[7] Leading the Yemenite revolt was Dhu Yazan, who sent appeals to Khosrow I (c. 534 CE) for military assistance. The king then met with his war council to solicit their decision on Dhu Yazan's appeal. The council advised Khosrow against military intervention, mainly out of concern for the internal state of Yemen, which was in disarray.

Upon the death of Dhu Yazan, his son Sayf also appealed for military assistance to Khosrow, who again consulted with the war council. This time the council ruled in favour of military intervention on behalf of Sayf bin Dhu Yazan, being swayed by the strength of the latter's appeal and Khosrow's sympathies for the Yemenite cause.[8] The council was evidently aware of the dangers of the

Abbysinian takeover of Yemen: upon doing so the Abbysinians would soon be able (especially with Romano-Byzantine assistance) to project their influence into the interior of Arabia. This would in turn endanger the Sassanian realm both economically and militarily. Economically, the Abbysinians might come to dominate the Persian Gulf trade and eliminate Sassanian maritime influence. Procopius reports that Romano-Byzantine emperor Justinian (r. 526–565) had dispatched an embassy to the Abbysinians to encourage them to sever the Sassanian Empire's maritime trade links with India. The war council had most likely realized the dire economic consequences of Justinian's schemes for the empire. Simply put, the Persian Gulf was (and remains to this day), Iran's main maritime economic artery for trade and commerce.

The second danger to the empire was military in nature. The growth of Abyssinian economic power could translate into anti-Sassanian military capabilities in the Persian Gulf. With Arabia under their sway, the Abbysinians (with Justinian's assistance) would be able to build naval forces capable of launching attacks into Iran's southern Persian Gulf coastline. This would allow the Romano-Byzantines to press their Sassanian adversaries into a two-front war in which the Abbysinians would engage in military action in the Persian Gulf with Romano-Byzantine forces attacking the empire from its western frontiers. There was even the possibility of a three-front war if enemies in Central Asia (i.e. Hephthalites) decided to coordinate their efforts with the Romano-Byzantines and their Abbysinian allies.

Despite agreeing on the urgency of the Yemenite crisis, Khosrow and the war council were hesitant to commit the major portion of the spah to their military venture. They decided to dispatch an army (composed of ex-prisoners by accounts such as Procopius) led by a commander named Vahriz in the endeavour to minimize losses to the main corps of the spah.[9] Vahriz's campaign was long and arduous but ultimately successful. Historians disagree as to the actual size of the original force dispatched to Yemen and how many actually reached there. Matofi reports 8,000 having been dispatched in eight ships (c. early 570s CE) with two having been lost at sea with all crew and troops. The *History of Al-Tabari* also reports eight ships having sailed from Persia with each transporting just 100 troops, with two vessels lost at sea with all hands, resulting in Vahriz's arriving in Yemen with just 600 troops. Another possibility is that Vahriz sailed towards Yemen with a large force (8,000 troops?) but reached the coast of Aden with a diminished force of just 800 men.[10] This force proved more than capable of achieving its mission, defeating the Abbysinians and allowing Vahriz to install Sayf bin Dhu Yazan as the marzban of the empire in Yemen (575–577 CE). The Abbysinians counterattacked shortly thereafter, slaying Sayf, but this success proved temporary. Vahriz engaged in a prolonged war, permanently expelling the Abbysinians from Arabia and (by 598 CE) supporting the ascension of Sayf's son, Ma'adi Karab, as ruler in Sanaa. Yemen was then thoroughly secured as a Sassanian province thus eliminating the threat of Byzantine influence in the region and the Persian Gulf. The Sassanian veterans of Vahriz remained in Yemen, with their descendants being known as the Abna.

The decision of the war council and Khosrow to dispatch a small expeditionary force to Yemen had proven militarily sound as it helped preserve the main manpower base of the spah. In addition, the dispatch of the Vahriz force meant that the empire was not obliged to weaken its military forces along the western (Romano-Byzantine) and Central Asian (Turks and Hephthalites) frontiers.

Evaluation of Commanders and troops

Prior to the outbreak of war, the war council and the king would carefully select and assign the most capable officers from the empire's leading clans to ensure that all military units were led into battle by seasoned and experienced officers. As the spah mobilized for war, the king and his advisors would review the existing complement of commanders leading the spah's various units of savaran, paighan and other units (elephant corps, archers, etc.).[11] The *Shahname*, for example, contains a passage describing the review of spah generals such as Bahram and Hormuzd at the time of Khosrow I.[12]

A candidate for command was evaluated[13] to determine if he possessed (1) a thorough understanding of military tactics and battlefield combat scenarios; (2) the ability to manage and supervise military organizations under his command and (3) the ability to think rationally and exercise caution, especially in militarily difficult situations. With respect to the third criterion, the commander was expected to study all possible outcomes of various tactical options and avoid (as much as possible) any rash actions that could jeopardize the military position of the army and morale of the troops. Lower-level officers and other professional warriors were also evaluated with respect to past combat performance and/or military reviews; they would then be assigned accordingly to the right, centre or left of the spah prior to battle.[14]

Experience of troops. Commanders were expected to factor in the battle experience of their troops in their tactical decision-making. According to Dinawari,[15] if the bulk of a commander's troops were battle-hardened, bold and experienced, then it was recommended to allow the enemy to attack first. Conversely, if his troops were largely inexperienced, then the commander was advised to attack the enemy first if battle could not be avoided.[16]

Numerical status. Dinawari further notes that a commander also had to factor in the numbers of troops available to him in his tactical decisions.[17] If a commander possessed between three to four times the number of troops available to the enemy, then he was advised to attack.[18] If the enemy were to attack it was recommended for the field army to possess at least (approximately) one and a half times more troops than the enemy;[19] in addition these troops would need to be proficient in close-quarter combat. However, the spah would often fight against numerically superior forces, especially when Iranian territory was imperilled or invaded.

Another interesting tactic with respect to numerical factors was the 'rotating' system, whereby a commander divided his primary forces into two 'rotating' ranks. One rank would engage the enemy in battle and then be withdrawn in favour of the second rank, which was bought forward to continue the engagement. The advantage of this technique was that a portion of the engaged forces would always be kept rested and thus more effective during a battle.

Geographical Factors in Battle Planning

Geographical factors were an integral part of the commander's battle planning, notably with respect to selection and control of the best terrain possible for one's army, climate and water supplies. These are discussed below.

Selection and control of terrain. It was of course imperative for the spah to have as much control over strategic terrain as possible. Dinawari highlights the importance of keeping enemy armies away from forested terrain and areas endowed with rivers.[20] The enemy was to be confined as much as possible in the open plains,[21] and it was preferred to fight him in such flat and open terrain. This was consistent with the spah's doctrine of relying on the savaran as the primary strike force, which was most effective employing the lance charge when operating on flat terrain.

The perils to the savaran when attacking uphill against enemy troops had already been demonstrated by the earlier Parthians in 40 BCE. In this encounter armoured Parthian knights charged uphill against the Roman forces of General Ventidus in the Tarsus Mountain range of Anatolia (modern Turkey). The knights' momentum was seriously compromised as they charged uphill. This was because the hill impeded the knights' charge and thus sapped their momentum and collective striking power. As a result, when the knights did reach Ventidus' positions, the power of their lance charge was weaker than it otherwise would have been had the attack taken place on flat terrain. The knights then became entangled with the formidable Roman troops in hand-to-hand combat. The Romans excelled in this type of fighting and the Parthian knights were repelled and forced to retreat towards Cilicia.

The *Strategikon* does make an interesting observation with respect to the spah's preference for rough terrain when facing 'pike men': 'When they are in battle against pike men it is their practice to place their main line in the roughest landscape and to use their bows in order that the attacks of the pike men against them are dispersed and easily dissolved by the difficult terrain.'[22]

In summary, the Sassanians were evidently aware of how different types of terrain affected the spah's military performance, thus obliging its commanders to factor this into their battlefield planning.

Climate. Dinawari also recommends that the commander factor climatic conditions before attacking. It is recommended that the sun and/or wind be situated to the backs of the troops rather than to the front.[23] Interestingly, the *Strategikon* also recommends that the Romano-Byzantine armies fight with the wind and sun at their rear.[24] The *Strategikon* also notes that, in the summer, the Sassanians 'like to make their attacks at the hottest hour, in order that through the boiling heat of the sun and the delay in time the courage and spirit of those lined up against them slackens'.[25] Interestingly, this shows the Sassanians' knowledge of combining various factors to psychologically and physically undermine the opponents' fighting spirit, including the sound of martial music (drums, trumpets, gongs, etc.), and the fearsome sight of the spah's armoured lance-wielding knights combined with extreme heat. Romano-Byzantine troops facing the Sassanians under these circumstances were undoubtedly steadfast, tough and resilient troops, a strong testament to their military professionalism and rigorous training.

Climate and weather was especially important as it could affect the performance of Sassanian arms during the course of battle. This was especially true of archery. The direction of the wind was a significant factor in undermining the efficacy of Persian archery against the Romano-Byzantines at the Battle of Dara in 530 CE (Chapter 9) and against the Arabo-Muslims at the Battle of Qadissiyah in 637 CE (Chapter 17).

Securing water supplies. Dinawari reports of specific protocols established by the Sassanians to secure water supplies.[26] What is of interest in this report is how the Sassanians factored psychological motivation in this battle scenario. Essentially the spah is advised to allow a nearby water supply to be secured by the enemy without interference.[27] The rationale is that battling against an enemy parched by thirst will result in heavy casualties, as that enemy will fight with desperation to secure the water supply for its survival. The enemy is to be allowed to satiate its troops, horses and transport animals first; only then is the spah allowed to attack the enemy. The reasoning is that a satiated enemy will fight with less intensity and vigour than one who is otherwise desperate (i.e. for scarce water supplies).[28] Conversely, it is deduced that the spah, with its thirsty troops, is more likely to fight with greater intensity against a satiated enemy. In such a scenario the Sassanians would be more likely to capture and retain the coveted water supply.

Vanguards and Reconnaissance

Vanguards advancing ahead of the main army are advised to move on even ground if possible and to occupy heights when resting and/or coming to a halt.[29] In addition, it is also advised to reconnoitre select territories prior to the passage of the vanguards and main armies.[30] Occupying strategic elevated sites is considered vital as the loss of such terrain to the enemy would allow him to observe the spah's movements.

Vanguards in the Sassanian army had other important military roles. In this regard Ammianus Marcellinus makes reference to the outbreak of hostilities between the Sassanian and Roman Empires in 359 CE in which the Roman General Ursicinus and his entire staff were very nearly captured by Sassanian advance elements at Nisibis.[31] As noted by Dodgeon and Lieu, Sassanian cavalry vanguards were tasked 'for the purpose of disrupting the Roman preparations for defence and confusing the defenders as to the exact direction of the main attack'.[32] Vanguards could also serve as reconnaissance elements and as Cossack-type cavalry raiders. In the latter capacity, these savaran elements would be entrusted with hit and run strikes; but, as Ammianus has noted, these savaran knights could also take advantage of unexpected opportunities, such as the capture of the command elements of the Roman forces. The exceptional mobility of these vanguard savaran units was partly contingent on them operating unencumbered by supplies and excess equipment. The *Shahname*, as noted by Dodgeon and Lieu, hints at this practice when it mentions how Shapur I 'dispatched a light-armed force [as far as Pauluina] without full supplies or impedimenta'.[33] This would be consistent with the spah's practice of employing vanguard cavalry forces for gathering intelligence, occupying strategic locations and/or heights and conducting raids and commando-type attacks.

Intelligence Gathering and Information Warfare

A.D. Lee of Cambridge University has provided an excellent synopsis of the importance of military intelligence for both the Romano-Byzantines and Sassanians. As noted by Lee, '[I]t is natural that historians should ... direct their attention towards the role of fortifications and military installations ... however it is possible to neglect another dimension of defence ... the role of military intelligence.'[34] The Sassanians, like their Romano-Byzantine counterparts, had a sophisticated intelligence-gathering system for conducting offensive operations and defending against an impending invasion, using spies, cultivating fifth-column elements in enemy countries, and employing ambassadorial missions for espionage duties.

Military secrets. Sassanian generals and professional warriors were well known for their ability to guard vital military secrets, even if captured by the enemy or enticed with bribes.[35] Military secrets were also very well guarded at the highest levels of the royal leadership. The *Toqi'ate Anoushirvan*, for example, cites a session where Mobads and Dastoors ask Khosrow Anoushirvan about his military goals in a particular campaign. Khosrow is reported as having stated that his ultimate goals in military campaigns are kept secret since 'I do not want the enemy to feel safe.'[36] This indicates that even as campaigns were initiated against either the Hephthalites or the Romano-Byzantines, the shah and the spah leadership did their utmost to keep their enemies guessing as to their ultimate objectives.

Spies and fifth-column elements. Subterfuge, spying and the cultivation of fifth-column elements were especially important, especially in sieges (Chapter 14). Spies and fifth-column elements would be paid a regular salary by the Sassanian state to engage in intelligence gathering on the state of the enemy's armed forces and war-making capabilities. In one notable case, for example, the Sassanians had sent 300 slaves (who were actually spies) as a 'gift' to the Romano-Byzantines.[37]

The spy's first mission was to infiltrate and blend into the enemy populace for the intent of obtaining access to militarily critical information. Having obtained as much information as possible, the spy would then return to the Sassanian realm to report his findings to the spah leadership. Despite their high level of loyalty to the Sassanian Empire however, Iranian spies could prove to be double agents who betrayed the spah's military secrets to its enemies.

Spies were also employed to monitor the conduct and performance of governors of Iranian provinces as well as conquered regions as a safeguard against high-level corruption. In the *Toqi'ate Anoushirvan*, for example, spies reporting to the shah in Ctesiphon describe how the governor of Ahvaz has engaged in excessive taxation of the local populace. The shah (Khosrow Anoushirvan) responds by ordering that the governor return to their owners all of the funds he had illegally acquired from unjust taxation.[38]

Propaganda. Propaganda was integral to the spah's war doctrine as it was intended to sap the willingness of the enemy to engage in battle. As noted by Jahiz, Sassanian kings went to war only as a last resort, preferring instead to first engage in any efforts – including, notably, propaganda and deception – that might 'prevent the spilling of the blood of the warriors and the expenditure of their riches in this endeavour. Only when these efforts failed then ... the sword would be drawn.'[39]

One tactic for the spread of alarmist and distressing (dis)information was to wrap a 'letter' around the shaft of an arrow and then fire the projectile into a besieged enemy fortress. The aim was to make the 'news' as believable as possible in order to sow doubt, fear and confusion and thus to (psychologically) undermine the military effectiveness of the defenders.

Control of information. Dinawari is very clear about the importance of controlling the flow of information within one's own army.[40] Simply put, falsified information could be just as harmful to one's own troops as it was to the enemy. The careful release of information to one's field army was of vital importance, since incompetent supervision of this process could result in the spread of alarmist news among the troops. The dangers entailed in releasing false information (e.g., rumours of the death of a commander) could very well backfire by undermining army morale.[41]

Control of information was also considered to be of utmost importance to the Romano-Byzantines. Procopius, for example, notes of General Belisarius' refusal to formally announce his military intentions, as these would surely reach the enemy.[42] The *Strategikon* also recommends that the Romano-Byzantines not deploy near heavily populated centres as this could lead to information of their army being leaked to their adversaries.[43]

Chapter 9

Tactics and Strategies along the Roman and Caucasian Frontiers

The main military adversaries of the spah along the western frontier were the Romans (later Romano-Byzantines). Roman forces were by no means static or monolithic in their development; they underwent a series of changes, notably in their (Romano-Byzantine) adoption of 'eastern' type armoured cavalry and archery technology such as the Hun-Avar bow. By the time of the empire's wars with Belisarius, Sassanian and Romano-Byzantine armoured cavalry forces bore similarities in equipment and tactics. The northern Caucasian frontier which faced nomadic intrusions was also exposed to Roman attacks through Anatolia, with Armenia being generally split between a pro-Iranian and pro-Roman faction. The southwest frontier and the Persian Gulf region were exposed to attacks by the Arabs. This chapter examines the battle tactics employed against Rome, the so-called tripartite doctrine, ambuscades, raids, pursuit of the enemy, ditches and traps, and tactics against invading forces. The spah's battles along the empire's northeast frontiers facing Central Asia will be discussed in Chapter 12.

Tactical and Military Distinctions between the Parthians and the Sassanians

Moghtader has drawn two major distinctions between Parthian and Sassanian tactics and warfare.[1] The first pertains to the evolution of Parthian tactics of rapid assaults by armoured horsemen (supported by horse archery) combined with the feigned retreat (and the Parthian shot). The Sassanians certainly inherited the Parthian style assault-feigned retreat tactics but with one marked difference: training regimens for the savaran appear to have placed greater emphasis on close-quarters combat (Chapter 4); the savaran for example were expected to engage in close-quarter combat in siege warfare (Chapter 14). The spah introduced professional combat infantry into its battle order as seen, for example, with Shapur II's 'gladiator' infantry of the fourth century CE (as described by Ammianus) and the later north Iranian Dailamites of the sixth century CE. The second Parthian-Sassanian distinction was in the evolution of Iranian knights with respect to armour, weapons (Chapter 6) and tactics. With respect to tactics, Moghtader notes that the spah was to increase in sophistication as it drew lessons from its battles against the Romano-Byzantines and the nomadic invaders of Central Asia.

Overview of Sassanian Battle Tactics

There are two general questions that may be posed with respect to Sassanian battle tactics. The first is whether the Sassanians were wedded to a limited series of tactics and formations. The second is whether Sassanian tactics changed over the centuries of their tenure. In a sense both questions (variety of tactics and tactical changes over time) are most likely interrelated. As noted previously, the early Sassanians appear to have had a 'Parthian'-type phase, but the military differences between the two forces were significant in their final showdown at Firuzabad in 224 CE (Chapter 6).

Savaran to the fore or rear? There does not appear to be an overall consensus of opinion among Western historians or even Iranian and Islamic-era sources regarding the question of tactics. In summary, descriptions vary according to sources consulted. Christensen, for example, notes that the Sassanians deployed their cavalry to the front of their forces with the battle elephants placed to their rear.[2] Relying on Anonymous (see below), Insotransev suggests that the savaran would be placed at the front for the attack but would then retire to the right and left flanks before making contact, allowing the attack infantry (following behind it) to then engage the enemy.[3] These descriptions suggest a 'savaran forward' tactical organization, but consulting other sources raises questions whether this tactical situation was always the case on the battlefield.

In the *Shahname* Firdowsi describes a battle between the mythical kings Kay-Khosrow and Afrasiyab in which the archers are deployed to the front line with the battle elephants placed at the rear.[4] Interestingly, Firdowsi then avers that 'Guarding each elephant are 300 Savar / All Warriors bearing lances'.[5]

According to Shahbazi, elephants were meant to stiffen the resolve of savaran troops.[6] The Firdowsi description then goes on to describe spear-armed infantry and shield-and-sword-equipped infantry as being situated to the rear of the 'elephant battle groups'. Positioned to the rear of the infantry were light cavalry or horse archers.

Dinawari's classification. Dinawari classifies Sassanian tactics as having been in two distinct categories: (1) tactics for set-piece battles against enemy armies, and (2) tactics for the capture of enemy fortifications, strongholds and cities.[7] The latter category will be discussed in a subsequent chapter. This chapter will provide an examination of Sassanian battlefield tactics, making clear that the Sassanian spah was beholden to numerous doctrines. It is also possible that certain tactical formations were preferred against different enemies. For example, the savaran is often at the fore of the attack against Romano-Byzantines, heavily supported by archery. Experiences against Roman forces in the fourth century apparently convinced the Sassanians to not use elephants as primary strike weapons, although this doctrine appears to have been abandoned somewhat during Julian's invasion of the Sassanian Empire in 363 CE. Elephants certainly played a decisive role in the spah's battles in Central Asia (Chapter 12).

Early Battle Tactics Against Rome: 233–296 CE

These wars may be characterized as those fought by Ardashir I and his son and successor Shapur I against the armies of Rome. Ardashir I prevailed at Ctesiphon (233 CE) against the armies of Emperor Alexander Severus (r. 222–235 CE) followed by the campaigns of Shapur I against Emperors Gordian III (r. 238–244 CE), Philip the Arab (r. 244–249 CE) and Valerian (r. 253–260 CE). These wars were concluded by Sassanian military success followed by the strong attacks of Odenathus of Palmyra against the spah.

Ctesiphon (233 CE). An early example of Sassanian horse archery can be seen in the battle of Ctesiphon in 233 CE in which the Roman forces of Emperor Alexander Severus (r. 222–235 CE) were defeated by the savaran of Ardashir I. According to Herodian:

> The Persian king [Ardashir] attacked the [Roman] army with his entire force catching them by surprise and surrounding them in a trap. Under fire from all sides, the Roman soldiers were destroyed ... in the end they were all driven into a mass ... bombarded from every direction ... the Persians trapped the Romans like a fish in a net; firing their arrows from all sides at the encircled soldiers, the Persians massacred the whole army ... they were all destroyed ... this terrible disaster, which no one cares to recall, was a setback for the Romans, since a vast army ... had been destroyed.[8]

The Ctesiphon battle in 233 CE raises the question of whether early Sassanian armies had 'Parthian' characteristics, despite their overall military distinctiveness from their Parthian predecessors whom they had defeated nine years previous at Firuzabad. One shared characteristic may have been in combining heavy cavalry with horse archery. The Parthians launched attacks with heavy armoured knights followed by horse archers firing missiles. The knights would attack their opponents with lances. They would either break through enemy lines or force their adversaries (i.e. Roman infantry) into tighter formations to prevent the knights from breaking through. The knights would then withdraw to allow the horse archers to unleash their volleys of missiles against the enemy. These tactics were applied with overwhelming success against the Roman forces of Marcus Lucinius Crassus at the battle of Carrhae in 53 BCE in which a Parthian force of 10,000 (including 1,000 knights; the rest horse archers) defeated a Roman force three to four times its size. The Romans, however, did succeed in preventing further defeats of this scale by adopting countermeasures (i.e. recruitment of horse archers). Additionally, Parthian military effectiveness was compromised by dynastic conflicts, rebellions in northern Persia, Persis and Media as well as conflicts in the northeast along the porous Central Asian frontier. Nevertheless, despite military challenges from the Romans, invaders from Central Asia and internal challengers, the Parthian armoured knight-horse archer system remained formidable. The question, however, is what types of 'horse archers' were employed at the Battle of Ctesiphon. Were Ardashir's tactics at Ctesiphon based on the classic Iranic practice of employing armoured knights in strike packages in concert with horse archery? It would appear that in this battle (as in the battle of Carrhae in 53 BC), the coup de grace was delivered by the spah's horse archers who, as Herodian noted, were 'firing their arrows from all sides at the encircled soldiers'. The Sassanians and later Parthians however apparently did not have the strict 'binary' armoured knight-(unarmoured) horse archer distinction: Sassanian and Parthian knights are seen carrying the tirdan (arrow case) at Firuzabad, suggesting that they were possibly capable of doubling as lancers and horse archers (Chapter 6).

It is also possible that Ardashir's cavalry at Ctesiphon (lancers and horse archers) was also employing an improved version of the Central Asian 'scatter-coalesce' technique. Jalali notes that a common military tactic by the spah was to (1) first deploy in a typical set-piece fashion (as in one army facing the other), then (2) 'scatter' in a number of different directions and (3) for all 'scattered' elements to coalesce at a pre-designated point facing the enemy army.[9] The 'coalescing' elements would then suddenly arrive simultaneously to attack the enemy.[10] A variation of this could certainly occur when the savaran and horse archers engaged in the feigned withdrawal, enticing their enemies to pursue them, and then scatter and coalesce at pre-determined points on the battlefield. As noted in Chapter 4, the spah's system of military music signalled movements to troops engaged in battle (i.e. move left, right, etc.). In addition, scattered elements that were coalescing were to do so in an ordered fashion and to join (or rejoin) their own units when signalled to do so. Perhaps Ardashir I defeated the Roman forces at Ctesiphon with variations of the scatter-coalesce stratagem. These same tactics were to be developed to near-perfection almost 700 years after the Sassanians by the Mongol armies of Genghis Khan who followed the dictum of 'march divided attack united'.[11]

Misiche (244 CE). The young emperor Gordian III attacked the Sassanian Empire, first defeating Shapur I in Rhesaina (in modern Turkey, located between Carrhae and Nisibis) in 242 or 243 CE.[12] This victory allowed Gordian to clear the spah out of Antioch, Harran, Carrhae and most of Nisibis. Gordian then prepared to deliver his final blow by crossing the Euphrates River to push towards Ctesiphon to crush the spah. At this decisive moment, Gordian suffered a personal setback when his father in law Timesitheus, who was accompanying him during the campaign, died of illness. This was a serious blow given Timesitheus' excellent military leadership skills, which had served Gordian very well thus far against the spah.

Gordian pushed on towards the Sassanian capital, determined to conclude his campaign. Shapur I and the spah met Gordian in battle once again at Misiche (vicinity of modern-day Anbar in Iraq) in 244 CE. There are contradictory versions concerning the outcome of the battle. The traditional Western view was previously based on reports of Classical sources such as Jordanes,[13] Festus[14] and Ammianus Marcellinus,[15] which generally assert that Gordian III was completely successful against the spah and defeated Shapur I, but met his death at the hands of Philip the Arab who was the Praetorian prefect. A new generation of Western historians[16] now strongly question this narrative of events. There are two reasons for this. First, there are other Classical sources such as the *Oracula Sibyllina*[17] and *Zosimus*,[18] which are clear in stating that Gordian lost the battle and was killed fighting against Shapur and the spah in 243 CE.

The second reason why Western historiography questions the claims of Gordian's 'victory' at Misiche has to do with the Iranian sources. The Shapur inscriptions at the Kaabe Zartusht (also known as Shapur Kaabe Zartusht, or SKZ) note that the 'emperor Gordian conscripted a force taken from the entire Roman Empire, the Gothic and German peoples and marched into Ashuristan and the Empire of the Aryans ... a great frontal attack took place along the borders of Ashuristan in Mishik [Misiche] ... Gordian was killed, and we destroyed the Roman army.'[19]

As noted by Dignas and Winter, 'The Shapur inscription was composed within thirty years of the events of 244 ... it would have harmed Shapur's credibility to deliberately create a false account; this would not have been in the Sassanian ruler's interest.'[20] In addition, the rock reliefs at Bishapur depict the unfortunate figure of Gordian III as lying dead and trampled under the hooves of Shapur I's steed.[21] In this regard there is a hint from Cedrenus, who reports that 'he [Gordian III ?] died after *falling down from his horse* and crushing his thigh.'[22] This detail will be revisited shortly below. In acknowledgement of Shapur I and the spah's great victory over Roman arms, Misiche was renamed as 'Pirouz Shapur', (lit. victorious Shapur).[23]

Loriot attributes the Roman defeat to Gordian III's tactical error in his choice of terrain which maximized the effectiveness of the savaran against Roman forces.[24] Gordian may have been confident that he was able to counter the savaran with his own cavalry contingents. With respect to Misiche in 244 CE, the SKZ reports that many of the Roman recruits were of 'Gothic and German peoples'.[25] It would appear that Gordian was using his Goth-Germanic cavalry as a way of countering the savaran. Perhaps the SKZ report that Gordian engaged his army in a 'great frontal attack' at Misiche may be in reference to a massive lance attack by the Gothic-Germanic knights. Bivar notes that Gordian's decision to use the Gothic-Germanic cavalry at Misiche led to a military 'disaster'.[26] The question that can then be raised is why were the Gothic-Germanic cavalry unsuccessful against the savaran? The SKZ does report of Shapur I's victory at Misiche[27] but fails to provide exact tactical details of the battle. The 'Sarmat-icized' Gothic-Germanic cavalrymen were well versed in lance warfare,[28] as these had learnt of mounted lance warfare and corresponding equipment through their contacts with the Iranic Sarmatians in Europe.[29] This may explain why the Roman military chose to recruit these Gothic and Germanic cavalry against the new type of (Sassanian) armoured knights. It is likely that the savaran knights outclassed their Goth-Germanic counterparts in lance warfare during the battle of Misiche. One reason may be because the armour of the savaran was more robust than that worn by their Gothic-Germanic counterparts. As at Firuzabad in 224 CE, the Sassanians were using a combination of mail and lamellar armour as opposed to their opponents who did not use mail. As noted by Boss, Gothic-Germanic knights wore scale armour, but even this was not of the same sturdiness and quality seen amongst the original Sarmatian models. The Germanic knights most likely carried small shields while still being capable of engaging in Iranian-style two-handed lance combat.[30] Thanks to their combination armour, the contemporary savaran horsemen had little need of shields at the time, but as to how much this afforded them a tactical advantage over their Germanic contemporaries is difficult to ascertain.

In addition to lance combat, consideration must be given to the possibility of close-quarter combat on horseback between the savaran and their Gothic-Germanic counterparts. There is little question of the bravery and hardiness of the Gothic-Germanic warrior; however he would have been facing the best of the savaran, who were highly trained and resilient. The Gothic-Germanic warriors wore helmets of the 'Spangenhelm' riveted type, but there were distinct differences in the swords of the protagonists on the battlefield at Misiche. The Gothic-Sarmatian swords are described by Boss as having been 'of cheaper construction suitable for mass manufacture for a large cavalry force'.[31] The Sassanian swords at the time of Shapur I were of the 'broadsword' type (Chapter 6) but were longer than the Kushan types, which were closely related to the Sarmatian and (earlier) Parthian models.[32] The scabbard tips of Sarmatian swords strongly differed from the Sassanians as the latter had scabbard tips which were wide and rectangular.[33] Further research is required to ascertain how these differences of sword types may have affected the course of the battle at Misiche.

There certainly were sharp differences with respect to archery; Germanic knights did not adopt the horse archery of the Sarmatians[34] and fought mainly with spear and sword.[35] The savaran were certainly lancers, however, as shown in the tirdan (arrow case) depictions at Naqshe Rustam (i.e. panel with Hormuzd II)[36] and Bishapur[37] (especially the depiction of Shapur I), the savaran had certainly not dispensed with horse archery. As a result, it is possible that the savaran would have held a clear edge over their Gothic-Germanic counterparts by being able to fire missiles at them from a safe distance during the battle of Misiche.

Revisiting Cedrenus' aforementioned narrative, it would be of interest to compare this with the reports of Malalas and Zonaras. According to Malalas, 'He [Gordian III] in the battle against the Persians was bought down from his horse and crushed his thigh.'[38] In this version of events Malalas writes that Gordian later died from his wound in his fiftieth year (and after his return to Rome from his Persian campaign). Zonaras' account is most interesting in that it is consistent with the reports of Malalas and Cedrenus that Gordian had fallen from his horse and suffered a crushed thigh, but also adds an important detail that may help explain the context of Gordian's situation. Zonaras notes that Gordian 'drove his horse forward in battle, exhorting his men and stirring them to feats of courage. The horse stumbled and fell on him, crushing his thigh. He therefore returned to Rome and died from his fracture after a reign of six years.'[39]

Perhaps, and as noted earlier, Gordian III had indeed fallen but the reason for this may be explained by his having led his armies forward as is suggested by Zonaras. This is also consistent with the SKZ's report of the Romans having launched a 'great frontal attack'. It would appear that Gordian was either leading the attack against the Sassanians in person or was among the lead elements in the attack. As he and his armies made contact he may have been unhorsed by a Sassanian knight's lance, an outcome which is consistent with Cedrenus and Malalas, who report the emperor as having fallen from his horse. Another possibility is that a Sassanian lancer hit the emperor's horse, which in turn unseated him.

Barbalissos (c. 253 CE). Philip the Arab became emperor of Rome following the death of Gordian in 244 CE. He set out to make peace with the Sassanians by paying them half a million *denarii* in ransom to ensure the repatriation of Roman troops who had been taken prisoner at Misiche. Philip also agreed to yield Mesopotamia and Armenia to Shapur I.[40] The terms of this treaty were considered a major humiliation for the Romans, with sources such as Zosimus complaining of Philip having concluded a 'most dishonorable peace'[41] with the Sassanians. This may help explain why the Romans soon broke the treaty Philip had worked so hard to conclude: Roman armies invaded the Sassanian realm by thrusting into Mesopotamia and Armenia in c. 252 CE. The Romans had timed their attack especially well as the spah was in the latter stages of its campaigns in the north and northeast of Iran. Shapur I was campaigning to secure the allegiance of the remaining Mede, northern (Giloi, Dailamite) and north-east (Khwarezmian, Kushan) Iranian peoples. The absence of the spah greatly aided Philip's advance into Armenia and Mesopotamia, which (according to Zonaras) caught the Sassanians by surprise.[42] Shapur, however, proved successful in the north and northeast of Iran and returned to the west with the spah, now augmented by the formidable Dailamite infantry warriors of northern Iran and Khwarezmian cavalry from the northeast. Shapur was ready to strike back, with the SKZ reporting: 'Caesar again lied and did wrong to Armenia and we attacked the Roman Empire.'[43]

Dignas and Winter note that the Sassanians overran much Roman territory in the Near East, inflicting heavy losses on Roman armies in 253 CE.[44] In that same year, the Sassanians scored a major victory by destroying a Roman army of 60,000 troops at Barbalissos.[45] So great was the magnitude of the Roman military disaster that, as Zosimus noted, 'the Persians could have conquered the whole of Asia had they not been overjoyed at their excessive spoils.'[46]

Edessa-Carrhae (c. 260 CE). After the victory at Barbalissos in 253 CE, the Sassanians had withdrawn from the conquered Roman territories.[47] Valerian, who became emperor in 253 CE, had led a powerful and successful counterattack, driving the Sassanians out of Antioch (c. 256). Shapur and the savaran deployed to the Carrhae-Edessa region, prompting Valerian to seek battle with him there (260 CE). The Sassanians would subsequently score an even greater victory. As noted in the SKZ:

> During the third campaign, when we advanced against Carrhae and Edessa and besieged Carrhae and Edessa, the Emperor Valerian marched against us ... with ... a force of 70,000 men ... on the other side of Carrhae and Edessa we fought a great battle with Valerian, and we captured the Emperor Valerian

with our own hands and the others, the Praetorian prefect and senators and officials, all those who were the leaders of the force … we made them all prisoners.[48]

According to the SKZ, the Roman army included a very impressive array of continental Europeans including Germania, Dacia (approximately modern Rumania), Pannonia (approximately modern Hungary), Hispania (approximately modern Spain), Moesia (in the Balkans), Raetia (roughly Switzerland, parts of southern Bavaria, Tirol, Lombardy, etc.), Noricum (portions of modern Austria and Slovenia) and Istria (encompassing modern-day Croatia, Slovenia and Italy). Tabari reports that the Romans lost 10,000 men in battle with 'a thousand and twice three hundred' made prisoner.[49]

The immediate consequence of this defeat was the fall (once again) of Antioch, Tarsus and Cappadocia, clearly indicative of the Sassanians' breakthrough into Syria and Anatolia. Perhaps of greater long-term significance was the impact of this defeat upon the prestige of Roman arms, especially with Valerian having become the only emperor in the empire's long history to have been captured in battle.[50] The military successes of Shapur and the savaran were commemorated in the rock-relief sites of Nagshe Rustam[51] and Bishapur.[52]

As at Misiche, the question raised is: what tactics were used in the battles of Barbalissos and Edessa-Carrhae? Archery certainly played a highly significant role in both battles. The *Oracula Sibyllina* alludes to archery's importance in a passage stating that Antioch and Dura-Europos fell to 'the arrow-shooting Persians'[53] in c. 256 CE. It is not clear if these 'Persians' are the armoured savaran or horse archers and, if the latter, whether they would have been of the armoured type. Nevertheless, it is certainly possible that the Sassanians deployed armoured horse archers; earlier Parthian armoured horse archers have been depicted at Dura Europos.[54] As noted previously, what proved decisive against the Romans at the Battle of Ctesiphon in 233 CE was evidently the delivery of the coup de grace by Ardashir I's horse archers. This would suggest that the Sassanian arrows were able to punch through Roman armour. Conversely, and as with Parthian archery at Firuzabad, Roman archery was evidently unsuccessful against the armour of the contemporary savaran. As a result, Shapur I's lance-wielding knights would have been able to charge into the Roman lines without much concern for Roman archery. Nevertheless, by the time of Belisarius, Romano-Byzantine armies were to adopt the more effective Hunnish bow, which was to prove highly effective against the savaran, as was demonstrated at the Battle of Dara in 530 CE (see discussion later this chapter).

As noted previously with respect to the battle of Misiche in 244 CE, the Roman employment of Gothic-Germanic armoured knights was a failure against the savaran. Lacking effective countermeasures (especially cavalry and archery) to neutralize the savaran, Roman forces were most likely vulnerable to repeated lance thrusts by the Sassanian horsemen. As Heliodorus noted (see Chapter 6), a savaran horseman could 'impale two persons in a single stroke'.[55] This capability would place Roman frontline troops at great risk, especially in light of the fact (and as noted by Cedrenus) that infantry comprised the core of Roman armies at the time.[56] That being the case, the emperor Valerian's decision to deploy his main army in the flat plains of Edessa-Carrhae in 260 CE[57] was especially inept as it simply served to maximize the advantages of the spah's lance-bearing savaran and archery against his infantry. Ironically, this was the same locale where Parthian knights and horse archers had destroyed the Roman armies of Marcus Lucinius Crassus in 53 BCE. Valerian's forces in 260 CE most likely succumbed to the deadly lance charges of the savaran supported by archery. The lance strikes and archery barrages against Valerian's army may partly explain why (according to Tabari) 'panic seized the hearts of the Roman warriors'.[58]

The main difference between the Parthian armies facing Crassus and the Sassanian spah facing Valerian was that the spah also included armoured infantry. With the repeated charges of the savaran lancers and the barrages of archery, Roman formations could have become sufficiently softened up to allow the Sassanian infantry to engage as well. Nevertheless, it is generally agreed that the chief instrument of the spah's victories was the savaran.

Odenathus (c. 260–261 CE). Shapur I's victory at Edessa-Carrhae brought large portions of the Roman Near East under Sassanian control. King Odenathus of Palmyra (r. 258–67 CE) was suitably impressed by Shapur's great victories by making peace overtures to him. He also made a personal appeal of friendship to Shapur, and to that end pointed out in a letter to the Sassanian ruler that 'he had done nothing against the Persians'.[59] These offers at friendship were contemptuously rejected by Shapur, who vowed to utterly destroy Odenathus and Palmyra. This prompted Odenathus to abandon his neutrality and adopt a fully pro-Roman policy. Just as the Sassanian army was returning from recently sacked Antioch, Odenathus struck at the spah's lumbering baggage trains, and apparently inflicted another defeat upon his enemies as they re-entered Persian territory. Odenathus then cleared the Sassanians out of Nisibis, Edessa and Carrhae.

Odenathus' successes were very much due to his highly efficient military machine. Barker has provided a comprehensive overview of Palmyran forces which were composed of archers, cataphracts and light cavalry.[60] Palmyra also fielded an excellent corps of infantry equipped with spears and small shields.[61] Palmyran foot soldiers also appear to have carried Roman-type swords: the Palmyran god Baalshamin is typically depicted as being equipped with a Roman-style short sword (*gladius*) and scabbard of the Pompeii pattern.[62] The Palmyran archer deployed the powerful composite bow (similar to the Partho-Sassanian bow) with his quiver suspended either on his shoulder[63] or from his belt.[64] Barker also notes that the Palmyran archers were 'numerically the most important troop type of the Palmyran army'.[65] The archers also carried swords or axes and (like the aforementioned) infantry carried small oval shields which could be suspended from the belt.[66] It is quite possible that Palmyran archers were able to hold their own against their Sassanian counterparts. This is also probably true when comparing Palmyran infantry to Sassanian armoured infantry. Assuming that Barker's statement regarding the numbers of Palmyran archers is correct, one may postulate that the Palmyran army, like the Sassanian spah, relied on massive and powerful archery barrages. Perhaps, like the Sassanians, the Palmyrans would precede their primary attacks with archery barrages. Given the similarity of their cavalry to Iranian cavalry, one may well conclude that archery barrages preceded Palmyran armoured cavalry lance thrusts.

The Palmyran cavalry was virtually an Iranian-(Partho-Sassanian) type force. Barker's description of the Palmyran armoured knight shows him to be virtually identical to the Sassanian savaran. The Palmyran knight wore a long hooded mail coat, with his torso protected by overlapping iron plates and his arms and lower legs protected by flexible ring armour. He also wore a helmet with iron or bronze face mask, gloves of mail, and iron shoes.[67] Much like his Partho-Sassanian counterparts, the Palmyran knight was equipped with a 12ft lance and carried a mace;[68] like the knights of Naqshe Rustam, the Palmyran knight carries no shield. Like the Sassanians, the Palmyrans fielded an effective light cavalry force. The horsemen carried bows with separate cases for their quivers (they did not have combined bow-quiver cases), swords and light spears.

When in battle against the Palmyrans, the Sassanians were fighting a highly efficient force which were very much familiar with contemporary Iranian war-fighting styles. The Iranian tactic of archery barrages followed by lance charges were countered by Odenathus' own archers (foot and light horse) and of course his armoured knights. Not only were the Sassanians pushed out of their recent gains inside Roman territory, they soon had to face Odenathus' forces at the very gates of Ctesiphon itself. Odenathus appears to have overstretched his forces when campaigning against Ctesiphon. What is known is that when news spread among the Sassanians of Odenathus' arrival at Ctesiphon, Sassanian military leaders sent reinforcements to the capital. These troops inflicted heavy losses on Odenathus' forces,[69] forcing them to withdraw. By this time, the Sassanians had most likely bought high quality Kushan cavalry from the empire's eastern marches. While tactical details are not clear as to how Odenathus was repelled from Sassanian territory, it is clear that he had failed to destroy the Sassanian army and free Valerian from captivity. Odenathus was unable to repeat his past successes against the Sassanians, who in turn could not topple Odenathus after the danger from Ctesiphon had been lifted. He certainly had saved Rome from complete disaster, driving the Sassanians back across their own borders. Even so, Rome had suffered heavy blows against the prestige of its armies. Rome now had to acknowledge that the Sassanian spah was a world-class military force on par with the Roman army.

The Battles of Galerius (295–298 CE). The Sassanian king Narseh (r. 293–301 CE) engaged in a massive attack against Rome by invading western Armenia in the Caucasus and ejecting Tirdad, the pro-Roman Armenian governor of Armenia, in 295 CE.[70] This success allowed the spah to once again roll into Syria to batter the Roman forces in that locale. The spah's campaign in Syria was assisted by local princes who sided with the Sassanians.[71] In response, Emperor

Diocletian (r. 284–305 CE)[72] dispatched his son-in-law Galerius to fight against the Sassanians.

Galerius' decision to fight the spah at al-Raqqah (Callinicum and Carrhae region) resulted in a crushing military defeat for Roman arms.[73] Galerius made the same error that Valerian had committed when he chose to fight Shapur in the same type of flat and open terrain. The decision was militarily maladaptive for the Roman military as their troops would be fully exposed to the dangerous savaran and horse archers, who would be able to fully exploit their rapid manoeuvring and tactical capabilities, thanks to the region's terrain which was ideal for Iranian cavalry warfare. Second, the terrain exposed Galerius' troops more openly to the massed archery unleashed by the spah's foot archers. Despite the lack of specific information on the actual tactics used by the spah, Dodgeon and Lieu in their study of classical sources report of 'arrow-holding quivers ... each held bow and spear in his hands ... the whole Nisean cavalry that fights on the plains was gathered together'.[74] The Roman army was once again crushed, much as it had been at Ctesiphon, Misiche, Barbalissos and Edessa-Carrhae.

The tactics of the spah were most probably those alluded to earlier, namely, massive archery salvos by foot archers followed by attacks by highly mobile mounted archers, both intended to soften Roman lines for the climactic assault by armoured savaran knights. As noted before, the Sassanians certainly had armoured and professional infantry, however the deciding factor must have been the savaran and horse archers operating in concert with foot archers. If the infantry was engaged in the fighting, it may have coordinated its attacks with the savaran during the battle against Galerius in 295 CE (see a description of such tactics in the *Chronicon Anonymum*).

The Emperor Diocletian's sole consolation after this military disaster was that Galerius and his surviving troops had evaded capture. Nevertheless Galerius was to soon reverse Rome's military fortunes against the spah. Three years (298 CE) after the debacle in Syria, Galerius, now reinforced by Roman contingents from Europe, was ready for a new war against the Sassanians. This time it was Narseh who committed a serious military blunder by choosing to fight with his main forces in Armenia in the Caucasus. In this endeavour, Narseh's geographical choice of the Caucasian terrain proved militarily adaptive for the Romans; the region features hilly and forested terrain which impeded the fluid manoeuvres and tactical options of the savaran and horse archers. In contrast, the Roman infantry was much better suited for combat in this theatre. Galerius' second campaign is of interest because of the victory he achieved. Assisted by local pro-Roman Armenian fighters, Galerius' army inflicted a crushing defeat on the spah.[75] Galerius then won another major victory in the Battle of Satala in 298 CE. In this clash the Romans captured many Sassanian nobles and even members of Narseh's family.[76]

What were the military reasons for Galerius' victory over Narses in 298 CE? It is almost certain that Galerius must have planned his new offensive well and drawn important lessons from his defeat in 295 CE. The Roman military staff must have realized that they had to find ways of minimizing the tactical advantages of the savaran and the deadly effects of Sassanian archery. Nevertheless, the terrain alone was not the only factor which blocked the success of the savaran and horse archery. Galerius' cavalry units were apparently able to counter the spah's cavalry formations sufficiently to neutralize their effectiveness against Roman front line (especially infantry) forces. With the effectiveness of the savaran and mounted archers somehow reduced by a combination of terrain and Roman cavalry, the Roman infantry were able to reach the spah's front lines to overcome the Sassanian foot archers. The latter would of course inflict casualties with their volleys at the approaching Roman infantry; however, the latter's rapid pace, determination, professionalism and discipline would have kept their ranks intact (irrespective of losses) as they closed in on the spah's front lines. Note that the armour worn by the infantry, along with their shields, would have obviated the effectiveness of arrows. In this context, Roman archery must have played a role in the Roman victory, although the level of its contribution to Galerius' victory is difficult to ascertain. Roman archers, for example, may have been able to at least partly cover the approach of the Roman infantry towards the spah's front lines by launching counter volleys of their own against Sassanian foot archers. It is therefore possible that the savaran horsemen were unable to launch successive lance charges and may have been forced into prolonged close-quarter hand-to-hand fighting against Roman troops, a type of combat for which the latter were very well trained.

Nevertheless it was not just the actions of the Roman infantry that must have contributed to Galerius's victory; Roman cavalry must have played a role. One of the depictions at the Arch of Galerius in Thessaloniki shows a melee in which Roman cavalry and infantry are engaged with Sassanian cavalry and infantry (one of the latter crouched on his knee, wearing what looks like a Spangenhelm helmet, holding a shield and straight sword). What is clear is that Galerius succeeded in negating the effectiveness of Persian archery and the savaran to defeat the spah in the Armenian campaign of 298 CE.

Battle Tactics against Rome: Fourth Century CE

The savaran's tactics in the late third to mid-late fourth century CE appear to have been very similar to those seen in the early days of the spah. Assaults by the savaran would be supported by massive arrow fire:[77] the archers' role was to soften up frontline enemy ranks in order to maximize the impact of the savaran assault. The deployment of archery as a primary weapon was part of the spah's philosophy of inflicting as many casualties as possible from a distance before the battle was joined between the opposing armies.[78]

Military changes to the spah. By the 350s CE (reign of Shapur II), the spah had introduced a series of new changes, notably the corps of 'super-heavy' savaran (Chapter 6). Sassanian cavalry during Julian's invasion of Iran in 363 CE were trained and equipped for close-quarter combat against Roman troops, yet retained the option of breaking off the assault to then engage in the traditional feigned retreat practiced by the Parthians. In such a scenario, pursuing Roman forces would then be subjected to the Parthian-shot tactic whereby the cavalry would shoot backwards as they 'retreated'. Julian and Ammianus Marcellinus have provided comprehensive analyses of the Sassanian battle order and tactics during the wars of Shapur II against the Roman Empire.[79]

Battle order of the spah as described by Ammianus Marcellinus. The savaran is described as being placed at the front of the spah. The savaran horsemen are fully armoured with their horses also protected. Infantry troops are described as having wicker-like shields; battle elephants are positioned (see Chapter 7) to their rear. The invasion of Persia by Emperor Julian (r. 361–363 CE), notably the Battle of Maranga (22 June 363) and the death of Julian (25 June 362) will be discussed later in this chapter.

The three-wave attack: Singara (350 CE). Roman sources describe an interesting three-wave model of attack by the savaran at the Battle of Singara in 350 CE.[80] In essence, this was an attack by a three-wave formation composed of lance-wielding savaran (first wave) horsemen, archers (second wave), followed by another (third) wave of lance-wielding savaran horsemen. The archers must have been mounted as these had to move at the same pace as the savaran. The rationale of the doctrine was as follows. The first wave of savaran horsemen would attack the Roman front lines to compel the enemy infantry to stand closer together in formation and thus prevent the savaran knights from breaking through. The knights would then break off their assault and retire to the left and right to clear the way for the arriving second wave of mounted archers. Having clustered to withstand the first wave of savaran knights, the Roman infantry troops now became vulnerable targets for deadly barrages of missiles being unleashed against them by the archers, who could be of the 'Parthian' lightly armed and armoured horse-archer type or bow-wielding armoured savaran knights. The missile barrages would presumably weaken the Roman infantry, leading the archers to retire to the left and right to allow for the (third wave) of savaran knights to mount their lance assault.

The main advantage of this type of three-wave (lance-missile-lance) attack was that it forced the defending infantry to rapidly switch their tactics in order to adapt to each type of (lance or missile) assault. Such a scenario would likely have been most effective against inexperienced troops, as well-trained and battle-experienced Roman infantry could, despite suffering losses, hold its ground.

Savaran-infantry tactic. This tactic involved combining a savaran assault with combat infantry. The main objective was to surprise enemy defenders who would be expecting to (exclusively) face savaran attackers during combat.

The *Chronicon Anonymum* provides the following description with respect to the savaran-infantry tactic:[81] the savaran horsemen would (1) advance toward the enemy battle line followed closely behind by the infantry; (2) as the savaran formation neared the enemy battle line it would split in two, with one section retiring to the left and the other to the right; (3) the infantry would move up to engage the enemy in close-quarters face-to-face combat.

This tactic clearly illustrates that while the savaran remained as the spah's primary strike arm throughout the dynasty's reign, the infantry was by no means insignificant. The *Chronicon Anonymum* certainly makes clear that primary assaults by the savaran could be combined with those of Sassanian infantry. It is important in this context to clearly distinguish what type of infantry is being discussed (recall Chapter 7). It is highly unlikely that Sassanian infantry would be of the type described by Procopius, namely troops that were poorly trained and ill-equipped for close-quarters combat; the formidable Roman troops would have little difficulty repelling and destroying them. The infantry employed for the two-wave assault were most likely of the armoured type, as seen with the early fallen Sassanian trooper at Dura-Europos or the later 'gladiator' type infantry described by Ammianus Marcellinus.

The Tri-Partite (Centre-Left-Right) Doctrine: Mid Sixth Century– Early Seventh Centuries CE

By the late Sassanian era the spah had adopted a standard three-section formation of a left wing, centre and right wing. The three-section formation had parallels with ancient Greek phalanx formations with their distinct *meymane-ye sepah* (right flank of the army),[82] *meysare-ye sepah* (left flank of the army),[83] and centre or *qalb-e sepah* (middle or 'heart' of the army).[84] Dinawari's *Uyun al-Akhbar* reports of specific battle rules for troops placed in the right, centre and left positions of the spah: rules for the commencement of battle, assessment of troops' experience, numerical factors, climate-geography and water supplies.[85] The analyses by Dinawari are of interest as these were made after the fall of the Sassanians in the seventh century and based on Pahlavi manuals that had survived the Arabo-Islamic invasions.

Like the *Uyun al-Akhbar*, the Greek-language *Strategikon* also reports of Sassanian military formations as being 'set up for battle in three equal parts, the centre, the right and the left'.[86] Attributed to the Byzantine Emperor Maurice (r. 582–582), the *Strategikon* was a military manual most likely written in the late sixth century to early seventh century CE.[87] Relying on Dinawari's *Uyun al-Akhbar*, Pigulevskaya has provided the following overall summary of Sassanian battlefield tactics:[88] (1) the savaran would stand ahead of the infantry prior to commencement of the attack; (2) the savaran would either commence the attack or part to the left and right to allow the infantry to assault the enemy; (3) the centre (or 'heart') and the right of the spah would engage in the attack; (4) the left of the spah would stand on the defence, entering the battle only at times of extreme necessity. The savaran apparently could be placed behind the infantry if deemed necessary by the commander. The *Shahname* does describe of one such instance: '[T]hus behind these [infantry] stood the savaran of war'.[89] In any event, the savaran was always decisive to the outcome of the battle. Bivar's succinct summary of the importance of the savaran in this context is clear: 'The whole issue of the battle, once an opening appeared, depended on the single overwhelming cavalry charge.'[90]

Centre or 'heart'. The centre was to be placed in an elevated location to act as the focal position holding the left and right flanks of the field army.[91] Placement upon an elevated position was also meant to ensure some protection against enemy attacks towards this position. The centre was considered highly critical as any serious weakening and damage to this position would seriously jeopardize the integrity of the field army and lead to its collapse. As long as the centre remained solid and intact, the left and right wings would not collapse, even if these were enduring heavy losses during the battle.[92]

The *Shahname* of Firdowsi states that the *lashgare ghalb* (heart of the army) must remain unwaveringly in its place, and should the heart waver 'you and the army will be displaced/come out of the place of heart' (*to ba lashkar az ghalbgah andaray*). Firdowsi also emphasizes the advantages of a successful attack by the field army against the enemy's centre. In a description of the legendary warrior Rustam, Firdowsi details his primary attack towards the heart of the enemy Turanian army. With the heart shattered by Rustam's assault, the left and right flanks collapse, allowing the warrior Guiw to become 'as a wolf towards the sheep [*chon gorg sooy-e barr-e*][93] with Gudarz tearing into the enemy's right flank.[94]

Maurice's *Strategikon* provides further details with respect to the centre of a typical Sassanian field army by noting that it was composed of '400 or 500 selected men'.[95] This may possibly be a reference to 'selected' crack troops entrusted with leading the attack from the centre. The *Strategikon* adds further information with respect to the nature of Sassanian battle formations in general and the role of the savaran within these by stating that 'they [the Sassanian spah] ... line up the cavalry in each unit in the first and second line or phalanx and to keep the front of the formation even and dense'.[96] This is consistent with the spah's battle philosophy since the early days of the dynasty of often placing the savaran as the primary strike arm at the front of battle formations.

If deemed necessary by the commander, troops from the centre and right flank were permitted to join the attacking forces (typically the savaran and other elite cavalry units), but were then to return in an orderly fashion to their original (centre and/or right) positions. Likewise if the field army were severely weakened during battle, the centre and the right flank were permitted to advance against the enemy, with the left flank being primarily defensive and expected to stay in place[97] (see below). Firdowsi also recounts the advice of Ardashir to his army commander by noting that the centre was allowed to move from its position only when the enemy's own centre had either moved or been displaced.[98]

A final question that may be raised with respect to the centre is the actual meaning of the term 'two chief parts' of the centre.[99] This is clearly distinct from the left and right flanks, so what is it that distinguishes the 'two chief parts'? It is possible that these 'parts' were actually lines or rows of fighting troops in which one is placed *behind* the other. In this regard, Ammianus provides us a clue by referring to the 'first line' of the Sassanian spah.[100]

The commander in chief and the centre. If the king were present to act as commander in chief, he would be preferably placed on an elevated position, seated on his throne. Ideally the throne was to be situated in the centre of the army to allow the king to have the best possible view of the battlefield. The king would have an elite contingent of troops and archers acting as his personal bodyguard, these being expected to defend the throne and national Drafsh Kaviani banner to the death. In addition, the king would always be accompanied by the *mobad* magi who would bring vessels housing the sacred Zoroastrian fires.

The Sassanian king would not only ride with the spah to war but even partake in hand-to-hand combat, one example being Shapur II who personally engaged enemy troops during his siege of Amida in 359 CE.[101] The practice of partaking in battle was meant to enhance the charisma of the king, who would demonstrate this though his gallantry and martial prowess on the battlefield to please the Iranic pantheon.[102] In a sense, the king would be demonstrating his *farr* (divine glory) by personally partaking in combat alongside his warriors. This topic is discussed further in the chapter on Sassanian military culture.

In practice, however, the king would not always be present to direct the battle, therefore it would be the top commander in the theatre who would occupy the throne in the king's stead.[103] Such a scenario, for example, occurred at the Battle of Qadissiyah in 637 CE, when the commander in chief, Rustam Farrokhzad, was seated on the throne while directing the fatal battle against the invading Arabo-Islamic army (Chapter 17).

The commander of the field army (either the king himself or the commanding general) was expected to give battle only in cases of extreme necessity,[104] after having exhausted all non-combat options, especially negotiations. The *Sirat Anoushirvan* even cites Khosrow I as having stated that peace is preferable to war when no threat of territorial loss is present.[105] Nevertheless, the *Sirat Anoushirvan* also notes that neither friend nor foe is to see the shahanshah in a fearful or agitated state.

Once battle is begun, the commander is then advised to protract the battle as long as possible, ideally for the duration of the day.[106] This is of interest as it matches descriptions by Procopius with respect to the timing of the Sassanian spah with respect to attacks and duration of battles. There are at least two distinct cases described by Procopius where the Sassanians attack around mid-day or slightly after, despite having drawn up their battle plans earlier around dawn.[107] Part of the rationale for delaying the attack from early morning to noon is explained as thus: Romano-Byzantine troops preferred having their main meal around noon, whereas the Iranians would dine in the evening. Timing the attack at noon would presumably be disruptive to the Romano-Byzantines as these would be forced into battle without having had a proper meal.

Right flank. The right flank was entrusted with the attack, especially with manoeuvres aimed at outflanking the enemy. In this endeavour, the savaran were the chief strike force and critical to the spah's success or failure in battle. Behind the savaran stood the infantry with battle elephants situated to its rear. The actions of the infantry and elephants essentially depended upon and/or followed the primary role of the savaran. Therefore, depending upon the tactical plans drafted by the commanders in the field, the infantry could attack first to prepare for the impending savaran assault, or even combine its assault with the savaran.

Left flank. Troops (typically archers and/or infantry) placed at the left would be responsible for defending their position at all costs to repel enemy attacks. So important was the role of the left flank in defence that it was referred to as 'the direction of the shield'.[108] This same 'shield' was responsible for protecting the field army from flanking attacks, just as the right flank was entrusted with out-flanking the enemy. The left flank, however, would enter the battle in situations of extreme necessity, especially if the enemy flanking movement was threatening to destroy the left flank. Nevertheless even this action is to be well timed and coordinated. Interestingly, evidence of this type of tactic is seen in earlier Sassanian armies facing the Roman invasion force of Julian in 363 CE. Ammianus, for example, notes of a situation where 'having compelled the left flank to fall back, the enemy began to rapidly surround us [the Romans] and conducted the fight with spears and every kind of missile weapons'.[109] By attacking, the left flank has in essence abandoned its strict defensive doctrine to prevent the entire field army from collapse.

Left-handed warriors, especially with respect to archery, were placed on the left flank due to their 'ambidextrous' ability to shoot at both the left and right sides.[110] Archers placed on the left flank were expected to keep firing as long as possible with their primary focus being to their front and towards the right, aiming at the enemy's centre. The archers would fire to their left in the face of an attempted flanking attack by the enemy.[111]

The rear guard. The rear of the army formation (or *sage-ye sepah*[112]) was critical to the force's integrity.[113] A successful breakthrough by the enemy into the rear would ensure the field army's collapse. A collapse of the rear could also endanger the king and the top military leadership. To head off this danger, experienced commanders were placed in the rear guard to ensure that it remained intact in case of surprise enemy attacks.

The tactical reserve. One of the measures undertaken by the commander was to avoid committing his entire force to the actual battle. As a result the commander took the precautionary measure of holding back a portion of his forces as a military reserve. This was necessary, especially in battles against highly resilient and well-trained enemy troops, notably the Romano-Byzantines. In encounters against equally matched foes where the battle's outcome was uncertain, a tactical reserve could be pulled into the fray in case the military engagement went awry. Elite units in particular would often be kept as a tactical reserve, as occurred with the *zhayedan/javidan* at Dara. The commander would then commit his reserve units, at what was judged to be the critical time, to the battle. The deployment of such units could prove critical to the battle's outcome, as was demonstrated at Dara (see below).

The *Shahname*: Examples of Tactics

Another valuable source of information pertaining to Sassanian tactics is the *Shahname*, which has been examined in the *Katsujinken* journal by Khorasani, et al.[114] There are some parallels between the examples of battle tactics described in the *Shahname* and the sources mentioned previously in this chapter, especially with respect to the lance charge discussed below.

Did horse archers accompany the lance charge? As noted in this chapter as well as in Chapter 6, the centre was pivotal to the success of the primary strikes. The centre formation was critical in breaking into and through the enemy's defences. It is generally agreed upon in Western and Iranian military historiography that the armoured lancers or savaran knights were critical in this role. Nevertheless, there is at least one hint in the *Shahname* that the primary armoured 'fist' may not always have been led by mounted armoured commanders. There is the case, for example, of a commander known as 'Karan the Bold', who was among the officers accompanying the mythical hero Rustam when the latter led a major charge into enemy lines. This type of attack involved the armoured lancers thrusting forward in a straight line, directly into the enemy ranks, with the intention of (at least) dislocating or even breaking through the enemy lines. The passage in the *Shahname* describing Karan's attack would indicate that not all commanders and cavalrymen within the primary charge were armoured knights: 'Karan overthrew ten warriors at each charge; now wheeling to the left, now to the right, and seeking to wreak vengeance on all sides.'[115] Karan's actions of being able to strike rapidly to his left and right indicates that he was a horse archer, not an armoured knight.[116] It is highly unlikely that Karan was unarmoured, as he was one of the top commanders in Rustam's strike. Instead, this passage appears to be a description of an armoured horse archer, although Karan slays the enemy commander with his sword.[117] Such armoured horse archers were also capable of making several archery passes before the enemy battle line before closing in to kill opponents with close-quarters weapons (e.g. swords, maces, etc.). At the very least, the possibility may be considered that not all of the savaran's armoured lance charges were composed exclusively of lancers, but may also have included armoured horse archers. The *Shahname* also makes reference to the participation of infantry in primary assaults.[118]

V-formation. In reference to the aforementioned *Shahname* passage, it may be deduced that the formation used in the primary charge was of the V-formation type.[119] This formation was used by the armies of Achaemenid Iran – for example, Classical sources describe Iranian cavalry attacking their foes in a 'wedge' formation. As noted by Sidnell, the Scythians are generally believed to have developed the wedge formation, this tactic then being adopted by the Thracians and Achaemenids and put into very effective use by the Macedonian cavalry of Alexander.[120]

The V-formation discussed in the *Shahname* would involve the top commanders, presumably with lances and heavily armoured, with Rustam described as leading the charge with the elite savaran horsemen riding just behind him. The commander, Rustam, leads the *Schwerpunkt* of the charge into what has been identified as the weakest possible point in the enemy formation. Once a successful breach has been achieved, the shahanshah orders the mass charge of the entire field army to destroy the dislocated enemy. This description seems to be at variance with the aforementioned instructions of the Pahlavi manuals which caution the commander against committing the left flank towards the offensive unless absolutely necessary. Nevertheless, if the field army was clearly winning the battle, the commander in chief may have committed the left flank to the final offensive. In such a scenario it was imperative to ensure (through intelligence and/or prior reconnaissance) that the enemy was not harbouring a hidden reserve force which could then be unleashed towards the army's right or left flanks.

Targeting enemy commanders. An interesting tactic engaged in during the frontal assault as described in the *Shahname* is the targeting of enemy commanders. In general, and as noted previously, the frontal assault entailed elite cavalrymen (both lancers as well as horse archers) attacking into the weakest

Table 4. Four parallels between *Kitab ol Ayin* and *Strategikon*.
(adapted from Hamblin, 1986; Insotrancev, 1926; Dennis, 1984)

	Kitab ol Ayin	*Strategikon*
Postponing Battles	'The commander ... should not wage battle against an enemy army unless under extreme necessity and in a situation where there is no choice but to give battle. In such a situation ... the commander exerts his full effort to postpone the battle until the last part of the day'. (p. 113, 1.2–3)	'... favourite ploy of theirs is to ... postpone the fighting'. (11.1)
Stakes and Pallisades	'... set ambushes in cover and in hidden places and throw out *hasak* [stakes or caltrops] in places where you fear to spend the night'. (p.113, 1.10–11)	'... they create a ditch and a sharp palisade around themselves ...' (11.1)
Three Segments of Battle Formation	'... for the heart [center of army] an elevated place ... be chosen ... if ... two chief parts [of centre] are beaten, the firmness of the right and the left wing is useless ...' (cited by Inostrancev, 1926, p. 13)	'... set up for battle in three equal parts, the center, the right and the left ...' (11.1)
Position of Cavalry	'Horsemen should be placed at front ... this is not observed during a mutual advance or flank movement ...' (cited by Inostrancev, 1926, p. 13)	'They ... line up the cavalry in each unit in the first and second line or phalanx ...' (11.1)

point of the enemy's lines to achieve a *Durchburch* (breakthrough). Critical to this endeavour was for the savaran to employ shock tactics, notably by targeting enemy commanders as the enemy forces were reeling in disarray.[121] This would in essence constitute a double blow as it would simultaneously damage (if not decapitate) the enemy's upper military leadership and demoralize the enemy troops.

Battle Tactics Against Rome (Late Fifth–Early Seventh Century CE)

By the beginning of the sixth century CE, the spah was fielding a new type of cavalry, known commonly as the 'composite' type (Chapter 6). Archery continued to play a dominant role as a battlefield support arm. General Belisarius fought a number of critical battles against the spah, notably at Dara (530 CE) and Callinicum (531 CE). These battles are of interest in that at Dara, a larger Sassanian force was defeated by Belisarius, whereas at Callinicum it was Belisarius' larger force that was defeated by the spah.

Dara (530 CE). Kavad I (first reign 488–495 CE, second reign 498–531 CE) fought a number of battles against the Byzantine Empire, in 502–532 CE.[122] One of these critical battles took place at Dara in 530 CE. Kavad had dispatched General Firouz towards Dara to capture this strategic city. Procopius identifies the commander as a certain Mirranes (Mehran?) which Hughes speculates may be 'possibly equating to the Marzban of the Persian army'.[123] The Sassanian army that crossed the frontier in June 530 CE towards Dara was most likely in a state of high morale given their successful military encounters against the Romano-Byzantines up to that time.[124]

Defending Dara was Belisarius, one of the Western world's finest military leaders. Aware of the capabilities of the Sassanian cavalry, Belisarius prepared a system of ditches. The apparent purpose of these was to channel the inevitable cavalry attacks of his adversaries.[125] As noted by Greatrex, 'The trench system was to play a key role [in preventing Sassanian] cavalry from engaging the unreliable Roman infantry.'[126] Belisarius placed his infantry behind the main trench, which certainly proved an effective defence against frontal savaran attacks. The main trench was also the central or focal position of Belisarius' formations. In support of the infantry behind the main trench were the cavalry forces of Belisarius and Hermogenes. To the left of Belisarius were the cavalry of Sunicas and Algan (600 troops) and to the right were the cavalry of Simmas and Ascan (600 troops). The name 'Ascan' is of interest as it is a close cognate to *Ashkan*, which is an Iranian term for 'Parthian'. Positioned on the left wing or flank (to the left of the infantry) were the forces of Bouzes and his Romano-Byzantine cavalry alongside Pharas in command of 300 Herulian cavalry. The right flank or wing was also composed of Romano-Byzantine cavalry. Belisarius was planning to allow the Sassanian knights to attack and drive back his own cavalry (on the left and right flanks) to then strike them unexpectedly in their flanks and rear. Belisarius' infantry ensured that the Sassanian centre remained pinned in place. The total available forces for Belisarius were reported at 25,000 troops, which included 1,200 Huns (most likely horse archers) and 300 Heruls.[127]

Upon their arrival, the Sassanian forces encamped a short distance from their Romano-Byzantine adversaries. The right flank of the Sassanian formation was led by Peteyak with the left flank commanded by Barsham (Barsamenes). Less clear is the nature of the Sassanian 'infantry', which was certainly present at Dara. Procopius' negative characterization of the infantry implies that it was composed of lightly armed and poorly trained peasant levies. The Sassanians did also field heavy infantry (see Chapter 7), but it would appear that such forces were not present at Dara. The 'infantry' must have included a large number of foot archers, given the critical role this arm would play in the ensuing battle.

In the early part of the first day no major military action took place. Instead, both armies engaged in a sort of 'sitzkrieg', being content to just observe each other. In practice, Firouz was aware that the Romano-Byzantines ate around noon, with the Sassanian troops being accustomed to dining later in the day. Firouz calculated that if he could attack the Romans when they were still hungry, then he could attack them when they were at their weakest. This deduction of course soon proved invalid. Firouz attacked Belisarius by unleashing the savaran on the Sassanian right flank led by Peteyak. The savaran attacked the Romano-Byzantine left and soon the cavalry of Bouzes and Pharas began to fall back, but Peteyak decided to halt.[128] Perhaps the 'easiness' of the assault and the willingness of the Romano-Byzantine left to fall back so quickly made the Sassanians suspect that Belisarius had planned a trap for them. Another possibility is that Firouz may have been attempting to gauge the fighting capabilities of Belisarius' troops. Whatever the reason for their reluctance to pursue, this hesitation was to cost Peteyak dearly. As noted by Greatrex, the forces of Bouzes and Pharas 'employed the Scythian technique of suddenly wheeling about to face their pursuers, having initially given ground'.[129] Peteyak and his force were thrown back, forcing them to return to their original positions on the Sassanian right flank.

Shortly after the conclusion of that opening engagement, a young Sassanian warrior named Ardazan (Ardazanes) came forth to challenge the best of Belisarius' men to a pahlavan-style duel (Chapter 15). The challenge was accepted by a German named Andreas, who killed his Sassanian counterpart and also another Sassanian challenger who came forth. The end of these duels signalled the cessation of hostilities for the first day of combat.

The second day of the battle was literally a war of letters. Commanders of both sides dispatched letters hoping to entice each other to simply retire or accept battle under more favourable circumstances. Evidently both sides appreciated the military strength of the other and hoped for some kind of negotiated settlement to avoid casualties. This proved impossible, given Dara's coveted strategic status. The 'war of the letters' between Belisarius and Firouz availed nothing.

By the third day the 10,000-man zhayedan or javidan (Immortals), an elite savaran contingent, had arrived to join the battle. Firouz kept these as his tactical reserve to be thrust into the battle during its most critical juncture. Thanks to the arrival of the javidan, Firouz was able to use his augmented numbers (now totalling 40,000) to adopt a new tactic. He divided his forces into two equal parts. The first part was to engage the Romano-Byzantines and then retire to allow the second 'reserve' force to resume the battle. In this way, Firouz would be able to constantly keep Belisarius' forces engaged while having the luxury of relieving a large proportion of his troops for employment as dictated by fluid battlefield circumstances. The deployment of the force remained as before: Peteyak commanded the right flank and Barsham commanded the left flank. Firouz held the centre with the zhayedan stationed in this position, to be shifted to the right or left flanks in accordance with the unfolding battle.

The battle was finally started in the afternoon with the Sassanians moving closer towards Belisarius' forces to unleash their archery barrages.[130] The Romano-Byzantines did respond with a counter-barrage of their own, but according to Procopius 'the missiles of the barbarians flew much more quickly'.[131] Fortunately for Belisarius, the wind that day 'blew from their [Romano-Byzantine] side against the barbarians, and checked to a considerable degree the force of their arrows'.[132] Archery barrages were critical to the Sassanian battle doctrine, and it is clear that at Dara, the efficacy of this arm had been compromised. Firouz had hoped that his archery barrage would soften up Belisarius' forces for his primary attack: a deadly lance thrust by the savaran of the right wing (Peteyak) into the Romano-Byzantine left flank.

Peteyak's attack made considerable headway; the power and momentum of the savaran lance thrust forced Belisarius' left wing (comprising Bouzes and his cavalry) to give way and approach collapse. Despite this shock to his forces, Belisarius had planned his own deadly stratagem. Prior to the battle he had wisely heeded the advice of Pharas to quietly take positions on a nearby hill with his 300-strong Herulian cavalry.[133] This deployment was accomplished without detection by Firouz, and was to prove fatal to the Sassanians. As Peteyak and the savaran pursued the retreating forces of Bouzes, Pharas suddenly thrust into Peteyak's (right) flank and rear. Belisarius' pincers movement was completed when he unleashed Sunicas and Aigan to thrust into Peteyak's left flank. These flanking attacks caught the savaran by surprise, resulting in the loss of 3,000 warriors.[134] The survivors of Peteyak's failed attack retreated into the ranks of their infantry.

Up to this point, Firouz had held the javidan back, but now these were shifted to the left flank led by Barsham, who was also reinforced with a number of troops from his second line. Firouz was now preparing to deliver what he hoped would be the decisive blow. Unfortunately for the Sassanians, this deployment was duly detected by Belisarius which proved fatal to the Sassanians' intentions. Belisarius now shifted the troops of Sunicas and Aigan to join Simmas and Ascan. These combined forces (1,200 cavalry) were placed behind the infantry of the right flank.

Barsham and the javidan attacked and were successful at first, inflicting heavy casualties but, as before, Belisarius had anticipated this action. Timing his counterattack with remarkable precision, Belisarius sent his 1,200 cavalrymen into the javidan's right flank, effectively trapping that elite force within the Romano-Byzantine formations. Despite being doomed, the javidan refused to surrender.

The Romano-Byzantines were forced to cut them down to the last man. Barsham was also killed. This phase of the battle resulted in the loss of another 5,000 Sassanian warriors.[135]

With the battle now lost, Firouz ordered his forces to retreat from Dara. The Romano-Byzantines continued their strikes, but Belisarius ordered a halt to further pursuit. This was due to his awareness of the Sassanian ability to quickly organize and launch counterstrikes even as they retreated.

It is certainly true that Belisarius had scored a great victory at Dara, but the defeated Sassanian army had not been destroyed. As noted by Hughes, 'The clash at Dara highlights one of Belisarius' favourite tactics when fighting a battle. He was primarily a *defensive* commander.'[136] Hughes' assessment is indeed accurate: it was Firouz who had launched every major attack, with Belisarius having successfully anticipated and prepared for each of those engagements. Hughes also attributes the success of Belisarius at Dara to two additional factors.[137] The first was terrain: with the Sassanians intent on capturing the town of Dara, Belisarius was able to maximize his advantages by digging trenches. These did much to channel the attacks of the savaran. Second, Belisarius was able to observe the actions of the Sassanians, thanks to his position on slightly elevated ground. This allowed him to quickly devise specific counter-moves in anticipation of every Sassanian attack.

But as Belisarius was soon to learn, the Sassanian spah was a completely different force than that of the Goths he had fought against in Europe. The Sassanians quickly drew lessons from their defeats and, like the Romano-Byzantines, worked hard to improve their military performance and adapt to new military foes. This was to be demonstrated by the spah at the Battle of Callinicum.

Callinicum (531 CE). The Sassanian military had crossed the Euphrates River in 531 CE in a determined thrust into Commagene (modern-day northeast Turkey). Once again, it was Belisarius who was entrusted with combating the Sassanian attacks. The Sassanian force, led by Azarethes, was an all-cavalry formation composed of 10,000 savaran knights accompanied by 5,000 of their highly effective Lakhmid Arab allies led by al-Mundhir.[138] Belisarius' force was larger with 20,000 troops, comprising both cavalry and infantry recruited from Romano-Byzantine and auxiliary contingents. Facing a larger force, Azarethes opted to withdraw into Sassanian territory, but Belisarius was insistent on pursuing Azarethes and destroying his force. Belisarius and his army arrived at Callinicum to meet the Sassanian invasion force. To reach the Sassanian force, Belisarius had been forced to engage his troops in exhausting forced marches. As Easter Sunday was near, his troops had also been fasting. These factors must have compromised the fighting qualities of Belisarius' troops.

The armies of Azarethes and Belisarius lined up to face each other on Easter Sunday, 19 April 531 CE, with the Euphrates River flowing to their east. The terrain rose at it stretched westwards. Azarethes was positioned at the centre of his army with the best of the savaran. Similarly, Belisarius and his cavalry were positioned in the centre of his army. Azarethes dug a trench in front of his positions, much as Belisarius had at Dara a year before. To counter the Lakhmids, Belisarius placed 5,000 of his allied Ghassanid Arab cavalry on his extreme right flank. Standing next to the Ghassanids were the Lycaonian (Phrygian highlander) infantry. Next to the Lycaonians were situated the cavalry forces of Ascan, a veteran of the Battle of Dara. To Belisarius' left were two other veteran commanders from Dara, Simmas and Sunicas, who together led the Hun cavalry. Next to the Hun cavalry and adjacent to the Euphrates River was the formidable Romano-Byzantine infantry commanded by Peter, one of Emperor Justinian's bodyguards. It was these troops who helped Belisarius escape in the disaster that was about to unfold.

The battle opened with a mounted archery duel. This time the wind favoured the Persian archers, blowing in the direction of the Roman-Byzantine forces and increasing the velocity and penetrating power of the arrows. Further enhancing the Sassanian advantage was the superior speed of their archery, resulting in the firing of more missiles. Employing Scythian-style tactics against Simmas and Sunicas,[139] the savaran knights distracted Belisarius as to the Sassanians' true battlefield intentions. Azarethes successfully shifted the best of his savaran contingents (possibly elite units such as Shahanshah, Janvespar, etc.) to the left wing close to al-Mundhir. At Dara, Belisarius had successfully detected Firouz's shifting of the crack savaran to the Sassanian left wing. Belisarius' failure to detect this shift soon cost him the battle and nearly his life.

Azarethes struck swiftly: Al-Mundhir's warriors attacked and destroyed their Ghassanid rivals, allowing the savaran next to them to quickly occupy the high ground. With this action, Belisarius' lines were open to destruction by the savaran. It was now up to the Lycaonians and Ascan to brace for the inevitable savaran lance charge. Ascan fought heroically but he and his men were slain, including the Lycaonian phylarch (tribal chieftain) Abrus.[140] Many of the surviving Lycaonians broke ranks and fled in panic. Belisarius' lines continued to unravel as the charge of the savaran broke through the Hun and Byzantine infantry contingents. With a complete disaster imminent, Belisarius ordered his remaining troops to reposition themselves 90 degrees with the Euphrates River running behind them. The infantry was now ordered to stand close together to form a virtual wall to block the lance charges of the savaran. The Romano-Byzantine infantry in the front row locked their shields together with the row behind them placing their shields over their heads. According to Procopius: '[S]tanding shoulder to shoulder they kept themselves constantly massed in a small space, and they formed with their shields a rigid, unyielding barricade.'[141] Greatrex notes that Procopius is describing the *foulkon* formation discussed in the *Strategikon*.[142] Hughes notes that this formation was the equivalent of the Roman *testudo* (tortoise) which was designed to defend against enemy missile assaults.[143] As further noted by Hughes, these troops had formed up in a U-shape, using the Euphrates River to close the top of the "U".

Greatrex considers it unlikely that Belisarius' troops would have placed their lances forward to repel the attacks of the savaran.[144] For this, Belisarius depended on his foot archers. As Belisarius' remaining troops stood their ground, Romano-

Byzantine foot archers inside of the 'U' provided missile fire to disrupt the attacks of the savaran.[145] As reported by Procopius, it is at this juncture that Persian archery proved faster but weaker than Romano-Byzantine archery – which Procopius described as slower but more powerful (this description is discussed and analysed in more detail in Chapter 5). The effectiveness of Romano-Byzantine archery certainly helps explain, at least in part, why the savaran, despite repeated charges, were unable to destroy the remnant of Belisarius' army.

Interestingly, Procopius also reports that the Romano-Byzantines banged on their shields to disorient the horses of the savaran. The shielding tactics of the Romano-Byzantine troops proved successful, as the savaran were prevented from breaking through Belisarius' line to reach the Euphrates. Belisarius had nevertheless lost the battle and could not hold out indefinitely. He and his surviving troops escaped to safety across the Euphrates.

Hughes attributes the success of Azarethes against Belisarius to the following four factors.[146] First, unlike Dara, the Sassanian army was not constrained in its tactics by trying to capture a city. Previously, Belisarius was aware that the Sassanian army intended to capture Dara and made his preparations accordingly. This entailed constructing ditches that would channel the savaran's attacks to his left or right flanks and to launch counterthrusts against the Sassanian horsemen. Belisarius' failure to secure an elevated observation point further contributed to his defeat. At Dara, Belisarius had been able to detect Firouz's shifting of cavalry to his flanks prior to each attack, but he could not do so at Callinicum. Azarethes shifted his savaran corps to support Al-Mundhir in the thrust against Belisarius' Ghassanids. As a result, when Azarethes struck, Belisarius had no counterattack prepared to stave off this attack. This related to the third failure of Belisarius: he did not have a reserve force in case his opponents succeeded in punching through his lines. Finally, Azarethes was able to count on the full mobility of his forces without being constrained by the vulnerabilities of the slower moving Sassanian infantry.

Nevertheless, despite Procopius' description of heavy losses to the savaran during the last stages of the battle, Zachariah casts doubt on this narrative. According to Zachariah, the Romans 'turned and fled before the Persian attack. Many fell into the Euphrates and were drowned, and others were killed.'[147] Malalas reports that Belisarius fled by boat while it was Sunicas and Simmas who dismounted along with their troops to join Peter's infantry in fending off the savaran assaults.[148] Procopius reports that Belisarius joined his infantry to fight off the savaran, to then withdraw with his surviving troops across the Euphrates. According to Hughes, 'it is believed that Procopius did not give the true version of events, possibly in order to defend Belisarius from criticism'.[149] It is possible that despite Belisarius' '90 degree' order, shielding tactics, and archery fire, a significant number of surviving Romano-Byzantine troops may have been lost during the final savaran charges. Another possibility is that Belisarius remained with his army so long as it was able to withstand the savaran's charges (and in doing so killing and wounding many of the attackers); but when the savaran broke the Roman-Byzantine line, Belisarius made good his escape across the Euphrates.

In any case, it is certain that Justinian was unsatisfied with the performance of his general. After an inquiry, Belisarius was dismissed from his post as *Magister Militum per Orientem*.[150] Despite the victory at Callinicum, Kavad too was dissatisfied with the performance of his general Azarethes, mainly due to the high cost in casualties.

Pursuit of the Enemy

The Sassanians and the Romano-Byzantines appear to have had similar rules concerning the pursuit of defeated adversaries. Specifically, and as evidenced in the writings of Procopius, both the Sassanians[151] and the Romano-Byzantines[152] respected the right of fugitives to escape a battlefield disaster; and, relatedly, both recognized that one should not endeavour to destroy the whole of a defeated army. It would seem that the antagonists had taken to heart an old maxim from the Caucasus: 'Never force the mouse into a corner for that same mouse will then transform into a lion.'[153]

Undoubtedly the experience of Pirouz, who recklessly pursued the 'fleeing' Hephthalite forces in Central Asia in 484 CE (Chapter 12), must have profoundly affected the formulation of Sassanian military doctrine. As noted earlier in Chapter 8, one of the virtues of a strong commander is his ability to exercise caution in battle. It is in this regard that Firdowsi, writing in the *Shahname*, provides a strong warning against reckless pursuit of 'defeated' enemies:

> *Cho to poshte doshman bebinee be chiz*
> *Mataz va mapardaz ham jaye tiz*
> *Nabayad ke iman shavi az kamin*
> *Sepah bashad andar daro dashto keen.*[154]

Firdowsi describes a situation where the enemy appears to be fleeing, i.e. when one sees the 'backs of the enemy' (*Cho to poshte doshman bebinee*). It is at this juncture that one must be cautious and refrain from charging the enemy (*Mataz va mapardaz*). Complacency is dangerous in this case in that 'one must not become/feel secure from ambush(es)' (*Nabayad ke iman shavi az kamin*) as the enemy forces are most likely at large (*Sepah bashad andar*). Interestingly, Procopius corroborates Firdowsi regarding the reckless pursuit, especially in the aftermath of the defeat and death of Pirouz in 484 CE: 'As a result of this experience [the defeat of 484 CE] a law was established among the Persians that, while marching in hostile territory, they should never engage in any pursuit, even if it should happen that the enemy had been driven back by force.'[155]

Ambuscades and Raids against Enemy Camps

The spah had developed a consistent doctrine with respect to the springing of ambushes against enemy forces. Favoured places of ambush would be typically well covered with foliage or other types of cover.[156] The ambuscade zone would also be favoured if it had ready access to water supplies, as this could prove vital over prolonged periods of time.

The action of springing the ambush against the arriving (and unsuspecting) enemy was to be as well-planned and calculated as possible in order to maximize its impact. It was also important that nearby animals should not be startled prior to the attack, as this could prematurely give away the ambush party's position and dangerously compromise its mission.

Warriors selected for ambuscade missions were to be of the highest calibre by being battle-experienced and courageous but also balanced with caution and clear thinking during battle. Such troops were to be especially resilient and not overcome by habits such as sneezing, sighing, coughing, yelling or crying out, as these could prove especially dangerous by alerting the unsuspecting enemy of an ambush. Likewise, the horses of the savaran on an ambuscade mission were to be of a select type not prone to whinnying and making other loud sounds.

The following four situations would prompt the ambush party to attack:[157] (1) failure of the enemy to send regular scouts; (2) dereliction by the enemy with respect to guard duties; (3) other types of overall carelessness by the enemy's vanguards and primary forces (i.e. allowing their steeds to roam and graze in an unsupervised fashion); and (4) extremities of the weather. With respect to the latter, the surprise attack could be sprung at extreme heat or cold, which could add to the enemy's commotion during the attack. Once the ambush was sprung, the attackers would form into groups. Each member of the ambush party was to be fully cognizant of his role, able to display exceptional speed at his task, and avoid any form of 'lingering or hesitation' in the performance of his duties.[158] With respect to 'lingering', Dinawari warns attackers against the taking of booty and spoils.[159] Put simply, the raiders were to strike as rapidly and decisively as possible without becoming bogged down or 'distracted' in activities unrelated to the mission.

In addition to ambuscades, the spah would dispatch personnel to partake in surprise 'commando'-type missions against the enemy camp. The best time to strike was judged to be at midnight or at the darkest time of the evening, when visibility would be at its lowest.[160] The 'commando' force would (in general) comprise two groups. The first was to remain at the periphery of the enemy camp with the second tasked with the more dangerous mission of quietly slipping into the centre of the enemy camp. Infiltration was also recommended if the enemy was encamped nearby a noisy river and/or in circumstances where a strong (and noisy) wind was blowing. Such natural sounds could help mask the sounds made by Sassanian infiltrators. The attack would be initiated by those infiltrating units already in place in the centre of the enemy camp. The sounds of commotion and fighting would be the signal for the warriors stationed at the periphery of the enemy camp to join in the attack. There are also recommendations for the attackers to engage in psychological warfare as they fall upon the enemy. This consisted of shouting in the enemy's language, e.g. 'O Warriors, hasten, hasten! He is already killed, your chief so and so! and many are slaughtered! and many are flying! ... Oh man! for God's sake have mercy on me!'[161] It is clearly evident that such 'messages' were meant to amplify feelings of distress and confusion in the enemy, who was presumably already in disarray as a result of the surprise attack.

Interestingly, an example of this type of Sassanian doctrine can be seen in the Safavid armies of Shah Abbas I (r. 1587–1629) in the military operation that liberated Tabriz from Ottoman Turkish occupation on 21 October 1603.[162] Shah Abbas selected his best troops to engage in a 'commando' operation, by tasking his men to quietly infiltrate occupied Tabriz and slay a number of Ottoman sentries. The Safavid commandos were then soon joined by another group of 500 crack warriors who had arrived in Tabriz wearing civilian clothes and pretending to be interested in commerce![163] These same 'merchants' succeeded in distracting the attention of the Ottoman garrison from Tabriz's peripheries, where Shah Abbas was assembling the main Safavid army. Having successfully penetrated Tabriz with his commandos and 'merchants', Shah Abbas unleashed his main army of 6,000 warriors. Abbas' attack was coordinated to take place after the commandos and 'merchants' had slain large numbers of Ottoman sentries at Tabriz's critical entrance gates. The main force entering the city was already facing an enemy in disarray as the commandos and 'merchants' had already been wreaking havoc among the occupying Ottoman troops. Tabriz was liberated in 21 October 1603[164] after twenty days of hand-to-hand combat in Tabriz's streets which led to the surrender of the remainder of the Ottoman troops.[165] Shah Abbas' tactics resembled Sassanian methods (albeit on a larger scale) in that he first infiltrated the enemy establishment with commandos and then unleashed the main assault force from the periphery once the commandos had already begun attacking the unsuspecting Ottoman troops.

Ditches and Traps

The formidable Romano-Byzantines were quick to exploit any opportunity where the Sassanians had been careless in the guarding of their military camps.[166] Army camps typically laid out iron traps in those places most vulnerable to enemy infiltration tactics or surprise attacks.[167] The Sassanians were cognizant of the threat of these types of attacks against their camps. They were also very adept at digging trenches which were strewn with concealed traps. Deep trenches or *khandaq* were dug on battlefields and also utilized for the defence of fortified structures, cities and even long 'Maginot'-type defence walls[168] (see Chapter 13).

This strategy of combining trenches with traps was used with considerable success against the troops of Belisarius in 528 CE during a military engagement in the Thannuris desert. As noted by Pigulevskaya, the Sassanians had prepared a series of 'triangular fences' that were artfully camouflaged to conceal them from the enemy's view.[169] When Belisarius ordered his forces to assault the Sassanian positions, they rushed forward in what appeared to be flat terrain only to fall into the Sassanians' prepared ditches strewn with traps. Belisarius and his troops fled the battlefield and the Sassanians mopped up in the ditches, killing any Romano-Byzantine troops who were caught in the traps.[170]

The use of traps can be seen in the very late Sassanian era during the empire's last stand against the Arabo-Muslims in the Battle of Jalula in 651 CE (see Chapter 17). To protect the mass of raw recruits now swelling the badly battered spah, General Firoozan had excavated a large ditch and filled it with iron spikes in what proved to be a successful bid to dissuade the Arab forces from attacking. After an eight-month 'sitzkrieg', the Arab commander, Numan, engaged in a brilliant strategy of guile by enticing Sassanian forces to abandon their defences in favour of pursuing a cavalry force. Numan's forces ambushed the pursuers, inflicting heavy casualties, and the surviving Sassanian troops fled back to their original positions, only to run into the very same defences that had been laid out to protect them![171]

Another type of battlefield defence weapon were caltrops – small metallic balls embedded with spikes.[172] It was a weapon which was probably adopted from the Romans. The use of caltrops constituted a sort of 'mine warfare' meant to make an area impassable to enemy cavalry.[173] When strewn across a field they could severely injure the hooves of cavalry horses.[174] According to Sami, caltrops were among the most effective weapons used by the Sassanians in the Battle of Qadissiyah in 637 CE, successfully blunting attacks by the Arab cavalry.[175]

Resisting Invasions: Scorched-Earth Tactics and Cavalry Raids

As noted previously by Dinawari, Sassanian commanders were advised to seek battle only after gaining numerical superiority over the enemy force. This recommendation, however, changed drastically if Iran itself was being invaded.[176] In the event of invasion it was acceptable for the army to undertake offensive action even if it was numerically inferior to the enemy.[177] The first line of defence against invasions could often be 'military colonists' that the spah had already settled along the empire's sensitive frontiers (Chapter 2 and 13).

As enemy forces advanced deeper inside the empire's territory, the spah had the option of engaging in scorched-earth tactics,[178] which could be applied in times of absolute necessity, especially when invaded by numerically superior foes. In such a scenario the Sassanians would destroy all food sources by burning crops and farmlands.[179] Dikes could also be opened to flood vast areas to impede the enemy's advance.[180] The Sassanians engaged in precisely such tactics against Julian the Apostate's invasion of 363 CE. As Julian's forces marched through the lowlands of Phissenia the Sassanians breached the local dams to transform the terrain into a marsh.[181] In practice, the Sassanians would often combine scorched-earth tactics with 'Cossack'-style hit-and-run cavalry attacks. Such tactics were also employed during Julian's invasion.

Julian the Apostate (363 CE): The spah defends the empire. Julian 'the Apostate' (r. 361–363 CE) began to make preparations for a massive invasion of the Sassanian Empire shortly after his ascension as emperor in 361 CE. A nervous Ctesiphon dispatched a diplomatic delegation (possibly *dabirs*) to discuss peace terms with Julian, who duly rejected them. After declaring that he would recapture Singara, Julian ordered the Armenian king Arshak to assemble a vast army and join him at a locale that had yet to be designated. Julian also ordered the construction of a powerful fleet at Samostasa. These ships would accompany his invasion force as the latter advanced towards Ctesiphon along the Euphrates and Tigris rivers.

Julian's primary strategy was to divide his invasion forces in two. Julian himself led a force of 35,000 men into the Persian heartland. The second force of 30,000 was led by Procopius into Armenia. Having assembled his forces Julian set out from Antioch on 5 March 363 CE. Reaching Callinicum on 27 March, he received a delegation of Arab chieftains the next day.[182] It would appear, however, that the majority of Arab scout parties and irregular parties may have sided with the Sassanians rather than the Romans.

From April through June Julian was basically on the march, joined by his fleet along the Euphrates. An interesting report notes that a hurricane struck and sank some of Julian's grain-ships[183] (12 April).[184]

Ferrill has argued that Julian's decision to divide his forces in two may have contributed to the disaster that was soon to befall the Romans.[185] Jalali highlights the importance of the elite savaran units (i.e. zhayedan/javidan, pushtighban, etc.) in the spah's ability to defeat Julian's invasion.[186] Ironically, the spah's savaran would now be fighting against former 'ex-savaran' comrades led by Shapur II's brother Prince Hormuzd. The latter and his savaran knights had defected to Julian during the reign of Constantine I (r. 306–337 CE) and would be an important component of Julian's 363 CE invasion force. Hormuzd would in fact lead the left wing of the Roman cavalry as Julian marched into Persia.[187] Julian may have calculated that Hormuzd would counterbalance the strengths of the Sassanian savaran. The first savaran-versus-savaran clash appears to have taken place sometime later in April (c. 22–24). In this encounter pro-Roman Prince Hormuzd had been leading a reconnaissance force which was then ambushed in a surprise attack by the spah's savaran led by a certain 'Suren' and pro-Sassanian Arabs led by Podosaces.[188] The term *suren* is in reference to the hereditary title of one of the Sassanian Empire's seven top noble clans (i.e. 'Suren-Pahlav'). This person had been entrusted with the post of second in command[189] or eiran-spahbod by Shapur II.

Julian's invasion went well, at first. He successfully entered into the Mesopotamian heartland, accompanied by a thousand-ship armada sailing alongside his forces on the Euphrates River towards Ctesiphon. Julian defeated a Sassanian army defending the capital, but Sassanian troops withdrew in good order into the safety of the city. It is not clear if the Romans had achieved a resounding victory. Ammianus (who was present at the battle) claims that 2,500 Sassanians were killed in exchange for just seventy Roman troops.[190] This is contradicted by Sozomen's *Historia Ecclesiastica* which states that 'at daybreak, the two armies engaged in battle, and after much bloodshed on both sides the Romans returned by the river, and encamped near Ctesiphon'.[191] Tabari reports that Julian actually captured Ctesiphon but was then ejected by Shapur II who recaptured the capital.[192] It is not clear why the reports of Ammianus, Sozomen and Tabari diverge so significantly, but it is possible that while the Romans had prevailed, their victory may not have been as spectacular as Ammianus had reported.

The core of the Sassanian spah, the elite savaran and Shapur II himself remained at large as they were not at Ctesiphon. The Sassanians opted to engage in a strategy of mobile and fluid defence. This was the most militarily sound strategy as Julian's forces had proven to be too formidable to engage in close-quarters hand-to-hand set-piece type battles; the Sassanian armoured or 'gladiator' type infantry at Ctesiphon had been overpowered by their Roman infantry counterparts and forced to retreat. Julian attempted to attack Ctesiphon but soon abandoned this effort given the strength of the city's defences (Chapter 13).

As events soon demonstrated, the Sassanians favoured method of combatting the Romans were Central Asian-style cavalry tactics of fluid movement combined with lance charges. It would appear that the Sassanians preferred these lightning lance strikes, which allowed them to quickly disengage and make way for the archers to do their work. Despite the Sassanians' reluctance to engage the Romans with the full weight of their army, Julian got his way and forced Shapur II into a major battle at Maranga on 22 July 363 CE. To avoid being flanked by the savaran, Julian's forces adopted a crescent-shaped formation. This tactic proved overwhelmingly successful, granting the Romans a clear tactical victory. Forcing their adversaries to fight them in close-quarters combat proved key to the Romans' success, and was precisely the type of engagement the Sassanians sought to avoid. The 'super-heavy' savaran knights were certainly formidable given their increased armour protection, however the efficacy of their lance charge was contingent on them being able to gain enough momentum before reaching the Roman lines. Instead at Maranga, Julian had succeeded in forcing the spah's super heavy savaran knights into prolonged stationary-style hand-to-hand combat against the Classical world's most formidable infantry forces, the Romans. However, as noted by Ammianus Marcellinus, Sassanian armoured knights, though dangerous and formidable, lacked long-term endurance during battle.[193] The knights were well trained and equipped for close-quarters combat, but these warriors were mainly intended as shock troops meant to dislocate enemy lines or break through them. Julian also negated the efficacy of the spah's armoured horse archers and foot archers; apparently the Romans did succeed in closing the distance between them and the Sassanian archers, forcing them to engage in close-quarters combat.

Mention must be made of the large numbers of Arab and Khazar auxiliary troops in Julian's cavalry.[194] The Turkic Khazars, well-accustomed to the steppe cavalry tradition, must have proved valuable to Julian as these could (at the very least) be highly effective in countering the savaran's horse archers. Roman infantry contingents had also devised tactics to counter the super heavy savaran knights. The Romans attempted to dive under the horses of the savaran just as they were bearing down upon their lines. The Roman infantry would then attempt to stab the lancers' steeds from underneath. Julian's Arab contingents were those who had survived Shapur II's counterstrikes against their earlier raids into Iran. While Arab light cavalry and infantry were incapable of defeating the savaran, these tough desert warriors could prove highly valuable in the role of auxiliary troops. In contrast, the Sassanian elephant corps does not appear to have made much of an impression on the fighting, although elephants could have been useful as elevated archery platforms.

Despite his success at Maranga, Julian had clearly failed to destroy the military power of Shapur II. The spah with the highly mobile savaran knights and horse archers simply retired after Maranga to regroup. From this point on the Sassanians would fight on their own terms. Jalali notes that 'Shapur II separated the elite Royal savaran units from the rest of the spah, probably 10,000 of these were then assigned to accompany Shapur II'.[195] The role of the elite savaran was to pursue Julian's forces and to strike at the Roman columns as they advanced, with the objective of throwing the invasion forces into disarray.[196] Shapur II had essentially withdrawn the combat infantry and foot archers of the spah in favour of the elite savaran knights, who became the primary strike force against Julian's forces. It is likely that by this time the majority of Roman combat losses had been due to Sassanian lance charges and missiles delivered from a safe distance on horseback.

Interestingly, Ammianus Marcellinus provides the impression that the Romans consistently beat off the savaran's attacks.[197] Other Classical sources provide a very different account of events. Festus, for example, reported that savaran horsemen were attacking Roman forces at the latter's 'front ... rear ... flanks'.[198] This would suggest that the savaran horsemen were attacking from multiple directions and then disengaging. Sassanian commanders would launch these forces at any time they chose, with Julian helpless to prevent their strikes from occurring. It would appear that at this stage the Sassanians were battering the Romans with 'Cossack-style' raids not unlike the attacks by Cossack units on Napoleon's Grande Armee during the French retreat through Russia in 1812. Augustine has provided a concise description of what Julian's increasingly beleaguered troops had to endure at the hands of the savaran: '[F]rom all sides the enemy was attacking the (Roman) soldiery ... to such an extent did the Persians have them [Romans] in their grip.'[199] The Sassanians had turned the tables against Julian: Shapur was now forcing Julian's army into a battle of attrition it could not win. Julian could choose to remain in Persia, but he would have to pay a heavy price: the ongoing savaran raids would continue to take their toll on his forces. In addition, it would only be a matter of time before Julian's supplies ran low with his constantly harassed forces stranded deep inside enemy territory. It was during one of these raids that the end came for Julian. Just four days after the Battle of Maranga, a force of savaran lancers attacked the Roman columns on 26 June 363 CE. The right Roman flank collapsed,[200] prompting Julian (sans armour) to lead a counterattack to beat off the savaran. In the ensuing battle, a spear was thrust at Julian, mortally wounding him; he died shortly afterwards. This forced the Roman army, now led by Jovian, to sign a humiliating peace treaty as the precondition for extricating themselves from Persia.

Julian's invasion had failed for almost the same reasons that previous Roman invasions had failed. While Julian's forces could defeat the Sassanian combat infantry and elephants, he, like other Roman emperors and military leaders who had failed before him, did not have the capability to dominate the savaran on the battlefield. In those instances when Roman arms had defeated the savaran, the Romans had either negated their mobility (e.g. Galerius in Armenia in 298 CE) and/or had succeeded in getting them to engage the Roman infantry in prolonged face-to-face combat.

One final point that may be discussed is the question of casualties. Sassanian losses are often reported as having been heavy during Julian's campaign, which is highly likely given the desperate situation the spah was facing in defending the very existence of the empire. A related question therefore is that of Roman losses during this adventure. These were heavy as well, at least according to John Lydus de Mensibus, who notes that on the day of Julian's death 'he [Julian] did not even have 20,000 men, when before he had led 170,000'.[201] Tabari does not give the total number of troops in Julian's army composed of Roman, Khazar and Arab contingents, but gives the very large number of 170,000 Arabs serving Julian.[202] These reports of large numbers of invading troops have yet to be accepted by Western historians. Whatever the actual numbers of Roman losses, the majority of these may have been due to the savaran raids and supply shortages.

Legacy of Shapur II. Scorched-earth tactics combined with cavalry raids were to be implemented centuries after the Sassanians by future Iranian armies. Such tactics were to reach their zenith during the Safavid era (1501–1722; nearly nine centuries after the Sassanians) against the invading armies of the Ottoman Empire. Like the Sassanians, the Safavids made very effective use of their crack *qizilbash* cavalry for harassing invading Ottoman forces, especially during the invasions of Iran by Suleiman the Magnificent (r. 1520–1566) in 1532, 1548 and 1554. The vast size of Ottoman forces invading Azerbaijan and the Caucasus (i.e. khanates of Irvan, Sheki, Baku, Nakhchevan, etc.) often forced the Safavid military to engage in scorched-earth tactics. This proved highly effective as the massive Ottoman armies would be left stranded inside Iranian territory with no food, water or shelter. The Safavids would poison wells, destroy crops as well as food supplies and demolish all dwelling places. These measures ensured that invading forces would be prevented from living off occupied Iranian territory. Shah Tahmasp (r. 1524–1576), for example, devastated a gigantic area spanning 160,000–200,000 square kilometres during the massive invasions of Iran from 1534 through 1555 CE by the Ottoman military machine.[203] Shah Abbas embarked on an even greater scorched-earth project against the Ottoman invasions of 1606–1607 in which the entire landmass between Tabriz in Iran's Azerbaijan province and Erzurum in eastern Anatolia was virtually depopulated of approximately 300,000 people including Azerbaijanis, Armenians and Kurds.[204]

Military colonists in border regions. Another effective tactic utilized by the Sassanians was to settle warlike tribes and even defeated and conquered enemy warriors along the empire's sensitive borders.[205] Khosrow I Anoushirvan, for example, did settle military colonists as part of his overall system of enhancing the empire's military effectiveness against invasions.[206] He settled the aforementioned Khazars as well as Alan and Abkhaz warriors in the Caucasus to help protect the empire's northern borders in that region,[207] which was also protected by the formidable Wall of Derbent (Chapter 13). The spah would also place its own regular garrisons among the recently settled foreign contingents.[208] Khosrow

Anoushirvan also drafted restless warlike tribes from Iran's interior for border guard duty, notably the Parizi tribe of mountainous Kerman.[209] This Sassanian technique of settling indigenous warlike Iranian tribes along sensitive borders was to be replicated by the Safavids. A prime example of this is Shah Abbas who settled Kurds from western Iran along Iran's northeast borders in Khorasan to guard against Uzbek raiders from Central Asia.[210]

Treatment of Noncombatants by the Spah in Wartime

Jalali has provided a succinct overview of the spah's policies with respect to non-combatants by noting that 'warriors were to advance in an orderly fashion and to refrain from violating the rights of the people and to avoid inflicting damages against the properties and possessions of individuals during their military campaigns'.[211] The *Shahname* provides a glimpse into the policies implemented during the reign of Ardashir I Babakan to ensure that citizen's rights and possessions would not be violated during the spah's campaigns. Note the following two verses in the *Shahname*:

> *Nabayad be heech Darveesh ranj*
> [No Darveesh [Sufi/mystic] must suffer
> *Har Ankas ke oo hast Yazdan-parast*
> [regardless of who that person is O worshipper of the Angels]

Such attitudes are essentially an extension of the ancient Iranian knightly pahlavan and *javanmardi* traditions as expostulated in Chapter 15. The spah would assign dezhban officers in each gund division to ensure that warriors would (1) inflict no harm upon urban civilians and farmers during the campaigns; and (2) to severely punish those troops who harmed and/or harassed noncombatants.[212] As noted by Tabari in reference to the dezhbans of Hormuzd IV, '[T]he army was ordered to keep away from farms and to avoid harming the peasants ... all who violated these orders were to be reprimanded.'[213] The *Toqi'ate Anoushirvan* even emphasized that 'as long as they [Christians and Jews] are not involved in mutiny or conspiracy they should be safe'.[214]

Unfortunately however, there were incidents in which the second and third principles cited by Tabari were violated. One example of this is seen in the late Sassanian era during the long war between the Sassanian and Byzantine Empires, when General Shahrbaraz conquered Jerusalem in 614 CE. Shahrbaraz and his local Jewish allies then engaged in the harsh treatment and massacres of the conquered city's Christians. However, modern scholarship (notably the archaeological survey of Gideon Avni) has questioned the accuracy of accounts claiming the widespread destruction of Jerusalem's churches following Shahrbaraz's conquest (see discussion in Chapter 16). In the overall sense, the spah had clear rules of conduct regarding the treatment of civilians, but the implementation (or violation) of these rules would depend on the decisions of the commander in chief in the theatre.

Chapter 10

Logistics and Support

The Sassanians developed a very sophisticated and effective system of logistics for the support of their troops, who could be called upon to fight on different fronts. The Sassanians also developed effective medical and veterinarian support systems for use in times of peace and war.

Logistics
The spah was often engaged in major campaigns in the Caucasus, Anatolia, Central Asia and the Roman Near East. The spah had to not only cope with vast distances but also with a diverse range of climates and terrain. These factors necessitated the formation of a highly effective logistics and support system for the provision of supplies, food, fodder and military equipment during the spah's campaigns. Care was taken to ensure that the armed forces would take necessary supplies as opposed to deploying with masses of redundant baggage and caravans carrying cargo of little military use.

Roads and transport. Each unit in general had three broad means for transport. These were chariots, wagons of several types, and a third group broadly composed of elephants or camels (or both).[1] Prisoners of war could also be pressed into service to assist in transport duties (see Chapter 11).

Foodstuffs. When the spah was on campaign, attention was given to the equitable distribution of food supplies such as milk, bread and beef.[2] Shares of food rations would be increased by at least one ration during actual battle days.[3] Mention must be made in this regard of the Persian innovation of the cylindrical clay oven, with origins dating to around 2,000 years ago. This was used to bake the *nagara* (Old Persian: naked) bread, which was to become known as *naan*, which means 'bread' in Persian. As noted by Marks, the *naan-e-sangak* (baked over heated river gravel) with its soft yet toasty-crunchy flavour, was 'For generations ... the standard bread of the Persian army. Each soldier carried a bag of flour and a small bag of pebbles, which could be heated alone or merged with those of other soldiers, on which to cook his dough.'[4]

Thus the naan-e sangak, which remains popular among Iranians, has its roots in the ancient military history of Iran. The naan-e sangak was in essence an efficient system of self-sufficiency for each soldier while on campaign, especially if logistics became strained due to long distances or enemy attacks on supply lines. Interestingly, Iranian soldiers were reported as carrying pieces of the naan-e sangak as well as small sacks of rice during the early days of the Iran-Iraq war as the Iranian army worked hard to reorganize its logistics system in the aftermath of the 1979 revolution.[5] The Persian naan has spread throughout the

Middle East, Central Asia and the Caucasus over the millennia in a great variety of breads and flavors.[6] Few realize its connections to the Sassanian spah and the Iranian armies of antiquity.

Access to food supplies may have been one of the factors that assisted the Sassanians' defeat of Julian's invasion of Persia in 363 CE. According to Kistler and Lair, just as the Roman army was running short of food supplies (after the Battle of Maranga), the spah was being regularly supplied from Ctesiphon,[7] which Julian had failed to conquer. The Sassanian retention of Ctesiphon allowed Shapur II to have access to vital food supplies. This was a major factor in allowing the spah to pursue and harass Roman forces stranded in Persia and to kill off stragglers from Julian's army. Kistler and Lair's analysis makes clear that no matter how well an army is trained and led, lack of provisions for supplies (in case things go awry) can spell doom. Dodgeon and Lieu have noted of the link between Julian's supply problems and Sassanian scorched-earth tactics.[8]

Offices of the eiran-ambaraghbad and zynpt. The Sassanians developed a system of *ambaragh* (magazines) and *ganz* (arsenals).[9] The eiran-ambaraghbad was responsible for ensuring that all magazines and arsenals were at their maximum level of efficiency and readiness to ensure that the spah would not be caught unprepared in case of attacks by the Romans or Central Asian nomads.[10] When the spah mobilized for war, the eiran-ambaraghbad was to supervise (a) the extraction and distribution of these weapons; (b) ensure their rapid delivery to military units; and (c) supervise the return of all weapons to their respective inventories.[11] The importance of this office is highlighted by the fact that persons designated for this post hailed from the seven upper noble clans of the Sassanian empire.[12]

The largest number of ambaragh, ganz and all other types of military storage and depot facilities were located in close proximity to the eastern (or Central Asian) and the entire western (Romano-Byzantines and the Arabs to the southwest) frontiers.[13] These military storage areas were critical to the spah's mobilization, especially when the intention was to strike into enemy territory. Given the strategic importance of these military establishments to Ctesiphon, the Sassanians often placed garrisons at these locales to provide maximum security. The civilian sector greatly benefited from this arrangement which in at least two cases led to the establishment of thriving metropolitan centres. One example is the city of Anbar located in modern day Iraq, which was a major storage depot for the spah's headquarters facing the Romano-Byzantines and the Arabs (to the southwest). Anbar was a major storage facility for weapons, foodstuffs and equestrian equipment and it was here where the spah would turn to distribute weapons to its troops in the western theatre when war with Rome was imminent.[14]

Interestingly, there was also a second city named Anbar located in close proximity to modern-day Balkh in Central Asia, which apparently performed the same military function as its Mesopotamian counterpart. The eastern Anbar however, was primarily a base against the Turks and their Hephthalite vassals by the late sixth and early seventh centuries CE.[15] Both the eastern and western Anbar facilities were so highly regarded by the spah that the supervision of these were placed under military leaders of the empire's top clans.[16] The word *anbar* means 'storage facility' or simply 'storage' in modern Persian.

Lukonin has identified another office entitled *zynpt* which was responsible for the Sassanian throne's imperial arsenals.[17] Jalali notes that the zynpt oversaw a very limited domain (imperial arsenals) as opposed to the eiran-ambaraghbad (responsible for the entire array of the spah's arsenals). It is possible that the eiran-ambaraghbad supervised the functions of the zynpt.[18] Interestingly, Tafazzoli uses the terms *zynpt* and *zenbed* interchangeably and translates both as meaning 'chief of the armaments'.[19] It is not clear if this definition denotes a wider category of responsibility (the entire armed forces and the imperial arsenals) or just the imperial arsenals, as Lukonin and Jalali have suggested.

Office of the akhorbad and akhoramar. The office of the *akhorbad* was responsible for the welfare, supervision and readiness of all of the military's inventory of animals: horses for the savaran, beasts of burden (i.e. mules, non-combat horses, etc.), and battle elephants. The akhorbad was expected to have all beasts combat-ready and at the maximum level of preparedness, even during peacetime. The akhorbad worked closely with the *akhoramar*. The latter was responsible for maintaining detailed files on all animals within the spah's inventory as well as all accounting-cost details related in their upkeep.[20]

Medical Support

The medical division of the spah was considered as one of the most important sections of that establishment.[21] The medical units were responsible for the provision of health care to troops in times of peace and war, treatment of wounds during battles, and veterinary care for horses and other animals (i.e. elephants) (see *stor-bizishk* below). According to Imam-Shustari:

> Medical and veterinarian personnel accompanied the Sassanian military during times of war ... in Iran there was a Divan [reference tome] known as 'Divan Iran Dorost-bad' which dealt with healthcare [and] instructions for doctors and treatment of diseases. A copy of this Divan would accompany every military division and doctors. The main duty [of medical units] besides treatment of wounds and healing the diseases of the troops was the supervision of the overall healthcare of all military personnel. This tradition of military healthcare was to continue into the Islamic era ...[22]

Medical doctors were often placed on military bases in peacetime and would accompany the spah during military campaigns. These doctors had readied support staff, medical instruments and tents to receive the wounded.[23] These facilities would be prepared to receive the wounded during and after battle for treatment of wounds by swords, spears, arrows, maces, etc.[24] As noted previously, the medical staff were also responsible for ensuring that the troops were in the best of health during peacetime, as the spah wanted its armed forces to be at its maximum level of battle readiness in case war broke out.[25]

Military doctors were often supervised by committees of the magi, who often hailed from the families of the nobility. There was also a cadre of herbal specialists who practiced medicine in the spah. Doctors and herbal specialists were generally of two types: (1) those whose knowledge derived from a master-apprentice relationship and practical experience; and (2) practitioners of more advanced methods of medicine and herbs whose knowledge had been obtained in the universities of larger cities located in Hamedan (in northwest Iran), Rayy (near modern Tehran) and the Persepolis region further south.[26]

Military medicine also benefited from Roman prisoners of war who were often put to service. Khosrow Anoushirvan also commissioned the translation of Indian, Aramaic, and Greek texts into Pahlavi, which greatly benefited Sassanian military medicine. These texts were used in conjunction with native Iranian medical practices in the major university of Jundi-Shapur which among many of its departments taught medicine specifically geared to the treatment of military personnel. Graduates from the latter programme at Jundi-Shapur were known as the *atravan* and were specifically trained to serve with the spah.[27] The tradition of military medicine was to survive the overthrow of the Sassanian empire and continue into the Islamic era.[28]

Stor-bizishk: veterinary care. The office of the *stor-bizishk* was responsible for the health care and vitality of the savaran's horses.[29] The Middle Persian term can variously mean veterinarian, draft-animal physician or veterinary surgeon. This made the office an especially important one as the savaran depended upon it for the delivery of powerful and healthy horses.[30] The stor-bizishk would accompany the spah in times of war and in peacetime visited all major military establishments to care for horses in need of medical attention.[31]

Interestingly, the stor-bizishk was well-versed in herbal remedies most beneficial for equestrian health.[32] In this endeavour, there was also a staff who worked with the stor-bizishk's office, notably specialists whose job was the collection and study of herbal substances best suited for equestrian health and medical care.[33] There were also schools in the empire's larger cities that provided training in veterinary medicine.[34]

Chapter 11

Post-Battle Scenarios and War Diplomacy

The spah had a number of doctrines that were implemented after the conclusion of a major war and/or battles. In the immediate aftermath of battles, the spah compiled casualty statistics. Measures were also taken, in the short and long term, against personnel who had deserted their comrades as well as those warriors who had failed to perform their duties during battles. Within this context, the spah operated a well-established judicial and prison system.

Accounting for Casualties

As noted previously, the spah had a sophisticated system of dabirs for military record keeping. Of particular importance for the spah was the keeping of records of battlefield losses.[1] For this process, there was an ingenious system for using arrows to account for battlefield casualties. Writing in reference to the aftermath of the Battle of Callinicum in 531 CE, Procopius has provided a comprehensive overview of this accounting system:

> [T]he king sits on the royal throne, and many baskets are set there before him; and the general also is present who is expected to lead the army against the enemy; then the army passes along before the king, one man at a time, and each of them throws one weapon into the baskets; after this they are sealed with the king's seal and preserved; and when this army returns to Persia, each one of the soldiers takes one weapon out of the baskets. A count is then made by those whose office it is to do so of all the weapons which have not been taken by the men, and they report to the king the number of the soldiers who have not returned, and in this way it becomes evident how many have perished in the war. Thus the law has stood from of old among the Persians.[2]

Procopius notes that each soldier deposits a 'weapon' into the royal basket, which was actually an arrow. Nevertheless the overall description by Procopius is highly accurate. Before the onset of battle, the king or acting commander of the field army would conduct a military review in which every warrior was to deposit an arrow into a large royal container. With the review concluded, a royal seal was applied to close the container. The seal would then be broken after the conclusion of the battle. Each of the surviving warriors would then pass by the open container and retrieve an arrow. The remaining arrows would then be officially counted; the final numbers would then give an accurate statistic on the losses incurred by the spah during the battle. The origins of this 'arrow-accounting' system most likely derive from an ancient Iranian mythological tradition (i.e. the *Avesta*), which places a heavy emphasis on archery. Usage of the 'arrow-accounting' system is also recorded among other Iranian peoples, notably the

Scythians and Sarmatians of ancient Eastern Europe who used this method for their population census.[3]

Another interesting note regarding the accounting of casualties pertains to the army's overall performance. Specifically, simply scoring a victory was not necessarily a vote of confidence for the commander; of paramount importance was the human costs incurred to secure that victory. Procopius notes that King Kavad was displeased with the victory achieved by his general Azarethes in the aftermath of the Battle of Callinicum (531 CE), especially after many (fallen) warriors failed to retrieve their 'weapons' (arrows) from the royal baskets. For this reason, Kavad 'demoted' Azarethes. Procopius writes that Kavad 'took away from him a decoration which he was accustomed to bind upon the hair of his head, an ornament wrought of gold and pearls. Now this is a great dignity among the Persians, second only to the kingly honour. For there it is unlawful to wear a gold ring or girdle or brooch or anything else whatsoever, except a man be counted worthy to do so by the king'.[4]

In summary, the casualty accounting system was for tabulating losses as well as evaluating the performance of commanders. Given their military manpower limitations, the Sassanians could ill afford heavy casualties. Therefore commanders were expected to be not only adept as warriors and tacticians, but to also be proficient at minimizing casualties.

Measures Against Desertions and Poor Military Performance

Abandoning one's comrades on the battlefield was considered as one of the greatest categories of disgrace in the spah. Troops who deserted their units or fled from the battlefield were dealt with in the harshest possible terms. In this endeavour, dezhban officers (see Chapter 2) were tasked with keeping watch on the rear areas of army units during campaigns to intercept troops attempting to desert the spah. In the *Shahname* Firdowsi notes that this office had existed from the days of the founder of the Sassanian dynasty, Ardashir I. If the dezhban caught a deserter in flight, he was authorized by the state to kill the absconder.[5] Deserters who did manage to escape the dezhbans were certainly not forgotten; thanks to the detailed record keeping of the empire's scribes (see *dabir* in Chapter 3) the dezhbans were able to keep track of runaways. Firdowsi, for example, notes of state tomes or divans which had detailed records of each trooper registered.[6] As a result, absconders could be tracked, arrested and brought to justice by the dezhbans, even years after the conclusion of the war.

Harsh measures would also be taken against those warriors who had been judged by dezhbans as having performed poorly during battle, although the nature of the punishment appeared to vary. Punishments of the 'milder' variety often involved ceremonies of disgrace. Typically the warrior would be forced to sit backwards on a horse to be led in a 'humiliation' ceremony attended by pahlevan knights and members of the nobility. One such measure, for example, was imposed upon General Firouz, who had failed in performing his duties against Belisarius during the Battle of Dara in 530 CE.[7] There were also punishments that were extremely harsh. Khosrow Anoushiravan, for example, ordered one of his generals to be flayed alive after his poor performance against Lazican fighters in the Caucasus.[8] Troops who failed to fight bravely in battle could also be subject to direct royal judgment.[9] Kavad, for example, would have troops executed for cowardice if they faltered in scaling ladders to fight Romano-Byzantine troops during the siege of Amida in 502–503 CE.[10]

The cost of rebellion by a professional warrior against his nation and comrades was public execution. Pigulevskaya cites the case of a rebellion against Ardashir I led by his son Anoushzad who was supported by a mix of military personnel as well as civilians. The rebellion was suppressed with Anoushzad and numbers of his followers captured. According to Pigulevskaya, Ardashir I provided amnesty to the civilian rebels but ordered the execution of the military members of the rebellion.[11] Ardashir I's final judgement shows a clear difference in the way justice was accorded to professional warriors and civilians.

Military Judicial System, Prisons and Punishments

One of the interesting aspects of the Sassanian legal code was the prestige it was accorded by the spah, which viewed its operation vital even during times of war. The code was also more stringent in comparison to other (non-military) classes when applied to military personnel.[12] The legal code was to be applied by the *spah-dadvar* to the entire array of forces during wartime, even when those forces were engaged outside of the empire's territory. Of note is the empire's prison system, which was under the supervision of officials with military backgrounds.

Office of the spah-dadvar. The *spah-dadvar* was responsible for all legal and judicial affairs of the spah's troops while on military campaign. Typically, persons assigned to these posts would be the mobad Zoroastrian priests or magi. The main qualification for these persons was to have at least ten to fifteen years of experience in judicial affairs.[13] The spah viewed it necessary to have the spah-dadvar assume responsibility for all legal issues pertaining to its troops in times of war. This allowed the spah's top officers to focus more effectively on strategy and related matters during military campaigns.

Office of the zendanigh. The zendanigh was responsible for the supervision of the empire's prison system. Jalali notes that this post was military in nature with the zendanigh required to have professional military training.[14] What appears from the sources is that the zendanigh was the supervisor of the 'Government Prison' known as the *gelkard* (Pahlavi: built of mud/soil). Western historians (e.g. Wiesehofer) also refer to the 'Castle of Oblivion' apparently in reference to the *Faramoushkhaneh*; its remains are situated along the banks of the Karun River in Susa (in Iran's southwest Khuzestan province).[15]

Treatment of Defeated Foes After Battles and Wars

Firdowsi notes that Ardashir I instructs his warriors to refrain from engaging in revenge against defeated foes. The warrior must refrain from bloodshed after he has achieved victory (*Cho pirouz gardi ze tan khoon mariz*) and he must also abandon his desire for vengeance (*kineh madar*).[16] Nevertheless, the defeated enemy would still be required to accept terms after his surrender, and the *Shahname* provides examples of Shapur I's demands after the surrender of Roman forces.[17]

Settlement of prisoners of war and civilian captives. Whenever the spah achieved victory, prisoners of war would be settled in the Sassanian Empire's cities. But the settlement process was not random; each prisoner would be assigned for settlement in locales in accordance to his military rank and social standing.[18] The areas of settlement typically varied according to the reign of the particular monarch. Shapur I, for example, settled the captured Roman emperor Valerian, his Praetorian Guard and other Roman officers 'in the empire of Eire-an, in Persis, in Parthia, Khuzestan, in Ashuristan [in modern Iraq] and in all the other provinces where we and our forefathers and ancestors had royal estates'.[19] The *Chronicle of Seert* also notes that Shapur I allocated housing and agricultural lands to the Roman deportees; many of these were Christians who succeeded in spreading their faith in Iran.[20] Deportations continued with Shapur II having mainly settled his Roman captives in Khuzestan;[21] his Arab captives (from the failed Julian campaign) were settled in Kerman.[22] The Roman garrisons of the cities of Singara and Nisibis (which had been yielded by Jovian to the Sassanians in negotiations following Julian's death) were allowed by Shapur II to return to the Romano-Byzantine realm.[23] In 395 CE, 18,000 captives were taken from Sophene, Cappadocia, Armenia, Syria and Mesopotamia, but as soon as they reached Iran they were freed and provided with food, with many of them settling in Koke and Veh-Ardashir.[24] Yazdegird I (r. 399–420 CE) allowed 1,330 to return to their lands of origin but 800 of these chose to stay in Iran. Examples of deportations are seen in the early sixth century with 18,500 inhabitants of the Edessa-Harran region having been sent to Iran in 501–502 CE during the reign of Kavad.[25] The latter's successor, Khosrow I, built an exact replica of the city of Antioch in modern-day Iraq named 'Weh Antioch Khosrow' (which Khosrow claimed was better than the original Antioch) in which to settle his captives from Antioch and other Roman cities.[26] One of Khosrow I's generals, Azarmahan, is variously reported as having brought anywhere from 92,000 to 292,000 captives from Apamea and its surrounding regions to Iran.[27] The practice of dispatching 'settlers' to Iran continued into late Sassanian times with General Shahrbaraz dispatching artisans and labourers to Iran after his capture of Jerusalem in May 614 CE[28] (see also Chapter 16).

The *Toqi'ate Anoushirvan* provides an interesting insight into another Sassanian facet with respect to the treatment of war prisoners. Evidently, Roman prisoners could be freed if the Sassanian administration received money.[29] This raises interesting questions, especially as to where the funds would be allocated and what sums would be required. It would be safe to assume that the cost of purchasing the freedom of higher-ranking Roman officers and dignitaries would be more than lower-ranking troops and auxiliaries.

Another interesting situation with respect to prisoners of war and the policies of Khosrow Anoushirvan is seen in the invasion of a Central Asian warrior people known as the Chuls. They had engaged in a ferocious attack from the eastern coast of the Caspian Sea in Central Asia into Gorgan. From there the Chuls wreaked havoc in northern Khorasan province. Khosrow and the spah counter-attacked with a powerful force of savaran knights. In the ensuing battles, the Chuls were virtually wiped out. The power of this counteroffensive ensured that the Chuls never menaced the empire again. In this campaign very few prisoners were taken. Khosrow perhaps intended to set an example for other Central Asian warrior peoples who may have contemplated similar ideas of raid and plunder against the empire. Khosrow spared only eighty of the Chuls, who were especially exceptional warriors. The shahanshah permitted these to live as long as they agreed to serve in the spah. The surviving Chul warriors agreed to Khosrow's terms and the shahanshah then assigned them to military service with the local spah garrison in the city of Shah Ram Pirouz.[30]

Use of prisoners of war for labour. Prisoners of war would be put to hard work, notably on construction and irrigation works and even on works of art. Shapur I, for example, used captured Roman engineers of Valerian's army after his victories in 260 CE to build numerous engineering works,[31] notably the bridge of Shushtar in Khuzestan,[32] whose remains are visible to this day. According to Tabari, the bridge was 'as continuous as a cable' and 'brought ... to completion within three years'.[33] The Louvre museum features Roman mosaic works made by captive Roman artisans for the Sassanian nobility at Nev-Shapur.

The king valued Roman engineers for their ingenuity in military architecture. Romans with engineering skills were captured in Singara (in 360 CE), a frontier city which had stood in the path of Sassanian invasions into Roman territory on a number of occasions. In this operation two Roman legions (I Flavia and I Parthica) as well as numbers of cavalry and other local troops surrendered to the Sassanians. Following a thorough inspection of the military architecture at Singara, Shapur II then allegedly brought a Roman prisoner by the name of 'Antoninus' and a number of other knowledgeable Roman prisoners to help in the construction of the fortifications of Siraf[34] (Chapter 13).

Military Diplomacy

As noted by Bullough, Romano-Sassanian military relations were shaped by the inability of either empire to completely subdue the other.[35] In this regard, Romano-Sassanian military issues were characterized by six general factors:[36] (1) the show of force; (2) engaging in small-scale land operations; (3) concluding alliances with third powers; (4) construction of military fortifications; (5) establishing military colonies; and (6) attempting to foment civil disturbances within each other's domains.

Even when the Sassanians decided to go to war, there were procedures in place to find means of avoiding military conflict. To that end, the Sassanian king would sometimes dispatch ambassadors to the enemy in the attempt to find means to resolve disputes and arrive at settlements. The *Shahname* reports that Ardashir I (r. 224–242 CE) 'dispatched a designated dabir, wise and with knowledge of science' (*ferestade bargozide-i dabir, kheradmand va ba danesh*) to negotiate a peace treaty with the empire's adversaries.[37] If the enemy was at an equal or superior position of military strength, the ambassadors would attempt to arrive at a favourable settlement without sacrificing the interests of the empire.[38] A clear case of an embassy being sent from Ctesiphon to the Romans to forestall war occurred in 362 CE. The Sassanians had discovered that a Roman invasion was imminent (intelligence sources had reported massive Roman military preparations on their borders) and had therefore dispatched their embassy to Antioch in hopes of concluding a negotiated settlement.[39] Upon the embassy's arrival in Antioch in late 362 CE, however, the emperor Julian simply rejected the Sassanian peace proposals and stated that there was no need for ambassadors as he would be meeting Shapur II at Ctesiphon.[40] With the failure of Shapur II's diplomatic mission at Antioch, the war council, already aware of the serious threat of a determined Roman invasion, finalized its decision to mobilize the spah for war.

If Ctesiphon's ambassadors or the king himself were negotiating from a position of perceived military superiority, they would attempt to force the enemy into surrendering concessions at the negotiating table.[41] Such a situation occurred after the conclusion of the *Pax Perpetuum* (lit. 'Eternal Peace') in 532 CE, between Emperors Justinian and Khosrow I. This allowed Justinian to shift the bulk of his military power to Europe to deal with military crisis in Italy and North Africa. By the same token the spah was left in a position of military superiority against the Romano-Byzantine Empire's eastern marches. This scenario may have prompted the Sassanians to reach out to the Gothic enemies of the Romano-Byzantines. It is also noteworthy that the Ostrogoth king Witiges, who was keenly interested in opening a second eastern front against his Romano-Byzantine enemies, had in fact sent his ambassadors to Sassanian Persia in 538 or 539 CE.[42] Items of earlier Sassanian origin (prior to 530s CE) have been discovered among Gothic tribes dwelling on the borders of the Roman Empire. One of these is an Iranian belt buckle found in Wolfsheim, Germany, bearing the name '*Ardashir*' in Middle Persian (Pahlavi) script; this was discovered alongside a coin of the Emperor Valens (364–378 CE).[43] The latter had been slain in the Battle of Adrianople, in which a Roman army was defeated by a force of Gothic warriors supported by Alan cavalry. It is quite possible that this belt-buckle was one of many items in a parcel of gifts brought by Sassanian diplomats (dabirs) to Europe for Gothic chieftains. Brogan, for example, has noted of a hoard discovered in Pietrossa (in modern Transylvania) that included two Sassanian vessels that he explains as 'presents in the course of diplomatic relationship between Goth and Persian'.[44] As noted previously, Goth-Sassanian diplomatic exchanges did take place, with Khosrow I receiving embassies from the Ostrogoths of Italy.[45] The latter had been under intense military pressure by the Romano-Byzantine generals, Narses and Belisarius. The Ostrogoths were evidently hoping to convince Khosrow to attack their mutual enemy and thus force the Romano-Byzantines to divert troops to the east. Khosrow I, already encouraged by the weakened Romano-Byzantine military presence to his west, certainly could not rule out the possibility of enhancing Sassanian territory at Constantinople's expense.

Finally alert to the real danger of a Sassanian invasion, Justinian dispatched Anastasius of Dara with a letter to Khosrow before spring 540 CE.[46] The letter essentially appealed to Khosrow I to desist from invading the Romano-Byzantine Empire.[47] Rejecting Justinian's appeal for peace, Khosrow I unleashed the spah against the Romano-Byzantines until 561 CE, when a new peace treaty was signed ending that war.

The situation was again reversed when Justinian's successor, Justin II (r. 565–574 CE) decided to reject the 561 CE peace treaty in order to launch his own attack against the Sassanian Empire. Khosrow I who had received military intelligence on Romano-Byzantine intentions, dispatched an envoy named Sebochthes to Constantinople. Interestingly, Menandor Protector claims that Sebochthes' embassy had been dispatched because Khosrow I 'was afraid that, on account of the major [Roman] preparations, [Justin] might mount an invasion'.[48] The Sebochthes mission was a failure as Justin II did indeed invade the Sassanian Empire, albeit with disastrous results. The spah (personally led by the aged Khosrow I) captured Dara in 573 CE, a loss which so shook Justin II that it caused him to go insane.

Chapter 12

The Spah in Central Asia: Warfare, Military Developments and Tactics

The armies of Iran have often been challenged by the formidable nomads of the steppes. The Medes had faced a Scythian invasion through the Caucasus in 650s BCE with their Achaemenid successors having had to face Scythian (Saka) warriors in Central Asia. Cyrus the Great (r. 559–540 BCE) lost his life in battle against the Massagetae; Darius the Great (r. 522–486 BCE) brought these formidable warriors to heel. As noted in Chapter 6, the Achaemenids were to be influenced by the heavy cavalry concept of the Central Asian Saka which they integrated into their military. The Parthians who succeeded the Achaemenids and overthrew the authority of the post-Alexandrian Seleucids from Iran were themselves of Saka stock. The Parthians often had to fight off military threats from Central Asia while having to face the formidable Romans to the west of the Iranian realms.

The Sassanians inherited the Parthian two-front strategic dilemma that led Ctesiphon's political leadership and the spah to develop the four-spahbod system. The military development of the spah was heavily influenced as a result of its military encounters in Central Asia. The displacement of the Iranian-speaking peoples of Central Asia led to the arrival of a series of Hun-Turkic peoples who would come to dominate the region. The first serious military threat posed by such warriors were the Chionites who forced Shapur II to abandon his sieges against the Romans in 337 CE. After his military successes against the Chionites, Shapur II recruited these as allies, most notably during his siege of Amida in 359 CE (Chapter 14). The Kidarites were to pose serious threats to the empire's northeast forcing Yazdegird II to campaign against them in 443–450 CE. The identity of the Kidarites is disputed, with historians variously identifying these as Turkic or Iranian-speaking Kushans. The most deadly challenge to the empire was made by the Hephthalites, whose identity is also debated, but it is agreed that these were an Altaic-speaking people.[1] It was in the aftermath of the spah's defeats against the Hephthalites that changes are seen in the military equipment of the savaran. The changes in the spah and the implementation of the four-spahbod system helped contribute to the dramatic successes of the spah against the Turks and their Hephthalite allies in 588 CE and 619 CE, leading to the military ascendancy of the Sassanians in Central Asia until the fall of the empire to the Arabs in 637–651 CE. This chapter provides an overview of the key battles fought by the spah in Central Asia and the military implications of these campaigns. Before these discussions, it is necessary to provide an overall sketch of the military proficiency of the Central Asian warriors.

The Martial Prowess of the Central Asian Warrior

The warriors of Central Asia were as formidable and dangerous to the spah as were the Romano-Byzantines along the western marches of the Sassanian empire. As noted by Sinor, 'inner Asia's contribution to the development of arts and science is relatively modest, the great influence it exerted on the history of mankind was through the excellence of its armed forces.'[2] Among the important contributions of Central Asian warriors, especially after the displacement of the resident Iranian speaking peoples by the Hephthalites, Huns and Turkic peoples, were innovations such as the lappet system for swords, archery (bow construction and the Mongolian draw), and the mastery of the feigned retreat.

Whenever the spah faced the armies of Central Asia, they were confronted by warriors who often matched them in training, archery and cavalry warfare. Central Asian warriors proved especially innovative with respect to tactics and weapons development. In their battles against the spah, they proved especially able to adapt to the tactics of their adversaries. Thus while the spah faced armies derived from a Western or Greco-Roman military tradition along its western frontiers, in Central Asia it would be fighting armies that bore many tactical and equipment similarities to itself. It is certainly true that the Romano-Byzantines would be strongly affected by the Iranian cavalry tradition (Chapter 19), but they were also heavily influenced by Hun-Avar military traditions (i.e. the Hun-Avar composite bow). Hence, the Central Asian military tradition exerted a highly significant influence upon the Iranians and the Europeans.

The military prowess of the Central Asian warriors was greatly respected by not only the Sassanians, but also the Romans and the Chinese. Speaking in reference to the Huns, Ammianus Marcellinus noted that 'they could be easily described as the most terrible of all warriors.'[3] The Hsiang-Nou, the eastern ethnic cousins of the Huns who faced the Chinese frontier, were greatly feared by the Chinese. The Chinese historian Ssu-ma Ch'ien wrote of the Hsiang-Nou that warfare was 'their natural disposition ... their business'.[4] Maurice's *Strategikon* reports that 'the Turks do nothing else but practice how to fight the enemy with courage'.[5] Perhaps the most detailed descriptions of the martial temperament of Central Asian warriors is provided by Juvaini (c. 1250 to early 1260s CE) with respect to Mongol warriors of the thirteenth century CE. Juvaini noted that the Mongol horde was 'peasantry in the guise of an army, all of them, great or small, noble and base, in time of battle becoming swordsmen, archers and lancers and advancing in whatever manner the occasion requires'.[6] It is also notable that despite being unpaid, Mongol warriors performed their military service with the utmost dedication and efficiency, and were fiercely loyal to their Khans. The Mongols were not simply a spontaneous military creation in the Islamic era; they were the heirs of a long-standing Hun-Turkic Central Asian martial tradition.

It is noteworthy that neither the Turkic nor the Mongolian languages have specific native (non-Arabic and non-Persian) words meaning 'soldier', just as these language groups lack native words for 'war' and 'peace'.[7] Combat was a way of life essential for survival, especially fighting in a collective as one unit for the benefit of the tribe, tribal confederation or any other form of political organization. Camaraderie was highly encouraged just as cowardice in battle was dealt with harshly.

Even as the ethnic and linguistic composition of Central Asia was transformed over the centuries due to migrations and invasions, the warrior culture and technological innovations of the region continued to develop. By the 500s CE Turkic peoples came to increasingly dominate Central Asia, displacing as well as absorbing the region's indigenous Iranian-speaking populations. The Turkish warriors proved especially fierce; so much so that their martial ardour is cited well after the fall of the Sassanians by the Persian poet Hafez (d. 1390): 'Oh Lord how bold are these young Turks for blood / Every minute they take another prey in their arrow-eyelashes.'[8]

Training and discipline. As in Sassanian Iran, military training in Central Asia began at a very early age, both at the individual and group levels. From the outset, the Central Asian warrior was taught to fight as a member of his collective. The aforementioned Chinese historian Ssu-ma Ch'ien wrote the following description of the military training regimen of young Hsiang-Nou boys: 'The little boys start out by learning to ride sheep and shoot birds and rats with a bow and arrow and when they get a little older they shoot foxes and hares ... all the young men are able to use a bow and act as armed cavalry.'[9]

There are strong indications that Central Asian warriors were every bit as disciplined as their counterparts in the spah. Concerning the Mongols, David of Ashby wrote in the 1270s that 'Never would you see a man shouting ... nor a horse neighing, for the horses are all well-schooled.'[10] Much like the spah, Central Asian armies based their primary strike forces on the cavalry with archery as battlefield support. It was this combination of constant training, strict discipline and constantly improving battle tactics that made the Central Asian armies forces to be reckoned with. This is in fact attested to by Theophylactos Simokattes (seventh century CE), who noted that the Mukri, who lived on the Chinese frontier, demonstrated 'great courage in armed conflicts because of experience gained in daily drills and steadfastness shown in the face danger'.[11] In reference to the Uighurs in Eastern Europe, Simokattes had very similar observations, noting that the Uighurs were 'among the strongest because of their number and the military drill they undergo'. It is also noteworthy that the horses of Central Asian armies were accustomed to the sounds of military drumming through specialized training.[12]

Cavalry. The heavily armoured savaran met its match against the Hephthalite Huns and it was not until the later sixth century CE that it finally got the upper hand against its Central Asian (Turkic and Hephthalite Hun) adversaries. The horse was integral to the Central Asian warrior's existence, a fact duly noted by Ammianus Marcellinus when he wrote that 'they are almost glued to their horses'.[13] The Central Asian horse was a relatively small and pony-like beast related to the Przewalski's Horse. This animal was exceptionally strong, resilient and capable of sustaining the warrior over long distances and dangerous combat situations. Sinor asserted that this very same horse was seminal to the military power of the armies of Central Asia.[14]

Where were stirrups invented? Coulston suggests that they were originally invented by Eurasian steppe peoples[15] with Sinor rejecting this by pointing to earlier representations of the stirrup in ancient Korea and Japan in the fourth and fifth centuries CE.[16] Bivar notes of the existence of the stirrup among Eurasian nomads (e.g. the Juan-Juan) as early as 560 CE.[17] The earliest Turkic stirrups shown in the Irkutsk and Frunze museums dated (earliest) to the 500s CE.[18] It is possible that stirrup technology had been adopted a number of decades earlier in Central Asia (c. 470s CE or earlier) but more research is required in this domain. Dien explains the stirrup as having been a Chinese invention traced to a representation of a triangular shaped set of stirrups from a Jin tomb in Changsha, China, dated to 302 CE.[19] There is an isolated representation of a Kushan engraved gem of a 'hook-stirrup' from early 100 CE, but this appears to be an isolated find and it is not clear if the Kushan device had any impact on later Chinese developments. Actual early Chinese stirrups have been found in the tomb of Feng Sufu (c. 415 CE) and an earlier stirrup of gilded bronze construction dated to about the mid-fourth century CE was found in one of tombs of Wanbaoting. Dien has written that the stirrup facilitated the drawing of a strong bow.[20] According to Dien, the introduction of the stirrup in northern China led to the rise of new military elites in the region[21] which was contiguous with Central Asia and its warrior societies. He also proposes that stirrups were the Chinese answer for enhancing the mounted stability of their *Tieji* or 'Iron Cavalry'.[22] In summary, while the issue of whether stirrups were invented by the Central Asians remains open, it is certain that they did adopt this technology and that peoples such as the Avars introduced it to the Romano-Byzantines. It was possibly adopted by the Sassanians sometime by the late-500s CE.

Parthian armies generally fielded separate and distinct cavalry types, the heavily armoured lancers and the lightly armed and armoured horse archers; however, there were also corps of *Shivatir-e Zrehbaran* (armoured horse archers). Coulston notes the following with respect to Central Asian cavalry: 'Steppe armies were less likely to have fallen tactically into clear-cut light horse-archer and heavy archer/lancer types. A shading off between the two, perhaps based more on age and experience than on wealth and class status, would have produced much looser and more mobile cavalry formations, coalescing and opening up with changing battlefield circumstances.'[23] This feature was highly indicative of the flexibility of military thinking with respect to tactics and weapons employment, based on battlefield circumstances, and of course the opponent's strengths and weaknesses. This is perhaps one of the key reasons why the Sassanians faced such great military challenges along the Central Asian frontier, as they confronted armies that were not necessarily bound to a limited series of tactics and formations. Instead the Sassanians faced enemies capable of adapting to the strengths and tactics of their heavy lancers and archery. The savaran's lance charges were often met with the flexible cavalry manoeuvres and horse archery of their Central Asian opponents who even if they could not repel the savaran, were able to inflict considerable damage though 'retreat' (or feigned flight). The tactics used by Central Asian cavalry would be the same as those practised by the spah such as ambushing at the flanks and rear, and destroying isolated units or groups of warriors.[24] Put simply, Central Asian warfare was cognizant of the dangers of the savaran's lance charges and devised tactics to repel these. In this respect, the Sassanians faced enemies in their northeast who were as formidable as the Romano-Byzantines to their west.

Archery. The savaran faced great challenges when locked in battle against Central Asian cavalry especially as the latter matched the Sassanians in one of their most powerful arms: archery. Jordanes sums up the skill of the Huns by stating they were 'excellent horsemen ... skilled in the use of the bow and the arrow'.[25] The Central Asian horse archer shot his missiles with deadly speed and accuracy. Sidonius Apollinaris noted of the Huns that 'shapely bows and arrows are their delight, sure and terrible are their hands; firm is their confidence that their missiles will bring death'.[26] In the spah's battles in the Central Asian theatre, battles were often characterized by the adversaries attempting to dominate each other in missile barrages and speed of missile delivery. Like the Sassanians, archery from horseback was a skill constantly honed and improved by Central Asian training, as noted in the *Strategikon* in its description of Turkic warriors.[27]

The compound bow has been described in detail in Chapter 5, but mention of it must be made here with respect to its employment by Central Asian warriors. The Central Asian bow was a powerful and versatile weapon, being constructed of horn and wood, stiffened with sinew that was glued to its wood core. An interesting feature of this weapon was its asymmetry, which resulted in the grip being placed below the centre of the bow. The bone arrowheads (crafted in the highest quality) of the Huns reported by Ammianus Marcellinus[28] were especially effective. These continued to be employed 900 years later by the Mongols.[29]

Close-quarters combat weaponry. Central Asian warriors were armed with weapons very similar to those of the savaran. Swords were their primary close-quarter combat weapon, with their lappet-suspension system being adopted by the Sassanians (Chapter 6). The sword held a status on equal footing with archery, along with lances and spears. The lasso was a highly prized weapon, as this could ensnare the opponent and even force him to be pulled off his horse, especially if he had been caught by the neck. Ammianus Marcellinus reported on the deadly effectiveness of the lasso as handled by the Huns, by noting that they 'throw strips of cloth plaited into nooses over their opponents and so entangle them that they fetter their limbs and take from them the power of riding or walking'.[30]

Battles were often decided by close-quarter combat, especially after missiles from the two sides had been exhausted. While the high level of horsemanship and archery of Central Asian warriors is hardly in dispute, what is less clear is how the spah's elite warriors were matched up with Central Asian warriors in close-quarter combat on horseback. Towards the end of the Sassanian era the spah was capable of fielding relatively small numbers of elite knights to defeat vastly larger numbers of Turkic and Hephthalite Hun warriors. While the reasons for these successes may be attributed to a number of factors (as described later in this chapter), one possibility is that the savaran had, by late Sassanian times, achieved new advances in close-quarter combats as a result of their training.

Armour. Turkic warriors from Central Asia and their Khazar cousins in the eastern European-north Caucasus theatre wore long and heavy lamellar armour featuring high collars.[31] Such military attire was also worn by Chinese heavy cavalry.[32] Taking advantage of their economic and industrial base, the Sassanians worked hard to produce effective armour.[33] Nevertheless, the question of 'better' armour did not rest on wearing more or heavier armour. It was a question of the effective construction of and combination of (types) of armours that proved most resilient. The departure from the 'super-heavy' cavalry concept towards cavalry wearing lighter armour may have been a response for better facing Central Asian cavalry.[34] The question of arms is addressed in more detail later in this chapter.

Martial music: battle kettledrums. Like the Sassanian spah, Central Asian armies used drumming for military coordination on the battlefield. Nikonorov notes that Central Asian kettledrums were possibly derived from the common cooking utensils of nomadic peoples.[35] The Mongols were famous for not commencing battle until having been given the signal by their military leader through the drumming of their *nakar* or *nagara*.[36] The early Turkic armies that faced the spah in the late sixth century CE were known to have had an array of military drums.[37] Turkic military drummers would often carry their drums by either suspending them on a waist belt or by means of a shoulder strap.[38]

Procurement and production of military equipment. The first question to be asked is how were the mobile cavalry forces of Central Asia supplied with such vast quantities of weapons during their campaigns. China, Sassanian Persia and the Romano-Byzantine world were able to maintain professional standing armies due to their sophisticated political, economic and agrarian infrastructures which were capable of sustaining permanent workshops and industries as well as pro-fessional craftsmen and specialists for the manufacturing of weapons. In sheer technological terms, Central Asia was every bit as capable in the invention and production of military equipment. For example, the shortage of iron was addressed by the use of bones for making arrowheads, horns and fabrics for the production of military equipment, etc.; but the shortage of iron could impose limitations. Mail, for example, could not be produced on a massive scale to equip entire armies due not only to the shortage of iron but also to what Coulston has described as 'the techniques of wire-drawing [which] required a sedentary base'.[39] The shortage of resources faced by Central Asian weapons builders led to highly effective solutions for the production of military equipment, notably missiles and arrowheads, lances, lassos, shields, armour, equestrian equipment and close-quarters combat weapons (especially swords).

Sinor has identified three sources of military supplies for Central Asia, namely, commerce, prisoners of war and taxation.[40] The first category, commerce, involved the silk route which traversed multiple routes between China and Iran, with Central Asia situated between the two empires. This was a source of revenue and became a major cause of friction between the Sassanians and the Turks, leading to war in the late sixth century CE (see below). The Chinese in particular were very sensitive to the export of iron to Central Asia. They issued official edicts forbidding the sale of iron to northern nomadic warrior peoples such as the Hsiang-Nou. Despite this, Chinese soldiers stationed along the northern frontiers often engaged in the sale of iron to warrior peoples such as the Hsiang-Nou. Even more interestingly, according to Yu, there were instances of Chinese soldiers stationed along the northern frontiers demanding that their government pay them in iron instead of money![41] Put simply, the armaments and iron embargo that the Chinese attempted to impose along their northern frontiers proved impossible to enforce. The illegal export of iron was probably one of the major economic factors that allowed Central Asian armies to consistently menace the north-eastern marches of the Sassanian Empire.

The second source of economic revenue for armaments production was the collection of prisoners or, more accurately, slaves. The northeast regions of the Sassanian Empire, notably Khorasan and much of modern-day Afghanistan, were vulnerable to hit-and-run raids by Central Asian warriors. The educated and skilled population of the Sassanian Empire's northeast would be a source of revenue, both in terms of the slave market as well as the forced labour of skilled professional craftsmen and weapons builders. The latter could be put to work for the production of weapons, with the other captured prisoners used as slaves or sold off for profit, which could be re-invested in the armaments sector. Slave raids into northeast Iran and modern-day Afghanistan continued well into Islamic times. Shah Ismail (r. 1501–1524), the founder of the Safavid dynasty, inflicted crushing defeats on Uzbek raiders in 1510,[42] but the Safavids had to continue battling these slave raiders into the 1530s[43] and even into the 1620s.[44] Central Asian raiders continued to capture Iranians for use as slaves as late as the 1880s, a fact recorded by Arminius Vamberry in his travelogues of Central Asia, Turkey and Iran.[45]

Slave procurement was not limited to raids into northeast Iran. Central Asian tribes could literally enslave each other. For example, if a particular tribal confederation gained military ascendancy over another tribal confederation, the latter could then be reduced to slave status. The slave tribe would then be forced to provide services and personnel as dictated by the requirements of its master tribe. An example of this is the Juan-Juan, which had forced the early Turks into the status of 'blacksmith slaves'.[46] The Gok (Celestial/Blue) Turks defeated and overthrew their Juan-Juan overlords to then create their own Turkic empires in Central Asia from the sixth century CE.[47]

The third means by which Central Asian armies could procure revenue was through the imposition of taxation on populations they had conquered. As seen later in this chapter, the Hephthalites captured much of Khorasan and Afghanistan after their victories in 484 CE. The Sassanians had been forced to pay a heavy annual tribute to the Hephthalites as a major condition of their peace treaty following the death of King Pirouz in 484 CE. The local conquered population of northeast Persia was also exploited by being forced into slavery, as well as being imposed with heavy taxes. All of this resulted in a sharp decrease in Ctesiphon's annual income, which also reduced its financial ability to rebuild and finance the spah.

The military recovery of the spah by the 500s translated into defeats for the Turkic and Hephthalite armies of Central Asia. This meant that Central Asian warriors could no longer collect slaves at will from northeast Iran or impose military taxation on the Sassanian Empire's northeast regions.

Weakness: overemphasis upon equestrian training? The heavy emphasis of Central Asian military training on horsemanship had serious drawbacks as well. As noted by Zosimus in reference to the Huns, the outcome of excessive reliance and training on horsemanship resulted in warriors who 'could not plant their feet firmly upon the ground'.[48] Concerning Turkic warriors, the *Strategikon* stated that 'having been bought up on horseback, their legs have become very weak'.[49] This meant that if the Central Asian warrior was caught on the ground without his horse, he would be severely handicapped in combat. Unlike Romano-Byzantine infantry, the horseless Central Asian warrior was highly vulnerable to the lance thrust, sword attacks and archery of the savaran. In addition, the Sassanians did field combat infantry, especially with the arrival of the tough Dailamites of northern Iran (Chapter 7). Horseless Central Asian warriors were probably at a disadvantage when forced into close-quarter combat against the Dailamites, a situation that may partly explain the victories of Bahram Chobin in 588 CE (see below).

Shapur II and the Chionites

The spah had engaged in the siege of Nisibis and Singara in 337 or 338 CE[50] (Chapter 14). After two months of intense combat, the spah abandoned its siege operations and vacated the theatre. The reason had little to do with Roman military action; the Sassanians were now faced with a very dangerous invasion of Khorasan and modern-day Afghanistan by the Chionites of Central Asia. The Chionites, of possible part-Iranian origins,[51] had acknowledged Sassanian authority at first but had then turned against them.

The military situation along the Central Asian frontier was desperate. Despite the presence of the spah in the region, the Chionites proved to be formidable warriors. By 350 CE, they had conquered Soghdia, a serious setback prompting Shapur II to intervene personally.[52] The tide evidently began to turn, but even so the fighting remained prolonged and probably hard fought. The spah and Shapur II finally secured a complete victory over the Chionites by 357 CE.[53] By 358 CE the Chionites had signed a peace treaty with Shapur II[54] and furnished him with warriors to join the spah in the upcoming siege of Roman-held Amida in 359 CE

Figure 10. Central Asian frontier (late sixth century to circa early-mid seventh century CE): (*left*) Armored East Iranian and/or Soghdian Warrior (seventh century CE); and (*right*) Gok-Turk officers of the type leading the Turco-Hephthalite armies which invaded Iran from the northeast in 588 CE and 619 CE (drawings by Farrokh, based on Reza originals). There were several shared features between Sassanian and Turkic warriors with respect to equipment, training and tactics, leading to a distinct Turco-Iranian military tradition in the post-Islamic era.

along the empire's western frontiers.[55] At Amida Shapur II was to be accompanied by Grumbates, the king of the Chionites and his son (who was killed during the siege).[56] According to Docherty, the joining of Grumbates with the spah against Rome probably spared India from a Chionite invasion.[57]

Bahram Gur (421 CE)

By the early fifth century CE the empire was faced with a new warrior people along its Central Asian frontier. These were the Hephthalites or 'White Huns', who had crushed Kushan authority and imposed their dominance by the first two decades of the 400s CE. By 420 CE, the Hephthalites felt confident in challenging the might of the Sassanians and proceeded to invade the empire's northeastern marches. The impact of these attacks reverberated across the Sassanian realm, but the Sassanian King Bahram Gur (r. 420–438 CE), maintained a cool and collected approach to the expanding military crisis.

In what can be described as guile, Bahram announced that he was going on a hunting expedition to Azerbaijan, with his brother Narses ruling as regent during the king's absence. Just as Bahram was departing for his 'hunting expedition' in 421 CE, Narses sent frantic appeals to the Hephthalites, offering them a vast tribute in exchange for their evacuation of occupied Sassanian territories. In practice, Bahram had other plans: he soon arrived with a small contingent of crack savaran cavalry at Adiabene in northern Mesopotamia (modern Iraqi Kurdistan). The *Akhbar al Tawwal* reports that Bahram then selected 7,000 cavalry who were ordered to ride with him on camels but were to bring their horses along as well.[58] While precise figures for Bahram's forces cannot be ascertained, it may be surmised that the force was meant as a small but highly trained and mobile strike force. Bahram's own cavalry contingents appear to have been royal units such as the gund shahanshah, zhayedan/javidan, jan-separan, or even the pushtighban. It is possible that these knights included lancers of the super-heavy type, as these had possibly not yet been discontinued as the advent of 'Composite' type cavalry was still decades into the future (possibly even the early sixth century CE; see Chapter 6). The Adiabene cavalry probably acted as support for Bahram and his elite savaran core by being able to engage in lance and close-quarter combat. It is also possible that the Adiabene corps was a light auxiliary cavalry formation whose horsemen specialized in archery support and javelin throwing, as the region's Kurds often provided both the later (Islamic-era) Ottomans and the Safavid Iranians excellent light cavalry in the sixteenth to the eighteenth centuries CE. It is also possible that Bahram and his savaran elites were to be the main strike force in the upcoming battle against the Hephthalites.

Bahram ordered his forces to bring 7,000 young (one-year old) horses and that 7,000 cows be killed to have their skins removed. Bahram was devising a clever stratagem, which soon manifested itself in battle. To avoid detection by the Hephthalites, Bahram and his army deployed from Adiabene into northern Iran, moving through Talysh, Gilan, Mazandaran and Gorgan along the southern edges of the Caspian Sea. This allowed Bahram to arrive unexpectedly in Khorasan advancing towards Sassanian regions occupied by the Hephthalites. Bahram worked hard to ensure that the movement of his forces went undetected by the Hephthalites, who were expecting to receive a massive tribute from Narses. The Sassanian strike force moved only at night to further camouflage its movement towards the empire's northeast. Bahram's tactics paid off: he and his army crossed Nysa and arrived at the oasis of Merv undetected by the Hephthalites. So secret had been this deployment that not even Ctesiphon was aware of Bahram's true whereabouts.

The Hephthalites had failed to take into account Sassanian guile and they soon paid the price for their overconfidence. As Bahram neared the Hephthalite camp, he ordered the 7,000 cow skins to be sewn and filled with rocks. Each of the 'rock bags' was then hung on the spare young horses that had accompanied Bahram's force. These 7,000 'rock bag' horses were now released into the Hephthalite camp. The arrival of the thousands of horses caused considerable confusion and panic, especially as the 7,000 rock bags combined to emanate a terrible sound.[59]

Up to this point the Hephthalites believed that they were soon to receive a Sassanian party bearing gifts and tribute. Instead, Bahram had begun his delivery of a crushing military strike.

With the Hephthalite camp in confusion and disarray as a result of the 7,000 'rock bag' horses, Bahram launched his attacks. Most likely his elite savaran corps moved towards the Hephthalite command centre with lances levelled. The Hephthalites were unable to stop the Sassanian knights and the Hephthalite king was killed. Bahram and his fellow knights most likely employed their bows with deadly effectiveness, thus wreaking further havoc in the Hephthalite camp. In this endeavour, Bahram's 7,000 Mede and Kurd cavalry may have supported his elite savaran with archery fire of their own.

Caught by surprise, the Hephthalites were unable to mount their horses; forced to fight on foot, they accordingly suffered huge casualties. As noted earlier in this chapter, Central Asian warriors may have been at their most vulnerable when caught on the ground, and if this was the case, then there was little they could have done against the lance-bearing savaran. The latter could have easily impaled their opponents on the ground, or have chosen to dispatch them with their swords, maces and other close-quarters combat weapons. This combined with their horse archery would have caused heavy casualties within the Hephthalite camp.

With the bulk of their army destroyed, the Hephthalite survivors of Bahram's assault began to flee for their lives. At this juncture, the lighter Adiabene cavalry would have proved indispensable in hunting down the escapees with swords and archery. Bahram in particular would have caused considerable havoc, especially if he drew upon his skills as a hunter, shooting at fleeing prey. As noted already in Chapter 5, Bahram was able to 'lock' the limbs of a fleeing animal with a single missile. It may be surmised that many more Hephthalites were killed as they attempted to escape. Despite the scale of their losses, a number of survivors from the Hephthalite army did succeed in escaping. Bahram was intent on finishing off the remnants of the once mighty Hephthalite force, as even a small proportion of their survivors could one day form the nucleus of a new army. Daniel notes that Bahram and his cavalry army crossed the Oxus River into Central Asia to continue their pursuit.[60] Now fighting inside their home territory, the Hephthalites stood their ground to meet Bahram in battle once more. A great battle took place in the vicinity of the oasis of Bukhara.[61] The outcome was again the same: Bahram decisively defeated the Hephthalites.[62] This is of interest as this time Bahram did not have the advantage of surprise and his enemies were prepared to face him and were familiar with Sassanian tactics. It would appear that the Hephthalites proved unable to counter Bahram's armoured lance charges supported by lighter cavalry. This would suggest that the Hephthalites had been overpowered by the lance thrusts, archery and close-quarters combat skills of their opponents. Hephthalite archery evidently proved unable to blunt the charge of the lancers. This may suggest that the armour and helmets of the latter were reasonably resilient against Hephthalite missiles. The Hephthalite rout was so pronounced that even the crown of the Hephthalite king was captured, to be subsequently hung as a trophy at the temple of Shiz in Azarbaijan.[63] The last of the Hephthalite fighters, realizing the futility of fighting against Bahram and his pahlavan knights, had no option but to request surrender. Bahram accepted their requests. He then forced the Hephthalites to acknowledge a pillar as marking the boundary between their domains and the Sassanian realm, a border which was not to be crossed again.[64] It is possible that Bactria had now fallen under Sassanian control.[65] These spectacular military successes soon led to the production of Bahram Gur's coins by the local rulers of Bukhara.[66] It is possible that Bahram's successes allowed him to wheel south towards northern India, but this possibility requires further research to substantiate.

Another factor that greatly aided Bahram's success was the Sassanian intelligence network. Matofi notes that Bahram benefited from an extensive network of informants not only inside occupied Sassanian territory but even in the lands of the Hephthalites, across the Oxus.[67] This may be explained by the fact that the Hephthalite Huns were recent arrivals into a region traditionally settled by Iranian speakers who had strong cultural and linguistic ties to their ethnic cousins in Sassanian Iran. Perhaps a segment of the region's indigenous population was disaffected with their Hephthalite overlords, thus proving to be willing recruits for Bahram's spy network. The population inside Sassanian territory that had been occupied by the Hephthalites would certainly provide Ctesiphon with spies and information as well. Most surprising, however, was the discovery by Bahram's network of an extensive pro-Hephthalite spy network inside Iran! Once this network had been exposed, its members were arrested and executed. The network may have owed its existence to adherents of the Manichaean faith who had been forced to go underground in the third century CE, to political disaffection among the Sassanians – the House of Sassan had its own internal rivals, willing to cooperate with any force that would help them seize power in Ctesiphon. Indeed, King Pirouz was to secure the help of the Hephthalites decades later during his own contest for power in 459 CE (see below).

Despite the vast scale and decisive nature of Bahram Gur's successes, the Sassanians' victories were to prove ephemeral. A major reason for this was the aforementioned resilience of Central Asian warriors and armies, who even after the most crushing defeats would again recover. The Sassanians would face new Hephthalite armies in the decades to come. These armies would prove even more formidable as by then they had absorbed the military reasons for their defeats at the hands of Bahram Gur. The Hephthalite armies of the future would certainly prove their mettle against the spah.

Yazdegird II and The Kidarites

Soon after the pacification of the Central Asian frontiers, the Sassanians faced a new threat. By the 440s CE, the Kidarites (also known as *Chuls*[68]) had crossed the Oxus and proceeded to attack Khorasan as well as Khwarezm farther north of Khorasan. The attacks were especially harsh as they involved looting, destruction and the capture of the empire's citizens to be carried off as slaves. The shahanshah, Yazdegird II (r. 438–457) and the military leadership convened the war council to discuss strategies for defeating these new threats to the empire's eastern domains.

A force of the savaran had been dispatched towards Nev-Shapur (Nishabur) along the eastern frontiers to face the Kidarite threat by 443 CE, but no decisive battle appears to have taken place. Instead, the Sassanians proceeded to build up massive walls at Gorgan and Khorasan (the walls of Tammisha and Gorgan, see Chapter 13). This proved to be a careful and prudent strategy, as Tammisha and Gorgan acted as powerful fortified bases for the assembly of savaran forces prior to undertaking offensives into Kidarite occupied territory. The war council had apparently ruled against a single 'all-out' offensive in favour of a series of carefully planned offensives that slowly unfolded in stages. Such tactics were possibly meant in part to assess the strengths and weaknesses of the Kidarites.

The phased offensives bore fruit seven years later to the extent that by 450 CE the spah had expelled the Kidarites from Sassanian territory. What remains unclear are the specific military details of the final battles against the Kidarites. At first glance it is possible to speculate that a combination of savaran lance charges, archery and close-quarters combat were the major factors in the spah's successes. Although the Kidarites were heirs to a long Central Asian cavalry tradition, the Sassanians may have employed superior tactics that tipped the balance in their favour. However, the exact nature of Sassanian tactics cannot be ascertained.

Following these successes, Yazdegird II built the fortress-city of Shahrestan-e Vuzurg (literally 'greater city' or 'locale'), which most likely was integrated into the fortress systems of the Gorgan Wall. Nevertheless, the Kidarites were far from finished. They retained the core of their military strength and continued to launch 'raid-and-run' attacks into Iranian territory, forcing Yazdegird to continue his campaigns against them to the latter days of his life. The Kidarite threat would be inherited by Yazdegird II's successor, Pirouz.

Pirouz and the Hephthalites (474–484 CE)

Following his passing in 457 CE, Yazdegird II's sons Hormuzd and Pirouz disputed the succession, plunging the empire into a civil war. The tide finally turned in Pirouz's favour when he took refuge among the Hephthalites in 459 CE to then enlist their military assistance to defeat Hormuzd and secure the throne in that same year.[69]

As soon as Pirouz ascended the throne he was faced with serious challenges in the Caucasus, notably the ongoing anti-Zoroastrian resistance movements in Armenia and Albania as well as the need to guard the Caucasian passes from Hun incursions. This often led Pirouz to request funds from the Romano-Byzantines, especially during the 460s CE.[70] Pirouz also had to face the highly formidable Kidarites, who had once again grown in power to menace the empire from Central Asia. He proved successful in crushing the Kidarites and announced his victory through an embassy to Emperor Leo (r. 457–474 CE) in Constantinople in 466 CE,[71] but the campaign was decisively ended in c. 468 CE when the Sassanians besieged and captured the Kidarite capital at Balaam in Central Asia (the exact location is uncertain).[72] The Hephthalites had supported Pirouz's military campaign by coordinating their military strikes with the Sassanians by attacking the Kidarites in Transoxiana in 466 CE.

The Hephthalite allies of Pirouz were to prove to be a deadly double-edged sword. They had recovered from their defeat at the hands of Bahram Gur by this time and stood poised to pose one of the greatest military threats faced by the Sassanians before the seventh century CE. This was a major reason why Pirouz's triumph against the Kidarites was to be short-lived. The defeated Kidarites had now given way to the Hephthalites by the late 460s CE.[73] Nevertheless the Kidarites were not completely wiped out, as elements remained in Kandahar in the late 470s CE;[74] and they did mount at least one unsuccessful attack against the empire in the time of Khosrow I. Nevertheless, the Hephthalites had replaced the Kidarites as a military power in the region and were now poised to attack along the empire's northeastern frontiers. The new Hephthalite state now ruled a vast swath of territory in Central Asia, which according to Kurbanov encompassed 'the eastern shore of the Caspian Sea, the deserts of Turkmenistan, areas around the Amudarya, extensive territory towards the eastern ward and along the upper course of the rivers Murgab and Tejen (Northern Afghanistan)'.[75] The Hephthalites also captured Balkh from the Sassanians,[76] which was for all practical purposes an act of war against the empire. Pirouz had another pretext for war, which according to Dinawari was the discontent of Tocharistan's local inhabitants against Hephthalite rule. It is fairly certain that Pirouz was organizing the spah for a major campaign against the Hephthalites in the 470s CE. The spah prepared for Pirouz's campaign by building a series of fortresses facing Central Asia. The Sassanians undertook three campaigns against the Hephthalites; all ended in disaster.

First Hephthalite war (474–475 CE). Pirouz launched his first campaign in 474–475 CE with an army comprising 50,000 troops.[77] The Hephthalites resorted to guile. A smaller portion of their forces engaged in a feigned retreat, luring the Sassanians deeper and deeper into their territory towards a gorge.[78] Realizing his predicament, Pirouz attempted to turn back, but it was too late. The greater portion of the Hephthalite forces who were in hiding up to this point sprang their deadly ambush and sealed Pirouz's egress route.[79] The Sassanians were now trapped[80] inside a valley with no way out. Pirouz, who had no means of escape, was forced to accept Hephthalite terms. The first was for the shahanshah to agree to give the Hephthalites a very large amount of gold, which was supplied by the Emperor Zeno (r. 474–491 CE). The Muslim historian al-Faqih (tenth century CE) described the failed outcome of Pirouz's first campaign:

> He [Pirouz] went [once] against them…he began to pursue to the waterless and fatal places. Then they attacked him and captured him, along with most of his court. Firouz asked the Hephthalites to give them and his captured soldiers freedom. He assured them [the Hephthalites] of God and firmly pledged that he would never overstep their boundaries. He has put between themselves and the Hephthalites a stone, which was made as border, and vowed that [he would not cross that border], calling as witnesses the Almighty God … Hephthalites

pardoned Firouz and gave him freedom and those who had been [in] captivity with him ...[81]

Other accounts describe a guide, who worked for the Hephthalites in secret, leading the Sassanians astray in the desert, forcing Pirouz to sue for peace terms from the Hephthalite king, Kushnavaz. But perhaps the greatest humiliation for Pirouz and the empire was in him having to prostrate himself before the Hephthalite king,[82] an action which was a profound blow to the prestige of the shahanshah. Kushnavaz also married Pirouz's daughter, but it soon was revealed that the bride was an imposter. Nevertheless, the spah had survived to return more or less intact back into Sassanian territories.

Second Hephthalite war (476–477 CE). Concerns over the rise of Hephthalite military power was most likely one of the reasons prompting Pirouz to break his treaty with Kushnavaz. The spah was once again mobilized for a new offensive against the Hephthalites; and Pirouz was once again defeated and captured by the Hephthalites in 476–477 CE.[83] Pirouz and his surviving troops were freed after having agreed to provide them a ransom of thirty mule-loads of silver drachmas.[84] But Pirouz could muster scarcely twenty mule-loads and, as a result, was forced to yield his son Kavad as hostage to the Hephthalites until such time that he could collect and pay the balance of the ransom to Kushnavaz. The cost of ransoming Kavad practically emptied the already strained royal treasury, thus placing severe economic burdens on the empire. Pirouz also promised (for the second time) to never attack the Hephthalites. By this time the region of Taleghan and Merv had fallen under the control of the Hephthalites.[85]

Third Hephthalite war (484 CE). Pirouz's decision to once again break his truce with the Hephthalites eight to nine years later proved disastrous. As events soon demonstrated, the spah had not absorbed the lessons of its previous defeats with respect to tactics, battle order, and military equipment. When the spah entered Hephthalite territory in force, Kushnavaz prepared his deadly stratagem. Procopius reports:

> [H]e [Kushnavaz] marked off a tract of very great extent and made a deep trench of sufficient width; but in the centre he left a small portion of ground intact, enough to serve as a way for ten horses. Over the trench he placed reeds, and upon the reeds he scattered earth, thereby concealing the true surface. He then directed the forces of the Huns that, when the time came to retire inside the trench, they should draw themselves together into a narrow column and pass rather slowly across this neck of land, taking care that they should not fall into the ditch.[86]

Kushnavaz's strategy in this campaign was similar to his previous campaigns. A smaller portion of his forces would again act as bait to lure the spah towards a locale of Kushnavaz's choosing. Pirouz once again rushed forward with his forces, apparently having failed to draw lessons from his previous battles against the Hephthalites. The bait force crossed, according to Procopius, over the safe passageway that had been constructed over the giant concealed trap. What transpired was one of the most disastrous defeats suffered by Iranian arms in the military history of pre-Islamic and Islamic-era Iran. According to Procopius:

> [T]he Persians, having no means of perceiving the stratagem, gave chase at full speed across a very level plain, possessed as they were by a spirit of fury against the enemy, and fell into the trench, every man of them, not alone the first but also those who followed in the rear. For since they entered into the pursuit with great fury, as I have said, they failed to notice the catastrophe which had befallen their leaders, but fell in on top of them with their horses and lances.[87]

Most of the Sassanian army perished in this assault,[88] although a small number of troops probably survived by halting before Kushnavaz's ditch. At this juncture Kushnavaz would have counterattacked first with horse archers followed by the main body of his army. Many Sassanian warriors who had avoided death in the ditch would have been cut down by arrows and the fearsome Hephthalite riders; a few would have been taken prisoner. Pirouz and seven of his sons were killed[89] in this battle; the shahanshah's body was never recovered.[90]

Consequences of defeat. The immediate consequence of this disaster was the loss of Khorasan to the Hephthalites.[91] Note that the territorial boundaries of Khorasan at the time would have been different than now, possibly including regions that are now located in western Afghanistan. The fortunes of the Sassanian Empire were at their lowest since the founding of the dynasty in the early third century. The spah had lost many of its top level officers[92] as well, and according to Tabari, much of Pirouz's entourage and family (including his daughter Pirouz-Dokht) were captured along with a number of high-ranking officers and government officials and a large portion of the royal treasury.[93] The loss of the latter had serious military consequences: there were no longer any funds left to rebuild and reequip the spah.[94] This was especially dangerous, as it meant that the ability of the Sassanians to defend the vast borders of their empire had been seriously weakened. The empire was rescued from complete military disaster by the efforts of Zor-Mehr 'Sokhra' of the Karen clan and Shapur-Razi of the Mehran clan, who in concert with various other nobles reorganized governmental authority in Ctesiphon to then usher in Balash in 484 CE as shahanshah of the realm.[95]

Military Reasons for the Spah's Defeats in 474–484 CE

Kushnavaz was evidently aware of the power of the super-heavy savaran. The sources do not mention close-quarter combat between Sassanian heavy lancers and Hephthalite troops. The giant Hephthalite ditch was intended to break the power of the savaran's charge and it succeeded in doing so, killing many Sassanian knights in the process. According to Procopius, the savaran knights were armed with lances,[96] indicating that Pirouz was evidently counting on the power, momentum and armour of his lancers to achieve victory. But as seen in previous chapters with respect to the super-heavy savaran knights, these formidable warriors suffered from serious battlefield limitations. By the same token, the more nimble Central Asian cavalry was capable of engaging in effective evasive manoeuvres to avoid the frontal assault of their savaran counterparts, and they benefited as well by the adoption of new military technologies such as (possibly) stirrups, lappet suspension, and improvements to their already powerful composite bows.

Stirrups. It is generally agreed that the Sassanians did not have stirrups, but it is possible that the Hephthalites were using this technology. If this is the case, this would at least partly explain why the Hephthalites were able to consistently prevail against the savaran, Kushnavaz's guile notwithstanding. If the Hephthalites did indeed have stirrup technology, they then would have had a significant advantage over the savaran with respect to battlefield manoeuvrability as a result of rider stability and equestrian control. The adoption of stirrups would have allowed Hephthalite heavy cavalry as well as lighter-armed and armoured horse archers to outflank their Sassanian (heavy cavalry and mounted archery) opponents. It is notable that in modern armoured warfare tank survival is contingent on three major factors for battlefield survival: firepower, (armoured) protection and mobility/manoeuvrability. Weakness in any one of these domains can spell the difference between survival and destruction during armoured combat between tanks; likewise, victory in cavalry engagements was often contingent on achieving just the right balance between armour, weaponry and mobility. The savaran knights possessed superior armour and were armed with excellent weapons, but the lack of stirrups proved a severe and often fatal handicap in any contest with the lighter-armoured but more mobile (possibly) stirrup-equipped Hephthalite cavalry. While these analyses provide a technical hypothesis for the Hephthalite successes, the latter's tactical acumen, battlecraft, combat skills and courage must have combined to produce Kushnavaz's victories over the armoured savaran knights.

Lappet suspension. The available accounts of Pirouz's wars with the Hephthalites provide few details on close-quarters combat. This certainly does not mean that the Central Asian cavalry at this time were not equipped or trained for face-to-face combat. An early 300s BCE battle scene at Xiaotangshan clearly depicts Chinese and Central Asian nomadic cavalry combating at close quarters with daggers and axes as well as archery. Few would question the Hephthalite ability to engage in close-quarter combat, but these formidable warriors may have deployed a new advantage over their opponents: the P-mount lappet suspension system discussed in Chapter 6. Hephthalite warriors would have been able to 'pre-adjust' the tilt of their swords for ease of access prior to battle whereas the scabbard-slide system of the Sassanians would have precluded them from doing so. As a result, when close-quarter clashes took place between the Hephthalites and the savaran knights, the latter would not have had the same level of efficient access to their swords, a factor which could have proven significant during such engagements.

The advantages of the lappet-suspension systems would have manifested in infantry combat as well. By 'infantry combat' we are referring to the dismounted savaran as well as the Sassanian heavy infantry of the 'paighan' or 'mirmillos' types. Had significant infantry clashes taken place, the Sassanians would have had the disadvantage of having to rest their hands on their sword hilts to 'tilt' these at an angle to avoid dragging their weapons on the ground.

The evolution of archery. As noted previously, stirrups provided horse archers with a more stable platform from which to discharge their missiles at a faster rate, with greater accuracy. In tandem with these developments was the evolution and improvement of the Central Asian bow itself. Put simply, this venerable weapon, known generally as the Avar bow in the West and adopted by the Romano-Byzantines, had evolved into a more powerful weapon capable of delivering missiles with greater penetrating power.

It cannot be proven with absolute certainty that the Hephthalites used Avar-type bows (or stirrups) during their battles with Pirouz, but if they did, they would have had a marked advantage over the archery of their Sassanian opponents. Such a weapon would have enabled the Hephthalites to wreak havoc among those surviving Sassanian troops who had avoided falling into Kushnavaz's ditch. It is possible (in contrast to Roman archery during the 350s to early 360s CE) that Avar-type bows were capable of damaging or even penetrating the armour of the super-heavy savaran, but this hypothesis had not been put to the test at the time of writing. If this were the case, however, it would partly explain the phasing out of the super-heavy savaran in favour of the more lightly armoured savaran of the 'composite type' by the sixth century CE (Chapter 6).

The question of armour. It is not clear how heavily armoured the Hephthalites were at the time of Pirouz's wars in 474–484 CE. Studies from the tomb of Tong Shou have indicated that Chinese heavy cavalry warriors of the mid-300s to early 400s CE wore amour of the lamellar type (not clear if this is hardened leather or iron), plumed helmets (protecting sides and back of head), short (sleeveless) mail coats featuring high necks and shoulder guards and chaps (not clear if these were of the classic Scythian type of 'armoured trousers') with the torso of the horses encased in armour and metallic horse-head shaped chamfrons for the horses' heads.[97] It is possible (though by no means proven) that the Hephthalites fielded heavy cavalry at the time of Bahram Gur in 421 CE and during their wars with Pirouz decades later. The question that may be raised here is whether the Hephthalites were wearing full-panoply armour of the Chinese (or contemporary savaran) type.

Another question pertains to horse armour: did the Hephthalites fit their horses in the torso armour of the Chinese and Iranian (especially Dura-Europos) type or had they devised their own innovations? A possible hypothesis may be derived from the later 'composite' savaran that appeared by the time of Kavad-Khosrow I. As noted in Chapter 6, these types of knights were influenced by the military experiences of the spah along the Central Asian frontier. The latest depiction of the Sassanian composite knight at Taghe Bostan clearly shows the steed to be partly armoured with protection for the animal's frontal area as well as being equipped with chamfrons. Was this new feature of decreased horse armour an indigenous Sassanian innovation or yet another case of Sassanian adoption of Central Asian technology? If the latter was the case, then perhaps the Hephthalites and other contemporary Central Asian warrior peoples (i.e. Kidarites) had developed this technology for the purpose of decreasing the overall weight of man and horse to increase mobility. Such a feature may have combined with other possible Hephthalite advantages in stirrups and P-mounts to give Kushnavaz's cavalry a decisive edge over the savaran in 474–484 CE.

Khosrow I: Destruction of Hephthalite Power (557–560 CE)

The heavy annual tribute imposed upon the empire by the Hephthalites had continued into Kavad's reign (r. 488–496 CE, 498–531 CE); Kavad was obliged to pay in Sassanian silver drachmas which were known in Bactrian documents as 'the Drachmas of Kavad'.[98] It is generally believed that it was after his battles against the Romano-Byzantines in the West and with the Khazars in the Caucasus when Kavad finally turned east to liberate Khorasan from the Hephthalites.[99] The crushing of Hephthalite power in Central Asia would be completed during the reign of Kavad's son, Khosrow I.

By the late 550s, Khosrow I had succeeded in stabilizing the western (Romano-Byzantine) frontier as well as removing potential threats in the south (Persian Gulf) region. Despite Kavad's campaigns to contain the Hephthalites, the latter remained at large in Central Asia with the potential to again slice into the empire's northeast Khorasan region.

Khosrow rejects the advice of the war council. Khosrow I, after having consulted with his war council, opted to act against its advice. According to the *Shahname*, Khosrow had to decide whether he should launch a military strike against both the Hephthalites and the khagan of China. As previously described, the Hephthalites had in 484 CE inflicted a catastrophic defeat on a large Sassanian army, killing King Pirouz and most of his troops.[100] Thus, 'The king [Khosrow I] got the assembly room ready in his palace, to which went the king-worshipping knights [savaran] along with the chief Mobad Ardashir and others such as Shapur and Yazdegird the scribe [Dabir], and all wise men capable of showing the way ... then having explained the situation the king asked them: What do you see in all this? What should we do?'[101]

The war council advised Khosrow I to refrain from launching a military attack. This clearly demonstrates that the war council was uncertain of the spah's ability to prevail in an all-out war against the Hephthalites. While Khosrow's military reforms had certainly been significant, these still required time to achieve full implementation – which may explain the council's hesitancy. Nevertheless, Khosrow opted for war. To that end, he had wisely struck an important military alliance with the Gok (Celestial/Blue) Turks in Central Asia, who were rivals of the Hephthalites.

Destruction of the Hephthalites. The spah, led by the savaran, struck the Hephthalites in 557–558 CE, with the Turks attacking the Hephthalites mainly to their north. The Sassanians achieved considerable success, such that by 560 CE Bactria had fallen under their influence. The Turks also seized control of

Hephthalite territory, making them the new Central Asian power in the Sassanian Empire's northeast. Khosrow's decision to make war against the Hephthalites in alliance with the Turks proved double-edged in the long-term as the Sassanians would later engage the Turks (and their Hephthalite vassals) in new wars in 588–589 CE and 619 CE.

Bahram Chobin (588 CE): The Spah Gains Supremacy

Khosrow I was succeeded by his son Hormuzd IV (r. 579–590 CE). Just two years before the end of his reign, Hormuzd IV faced a new and massive military threat from Central Asia. The defeated Hephthalites had now been incorporated into the armies of the formidable Gok (lit. Blue/Celestial) Turks. By this time the massive engineering works of the defensive walls stretching along the Central Asian frontier were most likely completed, or had neared completion (Chapter 13). This was part of the overall military reforms of the sixth century CE (Chapter 3). As noted by Howard-Johnston, the spah was now able to achieve a maximum concentration of force by positioning its forces at centrally located bases along the frontiers, enabling the Sassanian high command to rapidly deploy these forces to intercept invading armies 'at whatever point or points of entry' they chose.[102] The efficacy of these reforms would soon be demonstrated in the upcoming military engagements of the spah against the Turco-Hephthalite armies.

The Turco-Hephthalites invade (588 CE). While Chinese, Arabian and Persian sources agree as to the seriousness of the Turkish threat to the empire, they significantly vary with respect to the khagan's identity. Chinese sources identify him as Yang-Zu Dele as well as Asilan Dagan (Sinicized form of the original Turkic Arslan Tarkhan). Muslim historian An-Narshakhi calls the khagan Shir-e-Kishwar, which is Persian for 'Lion of the Nation'.[103] In Persian sources he is named Sawa Shah or Sawkh Shah. Turkish historians have identified the khagan as Il-Arslan,[104] an appellation which is adopted in this text.

The Gok Turks were formidable warriors who had benefitted from Chinese military-technical developments. The khagan was confident that he would prevail over the Sassanians. It would appear that he believed that his forces were superior to the spah especially with respect to cavalry warfare and archery. As well, the khagan must have known that the Sassanians were preoccupied with their western frontiers (see below), where the constant threat of war with the Romano-Byzantines compromised their ability to stem a Turco-Hephthalite invasion force.

The Turkish invasion went very well at first. The Sassanians, apparently alert to the danger, had stationed a very large force of 80,000 troops to guard the frontier.[105] The Turks crushed this force and quickly occupied Bactria (modern-day Western Afghanistan) and Khorasan. Those Sassanian troops that had survived the Turkish assault had opted to flee before the Turkish advance, compounding the unfolding disaster. The loss of such a large number of troops was a major blow to the spah. Especially hard-hit were the Sassanian infantry formations, which were completely overwhelmed by the Turkish onslaught.[106]

According to Tabari: 'Shaban, the great king of the Turks, advanced to Badqeis and Herat with 300,000 troops in the fifteenth year of his reign.'[107] The region of Herat had been invaded but the actual city of Herat had avoided capture. While estimates vary, the actual size of the Turco-Hephthalite invasion forces is reported as exceptionally large; estimates vary between 100,000 and 300,000 troops,[108] with Firdowsi reporting numbers as high as 400,000.[109] Most likely estimates of 300,000–400,000 troops are exaggerations, but few sources would dispute the fact that the spah was greatly outnumbered along the empire's north-eastern frontiers.

These dramatic victories clearly impressed the Turkish military leadership. The size and effectiveness of their forces would have most likely given them great confidence in their ability to decisively shatter the spah. Tabari reports the following message from the Turkish khagan, whom he identifies as 'Shaban' (Sheiban?) to Hormuzd IV regarding the Turco-Hephthalite invasion: 'Put in good repair the bridges over the rivers ... do likewise regarding all the rivers ... that lie along my route from your land to that of the Byzantines, because I have determined on marching against them from your land.'[110]

The khagan's letter conveyed two important messages. First, according to Reza, despite the khagan's stated intention to also 'march against' the Romano-Byzantines, the reality may have been different: the khagan may have been acting as an ally of the Romano-Byzantines, or at the very least had gotten their tacit approval for invading the entirety of Iran.[111] On the other hand, if the Turks really intended to attack the Romano-Byzantines after conquering the Sassanian Empire, then they were even more ambitious than their Hephthalite predecessors. This point pertains to the second message in the khagan's letter, namely his confidence in being able to defeat the armies of both the Sassanians and Romano-Byzantines and to conquer the entirety of their realms.

It would appear that the Turks had failed to appreciate that they had yet to face the cavalry elites of the savaran. In this endeavour, they would have underestimated the military developments of the spah, especially with respect to cavalry warfare, tactics and pyro-weaponry. These miscalculations were to lead the khagan's Turco-Hephthalite forces into a series of comprehensive defeats.

The war council and preparations for war. The seriousness of the threat led to the convening of the war council. Tabari reports that 'The decision was reached ... to move against the king of the Turks ... So Hormuz sent ... a man from the people of al-Rayy called Bahram, son of Bahram Jushnas, known as Jubin, with 12,000 men whom Bahram personally selected – mature and experienced men, not youngsters.'[112]

The Rayy region, close to modern-day Tehran, was the homeland of the Mehran clan, where Bahram originated. Bahram's nickname 'Chobin' (lit. wooden) may have been in reference to his tall and slender physique and/or to his prowess with the lance. The decision of the war council to select Bahram to lead the counterattacking force was a logical one as he had already distinguished himself by having led the savaran forces that captured Dara in 573 CE.[113] He had also served as the marzban of Azerbaijan and Armenia.[114]

The figure of 12,000 warriors is corroborated by Firdowsi[115] as well as Dinawari.[116] Bahram's selection of 12,000 savaran knights is of interest, especially in lieu of the evaluation processes of the spah for warriors prior to battles. As noted in Chapter 8, warriors were evaluated on the basis of their knowledge of military tactics, combat experience, and ability to maintain decision-making processes under the most difficult of circumstances. This may explain why the warriors of the crack force were reputedly 40 years old,[117] indicative of Bahram's intention to field the most seasoned warriors possible.[118] In this quest it is highly probable that Bahram had inspected a wide array of units and prestige units (e.g. the Shahanshah) to assemble his forces. It is also possible that Bahram's force was larger than his 12,000 'hand-picked' crack savaran warriors,[119] as he most likely also fielded supporting combat units such as battle elephants and the highly effective Dailamite infantry. As subsequent operations were to demonstrate, Bahram's forces also included siege engines and accompanying personnel.

Bahram's selection of warriors raises a number of interesting questions. Chief of these is why would Bahram select a relatively small force to confront a much larger force of Turco-Hephthalite warriors? The reasons may be twofold. The first factor may be found in the spah's endemic quality manpower problems (Chapter 16). The second reason may have been the dangerous and potentially volatile Romano-Byzantine frontiers along the western marches of the empire. Fighting had broken out between the Sassanians and the Romano-Byzantines as far back as c. 580 CE when the two clashed in the Mesopotamian and Syrian theatres during the reign of Tiberius II Constantine (r. 574/578–582 CE).[120] General Maurice managed to prevent the spah from prevailing in Anatolia, Syria and the Caucasus, where he scored a major victory. Maurice then became emperor in 582 CE and continued his battles with the Sassanians until 589–590 CE. These serious military threats on the western marches meant that the spah could not spare large amounts of professional manpower for the volatile Central Asian frontier. It would appear that while the spah could spare relatively modest forces to combat a Turco-Hephthalite invasion, it was willing to allow Bahram to select the highest quality troops for his crack force. Put simply, Bahram's strategy may have been to make up in quality for what he lacked in quantity. He also avoided marching directly towards Khorasan. To achieve full surprise and arrive unexpectedly, Bahram departed Ctesiphon for Ahvaz in Khuzestan in the southwest and from there marched into Khorasan to do battle.

The mission of Khorad-Barzin. Bahram Chobin resorted to guile and cunning to prevail against the vastly superior numbers of enemy troops. Before the battle a spy had been dispatched in guise of an ambassador to the Turco-Hephthalite camp with the apparent intention to discuss peace terms. In reality the 'ambassador' was a spy known as Khorad-Barzin.[121] Khorad-Barzin's mission was to also mislead the khagan as to the empire's true intentions. He showed a very conciliatory face on behalf of the empire, mainly to convey the impression that

Ctesiphon was very amenable to accommodate the khagan.[122] The 'ambassador' succeeded in carefully studying the Turco-Hephthalite camp, meticulously tabulating the enemy's apparent strengths, weaknesses and equipment. Having gathered all possible military intelligence, Khorad-Barzin quietly fled the Turco-Hephthalite camp at night to reach the encamped Sassanians and report his finds to Bahram.[123] The Sassanians now knew exactly where and how to strike the Turco-Hephthalite forces.

Bahram Chobin's strategy: 'commando' raid or military attack? Prior to his offensive, Bahram had issued strict orders to his commanders, notably Izad-Gushnasp and Narde-Gushnasp, to refrain from harming the non-military civilian population during the upcoming offensives into Central Asia. The spah had deployed from Nev-Shapur to confront the Turco-Hephthalites who were now in Khorasan. Bahram adopted a somewhat unorthodox tactical approach, at least in accordance with standard Sassanian military doctrine. He placed his cavalry in the centre, his elephant corps along the right and left flanks and the Dailamite infantry in front of the savaran.[124] This deployment would indicate that the Dailamites had been trained to repel frontal attacks by enemy cavalry, a feature often seen in Romano-Byzantine armies.

Central to Bahram's strategy was a surprise commando-style attack that would be part of his offensive. For this operation, Bahram relied on the very best of his warriors. According to Matofi: 'Bahram selected 100 Pahlavan warriors of the savaran and led them towards a hill where the Turkish king, who was seated on a golden throne, was observing the battle.'[125] Thanks to the earlier 'ambassadorial' spy operation, Bahram knew exactly where the khagan and his generals were located on the battlefield. Bahram was perhaps intending to decapitate the military leadership of the Turco-Hephthalites with one bold stroke.

Battle of Herat (April 588 CE). It is not clear where the battle actually took place; Baalami reports the region of Balkh, with Firdowsi and Tabari citing Herat as the battleground (Reza opines that Tabari and Firdowsi are correct).[126] The small but compact force of Bahram had arrived at Herat to face a reported total of 300,000 (or 400,000 according to Firdowsi) of the khagan's warriors. Like Bahram, the Turks were also employing battle elephants. According to Reza, the khagan had obviated his crushing numerical advantage by choosing to fight the battle in the vicinity of Herat.[127] To the north and south of Herat are situated the mountain chains of Zanjirgah and Amankuh respectively. The two mountain chains link up to the east of Herat. The Harirud River flows between the joining points of the two mountain chains. The Harirud River is not especially deep, but (excepting the summer and fall seasons) its current is too strong to allow for safe crossings. There is also a pass to the north of the river known as Bararan; it is approximately 8km long and wide enough for the passage of cavalry. It is here that the khagan committed a major military blunder. He chose to approach Herat through the Bararan Pass, but as the passage is too narrow he only managed to arrive with a portion of his forces and not with his full complement of 300,000 troops. Part of the reason for this may have been that the khagan was expecting to face the garrison of Herat rather than the actual strike force of Bahram. This assumption may have been reinforced by the earlier 'ambassadorial' mission of Khorad-Barzin. Reza's thesis is not supported by other Iranian military historians such as Safa and Matofi. According to Safa, the khagan had 40,000 troops protecting his throne, with 260,000 other troops assembled on the battlefield to face Bahram.[128] Citing primary sources (i.e. Dinawari) Matofi also concurs that the khagan had access to his full complement of forces in the upcoming battle against Bahram.[129] Reza's notion that Khorad-Barzin had possibly managed to persuade the khagan that Bahram's army was not in the vicinity may be questioned, especially in light of what Dinawari tells us. According to Dinawari, 'When news of the approach of the Iranian army reached the Khagan, he ordered the commander of his guards: 'go and bring this swindling Iranian to me.'[130] This makes clear that the khagan was (a) aware of the arrival of Bahram's army; and (b) had become suspicious of Khorad-Barzin's misinformation campaign. In summary, it would appear that the khagan had decided to deploy his full army (as per Dinawari), and he knew that he was facing the core of the spah's strike force rather than a weaker garrison force at Herat. Given how his numerical advantage had been a significant factor in his successes against the spah in his initial invasion of Iran, it is unlikely that the khagan would choose to yield that advantage when facing Bahram. While it is certainly possible that the battle did take place in the vicinity of Herat, the specific locale(s) where the actual battle took place may have been different than that proposed by Reza.

At first, as the armies squared off against each other, the khagan attempted to open negotiations. Bahram was offered the position of a high-ranking member of the khagan's court and to have his backing for the kingship of Iran. To sweeten the deal, the khagan offered one of his daughters as a wife for Bahram. All of these offers were rejected by Bahram, who proceeded to exhort his men to battle the invading khagan's host.

The khagan began the battle with an attack by his elephants into the Dailamite lines, but Bahram and the savaran counterattacked and repelled this assault. With the failure of this action, the Turkish cavalry attacked Bahram's savaran on the Sassanian left flank. Unlike their earlier breakthroughs into Iran, the Turks were now facing the best of the savaran who most likely would have proved especially adept in close-quarters combat, horse archery and lance combat. While the specifics of this clash are not known, the Turkish cavalry attack was defeated and forced to turn back. With the failure of his second attack, the khagan now unleashed his third assault: Bahram was now faced with a massive attack by 200 elephants.[131] Bahram is reported to have used 'naphtha throwers' (*naft-andazan*) against the elephants in concert with accurate archery aimed at the beasts' eyes and tusks.[132] The archers also shot flaming missiles at the elephants, many of whom had already been set on fire by the naft-andazan. The surviving and injured elephants now ran amuck, fleeing from the Sassanians towards the Turkish lines. Despite their best efforts, the Turks proved unable to maintain their cohesion, which meant that their advantage of numerical superiority was of little avail. It was at this juncture that Bahram launched his devastating counterattack.

The savaran apparently launched their attack first, which means that the Dailamite infantry standing to their front must have parted to allow their mounted
comrades to pass through. The battle elephants at Bahram's left and right flanks
were critical as they would have acted as the spah's 'mobile' missile platforms.
Given Sassanian battle doctrine (Chapters 6 and 9), these would have provided
covering fire to soften up the Turco-Hephthalite front lines, especially those
areas where Bahram and the savaran intended to break through. Once the breakthrough had been achieved with the savaran, Bahram and his 100 select pahlavan
knights peeled off to strike towards the khagan. Turco-Hephthalite forces were
most likely surprised by Bahram's attack, especially given the large disparity in
numerical strength in the khagan's favour. This factor is of interest, especially in
lieu of the Sassanian doctrine of the need for numerical superiority when engaged
in offensive operations (Chapter 9). The spah's battle doctrine also allowed this
proviso to be dropped in favour of attacking with numerically inferior forces
when enemy forces were occupying the territory of the empire.

As the savaran broke into the Turco-Hephthalite ranks, Bahram and his elite
knights acted quickly and succeeded in penetrating into the khagan's position. It
is not clear why the Turco-Hephthalite warriors failed to take advantage of their
numbers to stop Bahram. Their archery, if well-directed and coordinated, could
have wreaked havoc against Bahram's attack. This would suggest that disorgani-
zation within the Turco-Hephthalite camp had been very pronounced. By this
time Bahram's battle elephants would have most likely advanced toward the
enemy lines, with the archers riding the animals unleashing deadly salvos of missile fire against the stricken Turco-Hephthalites and thus preventing them from
reorganizing to counterattack. It is possible that Bahram may have directed his
elephant archers to target Turco-Hephthalite commanders as part of his 'decapi-
tation' strategy, but this hypothesis requires further research to substantiate.

The Dailamite infantry would have moved forward as well to engage the dis-
oriented Turco-Hephthalites in hand to hand combat. In a sense, this may
have been a 'mopping up' operation, but given the large numbers of Turco-
Hephthalite troops, the Dailamites would have most likely faced stiff opposition
from surviving elements of the khagan's armies. It would appear that the Dailamites overcame the Turco-Hephthalites in close-quarter combat, utilizing their
deadly skills with sword, dagger, axe and javelins. The savaran knights would
have wreaked havoc within the Turco-Hephthalite ranks, these also (like their
Dailamite comrades) pressing their attacks to engage in close-quarter combat.
Lance assaults as well as attacks with swords drawn in the 'Italian grip' style would
possibly have occurred, especially against surviving Turco-Hephthalite cavalry.
Citing Tabari, Safa reports that up to 30,000 Turco-Hephthalite warriors were
slain, 'the power of fire having all of them burnt'.[133] This appears to again be in
reference to a type of naphtha weapon hurled by Sassanian ballistae (Chapter 14).

As the Turco-Hephthalite soldiers reeled in disarray, Bahram with the support
of his pahlavan knights delivered his coup de grace: the khagan was killed.[134]
According to Tabari, 'Bahram killed Shaban with an arrow shot at him'[135] just as

the khagan had gotten up from his throne to mount his horse and flee the battle-field.[136] Bahram's pahlavan knights had engaged the khagan's bodyguards and killed them in close-quarters combat. The surviving Turco-Hephthalites began to flee the battlefield but Bahram ordered his warriors to pursue them, resulting in the slaughter of a large number of the late khagan's troops into the evening. Interestingly, Firdowsi mentions that many of the Turks were killed in a *tang rah* [tight/narrow pass/route] as they attempted to flee, with Tabari specifically iden-tifying this as the Bararan Pass.[137] It is very likely that the narrowness of the pass prevented the khagan's beaten army from fleeing en masse. By being forced to effect their egress through a narrow passageway, the Turco-Hephthalite soldiers would have fallen easy victim to the Spah's deadly massed archery barrages, which may have also included flaming missiles. If the latter were used, they may have also been intended as psychological weapons meant to amplify the despair and disarray in the fleeing host.

Battles with Yil-Tegin. With the khagan slain and his armies crushed, the imme-diate threat to the empire was over. Khorasan was saved from occupation and the city of Balkh that had fallen under the khagan's occupation was liberated by Bahram's warriors. Nevertheless, despite Bahram's overwhelming victories, the remnants of the Turco-Hephthalites were rallied by the late Khagan's son, Yil-Tegin. As with his father, Il-Arslan, the actual name of Yil-Tegin again varies with the sources. Persian and Islamic sources, for example, cite him as Narmud or Parmuda,[138] while Chinese sources identify him as Nili. Most likely the name Yil-Tegin (cited by Dinawari)[139] is a Turkic military appellation (like the 'suren' in the spah). Tabari records the exploits of the khagan's son, whom he identifies as B.R. Mudhah, as follows: 'B.R. Mudhah ... who was the equal of his father, marched against Bahram. Bahram attacked him, put him to flight, and besieged him in a certain fortress of his. Bahram pressed B.R. Mudhah so hard that he surrendered to him.'[140]

According to Safa's reports, the new Turco-Hephthalite armies stood at 500,000 troops, which, again, is probably exaggerated.[141] Nevertheless, Bahram apparently was concerned enough to augment his forces with reinforcements before facing down Yil-Tegin. Dinawari reports that Bahram proceeded to recruit warriors from Khorasan.[142] Most likely these men were of the East Iranian-type savaran (Khorasan, Soghd, etc.) referred to as the *savaran-e Khorasan* (Chapter 6). Despite this, Bahram's force was most likely still outnumbered, but once again troop experience, training and excellent generalship proved decisive.

The battle between the armies of Bahram and Yil-Tegin opened much like the battle with the late khagan: it was the Turks and their Hephthalite allies who attacked. This time Yil-Tegin chose to employ the Central Asian tactics of attack and feigned retreat, but these proved unsuccessful.[143] Yil-Tegin then launched a massive cavalry strike aimed at capturing Bahram, a gambit which nearly suc-ceeded.[144] Bahram evaded capture and his cavalry repelled the enemy horsemen. Yil-Tegin realized that the exclusive use of Central Asian cavalry tactics could not defeat Bahram and his knights.

After nightfall Bahram led the Sassanian counterattack,[145] and once again the Turco-Hephthalite troops were routed. It is also possible that Bahram employed naphtha-firing ballistae in this action. Yil-Tegin fled with 7,000 of his cavalry to the fortress of Avaze, where he made his last stand. Bahram and his army besieged and captured the fortress, forcing Yil-Tegin's surrender.[146] The immediate consequence of these Turco-Hephthalite defeats was the liberation of territories that had been originally overrun by the late khagan in 588 CE.

Battles with the eastern Turks. The great Turkish khanate had split into two distinct western and eastern khanates by the 580s CE. Bahram, who had completed his liberation of the empire's north-eastern territories now had to contend with the forces of the eastern khagan. Bahram crossed the Oxus River and was soon locked in battle with the eastern Turks. As with the battles against Il-Arslan and Yil-Tegin, Bahram's compact force emerged victorious. As noted by Czegledy, the eastern khagan was slain in battle.[147]

The spah had conclusively avenged its humiliating defeats during the reign of Pirouz. Central Asia was now secure for the empire with the Chinese gaining ascendancy over the eastern areas of the region. Bahram had also captured much booty during these campaigns, sending a haul of 300 camels to Hormuzd in Ctesiphon.

Smbat Bagratuni: The Savaran and the Naxarars Ascendant in Central Asia (619 CE)

The four-spahbod system for defending the empire from attacks on multiple fronts was put to the test once again in the early seventh century CE. The empire had been locked in a bitter war with the Romano-Byzantines since 603 CE, which diverted the primary attention of the Sassanians towards their western and Caucasian frontiers. Howard-Johnston highlights the spah's challenge of facing enemies on two fronts at this time, a dangerous situation and a difficult strategic dilemma which the Sassanians never fully solved.[148]

The long absence of a Sassanian military presence from the Central Asian frontiers provided the defeated Turco-Hephthalites and the Turkish khanates in general much needed time to recover from their crushing defeats in the late sixth century CE. The Gok Turk kingdom had also engaged in the building of a lucrative economic empire in conjunction with the Iranian-speaking Soghdian merchant class. This realm comprised a vast area from the Tien Shan mountains in the east westwards towards the eastern Caspian, encompassing Samarqand, Bukhara, Khashgar, Chach (Tashkent), Ferghana and the former lands of the Hephthalites bordering Iran.[149] Fielding a powerful Turco-Hephthalite army backed by a strong economy, the Turks took advantage of Ctesiphon's Romano-Byzantine wars to launch a major offensive into the empire's northeast. The attack took place just as General Shahrbaraz was entering Egypt in 619 CE.

The Turco Hephthalite armies tore into Khorasan and modern-day Afghanistan. Khosrow II summoned the Armenian general Smbat Bagratuni to the royal court and requested that he lead the counterattack force against the new invasion from the northeast. Armenian historian Sebeos describes the assembly of those warriors that formed the backbone of Bagratuni's forces:

> He [Khosrow II] gathered for him [Bagratuni] an army in fearsome array against the land of the Kushans in the east, and he bade him make marzipan whomever he might wish. So he departed, reached the nearby land of his former command, Komsh, summoned himself from Vrkan his own original army of compatriots and went directly to the east. These are princes of the Armenian nobles who [joined] him ... His troops were about 2,000 cavalry from that land.[150]

After being provided with a powerful army of savaran knights and other spah warriors by the Shahanshah, Bagratuni went to his Armenian homeland to gather his fellow Naxarar knights to join the spah against the Turco-Hephthalites. By this time the invaders were spread over the entire northeast including much of modern-day Afghanistan. When they received news of Bagratuni's arrival, the Turco-Hephthalites at first attempted to flee, but Bagratuni, determined to punish them for invading the Sassanian Empire, pursued them relentlessly. The Turco-Hephthalites abandoned their retreat, opting to make their stand against Bagratuni. Sebeos reports that 'they turned to face him in line of battle; they attacked each other in a mutual assault. The Kushan army turned in flight and was defeated by the army of Khosrov Shum. Many of them were killed and many fled.'[151]

Sebeos' account makes no mention of the tactics employed by the combatants, but it is clear that both armies had charged each other with combined-arms cavalry forces composed of mounted archers and lancers. It is likely that the Sassanians employed their standard tactics of beginning the battle with a massive archery barrage to soften up the enemy for a follow-up assault by savaran lancers. The Turco-Hephthalites, who themselves fielded excellent archery and cavalry contingents, probably did much the same. It is not known why the spah prevailed, but it is possible that the Sassanians' superior skills in close-quarter combat and the use of the lance proved decisive.

Despite this defeat, the Turco-Hephthalites remained a dangerous threat as the khagan was more than willing to provide them with reinforcements. Bagratuni first redeployed to Tus to then depart with 300 men to a walled village identified as Khrokht. At this point, according to Sebeos, a vast force of 300,000 troops arrived to replenish the battered Turco-Hephthalite ranks. This figure appears to be an exaggeration but nonetheless it is highly likely that the small Sassanian garrison was vastly outnumbered. Prince Datoyean, who was in command of the contingent of 300 troops, rushed bravely forth with his warriors to engage the enemy host. The Sassanian force was wiped out, but this action allowed Bagratuni to redeploy westwards to rebuild his forces. By now the crisis had reached epic proportions with the invaders having broken through as far as Rayy (modern-day Tehran) and Isfahan.[152] Despite these successes, the khagan was apparently unwilling to occupy Sassanian territory. The invaders, content with the vast plunder and spoils they had collected, returned to Central Asia.

Despite being engaged in the Romano-Byzantine war, the shahanshah had every intention of striking back at the Turco-Hephthalites. At issue was not simply a case for retaliation but the very real danger of a powerful Turco-Hephthalite force having the option to resume new invasions at times of its choosing. This threat had to be removed for two reasons. First, the collapse of the north-eastern frontiers could lead to the occupation of not just Khorasan but even regions of the Iranian interior. The recent raids by the Turco-Hephthalites had clearly demonstrated their potential to occupy even more land than the Hephthalites had after their victories over King Pirouz. The second reason Turco-Hephthalite power had to be destroyed was the prosecution of the Romano-Byzantine war. Put simply, the spah could not wage a full-scale war against two major enemies in a prolonged war. Therefore, the military strikes in the east had to be rapid and decisive. Sebeos provides a succinct overview of what transpired next: 'Smbat assembled the army and rearmed it. He also bought in many other troops to his support, and went to attack the nation of the Kushans and the Hephthalite king. The latter moved against him with a large force. They reached the battlefield and drew up their lines opposite each other.'[153]

Bagratuni had rearmed his warriors before the decisive battle with the Turco-Hephthalites, a process that would have involved the offices of the eiran-ambaraghbad who was responsible for the spah's entire array of magazines and arsenals (Chapter 10). As per Sebeos' reference to the 'nation of the Kushans', Thompson has noted that the Hephthalite king was a subject of the Turkish khagan.[154] As these forces assembled opposite of each other to do battle, the Turco-Hephthalite king challenged Bagratuni to a duel and was slain in the contest (for details of this duel see Chapter 15). This outcome shattered the morale of the Turco-Hephthalites who are described by Sebeos as having been 'terrified and turned in flight'.[155] Bagratuni now unleashed the naxarars and the savaran in hot pursuit of the fleeing Turco-Hephthalites. These cavalry attacks resulted in the slaughter of a large number of Turco-Hephthalites, with Bagratuni advancing as far as Balkh.[156] Bagratuni is also reported as having captured many Turco-Hephthalite fortresses which are described as having been 'burnt down'. This is perhaps an indication that Bahram Chobin-type projectiles with naphtha warheads may have also been deployed by Bagratuni.

The Central Asian Frontier After 619 CE
Despite their impressive victories over the Turco-Hephthalite armies, the spah could ill afford to permanently station a large force to guard the Central Asian frontier. As was the case after the Bahram Chobin offensives in 588 CE, the bulk of the spah's warriors were withdrawn towards the west. By now the empire was locked in a deadly struggle with its Romano-Byzantine rivals and could not sustain a prolonged two-front war. The Bagratuni-led offensives certainly devastated the Turco-Hephthalites, but the notion that the latter had been completely disabled militarily may be simplistic. The Sassanian northeast frontier was once again manned (at best) by a minimum retinue of warriors. According to Reza, the Sassanian Empire's northeast frontier was virtually defenceless from 620 CE

to the final days of the empire.[157] A new Turco-Hephthalite attack would have certainly caused serious problems for the Sassanians who by 626 CE were forced to face the counterattacks of Romano-Byzantine emperor Heraclius and his Khazar Turkic allies (Chapter 16). This raises interesting questions as to why the Turks of Central Asia chose not to invade Iran's northeast for a third time.

Reza attributes economic conditions as one reason for Turkish military inactivity. He notes that by this time the economic machine of the Gok Turk kingdom was in full swing, with secure control over the silk route trade.[158] The Soghdian merchants who played a key role in the Gok empire's commercial sector had no interest in a new war which they perceived as a threat to their bottom line. Reza notes that the Turkish leadership, seeing no threat posed to its control of the lucrative silk trade, saw no purpose in a new war. According to Reza, the Gok Turks were content to see their Turkic Khazar kinsmen take the war into Iran in conjunction with their Romano-Byzantine allies. Thus Sassanian Iran would be militarily and economically weakened, allowing the Gok Turks to expand their mercantile links without the need for military action against the spah. As noted by Sims-Williams, 'By this time [629 CE] Sassanian power had evidently waned once again and control of the region had passed to the Turks.'[159] It was only after the fall of Sassanian Persia to the Arabs that the Gok Turks would face a new military threat along their southern frontiers. Nevertheless the Turks too had been under severe Chinese military pressure and by 659 were on the verge of capitulation to the Tang Chinese.[160] Note that the Sassanian Empire had all but collapsed with the death of Yazdegird III (r. 632–651 CE) in 651 CE. As in their conquests of the Sassanian and Byzantine empires, the Arabs entering Central Asia were aided by the fact that their opponents were militarily spent. With the demise of the Sassanian Empire and the decline of the Turkish khagans, Central Asia was open to conquests by the Caliphate.

The second reason for Turkish inactivity was Chinese military pressure. Reza notes that the Tang dynasty in China had developed a keen interest in Central Asia. One of their leading generals, Li-Shi-Min, had begun a series of campaigns into Turkic controlled territories by 620 CE.[161] Hence increasing Chinese pressure was most likely another factor which dissuaded the Turks from launching any new military adventures against Iran after 619 CE.

Chapter 13

Military Architecture

Sassanian military architecture was a function of three distinct yet overlapping processes. First, it benefited greatly from the evolution of such architecture in the Iranian plateau since the times of the Elamites and Medes. Second, Sassanian military architecture was to become increasingly integrated into the spah's doctrine of defence of imperial territory and offence into enemy territory. It is notable that the spah's system of frontier defences was to be inherited by the Arabian Caliphs to form the *ribat* system in the Islamic era.[1]

This chapter will discuss the Sassanian Empire's military architecture, which was both extensive and formidable. There were numerous fortress systems, including frontier cities, wall defence systems, trench works or *khandaq*, etc. These were a cost-effective way of defending the empire, especially in being able to contain thrusts from enemies to then allow the spah to deploy enough troops to the threatened sectors to repel invasions, raids, etc. As noted in previous chapters, the empire had rationalized much of its defence around the 'quatro' or four-spahbod system, which depended heavily on fortresses and other defensive works. Military operations were often conducted out of fortresses, which meant that the empire spent considerable sums in the construction and improvement of such works. As will be seen later in this chapter, Sassanian military engineering was very much the equal of its Roman adversaries to the west.

Pre-Islamic Fortresses of Iran: Overview

Matofi traces Sassanian and post-Sassanian military architecture to the late Elamite and Median eras, roughly 3,000 to 4,000 years ago.[2] The development of military architecture on the Iranian plateau resulted in two distinct types of fortress: (1) those built in flatlands (few hills or mountains) and (2) structures built in mountainous regions. These are discussed further in this chapter.

Materials for the construction of Iranian fortresses would depend on the geography of the region. Therefore structures of the same type of design would often use different types of materials depending on where they were located. In general, fortresses in the interior of the Iranian plateau would often utilize hardened bricks and even hardened mud plaster whereas fortresses towards the north and in the Caucasus (see 'Wall of Derbent', below) would make greater use of various types of stones, limestone and other materials such as various types of chalks, etc.

Sassanian cities were essentially divided into two sections: (1) the *shahrestan* (civilian/residential section) and (2) the administrative and royal sectors in which the military leadership was concentrated. Sassanian builders made extensive use of mortar as well as unbaked bricks, stones and baked bricks (the latter three also utilized by the Romans).[3] Major Sassanian cities of this type would also be

Ardashir I (r. 224–241 CE) receives the diadem of *Farr* ('Divine Glory') from Ahuramazda at gshe Rustam. (*Photo: Amiri Parian, 2013*)

Triumph of Shapur I (r. 240/42–270/72 CE) at Nagshe Rustam: Emperor Valerian (r. 253–259 CE) oicted standing and grasped by Shapur; pleading and kneeling figure is believed to be Roman peror Philip the Arab (r. 244–249 CE). (*Photo: Mani Moradi, 2012*)

3. Close up of Shapur I at the triumphal
scene at Nagshe Rustam.
(*Photo: Saber Amiri-Parian, 2013*)

4. Panel featuring two equestrian joust-
battle scenes of Bahram II (r. 273–276 CE) at
Nagshe Rustam, known as 'Victory of
Bahram II'. (Photo: Mani Moradi, 2012)

Bahram II (r. 273–276 CE) surrounded by an audience of nobles and knights at Nagshe Rustam. (*Photo: Javad Chamanara, 2004*)

Narses (r. 293–303 CE) receiving the *Farr* ('Divine Glory') diadem from Warrior Goddess Anahita Nagshe Rustam. (*Photo: Saber Amiri-Parian, 2013*)

7. Enemy knocked off his horse by lance impact of Hormuzd II (r. 303–309 CE); the composition of this jousting scene is evidently derived from that of his great-grandfather Ardashir at Firuzabad. (*Photo: Javad Chamanara, 2004*)

8. Close-up of Hormuzd II and rear regalia of his horse at Nagshe Rustam. (*Photo: Saber Aniri-Parian*)

The Zoroaster cube at Nagshe Rustam. (*Chamanara, Kouchesfahani, Kial, Maddadi at Nagsh-e-Rustam, 2004*)

 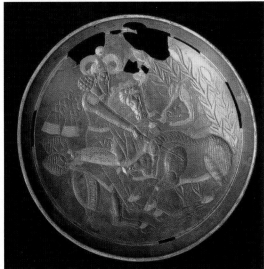

(*left*). Shapur III (383–388 CE) slays a leopard with his sword; on the reverse is a Soghdian scription, probably from the fifth century. (*Hermitage, inv. no. S-42*)

(*right*). A dismounted Bahram Gur slays a boar with his sword, fourth century CE; this was scovered in the village of Kerchevo in Perm province of Russia. (*Hermitage, inv. no. S-24*)

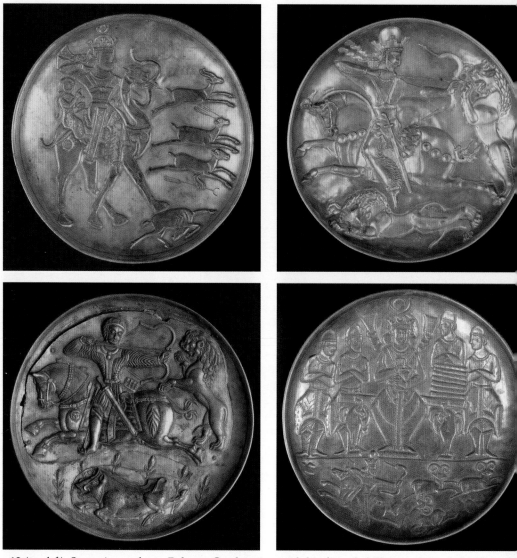

12 (*top left*). Sassanian archery: Bahram Gur hunting with his famed skills in archery; behind sits h[
companion Azadeh (seventh century CE). (*Hermitage, inv. no. S-252*)

13 (*top right*). Shapur II (309–379 CE) hunting lions with the Parthian shot. (*Hermitage, inv. no. S-253*)

14 (*bottom left*). Pur-e Vahman engaged in the Parthian shot against a pursuing lion. (*Hermitage, inv. no. S-247*)

Plates 13 & 14 both depict the Parthian shot in the early and late-post Sassanian eras. Despite the
surface similarities between the two plates, the two are profoundly different with respect to archery
techniques, sword suspension and stirrups. Archery: Shapur II draws the arrow with his right hand
Pur-e-Vahman apparently appears to be deploying the Mongolian draw but both warriors use the
Sassanian technique of 'pointing' their index fingers in the arrow's direction; Sword suspension:
Shapur wears the scabbard slide system versus Pur-e-Vahman's locket suspension system;
Equestrian stability: Shapur's horse features no stirrups while Pur-e-Vahman has the advantage of
stirrups.

15 (*bottom right*). The enthroned 'Khosrow I Anoushirawan' (lit. 'He of Immortal Soul')
(r. 532–579 CE) clasping his sword. The king is surrounded by four knights (probably the four maj[
Spahbods of the Spah). (*Hermitage, inv. no. S-250*)

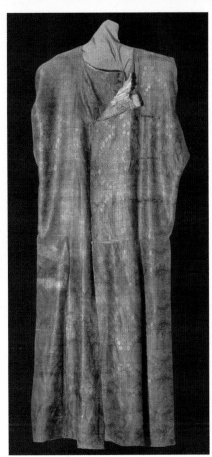

(*above left*). Close-up view of the sword clasped by the enthroned Khosrow I. (*Hermitage, inv. no. S-250*)

(*above right*). Late or post-Sassanian *brahmag e artesharih* (lit. 'costume of warriors') discovered in e Caucasus, a unique kaftan bearing the revered Sassanian *senmurv* motif. (*Hermitage, inv. no. Kz-6584*)

(*below left*). King Pirouz (r. 459–484 CE) in a hunting area, found in the town of Tcherdyne in the rm region (item dated to 460–480 CE). (*Hermitage, inv. no. S-216*)

(*below right*). Unidentified Sassanian king hunting ibex and gazelles, excavated at Ufa (Republic Bashkortostan in Russia, situated between the Volga River and the Urals). (*Hermitage, inv. no. S-297*)

20. Recreation of an *aswar* cavalryman from the third century, western Iran. He is equipped in a replica of the helmet found at Dura Europos and a mail hauberk, a relatively new style of armour i the third century. (*Courtesy of Nadeem Ahmad; photograph by Matt Body*)

21. Recreation of a Sasanian 'tanurigh' cavalry warrior, sixth to early seventh century CE. (*Courtesy o Amir Askari Yahyavi; photograph by Nadeem Ahmad*)

22. Recreation of a Spahbed from the late sixth or early seventh century. His armament is based on several museum examples and finds from Iran. The helmet is a copy of the one in the Metropolitan Museum of Art and finished with a *korymbos* and diadem made with five crescent moons as seen on the Spahbed seals. The sword (drawn in photo) would be suspended with two P-shaped fittings from a belt studded with pearls. (*Courtesy of Nadeem Ahmad; photograph by Matt Body*)

A Spahbed riding with his *redag* (page) from the late sixth or early seventh century; the arms and [ar]mour are based on several museum examples and finds and based on period artwork. Cavalry [for]ces such as these secured great victories for the Spah during general Shahen and Shahrbaraz's [thr]usts against the Roman-Byzantine Empire in the early seventh century CE before Emperor [He]racles' devastating counterattacks in concert with his Turkic Khazar allies in 627–628 CE. [Sas]sanian warriors such as these, operating in concert with Armenian Naxarar knights, combined to [def]eat a vast Turco-Hephthalite invasion from Central Asia in 618–619 CE. [Co]*urtesy of Nadeem Ahmad and Simon Weid; photograph by Matt Body*)

24. Sogdian armoured cavalry from Central Asia seventh to eighth century. (*Courtesy of Nadeem Ahmad; photograph by Eilidh Gilmour*)

25. Sassanian royalty hunting, using a courtly finger release. (*Courtesy of Nadeem Ahmad*)

Recreation of a Sassanian sword, dagger and pearl studded royal belt, late sixth to early seventh century CE. The sword has a hilt with an indentation for the first finger and is decorated throughout with a feather motif. Also visible is a coat of mail, made with iron links riveted together and butted copper alloy decorative rings. (*Courtesy of Nadeem Ahmad*)

A sword presentation *shapsheraz* ceremony of a nobleman presenting a sword to a King, with an armoured warrior in attendance. (*Courtesy of Nadeem Ahmad, Jamie Wright, and Amir Askari Yahyavi; photograph by dh Gilmour*)

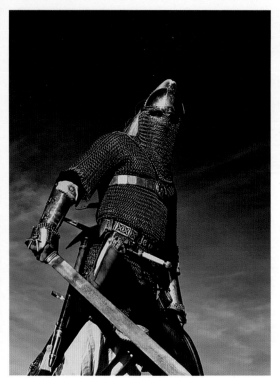

28 (*above left*). Dismounted Sassanian Savaran knight with sword with Kushan or East-Iranian type blade. (*Courtesy of Ardashir Radpour & Holly Martin*)

29 (*above right*). Dismounted Savaran knight engaged in archery as at the Battle of Anglon (542 CE). (*Courtesy of Ardashir Radpour & Holly Martin*)

30 (*below*). Detail of suspended *tirdan* (arrow-case). Note the lappet suspension system. (*Courtesy of Ardashir Radpour & Holly Martin*)

(*above left*). Savaran officer with lance. (*Courtesy of Ardashir Radpour & Holly Martin*)

(*above right*). Savaran officer engaged in horse archery. (*Courtesy of Ardashir Radpour & Holly Martin*)

(*below*). Close up of riveted Sassanian helmet with mail. (*Courtesy of Ardashir Radpour & Holly Martin*)

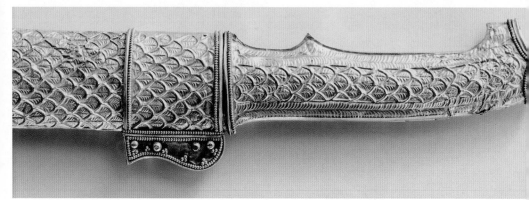

34. Late Sassanian sword with gold sheeting shown from (*top*) front and (*bottom*) rear. (*Riggisberg Abegg Foundation, inv. no. 8.I.63*)

35. Detail of the same sword; note 'pistol grip' design of handle and strap attachment for upper section of sheath for lappet suspension system; the feather-type motif decoration appears to be a tribute to ancient Iranian mythological bird motifs such as *Senmurv*.

36. Sassanian fingercaps: (*left row*) inv. no. 8.137.66; (*middle Row*) inv. no. 8.135.66; (*right row*) Riggisberg, Abegg Foundation, inv. no. 8.136.66. (*Riggisberg, Abegg Foundation*)

Shapur III (*left*) and Shapur
(*right*) posing with scabbard-
[sli]de broadswords at Tagh-e
[Bo]stan. Note stance with palm
[of] right hand placed on top of
[sw]ord hilt and left hand
[gra]sping hilt-handle. (*Courtesy of
[Sha]hyar Mahabadi, 2004*)

38. Relief at Tagh-e Bostan
depicting the investiture of Shapur
II (309–379 CE) or Ardashir II
(361–363 CE) at centre. To the left
stands Mithras with a ceremonial
sword or a Barsom (ceremonial/
religious bundle of twigs or rods);
possibly a depiction of a type of
honouring or 'knighting'
ceremony. To the right is Ahura-
Mazda or possibly a chief magus.
Beneath the feet of the king is a
trampled figure, possibly that of
Julian the Apostate. (*Photo: Shahyar
Mahabadi, 2004*)

[39.] Investiture scene above the
[lif]e Sassanian armored knight
[at] the vault at Tagh-e Bostan.
[To] the left stands Goddess
[An]ahita with her right hand
[rai]sed, bestowing a diadem of
[glo]ry or *Farr* towards Khosrow
[II] (at centre) who receives a
[dia]dem with his right hand
[fro]m Ahura-Mazda or the chief
[ma]gus. Anahita was a revered
[go]ddess of war among
[Sa]ssanian warriors. (*Photo:
[Sha]hyar Mahabadi, 2004*)

40. Tagh-e Bostan Royal Hunt at the right side of the grand Iwan. This shows a great deer hunt taking place within an enclosure or *pardis*. In one depiction, Khosrow II is provided shade with an umbrella handled by a courtier while he rests his hand on the sword handle, almost identical to Shapur I and his scabbard slide sword at Nagshe Rustam. Another depiction is that of a rider (possibly again Khosrow II or a nobleman) about to shoot an arrow downwards towards prey; the sword is suspended at an angle consistent with the lappet-suspension method of Central Asia. Herrmann has argued that the level platform of the rider's feet suggest that he was probably using stirrups. (*Photo: Shahyar Mahabadi, 2004*)

41. The late Sassanian knight at the great vault or Iwan at Taghe Bostan. The figure, generally identified as Khosrow II and his steed Sabdiz, provide valuable information on late Sassanian helmet featuring 'eyebrow' view slits, *bargostvan* (horse armour), mail, attire and the lappet suspension system. As the feet of the statue are broken off, it is not clear if the knight was using stirrups. The late Sassanians most likely deployed stirrups given the important but little known discovery of a pair of iron stirrups dated to the late Sassanian era in Iran's Marlik region.
(*Photo: Javad Yousefi, 2011*)

protected by a wall as well as ditches. The walls of Sassanian castles and fortresses would often feature long and vaulted corridors,[4] stepped niches and narrow rooms. The Sassanians could and did design very formidable walls, both for fortified structures and long defensive walls (see discussions on defensive walls later in this chapter). The wall of the fortress of Dastegerd for example was unusually thick at 16.6m![5]

There were also windows of the 'blind' type featuring arrow-slits (with triangle or horizontal coverings) with small niches that would be constructed within the facades of the walls.[6] The facades were not simply decorative but also military in function by allowing archers to discharge missiles. Sassanian military architecture also had interesting designs with respect to bastions, ramparts and semi-circular towers. One notable feature was bastions with pronounced extensions. The rampart system at Bishapur, for example, had been designed with semi-circular bastions that were separated by 40cm intervals.[7] The Ayvan-e Karkheh palace, famous for its long corridors, apparently featured a rampart section constructed of bricks arranged in an elaborate pattern. Ramparts of mud-brick construction were standard as seen in their utilization in the fortifications of the Sassanian capital at Ctesiphon,[8] which is further discussed later in this chapter. Dastegerd's semi-circular towers featured a unique pattern of inter-connectivity through a system of narrow corridors.[9] Prominent bastions often had gates placed between them. Another interesting feature was the placement of vertical shafts to connect the gate chamber with the defence platform placed above it.

Fortresses in pre-Islamic Iran and the Sassanian era in particular were of several types, notably circular, square-rectangular, and 'irregular' designs as well as designs particular to mountainous regions. There were also fortresses that featured unique types of technologies such as 'de-humidifiers'.

Square-rectangular system: the example of Siraf. The square-rectangular system, usually used for the defence of cities or towns, had their structures based upon the form of squares or rectangles. The typical design of such square-rectangle structures was the installation of four towers (one at every corner). These towers would be used for defensive purposes, guard duties and gate keeping. Examples of these types of fortresses can be seen in Iran at Qasr-e Shirin, Harsin and Siraf. The case of Siraf is of interest as this was also a coastal installation. The fort of Siraf was most likely established after the successful campaigns of Shapur II against Arab raiders who had menaced Iran's southern Persian Gulf coastline and interior. Primary excavations which began from the early 1970s found that the Siraf fort was of the traditional square type and more than 1km across.[10] On the south side of Siraf was a ceremonial-type entrance with a rectangular gatehouse. Hollow semi-circular towers protected that structure. Another circular tower acted as the reinforcement for the southeast angle of the structure. The structure housed a series of barrack-like rooms, at least some of which could have been used as magazines. Behind the outer walls was a fighting platform. It would also appear that the Siraf fort had a series of interval towers. Siraf housed a settled community as well as a series of narrow streets.

Whitehouse and Williamson were the first to speculate on a 'Roman connection' with Siraf.[11] The researchers note that a number of construction details at Siraf closely resemble those seen in Roman structures, especially at ancient Singara. Of note are the parallels that were discovered between the semi-circular towers at Singara and Siraf. Both Singara and Siraf feature arrow slits at their respective ground levels at shoulder-height or higher. Whitehouse and Williamson note that this is most likely the result of the arrival of Roman prisoners who were brought to the site as engineers by the Sassanians (recall discussion in Chapter 11).

Circular system: the case of Ardashir Khurra. The second type of land-based fortress (circular) identified by Matofi may in fact be traced to the Indo-European arrivals into the Iranian plateau in c. 1000–800 BCE, with the earliest possible introduction dating to the Scythians. As noted by Ghirshman, the 'design of [Partho-Sassanian] cities involved the robust circular design which was very efficient at defending against flank attacks ... western military engineers were to draw upon this concept in the Middle Ages.'[12] In practice the Parthians had at least three types of fortresses: circular, rectangular and polygon.[13]

Iranian circular fortresses would often feature building structures along both sides of their 'streets', not much different than a typical city street in antiquity.[14] The city of Ardashir Khurra ('Ardashir's Glory') at Firuzabad is typical of early Sassanian architecture utilizing the Parthian system of circular defence.[15] Ardashir Khurra's circular urban plan featured twenty subdividing lines which radiated outwards from the central tower, which then divided the fortress into twenty major sections.[16] There were two main (perpendicular) lines which also divided the city into four main quadrants with each having a gate of its own.[17] As noted by Matheson, Ardashir Khurra was surrounded by a ditch and earthen ramparts at a maximum diameter of 2km; the rim formed a virtually perfect circle with 'gateways at the four quarters'.[18]

There was also a tower known as the *tirbal* which was located exactly in the centre of the radial system. The tirbal allowed the entire plain to be observed, which explains its rationale, and most likely served as a lookout or military signalling post.[19] The function of the tirbal may have been more than just military. The tower featured a 2-meter-wide staircase (with a gradient of 13/30cm) with pieces of stucco still laying at the ingress of the tirbal's entrance. It is therefore possible that this tower had both a military and ceremonial/religious function.

It is notable that Ibn-Balkhi, reporting eleven centuries after the structure was originally built in the early third century CE, observed that the layout of Ardashir Khurra was 'as though drawn by compasses'.[20] Other military architecture features of note at Ardashir Khurra were bastions that had been built as part of its structure. The city centre, which may have housed official buildings, was surrounded by its own wall.[21]

'Irregular' fortresses: the case of Firuzabad. These types of fortresses were characterized by two features in that they were (1) of the 'combined' or 'blended' type which combined square-rectangular with circular designs; and (2) constructed on strategic heights. Four prominent designs of the 'irregular' type are those of Firuzabad, Turang Tepe,[22] Bishapur and the *atashgah* (fire locale/temple) of Isfahan.[23]

Ardashir's palace at Firuzabad is the classic example of this type of military architecture which combined the circular and square-rectangular systems in accordance with the proximate terrain to maximize its defensive capabilities. One end of the castle features a circular design followed at its rear with long curtain-type walls of the 'rectangular' type.

Fortresses with de-humidifier technology: the case of Dezh-e Shapur Khwast. This castle still stands atop a hill in Khorramabad, the provincial capital of Luristan in western Iran. Known today as the Falak ol Aflak, the Dezh-e Shapur Khwast was built during the Sassanian era. Materials used for the construction of this fortress were two types of bricks (mud-fired and mud) as well as mortar, wood and stones. The original fortress had a rampart of two layers. The total number of towers around the fortress was twelve, with only two of these standing today.

Perhaps the most interesting feature of the Dezh-e Shapur Khwast was the ingenuity of Sassanian engineers in installing what was essentially a 'dehumidifier' canal system. This was necessary as various materials of the fortress, especially stones and wood, are highly vulnerable to the region's humid climate as well as to the humidity emanating from the underground water in the area. To solve this problem, Sassanian engineers built the fortress on the highest elevation in Khorramabad. Then, the entire 'basement' area of the fortress was designed with 'de-humidifier' canals that stood at 1 meter-plus. With the fortress situated atop a hill, the wind would be constantly blowing into the 'basement dehumidifier canal system' which virtually eliminated the danger humidity would pose for the fortress's stone and wood materials. The case of Dezh-e Shapur Khwast is notable in that it demonstrates the Sassanians' determination to build fortresses that not only possessed powerful defensive capabilities but would also be resilient to the ravages of weather and time.

Mountain fortresses: the case of Bazz. Fortress design in mountainous regions often factored surrounding geography to help maximize the site's defensive capabilities. A typical example is the castle of Bazz in Iranian Azerbaijan which stands to this day. The foundations of this structure were built during the Parthian era, with the fortress being strengthened and improved by the succeeding Sassanians. Bazz was built at an elevation of approximately 2,500m and was surrounded by crevices that are narrow and deep (around a depth of 300m).[24] The crevices were flanked by rocky walls, making any attack against Bazz exceedingly hazardous. The narrow defiles leading to Bazz severely limited the number of troops that could be deployed against the castle. Attacking infantry forces could easily be 'channeled' into the rocky passes and exposed to archery and counterattacks. By the time any attacker neared Bazz, he would have to cross a meandering defile and then cross a very narrow defile just one person wide. The steep climb and narrow passes practically negated any advantages normally posed by cavalry forces. Even siege engines would be difficult to employ due to the rough terrain around Bazz. These advantages allowed Bazz to be held by a modest complement of troops. Bazz was to be the base for a major ninth century anti-Caliphate Iranian rebellion led by Babak Khorramdin[25] of Iranian Azerbaijan (795–838 CE). One major reason why Babak's rebellion lasted for so long was the castle of Bazz, which kept the armies of the Caliphate at bay for approximately thirty years (816–837).[26]

Ctesiphon (363 CE). One of the most important aspects of Julian's invasion of Sassanian Persia in 363 CE (Chapter 9) was his failed attempt to storm Ctesiphon. There are few details as to why this attempt failed, especially with respect to siege engines, Sassanian counter-siege operations, etc. Julian's massive invasion force must have had siege engines and anticipated the possibility of reaching Ctesiphon and besieging it. One little consulted source, Gregory Nazianzenus' *Oriationes*, may offer some clues as to the military architecture of Ctesiphon:

> Ctesiphon is a strongly fortified town, hard to take, and very well secured by a wall of burnt brick, a deep ditch, and the swamp coming from the river. It is rendered yet more secure by another strong place, the name of which is Coche, furnished with equal defences as far as regards garrison and artificial protection, so closely united with it that they appeared to be one city, the river separating both between them. For it was neither possible to take the place by general assault, nor to reduce it by siege, nor even to force a way through by means of the fleet principally, for he [Emperor Julian] would run the risk of destruction; being exposed to missiles from higher ground on both sides ... the danger that menaced him from the two garrisons.[27]

Coche (or Veh-Ardashir) had been built in the third century CE to replace the Hellenistic city of Seleucia.[28] Coche/Veh-Ardashir was on the right or western side of the Tigris River with Ctesiphon situated on the left or eastern side of the river. Gregory Nazianzenus makes clear that attacking Ctesiphon with a fleet along the Tigris was dangerous as the spah garrisons would fire their missiles upon them from both sides of the river (from Ctesiphon itself and Coche). The cities would most likely have had counter-siege batteries such as ballistae which could have inflicted severe damage upon any ships daring to enter the waterway between Ctesiphon-Coche. Ammianus Marcellinus reports, for example, of an 'arrow shot from an engine on the walls'[29] of Ctesiphon towards Julian as he was attempting a reconnaissance of the city. In any event, Julian burnt his fleet and made no attempts at a naval assault.

Gregory Nazianzenus' description of the defences of Coche-Ctesiphon is of interest in two respects: building materials and the use of moats/ditches. Ctesiphon's primary defensive structures are described as a 'wall of burnt brick', with Ammianus Marcellinus reporting the city as being fortified with walls.[30] The mention of bricks is interesting as Sassanian architects often used these in the construction of domes and vaults. Nevertheless, bricks could also be used in the construction of buildings as well, examples being locales such as Shiz, Ayvan-e Karkha, Dastegerd and even Ctesiphon. As noted previously, Ctesiphon's defences have been identified as the mud-brick rampart type, but these were most likely highly reinforced; it is possible that these walls were exceptionally thick. A hint of this is provided by Libanius' report of Ctesiphon's 'thickness of wall'[31] during Julian's time, but no further details are provided as to its actual dimensions. Recall the earlier mention of the unusual 16–17m thickness of the walls of Dastegerd; the 'thinner' wall of Gorgan facing Central Asia was 'only' 6–10m thick (discussed later this chapter).

Of equal interest is Gregory Nazianzenus' description of 'a deep ditch' surrounding Ctesiphon which was already flanked by the Tigris along its west. While exact dimensions for such a ditch in Julian's time are unknown, the standard width of Sassanian ditches is believed to have been in the 20m range (see discussion later in this chapter).

Frontier cities and military bases. Howard-Johnston notes that frontier cities often served as 'heavily fortified military bases'.[32] These needed to be garrisoned with regular troops (savaran, Dailamites, archers, etc.) along with support and logistics units. These frontier cities served in two capacities, defence and offence. In defence, the garrisons of the frontier cities would often be fighting to repel enemy attempts at capture and would have to hold out until the arrival of reinforcements. In the offence, frontier cities acted as staging posts for the spah's thrusts into enemy territory. In this endeavour, the local garrison would presumably be reinforced prior to the local force marching into enemy territory.

Military bases were also vital for a massive military machine facing multiple fronts. Essentially, the Sassanians required a permanent infrastructure system capable of housing troops, supplies, equipment, fodder and foodstuffs. These same bases were often built along critical roads, river and sea routes where the safe transport of supplies and intact communications was often critical in times of war.[33] In a sense this system of logistics, communication and troop deployments was dependent upon a massive system of military architecture which included not just frontier cities and military bases but even more massive construction projects such as wall-systems along dangerous frontiers.

Sassanian Wall-Systems for Frontier Defence: An Overview

Emperor Vespasian (r. 69–79 CE) had begun the construction of 'limes' (the Roman system of fortified and/or marked frontiers) in Roman-ruled Syria. The construction of limes was extended by Emperor Trajan (98–CE), such that by the time of the invasion of Parthian Persia, formidable Roman fortifications had become operational along the Euphrates River in Mesopotamia and the Caucasian theatre.[34] Roman fortifications were more or less completed by the time of Diocletian (r. 284–285 CE and 285–305 CE as co-emperor). As noted by Frye, the Roman system of defences gradually declined after Diocletian with the later (post-Parthian) Sassanians investing great confidence in the efficacy of their frontier defences right up to the times of the Arab conquests.[35] Defensive walls of course were nothing new to Near Eastern warfare; Xenophon, for example, reported that the Neo-Babylonians built a 'Median Wall' for the protection of Babylon against the Medes.[36]

Khosrow Anoushirvan's reforms rationalized the defence of Iran into four general zones of defence corresponding to the empire's western, northern, eastern/north-eastern and southern regions (Chapter 3). Khosrow constructed (and strengthened a series of existing) wall-systems of defence corresponding to northern, eastern/north-eastern and southern sectors. Each of these segments had a defensive wall for blocking potential invaders. In general there were two walls facing the northeast (Wall of Gorgan and Wall of Tammisha) to confront nomadic invaders from Central Asia (especially Turkic and Hephthalite-Hun warriors), the Khandaq-e Shapur facing potential Arab invaders from the south-west and the Wall of Derbent in modern day Dagestan entrusted with blocking Khazar invaders attacking from the northern Caucasus.[37] Each of the wall-systems had garrisons; however, given the empire's limited resources of professional military manpower, none of these could be permanently garrisoned with a full complement of troops. The barracks for these wall-systems could certainly be augmented in times of crisis, when the frontier region was being attacked or under threat of attack.

Interestingly, the empire did not construct a singular Maginot-type system on its western frontier facing the Romano-Byzantine Empire. This is of particular consequence as the Sassanian Empire fought a number of wars against the Roman (later Romano-Byzantine) empire from the early third century CE to the seventh century CE.

One interesting peace treaty, notably that between Khosrow Anoushirvan and Emperor Justinian (r. 527–565 CE) had a stipulation against the building of Maginot-type defences along their common frontier by stating 'neither state should erect ... in the border areas ... a wall so that this would not lead to accusations of trouble-making and cause a breach of the treaty'.[38] In the strict military sense the building of such walls by the Sassanians were most likely superfluous because they were less effective against the determined professional armies of the Roman-Byzantines who had an impressive inventory of siege weaponry with which to breach and/or scale the fortifications.[39] Instead of long Maginot-type defensive walls, the Sassanians relied on a system of powerful fortresses along the Romano-Byzantine frontiers for defence. The Romano-Byzantines certainly built strong fortresses of their own; one notable case being that of Emperor Anastasius (r. 491–518 CE) who built a series of fortifications along the Romano-Byzantine borders with the Sassanian Empire.[40] As noted previously, Ctesiphon, like Constantinople, had a very formidable defence-fortification system which enabled it to evade capture by the Emperor Julian in 363 CE (Chapter 9).[41]

Nevertheless, the term 'defence' is used with considerable licence here as fortresses were also used by the spah for the assembly of troops for impending offensives. The formidable city-fortress of Nisibis, for example, was used as an important base for the assembly of the spah's forces for launching its powerful attack against the Romano-Byzantine Empire in 603 CE. The Romano-Byzantines were well cognizant of the dangers posed by Nisibis as the afore-mentioned Emperor Anastasius had actually commissioned the construction of Dara-Anastasioupolis, which led to official protests from Ctesiphon as the locale was located just 28 *stadia* from Iranian-held Nisibis at the time.[42] The Sassanians had argued that the construction of Dara-Anastasioupolis was essentially in viola-tion of their treaty with the Romano-Byzantines.[43]

The case of Nisibis highlights an important military doctrine alluded to earlier: walls and fortresses were not exclusively used for defence in the Maginot Line sense; they could also be used for staging the spah's planned offensives into enemy territory. This was of course along the empire's western frontiers, but also along the Central Asian frontiers in the northeast, where, notably in this regard, the Wall of Gorgan had been built (see below). The system of walls and associ-ated defences was especially effective in that these provided terminus stations for troops shuttling from east to west and vice versa, to rapidly mobilize forces to face invasions and threats of invasion or to mobilize for attacks into enemy territory.

The system of defensive walls and city-fortresses was not simply a barrier to invaders; they were also responsible for safeguarding the very nerve system of the empire, namely its vital metropolitan centres and their citizenry, economic and agricultural centres as well as critical routes of communication and travel.

As noted in Chapter 10, military depots played a vital role in the spah's prepa-rations for war. The *ambaragh* (magazines) and *ganz* (arsenals)[44] were often part of, or possibly even integrated into, the defensive system. These ambaragh and ganz networks were (pre-) stockpiled with weapons and were under the super-vision of the eiran-ambaraghbad. The latter was also responsible for the rapid and efficient distribution of weapons and other stores to the spah's troops when war was imminent (Chapter 10).

An excellent overview of the two basic features of the spah's defensive walls has been provided by Frye. First, walls served a dual role by defending against both nomadic incursions and also against the desert and steppe terrain. Frye's hypo-thesis is based on observations of the Sassanians having done much work in culti-vation and agriculture, which in turn led to the development of new towns and cities. The agricultural system was vital in the maintenance of urbanization which in turn was critical to the empire's commercial activities. Ctesiphon therefore wanted to protect its agricultural investments from the encroachment of neigh-bouring steppe and desert terrain. The long walls therefore also served as 'geo-graphical' protection in addition to their strictly military role of blocking nomadic intrusions. The second point made by Frye pertains to military func-tion. Specifically, Frye notes that Sassanian walls were most effective against nomadic raiders who (unlike the Romano-Byzantines) were neither versed in siege warfare nor possessed the weapons and equipment necessary for reducing walls and fortifications. This is certainly the case with Khazar raiders attacking along the Derbent Wall or Turkic warriors encountering the Wall of Tammisha.

Finally, Howard-Johnston has provided four important observations with respect to the Sassanian design of defensive walls. First, the Sassanians took full account of their enemies and the nature of the terrain in the construction of their walls. Put simply, the Sassanians were not implementing a 'lego' system of engineering but taking into account the battle tactics and martial temperaments of their adversaries. In addition it is clear that studies would be made of the local terrain to utilize the most effective materials to construct the most durable defences possible. Therefore, depending on the terrain or geography, hardened mud-brick or stones would be used. Local geography would be incorporated as much as possible to maximize defences, examples being the walls of Derbent and Tammisha (see below). Second, the Sassanians were willing to invest very large sums from the state treasury to build, maintain and improve these wall systems. This may have been due to the perception of 'long term' economic savings. For example if no walls were in existence in Central Asia or Derbent, then nomadic armies could potentially break through into the Iranian plateau and wreak immense economic and manpower devastation with each raid and attack. With these walls in place, the spah could contain enemy attacks at the defensive walls to then counterattack and repel the invaders. Third, Sassanian walls were the equal of Roman walls in engineering sophistication, a topic which we will address later in this chapter. It is generally agreed that Sassanian walls were built to a high standard on any front they chose to construct them. Fourth, the Sassanian ability to build and maintain such massive military engineering works points to the existence of a strong imperial state machinery highly capable of organizing, funding and rationalizing such projects. In this regard, the Sassanians were much like the Romans, who constructed an impressive array of fortifications across the frontiers of their empire.

Wall of Derbent

The empire constructed and maintained Maginot-type defensive wall-fortress systems intended to stave off invasions from Iran's Caucasian passes. Known to the modern-day Lezgians as Krevar, the Sassanian Derbent or Derbend, the Deevar-e Darband or the Wall of Darband (*darband* = 'closed gate' in Persian) is also known as the 'Great Wall of the Caucasus'. This defence wall was situated on the empire's critical Caucasian passes defending the ingress routes in modern-day Dagestan into Albania (modern Republic of Azerbaijan),[45] Armenia and Azerbaijan to the south of the Araxes River.[46] Some have suggested that the first layout of the Derbent wall began with Yazdegird II (r. 438–457); however, its origins are generally attributed to Kavad I (r. 488–496, 498–530 CE) who fought a successful two-year war (489–490) to eject Khazar invaders rampaging though Armenia and Caucasian Albania.[47] With the expulsion of the Khazars back into the northern Caucasus, Kavad ordered the construction of a military wall of bricks in the Caucasus.[48]

The site of Derbent had also been an ancient Caucasian (Albanian) settlement since the eighth century BCE; Kavad revived and repopulated the town as 'Darband' (modern Derbent); the Sassanians were to repopulate much of Derbent with Armenian warriors and their families.[49] Nevertheless, much of the garrisons at Derbent were also Persians as noted by Islamic-era sources.[50] Kavad's son and successor Khosrow I (r. 530–579 CE) continued the construction of Derbent's walls.[51]

The total length of the Derbent wall is close to 70km, stretching from the Caucasian mountains (known as the 'Alan Pass' or 'Gates' in antiquity) in the west to the Caspian Sea in the east.[52] The Islamic historian al-Baladuri (d. 892) reported that Derbent's fortifications, identified in Arabic as 'Bab al-Bab' (Gate of Gates), consisted of gates to numerous mountain passes.[53]

The Derbent wall successfully sealed a narrow land strip that had allowed nomadic invaders from the north Caucasus to threaten the Sassanian Empire's northwestern marches. By the late sixth century CE, the northern Derbent wall had become a massive and formidable complex featuring two walls linked to a fortified harbour on the Caspian. The northern wall(s) then ran westwards to a fortress at the foot of the Caucasus. After that there was a single 20ft-tall lime-stone wall that connected a series of forts. By the end of Khosrow's reign the wall featured thirty military bases or castles facing the north, with these possibly having increased to forty by the late sixth century CE. It would appear that the type of stones used in the construction of the wall is identical to those used by the Sassanians for the stone wall at Shiz (Takhte Sulieman) in northwest Iran.[54] The 'northern wall' in the Caucasus ran for approximately 34–35km over hills and ridges.

The 'southern wall' was discovered in the Apsheron Peninsula region with the final (or fifth) wall being situated just north of Derbent.[55] This was shorter at approximately 29–30km. The wall was around 8m thick at various points and like the northern wall it extended from a harbour fortress on the Caspian to another fortress at the foot of the Caucasian mountains. A point that must be made regarding the Wall of Derbent is that there is evidence for five walls rather than just a single wall.[56]

This is suggestive of the possibility that the Sassanians had rationalized a 'back-up' wall defence system such that even if the front wall was somehow breached, attackers would simply become bogged down with the next wall(s). What is clear is that the Derbent wall became the empire's primary defensive line against not only the Khazars but all nomadic invaders from southern Russia who raided the southern Caucasus. Derbent was especially critical as it controlled the ingress from the southern Caucasus into Iran proper. The Sassanians were keenly aware of the importance of holding the line at Derbent as failure to do so would imperil not only Armenia and Albania but also Media Atropatene (Azerbaijan in north-west Iran) and the remainder of northern and western Iran. The Alans who invaded Media Atropatene in 75 CE during the Parthian era had first overrun Albania and Armenia where they destroyed the local Parthian-Armenian army.[57] The Scythians who invaded the Near East in the late 650s–early 640s BCE had also entered through the critical Derbent Pass. The Derbent wall was the Sassa-nian military answer to this ancient strategic threat against the northern Iranian realms. As noted by Archaeologist Murtazali S. Gadjiev (Daghestan Branch of the Russian Academy of Sciences), 'The Caspian plain narrows here [Derbent Pass] dramatically ... [which] made this a strategic point for millennia.' It is notable that no traces have been found of an actual wall prior to the Sassanians.[58]

The Wall of Derbent was also of vital importance in Khosrow I's expansion into the northwest Caucasus, notably into Colchis and Iberia (modern day Georgia).[59] It was here that Khosrow seized the port of Petra in an endeavor to install a Sassanian presence in the Black Sea region, an effort that the Romano-Byzantines eventually blocked (see Chapter 14). Interestingly, the Wall of Derbent was also of vital importance to the Romano-Byzantines as the fortification system held at bay dangerous nomads (i.e. Turkic, Hun, Khazar, etc.) who could just as easily use the southern Caucasus to launch raids into eastern Anatolia. As a result, Constantinople often had an interest in providing the Sassanian Empire financial support for the upkeep of the Wall of Derbent.[60] This Sassano-Roman strategic confluence is summarized as follows by Greatrex: 'Romans and Persians also shared a common foe – Huns from the area to the north of the Caucasus ... who would sally forth periodically and cause devastation in the Transcaucasus region, an area of interest to both powers.'[61]

Of special interest is a major Sassanian citadel of the Derbent wall known today as 'Narin Kala' which overlooks the town of Derbent as well as the Caspian Sea. The walls of the 8-acre Narin Kala fortress stand around 60ft in height, and despite the passage of over 1,500 years, have remained remarkably intact. There are two 20ft walls that stretch from Narin Kale to the Caspian Sea.

Spah doctrine for managing threats posed by nomadic warriors in the Caucasus: the Khazars. Despite the formidable Wall of Derbent, the sensitive Caucasus region, which bordered Eastern Europe to the north and the Romano-Byzantine world through its southwest, required constant military vigilance and diplomacy to maintain Sassanian authority. It is here that one may see how diplomacy combined with the show of arms achieved this aim. An overview of the *Sirat Anoushirvan*[62] and other Islamic-era sources by Mohammadi-Malayeri[63] reveal the overall policies that were followed by Khosrow Anoushirvan in the Caucasus to ensure that the Khazars were kept in check.

The first (and most critical) strategy was to militarily defeat those Khazars which were attacking the Iranian domains of the Caucasus. The spah and the shahanshah would deploy to Hamedan and Azerbaijan province in Iran's northwest to then cross the Araxes River to reach Derbent and the city of Firouz Khosrow. As the spah advanced, fortresses and military structures would also be inspected en route. Thus any structures in need of strengthening and/or repair would be attended to by the spah's engineers. The spah's deployment and the presence of the shahanshah also signalled to local governors and garrisons Ctesiphon's political authority and its ability to militarily support them in times of crisis. The spah would then deploy its forces to reinforce already existing garrisons (especially the Derbent wall) or any border region where the Khazars or other nomadic warriors may have broken through. The Khazars or other invaders would then be targeted for subjugation through military action. This action would not always prove necessary as the mere presence of the main spah force along with the shahanshah would lead invading nomads such as the Khazars towards diplomacy. Often, they would seek service with the spah (see 'Recruitment', Chapter 2). The shahanshah would then extend the hand of friendship by offering them military service under the supervision of sardars of the spah. Some local fortresses could then be turned over to the newly recruited Khazars (or other nomads) for garrison duty under the supervision of spah sardars.

Defensive Walls Facing Central Asia

The empire's eastern and north-eastern realms faced the vast steppes of Central Asia. This was the abode of the formidable Central Asian nomad warrior, one of Sassanian Iran's most dangerous and formidable foes. Nomadic armies were often able to crash into the open plains of Gorgan along the southeast coast of the Caspian or even into Khorasan and western Afghanistan. The vastness of this region led the Sassanians to rely on a multi-tier system of defence, which reached its architectural zenith by the sixth century CE.[64]

A number of Sassanian emperors had fought along the Central Asian front, notably Shapur II in his campaigns against the Chionites (Chapter 12) and Bahram Gur in his battles with the Hephthalites (421 CE) (Chapter 12). King Pirouz had lost his life in battle with the Hephthalites in 484 CE. The Sassanians' military fortunes gradually revived during the reign of Kavad. Subsequently Kavad's son and successor, Khosrow I (r. 531–579 CE), forged an alliance with the Turkish khagan (Sinjibu or Silzibul) to crush the Hephthalites, with the Turks appropriating the northern half of the conquered territories and the Sassanians absorbing the southern half.

Following the destruction of the Hephthalite kingdom the empire's relations with the Turks deteriorated. In response, the Sassanians constructed two walls in the north-eastern regions, the Wall of Gorgan and the Wall of Tammisha.[65] The latter was mainly intended to repel Turkic invaders attacking into northern Iran from the passes along the eastern rim of the Caspian Sea in Central Asia.[66] It is possible that the Tammisha wall acted as a second line of defence in case nomadic raiders succeeded in breaking through the Gorgan wall.[67]

The Wall of Gorgan, repaired and strengthened by Khosrow I,[68] protected a very large swathe of the north-eastern frontier against the defeated but still dangerous Hephthalites;[69] shortly after Khosrow's death in 579 CE, the wall played an important role in the defence of Iran's northeast against combined Turco-Hephthalite forces in 588 CE and 619 CE (see Chapter 12). The Gorgan and Tammisha walls were essentially part of the same overall defensive system that terminated at the city of Merv, which was the spah's military headquarters for Khorasan at the time.[70] The two walls are discussed in more detail below.

Wall of Tammisha. A very concise description of the Wall of Tammisha is provided by the Muslim geographic historian Yaqut Ibn Abdullah al-Rumi al Hamavi (1179–1229):

Tamisha is a city in the Tabaristan plain, at a distance of 16 Farsangs [approx. 160km][71] from Sari ... [and it] stands on the border between Tabaristan and the regions of Khurasan [Khorasan] and Jurjan [Gorgan]. At this place is a great portal ... it extends from the mountains to the [Caspian] sea [and is made] of baked brick and gypsum. It was Kisra Anusirvan [Khosrow I Anoushirvan] who built it as an obstacle against the Turks and their raids into Tabaristan.[72]

The Wall of Tammisha ran from the mountains to the seashore, thereby sealing the eastern marches into Mazandaran.[73] It was made of large bricks; Bivar and Fehrevari have noted that excavations along the Wall of Tammisha 'have revealed that the original fortifications consisted of a curtain-wall of large sized bricks probably of Sassanid date'.[74] Of special interest is Hamavi's description of the 'great portal' at Tammisha, indicating that a strong gate had been constructed to provide an ingress-egress route into northern Iran from the eastern Caspian marches.

The Wall of Tammisha was to be used well into the Islamic era. Maziyar, a contemporary and ally of Babak Khorramdin, destroyed much of the wall of Tammisha in 838 CE; it was actually Maziyar's brother Kuhyar who had been sent to undertake this task. According to Tabari, the wall was soon rebuilt by a certain Sarkhastan, who 'settled with his forces in [the city of Tammish] and around it he had a vast trench built together with towers for the garrison, and he had a strong gate built for it'.[75]

Note once again the reference to 'a strong gate' in the wall. This would allow a field army to deploy into Central Asia along the (eastern) shore of the Caspian Sea. Finally, an important observation made by Bivar and Fehrevari regarding the Wall of Tammisha was that it 'joins the "Long Wall" ... which extends right across the coastal plain'.[76] The 'Long Wall' is discussed below.

Wall of Gorgan. The ancient province of Gorgan[77] in northeastern Iran (specifically the plain of Gorgan) is a critical region commanding the ingress routes from Central Asia into Khorasan, northern Iran, and the Iranian Plateau. The *Deevar-e Gorgan* or Wall of Gorgan[78] provides a great deal of information on wall-type Sassanian military barriers. Like the Great Chinese Wall, the Gorgan wall was also built to withstand nomadic incursions from Central Asia. The Wall of Gorgan is the world's second-largest defensive wall; only the Great Wall of China is larger. The Gorgan Wall measures approximately 155–200km in length and spans 6–10m in width. The Gorgan wall begins on the Caspian Sea coast, then meanders to the north of Gonbade Kavoos. The eastern end of the wall is near to the Pishkamar district. This is essentially the 'Long Wall' alluded to earlier by Bivar and Frevahar.

The first serious excavations in the region took place in 1971 by an archaeological team led by Kiani, followed by more surveys in the 1990s. The general consensus by the Kiani team was that the Gorgan wall had its origins in the Parthian era. More recent excavations by a British-Iranian archaeological team[79] have challenged the notion of a Parthian origin. The findings of this team was reported by the Science Daily News (18 February 2008) which noted that the structure's origins are 'more than 1000 years older than the Great Wall of China, and longer than Hadrian's Wall and the Antonine Wall put together'.[80] The team has concluded that the wall provides 'compelling evidence that the Persians matched the Romans for military might and engineering prowess'.

The question is raised as to the state of the wall in Achaemenid times, especially in the period spanning Cyrus' defeat and death in Central Asia against the Massagetae (530 BCE) and the conquest of the Massagetae by Darius the Great (519 BCE). The capital of ancient Gorgan, Zadrakarta (later known as Astarabad) is in fact traceable to at least the Achaemenid era. Excavations were ongoing at the time of this writing, therefore it is possible that new research papers may address the nature of the Gorgan wall in the pre-Partho-Sassanian era.

The recent British-Iranian archaeological studies verify that the wall was significantly improved, strengthened and fortified during the Sassanian dynasty. Work on this structure was undertaken at least as early as the time of Yazdegird II who campaigned against the Chol-Huns in Gorgan and constructed a series of forts in that region.[81] Pirouz (r. 459–484 CE) continued the construction works of his father Yazdegird II, by building a fortress named 'Shahram Pirouz' in the vicinity of Abivard during his campaigns against the Hephthalites.[82] Khosrow I Anoushirvan is also recognized as having made improvements and repairs on the Gorgan wall.

Especially noteworthy was the Sassanian construction of a series of castles along the wall. The shortest identified distance between these castles is 10km with the longest being 50km. The thickness of the wall (cited earlier at 6–10m) varied according to the geographical circumstances of each particular region (climate, soil, terrain, etc.) traversed by the structure. The bricks used in the wall are said to have weighed 90–150kg (approximately 198–338lb)[83] with each brick measuring $65 \times 25 \times 10$cm.[84] Water for the castles was provided by a sophisticated system of water channels and aqueducts. Forty of these castles were built in the square-shape system,[85] featuring barracks capable of housing a total of 30,000–36,000 savaran knights.[86] But it is unlikely that the spah would be able to permanently station such a large force within the entire castle array of the Gorgan wall given the empire's military manpower limitations and potential threats posed by the Romano-Byzantines along the empire's western frontiers.

Wall systems and offensive warfare. The walls of Tammisha and Gorgan facing Central Asia also served an offensive function in times of military necessity. As noted in Chapter 10, the Sassanians had built a series of military storage facilities along the empire's defensive walls. Jalali has noted that these depots were critical in allowing the spah to mobilize its troops in a particular region in preparation for a powerful offensive into enemy territory.[87] As noted previously, the defensive wall at Gorgan already had a network of fortresses which were able to house large numbers of troops in times of military emergencies. As Howard-Johnston observes, spah units stationed in these castles could allow an enemy army to pass through the empire's first series of defences; the invading forces would then unknowingly advance into pre-designated 'kill zones' where the savaran would then counterattack.[88] A similar tactic would be to have the savaran conduct a feigned retreat, luring invaders into the 'kill zones' to be destroyed by the inevitable counterattacks.

The war council and the king were thus able to assemble their troops in the barracks of fortresses along the wall and quickly provide these troops with logistical support from the pre-stocked ambaragh (magazines) and ganz (arsenals) and other military supply depots. Nev-Shapur was a critical base, and it was from there that Bahram Chobin launched his overwhelmingly successful offensive into Central Asia against the Turco-Hephthalite forces in 588 CE (Chapter 12).

The empire's system of defensive walls, combined with a highly efficient logistics network empowered the spah's war council with efficient military options even if dangerous enemies such as the Turco-Hephthalites managed to break through into Khorasan. At first the invaders would certainly appear to be advancing, but eventually they would be brought to a halt, trapped between the defensive walls to their rear and the savaran cavalry assembling ahead of them in the Iranian interior. The Armenian general Smbat Bagratuni, for example, led his crack force of naxarars and savaran knights from Iran's northeast to repel a large Turco-Hephthalite force and then pursue it across the empire's borders into Central Asia, where it was destroyed (Chapter 12).

The *Khandaq* System: Ditches, Moats and Trenches

What is most interesting about the *khandaq* system is that this was both a system of military architecture as well as being one of the spah's methods for conducting sieges against enemy cities and fortresses (Chapter 14). Moats were definitely constructed by the Parthians, as seen in the excavation of such structures at Qaleh Kafar, Qaleh Soltanali and Qaleh Khandan at Gorgan.[89] Parthian and Sassanian moats were basically ditches that were constructed for the defence of fortresses, cities, villages, citadels and military camps.[90] They were often filled with water, and seeded with traps such as sharp iron and wooden spikes and spears. The moats could also be camouflaged with leaves, shrubs, branches, etc.[91]

In general, Iranian fortresses could be surrounded by moats that were typically about 20m wide. The soil extracted from digging the moat would often be 're-cycled' as thick earthen ramparts built to reinforce the fortress's walls. Of course, the dimension of moats varied according to the structures they surrounded. An excellent study by Ghasemi has provided a catalogue of Iranian moat engineering in the province of Fars.[92]

Facing the Southeast: Khandaq-e Shapur: Wall or Ditch or Both?

The southwest frontier of the Sassanian Empire was vulnerable to the raids of Arab Bedouin nomads. The first campaigns of Shapur II (309–379 CE) were undertaken to repel these tough Arab warriors who invaded much of the southern reaches of the Sassanian Empire and Iran's Persian Gulf coastline. The *Bundahishn* summarizes Persia's plight by noting that 'in the reign of Shapur [II] son of Hormuzd, the Arabs came and seized the banks of the River Karun [Ulay] and remained there for many years pillaging and attacking'.[93] Shapur II successfully organized the spah for a devastating counterattack. The savaran cleared the Arabs out of southern Iran and Mesopotamia and then drove them into the Arabian interior south of Mesopotamia. Arab foot soldiers, cavalry and camel warriors were decisively overcome by the charging savaran lancers. Being lightly armoured and equipped, the Arab cavalry and camel warriors found themselves severely disadvantaged in close-quarter combat with the heavily armed and armoured savaran knights. Savaran lance charges, already a great danger to the highly trained and professional Roman infantrymen of that time, were able to break apart opposing ranks of Arab infantry. The successful conclusion of Shapur II's campaigns are highlighted by the *Bundahishn*, which notes 'Shapur became of age and drove away those Arabs and took the land from them. He killed many rulers of the Arabs and scattered many of them.'[94] Those Arabs who had escaped the counterattack of Shapur II and the spah would soon join Julian the Apostate in his invasion of the Sassanian Empire in 363 CE (Chapter 9).

The success of the spah, however, could not alter the fact that the empire's southwest frontier was vulnerable to Arab raiders. The Arabs remained extremely capable and resilient fighters, being especially adept in conducting quick raids into southern Mesopotamia where the Sassanians held sway. Prior to Shapur II's counterattacks, Arab raiders had wrought much economic and demographic devastation to southern Mesopotamia and southern Iran. While Shapur II's victory was impressive, it would only be a matter of time before the Arabs recovered sufficiently to resume their raids and thus threaten the empire militarily and economically.

The Sassanians apparently tried to deal with the Arab threat by constructing a defensive barrier against their incursions. It is not known, however, where this barrier was located or what form it took. Mahamedi has suggested that the barrier consisted of a man-made moat or large ditch facing the Arab side of the border (identified by Mahamedi as *Xandaq-e Shapur*) and a wall (on the Iranian side) which could possibly be the *War-e Tazigan*.[95] Mahamedi also suggests that the wall was first built by Ardashir I and either completed or even rebuilt by Shapur II.[96] Nevertheless, it is important to note that archaeological evidence for an actual wall has yet to be discovered at the time of writing. The construction of a wall and moat, at least during the time of Shapur II, is certainly possible given the dire military threat the Arabs posed to the empire.

The existence of an actual moat has been attested to by Islamic-era sources. Al-Hamavi for example, provides a highly informative account of the location of the moat and the nature of its defences:

Xandaq-i Sabur is in Bariyat al-Kufa, and was dug by the order of Sabur to separate his realm from that of the Arabs, for fear of their raids. Sabur, the lord of the shoulders,[97] built and made frontier watchtowers to protect the areas that lay near the desert, and ordered a moat [*xandaq*] to be dug from the lower region of the desert to what precedes Basra, and is joined by the sea. There he built turrets and forts and arranged frontier watchtowers, so that the moat could be a barrier between the inhabitants of the desert and the people of as-Sawad.[98]

In this passage Hamavi is clearly describing military architecture; what is less clear however, is whether actual walls were built to link the turrets, forts, and watchtowers he mentions. Here one would note that the Pahlavi term *war* can mean 'wall', 'enclosed space' or 'surrounding'. Note also that the specific word for 'wall' in Pahlavi is *dewar*, which has cognates in modern Kurdish (*diwar*) and Persian (*divar*).

From this one may conclude that *War-e Tazigan* could be translated as 'Wall of the Arabs'. Nevertheless, *war* (but not *dewar*) can also mean 'sea', 'body of water', 'bay/fjord' or 'lake'. Mahamedi is correct in noting that the name should not be translated as 'Lake/Sea of Arabs',[99] especially as 'It is unlikely that before the Arab conquest, Persians referred to the Persian Gulf as "Lake of the Arabs"',[100] with the name 'Persian Gulf' corroborated by Classical sources.[101] It must also be noted that the term *frawar* in Pahlavi means 'bastion' and in Armenian *patuar* denotes 'wall'.

Also at issue is when the foundations of the southwestern barrier were laid. Were they built during the time of Shapur II, or earlier? As noted previously, al-Hamavi attributed the moat and military structures to Shapur II; however, another Islamic-era source, al-Bakri, disagrees, asserting that Khosrow I Anoushrivan built these defences.[102] In practice, it is possible that Mahamedi as well as the Islamic sources (i.e. al-Hamavi, al-Bakri) are all correct, as the defences in the southwest had been a work in progress since the early days of the dynasty. As previously noted, Shapur II certainly appreciated the value of these defences and proceeded to strengthen them, hence the appellation of *Khandaq-e Shapur* (Moat of Shapur). Khosrow I, whose primary role in strengthening the empire's defensive walls in the Caucasus and those facing Central Asia have been discussed earlier in this chapter, would have most likely engaged in improving and strengthening the empire's defences in the southwest as well. Khosrow I had rationalized the defence of the empire into four equally important military zones. He proceeded to build up and improve the defences of the region after a series of serious Arab raids, as described by al-Hamavi:

> [W]hen Anushirvan ruled he was informed that certain tribes of the Arabs were attacking what was near the desert of the Sawad. Then he ordered the making of a wall belonging to a town called al-Nasr which Shapur [II] had built and fortified to protect what was adjacent to the desert ... he ordered a moat dug from Hit and passing through the edge of the desert to Kazime and beyond Basra reaching to the sea. He built on it towers and pavilions and he joined it together with fortified points.[103]

It is clear from this that the construction of fortified structures and walls was underway at the time of Khosrow I, who obviously took the threat of Arab raids very seriously.

The *Khandaq-e Shapur* and its associated fortifications are generally believed to have been located on the border between the desert near Kufa and the cultivated lands of the Sassanian Empire.[104] The moat was most likely filled with water brought to it from various sources through a system of channels.[105] Given the above descriptions and the analysis of Mohammadi-Malayeri, it may be assumed that the forts, watchtowers, pavilions, etc. were equidistantly located from the giant moat.[106] As noted by Baladuri, these marches were held by Arab garrisons who had been granted lands and made exempt from taxation by the Sassanian Empire since the time of Shapur II.[107] In this endeavour, the Lakhmid Arabs became a vital military force in the spah, entrusted with safeguarding the empire's southwestern marches against raiders from Arabia and especially from the pro-Romano-Byzantine Ghassanids.[108] It is known that Shapur II had appointed Imr'ul Qais as the governor of Hira; Qais' son Nu'man served as the Sassanian Emperor's Ward; Nu'man raised Bahram V 'Gur' (r. 388-399 CE) in his court at Hira.[109] Interestingly, excavations at the Lakhmid capital, Hira have revealed that the city had no actual defensive walls which according to Frye is '. . . presumably because the long wall and moat took their place'.[110] When the empire neglected its southwest defences or *limes* by the early seventh century during the reign of Khosrow II Parveez (r. 590–628 CE), this significantly contributed to the weakening of that frontier, just as Arab military strength was rising under the banner of Islam. It was from this very sector that the final doom for the empire came in the form of an Arab invasion in 637–651 CE (Chapter 17).

Troops Garrisoning Frontier Defences: An Overview
Troops entrusted with manning frontier defences such as those of Derbent, Central Asia or Iran's southwest were especially esteemed by the spah. Iranian military historians note that these were considered *pishmarg*, or those who were first or at the forefront of sacrificing their lives against invaders entering the empire's territories.[111] Put simply, invaders often had to target these pishmarg troops and their fortifications before being able to break into the Iranian interior. Interestingly, the Kurdish term *peshmarga* is analogous to its Persian counterpart in that it denotes the front-line guerrilla fighter who is willing to sacrifice his life. A more popular military term used in reference to the spah's garrison troops, however, was *neshastegan*.

Neshastegan. Kramers defines neshastegan as 'somebody who has been made to dwell in a certain place ... a garrisoned warrior'.[112] The term 'neshastegan' broadly describes troops stationed in fortresses and bases situated along critical border areas, especially those facing the Caucasus, Central Asia and the western Romano-Byzantine frontiers. Mashkoor notes that neshastegan became synonymous with 'military base' in Pahlavi (Middle Persian),[113] however the term *neshast* is translated by Amid as 'a person or thing that is located in a place'[114] with *gan* often being a titular appellation.[115] Khosrow I made prodigious efforts to clearly delineate the military role of the neshastegan, especially when he placed battle-experienced troops to man the Wall of Derbent in the Caucasus.[116] These 'frontier troops' were highly regarded by the king, who provisioned them with 'soldiers' fiefs'.[117]

Welfare of the neshastegan. Tabari has provided valuable insight into the level of the spah's appreciation for the welfare of the empire's front-line garrison troops.

According to Tabari, Shapur II had received reports by his military advisors regarding the state of his front-line troops stationed in the spah's defence works along the empire's frontiers.[118] The advisors informed Shapur that troops that had been stationed for extended periods along the frontiers had become distressed and demoralized. Shapur II ordered that letters be written to the troops in those garrisons stating that all those who longed to visit their families and relatives were allowed to go on leave, and were to return to garrison duty when required to do so.[119] What the Tabari report makes clear is that the king and the spah were sensitive to the morale of their professional troops and realized its military importance for the defence of the empire's borders. Any slackening of motivation among these front-line troops could prove deadly for the empire, as enemies (especially nomadic warriors) were keen to exploit any possible weakness to launch attacks. It is possible that the massive breakthrough by the Turkish khagan across the north-eastern defences and into Iran in 588 CE was at least partly due to such demoralization.

Chapter 14

Siege Operations

The battles of the spah against forces of the Romano-Byzantine Empire were not simply of the set-piece battlefield type discussed in Chapter 9. Many of the most important operations undertaken by the spah against the Romano-Byzantine Empire was in siege warfare. This chapter focuses on the Sassanian spah's siege technologies, tactics and operations. Siege warfare was an integral part of the spah's military doctrine as any attempt at expansion into Roman territory involved taking cities by siege. Unlike the Parthians who were not known for a high degree of skill in siege work, the Sassanians were to develop siege warfare to levels matching their Roman adversaries. The Sassanians also demonstrated their ability to maintain an efficient supply-logistics system, enabling them to maintain sieges over long periods of time. Writing in late Sassanian times, Emperor Maurice commented in his *Strategikon* that the Sassanians 'are awesome when they lay siege, and even more awesome when they are besieged'.[1]

This chapter provides an overview of Sassanian siege tactics and weaponry in the *Ayin-nameh*, *Shahname* and the analyses of Pazoki and Lukonin. Reconnaissance, spies/fifth-column elements, siege weaponry and tactics, the role of spah personnel during sieges, the savaran and war elephants are also discussed. The chapter will then examine a number of battles in which the spah engaged in siege operations followed by battles when the spah was besieged.

The Ayin-nameh
The *Ayin-nameh* has provided some interesting details of Sassanian siege warfare.[2] The spah is advised not to lay siege to an enemy city or fortress without having first engaged in detailed reconnaissance. Emphasis is placed on collecting critical intelligence on a targeted fortress's strong and weak points before placing it under siege. The employment of spies and fifth-column elements within the fortress is also discussed (see also Chapter 8). Interestingly, the *Ayin-nameh* also recommends that fires ignited at or under various structures of the enemy fortress are most effective when their placement is guided by prior intelligence, especially information obtained from spies inside the fortress. Similarly, the *Ayin-nameh* recommends that prior intelligence be used to determine the placement of scaling ladders against the enemy's walls.

Pazoki's Analyses of Sassanian Siege Tactics
Pazoki cites four distinct methods used by the spah for capturing cities.[3] The first was the set-piece battle in which the spah engaged the enemy forces outside of their city. In this scenario, the city was captured following the comprehensive

defeat of the enemy army, who then yielded the city as a condition of its surrender. The second method, which was most frequently used against the Romans, was the employment of siege engines and associated tactics to force the submission of an enemy fortified city. This was a typical scenario as enemy forces tended to conserve their strength by taking refuge behind strong fortifications. The besieging of Roman fortifications was a formidable task for the spah, as the Romans were adept in conducting counter-siege operations. The third method of capture was by the digging of tunnels and mining operations. Tunnelling beneath the enemy's fortifications enabled the attackers to penetrate, undetected, into the city's interior. The fourth method was the use of pyro-techniques and especially setting the enemy's walls on fire. The heat generated by the fires would weaken and eventually collapse the walls, creating gaps through which the attackers would charge. Pazoki also cites two non-combat methods for taking an enemy fortress. The first was by way of intrigue and subterfuge and the second by way of negotiation, compromise and offers of friendship to the defenders.[4]

Lukonin's Analysis of Sassanian Siege Tactics

Lukonin has provided the following overall summary of Sassanian siege tactics,[5] namely (1) encirclement of the enemy installation or city; (2) deployment of siege equipment; and (3) infantry, archery and savaran assaults. The first phase (encirclement) entailed the achievement of two basic objectives, namely to prevent any means for the defenders to escape and to bar any supplies and relief forces from reaching the besieged. Once encirclement was achieved, siege engines and equipment would be strategically placed to maximize their effectiveness against the enemy walls, towers, gates and other structures in the interior of the town or installation (i.e. barracks, storage buildings, etc.). The infantry would then advance with large shields towards the enemy walls and gates. In the course of advance attempts would be made to find weaknesses in the enemy's walls, gates, towers, etc. The advance could also be made with personnel bringing ladders which would be placed against the enemy's walls. Archers would cover the infantry's advance, using barrages to counteract the enemy's archery. If the ladders could be successfully placed against the enemy's walls, the infantry and dismounted savaran knights would ascend to the top of the walls to engage the defenders. In practice however, this could prove extremely difficult, especially when fighting Roman defenders who were especially skilled in repelling such assaults with archery, naphtha, etc. In practice when fighting against besieged Roman forces, the Sassanians often resorted to deploying mobile towers and raising earthen mounds for their archers (see below). Lukonin notes that savaran assaults, conducted 'under the protection of a hail of archery'[6] and siege weapons, were critical in allowing the spah to break into the enemy installation or city.

Siege Weaponry and Techniques

Most Iranian military historians[7] would concur with their Western counterparts that much of the original technology and tactics of Sassanian siege warfare was initially borrowed from the Romans.[8] The Sassanians however, soon began building their own siege machinery and were to also incorporate Chinese technologies. By the late third and early fourth centuries CE, Sassanian siege technologies had so progressed that, according to Oates and Oates, the Romans were obliged to build 'more elaborate systems of fortification ... [Roman] fortress cities began to play a more dominant role in frontier strategy'.[9] As will be seen later in this chapter, Sassanian offensives into the Roman-held Near East often resulted in clashes with fortress cities, such as Nisibis, Singara and Dara. The *Ayin-nameh* provides interesting information on the types of siege weapons and implements developed and employed by the spah. Procopius[10] and Ammianus Marcellinus[11] also provide information on Sassanian siege weaponry.

Reconnaissance. Enemy fortifications, especially gates and ingress/egress points, were to be critically examined before initiating a siege. This process was critical to maximizing the effectiveness of the spah's ballistic weapons and battering rams.[12] Presumably the quick destruction of an entrance point (i.e. gate) or weak wall/barrier would allow the spah to pour its troops into an enemy fortress sooner. Lack of intelligence on the strengths and weaknesses of an enemy fortress's entrance points and walled structures would minimize the effectiveness of the spah's employment of battering rams and pyro-techniques, leading to the prolongation of the siege as well as higher casualties.

Reconnaissance was also of prime importance in gathering information on possible blind spots in the enemy's defences, especially potential entrance routes that could be used to infiltrate close to the enemy's fortifications without detection.[13] Knowledge of such routes was especially critical, as these could be used to mount surprise attacks during prolonged sieges.

Sassanian Ballistae and the Charx. The spah deployed a variety (of varying sizes and power) of *kashkanjir* (Persian: ballistic weapon[s]). These would be used to launch missile or arrow-type projectiles with shafts constructed of wood.[14] In practice, Sassanian ballistic weapons were typically propelled against enemy towers, walls, and defending enemy personnel.[15] The *Lexicon of Arms and Armor from Iran* defines the *charx* as follows:

> a type of a bow with large arrows ... a type of ballista, resembles a large crossbow and shoots heavy darts. The dart used for this type of bow was as big as a big spear. This type of bow was used to shoot these long arrows in the cities under siege or among enemy ranks to create fear and disorder. The string was drawn via wheel with two handles that were drawn by two strong men. By turning the wheel, the string was drawn via a rope that was fastened in the middle of the string and this rope was turned around a wheel.[16]

Ammianus Marcellinus provides a glimpse of Sassanian ballistic weapons during Shapur II's siege of Amida (see below): 'They shot out heavy wooden javelins with great rapidity, sometimes transfixing two of our men at one blow, so that many of them fell to the ground severely wounded, and some jumped down in haste from fear of the creaking engines, and being terribly lacerated by the fall, died.'[17]

While the above description certainly illustrates the power and efficacy of Sassanian ballistic weapons, the engineering methods of their construction, their precise sizes, weights, and methods of launch remain unknown.

The Iranians apparently continued their evolution of siege ballistae centuries after the fall of the Sassanian Empire. Islamic-era Iranian sources also refer to the kashkanjir[18] which was capable of launching the same type of projectiles as the ballistae already described. The term *kashkanjir* is derived from *kooshk* (castle/fort) and *anjirdan* (to penetrate/to make holes), suggesting that the design of its bow-like launching device was specifically aimed at launching projectiles that were capable of penetrating enemy structures. There are also references to *khaar-kaman* (giant bow) in Islamic-era Iranian poetry.[19]

There are also reports for example of a certain Alao-wa-ding (or Ala-e-din, c. 1312 CE)[20] who served as a mangonel specialist in the armies of Kublai Khan during his campaigns against the Song dynasty of southern China. Bradbury provides a description of Persian mangonels in medieval times:

> The Persian mangonel had a power of 50 pounds; its base was shaped in a cross. This appears to be a complicated machine, using both tension of a crossbow for the initial power, perhaps as a kind of trigger, and then a counterweight. It involved a machine of the crossbow type, in which the operator 'takes the bow and shoots and releases the shaft', but it is interesting that a shaft of stones is used to draw the bow, which indicates a move towards the trebuchet.[21]

What is interesting in this description is the bow-like or 'crossbow' mechanism described earlier with the term 'kashkanjir'. In the latter case the bow mechanism is the primary launch mechanism of the projectile, with Bradbury's description noting that the bow mechanism was integrated with other components.

Finally, mention must be made of Matofi's report from Persian literary sources of a carriage installed with large bows constructed with metallic materials.[22] The bowstrings were pulled back by a wheel to be positioned in front of a metallic sheet filled with holes. Each of those holes held an arrow. The weapon system was designed such that all arrows could be shot simultaneously, a design reminiscent of Leonardo da Vinci's twelve-barrelled gun. It is not clear if such a weapon was used against the Romano-Byzantines, but if this was deployed on the western frontiers, it may have been in the late Sassanian era. The carriage allowed for mobility, making the weapon useful for both set-piece battles and siege operations. In the latter case, it could assist the regular archery barrages of the field army against a defending stronghold. In set-piece battles, such a weapon could assist in blunting attacks by enemy cavalry (heavy lancers or light horse archers) as well as infantry.

Aghrab or scorpions? Jalali notes that the spah employed a variety of *aghrab* (of varying sizes and power) to launch 'stone bullets' (presumably shaped like cannon-balls) against besieged enemy personnel as well as enemy structures (i.e. towers, gates, walls, etc.).[23] The term 'aghrab' is the Persian term for 'scorpion'.

The Roman *scorpio*, however, appears to have been a different weapon: a ballistic weapon for launching missiles possibly suitable for the 'sniping' role rather than for heavy siege work. But the Roman scorpion at least as encountered by the Sassanians in the fifth century CE was indeed a stone-hurling weapon as described by Ammianus Marcellinus, who reported these as operating 'with their iron slings, hurling huge round stones'.[24] While it is generally agreed that the Sassanians did borrow much of Roman siege technology, the aghrab, in being a stone-hurling weapon, was technically a different weapon than the Roman (ballistic launching) scorpio.

Sassanian catapults: manjeniq and aradeh. As noted by Matofi, there are two types of catapults in the Sassanian inventory of siege engines, which the *Shahname* defines as the *manjeniq* and the *aradeh*.[25] The *Lexicon of Arms and Armor from Iran* defines the manjeniq as a 'catapult; instead of shooting an arrow, these machines threw giant stones by flinging them using a wheel'.[26] Note that the manjeniq deployed a wheel to launch its ordinance versus the aforementioned aghrab, which used 'iron slings' for the launching of its ordinance.

Of interest is Firdowsi's reference to the spah having set up the manjeniq 'from four directions' (*az chahar soo Manjeniq*).[27] This is probably in reference to a Roman square or rectangular fortress being surrounded and then subjected to bombardment by the manjeniq.

The aradeh is defined by the *Lexicon of Arms and Armor from Iran* as 'a small catapult that throws stones and is smaller than a Manjeniq'.[28] A question posed here is what was the range and power of the aradeh compared to the larger manjeniq. The *Shahname* notes that the aradeh was employed by placing it over walls (*Be deevar Aradeh bar pa-y kard*),[29] which suggests that Sassanian engineers built some sort of wall or barrier upon which these weapons would be placed during a siege. The *Shahname* notes that up to 200 manjeniq and aradeh would have been loaded with rocks for launching against Roman forces.[30] Perhaps this may have been a Sassanian strategy for hurling rocks of various sizes for different purposes. Possibly the larger rocks of the manjeniq were meant to smash larger and more powerful structures such as gates, towers, etc., with the smaller aradeh intended for use against smaller targets such as defending enemy troops.

Trenches and ditches. The spah was especially proficient in the use of trenches and ditches during siege operations. Ditches could be dug around a particular fortress or city (see Petra later in this chapter) and could then be filled with water depending on the tactics devised by the spah's commanders (see Nisibis later this chapter). Ditches could in turn be seeded with deadly iron traps,[31] which could certainly dissuade surprise sorties out of the fortress against the spah's positions. Roman forces certainly did take advantage of the absence of such ditches and barriers when they unleashed their Gallic cavalry in a deadly surprise raid against the besieging camps of the spah during Shapur II's siege of Amida in 359 CE[32] (see below).

Saket and Yahaghi describe an effective tactic employed by the Sassanians which involved the use of ditches. This entailed the digging of a deep trench around an enemy fortress or city and then filling the trench with wood sprayed over with flammable substances.[33] The wood would then be set alight, thus encircling the enemy stronghold with fire. Then the charx and manjeniq siege batteries would open fire, launching a massive barrage of heavy stones and ballistic missiles (including flaming projectiles). The fire in the ditch would dissuade attempts by the garrison to launch counterattacks or to try and escape. Once a breach had been effected, the besiegers would put out the fire in front of the breach. Then the savaran and infantry would be sent through the breach to storm the enemy stronghold. Alternatively, the surrounding fires could help mask the digging of tunnels by the Sassanian besiegers under the enemy's walls for yet another route of ingress into the enemy stronghold.

Suffusion and mining strategies. Suffusion strategies were critical to the spah's prosecution of sieges.[34] These were techniques for digging under fortress walls, creating passages that would enable the besieging troops to break into the interior of the enemy fortress.[35] Ideally, a number of such tunnels would be dug to create multiple ingress routes into the fortress and thus enable the Sassanians to break into the interior of the structure from multiple directions. Roman forces, who themselves were adept at such strategies, were often able to detect the spah's suffusion efforts and implement countermeasures (i.e. collapsing enemy tunnels, pouring in troops to block incoming Sassanian troops, etc.). Dara, for example, was very nearly captured by Khosrow I in 540 CE by a Sassanian mining operation dug from the eastern side of the city but was blocked by Romano-Byzantine countermining operations.[36] What is of interest in this operation is that the digging had begun from one of the Sassanian trenches but as this was done at a deeper level, it had gone unnoticed by the Romano-Byzantine defenders at first.[37] Khosrow I's second siege of Dara in 573 CE however proved more successful as the Romano-Byzantines failed to counter the spah's siege operations that resulted in the Sassanian capture of the city. Notable during the operation was the use of Roman siege engines that had been captured earlier by Khosrow at Nisibis.[38]

Sandbags and buckets. The spah often made great use of sandbags as well as sand-filled buckets to act as temporary defensive walls or shields for their military personnel.[39] These could also be used to partially mask other impending activities such as the digging of tunnels, etc. Sandbags and sand buckets would also be used to fill in sections of water-filled moats surrounding an enemy fortress.[40] This task was of course fraught with great risk as personnel engaged in such actions would be subjected to severe countermeasures, most often the besieged troops' use of archery.

Mounds. Artificial hills or mounds could be erected close to the enemy's defensive walls. These provided two overall advantages:[41] (1) archers positioned on the artificial hills could direct more accurate fire at closer range against defenders (especially if the hills were at a higher elevation than the defending walls); and (2) the hills could be used as platforms to attempt landing troops into the enemy's

defensive walls to engage in hand-to-hand fighting. Nevertheless, the employment of the 'mound technique' against the Romano-Byzantines was not always
successful. When Khosrow I besieged Edessa in 543 CE, his engineers undertook
to build a mound that would overlook the city's walls. Edessa's defenders however, destroyed that mound by setting fire to it.[42]

Mobile towers. Sassanian engineers also constructed mobile towers[43] for use by
archers.[44] Mobile towers are reported as being of metal,[45] however it is not known
whether references to their metal construction mean that metal plates were
applied as armour upon towers whose chassis were (presumably) built of wood. At
the very least, such armour could protect its personnel against enemy archers. The
towers could be placed before mounds to provide additional protection against
enemy countermeasures.[46] Of interest in this regard is Ammianus Marcellinus'
report of Shapur II's siege of Amida, where 'ballistae of the enemy [the spah],
placed on their iron towers, and pouring down missiles with great power from
their high ground on those in a lower position, spread a great deal of slaughter in
our ranks'.[47]

The devastating impact of the ballistae with their mechanical propulsion
systems were multiplied when shot downwards, wreaking havoc among defenders.
In a sense these types of mobile 'tower-ballistae' weapon systems were the
Classical era's closest equivalent of mobile mechanical warfare. Nevertheless, the
armour and structure of the Sassanian towers were vulnerable to high-powered
siege (or counter-siege) weaponry. Ammianus notes that the Roman defenders
of Amida deployed (heavy) stone-hurling scorpions against the towers which
destroyed those structures[48] along with their mounted ballistae and personnel.
It would be safe to assume that Sassanian towers could also be vulnerable to
ballistae.

Battering rams. The spah was very adept at the use of battering rams when
besieging Roman cites and fortified structures. Sassanian battering rams were
evidently well designed, and their effectiveness has been noted with respect to
the damage they could inflict upon enemy walls and gates. During Shapur II's
siege of Bezabde in 360 CE, the besieged Roman defenders had proven especially
obstinate in their defence. Shapur II's commanders then bought forward their
primary battering ram, which was protected from incendiary missiles. As noted
by Ammianus:

> One battering-ram was higher than the rest, and was covered with bulls' hides
> wetted, and being therefore safer from any accident of fire, or from lighted
> javelins, it led the way in the attacks on the wall with mighty blows, and with its
> terrible point it dug into the joints of the stones till it overthrew the tower. The
> tower fell with a mighty crash, and those in it were thrown down with a sudden
> jerk, and breaking their limbs, or being buried beneath the ruins, perished by
> various and unexpected kinds of death; then, a safer entrance having been thus
> found, the multitude of the enemy poured in with their arms.[49]

Amminanus' account is of interest in a number of respects. The first is in the usage of the different 'calibres' of battering rams. The spah had first attempted to deploy what may have been a more 'standard' ram to hammer at the enemy's walls, only to be repelled 'by the vast weight of millstones, and all kinds of fiery missiles hurled against them'.[50] With the failure of their 'regular' battering rams, the spah then resorted to deploying its on-site *Wunderwaffe*. Second, there is the question of Ammianus' description of that battering ram's 'terrible point'. This in itself raises more questions. The first question is what type of metal (or metals) had been used in the construction of the ram's head? While obviously robust and sturdy, the second question is what type of metallurgical engineering methods had been used in its construction to make it so effective against Bezabde's walls? One possible hint of what the head of the battering may have been is again pro-vided by Ammianus Marcellinus, who describes an older battering ram of Persian manufacture that was later used by the Romans (the weapon had been left by the Sassanians at Antioch after they had used it there in one of their earlier sieges of that city). The head of that weapon is described as having had a 'projecting iron head, which in shape was like that of a ram'.[51] This, however, does not necessarily imply that all Sassanian battering rams were of this shape and manufacture, but what is clear is that the metallic materials used in its manufacture were highly robust and resilient upon impact, especially given Ammianus' report that the 'Persian' ram that the Romans were using was already 'old',[52] although the exact age of the weapon is not known.

The third question that may be raised with respect to the ram's head is one of shape. Was it shaped like a giant bullet? As noted previously, bullet-shaped pro-jectiles have been discovered at Dura-Europos, therefore such technology was alien to neither the Romans nor the Sassanians. Whatever the shape of the ram's head, it clearly punched through the walls with such force that it led to the col-lapse of an entire tower, which opened a gap of sufficient size to allow for Sassa-nian infantry and other warriors (esp. dismounted savaran knights) to storm into Bezabde.

Finally, there is Ammianus' description of the tower's collapse after the impacts of the battering ram relating to the 'location' of the impact. It would appear that Shapur II's forces were following the *Ayin-nameh*'s recommendation that batter-ing rams are most effective when used against the weakest points of the enemy's fortifications.[53] Ammianus' note that the battering ram 'dug into the joints of the stones' may perhaps indicate that the Sassanian besiegers had detected some sort of weakness at that location and possibly realized that it was a vulnerability that could be exploited.

Procopius has also described Sassanian mobile towers almost two centuries after those seen in Ammianus' time. These are described as 'battering towers',[54] which presumably combined mobile towers with battering ram technology. Roman defenders were quite resourceful in defending against Sassanian battering rams. For example, during Kavad's siege of Amida in 502 CE, Roman defenders 'constantly broke off the heads of the rams by means of timbers thrown across them'.[55]

Hydro-engineering: 'water battering rams' and 'siege battleships'? The tactic of utilizing rivers as a weapon of war was an ancient Iranian military tradition dating back to Achaemenid times.[56] Shapur II's first siege of Nisibis in 337 or 338 CE is notable with respect to reports of the Sassanians employing hydro-engineering siege techniques. The Sassanian strategy had been to harness the power of water currents (esp. that of rivers) as a weapon by building dams or dykes. Once the water was collected, Sassanian engineers opened the dykes to propel the water against one of Nisibis' strong fortress walls.[57] Theodoret has provided an excellent description of this aspect of Sassanian military engineering:

> Shapur stopped up the course of the river which flowed past the city and when as vast an amount as possible of the accumulating water had piled up behind the dam he released it all at once against the walls, using it like a tremendously powerful battering-ram. The wall could not withstand the force of the water, and indeed, badly shaken by the flood, the whole stretch of that side of the city collapsed.[58]

Dodgeon and Lieu have noted that the Sassanian dam must have been of 'enormous height' to allow the water to attain sufficient pressure before its release as a battering ram.[59] The conversion of water's potential energy into kinetic energy against Nisibis for use as a 'battering ram' would suggest that the Sassanians had a sophisticated corps of military engineers who would have accompanied the spah during its campaigns.

Western experts have questioned the historical validity and scientific reliability of the Nisibis operation, but a precedent for these types of operations can be seen around five centuries before the Sassanians in Chinese military history. Chin Shih Huang-Ti (259–210 BCE) who campaigned to unify Northern China, is known to have diverted rivers to undermine his enemies' defences. Given recent reports of Iranian-Chinese contacts dating to the era of Emperor Huang-Ti,[60] approximately five centuries before the Nisibis operations, it is possible that the Iranians were cognizant of Chinese military hydro-engineering technology.

The Mygdonius River was once again utilized by the spah against Nisibis in 350 CE. In this instance, a large ditch had first been dug around the city and filled with water channelled from the Mygdonius, to then surround the city with water. This use of water is interesting inasmuch as it prevented the defenders from launching sorties from inside the city against the besieging army. It was here that the spah sprang an interesting surprise against the Romans. According to Julian, Shapur II besieged the city 'by bringing up ships with engines on board. This was not the work of a day, but I believe of almost four months.'[61]

Evidently, Sassanian engineers had constructed 'siege battleships' that most likely carried varieties of scorpions (aghrab), catapults (manjeniq and aradeh) and ballistae (charx) to attack the city. This raises two questions. First, were the ships assembled during the siege at Nisibis and then launched? This would seem more practical than hauling already built vessels by land to Nisibis. Perhaps the spah had bought forward pre-assembled 'kits' to then make the final assembly once they had surrounded the city with water. The kits may have been the siege batteries themselves which were then mounted on the ships which were presumably assembled from various components transported to the site. The second question is the actual size of these 'battleships'. They were probably more like large boats than actual 'ships'. Here is where Julian offers a clue. When the siege was underway, Julian notes that the Romans 'from the wall they hauled up many of the ships'![62] While no information is provided concerning the weight of the vessels, it is safe to assume that the 'ships' were probably not so heavy. Calculating the size and weight of the ships requires knowledge of the width and depth of the water channel. This would then allow for estimates to be made as to the size and power of the siege engines that had been mounted on these 'battleships'.

Roman defences certainly took a deadly toll of the 'siege battleships' at Nisibis. Roman countermeasures that proved effective in destroying the siege engines included the hurling of large stones and missiles with catapults and ballistae respectively, as well as the employment of what Julian describes as 'fire darts'.

Scaling walls. Sassanian besiegers are often described bringing forward ladders when attempting to scale the enemy's walls.[63] Less clear are the specific dimensions of the ladders, especially if they were built in a series of varying heights to accommodate various types of defensive walls encountered during sieges.

Protection – shielding for troops. The spah employed mobile sheds or 'cabs' that were used for the protection of (1) personnel who were moving battering rams forward; and (2) infantry or dismounted savaran knights moving toward the enemy's walls or gates.[64] The actual dimensions and protection capabilities of the 'cabs' are open to speculation but it would be safe to assume that they could provide protection against enemy archery. It is not clear, however, how resistant the 'cabs' would be to enemy countermeasures such as heated liquid substances being poured down by the defenders or the dropping of heavy stones. Islamic sources mention two distinct types of mobile shed, the *darraga* and the *dabbabat* (Table 5). The darraga was used to protect besieging troops as well as personnel operating battering rams. It is described as being a sturdily built enclosure made of wood and covered with hide. It is possible that in some cases these devices were built in the battle theatre in accordance with the specific siege operation requirements.

There is also a reference to 'wicker screens' being used for protection by Sassanian troops during sieges.[65] This may possibly be in reference to standard Sassanian infantry shields of the wicker type (Chapter 7). If the reference is to this type of shield, then it may be possible to speculate that Sassanian infantry may have adopted the Roman 'testudo' method. If this Roman tactic was adopted (as the spah had certainly adopted Roman siege methods and technology), then the troops in a besieging Sassanian infantry formation would have their shields placed above their heads, front, sides and rear for protection as they advanced close to the enemy's walls. Another type of shield used by besieging infantry was what Raspopova has reported as being 'a siege shield made of slats'.[66] This type of

Table 5. Sassanian siege warfare equipment as reported by Arabian sources with (mainly) Arabic terminology.
(sources: Al-Jahiz, vol. 3 (Beirut, 1968); Inostransev (1926, pp. 50–52); Taffazoli (1993, pp.194–195); Matofi (1999, p. 221); and Khorasani (2010, pp. 101, 225))

scorpion	*rutaila*; New Persian: *aghrab*
mobile shed for besieging troops and/or battering rams	*darraga*
a more powerful mobile shed for sieges	*dabbabat* (constructed of wood and covered with hide); New Persian: *Xarak/kharak*
naphtha-hurling engine	*naffata* (New Persian: *naft-andaz*)
catapult	*manjeniq/manjaniq* (giant stones hurled by a wheel-device)
small catapult	*aradeh* (for hurling smaller stones)
possible bow-like device for launching projectiles	*kashkanjir*
type of a bow resembling a large crossbow capable of shooting giant heavy darts as large as spears	*charx*; Islamic-era references also to *khaar-kaman* (giant bow)
iron traps	*hasak*; note similarity to Middle Persian *xasak* (thorn)

'slat' shield would be used by the infantryman to move closer towards the enemy's walls for digging mines or other forms of siege action.

Pyro-techniques and 'Firearms'

The spah employed pyro-techniques to weaken the enemy walls, gates and towers.[67] Arrows coated with flammable materials such as naphtha were shot by foot archers positioned on the ground or in mobile towers. The aforementioned ballistic weapons were capable of shooting naphtha and other flammable materials. Structures struck by such weapons might either collapse or be weakened to allow the successful use of other siege weaponry. For example, if an enemy wall was weakened by high-temperature fires, battering rams and ballistic weapons could be used to collapse them.

'Firearms' of Bahram Chobin. Safa has reported on the use of naphtha ballistic weapons by Bahram Chobin during his campaigns against the Turco-Hephthalite invasion of the northeast regions of the empire in 588 CE.[68] The weapons shot what were essentially large arrows or 'missiles' tipped with a container filled with naphtha. The latter substance came from the oil deposits of Badkobeh (modern Baku in the Republic of Azerbaijan), with the catapult device designed by the spah's engineers. The standard complement of such naphtha-projectile batteries stood at five men. Two men operated a bow-like torsion device to launch and propel the projectile. The third and fourth were responsible for filling the container with naphtha and igniting the fluid, and the fifth person aimed the weapon. It is very likely that Bahram Chobin's overwhelming successes against the invading Turco-Hephthalite armies were at least in part due to the employment of this weapon.

Role of Spah Units in Sieges

Building siege works was often the job of peasant conscripts as well as the personnel who operated the siege weaponry and equipment. Savaran knights, *paighan*
heavy infantrymen, and archers also performed critical roles. The successful
prosecution of sieges was thus contingent on the proper coordination of these
various spah units and personnel.

Paighan and peasant conscripts. The *paighan* were the empire's heavy infantry,
described as the armoured gladiator type (or *mirmillos*) by Ammianus in the early
360s CE.[69] In contrast to the paighan, the peasant infantry were poorly trained
and equipped for close-quarter combat (Chapter 7). The peasant infantry were
used to create siege works such as digging ditches, tunnels, etc. and were of little
use when caught at close quarters by the professional Roman infantry. When
breakthroughs were effected into the enemy's fortifications, the paighan were
the empire's main infantry force capable of close-quarter combat. By the sixth
century CE, the Dailamites were most likely entrusted with this role as well.

The savaran. Siege warfare also involved the direct intervention of the savaran.
As noted by Inostrancev, the savaran knights were well versed in siege tactics and
were well trained in employing siege warfare equipment.[70] Savaran knights were
involved in three critical tasks during sieges. First, they partook in the coordination of siege weaponry and the construction of siege works.[71] Second, they
were responsible (along with infantry and archers) for protecting and defending
siege batteries and personnel against enemy sorties.[72] If the walls of enemy installations were relatively short (i.e. ranging approximately 2–3m in height) the
knights could shoot arrows into enemy compounds and against defending enemy
troops in attack-retreat manoeuvres aimed at exhausting their besieged adversaries. Finally (as noted earlier by Lukonin), savaran knights were expected to
engage in hand-to-hand combat when breaking into enemy installations.[73] This
would occur when enemy fortifications had been breached, allowing the knights
to support the besieging infantry's assault into the fortress or city. This is seen for
example, during Shapur's campaigns in 256 CE when the Sassanians demonstrated their advanced skills in siege craft, especially in the capture of Antioch and
Dura Europos.

War elephants. Like the savaran, infantry and archers, war elephants were an
integral element of the battle order of the spah, both in set-piece battles as well as
sieges (Chapter 7). Zoka has suggested that the Sassanians may have used their
elephants as a kind of mobile siege tower for attacking enemy fortresses and
cities. They could be quite effective in this regard, given their ability to allow
archers to fire from elevated positions.[74] Elephants were most effective when
attacking towns and installations with shorter walls (i.e. 3–5m in height). But
the beasts were vulnerable to Roman counter-siege techniques such as the use of
fire arrows (see Amida, below); they were certainly vulnerable to heavier Roman
siege weaponry. At Nisibis (350 CE), for example, Theophanes reports that the

besieged Romans 'slew the majority of the elephants with catapults'.[75] Presumably these were clothed in armour of the laminated type, which would have been of little avail against projectiles propelled by powerful catapults.

Archery. Archers supported the savaran in sieges as they did on the open battlefield, by softening up the enemy prior to the savaran's attack with a deadly shower of arrows. In sieges, the archers would target defending archers and other personnel as the savaran approached the enemy city,[76] especially if a breakthrough through a breach or damaged gate was imminent. Archers in fact played a key role during breaching operations. At the third siege of Nisibis (350 CE), for example, Julian reports that 'the Parthian king [in reference to Sassanian king Shapur II] divided his archers into companies and ordered them to relieve one another and to keep shooting at the breach in the wall, so that the besieged could not rebuild it.'[77]

This was in essence the Classical equivalent of modern warfare's 'suppressive fire' against enemy engineers attempting to rebuild a bridge for vehicle crossings, etc. The 'rotation system' ensured that archers would not become fatigued and also allowed the resting archers to replenish their supply of arrows. Meanwhile, even as enemy troops working to repair the breach were being suppressed by archery, the Sassanian siege engines would be inflicting further structural damage against the enemy's fortifications. The critical role of archery during sieges will be further discussed later in this chapter.

Observation of operations. Siege operations were observed from an elevated position by the shahanshah and his military leaders. Khosrow I, for example, placed himself on elevated positions or hills to observe the interior of the besieged cities at Petra (541 CE), Edessa (543 CE) and Dara (573 CE).[78] In attendance with the shahanshah were scribes (Sassanian: 'dabir') who would observe and record the performance of the warriors (Chapter 2).

'Non-combat' Methods for Capturing Enemy Cities

The Sassanians did attempt to use a variety of 'non-combat' strategies to facilitate their capture of an enemy city or fortress. These methods typically rested on the use of spies, psychological warfare and fifth-column elements.

Spies. Once the enemy city or fortress had been surrounded by the spah, Sassanian military commanders would seek ways to demoralize the besieged population. The Sassanians were especially keen on using spies and subterfuge as a means of minimizing casualties.

Attempts would be made to send spies and agitators into the enemy city or fortress in an attempt to influence the mind-set of the opposition; the primary aim was to use psychological tactics to demoralize and confuse enemy civilians and combatants. Dinawari notes that spies would seek out just one or two people who could provide information on structural weaknesses of the fortifications.[79] Armed with this information, the spies would then manipulate it in an attempt to influence the besieged civilians and military personnel in order to sow hopelessness, discord and defeatism.[80]

Psychological warfare and fifth-column elements. This entailed the creation of fear among the defenders by the dispatch of messengers to 'advertise' the spah's military capabilities, especially with respect to specific weapons systems (pyrotechniques, scorpions, etc.) and the havoc and casualties these could create.[81] Conversely, the enemy could be enticed to join the Sassanians by offers of friendship, material rewards, titles, etc. The system of 'buying off' influential enemy military personnel or officials within a besieged city was also meant to create a pro-Sassanian fifth column.[82] In ideal circumstances members of the fifth column would even endeavour to militarily assist the spah during a siege. Cultivation of such treachery required that spies locate and recruit individuals who were motivated by greed, personal vendettas, ambitions of power, or any combination of these.

Other means of sowing fear among the defenders was to awe them by engaging in spectacular manoeuvres in which the Sassanian king was prominent.[83] This technique was clearly employed by Shapur II during the siege of Amida in 359 CE; the king believed that at 'the moment he made his appearance the besieged would be suddenly panic-stricken, and have recourse to supplication and entreaty'.[84] Shapur II hoped to induce the garrison to surrender with the spectacular display of himself and his formidable host. Another example of the use this technique occurred during Khosrow's campaign in 576 CE, in his effort to take Theodosiopolis. Capture of this city would be of great geostrategic value as it would enable the Sassanians to gain greater control over the western Caucasian regions, namely Armenia and Iberia. Khosrow's campaign timetable, however, prevented him from implementing a full-scale siege against Theodosiopolis. Instead, the shahanshah conducted manoeuvres intending to awe the city's garrison and thus inducing them to surrender. Menander describes how Khosrow assembled his army outside the walls of Theodosiopolis and then joined the parade on his horse.[85] Iranian historiography also emphasizes the role of martial music during such manoeuvres.[86] The martial music which accompanied these military displays of king and spah was meant to both demoralize the enemy while simultaneously boosting the morale of the besieging host (see Chapter 4).

Shapur I and the Fall of Dura-Europos

Dura-Europos had been one of the Roman cities to fall to the armies of Shapur I in c. 256 CE (exact dates are disputed at the time of writing). Dura-Europos changed hands several times between the Romans (later Romano-Byzantines) and Partho-Sassanians in the course of the wars they fought. The site has generally been of great interest to military historians especially with respect to pictorials depicting Parthian armoured knights, horse armour for chargers and the remains of the fallen Sassanian soldier.

The Sassanians at this time were much more adept at siege warfare than their Parthian predecessors, a fact which may have (at least in part) caught the Romans by surprise. It would appear that the Sassanian armies of Shapur I were using a combination of strategies such as bombardment with heavy siege engines (e.g. mangonels) and the employment of siege towers. Ballistae were most likely employed during this operation. Wooden artillery projectiles have been retrieved from Dura Europos. At least two dozen projectiles, along with around fifty iron projectile heads (including a unique incendiary head) have been retrieved from the site. It is also highly likely that the Sassanians captured Roman siege engines to not only use these against their former owners but to also study these machines to build versions of their own.

'Chemical weapons' or smoke inhalation in confined tunnels? Both Romans and Sassanians were highly proficient in mining and countermining operations. Put simply, the besieging army would dig mines under the enemy's walls in an attempt to burrow into the city itself; the besieged would in turn dig counter-mines to block the enemy's tunnels. The struggle between mines and counter-mines would often result in bitter, close-quarter, hand-to-hand fighting in the confined spaces underground.

Simon James of Leicester University (a leading archaeologist and expert on Dura-Europos) has provided a alternative explanation as to what may have occurred in one of the Sassanians' mines at Dura-Europos. According to James, the Sassanians had deployed burning bitumen and sulphur crystals resulting in the asphyxiation of a number of troops in one of the mines. According to James, the 'use of such smoke generators in siege-mines is actually mentioned in classical texts, and it is clear from the archaeological evidence at Dura that the Sassanian Persians were as knowledgeable in siege warfare as the Romans; they surely knew of this grim tactic.'[87]

Interestingly, reputable mainstream media outlets began issuing sensationalist reports that appeared to be taking James's studies out of context, notably the BBC's headline 'Ancient Persians gassed Romans' (19 January 2009).[88] Such reports even provided the nuanced impression that the Sassanians relied on 'chemical weapons' or even 'gas warfare' while the Romans did not. First, as noted by James, both the Romans (and later Romano-Byzantines) and the Sassa-nians were cognizant of a variety of siege warfare techniques, including the use of burning sulphur crystals and bitumen. The later Romano-Byzantines, for example, employed a rudimentary form of napalm known as 'Greek fire' in naval warfare. Second, sulphur crystals and bitumen can be deadly but only in very narrow and confined spaces with no exit points or ventilation. Such scenarios often occur during house and building fires where smoke inhalation can lead to death, but this is not the same as 'chemical warfare', where weaponized chemical agents are employed against enemy troops in open spaces. It is certainly true that burning sulphur crystals and bitumen give off deadly smoke and fumes as James avers, but these are not the same as modern-day (human manufactured) tabun, sarin, mustard, or nerve gasses as Saddam Hussein had used against Iraqi civilians and Iranian troops in open spaces during the Iran-Iraq war (1980–1988).

Iranian academics such as Khodadad Rezakhani (Department of History, University of California, Los Angeles) and Reza Yeganehshakib (Department of History, University of California, Irvine) have disputed the conclusions of James and the BBC reports. Rezakhani and Yeganehshakib (who also holds a bachelor of science degree in chemical engineering and a master of science degree in environmental sciences) made the following three points in an interview with *Payvand News* of Iran.[89]

First, a blockage at the mouth of the tunnel, caused by a cave-in at that location, may have choked off the tunnel's oxygen supply, thus asphyxiating the Roman soldiers. But the dimensions of the tunnel as well as the properties of the soils and the materials used to shore up the tunnel need to be analysed to determine whether a collapse could have occurred.

Second, one must consider the necessity of lighting inside dark tunnels during siege work and combat. Simply put, without lighting neither the Roman nor Sassanian troops could operate inside the tunnels. Sulphur crystals and bitumen were the standard chemicals used for the creation of torchlights in very dark environments, and the gases they produce when burned are poisonous. It is possible that these gases accumulated, with fatal results for the workers, as the result of physical blockage at the tunnel's ingress or egress points. The researchers also state that the accumulation of the deadly gases could have been due to:

> the air pressure difference between the inside of the tunnel and the outside air pressure particularly at the mouth of it. If the outside air pressure was higher than that of the inside, then the gases inside could not be released to the outside and would accumulate there. The elevation difference of the tunnel and its entrance is a crucial factor, as the air density and pressure in the higher altitudes is lower than that of lower altitude.

If the Sassanian tunnel had been excavated at a lower elevation with an open entrance to allow oxygen to enter, then any open area (or hole) could have connected the Sassanian and Roman tunnels. In such a scenario, the oxygen or air in concert with the toxic gases of the torchlights could have rapidly risen and entered the Roman tunnel due to differences in air pressure. The situation would become especially dangerous if, for whatever reason, the mouth of the Roman tunnel had been sealed.

The third point to consider is the scientific role of chemistry in this scenario. Burning processes require sufficient quantities of oxygen, fuel and temperature. It is possible that the right amount of temperature would have been produced by the initial ignition of the sulphur crystals, but the gases produced due to combustion could only be proportionate to the amount of available air and fuel. To arrive at definitive conclusions, one must ascertain the quality and amount of fuel, a very difficult task. With such scientific data, the amount of the gas released through the creation of an energy-mass balance for the chemical reaction of the combustion may be determined. This would allow for the objective quantification of the actual quantity of poisonous gases, and whether these quantities were capable of killing twenty Roman soldiers and one Sassanian trooper. What must also be determined is the amount of air or oxygen in this scenario, and whether this was sufficient to propel the combustion.

As a result, the allegation of 'chemical weapons' tactics could have been a case of lethal gaseous by-products of torchlights used for lighting the tunnels. The same torchlights would be of little danger in an outside-open environment. In an interview with *BBC-Persian* (20 January 2009)[90] Ali Asghar Ramezanpour (Anthropology and Genetics, Plymouth University, UK) speculated that the Roman soldiers were killed in subterranean clashes with Sassanians soldiers. Ramezanpour noted in this regard that the tunnel was wide enough to accommodate four men standing (or crouching) shoulder to shoulder. Ramezanpour also questioned the scientific basis for the 'chemical weapons' hypothesis. In practice, objective scientific data has yet to be produced to sustain the hypotheses of James and the BBC. This may partly explain why the 'chemical warfare' hypothesis has yet to be accepted by scholars in the domain of Sassanian military history. This and other aspects of the siege of Dura Europos are likely to be subjects of study for decades to come.

Siege Operations of Shapur II
Shapur II fought a number of battles against the forces of the Roman Empire over the course of some twenty-two years (c. 337 or 338–359). Many of these battles were notable for the display of Sassanian military skill in siege operations. When Sassanian forces crossed the Tigris in 337 or 338, they simultaneously besieged the cities of Nisibis and Singara.

Nisibis (350 CE). Shapur II's first siege of Nisibis is of interest because it saw the first recorded use by the spah of battle elephants against the Romans.[91] As noted previously, the spah had attempted to utilize the power of the waters of the Mygdonius River as a siege weapon against Singara. Prior to this action, Shapur II had built towers and placed his archers in them to fire at the defenders on Singara's walls while his engineers tunnelled beneath them.[92] Despite these efforts the Romans held on to Singara, inflicting heavy casualties on the attackers. The Sassanians suffered the same lack of results, as well as substantial losses in men, at Nisibis. Just two months into the siege operations the Sassanians had to suspend operations against the Romans to confront Chionite invaders threatening the Sassanian Empire's northeast. Nisibis was attacked for a second time but the city resisted capture once again.

Some thirteen to fourteen years later, following the pacification of the Central Asian frontier, Shapur II resumed hostilities against the Roman empire. Once again, his forces crossed the Tigris and laid siege to Nisibis in 350. Supporting the heavily armoured savaran knights at Nisibis were battle elephants and 'hoplite'-type armoured infantry.[93] Interestingly, the 'armoured elephants'[94] are described as advancing 'in a battle line ... and hoplites filling the spaces between'.[95] This force was entrusted with the task of continuing the spah's assaults following heavy losses suffered by the savaran.[96] Roman missiles proved effective in repelling the spah's elephant-hoplite assaults. Some of the wounded elephants sank into the muddy terrain; other elephants panicked and crashed into their own (Sassanian) ranks. Roman sources claim that this 'elephant panic' resulted in the deaths of up to 10,000 Sassanian troops.[97] As noted previously in this chapter, the Mygdonius River had again been put to use in the siege operations against the city.

Amida (359 CE). By the time Shapur II invaded eastern Anatolia in 359 CE, the Central Asian frontier had been pacified with the Chionites accompanying the Sassanians as allies. Crossing the Zab River on a pontoon bridge built by Sassanian engineers, Shapur II and the spah entered eastern Anatolia and punched towards pro-Roman Amida (modern Diyarbakr). As Sassanian forces advanced towards Amida they also captured the fortresses of Busa and Rema.[98]

When the Sassanians reached Amida Shapur II ordered his army to surround the city. The Greco-Roman warrior-historian Ammianus Marcellinus, who was a member of the Roman military staff of General Ursicinus, has provided detailed descriptions of Shapur II's siege of Amida. At the eastern gates of the city stood the Chionites of Central Asia while the Saka cavalry of Iran's Seistan-Baluchistan was posted at the western gates, the cavalry of Albania (modern-day Republic of Azerbaijan) took up positions at the northern gates and Shapur II and the elite savaran corps deployed to the south of the city.[99] Ammianus observed that the spah was also employing Sassanian battle elephants against Amida. He evidently first witnessed the slow march of 'lines of elephants ... loaded with armed men' at Amida's western gates.[100] This is of interest as the elephants were being deployed from the same position as the Saka contingent.

Siege engines were quickly operationalized allowing powerful projectiles to be hurled into Amida. These inflicted heavy casualties among combatants and civilians alike. Shapur II then followed up with messages of peace that were rejected by Amida's leadership. Sassanian siege batteries then resumed their deadly barrages. Shapur II then led his elite savaran corps in major assaults against Amida's gates, which had most likely been damaged by the Sassanian siege batteries. According to Ammianus, Shapur II 'rode up to the gates attended by his royal escort, and while with too great assurance he came so near that even his features could clearly be recognized'.[101] Nevertheless, each of Shapur's assaults was beaten back by the defenders, who evidently waited until the attackers had approached to within 100m of the gates before unleashing a powerful barrage of missiles into their compact formations. Heliodorus wrote that the armour of the savaran knights was 'proof against any missiles',[102] but this was not the case at Amida; at close range their armour could be, and was, penetrated. The defenders were also apparently in possession of mechanical ballistic weapons capable of discharging projectiles at high velocities with great penetrating power. The son of Gumbrates (the Chionite king) was killed by just such a weapon as he and the Chionite contingents launched an assault against the city's eastern gates.[103] The Romans also found ways of countering Shapur II's elephants by hurling flames against the animals, making Sassanian elephant drivers 'unable to control them'.[104]

On the third day of the siege, Shapur II's commanders methodically reorganized his forces for a fresh round of assaults. As before, the eastern gates were faced by the Chionites, the western gates by the Sakas, the northern gates by the Albanians and the south with the Gelai (modern-day Gilan in northern Iran).[105] The presence of the Gelai, who were excellent infantry fighters, indicated that the Sassanians expected to break into Amida to engage its desperate defenders in close-quarter combat. A 'wall of infantry' five rows deep now surrounded Amida.[106] Shapur II ordered fresh assaults of infantry and cavalry supported by the concentrated barrages of Sassanian foot archers. Despite the ferocity of the assaults, the Amidans again repelled the attackers with a combination of missiles, ballistic weapons, lances and scorpions.

While the Sassanians had certainly suffered heavy losses, their siege engines had exacted a heavy toll on Amida's defiant defenders. The Sassanians were also employing Roman siege batteries captured in earlier campaigns. Amida's 20,000 inhabitants had suffered terribly during the siege and the seven Roman legions defending the city were running out of land in which to bury their dead.[107] The Sassanians intensified their efforts by installing mangonels and armoured towers at key locations around the city. Ballistic weapons were mounted on the towers to suppress the fire of Amida's archers and ballistae and thus allow the Sassanians to attack the city's gates without suffering the heavy losses incurred in previous assaults. Sassanian engineers also constructed a large mound that was to prove its effectiveness in finally turning the tide in Shapur II's favour.

Another stratagem was the successful infiltration of seventy elite archers onto Amida's southern walls with the assistance of a Roman deserter. The archers then fired their arrows against Roman troops in the city, but when their quivers emptied they were all cut down by Roman troops. The Romans also launched a sortie of their own by sending their Gallic troops on a raid against the Sassanian camps.

Sassanian and allied infantry and cavalry resumed their attacks but these (and the battle elephants) were all repelled by the devastating fire of Amida's archers, ballistae, slingers and scorpions. Sassanian ballistic towers, however, were now placing the Amidan defenders at great risk. This prompted the Romans to launch heavy 'round stones' which accurately struck at the joints of the towers, causing their collapse.[108] Shapur II responded by launching yet more attacks lasting into the night and even participated in these dangerous assaults in person.[109] The mound already erected as high as Amida's towers by the Sassanians now proved decisive. Sassanian engineers placed makeshift 'bridges' connecting their mound to Amida's walls. This allowed Sassanian infantry, dismounted savaran knights and allied forces to pour into the city to subdue its defenders. The fighting was very bloody with the dead of both sides piling into the trenches, and with Shapur II engaging in hand-to-hand combat with sword and dagger.[110] With Amida now clearly doomed, the survivors sued for peace, allowing Shapur II to officially enter the city as its conqueror.

Singara (360 CE). Shapur assembled a formidable army in 360 CE,[111] crossed the Tigris River to then arrive at Singara to besiege it.[112] The defenders quickly organized their defence by sealing the gates of Singara. They placed their siege (or counter-siege) batteries in position with their troops taking their positions on the battlements and towers. Shapur II attempted to avoid combat by appealing for a negotiated settlement but this failed to achieve results. Determined to repel Shapur II's attempts at taking over their city, the defenders of Singara remained defiant. The Sassanians would soon be in for a tough battle.

Shapur II gave his army a day to rest. On the next day a red or 'scarlet' flag was raised which signalled the attack. Very quickly troops surrounding the city bought forth ladders to scale Singara's walls. Sassanian siege engines were installed and protective works were built to shield their crews. Attempts by the Sassanians to move forward were repelled by heavy barrages of missiles and stones. This pattern repeated itself for several days without gains and resulted in heavy casualties for both sides. The Sassanians now revised their strategy by bringing forward a large battering ram against one of the city's rounded towers. Apparently there was a weakness in the tower's foundation; the structure had undergone repairs and the mortars and cement were still in the process of curing. It is possible that the Sassanians had sent reconnaissance teams to study Singara's foundations in search of weak spots. Whether this was the case or not, the Sassanians had chosen their strategy well, as the defenders did their utmost to repel the attacks of the battering ram with missiles, 'bullets'[113] and flammable substances. Despite the ferocity of their efforts, the Singarans failed. Ammianus reports that 'the keenness of the ram prevailed over every means of defence, digging through the mortar of the recently cemented stones, which was still moist and unsettled'.[114] This created a dangerous breach and it was from here that the final doom came for Singara. The defenders, despite their stubborn defence, were forced to give way by the Sassanian assailants who were now pouring into the breach. The assailants were most likely dismounted savaran and paighan troops, with archers providing support. Sassanian combat troops now made a clear breakthrough and fanned out across the city. As noted by Ammianus:

> A very few of the inhabitants were slain, and all the rest, by command of Sapor, were taken alive and transported to the most distant regions of Persia ... the First Flavian [Legion] and the First Parthian [Legion], and a great body of native troops, as well as a division of auxiliary cavalry which had been shut up in it through the suddenness of the attack made upon it. All of these, as I have said, were taken prisoners.[115]

The Sassanian troops must have engaged the formidable Roman troops (in this case the First Flavian and First Parthian Legions) in hand-to-hand combat, but Ammianus' description of their surrender makes clear that they had been overpowered.

Siege operations of Khosrow I: The case of Antioch (540 CE)

Khosrow I and the army had crossed the Euphrates in 540 CE to attack into Roman-held Syria. The army had bought siege equipment as Khosrow intended to besiege a number of Roman cities along his line of advance. It is not clear how many troops the spah employed in its subsequent capture of Antioch, as

Procopius has provided no actual numbers. The only information provided by Procopius is the fact that it took Sassanian forces three days to cross a temporary (pontoon?) bridge across the Euphrates river as they returned home to the Sassanian empire.[116] As Downey has correctly pointed out, this information is insufficient to estimate with any degree of precision the size of the spah during the 540 CE campaign as no data is provided with respect to (a) the size of the bridge; (2) whether the spah was crossing that bridge in formation, and if so, what type of formations were used; and (c) how many hours were spent in each of those three days to cross the bridge.[117] Tabari has reported Khosrow as having employed 90,000 men in the campaign that led to the capture of Antioch. While the number may have been exaggerated by Tabari, it is very likely that a large proportion of these were peasant levies that had been recruited for siege work (labour, digging ditches, etc.). When Khosrow besieged Dara later in 573 CE, his forces were composed of 23,000 savaran knights, 40,000 infantry and 120,000 labourers for the purpose of siege work. Essential to the subsequent fall of Dara was the employment of Romano-Byzantine siege engines which Khosrow I had captured at the siege of Nisibis.

The commander of Romano-Byzantine forces in the Syrian theatre was Bouzes, who failed to halt the spah's advance. Zenobia avoided capture[118] but the spah then advanced to Sura and captured it.[119] The inhabitants of Antioch had initially hoped to negotiate with Khosrow to avoid a siege, and sent an emissary named Megas (the Bishop of Borea) to meet Khosrow. After his meeting Megas went to Antioch to discover that all direct negotiations with Khosrow had now been forbidden by Byzantine officials.[120]

Meanwhile, as part of his thrust into Syria, Khosrow I had entered the city of Borea and virtually destroyed it. This was because the inhabitants had failed to produce the ransom that had been set by Khosrow (they had paid him only half of the originally demanded 4,000lb of silver). The defenders of Borea then took refuge in the city's acropolis, which Khosrow besieged. The defenders in the acropolis soon suffered from critical water shortages.[121] Megas came again to the Sassanian camp and managed to persuade Khosrow to accept the offer of 2,000lb of silver and lift the siege. Khosrow actually complied, but when Megas informed him of the change of attitude by Antioch, he moved his forces to that city.

The defences of Antioch had already been examined by Germanus, who had been dispatched to the locale for this purpose by Justinian.[122] Germanus found the main part of Antioch's defences secure but was very concerned about a nearby mountain which rose above the city. The main danger with that mountain was a rock which 'spreads out to a very considerable width, and rises to a height only a little less than the fortifications'.[123] Germanus' solution for this problem was to isolate the rock by either altering the facing wall to 'fit' the rock into it or to dig a large ditch along the wall. The engineers protested that there would not be enough time to complete such a project. They argued that the rapidly marching spah would arrive quickly at Antioch while these engineering works were still under construction. The Sassanians would then quickly realize the weakness imperilling Antioch and seek to take advantage of it. Germanus grudgingly accepted the logic of these arguments, apparently hopeful that a large force would soon be sent by Justinian from Constantinople.[124] But in the event, no large army came to the rescue of Antioch. Instead, 6,000 troops led by Theoctistus and Malatzes arrived from Lebanon to reinforce Antioch in anticipation of Khosrow's arrival.[125] As events soon demonstrated, Germanus' fears of the rock platform being a dangerous liability proved warranted.

Khosrow and the spah arrived at Antioch and encamped in the city's environs along the Orontes River. It is clear that at this juncture Khosrow was hoping to avoid a military showdown by negotiation. Khosrow demanded 110 centenaria (11,000lb) of gold to forego besieging Antioch; Procopius stated that the shahan-shah would have accepted less.[126] Negotiations were begun but the following day the populace of Antioch hurled insults at the Sassanian monarch.[127] Khosrow responded by initiating military action.

The spah deployed to assail the wall and launched attacks from a number of points along the river. Just as Germanus had feared, 'he [Khosrow I] himself with the most of the men and best troops directed an attack against the height. For at this place ... the wall of fortification was most vulnerable.'[128]

The structure upon which the Romano-Byzantines were to stand and fight was very narrow, which obliged them to devise an ingenious strategy. They bound together long timbers and suspended them between two towers to make 'these spaces much broader, in order that still more men might be able to ward off the assailants from there'.[129] The timbers were apparently assembled in haste, as the engineers had seemingly failed to account for the stresses and weight the timbers could withstand. These engineering errors would contribute greatly to the disaster that was about to befall Antioch.

The Sassanian warriors pressed their assaults on all sides with their archery discharging massive volleys of missiles, 'especially along the crest of the hill'.[130] The Romano-Byzantine defenders stood their ground and fought bravely, joined by the youth of Antioch. But they could not stop the Sassanians, who were being exhorted by Khosrow himself to fight at their best. The problem, from the stand-point of the Romano-Byzantines, was the broad and high rock which was prac-tically right up next to Antioch's fortifications: it allowed Khosrow's troops to fight the defenders on what was essentially a flat surface. In the meantime Persian archers continued to discharge their deadly volleys.

The turning point came when the timber platform suspended between the two towers collapsed, plunging to the ground along with the defenders who had stood upon it. This caused panic among the troops of Theoctistus and Malatzes, who took to their horses to escape. As the Romano-Byzantine troops rode out of Antioch, their horses trampled and killed a number of Antioch's non-combatants. The Sassanians quickly took advantage of the disruption caused by the timbers' collapse by bringing ladders against the walls. The walls were then scaled with very little difficulty. Upon reaching the battlements, the Sassanian warriors clearly witnessed the flight of the Roman-Byzantine troops. Instead of shooting arrows at them or pursuing them, the Sassanians gestured at their Romano-Byzantine counterparts, indicating that they should immediately flee. The

Romano-Byzantines then escaped through the gate leading to Daphne (a suburb), and the Sassanians did not attempt to block their flight. In the meantime, however, the Sassanians lost no time in securing Antioch's other gates. As noted previously in Chapter 9, the spah's battle doctrine did allow defeated foes to escape, in recognition of the dangers of attempting to entirely destroy a defeated army. Had Khosrow ordered his warriors to block the gate leading to Daphne, the fleeing Roman-Byzantines would have been forced to stand and fight for their very survival. This would have made them especially formidable in hand-to-hand combat, which would likely have resulted in heavy Sassanian casualties. As events soon demonstrated, Khosrow's decision to leave the Romano-Byzantine flight unmolested proved militarily wise.

In contrast to the troops commanded by Theoctistus and Malatzes, the young men of Antioch's circus factions, organized into armed militias, stood their ground and fought tenaciously. Despite holding their own against the Sassanian warriors (presumably infantry and dismounted savaran knights), Antioch was doomed. Some of the defenders wore heavy armour but many others had scarcely any equipment or weapons and used stones to fight the Sassanians. With the arrival of fresh Sassanian troops the defenders were finally overcome and put to flight.[131] The Sassanians then proceeded to sack and burn the city. Khosrow then re-built a new version (or near-replica) of the city of Antioch inside the Sassanian Empire where he settled the captives of the original Antioch.

Siege Operations of Khosrow II

The long and devastating war with the Byzantine Empire very nearly eliminated the latter as a major threat to the Sassanians. The war's first phase entailed a lengthy but successful campaign, from 603 to 609/610 CE, to dismantle the elaborate Romano-Byzantine system of defence in depth along the western frontiers (see Chapter 16). The destruction of the defensive system enabled the Sassanians to penetrate into the Byzantine Near East and Anatolia. Dara was the first of the strong Romano-Byzantine cities to fall, and in 614 CE the Sassanians captured Jerusalem. Twelve years later, in 626 CE, the Sassanians laid siege to but failed to take Constantinople itself. These campaigns are briefly examined below.

Dara (603 CE). Emperor Maurice (r. 582–602), who had helped Khosrow II regain his throne from Bahram Chobin, was assassinated in a palace coup in 602 CE. He was succeeded by Phocas, prompting Khosrow to renege on his territorial concessions to Maurice and then attack the Byzantine Empire. The war with Byzantium opened with Khosrow II marching on Dara in November 603. Phocas dispatched General Germanus to attack Khosrow II and his besieging forces, but these were soundly defeated; Germanus, wounded in battle with the Sassanians, died shortly thereafter. In the meantime, a Byzantine general named Narses had rebelled against Constantinople and seized Edessa. Realizing the seriousness of the threats to his newly gained authority, Phocas decided to dispose of the greater threat first. He dispatched a new army to crush the Sassanians and eject them from his realm. The battle was joined at Arxamus (Arxamoun). The result was another crushing defeat for the Romano-Byzantines. Of special interest are Theophanes' reports of the Sassanians having captured Romano-Byzantine prisoners.[132] Also of interest are reports that the Sassanians had assembled 'a fort with ... elephants'.[133] The specific tactical nature of this 'fort' and others like it is not known, but it is possible that the elephants were used for transporting archers. Perhaps the Sassanians used formations of elephants equipped with 'forts' in the siege of Dara; if so, the elephants may have been protected from dangerous countermeasures such as naphtha and enemy missiles (especially incendiary missiles). At the battle of Arxamus, the elephants would not have been sufficient to defeat Romano-Byzantine troops, but acting in coordination with the savaran, these could have functioned as 'mobile mini-archery forts'. Dailamite infantry would most likely have been present, and they may have followed the savaran knights when the latter charged the enemy with their lances.

What is certain is that the defeat of Phocas' armies doomed Dara; Khosrow II captured the city after a nine-month siege in 604 CE. Khosrow II had originally yielded Dara to Maurice in exchange for his assistance in toppling Bahram Chobin who had seized power at Khosrow II's expense. With this important and strategic fortress-city in Sassanian hands, Ctesiphon could once again penetrate into Roman-held Mesopotamia and Anatolia. Khosrow II now left the field and handed over command of his armies to his generals.

Jerusalem (614 CE). After the destruction of the Byzantine defensive system, General Shahrbaraz captured Edessa in 610 CE. These operations along with the consolidation of Syria allowed the Sassanians to thrust into Palestine towards Jerusalem in 614 CE. The capture of Jerusalem and control of the Palestinian coastline would provide Ctesiphon access to the Mediterranean. The Sassanians would then have the option of constructing a fleet in an attempt to wrest control of the Mediterranean from the Romano-Byzantines, much as the Achaemenids of old had attempted against the Greeks.

General Shahrbaraz besieged Jerusalem in 614 CE and captured it in just eighteen to twenty days.[134] The Sassanians' success in breaking into and capturing Jerusalem was achieved by way of the suffusion and mining strategies discussed earlier in this chapter. The Sassanians dug tunnels under walls near the Church of Saint Stephen (near the Damascus Gate).[135] The Romano-Byzantine defenders failed to block this penetration and were soon overpowered by Sassanian troops, leading to the capture of Jerusalem. Romano-Byzantine troops had arrived from nearby Jericho but then fled the theatre instead of joining the defence of Jerusalem against the Sassanians. This may partly explain why the Sassanians did not face prolonged resistance in the battle for Jerusalem.

The Sassanian Empire's Jewish allies may have helped the Sassanians capture Jerusalem. At the onset of the Sassanian-Byzantine war in 603 CE, Khosrow II struck a military alliance with Nehemiah ben Hushiel, son of the Jewish Exilarch. Some 20,000 Jewish troops were then recruited to fight alongside the Sassanians as they struck into the Byzantine-ruled areas of the modern-day Middle East.

A key success was the capture of Antioch with the aid of Nehemiah ben Hushiel's Jewish troops. As the Sassanians marched towards Jerusalem, it was joined by more Jewish volunteers and later by a number of Arabs. The Jews who joined the spah were rebels led by Benjamin of Tiberias, who had already led a powerful revolt against Emperor Heraclius. Benjamin succeeded in recruiting more Jewish troops from Galilee, Nazareth and Tiberias.

When the Sassanians besieged Jerusalem in July, they were also supported by a pro-Sassanian force within the city. The Sassanians thus achieved one of their objectives necessary for prosecuting sieges: enlisting allies within the enemy city. The Sassanians rewarded the Jews by appointing Nehemiah ben Hushiel as governor of Jerusalem. This was part of a Jewish autonomous region that was set up within the Sassanian empire. Shahrbaraz trusted the Jews of Jerusalem; according to Strategius, 'the Jews were left in Jerusalem'. This was broadly consistent with the overall historically constructive relations between the Jews and the Iranic world since the times of the Achaemenids. Jews, for example, had supported the Parthians during their attacks against Roman forces in ancient Palestine in 40–39 BCE.[136]

Traditional sources often report of the mass destruction that was then wreaked upon Jerusalem by the Sassanians. According to Antiochus Strategius:[137]

> Holy churches were burned with fire, others were demolished, majestic altars fell prone, sacred crosses were trampled underfoot, life-giving icons were spat upon by the unclean ... when the people were carried into Persia and the Jews were left in Jerusalem, they began with their own hands to demolish and burn such of the holy churches as were left standing.

A comprehensive archaeological survey by Gideon Avni questions the accuracy and authenticity of the above statement. As noted by Avni, 'Many sites that had been supposedly destroyed by the Persians continued in use into the early Islamic period.'[138] The comprehensive study can be summarized as follows: (1) excavations made in the sites of Byzantine monasteries fail to reveal evidence of destruction in the early seventh century CE; and (2) Jerusalem's residential areas and streets continued to function during the early days of the Islamic conquests. The validity of previous studies suggesting that the Sassanians had destroyed numerous sites in Jerusalem can now be seriously questioned. Detailed excavations and studies of sites such as the upper slope of the City of David or the area south of the Temple Mount, the Byzantine Monastery of Saint George, the churches of Eleona and Gethsemane, the New Church of Theotokos and the Church of Probatika had not been destroyed by the Sassanians.[139] Even the Church of the Holy Sepulchre which 'according to most sources ... was set on fire and badly damaged ... [and] later repaired by Modestus ... reveals no evidence of significant damage or destruction'.[140]

In summary, investigations made in the last three decades reveal that urban life and settlement in Jerusalem and the rest of Palestine went virtually uninterrupted during the fourteen-year Sassanian domination followed by the early Islamic conquests. In contrast the archaeological evidence which outlines the Roman destruction of Jerusalem in 70 CE reveals this to have been extensive and significant, with much of the city (especially the Jewish quarter) having been destroyed by the Romans.[141]

Nevertheless, there is evidence of destruction in at least three areas in Jerusalem that appear to be consistent with a military siege. The first is the area of the Damascus Gate, where several ash layers outside the walls were attributed to Shahbaraz's capture of Jerusalem.[142] A second structure is that of a large building near the Dung Gate south of the Old City which was destroyed as a result of the Sassanian siege. What is of interest in this case is the discovery of a hoard of 264 Byzantine gold coins in one of the rooms of the destroyed building. These coins were from the time of Emperor Heraclius (r. 610–641 CE) and had been minted in 610–613 CE, right before the fall of Jerusalem to Shahrbaraz in 614 CE. The coins were virtually unused, which has led to suggestions that this hoard of coins had been hidden by Jerusalem's citizenry just prior to the city's fall to the Sassanians.[143] The Church of Holy Zion on Mount Zion was damaged in the fighting but quickly repaired after the Sassanians captured the city.[144]

There is plenty of archaeological evidence corroborating the claim of a large number of Christians having been slain after the capture of Jerusalem. Strategius has cited thirty-five mass burial sites of Christians slain after the city fell, with at least seven such sites having been identified with archaeological evidence thus far.[145] These seven sites are all located outside of the Old City and associated with the Byzantine era. The most significant of these is the mass-burial site at Mamilla (approx. 120m from the Jaffa Gate), which is a rock-cut cave. The site has yielded hundreds of skeletons of young people who met a sudden death.[146] The manuscripts, however, assert that between 4,518 and 24,518 were killed at Mamilla. Avni cautions that 'Even if the numbers of deceased ... were highly exaggerated ... several tens of thousands of people, almost equals the whole Jerusalem population ... seems highly unlikely'.[147] What is clear is that these killings, the capture of the Patriarch Zacharias, and the carrying away of the true cross to the Sassanian empire must have helped Heraclius to subsequently galvanize what was essentially a defeated Romano-Byzantine empire towards a type of 'crusade' against the (Zoroastrian) Sassanian empire.

Constantinople (626 CE). Marching across Anatolia, Shahrbaraz reached Constantinople and placed it under siege in c. 626 CE. Having reached the shores of the Bosphorus, the armies of Iran were once again looking towards the European mainland as they had in the times of Darius and Xerxes. Shahrbaraz now made contact with the khan of the Avars for the purpose of forging an anti-Byzantine alliance. Constantinople was now besieged by the Avars and their Slavic, Bulgar and Gepid subject peoples from the European side, with Shahrbaraz and the spah besieging the city from the Asiatic side. The siege tactics used by Sharbaraz are not known, but it is certain that he was unable to overcome the powerful defences of Constantinople.

Avar operations against Constantinople were characterized by sophisticated siege tactics.[148] The Avars employed rope-pulled trebuchets (originally of Chinese design) capable of launching heavy projectiles and firing them in rapid succession. They also constructed twelve siege towers. It is not clear if Shahrbaraz provided the Avars with Sassanian military engineers to act as 'advisors' in their siege operations. There is general agreement, however, that Constantinople was first subjected to a massive bombardment by Avar siege engines followed by a furious two-day assault; but Constantinople's strong walls and resilient Greek defenders simply could not be overcome, compelling the Avars to cease operations.

Additional setbacks for the attackers were the Byzantine navy's success in sinking a fleet ferrying Avar-Slavic troops to the theatre, and the sinking (in a separate engagement) of a Sassanian fleet ferrying Sharbaraz's troops. Shahrbaraz could not send any of his crack savaran knights and other troops from the Asiatic side of the Bosphorus to assist the Avars, thanks to the menacing presence of the Byzantine navy. With no hope of any Sassanian army landing on the European side to help them and beset by critical supply shortages, the Avars abandoned the siege. They soon paid dearly for their failure, when their subject Slavic, Bulgar and Gepid peoples rose against them in revolt.

Irrespective of his successes against the Avars, Heraclius did not risk a set-piece battle against Shahrbaraz's formidable army. The latter withdrew following the emperor's skilful 'Byzantine' diplomacy, by which he persuaded the Sassanian general to call off the siege and withdraw from Anatolia.

Defense against Sieges

As Emperor Maurice remarked in *Strategikon*, the Sassanians were equally (if not more) formidable defending their cities and fortresses against sieges: they resisted doggedly, even when facing hopeless odds. The sieges of Bezabde (360 CE) and Petra (551 CE) described further below highlight how ferocious Sassanian resistance could be when defending against besieging forces.

Besieging troops and their siege machinery would be countered by Sassanian ballistae launching varying sizes of wood-shaft 'missiles', aghrabs would hurl stone 'cannon balls' and catapults would throw heavy stones (or boulders).[149] Attacking enemy troops and siege batteries would also be subjected to petroleum and naphtha attacks hurled by ballistae; pyro substances would also be poured on enemy troops attempting to scale the walls of the Sassanian fortress or city.[150]

Bezabde (360 CE). After Shapur II captured Bezabde, Roman Emperor Constantius II (r. 324–361; co-emperor 337–350) marched with a powerful army to recapture the city from the spah. The account by Ammianus Marcellinus of the battle for Bezabde provides an excellent overview of Sassanian tactics and fighting methods when besieged. After capturing Bezabde the Sassanians repaired the city and garrisoned it with a cadre of professional fighting men in case the Romans counterattacked.

When Constantius arrived at Bezabde he first engaged in negotiations with the Sassanian garrison. The Sassanians rejected Constantius' offers of rank, rewards and Roman citizenship, obliging the Romans to capture the city by force. The first attack was an all-out assault that saw the Romans attacking Bezabde from all sides. The Sassanians repelled the Romans with 'all kinds of missiles ... poured down upon them [attacking Roman troops], which disjoined the union of their shields, [and] they fell back, the signal for a retreat being given'.[151] After a truce, the Romans again assaulted the city. The Sassanian defenders:

> hurled down stones and javelins on their assailants below ... And while the wicker penthouses were advanced boldly and brought close to the walls, the besieged dropped upon them heavy casks and millstones, and fragments of pillars, by the overpowering weight of which the assailants were crushed, their defences torn to pieces, and wide openings made in them, so that they incurred terrible dangers, and were again forced to retreat.[152]

The first Roman attack was repelled with missiles, the second with javelins and stronger measures such as 'heavy casks and millstones, and fragments of pillars'; in the latter, the attacking parties were clearly using better protection such as 'wicker penthouses'. This would indicate that Shapur II had installed batteries and/or engines of sorts (i.e. catapults) at Bezabde after his capture of the city.

With two major attacks repelled, Constantius now resorted to employing the same battle-winning weapon used earlier by Shapur II in his capture of Bezabde – a massive battering ram. The irony of this was that the battering ram was a Sassanian weapon that had been used in an earlier spah siege of Antioch; the weapon had been left there and never bought back to the Sassanian empire. The Romans had 'borrowed' this Iranian weapon for their own siege against the Sassanians! However, the weapon was old and had been broken down into parts by the Romans for ease of transport to Bezabde. The Roman engineers thereby needed time to assemble the battering ram, a weakness which the Sassanian garrison was to take full advantage of. While the Romans were assembling the battering ram, Sassanian troops launched fierce raids aimed at destroying the weapon, aware that their own capture of Bezabde had also been made possible by the use of a battering ram. These battles were especially bloody as both sides fought hard, with missiles and stone-hurling batteries taking a heavy toll on Romans and Sassanians alike.[153] Sassanian archers also sniped at Roman troops who had taken off their helmets during battle so as to be recognized for their valour by their emperor.

The Romans, however, had been devising ingenious stratagems for turning the tide of the battle. Their engineers had been steadily building mounds which would soon pose a great danger to the Sassanian garrison.[154] The defenders attempted to prevent the giant 'Persian' ram from being used against Bezabde's primary tower; they:

> entangled its projecting iron head ... with long cords on both sides, to prevent its being drawn back and then driven forward with great force, and to hinder it from making any serious impression on the walls by repeated blows ... they poured on it burning pitch, and for a long time these engines were fixed at the point to which they had been advanced, and exposed to all the stones and javelins which were hurled from the walls.[155]

Once again, the spah's garrison responded with boldness, launching an unexpected attack against the Roman front lines out of the city's gates. Reportedly, the attackers 'with all their might hurled firebrands and iron braziers loaded with fire against the rams...'.[156] It is not clear if the attacking force consisted of infantry, savaran contingents, or a combination of the two. The savaran was most likely involved as Shapur II had stationed at Bezabde members of the nobility who were battle-experienced veterans.[157] The Romans, however stood their ground and engaged in fierce close-quarter combat against the spah's warriors, who were driven back towards Bezabde's walls. The Romans also applied countermeasures against the Sassanian pyro weapons, by quickly extinguishing all fires hurled against their engines. But this Roman success proved ephemeral as the Sassanian warriors renewed their assaults, once again determined to set fire to the Roman engines. The Sassanians came at the Romans 'bearing torches, and iron baskets full of fire, and faggots; and all kinds of things best adapted for setting fire to the works of the besiegers'.[158] This time the Sassanian warriors achieved success, setting all of the Roman engines on fire. The big 'Persian' ram, although not disabled, was partially burned.

The battle, however, was far from over. Constantius' troops placed powerful ballistae on the mounds, and with these machines providing cover the Romans attacked in a three-tier formation, bringing ladders with them to scale the walls. The Sassanians beat them back; the Romans brought up a battering ram and also employed spades, levers and axes in a desperate attempt to hack through the city's walls. Ladders were again bought forward in yet another attempt to scale these walls but the embattled Sassanian defenders held firm.[159]

The Sassanians who once again launched a raid against the Roman lines aimed at destroying the enemy's ballistae. The defenders are described as having 'rushed forth valiantly with drawn swords'[160] with their other comrades bearing pyro weapons. As Sassanian warriors engaged in fierce hand-to-hand combat against the formidable Roman troops, those troops bearing pyro weapons 'pushed the burning coals in among the interstices of one of the mounds, which was made up of branches of trees, and rushes, and bundles of reeds. This soon caught fire and was utterly destroyed.'[161]

This action proved to be the turning point in the siege as those Roman troops who had been caught in the fires were now forced to flee, unable to rescue their ballistae. The boldness of the Sassanian warriors and the success of their final strike finally convinced Emperor Constantius to abandon the siege and retire with his army to Antioch in Syria.[162] Bezabde remained in Sassanian hands.

Petra (541–551 CE). Khosrow I had entered Lazica (modern Republic of Georgia) along the Black Sea coast in the Caucasus in 541 CE.[163] This allowed Khosrow to dispatch the spah to capture the Romano-Byzantine held fortress of Petra. Sassanian general Mehr-Mihroe surrounded Petra with a ditch, thus cutting it off from all sources of supply. Petra's garrison surrendered and its troops joined Mehr-Mihroe.[164] Khosrow, however, was forced to withdraw the bulk of his forces from the Caucasus due to a combination of attacks against the western regions of the Sassanian Empire by the Al-Harith Arabs and General Belisarius.[165] Khosrow's hold on Lazica was now precarious as the only Sassanian force there was the garrison at Petra.[166] By 547 CE Lazic-Sassanian relations had deteriorated leading to the breakout of several anti-Sassanian rebellions. Byzantine emperor Justinian dispatched an 8,000-man force led by General Dagisthaeus to support the Lazic king, Gubarzes. The two attempted to recruit Alan and Sabir warriors for their campaigns to drive the Sassanians from the Caucasus. To achieve this, the 1,500-man Sassanian garrison in Petra had to be captured. The Sassanian troops were most likely a combination of Dailamite infantry and savaran knights. Dagisthaeus' powerful assault against Petra resulted in the loss of 1,200 Sassanian troops, but the remaining Sassanian warriors refused to surrender. Just as the situation appeared hopeless for the Sassanian garrison, a relief force of 30,000 fresh troops led by Mehr-Mihroe reached Petra. Dagisthaeus retreated and Mehr-Mihroe placed 3,000 troops to hold Petra. Nevertheless, the Sassanian position in the Caucasus remained uncertain. Thanks to Byzantine-Lazic attacks and supply shortages, Mehr-Mihroe was obliged to withdraw his forces back into Iran. Determined to hold onto Lazica, Khosrow I dispatched a new force led by General Khworian into Lazica in 549 CE. After a series of inconclusive cavalry engagements Khworian was defeated and killed;[167] however, these battles allowed for a Sassanian supply column to get through to the Petra garrison.

The Byzantines besieged Petra for the second and final time in 551 CE. The 3,000-man Sassanian garrison beat back a number of Byzantine assaults by successfully combining massed archery with the hurling of pyro substances (i.e. naphtha) against the attacking Romano-Byzantine troops.[168] Nevertheless, the ferocity of the Byzantine assaults had resulted in the loss of 700 Sassanian fighters. Byzantine military engineering resulted in the collapse of two of Petra's walls, allowing the Byzantine force to break into the fortress. Even so, the doomed Sassanian garrison refused to surrender, forcing the Romano-Byzantine troops to engage in savage hand-to-hand combat that drove the defenders back to Petra's citadel. The Sassanians lost another 1,075 troops in the struggle. Some 500 surviving Sassanians retreated into Petra's citadel and fought to the last man. The intensity of Sassanian resistance is indicated by the haul of Sassanian prisoners, all (except eighteen) of whom were severely wounded and unable to offer further resistance and evade capture.

Chapter 15

Sassanian Military Culture

Sassanian military operations and tactics discussed thus far were closely linked to an elaborate and sophisticated military culture. Excellent studies by Iranian and Western historians in combination with discoveries of Islamic-era texts on the subject provide an interesting overview of Sassanian military culture.

The Shahanshah before Battle

There were specific rituals that the shahanshah would follow in preparation for war. First, when war was imminent, the king would suspend his regular tasks as monarch to prepare for the task of war. Second, the king would adopt very specific customs prior to and during the prosecution of war. Lavish dining would give way to simple and humble meals.[1] Perhaps this custom was one way of 'humbling' the monarch by bringing him closer to his commanders and troops. On the other hand, Al-Jahez's *Taj* reports that only three of the empire's high notables were allowed to sit and dine with the king: the aswaran-sardar or framandar savaran, the mobadan mobad and the eiran-dabirbod.[2]

The Mobads before Battle

The role of the magi or mobads in the spah has been outlined in Chapter 2, however the importance of their function to the troops just prior to battle requires a brief explanation. Mobads were entrusted with a distinct 'mystical' role, especially astrology before battle. Specifically, mobads were responsible for finding the most favourable alignment of the stars and associated hours of the day which could most auspiciously affect the course of battle.[3]

Mobads exhorted troops to fight without fear of death against their unbelieving (or non-Zoroastrian) enemies. This was done by appealing to the supreme god Ahura Mazda, who through Mithra would channel courage, endurance, resilience and martial ardour.[4] Following prayers, the warriors would collectively pull their swords out of their sheaths, hold them aloft and shout the name of Mithra in unison.[5] The calls of the magi for warriors to maintain their valour necessitated the battlefield participation of the magi themselves. As noted in Chapter 2, this also allowed the magi to observe the battlefield exploits of the warriors, which were then recorded by scribes. The valiant warrior who survived the battle would be rewarded with honour and spoils and if he were killed then he would be ranked among the honoured dead in the afterlife. The magi played a critical role in ensuring that the troops maintained their cohesion and cooperation during battle and ensured that they would obey their commanders under any circumstances.[6]

Just prior to the outbreak of battle, 'holy water' would be sprinkled, followed by the shooting of a symbolic arrow. Following this ritual, the enemy would be exhorted to submit to the shahanshah and to embrace the faith of Zoroaster.[7] The symbolic arrow was also used when demanding the enemy's surrender. In these situations a summons-to-surrender letter would be attached to the shaft of the arrow that was then fired into enemy lines. The same ritual is seen in the Romano-Byzantine armies as reported by the *Strategikon*.[8] The arrow shaft was considered to be a 'sacred branch'.

Darb-e Mehr and the Warriors

Before assembling with the shahanshah on the battlefield, warriors would congregate at sacred fire temples to engage in prayers. Zoroastrian fire temples are referred to as *darb-e mehr*, or the gateway/door/temple of Mithra (see below). The warriors arrived fully armed and armoured at the fire temples to be led in their prayers by the mobads. This rite was also observed by the shahanshah, who like other warriors appealed for victory to Ahura-Mazda. The sacred fire was not simply abandoned as the warriors concluded their prayers to then depart for the battlefield. The magi would bring portable containers harbouring the sacred fire along with the army during its campaign.

After the conclusion of a campaign, warriors would return to the temples for prayers. A major temple was that of Azargoshnasp in Azerbaijan (Iranian province of Azerbaijan below the Araxes River). After his successful campaign against the massive Turco-Hephthalite invasion of 588 CE, Bahram Chobin brought much of the captured booty to the temple.[9] Azargoshnasp was a very important temple for Sassanian warriors, as it was believed that a special sacred fire for the pahlavans was maintained at this locale.[10]

Mard o Mard: Man-to-Man Duels

Prior to the outbreak of battle the Sassanian commanders would select a pahlavan (lit. brave, intrepid) champion from the savaran to challenge the most formidable warrior of the enemy in a man-to-man duel. The primary objective of this was for the pahlavan to demonstrate to the opposing army the bravery, resilience and hand-to-hand fighting skills of not only himself but of all of his comrades. The pahlavan champion selected for the duel-joust was known as the *yalan-yalbod*, and considered as among the bravest and most capable of the pahlavan knights.[11] Instances of Iranian knights challenging the Romans have been reported by Classical sources (Chapter 19).

As noted in Chapter 6, the notion of the chivalry style joust-duel was an ancient tradition going back to the earlier Iranic (Medo-Persian and Scytho-Sarmatian) martial tradition. Nevertheless the chivalrous joust-duel had become highly sophisticated, both in terms of ethical codes and regulations, by Sassanian times.[12] So great was the prestige of the shahanshah as victor of a joust-duel that reliefs would be created in his honour and illustrated with single combat motifs. Interestingly, physical appearance coiffure played a significant role in the projection of the pahlavan's prowess during the joust-duel, especially with respect to his moustache, which was grown relatively long and thick,[13] as seen on the statue of the Parthian nobleman housed at the National Museum of Iran.

Man-to-man duels are an integral aspect of the *Shahname*, and thus indicative of its high level of importance in ancient Iranian military culture. Vivid descriptions are provided as to the rituals, usage of weapons and the processes of combat. One example is the tragic father-son duel of Rustam and Sohrab, which is perhaps one of the most detailed and vivid accounts of single combat in the Islamic-era Persian-language literature.

The Shahname and the duel. The *Shahname* not only features many accounts of duels, it contains detailed descriptions of the weapons, fighting techniques, rituals and motives for duels. A seminal article in *Katsujinken* journal has provided a comprehensive compendium of the duel in Iranian military culture. The authors describe the motives for the duel, general features of duels, and the order in which weapons were used in the course of the duel.[14] The first motive for the duel is vengeance (e.g. Guiv/Guiw taking revenge against his brother Bahram). The second is intervention to rescue a warrior from a more powerful opponent (e.g. Rustam rescuing his brother Zavareh in the duel against Alkus). The third motive for the duel is to serve as a prelude for set-piece battles between armies, and perhaps as the deciding clash that would settle the issue. It would appear that there were instances in which duels were used to determine the outcome of the conflict. This served to reduce the casualties that would otherwise have been inflicted upon both armies had a full clash between all warriors taken place.

A duel fought for this purpose may have decided the issue at Firuzabad in 224 CE. Mard o mard duels could also happen after the main battle had started. This happened, for example, at the Battle of Dara, where a number of duels were fought in the evening after the conclusion of the first day's military engagements. The victor of a duel would by virtue of his achievement certainly boost the morale of his army, thus enhancing its combat effectiveness before the start of the battle. By the same token, if the pahlavan was defeated and killed, morale could be damaged.

As noted by Khorasani et al., there were four general features of the duels described in the *Shahname*. First, warriors engaged in the duel were cavalrymen savaran and fought from horseback. Second, the participants used psychological tactics to undermine their opponents. Typical in this regard, the opponents would question each other's martial prowess prior to the start of combat. The third feature was the opponents' agreeing to rest, especially if the duel was very evenly matched and prolonged. The fourth feature concerned the nature of the duel itself, notably the usage of weapons. For example, warriors might employ a variety of weapons (sword, dagger, lance, mace, lasso and bows) and change these as circumstances dictated during the duel. Opposing champions are often described as being evenly matched with respect to weapons, combat skill and valour.

The duelling tradition on display in the *Shahname* has several parallels with Central Asian traditions. Mode's detailed examination of the battle scene exhibited on one of the bone plaques from the Orlat cemetery in modern Uzbekistan is of interest as it believed to be dated to the Hun-Turkic invasions of Soghdia.[15] Dates are disputed as some believe the object to be dated to the first century CE with others citing the fourth/fifth centuries CE as the correct date. Of interest are the pictograms on the plaque and its representation of the death of the main hero. There are fifteen pictograms or 'frames' detailing the battle step by step, but its main thrust may be summarized. The hero is struck in the eye by an arrow, but proceeds to single combat against his opponent with his lance. The lances of the antagonists meet but it is the hero whose lance breaks and who is pierced by his opponents' lance. The hero falls from his horse, casting away his broken lance. Having been lanced, he grasps his scabbard with his left hand and draws out his long sword with his right hand. The hero is then struck in his remaining good eye by an arrow.

An interesting passage in the *Shahname* concerns one 'Karan the Bold'[16] who charged repeatedly into the ranks of the enemy. As recounted by Firdowsi, 'Karan overthrew ten warriors at each charge; now wheeling to the left, now to the right, and seeking to wreak vengeance on all sides ... Seeing Shamaras, who raised the war-cry lion-like, he charged, unsheathed his sword, smote his foe's head, and shouted: The famed Karan am I.'[17]

This account of Karan's exploits describes an attack by one man against many, rather than single combat between two champions; as such, therefore, he is not, strictly speaking, engaged in a duel. Even so, his actions achieve the same ends as a duel, namely to prove his valour and bolster the morale of his troops. Karan's action of striking his opponent's head with his sword is virtually identical to the actions of the Armenian Naxarar knights.[18]

The duel of Smbat Bagratuni. Another instance of the duel of a Sassanian-type knight involved the Armenian general Smbat Bagratuni who led the spah in the 619 CE war against the Turco-Hephthalites. According to Sebeos, just prior to a major battle between the spah and the invasion forces, the Turco-Hephthalite king challenged Bagratuni to a man-to-man duel:

> 'Come, let me fight you alone. I shall come as a champion from my side, and you from yours, so that today my valour may be known to you.' Then putting his hand on his heart he said: 'Behold I am ready to die'. Coming out from either side, they rapidly confronted each other. They were not able immediately to overcome the other, because they were both men of gigantic strength and fully covered in armor. But help came from on high: the armor of the K'ushan king, chain-mail from Bahl and a solid cuirass was split by Smbat's lance, and he powerfully struck him as a corpse to the ground and slew him.[19]

In this duel, both warriors were evenly matched and both were clad in armour that was described as being very strong. Perhaps they had first clashed with swords and even battle-axes, but the outcome was decided by a lance duel. Bagratuni succeeded in finally penetrating the armour of his opponent, thus unseating him from his horse and slaying him in front of his army.

Sassanian kings also engaged in duels. Two panels at Nagshe-Rustam depict Bahram II duelling with adversaries; the upper panel portrays Bahram unseating the Roman Emperor Carus (r. 282–283 CE) with his lance and the lower panel shows Bahram employing his lance to defeat a Sassanian rival.[20]

The Sassanian lance joust is part of a broader and older Iranian martial tradition. For example, mounted lance combat between the eastern Scythians or the Saka of Chorasmia[21] and the 'European' Scythians is depicted in a combat scene on the famous golden comb discovered at the Solokha royal burial mound (fourth century BCE): the illustration shows a Scythian warrior about to thrust his spear into a prostrate opponent. Sarmatian mounted warriors engaged in lance combat are depicted on the Kosika vessels (c. first-second centuries CE); and a lancer is depicted on the marble stele of Tryphon (c. third century CE), discovered in the ruins of the Bosphoran city of Tanais along the Don River.[22]

The lance joust and the duel: Firuzabad. The Firuzabad panel near Ardashir's palace depicts a lance joust between the early Sassanians and the late Parthians. The panel portrays three Sassanians locked in combat with their Parthian adversaries.[23] The first panel to the right shows Ardashir I having lanced his opponent, Parthian king Ardavan V, whose horse topples backwards. The second panel (to the left of Ardashir) shows prince Shapur, who has also lanced his adversary, possibly the Parthian vizier Darbandan. Finally, to the left of Shapur an unidentified Sassanian and Parthian are wrestling on horseback, with the Sassanian having the upper hand by having trapped his opponent in a headlock.

Perhaps one of the most interesting aspects of the Firuzabad joust is its representations of 'ranked combat': Ardashir versus Ardavan, Shapur versus Darbandan, etc. These strict rules of ranked combat would of course be adapted at times of national crisis when the empire was being invaded by dangerous enemies such as the Romans or Central Asian warrior-nomads. The spah would apply its war-making doctrines by first convening a war council to discuss strategy whereby the entirety of the savaran, infantry and other auxiliary units (i.e. battle elephants) would fight collectively as comrades-in-arms against the entire spectrum (ordinary troops to commanders) of enemy troops (Chapter 3). A striking parallel is seen in Medieval Japan where the lower class *bushi* foot soldier and higher class samurai (mounted and dismounted) fought side by side against Mongol invaders in 1261 CE.[24] In like manner the elite savaran knights would be fighting alongside 'lower class' infantry.

Brahmag e Artesharih: 'Costume of Warriors'

The nobility who formed the core of the Sassanian knights, could be distinguished by their particular dress, known as *brahmag e artesharih* (costume of warriors) with purple and red often being the colours of distinction. This is attested to in the Dinkard: 'And among the clothes, the garment which is red and wine coloured, adorned with all kinds of ornament, with silver and gold, chalcedony, ruby belongs to warriors'.[25]

Interestingly, there appear to be parallels between the brahmag e artesharih and the dress of the ancient Achaemenid warriors. In his description of the armies of Darius III deploying towards the battlefield, Quintus Curtius Rufus (writing in the first century CE) noted that the magi were 'followed by 365 young men clad in purple robes'.[26] This may suggest that the military attire in the Sassanian era may at least in part be inspired by pre-Sassanian military traditions. The *Bundahishn* corroborates the statements of the Dinkard in a description of a Sassanian warrior named Vay: 'Vay, the Good, donned a gold and silver garment, adorned with precious stones, purple and multi-coloured the Brahmag e Artesharih [Costume of warriors].'[27]

According to Sekunda, the ancient Achaemenids introduced uniformity in military dress at an earlier date than the Greeks, who did so by the fourth century BCE.[28] Classical sources have suggested that the Sassanians looked to the ancient Achaemenids for inspiration in the design of their brahmag e artesharih. Julian, for example, noted that Sassanian warriors 'imitate Persian fashions ... [and] take pride in wearing the same ... raiment adorned with gold and purple ... [that] their king [Shapur II wore] ... imitating Xerxes'.[29] Nevertheless, as alluded to in the introduction, the notion of Sassanian cognizance of Achaemenid military practices is disputed by a number of Western historians.[30] What can be observed in the overall sense is the remarkable continuity of the Iranian riding costume (cap, tunic, leather boots, trousers, belt, etc.) since antiquity. This was the traditional Iranian riding costume seen among Iranian-speaking peoples such as the Sarmatians and Scythians of Central Asia and Eastern Europe as well as among the Medes, Persians and Parthians of Persia. By the time of the Sassanians this type of dress was most likely varied with respect to both ceremonial and military uniforms, with possible distinctions made according to military rank and clan membership.

Early versions of the brahmag e artesharih. Late Parthian dress is remarkably well represented in the Sassanian era, especially during the dynasty's earlier years. This was due to the fact that after the Battle of Firuzabad many of the major Parthian clans invested their support in the new Sassanian dynasty. Perhaps one of the most vivid depictions of the Partho-Sassanian-type dress is seen among the three magi at Chiesa di S. Apollinare Nuovo in Ravenna, Italy.[31] Notable are the Iranian style of richly coloured and decorated trousers, cloaks (typical of the nobility), red caps and footwear. The trousers of the magi at Ravenna are typically Iranian in having a tight fit right down to the ankles. The Parthians wore such trousers and like the Ravenna magi, stripes were applied which reached all the way to the foot. This striping system may have signified military, religious or royal rank. The Parthians and Sassanians appear to have been keen on colours such as red, green and blue, with the later Sassanians increasingly introducing 'Achaemenid' colours such as varieties of purple, crimson and brown. Perhaps the best-known Parthian dress is the tunic in which the right tunic breast lays over the left, with long sleeves and a v-shaped neckline.

There are four general depictions of early Sassanian brahmag at Firuzabad, Nagshe Rustam, Naghse Rajab, Salmas and Persepolis. Table 6 provides a list of Sassanian terms in reference to apparel pertaining to the brahmag e artesharih. The costumes depicted in Persepolis, on what is known as the 'Persepolis Graffiti', are of interest as these show an inheritance of Parthian styles. The graffiti show knee-length belted tunics with side vents for ease of riding, baggy trousers with 'disco 1970s style bell bottoms', galoons, cuffed as well as narrow sleeves, the tall (rounded or peaked) cap or *kulah* featuring neck covers and lappets, and footwear of the soft one-piece type (without soles), again suitable for cavalrymen.[32] Three of the figures have their hands on long swords of the scabbard-slide type with one standing with hands crossed.

Mention must also be made of cloaks worn by the nobility. There appears to have been two different types of mantles worn by the Sassanians. One was a more 'ceremonial' type which was a wide cloak without sleeves. A round fibula was used as a clasp to hold the mantle in place at the centre (roughly in middle of the upper chest area) or at the right shoulder. Examples of such mantles can be found in the aforementioned representation of the three magi at Ravenna. The second type of mantle was the 'fluttering' type worn by Sassanian horsemen which was held in its place by a clasp on the right shoulder.

While the Firuzabad, Nagshe Rustam, Naghseh Rajab, Salmas and Persepolis sites do show the overall consistency of the brahmag e artesharih, it is also likely that there were stylistic variations among the different factions of the spah. The heads of the leading clans and families are believed to have had their own variations which were consistent with the attire of a particular region,[33] not unlike the variations seen today for example between Iran's western (i.e. Lurs, Kurds), northwest Iran (Azaris) and southeast (Baluchis) regions.

In the victory scenes of Shapur I at Bishapur, numbers of knights can be seen clothed in the wide Iranian *shalvar* trousers and leaning on their scabbard-slide broadswords. One panel of interest at Bishapur (bottom right, depicting the mounted Shapur I triumphing over Valerian, Philip the Arab and Gordian III) shows what appears to be Mede warriors wearing more tightly fitting trousers. The observation that the warriors have long hair may be incorrect: they may in fact be sporting false hair (ceremonial wigs), a tradition found amongst the Medes since at least Achaemenid times.[34] The Medes are also seen carrying their swords in scabbard slides and resting their hands on the sword hilts. Another panel of interest at Bishapur is one featuring five rows; at the third row (from top) of that relief are five knights situated to the left of Shapur I, who is receiving a diadem from a figure to his right. The five knights have hair styles that are similar to that of their king with their headgear different from the other knights behind them as well as those of the other four rows. It is highly probable that they are elite cavalry commanders, perhaps hailing from the top seven families of Persia. The fourth cavalryman behind Shapur wears headgear in the shape of a pointed or 'beak-like' figure, which may indicate that he is of the Suren-Pahlav clan. The same 'beak-like' hat can be seen in the aforementioned panel of a triumphant Shapur (over Roman enemies) in which an Iranian knight (most likely an elite commander and/or nobleman) is seen standing to the right of the king. Top family members would assume command positions amongst the elite cavalry and other military units. This may partly explain the tendency by Roman historians to confuse Iranian clan names such as 'Suren' with military titles.

A very interesting 'apron'-style overcoat was to appear in the fifth and sixth centuries CE, as seen in the Sassanian metalworks at the Hermitage displaying King Pirouz hunting wild game on foot (Hermitage, Inv. S-216) and a figure of Khosrow I flanked by four nobles (Hermitage, Inv. S-250), who may be the four spahbods of the spah. In this design, the overcoat or tunic would 'bundle up' into an apron-like shape at the sides. Interestingly the exact same type of Sassanian style 'apron' overcoat is seen among the Armenian Naxarar knights, as depicted in the figure at the Surp Nshan Basilica in the Republic of Armenia. Contemporary to this era is the design seen on the 'cup of Khosrow I' which depicts the monarch with a tight-fitting long sleeved robe decorated with rich designs.

One feature of note is the chest harnesses worn by Sassanian warriors. Goldman has classified these into four general categories.[35] The first category has strap ends and the breast band joined together at the centre end. An example of this can be seen with the rock relief of Ardashir I at Firuzabad. The second category has the shoulder straps attached to a circular breast band on both sides of the centre clasp, rather than being attached to the clasp. An example of this can be seen with Sassanian metal works depicting Pirouz (or Kavad) and Khosrow I. The third category generally has various types of decorative motifs with shoulder straps attached to the breast band. An example of this can be seen with the metal bowl showing a Sassanian king (possibly Khosrow II) engaged in the hunt. The fourth and final category bears no apparent decorative motifs. Examples of this can be seen on the Cincinnati and Klimova plates.

Late versions of the brahmag e artesharih. Late Sassanian brahmag continued to incorporate the traditional features of Iranic riding and military costume. The site of Taghe Bostan is of prime interest as it shows the appearance of late Sassanian brahmag. Like Central Asian styles, the Sassanian brahmag was composed of riding trousers and a long tunic or overcoat or kaftan. The chief riders and nobles at Taghe Bostan wear long-sleeved and tight-fitting garments belted at the waist.[36] Of particular interest is the 'hunting cap' of Khosrow II in the Taghe Bostan hunt scene: a small, square Central Asian flat cap. Trousers in the late Sassanian era could be highly decorated as indicated by the investiture scene of Khosrow II at Taghe Bostan which shows the monarch wearing trousers studded with jewels. An indication of late Sassanian costume is given by Tabari, who describes the costume of Hormuzan, one of the spah's leading nobles, after his capture by the Arabs during their invasion of the Sassanian Empire in 637–651 CE. The descriptions are remarkably similar to the information provided below.

The Taghe Bostan boar and stag hunting scenes show the kaftans covered by elaborate design patterns. Holmes-Peck traces the origins of the kaftan to the Kushans,[37] but it is certain that this item became widespread across Iran and

Central Asia. Even with the arrival of the Turkic-Hun peoples into Central Asia, the kaftan remained popular after the fall of the Sassanians. The material was most likely silk. The Sassanian kaftan was distinguished from its Central Asian counterparts in two ways. The first was that these often had high, embroidered and stiff collars. This style was certainly known in Central Asia; a similar collar design is seen with the rider displayed at the Pazyryk carpet of the fourth century BCE. Perhaps this 'decorative' style was popular in Central Asia in pre-Sassanian times and introduced into Iran by the Parthians, a fashion continuing into Sassanian Iran. While the 'decorative' collars may not have been as popular in Central Asia by late Sassanian times, late east Iranian and Central Asian armoured tunics or 'long tunics' had high neck guards for protecting the neck against sword strikes. The second distinguishing feature of Sassanian kaftans was in the variety of designs decorating them. At Taghe Bostan the kaftans feature various floral designs, birds, moon-crescent, circle motifs, ibex, etc. There is also what appears to be (with the detail of the king at the boat hunt) the *simurgh* or *senmurv* motif (winged mythological entity combining gryphon, leonine and canine beasts) woven in the upper (torso) section of the kaftan alongside the four-petal designs. A sample of a long type of Sassanian kaftan has been uncovered in the northern Caucasus by Russian archaeologists and is presently housed in the Hermitage Museum at St. Petersburg (Inv. Kz.6584). This has the simurgh motif featured all across the garment. Colours in general appear to have varied in the ranges of 'colder' types such as blue, green, etc. and 'warmer' colours of red, orange, yellow, etc. It was this long type of Sassanian kaftan which may have eventually evolved into the Caucasian 'Cossack' type of overcoat in later centuries.

Mention must be made of the general length of the Sassanian kaftans. These could reach up to 200cm, indicative of the overall height of the professional Sassanian warriors of the time. The aforementioned kaftan uncovered in the Caucasus (Inv. Kz.6584) broadly fits into this longer type of garment. In short, warriors wearing such kaftans were above-average in height, even by modern-day standards. Long kaftans can also be seen in Central Asia. One clear depiction of this is with Chinese envoys and their Turkish guards in the Soghdian wall paintings of Afrasiyab, dated to the seventh-eighth centuries CE,[38] after the fall of the Sassanians. There were also shorter versions of the Sassanian kaftan, which like the Central Asian versions (notably the Tocharian knights or nobles at Qizil, Tarim Basin) would reach around 140–150cm in length.

Late Sassanian brahmag show another distinct feature shared with Central Asia, especially with respect to high boots reaching up to a point just below the knee.[39] While it has been suggested that the high boot was of Kushan origin, this type of footwear was already in place during the early Sassanian period, as indicated by the finding of a male mummy and his knee-high (left) boot at the Chehr Abad salt mines. Interestingly, the noblemen at the side panel at Taghe Bostan are seen with boots decorated with drawings of heraldic birds. Nevertheless the high boot is seen in the aforementioned depictions of King Pirouz as well as Khosrow I and the four nobles[40] before the Taghe Bostan depictions. As noted by Goldman, the *Book of Ayin* contains a passage describing the 'royal Persians shod in soft boots of scarlet or purple ornamented with gems, pearls, and gold embroidery, and decorated with eagles'.[41] In short, the decorative patterns of birds and eagles on the boots was a favoured Sassanian feature. The high boot continues to be displayed into post-Sassanian times (seventh or early eighth centuries CE), as seen in the hunting scene with Pur-e Vahman (Hermitage, S-247).

Belts of warriors. Integral to the brahmag e artesharih (early and late Sassanian eras) was the belt or, in practice, belts. Broadly speaking, there was the *kustik* and the *kamar*. The kustik was a religious strap worn in the Zoroastrian fashion. This was most likely some type of cord rather than a 'belt', as seen today among Zoroastrians. The kamar was essentially a sword belt, with those of upper nobles and high-ranking officers being richly decorated. This was often used for the ceremonial scabbard-slide 'broadsword'-type swords which were militarily obsolete by the late fifth century.

Central Asian influences can be seen in the belt-wear of the nobility by the early seventh century CE, especially in the depictions at Taghe Bostan. These types of belts have decorative lappets ending with tongues of metal. As noted by Widengren, the appearance of this type of belt at Taghe Bostan is indicative of the contacts that were taking place between the Sassanian Empire and Central Asia at the time of Khosrow II.[42] These belts were typically worn around the waist just above the functional (weapons) belt which was suspended around the hips. This type of belt had vertical lappets which signified the person's rank and status. Nevertheless, this 'status' belt could also contain lappets for the suspension of weapons. Despite the Turkic origin of this type of belt, the Sassanian method was to have the lappets placed closely to each other with all lappets being of equal length. The Sassanian version is also of interest as there are an equal number of lappets on the left and right sides. The higher the person's status, the more lappets he carried on his belt. The Taghe Bostan hunting scenes clearly show this with respect to the shahanshah, who has the most number of lappets (eight to ten), followed by the nobles (usually six) and men of lesser ranks. The Sassanian 'status' belts were also notable for their handsomely decorated lappets and belt buckles. The belts of professional officers in particular were often highly decorated with precious gems and jewels, with that of General Shahrbaraz being described (after its capture at Salbalon in the Caucasus) as a 'gold belt set with precious stones'.[43] Belts of gold signified the warrior's oath of service to the shahanshah.[44] Overlaet's description of Dailamite military gear from northern Persia also revealed a set of gold ornaments for belts from the Amlash region which were decorated with granulations and pearl wire in what appears to be a distinctly 'Celtic' style of spiral and circular designs.[45]

Medallions, *Drafsh*, Military Ranks and *Neshan*

In addition to their brahmag e artesharih, the heads of the different clans who led the Sassanian military machine were also distinguished by their system of medallions, ranks and *neshans*. The higher the person's status in the spah the more elaborate would be his medallions, etc., which would often be used to adorn his brahmag e artesharih as well as his (ceremonial) headgear or helmet.

Headgear and sar designations. Medallions could also be displayed on the helmets and headgear of the empire's leading nobles who led the Sassanian spah. Jalali has identified two distinct symbols, the *afa-sar* and the *mah-sar* that were displayed on the headgear of the empire's leading generals who hailed from the upper nobility.[46] The term 'sar' is old Iranic for 'head', and is seen in West Iranian languages such as modern Persian as well as in Ossetian (a northwest Iranian language). Afa-sar was essentially a sun symbol (*aftab* which generally designates 'sun/sunny' in Persian) which would be worn either on the headgear (or helmet) or pinned like a medallion on the brahmag e artesharih.[47] It is notable that the term 'afa-sar' has undergone a lexical transformation such that in Modern Persian it means 'officer'. The mah-sar was a moon symbol which like afa-sar was also either worn on headgear or pinned upon the brahmag e artesharih.[48]

Drafsh. Savaran and other elite cavalry units each bore their own distinct *drafsh* (banner). In practice this was a coat-of-arms system of unique symbols which could also be displayed as battlefield banners. There were also various banners which appear to have had a 'higher' designation than that of a particular military unit or clan. These included the symbol of Zoroaster, Mithra, etc.

Table 6. Sassanian terms in reference to *Brahmag e Artesharih*.
(adapted from Widengren, 1976)

Term	Sassanian Pahlavi	Notes
boot or shoe	*mok* or *mocak*; *kafshak*	*Mocak* may have meant 'half-boot' by end of Sassanian era; *kafshak* meant 'shoe'.
trousers and/or leggings	*shalvar*	Older Zoroastrian literature makes references to *ran-pan/ran-ban* and *ran-varten*.
tunic	*kurtak*	*Kurtak* could also be accompanied by a *sapik* (sacred undershirt) worn under *kurtak*.
outer garment	*kapah*	Modern Persian *qaba*, also a loan-word into Arabic.
long coat	*pargoo*	Luxurious garment decorated with rich jewels and gold. *Pargoo* is also a loan-word in Jewish Talmud text.
sacred belt	*kustik*	Religious girdle worn in Zoroastrian fashion. *Kustik* was most likely a cord of some type, as seen today among modern-day Parsees.
sword belt	*kamar*	Often decorated with pearls and jewels. Possible that there were more terms in reference to the sword belt, possibly in references to different types of sword belts. One example is *hamyan*.
rounded cap	*kulah*	*Kulah* is in reference to the rounded caps worn by knights and nobles in retinue of Shapur I. The term means 'hat' in modern Persian.

The Sassanians directly inherited the drafsh system from the Parthians. Nevertheless, the drafsh could also be the symbol of a particular clan (i.e. the Suren-Pahlav) which often was concomitant with that particular military unit. Iranian armies had used banners and designations of various sorts from Achaemenid times with the north Iranian tribes of Eastern Europe being known for their Tamgas (sing. Tamga: seal, stamp, insignia, symbol), which often designated clan, status or abstract religious or mythological symbols.

Information regarding Sassanian drafsh is mainly derived from Sassanian rock reliefs although there are some Roman references to them (see *Draconis Persicus*). The draco standard (which was in use by the Parthians) had already been seen by the Romans during the north Iranian arrivals into Central and Western Europe in the fourth and fifth centuries CE. Another excellent source of information on the drafsh is the Islamic-era *Shahname* which Christensen makes clear is derived from Sassanian sources.[49] There were a very large number of drafsh, examples including gazelles, bears, lions, wolves, elephants, eagles, ibex, tigers, boars, serpents, dogs and even mythological beasts. There are at least two types of 'royal' drafsh also reported in the *Shahname*.[50] The first is that of the sun emblem with a moon symbol above it and the other is a lion wielding a gurz (mace) and a sword. The red banner would be displayed right before the Sassanian army was to engage in battle.[51]

The symbol of the drafsh could also be worn as medallions and emblems, which would suggest that these were military designations as well as clan symbols. On the battlefield, the drafsh would be often displayed on a crossbar or pole but the drafsh symbol could also be worn on tunics or even displayed on the shield bosses of the warriors.[52]

Drafsh Kaviani. Perhaps the empire's most important banner was the Drafsh e Kaviani, commonly known as 'the Banner of Kaveh'. Mehreen (Shushtari) describes the prime importance of the ceremonial display of the Kaviani, especially in the aftermath of successful battles and the capture of cities.[53] Jalali notes that during peacetime, the Drafsh Kaviani was housed in a special (or holy) abode (or temple).[54] When war was imminent, five mobads were entrusted with bringing the Kaviani from its resting place to the military barracks or place where the army was assembling, a process replete with specialized ceremonies. The safety of the Kaviani was entrusted to a high-level military commander who, along with his men, was expected to defend it to the death. According to Hekmat, that commander was to surrender the Kaviani after the battle to the king's treasurers who would then deliver it to the king's personal treasury.[55] Presumably the Kaviani would have then been moved back to its own housing area.

According to Sami the Kaviani measured 7×5m (23×16ft) and was adorned with jewels.[56] The ascension of a new king often meant that new jeweled adornments would be added to the Kaviani.[57] According to Iranian mythology, the Kaviani has its origins in the person of Kaveh Ahsengar (New Persian: *ahangar*, ironsmith). Kaveh placed his *pishband* (leather apron) atop a spear to rally the oppressed Iranians against their evil serpent-shouldered oppressor, Zahak. In practice, the origins of the Kaviani may have its roots during the Parthian era, and was passed on to the Sassanians who accorded it increased status.

Nevertheless, it is not yet possible to draw clear-cut conclusions that the Kaviani was a Parthian banner passed onto the Sassanians, as prior to their rebellion in Persis banners resembling the Kaviani were already in existence in local temples and inscribed on local Persis coins.

The symbolic power and prestige of the Drafsh Kaviani was also double-edged. The death or wounding of the standard bearer(s) could potentially demoralize the troops during combat, even if they were winning the battle.[58] Loss of the Kaviani banner could prove catastrophic, as it did when the Arabs captured it in the aftermath of the disaster at Qadissiyah in 637 CE (Chapter 17). It is possible that the shock of the loss of this national symbol was one factor that severely diminished the will of many Sassanian troops to resist the Arab invasions.

Epaulets and rang. The spah had a defined system of military decorations. Boss has noted that military coloured shoulder tufts 'have a Persian ancestry'[59] (the *Strategikon* has also described these). Perhaps the most vivid displays of shoulder tufts are seen at Taghe Bostan showing Sassanian noblemen wearing rather 'modern'-looking rectangular epaulettes[60] of a type seen on contemporary military officers. Like the late Sassanian uniforms discussed earlier, these may also have a Central Asian ancestry; e.g. the wall paintings of Panjikent also portray officers wearing such insignia.[61]

Honoring Ceremonies for Successful Generals: Sebeos' Description of Smbat Bagratuni

Sebeos provides a detailed description of Sassanian military culture and its rituals for honouring distinguished military commanders, especially in reference to the Armenian general Smbat Bagratuni. As noted previously in Chapter 12, Bagratuni had been instrumental in crushing a dangerous Turco-Hephthalite invasion from Central Asia and rescuing the empire's eastern marches. Khosrow II conferred the highest military honours upon the Armenian general.

After a formal summons by letters, Bagratuni arrived to be received by Khosrow II at Dastegerd. When the shahanshah arrived to receive Bagratuni, Sebeos reports the following rituals as having taken place: '[T]he king bestowed on him the office of Tanuter, called Khosrov Shum, robed him splendidly with a hat and robe of silk woven with gold, exalted him tremendously with a collar set with gems, a necklace and silver cushions ... He gave him four-keyed trumpets and guards for his court from among the Royal retainers.'[62]

Sebeos' description of Khosrow II's gift of a robe may be in reference to a high-ranking brahmag e artesharih with the necklace possibly also being a sign of high military rank in the spah. The granting of royal trumpeters and retainers was possibly one of the highest military honours that could be bestowed by the empire, a distinction reserved in the main part for the highest nobles. The term 'Khosrov Shum' is defined by Thompson as Armenian for 'Joy of Khosrow'.[63] After his final victory over the Turco-Hephthalites, Khosrow II once again conferred more honours on the Armenian general as well his son and Naxarar knights. According to Sebeos:

> King Khosrov ... ordered a large elephant to be decorated to bring him to the hall [of the palace]. He also commanded his son Varaztirots to be promoted, who was called by the king, Javitean Khosrov. He ordered treasures to be distributed to his host ... When he had approached within a day's journey of the Royal court, the king ordered all the nobles and the army to go out and meet him. He commanded the auxiliaries to meet him with a fine horse from the royal stable with royal equipage ... On seeing him [Bagratuni] he [Khosrow II] welcomed him with joy, and stretched out his hand to him ... He [Bagratuni] was the third noble in the palace of king Khosrov.[64]

The elevation of Bagratuni as third noble of the royal court was a high distinction for one not hailing from the noble families. Sebeos' report of Bagratuni's son Varaztirots being given the title of 'Javitean Khosrov' may perhaps be in reference to him having been made a member of one of the empire's premier elite savaran units, the 'Javidan' or 'Immortals' (Chapter 6). As Sebeos makes clear, upon their arrival to the royal palace, Bagratuni and the Naxarar knights were ceremoniously honoured by the spah, nobility and the shahanshah. The honouring by the spah and the shahanshah of the Naxarar knights in Sassanian service was an established Sassanian military custom.

Duties of Pahlavan Knights

Pahlavan knights were held in very high esteem in Sassanian society, surpassed in stature only by the magi and the person of the shahanshah. An indication of the favoured status of the Sassanian warriors is provided to us by the *Letter of Tansar* which states: 'As for the ... fighting men, he [the Shahanshah] has conferred positions of honour and favours of all kinds upon that group, because they are ever sacrificing their own lives and possessions and followers for the welfare of those who labour, devoting themselves to combat with the country's foes.'[65]

Honar in defence of Eiran-Shahr. The pahlavan knight's most important duty was to defend the Iranian realms against military aggressors.[66] The *Menog e Xrad* is clear and specific regarding the primary role of the *arteshtaran* (warriors) in stating that 'The duty of the Arteshtaran is to strike the enemy and to hold their own country secure and tranquil.'[67] The *Avesta* elevates this role at the theological level by declaring that the warrior 'who does battle and whom they kill in battle is blessed'.[68] A fundamental characteristic of the Iranian warrior's capability to wage war was his *honar*, translated in Middle Persian as 'valour', with the *Shahname* defining this as 'skill in the affairs of war, bravery, manliness'.[69] Interestingly, in modern Persian 'honar' is broadly defined as 'talent' (usually in the context of creativity and the arts). It is also notable that the pahlavan warrior is warned to never underestimate the honar of his battlefield opponents,[70] presumably in reference to the Romano-Byzantines and the warriors of Central Asia.

Extrapolating from the *Shahname*, Khaleqi-Motlagh notes five general martial qualities expected from the pahlavan.[71] The first was to be bold and skilled in close-quarters combat; the second was to be thoroughly familiar (or well trained) in the usage of weapons; the third was for the warrior to maintain a high level of physical strength, an aspect which was thoroughly discussed in Chapter 6 with respect to Sassanian military training; the fourth was for the warrior to never shirk his enthusiasm for and perseverance in battle, even under unfavourable circumstances (note in this regard that honour and rank were obtained in proportion to one's valour and steadfastness on the field of battle). The fifth and final quality is best summarized by Khaleqi-Motlagh: '[B]etter for the pahlavan to die with a good name rather than existing in infamy.'[72] There are numbers of sayings among Iran's tribal peoples that are apparently a continuation of this pahlavan tradition. An old saying from the Boyer-Ahmad clan, for example states that it is 'better to die in battle rather [than] of old age on the death bed'.

Defence of frahang. *Frahang* is broadly defined as learning and culture.[73] The military role of the knights was not restricted to defence of Iranian territory but also the preservation and defence of *frahang*, or the Persian culture and tradition of learning. Tafazolli has discussed the role of these knights with respect to not only culture but also the importance of their defence of Iran's learning tradition.[74] The *Shahname*, for example, notes the importance of pursuing learning and knowledge and sending children to school (*dabestan*).[75] In summary, learning was an important element of the culture of Iranian knights.

Thousands of years later, the Iranian martial tradition would cause grave concerns for Tsarist Russia. Despite their more advanced weaponry, the Russians had been forced to fight two hard-fought wars against the poorly equipped armies of nineteenth century Persia for possession of the Caucasus. Zenkowski has noted that for imperial Russia, the culture of ancient Iran, especially its ancient martial tradition, and its legacy in the Caucasus posed a mortal threat to Russian domination of the region. The Russians undertook to wipe out Persian culture in the Caucasus, especially with regard to the pre-Islamic martial tradition as recorded in the *Shahname*, by instituting destructive 'educational' policies.[76] These policies were continued by the succeeding Soviet regime in Russia.[77]

Shahanshah as defender of frahang. Like the knights discussed above, the shahanshah was also seen as the military defender of frahang and wider civilization. The Sassanian shahanshahs actually acknowledged the Roman Emperors as partners in the defence of civilization against the barbarian hordes. King Narses (r. 293–302 CE) for example dispatched the following message to Galerius through the envoy Afraban:[78] 'The whole human race knows that the Roman and Persian kingdoms resemble two great luminaries, and that, like a man's two eyes, they ought mutually to adorn and illustrate each other.'

Similar sentiments were expressed in the correspondence of Shapur II and the emperor Constantius. Shapur II addressed Constantius as 'my brother Constantius Caesar' to which the emperor replied 'my brother Shapur'.[79] While outside the scope of this book, the Romano-Byzantine and Sassanian Empires did engage in several domains of cultural exchange (i.e. arts, architecture, medicine, etc.).[80]

Shahanshah as battlefield pahlavan knight. Despite the passage of over thirteen centuries since the fall of the Sassanian Empire, Iranian military culture maintains the concept of *jangidan doosh ba doosh-e hamrazman*, broadly translated as 'fighting shoulder-to-shoulder alongside one's *hamrazman* (comrades in battle)'. Therefore, while the military ranking and social status of the commanding general would be higher than the lower-ranked warriors and other troops, his entrance into combat was meant to signal two messages to the warriors. First is the concept of *hamrazm* where the military leader is clearly letting his troops know that he is their comrade-in-arms. The second was to set the example of the pahlavan ethos in the battlefield. Sassanian kings from Ardashir I to Khosrow I Anoushirvan did take to the field and engage in combat alongside the spah's warriors. Shapur II, for example, engaged in close-quarter combat during the siege of Amida in 359 CE. As noted by Ammianus Marcellinus, Shapur II 'rode up to the gates attended by his royal escort, and while with too great assurance he came so near that even his features could clearly be recognized'.[81]

The 'royal escort' of Shapur II during these charges to Amida's gates was of course the elite savaran armoured knights, possibly of the brigade of the Pustigh-ban (Chapter 6). The charge was made against the powerful ballistae and missile barrages of Amida's defenders. Shapur II's actions at Amida prefigured those of Safavid king Shah Ismail (r. 1501–1524 CE) who led his small force of Qizilbash cavalry against the awesome firepower of Ottoman musketry and cannon at the Battle of Chaldiran in 1514.

After the shattering of his siege towers by the Amidan defenders, Shapur II opted to once again engage in close-quarter combat: '[T]he king of the Persians himself [Shapur II], who is never expected to mingle in the fight, being indignant at these disasters... sprang forth like a common soldier among his own dense columns; and as the very number of his guards made him the more conspicuous to us who looked from afar on the scene, he was assailed by numerous missiles.'[82]

There was special emphasis on the regal aspect of Sassanian military culture, especially before the onset of battle. Before Shapur II began his siege of Amida, he engaged in a spectacular military manoeuvre outside of the city's walls. Ammianus Marcellinus, who was trapped in Amida, reports the following with respect to Sassanian military display:

> [E]verything as far as the eye could reach was filled with glittering arms and mail-clad cavalry filled plains and hills. The king himself [Shapur II], mounted on a horse and higher than the rest, rode before the whole army [Spah], wearing in place of a diadem a golden image of a ram's head set with precious stones, distinguished too by a great retinue of men of the highest rank and of various nations.[83]

Ammianus' description highlights the powerful bond between martial ardour and regal military rituals among the Sassanians.[84] Another instance of such behaviour by a Sassanian king occurred when Kavad drew his sword at the foot of a scaling ladder during the siege of Amida in 502 CE. In doing so Kavad meant to urge his men to go up the ladder and fight the Romans hand to hand. The importance and symbolism of the sword (sheathed and drawn) in stirring the martial ardour of Sassanian troops is discussed below.

The respect of the Sassanian nobility and military leadership for the king who led his armies in person was extended even to Emperor Heraclius (r. 610–641 CE), who accompanied his army in its advance to Ctesiphon in December 627 CE. The Sassanians were well aware that Khosrow II had not led any of his armies in war since 603 CE, whereas Heraclius had risked his own life in leading the Romano-Byzantine armies in person.[85]

The regal presence of the king with the spah at war (even if he did not enter the fighting himself) did often have the effect of raising the military performance of the troops on the battlefield and in sieges.[86] The presence of the shahanshah with the field army was also a source of great distress to Romano-Byzantine troops, as they realized that the Sassanian warriors would fight much harder as a result.[87]

Another ritual observed by the shahanshah was his selection of weapons. The weapons could be of gold if the shahanshah was about to partake in ceremonial functions which could be religious or observing troops in military reviews. Gold was chosen as it symbolized the divine fire of the heavens.[88] If the king was about to partake in more 'earthly' affairs such as combat, he would enact another ritual where he would select his own distinctive helmet, sword, armour and archery equipment from arrays of weaponry presented to him in a designated arsenal.[89]

Warning against character flaws. The *Menog-e Xrad* warns warriors against moral decay by noting that the 'vices of the Arteshtaran are oppression, violence, breaking faith, lack of remorse, whoring, arrogance and contempt'.[90] Apart from the 'spiritual' aspect of this admonition, the linkage is between moral character and military performance. Corruption of character could lead to dereliction of duty, decline of military discipline and neglect of consistent and vigorous training. The *Andarz-e Oshnar-e Danag* (*Advice/Counsel of the Wise Oshnar*) identifies the four sources of moral corruption as 'Drinking too much wine, lusting after women, playing too much backgammon, and hunting without moderation'.[91] Balance and moderation are important characteristics of a pahlavan knight.

Interestingly, the *Shahname* also strongly admonishes against gluttony and drunkenness, describing these as vices that downgrade the pahlavan's martial spirit and moral character.[92] The link between the warrior's moral character and battlefield performance is perhaps best expressed by the ancient local lore of Iran's Azerbaijan's province, which states that 'the chaste warrior is the Pahlavan who wields his sword with a grip of steel on the battlefield, even as he suffers from terrible wounds and is outnumbered by the enemy'.

The Aryan Class System: Could 'Lower Classes' Become Arteshtaran?
Darayee has provided a comprehensive explanation of the division of classes (*pesag*) in the Sassanian Empire.[93] There were four classes in the empire with the

asronan (priesthood) being the top or first caste. These were actually subdivided into the mobads (chief priests or Magi), herbadan (priests attending the sacred fires), dasturan (theologians), dadwaran (judges), and radan (learned priesthood). As noted in Chapter 2, the mobads would accompany the warriors of the spah during military campaigns and would even enter close-quarter combat. The second class was the arteshtaran, the third was composed of dahigan (farmers) and wastaryosan (husbandmen), with the lowest and fourth class being the hutuxsan (artisans). The subdivisions of the arteshtaran has been described in this text, but like the asronan, the third and fourth classes had their subdivisions as well. The primary question would then be this: could members of the lower classes, notably the dahigan (farmers), wastaryosan (husbandmen), and hutuxsan (artisans) somehow become promoted into the arteshtaran? At first glance, given the general rigidity of social class traditions, this would seem improbable; however, there appear to have been exceptions or caveats to the permanence of one's membership in a certain 'lower' class. Jalali[94] and Sami[95] note that if a member of a lower class demonstrated bravery, combat skill and aptitude in battlefield situations, then that person could be promoted to the arteshtaran on the basis of their demonstrated martial merit. For example, if a peasant labourer or baggage handler demonstrated exceptional martial prowess against the enemy which had broken into the Sassanian camp, this could be reason for his recommendation into the arteshtaran as that person had performed outside as well as above and beyond what would normally be expected from him. Sami notes that such 'promotions' were more the exception rather than a common occurrence as the Sassanian class system remained for the main part highly conservative.[96]

Mention must also be made of the demotion of warriors who failed in their martial duties. The shahanshah had the authority to strip the warrior of his titles and privileges, especially if he had failed to perform at his best on the battlefield.[97] Martial qualities were so esteemed that they were valued above education. The *Shahname* describes a mobad who inquired of Khosrow I as to whether a pahlavan was obliged to pursue higher education. Khosrow reputedly replied that the fundamental duty of the spah warrior was being an excellent fighter and to be willing to risk his life in battle.[98] Therefore if the warrior chose not to pursue higher education, he would not be judged unfavorably.

Military Ceremonies and Court Customs

Hamza Isfahani studied a text from the Sassanian era featuring detailed illustrations of twenty-six Sassanian kings (Isfahani claimed that this is the same book that Al-Masoudi studies; Christensen believed it was the *Taj Namag*).[99] The throne of the kings is variously described as being built of ivory and decorated with pearls and designs of wolves, lions, and other wild animals. Of special interest are references to four pillows symbolizing the four regions of the empire's defence.[100]

There are a number of representations of enthroned Sassanians kings which have survived. One of these is the rock relief attributed to Shapur II in the Bishapur gorge where the monarch is seated with feet pointed outwards and holding a broadsword with both hands. Another example is a metalwork plate with an image of Khosrow I who is again holding a broadsword with both hands (Hermitage, Inv. S-250). The Isfahani descriptions of enthroned Sassanian kings describe them as having wielded a series of ceremonial weapons at court, these being mainly swords, spears, bows, maces and axes.[101] There are also some references by Isfahani of kings having wielded weapons with two hands. The crowns of the kings as cited by Isfahani are described as being either green or blue or a combination of green and blue, and in all cases blended with gold. The tunics and trousers of the kings are described by Isfahani as being, usually, blue, green, red and crimson, with yellow and black being especially rare.

In addition to the throne of the shahanshah, there were also a number of other ceremonial thrones in the Sassanian court. According to Ibn Balkhi the court of Khosrow I had three thrones in addition to that of the shahanshah. These three thrones were ceremonial and were reserved for the emperors of the Khazars, Rome and China. This is indicative of the Sassanians' respect for the military might of their Roman, Khazar and Chinese contemporaries. Ibn Balkhi mentions other 'lesser' thrones assigned to a certain 'buzurgmehr', the mobadan mobad (chief of the magi), and others belonging to the various buzurgans and marzbans.[102] These thrones were all assigned to those of specific rank and no one of 'lesser' ranks was allowed to occupy them.

The Royal Hunt and the Royal Banquet

The royal hunt was an integral aspect of Sassanian military culture. This was as much an arena for training (Chapter 4) as it was for testing one's martial mettle, bravery, strength, valour and skill against dangerous beasts. Sassanian depictions of the hunt are also meant to symbolize the triumph of the hunter-king, who is the defender of arta (truth) and order over evil, falsehood and chaos as represented by wild beasts.[103] Hanaway has noted that the Iranian conception of the hunt as the opposite face of war may have deeper roots within a more ancient Indo-European tradition that views the king as a warrior-god.[104]

Representations of the lion hunt on horseback can be seen in at least three metalwork plates, notably of Shapur II (Hermitage, St. Petersburg, Inv. S-253) and two unidentified Sassanian kings (British Museum, Inv. BM.124092 and the Sari dish in the Tehran Museum). The theme of confronting dangerous feline beasts can be seen in a representation of Bahram II carved into a mountain at Sar Mashad. This panel shows Bahram II slaying lions to defend his queen Shapurdukhtat; the magus Kartir stands between the queen and Bahram. Sassanian hunters also engage in the chase dismounted, as seen in representations of Sassanian warrior-kings on foot hunting (Hermitage, St. Petersburg, Inv. S-216 and private collection of Leon Levy and Shelby White in New York), and Shapur II hunting a leopard.

The hunting of boars on horseback is also a common theme, and is depicted, for example, on a drinking bowl showing Pirouz or Kavad (Ghirschman private Collection, 1962). Perhaps the grandest depiction of a boar hunt (and all Sassanian royal hunts in general) appears on the left side of the grand iwan at the entrance to the vault at Taghe Bostan. Here the king is prominently shown with other nobles engaged in the hunt against a large number of boars, whose carcasses are then carried off by elephants. The hunt is also accompanied by musicians playing various instruments, as seen in both the right and (especially) left panels (Chapter 4). Theophanes has also described Khosrow II's royal hunt 'theme park' at his favorite palace in Dastegerd, which featured ostriches, pheasants, peacocks, onagers, and antelopes.[105]

The royal hunt is also depicted in the context of hunting several dangerous beasts on the same expedition. One metal plate, for example, shows an unidentified king hunting lions, boars and a bear (Museum für Islamische Kunst, Berlin. Inv. I.4925). There is a similar depiction of the post-Sassanian figure of Pur-e-Vahman hunting lions and boars (Hermitage, St. Petersburg, Inv. S-247).

The banquet or feast was, as noted by Whitby, 'the natural complement to the hunt'.[106] The link between the royal hunt and the royal banquet is symbolized in a Sassanian bowl (housed at the Walters Art Gallery in Baltimore) showing a royal couple enthroned in *farr* (divine glory); strewn at the base of the regal throne are three boar heads signaling the king's return from a successful hunt.[107] Xenophon provided a description of a Persian banquet in Achaemenid times, explaining how wine was poured into royal goblets 'without spilling a drop'.[108] Proper conduct expected of military officers is reported in the *Cyropedia* which advises that 'a banquet ... [is] in no case ... a moment for gluttony and drunkenness'. The Caucasus was to be heir to Sassanian Iran's martial culture well into the Islamic era. As noted by Chardin, Iran's pre-Islamic martial tradition was to resonate in post-Islamic Georgia with examples such as Persian style mansions, welcoming ceremonies for guests of the court, royal and wedding banquets, Partho-Sassanian style posture and stance, and even bejeweled drinking vessels in the Achaemenid-Sassanian style.[109] The military aristocracy of Armenia shared the same concept of the royal hunt followed by the royal banquet.[110]

Dogs were sacred in the Zoroastrian tradition and may have had an important role in the royal hunt. An indication of the importance of the dog to the hunt is found very late in the Islamic-era tradition of Attar's *Manteq al-Tayr*, which makes reference to a king who went hunting 'with an elegantly accoutred dog'.[111] A final point of interest with respect to the hunt in the Iranian milieu was the notion of mercy towards captured beasts. Put simply, beasts that had been captured during the hunt but not killed were to be spared and set free. This tradition is seen very late into the Islamic era at the time of Shah Abbas (1588–1629) who had his men brand and attach earrings (with the royal seal) to captured animals before setting them free.[112]

Military 'Museums'

One of the most distinct features of the Sassanian spah was how it sought to preserve its military legacy and history. The storage of captured enemy standards and weapons can be seen as far back as the Parthian era. Following the defeat of the Roman legions of Marcus Lucinius Crassus by Parthian general Surena in 53 BCE, the Parthians placed captured Roman aquilae (legionary battle standards) in temples at Ctesiphon. These were repatriated to the Romans following negotiations with Emperor Augustus (r. 27 BCE–14 CE).[113]

Ctesiphon was apparently a major centre for the display of captured enemy equipment, although it is not clear if these were specifically stored in public 'museums' or placed in temples (or a combination of both). Nevertheless Ctesiphon was not the sole locale for the storage of captured enemy prestige weapons. As noted previously, the temple of Azargoshnasp in Iranian Azerbaijan was a major locale for the storage and display of captured booty. Following his victory in 588 CE over the Turco-Hephthalites, Bahram Chobin donated the late khagan's handsome sword decorated with precious jewels to the temple at Azargoshnasp.[114] One of the final prestigious military items captured by the spah and put on display in Ctesiphon was the sword of Heraclius that had been captured during the long Byzantine-Sassanian wars of 602–627 CE. When Ctesiphon fell to the Arabs in 637 CE, they captured that sword along with countless other Sassanian state treasures,[115] including the ceremonial broadswords of Kavad, Bahram Gur and Khosrow II.

Cult of the Broadsword

The 'classical' or early Sassanian sword (Chapter 6) of the long, straight 'broadsword' type was an important military and mystical symbol that exemplified the king's farr (divine glory) as supreme commander of the spah. A distinct representation of king-broadsword is seen in the rock relief of Shapur II at the Bishapur gorge. Here, Shapur is seated on his throne, with his left hand resting on the pommel of a broadsword with his right holding what appears to be either a staff or lance. There is also the image of a seated Khosrow I on a metallic plate clasping a broadsword (left hand resting on pommel, right hand grasping handle) (Hermitage, St. Petersburg. Inv. S-250).

The shamshirdar/shapsheraz. The role of the *shamshirdar* (New Persian: Sword bearer) or *shapsheraz* (Pahlavi: he who bears/brandishes the sword) was not a purely ceremonial title. The shamshirdar/shapsheraz was the personal bodyguard of the king; however his function was also ceremonial in the Sassanian court.[116] The shapsheraz is clearly alluded to as early as the time of Shapur I in the inscriptions of the Kaaba Zartusht.[117] This is corroborated by Faustus of Byzantium who describes a 'sword bearer' dressed in a military uniform who, at official court receptions, holds the 'king's sword in a golden scabbard, with a belt decorated with stones and pearls'.[118] The sword-bearing shahpsheraz was essentially a ceremonial military office who took part in the annual ceremonies of *Nowruz* (Iranian new year, 21 March) and *Mehregan* (Festival of Mithra). During these ceremonies another essential ceremonial office was that of the *karframandar* (court steward).[119]

The Sword of Khosrow II. The depiction of the broadsword in the late sixth and early seventh centuries is significant as this weapon had become militarily obsolete (Chapter 6). Its demise as a battlefield weapon came as a result of changes to swords, notably the P-mount system of lappet suspension (Chapter 6). Such developments, however, did not phase out the broadsword from Sassanian culture; it continued to be an important ceremonial weapon. The latest representation of such a ceremonial weapon is seen at the upper panel in the inner vault (or sanctum) or Iwan at Taghe Bostan near Kermanshah. On the floor of the vault is a mounted armoured knight of the late 'composite' type, believed to be Khosrow II, who is equipped with typical late Sassanian military gear, notably the lappet suspension system (Chapter 6).

In contrast to the knight armed with contemporary military equipment, the upper panel of the vault at Taghe Bostan shows Khosrow II standing with a ceremonial broadsword. The weapon is sheathed within a scabbard inlaid with what appears to be pearls; the king stands with his left hand resting on the broadsword and his right about to grasp a diadem (symbolic of *farr* or divine glory) from Ahura-Mazda (dressed like a Sassanian nobleman or mobad) standing to the left of the king; the goddess Anahita with right hand raised towards Khosrow stands to his right. According to Lerner, the P-mount sword 'was probably deemed too barbaric for the highly religious scene of divine investiture'.[120] This observation is consistent with Overlaet, who concurs that Khosrow II's sword in this context is an accurate portrayal of a ceremonial weapon.[121] Judging from later Arab accounts (written after the Arabs captured Ctesiphon and its military museum), the ceremonial sword was a handsome weapon.

The Warrior Cults of Mithra and Anahita

In addition to Ahura-Mazda, Iranian warriors also invoked the god Mithra and the goddess Anahita for strength in battle. As noted by Nigosian, in the Zoroastrian faith 'no distinction is made between the genders … both occupy the same place of honour … on the same level in … power'.[122]

Mithra. Mithra played an important role as the protector of the Parthian army. The worship of Mithra was widespread in the Parthian empire with several prominent Parthian kings having adopted his name (e.g. Mithradates I (r. 171–137 BCE), Mithradates III (r. 57–55 BCE), etc.). He is very much a god of war, fate and victory.[123] The *Yasht* states 'I shall worship the powerful God, strong Mithra, strongest in the (world of) creatures.'[124] In the ancient Iranian pantheon Mithra is described as driving a chariot drawn by four horses.[125] The warrior nature of Mithra resonates among the Zoroastrian magi to this day; they carry a symbolic gurz (mace) of Mithra as part of their priestly oath to make war against evil.[126] As lord of the light who fights against evil,[127] Mithra is the enemy of all vice, lies, impurity and darkness. As noted by Taraporewala, 'Mithra leads the hosts of heaven against the hordes of the Abyss. In a sense, Mithra is the prototype of the Archangel Michael.'[128] Mithra was also the lord of fecundity and wild pastures, the giver of life, the god of the social order and justice, abundance, progeny and herds.[129] A critical role of Mithra was him being the god of contracts; so important was this to Iranian warriors that Iran itself was regarded as the land of contracts by its inhabitants.[130] Making a contract or oath was considered sacred and one who broke this was judged to be *Mithra-druj* (sinners/liars against Mithra).[131] Hence the Sassanian warrior's oath to his nation, fellow warriors and the shahanshah was not just a matter of word, but a sacred spiritual bond for life. Mithra severely punished those who broke their oath but also protected those who maintained their loyalty to the contract.[132] Hinnells avers that before going into battle against the 'anti-Mithraic countries' Iranian warriors would pray to Mithra at the manes of their horses.[133] Interestingly, Quintius Rufus Curtius in his *History of Alexander* observes that before entering battle the Persian king 'with his generals and staff passed around the ranks of the armed men, praying to the sun and Mithra and the sacred eternal fire'.[134]

Perhaps the most salient representation of Mithra is seen at Taghe Bostan where a panel depicts a monarch (most likely Ardashir II) who is flanked by the figure of Mithra to the left (of the panel). Most interesting is the way in which Mithra wields what appears to be a ceremonial sword or a *barsom* (ceremonial/religious bundle of twigs or rods); this may have been a type of honouring or 'knighting' ceremony. Mithra's image became especially pronounced in the Median realms outside of Persis during the fourth century CE.[135] It is ironic that Mithra, the Iranian god of war, came to be worshipped by Roman soldiers.[136]

The Goddess Anahita. The temple of Anahita at Istakhr and its popularity as a war-cult became especially pronounced during the Parthian dynasty (247 BCE–224 CE).[137] It is noteworthy that Babak, the father of Ardashir I, was a priest at the temple of Anahita at Istakhr in Persis, which as noted by Daryaee: '[The temple] must have been a stage for the rallying of the local Persian warriors who were devoted to the cult of this deity ... in early Sassanian Persia we have a king who is the caretaker of the Anahid [Anahita] fire temple which was also a warrior of a cultic centre.'[138]

Sassan, Ardashir I's grandfather, had also been a high priest or dignitary at the Temple of Anahita.[139] During his ascent to power of the Iranian realms, Ardashir I sent the severed heads of Ardavan V and his enemies to the temple of Anahita.[140]

It is clear that Anahita was a major entity providing legitimacy for the Sassanian kings.[141] The Taghe Bostan depictions of Anahita, Khosrow II and Ahuramazda resonate with themes unique to Sassanian military culture. As noted previously (see Chapter 2), the mobads played an important role in Sassanian military culture, including presiding over rituals prior to the commencement of battle to the supervision of warriors during the battle. This would at least partly explain (from the aspect of Sassanian military culture) the presence of the 'supreme mobad' Ahura-Mazda to the right of the king. Taghe Bostan's Anahita stands to the left of the sovereign and raises her right hand towards that sovereign. There is at least one earlier depiction of Anahita as seen in the Sassanian rock reliefs at Naghshe Rustam where the goddess stands beside King Narseh (Narses). Anahita is in fact much more than just a 'fertility' goddess; she is also integral to Sassanian military culture. Anahita has been proposed as being the female counterpart of Mithra (Mitra).[142,143] The primary importance of Anahita to the warrior-king can be seen in the inscriptions of Artaxerxes II in the fifth century BCE who in addition to his worship of the supreme lord Ahura-Mazda also invokes the names of both Mithra and Anahita.[144] It is therefore interesting that Iranian military culture during the Sassanian era was to return to the 'Achaemenid-like' reverence for all three entities (Ahura-Mazda, Mithra and Anahita) at Taghe Bostan.[145]

Like Mithra, Anahita was seen as one who would come to the aid of her worshippers in times of distress. Warriors would offer sacrifice to Anahita in search of beneficence and pray to her (as they did to Mithra) to receive life and victory. Mithra's additional role of 'lord of the pastures' provides him an additional link to Anahita who is the mistress of the waters.[146] Daryaee describes Anahita's warlike nature as being a symbiosis of the Iranian tradition along with ancient Near Eastern (Ishtar) and Hellenic (Anaitis/Athena) themes.[147] Like Mithra, Anahita also drives a chariot pulled by four horses.[148] Anahita (much like Mithra) is seen as 'efficacious against the Daevas [demons]'.[149] This delineates a clear linkage between the sovereign or warrior-king and the goddess Anahita in Iranian mythology.

Chapter 16

Military Weaknesses of the Spah

This chapter examines the military factors (especially weaknesses) that led to the downfall of the Sassanian military machine in the seventh century CE. Even before the empire's last major wars, the spah was beset by major weaknesses notably in the 'quatro' four-spahbod system of defence as well as critical weaknesses that undermined Sassanian military performance. While this chapter's main emphasis is upon military factors, brief mention must be made of non-military factors that also contributed to the empire's demise.

The Sassanian Empire was facing severe economic difficulties by the 630s CE. Severe floods had destroyed much of the crops and harvests prior to the Arab invasion, imposing food shortages and economic hardships on the population.[1] The empire was also riven by internal dissensions primarily propelled by the inequitable distribution of wealth resulting in sharp gaps between the rich and poor. These social inequities had been last expressed in protest by the Iranian prophet Mazdak (d. 524 or 528 CE) during the late fifth and early sixth centuries CE with this movement finally being suppressed by the Sassanian dynasty.[2] These serious socio-economic issues remained unaddressed until it was too late. This combined with rifts within the upper political and military leadership, especially after the wars with Byzantium, made Iran militarily vulnerable to attacks, and eventually conquests, by Arabs imbued with the zeal of the religion of Islam.

Weaknesses in the Sassanian Order of Battle

The Sassanian military order was beset by a number of serious weaknesses.

Peasant auxiliaries. Note that in Chapter 7 the term 'infantry' was shown to refer to not just a monolithic force but actually a number of distinct services. These included foot archers (Chapter 5), neyze-daran (spear-bearers), paighan, Dailamites and auxiliary peasant recruits. It was the latter who often proved to be the Achilles heel of the spah, especially if the battle went badly, as occurred at the battle of Dara (530 CE). The peasant recruits were pressured into service of menial tasks, often used for siege works, digging of trenches, etc.; but they had little military training and adequate equipment for face-to-face combat against enemy professional troops. Morale was often low, possibly due to two factors. They were unpaid and forced into service by their overlords, who often were members of the elite savaran corps or the military leadership. Second, they were regarded as inferiors by the 'higher classes' of the military, notably officers, etc. As a result they would prove especially vulnerable to the egalitarian messages of Islam during the Arab invasions of Iran in 637–651 CE.

Conflicts within the upper leadership. Perhaps one of the most critical problems plaguing the empire was disunity which seriously undermined the political leadership at the eve of the Arab invasion. These had serious repercussions within the upper military leadership and significant consequences for the spah's military performance. The Sassanian dynasty was essentially a federation between the great Parthian and Sassanian clans which were the military backbone of the empire. As noted in earlier chapters, many of Iran's top elite families were Parthian in origin and it was these who furnished the spah with some of its finest cavalry for the savaran corps. While it is true that the reforms of the sixth century CE did create a new and significant corps of dehkans, these did not decrease the military importance of the elite families of Parthian origin. The rebellion of Bahram Chobin after the Turco-Hephthalite wars in 588 CE against Hormuzd IV (r. 579–590 CE) and then his son Khosrow II (r. 590–628 CE) is of major significance as Bahram had challenged the very legitimacy of Sassanian authority. While Bahram's rebellion was crushed, the sense of distinctiveness among the Parthians from the Sassanians certainly did not disappear. It would appear that these clan-type rifts only widened in the aftermath of the wars with Byzantium.

Pourshariati's comprehensive study has noted that conflicts between the Parthian and Sassanian houses were a key reason for undermining the military and political leadership of the Sassanian spah at the eve of the Arab invasions.[3] Interestingly, many of the dehkans chose not to battle the Arabs as they entered Iran and even joined the banner of Islam, a strong indication that loyalty to the Sassanian dynasty had plummeted significantly, especially after the wars with the Romano-Byzantines.

Loyalty. Readers are reminded of a quotation by Ammianus Marcellinus, cited in Chapter 1 of this book: 'In military system and discipline, by continual exercises in the business of the camp ... they [Sassanian spah] have become formidable even to the greatest armies ... so brave is it and so skilful in all warlike exercises, that it would be invincible were it not continually weakened by civil and by foreign wars.'[4]

Of special interest is the reference to 'civil' conflicts. Note that we are not discussing the Parthian-Sassanian rivalry, but the issue of loyalty to the country as a whole. Despite the steadfast loyalty of the vast majority of the troops and leadership to the latter days of the empire, there was also an element of opportunism which often greatly endangered the Iranian state. One example is the defection of Prince Hormuzd to the Romans with crack units of the savaran against the Sassanian Empire in 363 CE (Chapter 9). Hormuzd had engaged in this action due to his dispute with Shapur II over the question of who was to be shahanshah. The consequences of Hormuzd's betrayal of the spah were profound for Iran. Hormuzd's savaran entered Roman service against Iran and may have been influential in the development of Rome's own 'Persian'-type cavalry units (Chapters 9 and 19). During Julian's invasion of Iran in 363 CE, the savaran were also forced to fight their former comrades who were now in Roman service. Thus Hormuzd was willing to endanger the safety of his nation and even sacrifice its independence just to become shahanshah. Interestingly, similar actions were to occur in Iran as late as the early nineteenth century CE when imperial Russia began invading Iranian territories of the Caucasus during the reign of the Qajar dynasty (1794–1925). Just as the Iranian army was locked in mortal combat to defend its territories in the Caucasus, numbers of Qajar princes and various khans rebelled against the ruling Qajars in Tehran, thus undermining Iranian military performance.[5] There were even cases of important local military leaders (i.e. Ibrahim Khalil-Khan Javanshir of the Karabakh Caucasian Khanate[6]) switching allegiance to the Russians for the sole purpose of increasing their personal power and prestige at the expense of their nation.

Reaction to battlefield defeats. Despite being a formidable military force, the field armies of the spah could become unreliable upon suffering battlefield defeats. Jalali notes that Sassanian forces could often lose their battle cohesion, or even flee the battlefield, when the spah was defeated or when defeat was inevitable.[7] Jalali also notes that Iranian warriors often over-emphasized the importance of their military leaders in battle, such that if one of their leaders was slain or chose to flee, the regular troops would often flee as well, without regard to the consequences of their actions.[8] The tendency of Sassanian forces to lose cohesion when they were nearing defeat did lessen somewhat during the later stages of the Arabo-Islamic invasions of Iran, but by then much of the spah had been severely weakened and completely destroyed by 651 CE.

Lack of a charismatic warrior-king. In contrast to earlier Sassanian kings such as Ardashir I, Shapur I, Shapur II, Bahram Gur, Pirouz, Kavad and Khosrow I, later Sassanian kings did not, in general, personally lead their armies in battle. It is true that Khosrow II (r. 590–628 CE) did open the war against the Romano-Byzantines and even captured the fortress of Dara after a nine-month siege in 604 CE. But after this, Khosrow II gave command of the spah forces to generals such as Rasmiozan or Farrokhan Shahrbaraz (lit. 'Boar of the Kingdom') as well as Shahraplakan and Shahen. Khosrow II did not take part in any subsequent campaigns, leaving his generals to plan, lead and conduct their own battles.[9]

The lack of participation in battles could be seen with Khosrow II's father Hormuzd IV (t. 579–590 CE) who, despite several military threats posed by both Romano-Byzantines and Central Asian warriors, never actually took to the field himself. Hormuzd IV's own father, Khosrow I (r. 531–579 CE) had stopped campaigning in 576 CE, having reached the advanced age of eighty.

Khosrow II was not an accomplished warrior-king as was his grandfather Khosrow I or any of his aforementioned predecessors. Though nominally in command of the combined Sassanian-Armenian-Byzantine force which secured him the throne of Ctesiphon, Khosrow II made very little military impression during the campaign with respect to planning, strategy or personal combat.[10] His earlier attempt to face down the rebel Bahram Chobin at the Nahrewan canal near Ctesiphon had ended in disaster. Even at the siege of Dara, Khosrow II was very nearly captured by a Romano-Byzantine warrior who had managed to ensnare him with his lasso.[11] When Heraclius was closing in on Ctesiphon in 628 CE, Khosrow II had no forces in the theatre to oppose him, nor did he have the allegiance of the large and powerful force of General Shahrbaraz who had withdrawn from the war.

Shortage of professional military manpower. A distinct and characteristic weakness of the savaran which undermined the spah was the shortage of quality professional manpower. This was a problem that the spah had inherited from the Parthian era. This problem was also shared by the Armenian military which had close doctrinal and equipment ties with the Iranian world (as discussed previously). At the Battle of Tigranocerta, for example, the armies of Tigran could only field 17,000 armoured knights[12] with Artavazdes II leading 10,000 knights.[13] The Parthian armies facing the Roman army at the Battle of Carrhae in 53 BCE, had only 1,000 armoured knights available.[14] The maximum number of armoured cavalry that the Parthians were able to recruit is estimated to have ranged between 50,000 and 60,000 knights.[15]

This problem was recognized by Ardashir Babakan and he tried to solve it, notably by raising the javidan cavalry elite corps, but ultimately he failed, despite his best efforts, to significantly enlarge the savaran.[16] The problem largely derived from the structure of Iranian society itself where the knights could only come from the select upper noble clans of Aryan descent. This significantly limited the population base upon which the spah could draw for recruitment. Even after the reforms of Khosrow I and the creation of the dehkan corps from the 'lesser nobility' two and a half centuries after Ardashir I to augment the ranks of the savaran, the number of professional savaran warriors along the Western frontiers stood at a modest total of just 60,000 to 70,000 warriors. These numbers appear to have finally increased towards the end of the sixth century CE, most likely as the result of the long-term effects of reforms, but even then the numbers were not impressively greater. This can be seen in the final encounter between Khosrow II and Bahram Chobin in 591 CE at Atropatene (Azerbaijan province in Iran). During this engagement Khosrow II fielded a total of 60,000 warriors, including Byzantine cavalry furnished by Emperor Maurice. Howard-Johnston notes that the majority of the troops would have been Khosrow II's loyalist troops (especially from the garrison at Nisibis) with Bahram Chobin's forces at a maximum of 40,000 knights.[17] By factoring out the non-Iranian elements in Khosrow II's forces in 591 CE, the combined total of Iranian warriors (supporters of Bahram Chobin and Khosrow II) appears to have been about 90,000. While this would seem impressive at first, such numbers were far from adequate to repel simultaneous attacks on several fronts, especially the western (Romano-Byzantine) and Central Asian fronts. While estimates of the size of Roman forces vary, it is generally agreed that the Romano-Byzantines had double the manpower available to the Sassanians.[18] As the events of 588 CE and 618 CE demonstrated, the Sassanians were also vastly outnumbered along the Central Asian front. Manpower shortages also imposed economic challenges, as the empire was forced to recruit more able-bodied men to the spah and to spend more of the state treasury on the military.[19]

As noted previously in discussions of the 'quatro' system, the strategy for coping with limited numbers of professional troops was to prioritize: focusing the bulk of the spah's resources on the more critical sector while dedicating just the minimum force necessary to avert disaster in the 'less critical' sector. Another means of coping with the manpower shortage problem was to improve and increase the capabilities of the troops themselves, especially through training in weapons employment and battlefield tactics. When the empire was threatened by a massive Turco-Hephthalite invasion force numbering in the hundreds of thousands in 588 CE, the empire was able to dispatch a very modest force of just 12,000 savaran knights led by General Bahram Chobin (Chapter 12). Bahram's spectacular victories over the Turco-Hephthalites in 588 CE was the result of the spah's very heavy emphasis on rigorous training and professional military leadership.

The danger to the empire stemmed from the fact that the spah had to be ready to engage potential enemies to the north, south, east or west, with the real possibility of facing combined (or even coordinated) attacks along any of those fronts. These scenarios were fraught with the real possibility that the spah would be faced with very high losses of professional warriors which could not be replaced in the short term. This would then lead to a dangerous military vacuum. It was precisely this vacuum which the Arabo-Islamic invaders of 637–651 CE successfully exploited in the aftermath of the long and devastating Sassanian-Byzantine wars of 603–628 CE.

Weaknesses of the Four-Spahbod system

The reforms of the sixth century CE resulted in the rationalization of the empire's defence along a 'quatro' system of four spahbods, each of whom was entrusted with the command of major sectors generally corresponding to the empire's north, south, west and east axes. There were two critical weaknesses in this system. The first was a question of strategic doctrine, namely whether the four-spahbod system was primarily offensive or defensive. The second was the question of the spah's military strength on the empire's frontiers in comparison to the interior of the empire. These are discussed below.

An offensive or defensive doctrine? This system had been designed to allow the spah to simultaneously combat invasions launched against the empire from multiple fronts. This would suggest a primarily defensive rather than offensive doctrine. It is true that the system did allow for the spah to assemble for strikes into enemy territory (Chapter 3) but there are no indications that the four-spahbod system had been designed to sustain a major military offensive for the permanent securing of a vast territorial area. Essentially, the system did allow for attacks into Roman-held areas closer to the frontiers such as those in the Caucasus, Anatolia, Mesopotamia and even Syria, but the doctrine had apparently failed to factor in the scenario in which the spah would be required to engage in a costly and prolonged war for the express purpose of ejecting the Romano-Byzantines from their territories in Anatolia, Mesopotamia-Syria, the Levant, Egypt, etc. It is true that the spah could and did engage in attacks against Roman-held territories during the reigns of Ardashir I, Shapur I, Shapur II, Kavad I and Khosrow I, but few would argue that these monarchs had intentions of overthrowing the Roman (later Romano-Byzantine) Empire.

Put simply, it would appear that the four-spahbod system was a military system for preserving the contemporary boundaries of the Sassanian Empire rather than being designed as a primarily offensive doctrine for the overthrow of the Romano-Byzantine empire. The major offensive of Khosrow II in 602 CE was no less than an attempt to restore the frontiers of the Achaemenid empire. Khosrow II's offensives obliged the bulk of the spah to move outside of its designated spahbod zones. This action would constitute a major threat to the security of the empire against invasions as the four-spahbod defensive zones were now reduced in military strength. To minimize that threat, the spah was obliged to take the following three critical factors into consideration: (a) duration of campaign; (b) extent of territorial expansion; and (c) capacity or limit for absorbing losses.

The first category (campaign duration) was especially important for one simple strategic reason: the longer the bulk of the spah was engaged in one theatre, the greater the possibility that enemies near the empire's other borders would seek to take advantage of the spah's absence. For example, if the bulk of the spah was campaigning in the west against the Romano-Byzantines, then the empire's enemies to the northeast, namely the Hephthalite Huns and the Turks in Central Asia, would seek to take advantage of the spah's military preoccupations to their west. The Central Asian frontier had been militarily pacified during the campaigns of Bahram Chobin in 588 CE, but this did not deter a massive Turco-Hephthalite invasion in 619 CE, which took place seventeen years after the spah's major invasion of the Romano-Byzantine Empire. Recall that Shapur II's siege of Nisibis in 337 or 338 CE had to be suspended after two months due to an invasion threat to Iran's northeast by the Chionites in Central Asia. The four-spahbod system, combined with the brilliant leadership of Smbat Bagratuni, averted disaster in the east, but it is likely that such a scenario may not have occurred had the spah not been engaged in its prolonged war with the Romano-Byzantines. The second critical factor was directly correlated with the extent of the spah's military success in securing territory. While certainly impressive, the capture of large swathes of territory also posed a major liability for the spah because it lacked the manpower to permanently garrison large bodies of troops to both retain recently captured territories and to maintain overstretched communication and supply routes. Not only had the four-spahbod system failed to account for such a scenario, it had also failed to make preparations against Romano-Byzantine naval landings from the Black Sea onto the west Caucasus coast. It was along these very same 'blind spots' in land mass and coastal regions where Heraclius and his Khazar allies began their counteroffensives against the spah in Anatolia and the Caucasus.

Powerful along the frontiers but weaker in the interior. The significant rise in
the spah's efficiency had also contributed to a major strategic weakness. As noted
by Frye, the spah's doctrine of placing the bulk of its forces in the spahbod-
commanded frontier regions meant that the interior of Iran was sparsely garrisoned by professional troops. This would not appear as a problem at first,
especially if the frontier defences and garrisons could successfully repel enemy
invasions. On the other hand, if the enemies did succeed in breaking through any
of the spahbod-manned regions, then they often could push their troops far into
the Iranian interior against little serious opposition. This in fact happened during
the Turkish khagan's invasion of the empire from Central Asia. As discussed in
Chapter 12, the khagan's troops broke into very large swathes of Iranian territory,
especially after they overpowered and destroyed Sassanian forces that had been
entrusted with guarding the Central Asian frontier. This was a very dangerous
situation, one which the Romano-Byzantines could have potentially exploited
along the empire's west. The sheer size of the empire itself, which translated into
long frontiers and extended communication lines, was already a major source of
vulnerability. This could pose a serious problem whenever the empire had to face
a Roman-Turkic military alliance, especially as the spah lacked the manpower
resources to match the potential numbers of troops that could be fielded by such
a military (Roman-Turkic) *combinazioni*.

As noted previously, the spah had available excellent elite savaran troops, who
under Bahram Chobin's brilliant leadership succeeded in staving off the Turco-
Hephthalite invasion. But despite this success, the Central Asian frontier
continued to be vulnerable to invasion, as demonstrated again by a new Turco-
Hephthalite invasion in 619 CE. This too was dangerous given the spah's military
preoccupation with the Romano-Byzantines in the west. Once again, the deployment of smaller numbers of highly trained elite troops, this time led by Armenian
general Bagratuni, saved the empire. But what would happen if nomadic warriors
broke through into the interior of Iran in the aftermath of a long war which had
wiped out a large proportion of the empire's elite troops?

It was precisely this scenario that had developed when the Caliph Omar chose
to strike Iran. A resourceful and intelligent military leader, Omar was cognizant
of the fact that the spah had lost a major portion of its best troops in the futile war
against Byzantium. Omar exploited this weakness to the full by unleashing his
Arabo-Islamic armies, which broke into the interior of Iran after 637 CE. Frye
has noted that when the Arabo-Islamic forces broke through, there were no fresh
garrisons in Iran's interior to repel the invaders.[20] Interestingly, Armenian
sources report that the creation of the four-spahbod system weakened the Sassanian Empire, but fail to provide specific military reasons as to why this was the
case. Most likely, Frye's thesis provides an accurate insight as to the specific
weaknesses of the four-spahbod system. The empire's sixth century military
reforms and subsequent Sassanian war councils had failed to address the need to
permanently station a professional military reserve in Iran's interior in case of
breakthroughs by invading forces. This failure proved to be one of the major
factors that led to the demise of the Sassanian Empire by 651 CE.

From Victory to Disaster: The Wars with Byzantium (603–628 CE)

The decades-long war between the Sassanian and Byzantine empires has been thoroughly examined and detailed by Western historians, especially in the works of Greatrex and Lieu (2002), Howard-Johnston (1999) and Metzger (2002).[21] The main focus here is the examination of (1) the failure of the four-spahbod system and (2) the possible military (battlefield) reasons why Heraclius finally prevailed and rescued the Byzantine Empire from defeat.

Four spahbod system put to the test: battles on several fronts (603–628 CE). The four-spahbod or 'quatro' system functioned perfectly during the reign of Khosrow I, enabling the comprehensive defeat of a Tukish-Byzantine alliance acting in concert with (dissident) Armenians, thus rescuing the empire from a serious multiple-front threat (Chapter 3). Despite Khosrow I's successes, the aforementioned weaknesses with the quatro system had not been addressed. The four-spahbod system was to again be tested along its western, northern, southern (or southwest) and Central Asian fronts in the early seventh century. The quatro system did perform well at first, especially during the initial phases of the spah's offensives against the Byzantine Empire in 603–627 CE; and, as in 588 CE, a massive Turco-Hephthalite invasion was defeated by 619 CE (Chapter 12). Nevertheless, the quatro system was finally broken along the north and west when Emperor Heraclius of Byzantium struck a military alliance with the Khazars. The spah was outflanked, with Sassanian possessions in the Caucasus overrun and Azerbaijan penetrated by 627–628 CE. Below is a brief sketch of that war, especially in the context of the four-spahbod system.

The first phase of the war was characterized by the spah's campaigns to reduce the massive in-depth defensive system along the western frontiers that protected the Byzantine Near East and Anatolia. First to fall was Dara in 603–604 CE. By the winter of 609–610 CE, the entire Byzantine defensive system had been overcome, allowing the spah to break into the Byzantine Near East and Anatolia.

Conquest of Cappadocia, Syria, Palestine and Jerusalem (613–614 CE). The spah's operations were split into two axes: north and south. The northern axis was led by General Shahen who deployed out of Armenia into Cappadocia, which was cleared of Romano-Byzantine troops. The southern axis was led by General Shahrbaraz, who captured Emesa, Apamea and Antioch in 613 CE. Heraclius led the Romano-Byzantine armies in a powerful counterattack against Shahrbaraz but was defeated.[22] Following the rejection of his peace overtures to Khosrow II, Heraclius prepared for new counteroffensives. General Phillipicus was sent to the Caucasus where he entered Armenia, to then withdraw. The intention of Phillipicus' manoeuvre was to distract the Sassanian war council as to Romano-Byzantine intentions in Syria. Heraclius, his brother Theodore and General Nicetas were moving into Syria to crush Shahrbaraz. The Phillipicus ruse failed in its purpose to divide the attention of the spah, which was all too aware of what was transpiring in Syria. Shahrbaraz engaged and defeated the armies of Heraclius, Theodore and Nicetas in separate battles. Heraclius was again defeated at the Cilician Gates in northern Syria by Shahrbaraz, who then entered Damascus and captured a large number of Romano-Byzantine troops.[23] These victories allowed Shahrbaraz to lead the spah in consolidating his gains in Syria and to then enter northern Palestine by the end of 613 CE. This led to the siege and capture of Jerusalem in 614 CE (Chapter 14). What was remarkable in this operation was the fact that the Romano-Byzantine garrison at Jericho had been originally sent to defend Jerusalem, but upon approaching the city and witnessing Shahrbaraz and his troops, the Jericho garrison simply fled the theatre.[24] This action by the Jericho garrison allowed the spah to capture the city in eighteen to twenty days (Chapter 14).

Crisis in the East (618–619 CE). The quatro system was now dangerously vulnerable. Khosrow II's war with Byzantium had forced the spah to deploy the majority of its forces to the West. The immediate impact of this was the weakening of the quatro system's eastern/northeastern front. During the time of Khosrow I and Hormuzd IV, the war council had factored in all sectors or fronts during their wars, which meant that crises along all fronts were prioritized, thus allowing for the rational allocation of military resources to various sectors in accordance to their level of importance. For example, if the western and Central Asian fronts were simultaneously dangerous, the war council would implement its aforementioned 'Schlieffen plan' approach to first deal offensively with what was considered as the greater threat, while simultaneously keeping just enough forces to ensure that the other threatened front was not penetrated. By the 610s CE however, it would appear that this balanced type of planning and resource allocation was no longer being adequately considered by the war council. This was at least in part due to the person of Khosrow II whose singular focus against the Romano-Byzantine Empire led to the spah's reduction of strength along the Central Asian frontier.

As noted in Chapter 12, the empire faced a renewed invasion by 619 CE. The Turco-Hephthalites had at one point reached Isfahan and Rayy (modern Tehran). If swift action was not taken, the advancing Turco-Hephthalites could most likely have alleviated the military pressure on the Romano-Byzantines, which could possibly have also led to an alliance between them. As noted by Howard-Johnson, 'The whole Iranian interior was thus shown to be vulnerable to attack, if too much of Persian fighting strength was concentrated to the west.'[25] Howard-Johnson's point makes clear that Khosrow II's successes thus far against the Romano-Byzantines had come at the price of weakening the Central Asian front, which undermined the quatro system and endangered the very survival of the empire itself. The Sassanian empire was now in danger of being pressed on two fronts and forced to sue for peace on the most unfavorable terms or risk complete collapse. It is possible that the empire could have collapsed as early as 618–619 CE had Bagratuni not been in service at that time. So, while disaster had been averted, the quatro system had very nearly failed in 618–619.

Conquest of Egypt (619 CE). As Shahrbaraz entered Egypt, Anatolia was also being menaced by the spah. In Egypt, Shahrbaraz no longer had to face the scale of military opposition Sassanian troops had faced in Anatolia, Syria and Palestine. Based on studies of Egyptian papyri, Hardy has provided the following valuable information on the state of Romano-Byzantine forces which had to face the arrival of Shahrbaraz and the savaran:[26] (1) the Romano-Byzantine governors of Egypt had at their disposal few mobile troops; (2) the major garrison in Egypt had been divided into smaller detachments for distribution in Egypt's cities; (3) garrison troops were not well equipped for major battles and were mainly intended for maintaining order in the cities; and (4) excepting Alexandria, the Sassanian armies faced no meaningful military opposition. Hardy further notes that Shahrbaraz's forces were in fact welcomed as liberators and that no rebellions occurred against the Sassanians during their ten-year occupation of Egypt. This was due to the fact that the Egyptians felt little loyalty to the Romano-Byzantines. Even after the departure of the Sassanians, the Egyptians, who were disaffected with the rule of Constantinople, were to again welcome the Arabs as liberators.

Naxarars abandon the Sassanians (618–619 CE). One of the greatest blows to befall the spah was the departure of the formidable naxarars from the battle order of the savaran. As noted by Sebeos, 'they [the Naxarars] rebelled and submitted to the great Khak'an, king of the regions of the north ... they went ... to join the army of ... the Khak'an. Passing through the Pass of Chor with many troops, they went to assist the king of the Greeks.'[27]

Smbat Bagratuni, who had been honoured by Khosrow II for his great victories over the Turco-Hephthalites (Chapter 12), had been allowed to retire in comfort and splendour in the Sassanian court. When Smbat passed away, the naxarars bought his body to his native Armenia and interned it in his ancestral sepulchre in the village of Dariwnk in the province of Gogovit. Then the naxarars chose to break off their alliance with Khosrow II. This was followed by their switch of allegiance to the Khazar Turks, whom they were to accompany in their attacks into the Caucasus and Iran. The departure of the naxarars from the spah's battle order to join the Khazars and ultimately the Romano-Byzantines would prove to be of great tactical value to Heraclius, especially in his offensives into Iran.

Khosrow II's 'final solution' (614–616 CE). It is generally agreed that Khosrow II had decided to eliminate the Byzantine Empire sometime in 615–616 CE.[28] This was not just an attempt to restore the boundaries of the old Achaemenid Empire. This was also in a sense, Khosrow's solution to eliminating a dangerous military rival that posed great challenges for the 'Quatro' system's western flank. If Byzantium were somehow 'eliminated' the spah would then be able to balance its complement of troops more evenly along its east/northeast, southern and northern sectors in the face of potential Turkish, Arabian and Khazar attacks. As long as the Romano-Byzantine military remained in existence, the spah would be forced to station the bulk of its best forces along the Western frontiers, at the risk of weakening the defence of other (east, north, south) sectors.

Byzantine counterthrusts into the Caucasus (622–625 CE). Heraclius had proceeded to rebuild the shattered Byzantine armies. He then launched a successful attack into the Sassanian portion of Armenia, defeating a Sassanian force.[29] Shahrbaraz marched to confront Heraclius but was defeated. These were the first significant successes of the Romano-Byzantines since the onset of the war, but Hercalius had to withdraw from Armenia towards Western Anatolia as the Avars were now streaming into the Balkan regions and threatening the Byzantine Empire from its western (European) flanks. Hercalius returned to Armenia once more from his staging post in Cappadocia in 624 CE. After entering Armenia once more, Heraclius wheeled into Nackchevan (just north of Azerbaijan province in Iran) and Dvin, causing much devastation in his wake. Heraclius then marched into Atropatene (Iran's Azerbaijan province) and drove towards Ganzak where a Sassanian force of 40,000 troops simply scattered.[30] Takhte Suleiman was also attacked, but after a Sassanian force engaged in pursuit, Heraclius withdrew across the Araxes river into Albania. By now Heraclius had sent appeals to the Khazars north of the Caucasus, inviting them into an alliance against the Sassanians. Heraclius had also sent appeals to the Christian leaders of the Georgians and Armenians to join him against the Sassanians.

The war council dispatched three armies towards the Caucasus, led by Shahrbaraz, Shahen and Shahraplakan. The latter included the elite *Khosrowgetai* and *Pirouzetai* units and another unit led by *Granikan-Salar* (the term may possibly designate a military title). Shahraplakan caught up with Heraclius and defeated him, forcing him to retire from the Caucasus into Anatolia.[31] The costs of Shahraplakan's victory were apparently high, with Heraclius having been able to extricate the core of his forces from destruction, which meant that he remained a serious threat to the Sassanians in the Caucasus. Shahrbaraz arrived and joined Shahrplakan to pursue and finish off Heraclius. When the battle was finally joined, Heraclius emerged victorious over the combined force. Shahraplakan was killed but Shahrbaraz managed to escape. Sebeos' account is different as he reports Shahrbaraz having joined Shahen, resulting in a total of 30,000 troops who were defeated by Heraclius' 'elite force of 20,000 men'.[32] What is generally clear is that the war council detached a force of 50,000 troops to join Shahen. Shahrbaraz then deployed into Western Anatolia apparently in an endeavour to join the Avars, who were now menacing the Byzantines in the Balkans. Just as Heraclius was attempting to outflank the Sassanians from their north, the war council determined to outflank Heraclius by attacking the Byzantine capital. Heraclius divided his forces in three to counter this crisis: one portion was to be led by his brother Theodore against Shahen in the Caucasus, another was to deploy to Lazica along the Black Sea coast and the third portion (to be led by Heraclius himself) was to rush back to defend Constantinople. Theodore met Shahen in battle and emerged victorious, but specific tactical details of this battle remain unclear. One account attributes Shahen's defeat to a hailstorm that began just as the Romano-Byzantines were advancing.[33] Most likely new tactics may have been developed by this time to counter the savaran and archer-manned battle elephants.

While the Sassanian Empire still had the upper hand by occupying the Byzantine Near East and Egypt, the core of the Byzantine empire remained intact.

First, Heraclius' successes in the Caucasus had undermined the security of the northern flank of the Sassanian empire's quatro system. Also, as much of the spah was dispersed campaigning for so long outside of the empire's frontiers, the quatro system was potentially vulnerable along its western frontiers, especially if the Romano-Byzantines could succeed in neutralizing major forces such as those of Shahrbaraz. In such a scenario, the empire would be vulnerable to attacks from its northern (already weakened and vulnerable) and western sectors. Not only would Ctesiphon be threatened but the Arabs along the southwest could contemplate some type of military action or raids at the very least. As noted previously, the Sassanians lacked a reserve force inside the empire to either bolster weakened sectors of the quatro system or to defend the interior of the empire in case of invasion(s)

Four spahbod system penetrated: the empire attacked on several fronts. (626–628 CE). Shahrbaraz besieged Constantinople in 626 CE, but was unable to overcome the city's powerful defences. Conversely, Heraclius did not risk a set-piece battle against Shahrbaraz's formidable army, opting to use diplomacy instead of military action to persuade Shahrbaraz to not only lift the siege but to withdraw entirely from the war. Heraclius had apparently persuaded Shahrbaraz that Khosrow II was plotting to assassinate him. The impact of the withdrawal of Shahrbaraz's brilliant military leadership and his formidable army was a major military blow against the spah. This became especially critical when the empire soon became besieged by attacks launched from several fronts.

Despite their failure at Constantinople, the Sassanian alliance with the Turkic Avars left a profound impact upon Heraclius. The latter decided to recruit Turkic allies of his own, thus reaching out to the Sassanians' traditional enemy in the northern Caucasus: the Khazars. Reza notes that the Byzantine-Khazar alliance was also joined by China which wished to wrest full control of the Sassanian share of the Silk Route trade.[34] Reza further avers that the Sassanians may possibly have dispatched ambassadors to the eastern Turkic khanates in Central Asia in an endeavour to form a common front against China. According to this thesis, the eastern Turks of Central Asia were already concerned with the rise of Chinese military power. Kut-Ilkhan, the leader of the eastern Turks, apparently took advantage of China's internal difficulties to launch attacks resulting in the capture of Shanxi province in 622 CE followed by a large but inconclusive battle in the fall of 624 CE. In the following year Kut-Ilkhan launched an attack by two armies: one of these was successful but the other was defeated.[35] China's military fortunes greatly improved by 626 CE, with further Turkish offensives having apparently been either contained or repulsed. By 629 CE the Tang dynasty had succeeded in uniting much if not all of China, which further increased Chinese military power vis-à-vis the Turks. There are no records of Chinese armies attacking Iran, but it is possible that the Chinese were achieving military ascendancy over Central Asia's Turks by the late 620s CE.

The spah was now faced with not only the absence of Shahrbaraz, but the impending military alliance of the Romano-Byzantines with the Khazars. With the alliance in place, Heraclius sailed with a revitalized Romano-Byzantine army (most likely trained with Turkic-Khazar assistance; see Karantabias, below) to land along the northwestern shores of the Caucasus. It was here that he was joined with his Khazar allies. By this time, the armies of Shahen and Shahraplakan had already been destroyed. The Byzantine-Khazar alliance sprang into action. The combined Khazar-Byzantine forces were vast, totalling some 120,000 troops. The spah simply did not have the manpower base to quickly raise such a large number of professional troops along the northern front. Attacking along the empire's northern frontier, the Khazars broke through Sassanian defenses into Albania (modern Republic of Azerbaijan), where they reportedly massacred the local Albanian population.[36] The next stage was an attack on Georgia, where the armies of the Khazars and Heraclius would link up. The empire was now paying the price of committing the bulk of its military resources along a single front (the western) for so many years. Now there were too few professional warriors available to enable the high command to fight effectively on several fronts simultaneously. As the Khazar and Romano-Byzantine armies closed in on the Georgian capital, Tbilisi, the spah managed to dispatch a token force of 1,000 savaran knights to Georgia to fight the invaders.[37] Outnumbered virtually 120:1, the savaran contingent was doomed from the start, and could do little to stop the Khazars and Heraclius from linking up in Tbilisi. This was a major blow as the Khazars and Heraclius could now thrust south to conquer Armenia and then cross into northwest Iran to attack Aturpatekan (Azerbaijan).

The Khazar-Byzantine forces now struck into Armenia. Recall that the crack naxarar knights who had fought alongside the savaran knights had now joined the Khazars against their former comrades. The naxarar knights were most likely accompanying the Khazars and played a critical role in convincing the local knights in Armenia to join the Khazars and the Romano-Byzantines against Iran. With the addition of Armenian warriors to the forces of his Khazar allies, Heraclius thrust into northwest Iran's Aturpatekan region. This was a disastrous blow which allowed Heraclius to wheel into northern Mesopotamia. Khosrow dispatched General Razutis to halt Heraclius' advance and the battle was joined at Nineveh in December 627 CE. Hard fighting ensued and Razutis appears to have had the upper hand, at least at the outset. But when Razutis and three of his commanders were slain the Sassanian army was overwhelmed and destroyed, resulting in the deaths of 50,000 savaran knights – a catastrophic strategic blow for the empire. With the loss of Razutis and his forces, Khosrow II now had no armies left to oppose the advance of Heraclius and his allies.[38] As Heraclius advanced towards Ctesiphon, Khosrow II was assassinated in a palace coup, followed by a peace treaty shortly thereafter. The war had certainly ended in Heraclius' favour, but the end result was that both empires had become severely weakened militarily.

Military Reasons for Heraclius' success: adoption of Turkic-Hun military tactics and technology? Karantabias has provided two general reasons as to why the forces of Heraclius were able to militarily prevail after their successive defeats in the first two decades of the war.[39] The first is explained as the Byzantine willingness to adopt Turkic-Hun military equipment, notably the iron stirrup and the 'Hunnic' compound bow as well as its associated 'Mongolian draw', which utilized the thumb for drawing and releasing the arrow. The iron stirrup would have provided the rider with much greater stability, translating into a much more effective missile launch. Increased rider stability in combination with the Hunnic compound bow/Mongolian draw would then have translated into a more powerful missile delivery over longer ranges in comparison with their Sassanian counterparts. The stirrup would not only increase the effectiveness of horse archery but also enhance the effectiveness of the lance charge as well as close-quarters hand-to-hand combat with swords.

Karantabias is essentially correct with respect to the Byzantine adoption of the iron stirrup, compound bow and even the Mongolian draw. The Byzantines had developed an extremely efficient military machine in the Roman tradition and proved open to new military ideas, including those of their neighbours and adversaries. The compound bow was already in use by Justinian's forces against the Sassanians at the Battle of Callinicum (531 CE) (Chapter 9); therefore the use of the Mongolian draw is certainly possible as well. However Karantabias' assertion that this bow and Mongolian draw produced superior archery to that of the Sassanians may be questioned, especially in view of the discussion in Chapter 5. Tests conducted by Karasulas have failed to find that the Sassanian method of the draw (three fingers with index finger pointed) was inferior to the Mongolian draw (propulsion power and missile range). In addition, as noted already in Chapter 5, the Mongolian draw was most likely known to the late Sassanians and the spah may well have used it. Evidence for this is provided by the early post-Sassanian depiction of Pur-e Vahman, who draws his bow in the Mongolian fashion (Hermitage Museum, St. Petersburg, Inv. S-247). In addition (noted already in Chapter 5), following the reforms of the sixth century CE, Sassanian bows acquired more 'Hun'-type features such as shorter ears and longer limbs (in proportion) with possibly wider limbs.[40] Not only can Karantabias's proposal that the Sassanians did not use the Mongolian draw be questioned, the thesis of the Mongolian draw being superior to the Sassanian draw requires further field studies (esp. scientific measurements of missile range and force of impact, etc.). In addition it must be noted that the Sassanian archery inventory was not confined to standard bows; there were other varieties of archery weaponry such as the panjgan and nawak (Chapter 5).

Karantabias' notion that 'Persian conservatism'[41] prevented the adoption of steppe equipment may also be questioned. First, the Sassanians did adopt the lappet suspension system and P-mounts for their swords (Chapter 6). The scabbard-slide or traditional 'broadsword' was a sacred weapon in Iranian military culture (Chapter 15) and, as noted by Lerner, remained as a ceremonial weapon even after the adoption of the steppe system for sword suspension.[42] Why would the Sassanians discard their most sacred weapon in favour of its steppe counterpart but choose to reject other innovations such as the stirrup? In addition, the assertion that the Sassanians failed to adopt the stirrup is simply untenable. First (recalling Chapter 6), a pair of iron stirrups dated to the late Sassanian era or the sixth–seventh centuries CE (neatly fitting into the chronology of the war) has been discovered in Iran's Marlik region (Römisches Germanisches Museum, Mainz, Germany, Inv. 037985 and Inv. 037986). Second, the assertion that 'at Taghe Bostan ... Khosrow II is portrayed in his heavy armour, yet the stirrup is absent ... leads us to assume that ... [the] Sassanid army must not have stirrups' is misleading. First, the feet of the rider (Khosrow II) are not visible as these have been broken off over time; therefore, this statue provides us with no clue as to whether a stirrup had been depicted or not. Second, Herrmann has noted that the hunting scenes at the ingress into the vault where Khosrow II is displayed shows riders' feet depicted in a way consistent with the use of stirrups.[43] In addition, Herrmann has observed that the support situated to the rear of the Taghe Bostan knight's saddle is suggestive of stirrups having been used. Nicolle also reports one of the Sunni Hadiths which cites the Prophet Muhammad's observations of the Persians and the stirrup.[44] Note that the prophet would have made this observation during his lifetime which corresponded to the long Sassano-Byzantine war of 603–628 CE. In summary, Karantabias' thesis of the stirrup being wholly absent in late Sassanian armies may be challenged.

The second reason for Heraclius' success, explains Karantabias, has to do with his implementation of highly effective and rigorous training exercises for the battered Byzantine army at Caesarea Mazaka.[45] This training had three major impacts on the Byzantine military. The first was the transformation of the Byzantine force's defensive doctrine into an offensive one. The second was the aforementioned greater level of integration of Turkic-style military equipment. The third appears to have been the possible adoption and integration of steppe nomad tactics into the Byzantine battle order. The incorporation of significant numbers of Turkic Khazar cavalry into Heraclius' force may have significantly affected, or complemented, Romano-Byzantine military training. Noting that while no direct evidence has yet surfaced, Karantabias has suggested that 'The expertise of the Turkish cavalry may eventually have contributed to the education of the Eastern Roman cavalry ... the training at Caesarea was thus complete with the supplement of troops from the steppes.'[46] The integration of Turkic warfare methods into the Romano-Byzantine military tradition would certainly explain the rise of a wholly different yet devastatingly effective force. Thanks to Turkish military training at Caesarea, Byzantine cavalry were now able to effectively employ tactics such as the feigned retreat and fluid horse archery. It is possible for example, that the Byzantine victory at Nineveh in 627 CE was at least partly due to Heraclius' deployment of the Turkic steppe tactic of luring a major portion of the Sassanian force towards a pre-designated area to then engage in an outflanking manoeuvre.[47] The development of such tactics, thanks to the Khazar Turks, would have greatly enhanced the Romano Byzantine army which already possessed lancers on par with the savaran and a large and excellent infantry force which the Sassanians could never fully match. Classical sources make clear the decisive role of the Turks; Theophanes reports of a very large force of 40,000 Turkic Khazars having entered Heraclius' army.[48]

When Heraclius unleashed this new 'Turkified' force against the spah, he achieved complete tactical surprise. The elite savaran knights were no longer able to dominate the battlefield and the Sassanian generals were equally unable to cope with an enemy that successfully integrated western (Romano-Byzantine) military training with that of the steppes. The spah had primarily fought warriors of the steppe tradition on its non-western frontiers, especially Central Asia. This is demonstrated by the spah's victories in 588 CE and 618–619 CE. Now, in addition to the Byzantine-Turkic forces of Heraclius, the spah faced a massive pincer movement through the Caucasus. The Khazar allies of Heraclius supported him by penetrating the four-spahbod system in the empire's north. As noted previously, the empire simply did not have the military resources to fight a massive two-front war.

Military weaknesses of the Sassanian Empire after the Heraclius-Khosrow Wars

As noted earlier in this chapter, the spah was beset by a number of serious military weaknesses. The impact of the decades-long Khosrow-Heraclius wars resulted in two additional weaknesses which further undermined the ability of the spah to defend the empire against future invasions.

Morale. The long war with Byzantium was most likely one of several critical factors that profoundly undermined the morale and martial spirit of the spah. This state of affairs is well summarized by Mackey who observes that the 'spirit' of the spah had been 'drained off in the futile campaigns against Byzantium'.[49] This would prove especially dangerous if and when a determined enemy force subsequently invaded Iran. Nevertheless, when the Arab invasions commenced in 637 CE, the spah, or what was left of it after the wars with Byzantium, did its best to put up a determined resistance against the invaders, especially at Nahavand in 651 CE.

Professional warriors. Iran remained capable of producing vast stores of weaponry which were duly housed in military depots. The Achilles heel of the spah was now in its complement of professional personnel. The Byzantines too had suffered horrendous losses. Gabriel and Boose provide a sobering analysis of the state of the Byzantine military by noting that their total losses had amounted to 200,000 men.[50] The Sassanians must have lost at least an equal number of warriors, especially during the final stages of the war. Between them, the Sassanians and the Romano-Byzantines may have lost between 400,000 and 500,000 professional warriors. The sheer scale of these losses would be seen perhaps well into the 1860s during the American Civil War in which the Union and Confederacy lost over 600,000 men.

The loss of a large proportion of the empire's veteran warriors affected the spah in two ways. First, these losses would take time to replace, leaving the empire highly vulnerable to an Arab invasion from the southwest. The Sassanians simply did not have the warriors of quality necessary to repel the coming Arab invasions. Second, the loss of such large numbers of veterans meant that many of the new recruits would not receive critical instruction from seasoned veterans in military tactics and codes of professional discipline. While true that the spah still had an intact force of battle elephants as well as crack units such as the Dailamite infantry and savaran units such as the sarhangan, these simply were no longer available in the quantities seen before the Khosrow-Heraclius wars. Time was needed to replenish the ranks with professional troops, re-organize the spah and to re-instill the organization's traditional esprit de corps. Matofi notes that the state of the spah's troops was one of 'widespread chaos, hopelessness, dereliction of duty, lack of discipline'.[51]

The empire was relatively safe from the Byzantine frontier as Constantinople, like Ctesiphon, had yet to recover its full strength as a result of its wars with Persia. The Central Asian frontier appeared relatively calm in large part due to the successful military campaigns of Bahram Chobin and Smbat Bagratuni against the Turks and Huns in 588 and 618–619 respectively. Iran's chronic manpower problem meant that it would take at least a generation for the spah to recover from the terrible devastation of the Khosrow-Heraclius wars. But time was a luxury the empire could ill afford. The Arabs now united under the banner of Islam were well aware of the military weaknesses of both Persia and Byzantium. The second Caliph Omar fully realized that the moment had come for the Arabs to strike at Persia and Byzantium.[52] Put simply, Omar had no intention of taking his time to allow the spah (or the Romano-Byzantines) to recover. The Arabs now invading Iran would be facing a Sassanian military that was a mere shadow of its former self.

The Arabian (southwest) frontier: a new weakness in the four-spahbod system.
Just before his major attacks against the Byzantine Empire, Khosrow II committed a major blunder by removing the Lakhmid king Numan III in 602 CE.[53] He worsened the situation by alienating more local Arabs, notably the Bani Sheiban, who with their allies mobilized to fight the empire. This process was completed by 610 CE, just as Heraclius had come to power. Ctesiphon dispatched a force of 2,000 savaran knights and 3,000 Arab allies to combat the Bani Sheiban-led forces. The two armies met in battle in what is known as the Battle of Dhu Qar (610 CE), and the Arabs emerged victorious. Despite the seriousness of this defeat, Ctesiphon and the high command seemed unconcerned and failed to seriously address the reasons for their defeat at Dhu Qar. While this was most likely due to the spah's preoccupation with the Byzantines, the failure to appreciate the formidable martial skills of the Arabs would cost the empire very dearly less than three decades later.

Khosrow II appears to have contributed in two ways to the empire's downfall. First, he practically dismantled a vital military sector that had been established to guard the critical (southwest sector) of the empire's western portion of the four-spahbod system facing the formidable warriors of Arabia. Compounding the strategic crisis was the derelict state of the Khandaq-Shapur system of ditches which were in desperate need of repairs and rebuilding. But no initiative was to be shown by the high command in this regard. It is thus ironic that the greatest resistance against the impending Arabo-Islamic invasion of the Sassanian Empire was to be offered by various Arab tribes, notably the Bani Hanifah.[54] The Sassanian tendency to under-appreciate Arab martial ardour was especially inept. The Lakhmids were formidable warriors who had proved their mettle beside the savaran (Chapter 9). Other Arab warriors could have supplied the spah with light cavalry, much as the Ghassanids had done for the Romans. Such forces had a greater appreciation and understanding of the style of warfare practised by their Arab cousins invading from Arabia. Had Khosrow II realized the wisdom of his predecessors in continuing to support the Lakhmids (as well as other supportive Arab tribes) and maintained the Khandaq system, the Arabo-Islamic invaders may have experienced much greater difficulties in breaking into Mesopotamia and southwest Iran.

Second, as noted already, Khosrow II's war against Byzantium greatly weakened the military potential of the spah. Instead of agreeing to a favourable peace with Heraclius when the spah was ascendant, Khosrow II opted to eliminate the Byzantine Empire. The final blow which swept away the Sassanian Empire was to come not from the militarily exhausted Romano-Byzantines or the Khazars, but the hardy warriors of Arabia. Soon, the empires of the Sassanians and Byzantines as well as the Turkic warriors of Central Asia and the northern Caucasus would be confronted by the new military power of the Caliphate.

Chapter 17

The Fall of the Spah and the Empire

The Sassanian Empire's war with Byzantium in 602–628 seriously undermined the spah's military strength as well as its four-spahbod defensive system. The military rise and unity of the Arab Bedouin tribes of the Arabian Peninsula was to prove fatal for the Sassanian and Romano-Byzantine Empires. While the two empires were exhausting each other in a war lasting over two decades, the Arabs had in the meantime developed critical military strengths which proved key in their overthrow of the Sassanian empire and the ejection of the Romano-Byzantines from Syria, Palestine, Egypt and even parts of Anatolia.

Overview of Military Reasons for Arab Military Successes against the Sassanian Empire

While it is true that conflict between the Sassanians and the Byzantines proved militarily destructive for both, the notion that this was the only military reason for the Arab successes may be simplistic. Put simply, the Arabs did not simply 'walk in and take over' the Sassanian and Byzantine realms. Donner dubs this interpretation 'the accidental thesis' which is favoured by a number of Western historians. According to Donner, this is the notion that 'the Arabs "found" themselves in possession of vast domains, that as an afterthought, they stitched together into an empire'.[1] The author would concur with Donner that the 'accidental thesis' fails to provide adequate explanations for the military successes of the Arabs against both the Byzantine and Sassanian Empires. Instead of having '"found" themselves in possession of vast domains', the Arabs had to engage in serious and sustained warfare against both of those empires in the course of their conquests, and much research remains to be done with respect to Arab military tactics and capabilities.

Thanks to the work of Western scholars, a more cogent and comprehensive overview is emerging with respect to the forces of the early Arabs, especially on the eve of their invasion of the Sassanian Empire. In general, the topics that need to be addressed with respect to Arab military capabilities at the eve of the conquests are leadership, types of warfare, Arab archery, and logistics.

Arab military leadership. It is notable that despite their close contacts with Sassanian Iran and Byzantium, the Arabs chose not to adopt their strict hierarchical models of military organization. Even more interesting was how Arab-Muslim military leaders were selected. As noted in earlier chapters, military leaders of the spah were selected from the upper nobility. This was not the case with the Arabs. Arab military leaders were often appointed by a process of collegial consultation between members of local communities. What mattered most was military merit, not whether the appointee hailed from a 'low class' or 'upper family'. In fact, social class was of little consequence in the decision-making of the Arabs at this time. While certainly true that the spah did do its best to select officers of the best calibre for upcoming battles, the very nature of Sassanian society (with its clearly defined stratified and hierarchical social structure) undermined the process of selection for the military leadership. The fact that it was (for lack of a better term) a 'sacred rule' that military leaders could only be selected from the nobility severely limited the pool of qualified applicants for the (military) tasks at hand. The Arab communities were more loosely organized, which meant that persons from a wide variety of social classes would have the opportunity to converse collegially as equals in collective decision-making processes, especially with respect to military matters. In Sassanian Persia, the opinions of more 'lowly' persons would be of no consequence in the decision-making processes of the war council, which was essentially composed of a select few of the shahanshah and the empire's elites.

The Arab system of appointing military leaders proved to be a critical advantage against the Byzantines and Sassanians. Military leaders could be selected on the basis of who would be most suitable for a particular campaign. Sometimes, there was also the principle of *tasanud*, whereby multiple persons could be appointed as leaders for the prosecution of a particular campaign. Put simply, the criterion for selection was military acumen. Thus, according to Landau-Tasseron, 'the commander in the field had a measure of autonomy, while at the same time his own authority was not firmly established ... the commanders were not distinguished from the men in the ranks in any way.'[2]

This is an interesting observation as it demonstrates the high tolerance for differences of opinion regarding military strategy. As a result, an attacking force would have the benefit of considering a wide range of military options both before and during the battle. This resulted in greater flexibility of response to fluid battlefield conditions. Also, even if an Arab army suffered a military defeat, the reasons for the setback could be discussed and addressed in a collective and collegial fashion. This would often have the effect of improving military performance and limiting liabilities for future military engagements.

Arab warfare before the conquests. Landau-Tasseron has highlighted five distinct means by which the Arabs acquired valuable military experience prior to their attacks against the Sassanian Empire: caravan looting, raids against rival Arab tribes, attacks on settled communities, frontal encounters and defensive warfare.[3] The first category, caravan looting, was one of the principle means of gaining military experience for Arab warriors, who (for the most part) had had little formal military training. The raiding of caravans not only secured supplies, but was also relatively easy to conduct, especially for persons lacking in military experience. As Meccan caravans were not defended by military escorts, these raids required only small numbers of warriors to prosecute. It was these very same small-scale raids that provided the initial basis of Arab military experience. The Arabs soon refined their tactics by factoring in routes and locales most convenient for their attacks. The importance of raiding tactics is highlighted by the fact that the Battle of Badr was essentially, at first, a caravan raid.

The second category, raids against rival Arab tribes, was also an important arena for military experience. Prior to the Muslim conquest of Mecca in 630 CE, it is generally known that the Bedouins intended to strike at Medina. This was apparently aborted by a 'pre-emptive' strike by the Muslims. In general however, raids against the Bedouins involved small parties and quick raids against Bedouin camps for the purpose of capturing booty, livestock, etc. In practice this type of warfare entailed hit-and-run raids and the avoidance of pitched battles. When engagements did occur, they typically took the form of skirmishes. These raids also helped the Muslims to secure control over roads and select territories.

The third category, attacks against settled communities, was often accomplished successfully by the early Muslim Arabs. This is remarkable given the relatively limited amount of resources they had available to them. In the conquest of Mecca for example, the Prophet Mohammad is reputed to have mobilized 10,000 troops. Arab towns that had submitted to the Muslims would then provide new recruits for the growing Muslim military force. In the case of subjugated Jewish towns, the Muslims acquired large stores of weaponry as well as immense wealth that far surpassed anything that could be acquired through raids against caravans or the Bedouins. Thus, in summary, the Muslims expanded their economic, political and territorial foundations and increased their armaments as well. On the other hand, the relative ease with which they acquired the settled areas of Arabia meant that the Muslims had yet to learn about the conduct of siege warfare. This certainly posed challenges during the Arab conquests of the Byzantine and Sassanian Empires but did not hinder the expansion of the caliphate. The capital of the Sassanian Empire, Ctesiphon, did fall to the Arabs (see below) but Constantinople evaded capture.

Frontal encounters (fourth category) were relatively few, but the Muslim Arabs were to learn a great deal from such engagements. In general, major frontal encounters are recorded as having taken place at Badr, Uhud, Mu'ta and Hunayn. The Muslim Arabs actually won two of these battles (Badr and Hunayn). The success at Badr may have been partly due to the lack of organization and overall confusion of the Quraysh tribe. At Mu'ta, the Muslims suffered a severe defeat, but the presence of Byzantine troops in that battle enabled the Arabs to experience Byzantine fighting methods and tactics first hand. Uhud was also a defeat for the Muslims, believed to be the result of fighters who abandoned their posts and archers who had chosen to focus their efforts on acquiring booty. This defeat taught the Muslims several valuable lessons, namely the need for military discipline and organization, and for better coordination between commanders and troops. In the battle of Hunayn, the Muslims were better armed and more confident in their military capabilities. The battle was hard fought, but resulted in a Muslim victory. What is significant is that in victory or defeat, Muslim armies would emerge more formidable than before. The Muslims would in each instance examine the reasons for their successes and shortcomings. This is one factor which probably led to their rapid rise as a highly fluid yet formidable fighting force.

The fifth category, defensive warfare, was already known to the Muslim Arabs. The prophet Mohammed accepted the advice of Roozbeh son of Marzban (who became Salman the Persian after his conversion to Islam) to use the Sassanian tactic of khandaq military ditches to defend Medina against Meccan attackers. Then, the Muslims, like the Sassanian spah, could fire arrows at their attackers from the safety of the khandaq. So at least in this sense, the Arabs had already adopted one of the spah's methods of warfare prior to their invasion of the Sassanian Empire. This raises the role of non-Arab influences in the evolution of early Arabo-Islamic armies. It is known that anti-Sassanian Iranians had moved to Arabia and adopted Islam; the most famous of these was the aforementioned Salman, who was clearly cognizant of sophisticated Sassanian military tactics. The military role of Roozbeh or Salman in Arab service was especially significant. Zakeri has outlined Salman as having been from the elite dehkan (or marzban) aristocracies of Iran as well as having served as a member of the savaran.[4]

As will be seen later in this chapter and in the following one, the arrival of large numbers of Sassanian warriors had a profound impact not only upon the early Islamic armies but also the later armies of the Abbasid Caliphate. The role of former Romano-Byzantine troops fighting within the ranks of the early Arabo-Islamic armies is also significant.

Arab Archery: The Jandora Hypothesis. Jandora has written a very seminal critique of early Arab archery. Jandora challenges the common narrative of the sources that the Arabs defeated stronger foes such as the Sassanians and Romano-Byzantines with modest resources, noting that the authors of such accounts wrote 'salvation history, not military history'.[5] Jandora suggests that 'early battlefield successes [of the Arabs] should be attributed to the employment of foot archers in tight formations[6] ... [the] mainstay of the early Islamic battle-array was a close order formation of foot-soldiers, most of whom employed bow and arrows'.[7]

To bolster his hypothesis, Jandora refers to rock reliefs in Oman and Yemen which depict Arabs using the bow.[8] Numerous archival sources provide further support. For example, the Hadith quotes in the *Jihad* and *Maqhazi* sections in al-Bukhari's *Jamih al-Salih* make references to the key role played by Arab archery. One of these, the *Jihad*, refers to the Battle of Badr (624 CE) where the Prophet Mohammed commanded the Muslims: 'When they close on you, [strike] at them arrows.'[9] The *Maqhazi* offers a variation of this by stating that the prophet commanded 'shoot at them, but use your arrows sparingly'.[10] Jandora makes four interesting references to the importance of archery in the early Muslim battles in Arabia. The first is Saad bin Waqqas' firing of missiles at Thaniyat al-Murra, which is cited as the first case of a Muslim archer firing at the enemy. It is notable that Waqqas, who defeated the Sassanian military at Qadissiyah (see below), was renowned for his excellence in archery. The second is that of Hamza's campaign along the Arabian coast where he and the Muslim forces stood a bowshot apart from their enemies. The third is that of the warriors of al-Qara, who were recognized as excellent archers. Fourth is Al-Masoudi's reference to the Arabs having adopted archery from the Nubians.

Al-Tabari's reference to the Arab formations is of special interest, as this refers to ten-man units or the *irafa* at the time of the Prophet Mohammed.[11] References do exist to the *rajjala-rumah* (infantry vice archers) which may suggest the lack of a clear distinction between archers and infantry in early Islamic armies.[12] This attests to the flexible nature of early Islamic armies. Other sources cite these archery/infantry units as being grouped in multiples of seven (i.e. 70, 700, 7,000).

By the time the Arabs were invading Iran from the mid-630s CE, their armies appear to have adopted a highly flexible yet devastatingly effective battle formation. While cavalry formations did exist with the tough Bedouin foot soldiers being especially formidable in close-quarter combat, it was their archery that may have been the key to victory over the late Sassanian armies. The Arabs demonstrated the devastating effectiveness of their archery at the Battle of Qadissiyah (see below). Nicolle notes that during this battle the Arabs were shooting large arrows which the Sassanians initially derided as 'spindles'.[13] This attitude changed as the battle progressed. Nicolle further cites a Sassanian warrior who survived Qadissiyah and reported:[14] 'These spindles continued to shower upon us until we were overwhelmed. Our archer would send an arrow from his Nawak bow but it would merely attach itself to an Arab's clothes whereas their arrows would rend the mail hauberk and mail cuirass we had on.'

This passage is indicative of the power of Arab archery: they had powerful bows, launching methods and missiles capable of penetrating Sassanian and Romano-Byzantine armour. It is also of interest as to why the same nawak bow (Chapter 5), which was effective against the Turkic warriors and Romano-Byzantines, failed against the Arabs at Qadissiyah. The answer may partly lie in Arab clothing as described by the Sassanian veteran, but as to what type of garments these were and how they minimized the effectiveness of the nawak is open to speculation. Perhaps some of the Arabs were wearing some type of armour underneath their garments, but many of the Arabs still lacked heavy armour at this time. It is clear that the Arabs had found a method to cope with the Sassanian ability to rapidly launch large volumes of missiles during battles.

Arab battle formations. Jandora has proposed the following configuration for early pre-Islamic battle formations known as the irafa:[15] (1) these were formed in tandem files of five men each (note: their orientation perpendicular to front of formation); (2) men of each file in the first position (collectively) form the first rank of the battle line, with men of each file in the second position (collectively) forming the second rank of the battle line – all the way to the men of the fifth position; (3) the majority of foot soldiers in the irafa would have carried bows; (4) the first (and possibly second) rank (or position) troops were probably equipped with sword, spear and some type of body armour; (4) frontline troops may have had some type of 'wall' placed for protection; and (5) the troops in the fifth or last rank probably carried more weapons. This thesis helps explain how the forward ranks of the irafa were able to withstand attacks by cavalry and infantry. Frontline irafa were equipped for hand-to-hand combat in case the enemy attempted to close in; therefore these troops probably were also equipped with large shields. This irafa system was to become more streamlined, specialized and devastatingly effective by the Battle of Qadissiyah.

Supplies and logistics. In general, the ability of Muslim armies to consistently provide food and weapons for their troops campaigning outside of Arabia had yet to be developed. This was mainly due to the Arabs' lack of generational experience with logistics during military campaigns. In the early years of Islam in Arabia, it was generally the warrior's responsibility to arrange for his own food supplies, although wealthier Muslims would make donations for the greater cause. Arab warriors could also engage in the hunt to secure food. Such measures proved sufficient at compensating for the lack of an organized logistics system typical of the armies of the Romano-Byzantines and the Sassanians. In short, the lack of a centralized system for food supplies meant that early Muslim raiders in Arabia would often resort to sharing food, and could even go hungry during campaigns. Nevertheless, by the time of Caliph Omar (r.634–644) attempts had been made to centralize the organization and distribution of food supplies for troops. The commander of Arab troops in Egypt in 634 CE, for example, made efforts to organize food supplies. Interestingly, local Egyptians would provide food supplies to the Arabs as payment of taxes. In Iran, such arrangements may not have always been possible, given the hostility of the resident population against being forcibly incorporated into the caliphate. By the time of the Ummayads (661–750 CE) food storage depots for military use had been created. By the eleventh century CE, the Abbasid Caliphate's (750–1258 CE) military commanders were expected to plan for the provision of supplies for their troops and animals (i.e. horses, mules). The diet of Arab troops invading the Byzantine and Sassanian Empires was often dates and barley gruel, with meats and breads prepared en-route.

The question of the armaments of Muslim warriors remains complex, given the multiplicity of accounts from the sources. One key question is how much of captured enemy weaponry and armour would be immediately distributed among the troops. It is possible that the question of whether or not a warrior was entitled to the enemy's captured war spoils such as mail, swords, lances, etc., was at the discretion of the supreme leader. If this were the case, then this raises the possibility that there were storage facilities for the keeping of such captured weapons, at least during the lifetime of the Prophet Mohammad. Nevertheless, no firm guideline can be established for the provision of weapons to early Muslim warriors, especially at the eve of the invasions of the Sassanian Empire and Byzantium. Reports vary, with suggestions that some warriors received their weaponry through private donations and/or that warriors were responsible for the provision of their own weapons, meaning that they had to privately purchase the equipment themselves. Conversely, there are also reports that the Caliph Abu Bakr (r. 632–634 CE) used public funds to purchase weapons and horses for Muslim warriors. Prior to his death the Caliph Omar had instituted a plan to pay each Muslim warrior 4,000 dirhams, which would be spent as follows: 1,000 for weapons, 1,000 for supplies, 1,000 for family expenses and the remaining 1,000 for 'such and so'.[16] Although the plan was clearly proposed at the height of the Arab invasion of Iran, it was not implemented after Omar's passing. Despite this, Omar's plan makes clear that the caliphate was cognizant of the need for the regularization of the system of supplies, weapon distribution and rationalization of payments for regular troops. On balance it would appear that by the time the conquest of Iran was in its later stages (c. late 640s CE), Muslim warriors were probably equipped with weapons in a combination of personal procurements as well as organized distribution. Clear cases of the latter are demonstrated during the battles of the Arabs in Transoxiana where local Iranian aristocracies and the Turks resisted the caliphate. In one case, the commander of Arab forces in theatre, Qutayba ibn Muslim, obtained permission from his superior, the governor al-Hajjaj, to distribute weapons from Persian (or former Sassanian) armouries. Another case of organized delivery of weapons occurs in 730 CE when the Caliph Hisham dispatched 30,000 coats of mail and 30,000 lances for warriors fighting in Central Asia. It would appear that by this time the caliphate was storing much of its weaponry in the *bayt al-mal* (state treasury). Mosques could also be used for the temporary storage of weapons.

Command, coordination and control during the conquest of Iran. One key issue that requires investigation is the question of command, coordination and control by the caliphate over its forces engaged in the full-scale invasion of the Sassanian Empire in 637–651 CE. Donner has attributed the Arab successes to the centralized coordination of the various war parties fighting on several fronts, especially with respect to tactics, communications and logistics.[17] The aforementioned 'accidental thesis' for Arab successes fails to address the following questions: (1) if the advances were conducted by scattered war parties strategically unconnected to each other and bereft of centralized command, then how did the Arabs succeed in penetrating not just the Syrian and Iraqi fringes to the north of the Arabian deserts, but deep into the Sassanian and Byzantine Empires? (2) if the caliphate had been formed by scattered war parties, then why would those same parties not engage in civil wars and disputes as the caliphate rose as an empire upon the ashes of the Sassanian Empire and the Byzantine holdings in the Near East and Egypt? These successes in empire building are more likely explained by Arab cooperation and coordination rather than uncoordinated divergence.

The First Arab Raids and the Battle of the Bridges (633–634)

Sassanian military weaknesses had been duly noted by Caliph Omar. The heavy losses to the professional core of the spah, the dismantling of the Lakhmids, and the deteriorated state of the Khandaq Shapur meant that the Arabo-Islamics could conduct attacks and raids into southern Mesopotamia, thus easily penetrating the empire from the southwest. The Arabs grew increasingly confident, prompting Omar to dispatch a force of 6,000 warriors led by Abu Ubeidah to cross the Euphrates. Omar may have been intending to force the militarily diminished

Sassanians into a major military showdown. Abu Ubeidah and his forces arrived at the western side of the Euphrates by November 634. Sassanian general Bahram arrived with a force of 4,000 savaran knights supported by battle elephants and archers. Interestingly, the Sassanian force had arrived with the national Kaveh standard (Drafsh-e Kaviani), an indication of how seriously the empire now viewed the Arab threat.

Bahram did not initiate any major offensives. In contrast, Abu Ubeidah hastily crossed the Euphrates with his forces, indicative that the Arabs were now highly confident of being able to destroy any Sassanian forces they encountered. Bahram, however, was waiting for them. He first unleashed a combined armoured elephant and savaran lance charge against Abu Ubeidah. The Arabs were overpowered, partly because Bahram attacked quickly, not allowing them to organize their forces once they had landed on the Sassanian side of the Euphrates. The elephants also featured archery cabs which in conjunction with Bahram's foot archers wreaked havoc in the Arab ranks. Bahram continued to pummel the Arab force, with one account stating that Abu Ubeidah was trampled under an elephant.[18] The battered Arab force was now cut down on the eastern side of the Euphrates with its survivors forced to flee back to the western side of the river. Donner cites Arab losses at 3,000 (1,000 killed in battle and 2,000 by drowning); some 3,000 survivors retreated.[19] The Arab defeat at the Battle of the Bridges clearly demonstrated that Arab cavalry and infantry could not stand up to the savaran in open battle characterized by fluid movements.[20] The harsh lessons of this defeat were absorbed by the Arab commanders, who soon demonstrated that they were indeed splendid warriors. The Battle of the Bridges would be the last major set-piece battle in which the spah emerged victorious.[21]

Battle of Qadissiyah (637 CE)

The Caliph Omar bin al-Khattab (r. 634–644 CE) had ordered reinforcements and supplies to be sent to the Arab commander Saad bin Ebi Waqqas, who was famed as 'The Archer of Islam'. Waqqas was invading Sassanian Mesopotamia or modern-day Iraq. After the Arab victory in the Battle of Yarmuk against the Romano-Byzantines in Syria in 636 CE[22] Omar shifted his main military efforts towards Iran. The objective was the complete conquest of the Sassanian Persian Empire.

Numerical factors. General Rustam Farrokhzad was in overall command of Sassanian forces in Mesopotamia. He crossed the Euphrates with an army composed of Dailamites, surviving veterans of the Khosrow-Heraclius wars and raw recruits untested as yet in battle. Rustam and his forces arrived at a site near Kufa known as Qadissiyah where the Arabs and their commander Waqqas had encamped.[23] While the numerical difference between the two sides is more difficult to ascertain,[24] it is generally agreed that the Arabs were outnumbered three to one by the Sassanians. Balazi, however reports of just 10,000 Arab troops against Tabari's citation of 120,000 Sassanian troops (including 13,000 noble-men).[25] Sassanian forces also included at least thirty battle elephants.[26]

The spah before the battle. The two armies faced each other for four months as Rustam sent emissaries to the Arab camp in search of a peaceful resolution. Attempts at negotiation failed as Waqqas had no desire to vacate Sassanian territory and sought the complete subjugation of all of Persia, obliging Rustam to make preparations for the inevitable battle. The ensuing four-day battle is known as the Battle of Qadissiyah.[27]

The Arabo-Islamic preparations. Waqqas had organized his forces into six sections[28] and had evidently devised an excellent strategy of defence and offence. To avoid being outflanked by the dangerous savaran in the open terrain, Waqqas placed his Arab fighters in an excellent defensive position. The Arabs were based in a patch of land that was virtually impervious to flanking as it was protected by a river to its front, swampland to its right, a trench to its rear, and to the left a lake and the Atik canal. Rustam was thus prevented from engaging in flanking manoeuvres against the Arabs. He would be forced to attack frontally by crossing the Atik canal. It would appear that Waqqas had also ensured that his warriors would be anchored to a defensive structure known as the Fort of Qudays. From what can be surmised, Qudays featured a tower and was surrounded by a 30m wall on each of its sides.[29] With Waqqas' fighters ensconced in the tower, the Arab flanks could be effectively defended, especially if these were in danger of caving-in to Rustam's forces during the upcoming battle. Rustam apparently intended to neutralize the tower of Qudays, which helps explain his subsequent deployment of battle elephants for this task.[30]

Waqqas also established a very effective line of defence with his foot soldiers, which were now divided into distinct close-quarter combat infantry and archery formations. The infantry and the archers were to be known in later Muslim citations as the *muqatila* and *muramiya* corps respectively.

First day of battle. Rustam opened the first day of the battle[31] with a powerful charge of the savaran knights attacking in concert with the battle elephants. The Arabs, though at first shaken by Rustam's attack, held their ground and overcame the Sassanian battle elephants. This was mainly due to their ability to overpower the infantry escorting the battle elephants. The Arabs then tore the girths of the elephants, resulting in their archery cabs tumbling onto the ground. Surviving Sassanian archers were then slain by the Arabs. Sassanian knights were successfully prevented from supporting the elephant corps, mainly due to massive firings of missiles. These proved instrumental in blunting the coordinated strikes off the Sassanian cavalry. This allowed the nimble Arab infantry to close in on the disorganized ranks of the savaran and overcome the knights in close-quarters combat. Waqqas had also successfully negated the effects of the Persian archers, most likely by rushing at them from multiple directions and then overcoming them in close-quarter combat. Facing certain defeat, Rustam then pulled back his troops to regroup, thus ending the first day of battle.

Second day of battle. The second day of the battle[32] began with Rustam sending in his best warriors to challenge the Arabs in one-to-one duels. Rustam's decision was unsound as the empire's best warriors (savaran knights and Dailamite infantry) had mostly been killed or disabled during the Khosrow-Heraclius wars. The warriors chosen were certainly motivated to fight for their homeland against a tenacious invader, but the end result was the Arabs winning all of the duels. Rustam had miscalculated the religious fervour of the Arabs fighting for what they believed to be a divine cause. Rustam had also evidently underestimated the fighting prowess of the tough Bedouin warriors. The defeat of the Sassanian champions damaged Sassanian morale, which would help explain why the Arabs won the ensuing clash, obliging Rustam to once again withdraw his forces, thus ending the second day of battle.

Third day of battle. The third day of the battle opened with Waqqas making a determined push to destroy the savaran, the elephant corps and the remainder of Rustam's forces. Waqqas now held two distinct advantages. First, his army had been joined by ex-Byzantine infantry trained to disable Sassanian elephants by hurling javelins into their eyes. Second, Sassanian deserters had entered his camp to inform him of Rustam's planned tactics, weaknesses and strengths. Facing the prospect of total defeat, Rustam again withdrew his forces and retired across the Atik Canal. Waqqas held the field but had yet to destroy the Sassanian army before the Arabs could storm Ctesiphon. Waqqas, however, was unwilling to give Rustam the opportunity to rest and re-organize his forces. This led to the launching of a number of commando-style raids against Sassanian forces across the Atik Canal in a bid to goad them to launch a general attack against Waqqas' camp.

Final day of battle. The next (fourth) day witnessed a powerful and successful attack by Rustam's forces across the Atik Canal. This time the savaran held the upper hand, perhaps having learned to adapt to the fluidity of Arab tactics on the battlefield. The Savaran (and Rustam's forces in general) had probably abandoned the elephant-infantry battle group doctrine in favour of looser Cossack-style cavalry tactics of harassment and hit-and-run attacks. Rustam's forces had also successfully used caltrops to disrupt Arab attacks during the Qadissiyah battles but these had failed to turn the tide in his favour. A second possibility is that Rustam had finally found a way to prevent the Arabs from closing into his lines, thus preventing them from engaging in close-quarters combat. Cossack-style tactics for example, may have been able to disrupt Arab frontal attacks. This would partly explain why the Arabs failed to overcome Rustam's elephants at this juncture of the battle. With their elephants protected by infantry, Sassanian archers riding in the elevated platforms on the animals would be able to fire their deadly missiles into the Arab ranks. Waqqas' forces began to be pushed back by the Sassanians. Sassanian infantry archers also held the upper hand at this stage, wreaking havoc in the Arab ranks. By noon the battle was nearly won by the Sassanians. However, just as Rustam was about to deliver his final blow to crush Waqqas and the Arabs, a violent sandstorm broke out, blowing large volumes of sand into the faces of Sassanian troops. This resulted in the loss of cohesion among the Dailamites, savaran, elephant corps, archers and other Sassanian troops. A gap then developed in one of Rustam's wings commanded by General Hormuzd. Waqqas quickly seized on this opportunity and rushed his remaining forces into the gap. Waqqas' strike was so successful that he tore right into the command centre of the Sassanian army. Rustam was then killed by one of the Arab warriors known as Hillal who reputedly shouted 'By the lord of Kaaba, I have slain Rustam.' Surviving elite units (archers, savaran, Dailamites, etc.) fought hard to defend Iran's primary standard, the Drafshe Kaviani, but despite their best efforts the Arabs captured it. Mention must also be made of military exploits of the Arranian/Albanian Mehranid king, Javanshir, who fought alongside the Sassanian army with his Albanian cavalry. Armenian historians Sebeos and Moses of Dasxuranci's tenth century CE text, *History of the Albanians*, also report of the battlefield exploits of the *sparapet* (Armenian: marshal) of Albania during the Battle of Qadissiyah.[33]

The destruction of Rustam's forces meant that the entire Sassanian military position in southern Mesopotamia had collapsed.[34] According to Masoudi, the Sassanians had lost up to 40,000 killed,[35] which would mean the loss of at least one-third of the Sassanian force. These would have undoubtedly included a high proportion of professional troops. Actual losses, however, were much higher as unspecified numbers of troops had suffered mortal injuries. In addition, numbers of Sassanian troops had chosen to join the Arabs. Up to 4,000 first-rate Dailamite troops who had served with the armies of Khosrow II switched their allegiance to Waqqas. These troops[36] along with other defecting savaran troops[37] would prove highly effective in supporting the Arabs in conquering Iran. Dailamite troops, for example, were to greatly assist the Arabs in later capturing Ctesiphon and in the upcoming battles of Jalula and Nahavand.[38] The Arabs in turn rewarded these ex-Sassanian troops with greater pay than regular Arab troops.[39]

Fall of Ctesiphon (638 CE)

The Arab victory at Qadissiyah had taken a heavy toll on the caliphate's forces, perhaps up to one third of the entire Arab force.[40] This led to a suspension of Arab operations for almost a year. The Sassanians, however, failed to utilize this time for building up their forces for a major attack to expel the Arabs from Sassanian territory. As events soon demonstrated, the Sassanians had also failed to devise a coherent strategy for defending against Arab thrusts into northern Mesopotamia. By 638 the Arabs had resumed their advance towards Ctesiphon with no Sassanian forces to oppose them. Yazdegird III and his generals mustered the remaining Sassanian forces in the aftermath of Qadissiyah for the defence of the capital. Saad, the Arab commander, who was advancing with 15,000 troops, easily occupied key centres along the route to Ctesiphon, namely Najaf and then Burs. The small Sassanian force at Burs was defeated, obliging it to retreat to Babylon. The Arabs pursued them, crossing the Euphrates and placing Babylon under siege. The local Sassanian commanders (Firoozan (a veteran of Qadissiyah), Mehran, Nakhirzan and Hormuzan) failed to combine their efforts against the Arabs. General Hormuzan pulled his forces back to his home city of Ahvaz in

Khuzestan with Mehran, while Firoozan and Nakhirzan withdrew their respective forces to the north. This led to the easy capture of Babylon by the Arabs. They then pursued and defeated a Sassanian rear guard at Sura. The remnants of that force fled to Deir Kab to join the local Sassanian garrison there but this combined force was also defeated by the Arabs. The last Sassanian force to oppose the Arabs before Ctesiphon was at Kusa, approximately 20km from Ctesiphon. This force was defeated with its local commander Shahyar killed in a duel against an Arab challenger.[41]

Yazdegird had decided to retreat from Ctesiphon to prepare for his last stand in the mountains of Kurdistan and Azerbaijan in Iran's northwest. This decision may have been tactically inept as Ctesiphon was a formidable city with powerful defences.[42] Yazdegird had already stationed numbers of the survivors of the battle of Qadissiyah to support local citizens at Ctesiphon, but they ultimately failed to prevent the Arabs from capturing the city. Had Yazdegird managed to spare more troops for the city's defence, more time could have been bought for the Sassanian military to organize and strengthen its defences in the north and east. If Ctesiphon's garrison had held out against the Arabs, the Sassanian military could have regained enough strength to return to the city to defeat the Arab siege. The Arabs would have already exhausted much of their military resources to take the city. The Sassanian military was very proficient in withstanding sieges, a mode of warfare in which the Arabs lacked proficiency at the time. In practice, the burden of Ctesiphon's defence fell upon local citizens who held off the Arabs for over a year.

Ctesiphon was actually a metropolis composed of districts (or sub-cities) situated on both banks of the Tigris River. Darzejan, Seleucia, Mahroze, Sabat and Veh-Ardashir were situated on the west bank with Astanbar and Ctesiphon on the left bank. The Arabs first reduced (most but not all of) the western bank and then focused their attentions upon the eastern bank. Ctesiphon's defenders had already destroyed the bridge connecting the western and eastern banks of the metropolis. This allowed the citizens to hold off the Arabs, but the situation changed when the Arabs built a bridge of their own. By this time, numbers of anti-Persian Babylonians had joined the Arabs to provide them with critical engineering support (i.e. building bridges, etc.). The building of the bridge allowed the Arabs to finally attack Ctesiphon directly. Local citizens with a handful of Sassanian troops led by General Khorrazad (brother of the late Rustam of Qadissiyah) refused to surrender. They made effective use of catapults and ballistae with a detachment of Sassanian cavalry fighting to prevent the Arabs from crossing the Tigris. The Arabs defeated all of these efforts to finally break into Ctesiphon. The remaining citizen fighters and Sassanian detachments made their desperate last stand at Veh-Ardashir, but their cause was doomed. The battle for Ctesiphon was finally over.

As the Arabs stormed Ctesiphon they engaged in much looting and destruction. So great was the looting of Ctesiphon that every Arab soldier appropriated 12,000 dirhams worth of goods from the metropolis[43] (approx. US$250,000 in modern currency). Nearly 40,000 Sassanian noblewomen were captured and taken to Arabia to then be sold as slaves. The Arabs also captured key symbols of ancient Persia's splendour, namely the ceremonial swords of Khosrow II, Bahram Gur and Kavad.[44] The Arabs also captured the crown jewels and royal garments of Khosrow II and even the sword of Heraclius, captured earlier by the Sassanians.[45] The gigantic 'Royal Carpet of Persia' measuring 30×30m and woven with rare jewels,[46] gold, and silver[47] was sent to Omar in Medina who tore the carpet into pieces for distribution to local citizens.[48] Newark has provided a summary of the actions of the victorious Arabs at Ctesiphon.[49] In one case for example, the Arabs tore up priceless carpets studded with jewels and shared them among each other.[50] The very royal standard of the Iranian realm, the Standard of Kaveh, was also sent to Arabia; this was sold for 30,000 dirhams[51] (approx. US$600,000 in modern currency). Omar was to receive one-fifth of all goods looted from Ctesiphon. Persia's ancient learning traditions were also targeted for destruction, with the Arabs destroying stores of books and libraries under the pretext of religion.[52] Mackey has noted that the Arabs also vandalized the surviving structures of Persepolis, the ceremonial capital of the ancient Achaemenid dynasty.[53] The spah's failure to address its weaknesses and its heavy losses during the wars with Byzantium in 603–628 CE had resulted in serious military weaknesses that allowed the Arabs to conquer Iran. As noted by Litvinsky, Jalilov and Kolesnikov, 'The Arab conquests ... [were] responsible for many deaths and destroyed urban life. As a result of military action and fierce battles, irrigation systems ... fell into ruin ... works of calligraphy, architecture and art were destroyed.'[54]

Battle of Jalula

The fall and sack of Ctesiphon came as a profound shock to the empire, resulting in further demoralization among the military leadership, nobles and regular populace. Despite the magnitude of this disaster, Yazdegird made every effort to revive the beaten Sassanian spah to resist the Arabs. These efforts resulted in the assembly of 120,000 troops led by General Mehran at a site near modern-day Jalula or Holwan. This force was confronted by an Arab force led by al-Hashem. The Arab forces were reputedly just one-tenth the size of Sassanian forces, or 12,000 men. Of these at least 4,000 would have been non-Arab Iranian Dailamite troops who had already defected to the Arabs at Ctesiphon. Whether the actual Sassanian-to-Arab ratio was 10-to-1 is difficult to ascertain as the figures may be equally representative of the facts or contemporary propaganda. Sassanian numerical superiority, however, is possible as Yazdegird was mostly drawing upon a population base of peasants and farmers. While large numbers of these could be mobilized, these men often lacked training and military discipline. By this time Iran had lost much of its professional military base as a result of the Khosrow-Heraclius wars and more recent losses and defections to the Arab invaders. Iran's remaining savaran elite cavalry and Dailamite infantry worked hard to instill a professional esprit de corps, however time was too short to wield these raw recruits into a cohesive military force. Yazdegird's army was inferior to its predecessors with respect to training, weapons, leadership and tactical acumen.

Nevertheless, these same raw recruits were to more than make up in nationalistic ardour for what they lacked in professional military training.

Mehran opted for a static defence strategy, acutely aware of the deficiency of his forces in rapid movement and manoeuvre. A large ditch filled with deadly iron spikes was dug in front of the Sassanian forces (Chapter 14). This practically negated any possibility of a frontal assault by Arab camel and cavalry forces. By this time former Sassanian savaran warriors were most likely fighting within the Arab ranks. Mehran's static defence kept al-Hashem at bay for at least eight months. The stalemate was then broken by an ingenious stratagem whereby an Arab cavalry force led by Amro Bin M'aadi Karab succeeded in luring the Sassanians away from their defensive positions. This now left the highly motivated but militarily raw Sassanian troops exposed to the deadly and nimble assaults of Arab cavalry, camel and infantry attacks. The latter (infantry) were led by Tolohiya Bin Khoyaled, whose contingents most likely included the now pro-Arab Dailamites who had defected earlier to the Arabs. Nevertheless the Iranians fought with bitter determination. Matofi notes of the battle that 'all arrows were exhausted, all spears broken and fighting by swords proceeded. The swords also broke or were damaged ... then iron maces were used.'[55] Hashem's forces appear to have had the advice of former Sassanian savaran and Dailamite contingents as the Arabs knew where to strike fatally against the Sassanian forces.

As the tide of the battle swung in Hashem's favour, the remnants of Yazdegird's forces attempted to flee towards the sanctuary of their defensive positions to their rear. The retreat of the Sassanian infantry and cavalry resulted in a disorderly flight leading them into the deadly traps (especially iron spikes) originally intended for use against attacking Arab forces.[56] According to Tabari, the Arabs pursued and slew 100,000 fleeing Sassanians.[57] The end result was yet another major military defeat for the Sassanians, leading to the Arab capture of much booty as well as the wives and children of slain Sassanian warriors.[58] General Mehran was pursued by the Arabs and finally killed at Khaneqin[59] (in modern Iraqi Kurdistan). Further Arab advances were temporarily halted due to disputes among them regarding shares of captured spoils (i.e. estates, jewelry, etc.).[60]

Yazdegird evaded capture and reached Rayy (near modern Tehran), which became the new Sassanian capital. During this time Yazdegird had ordered General Khosrowshonum to hold the fortress city of Holwan at all costs.[61] Holwan was critical as it commanded a key ingress route from those lands east of the Tigris projecting into the Iranian plateau. The Arabs, however, also captured Holwan, which was yet another critical blow against the battered Sassanian Empire. The Arabs now punched through to the major Sassanian base of Mahrod, where the local cavalry force surrendered to Hashem without offering any resistance.[62]

Fall of Southern Iran
As Yazdegird retired to Rayy after the defeat at Jalula, a portion of the battered remnants of the Sassanian spah were deployed into Khuzestan and Persis in south and southwest Iran.[63] The efforts of the Sassanian military failed in Khuzestan as

the Arabs captured the city of Ahwaz.[64] This allowed the Arabs to break into the heartland of Persis, which was already being menaced by the Arabs in the Persian Gulf who had landed on Bahrain Island. Bahrain was soon used by the Arabs as a naval base to land more troops into Persis.[65] The Arabs then engaged in a major battle in Persis (known as the Battle of Tavoos) which led to the capture of the city of Istakhr.[66] The battle for Persis, however, was far from over with General Shahrak rallying the remnants of Sassanian forces and local citizens to resist the Arabs. Despite these efforts the Arabs continued to prevail.[67] The Sassanian strongholds at Shushtar, Tustar, Ramhormuz, and Manadir were all captured by the Arabs.[68] Ramhormuz and Manadir had been quickly captured but Shushtar and Tustar had bitterly contested the Arab invaders.[69] Shushtar had been a key military base for not only the defence of Persis, but all of southern Persia. Hormuzan (military commander of Sassanian forces in the empire's southwest) had established his headquarters at Shushtar, which had become the empire's last base for defending Persis and Khuzestan.

Abu-Moussa, the Arab commander, had reached the environs of Shushtar, prompting Hormuzan to deploy his forces outside of the city to face the Arabs. Hormuzan, however, was defeated, losing 1,000 dead and 600 prisoners who were all executed. Hormuzan and his few remaining troops retreated back into the city to prepare for Abu-Moussa's siege. Hormuzan's defence, however, was soon undermined by treachery. One of the city's nobles had organized a small fifth column to support the Arab onslaughts. The conspirators slew the sentries and opened the gates of Shushtar and surrendered it to Abu-Moussa. Refusing to surrender, Hormuzan and his remaining troops retreated into the city's citadel for the final battle. In the end it was the exhaustion of supplies which forced Hormuzan and his soldiers to ask Abu-Moussa for peace terms.[70] The fall of Shushtar then allowed the Arabs to fan out across the remainder of Persis and Khuzestan, where they continued to encounter stiff resistance.

Battle of Nahavand (651 CE)
Following the string of military disasters and loss of Mesopotamia and southern Iran to the Arabs, Yazdegird and the Sassanian leadership had worked hard to rebuild the crumbling Sassanian military machine. Despite the catastrophic military losses since the 620s, Yazdegird and the Sassanian military leadership succeeded in assembling up to 150,000 men for the upcoming battle against the Arabs. These had been recruited mainly from Iran's northwest, north and northeast. Arab sources reveal that the caliphate was concerned by the presence of savaran cavalry in Yazdegird's forces.[71] The Sassanian populace, political leadership and surviving military units were now fighting against Arab attempts to reduce Iran into a conquered province.

The Arab army of the caliphate had now expanded to a force of up to 100,000 troops.[72] This was due to two factors. First, the Arabs had appropriated much wealth from Persia, especially in the aftermath of the battles of Jalula and Shushtar. Specifically much of the wealth of former Iranian cities had now been confiscated by the caliphate along with vast stocks of weapons from captured

Sassanian arsenals.[73] These helped to equip larger numbers of Arab troops and to provide the necessary finances for the conquest of Persia and other territories further west, especially Spain. The second factor that led to the expansion of the Arab army was the recruitment of more and more professional troops, especially ex-Sassanian (i.e. savaran) and possibly some ex-Byzantine and other troops from conquered non-Arab lands.

Yazdegird and his generals chose modern Malayer (near Nahavand in north-west Iran) to make their do-or-die stand against the Arab armies. Malayer is a critical strategic nexus point connecting Luristan, Kurdistan and Azerbaijan. The Arabs would have to cross this region in order to break into northwest Iran to then storm the Caucasus and northern Iran. If the Sassanian military could finally defeat the Arabs at Malayer, they would then be able to thrust into Arab-conquered northern, central and southern Mesopotamia. The Arabs could also be cleared out of southern Iran should the battle at Malayer prove successful. Yazdegird had placed General Firoozan in command of the army.

The Arab force of 30,000 arriving at Malayer was led by Numan. Despite out-numbering the Arab forces, Firoozan (who had battled the Arabs at Qadissiyah) chose not to attack Numan as he assembled his forces. This was probably due to the fact that the mass of the new Sassanian army was now composed of raw recruits who lacked the professional military training of the now much-diminished savaran and Dailamite forces. The Arabs were especially proficient in rapid and fluid movements on the battlefield, a capability which Firoozan must have appreciated through previous battle experience. Firoozan had chosen a defensive position. Extrapolating from surviving Sassanian military literature, it is possible to speculate that Firoozan had built very powerful defensive positions (i.e. traps, etc.).[74] Arab troops attacking Sassanian positions would first be exposed to the deadly archers who would be safely positioned behind Firoozan's defences. Surviving Arab troops who would reach Sassanian lines would then be ensnared in its deadly defences, allowing Firoozan to unleash his remaining savaran and Dailamite contingents to wipe out Numan's forces.[75] In such a scenario Firoozan's professional troops would most likely be facing former (Iranian) comrades who had by now joined the Arabs.

Numan however refused to initiate the offensive, most likely having realized that Firoozan's well-prepared defence works, stratagems and large numbers of recruits would have taken a heavy toll of any direct Arab offensive. The Arabs were also concerned with the deadly effects of Persian archery, especially when firing from well-prepared static positions.[76] The Sassanians were still able to rapidly unleash large numbers of deadly missiles, thereby taking a heavy toll of any attacking force. As Numan had no countermeasures to counteract Persian archery, he opted to stay in place to devise strategy with his commanders. This resulted in a stand-off or 'sitzkreig' in which the two sides simply observed each other for two months.

Firoozan benefited from Numan's refusal to attack. The caliphate's supply lines were now increasingly stretched in its campaign to subdue Iran. The Sassa-nian logistics system appears to have remained operational as late as the early

650s CE, with the Arabs having yet to develop a comparable system of their own.[77] As more troops arrived to join the Arabs, Numan's situation with supplies became increasingly precarious. The longer Numan waited, the more he risked depleting his meagre supplies. Firoozan appears to have realized Numan's predicament, as no Sassanian attack took place.

To break the stalemate, Numan and his commanders resorted to guile. The Arabs spread false rumours that Caliph Omar had died and that they were now withdrawing their forces. To accentuate the deception, Numan ordered that a 'withdrawal' be organized to further deceive the Sassanians. The gambit succeeded with Firoozan abandoning his well-prepared defensive positions to pursue Numan's 'withdrawing' troops. As Firoozan caught up with the Arabs, he realized that he had fallen into a trap; the Arabs were waiting for his forces in disciplined ranks. Numan's forces then attacked in a highly determined and organized thrust.[78] Despite being caught unprepared, Firoozan's surprised forces stood their ground and fought back against the Arab assaults. The battle proved especially bloody, with casualties on both sides. The ferocity of the battle is indicated by Numan himself having been slain by a Sassanian arrow during the battle.[79]

Firoozan and the Sassanian forces refused to give ground, placing the Arabs under considerable strain. The Arab armies, however unleashed their cavalry, which swung the tide of the battle effectively in their favour. Note that large numbers of now ex-Sassanian savaran knights had already joined the Arab invasion since 637–638 CE with many of these now supporting the Arab cavalry at the Battle of Nahavand. While precise numbers cannot be ascertained, the ex-Sassanian savaran knights were well-cognizant of the tactics and fighting methods deployed by the savaran horsemen and professional Dailamite infantry on the Sassanian side.[80] This meant that any tactical advantage wielded thus far by Firoozan's professional troops (savaran and Dailamites) was now effectively negated by the caliphate's cavalry. With the destruction of his professional core of troops, Firoozan's mass of recruits lost cohesion, resulting in heavy losses.

The consequences of the Sassanian defeat at Nahavand were as catastrophic as they were final. Iran had lost its final chance to stem the Arab invasion and to preserve its independence. The Arabs soon marched to Rayy (roughly modern Tehran) and captured it with little difficulty.[81] With these events, the remaining marzbans in Iran chose not to resist the Arabs and to provide them with professional troops as well as access to large stores of weapons. Nevertheless, the remnants of the savaran and Dailamite units refused to submit to the caliphate. Many of these took refuge in northern Persia, which remained unconquered at this time.

Chapter 18

Post-Sassanian Resistance and Rebellion against the Caliphate

Rebellions did break out despite the finality of the Arabo-Islamic conquests; much of the Iranian population refused to submit to the caliphates. Though conquered, Iranian cultural identity and military culture continued to endure.[1] This may explain why the Ummayad Caliphate (661–750 CE) had instituted a number of discriminatory anti-Iranian measures aimed at the elimination of Persian language and culture. Arab sources even report of harsh measures taken against citizens daring to speak Persian in public. Non-Arabs were considered as an inferior race[2] with Clawson noting that the Iranians 'chafed under Arab rule'.[3] While Arabic culture and language began to dominate ancient Egypt, North Africa, Syria, Mesopotamia and even Arab-occupied Spain by the tenth century, the Iranians resisted cultural assimilation, resulting in a number of anti-caliphate (Ummayad and Abbasid) revolts. These have been recorded by Arab historians, notably Ali Ibn Ahmad Ibn Hazm (994–1064 CE), who notes in his *Al Fasl fil Milal Ahwz n Nihal* that 'the Persians ... were greater than all of the people ... after their defeat by the Arabs, they [the Persians] rose up to fight against Islam ... among their leaders were Sunbadh [Sindbad], Muqanna, Ustasis, Babak [Khorramdin] and others.' Negative Iranian sentiments against the caliphates forced Arabization policies are evident as late as the eleventh century, when the Iranian poet Firdowsi (940–1020 CE), in his epic *Shahname*, quoted an Iranian general fighting against the invading Arabs as having stated 'Damn this world, damn this time, damn this fate, that uncivilized Arabs have come to make me Muslim.'[4]

Prince Pirouz and the Last Sassanians

Despite the fall of the Sassanian empire by 651 CE, the remnants of the Sassanian dynasty had escaped from Khorasan into Central Asia to arrive in China. Yazdegird III had died at the hands of a Christian miller in 651; however his son, prince Pirouz III (who was a child at the time), managed to escape with the remnants of the Sassanian administration and military leaders from Central Asia through the Pamir mountains (in what is now Tajikestan) to arrive in Tang China. As the sister of Pirouz was married to the Tang emperor Gaozong (r. 649–683 AD), Sassanian refugees were welcomed into China.[5] Pirouz intended to build a military force with Chinese military assistance as early as 661 to re-enter Iran and liberate it from caliphate occupation.

After Pirouz's request for Tang military assistance in 661, he was given control of a Persian command in the region of modern-day Zaranj, Afghanistan. It was sometime in 670–674 when Pirouz arrived at the Tang court where he was bestowed the title of *Youwuwei Jianggium* (Martial General of the Guards of the Right Flank). It was sometime in 678 when Pirouz was escorted by the Tang official Pei Jinggian (Tang deputy state secretary for personnel) for a military mission into Persia against the Arabs. The expedition failed to reach Iran with Pei Jinggian returning after the force reached Tokmok, Kyrgyzstan with Pirouz and several thousand of his troops then staying in the Bactria-Tocharistan region for nearly two decades. The Tang court bestowed the title of *Zuoweiwei Jiangjun* (the Awe-inspiring Commander of the Guards of the Left Flank) on Pirouz in 708 CE. With the failure of Pirouz and his successors to launch a military campaign against the Arabs, the last of the Sassanians in China were to be assimilated into mainstream Tang Chinese society.

Resistance in Central Asia: Early 700s–Late 740s

Despite Pirouz's failure to launch his campaign against the Arabs, the Ummayad caliphate continued to face resistance in Central Asia and Northern Persia in the late 600s CE. Despite a significant Buddhist legacy and the Arabo-Islamic arrivals, the practice of a local variant of Zoroastrianism remained strong in Central Asia.[6] The endeavour to preserve their Iranic heritage and languages (esp. Soghdian) led to a serious anti-Ummayad resistance movement among the Soghdians in Central Asia in 720–722 CE. The caliphate dispatched an Arab force led by al-Harashi, who engaged in both a military and a 'punishment' campaign to ensure that the local populace would never again dare rise against Arab rule. One of al-Harashi's notable actions was the killing of up to 3,000 Karzanj farmers in Khojand for their pro-Soghdian sympathies.[7] Al-Harashi then focused his military campaign against the main Soghdian force led by a leader known as Divashtich, whose base was the Abargar castle (known also as the castle of Mug). Located approximately 120km from Panjikent, Abargar/Mug was Divashtich's main base for his anti-Arab campaign, a powerbase which al-Harashi was determined to destroy. The Arabs approached Abargar/Mug in 722 CE, and Divashtich led his forces in a major battle against al-Harashi approximately 6–7km from the fortress. Al-Harashi defeated the Soghdians and captured Divashtich, who was executed in the autumn of 722 CE. The Arabs also pillaged and destroyed Abargar/Mug castle. Had Pirouz's original campaign in the late 600s CE succeeded in reaching Central Asia, he may have been able to link up with the local Iranic population to support them against the caliphate and enlist their support for his drive into Iran proper.

Despite the punitive campaigns, Central Asian sentiments against the caliphate remained undimmed. Just six years after the death of Divashtich, a new rebellion broke out in the entirety of Transoxiana in 728 CE. In that same year (728 CE) the Arabs were driven out of most of Central Asia. Al-Sulami, the Ummayad governor of Khorasan, was forced to engage in very hard combat, with his only success being the capture of the city Bukhara in 729 CE. By this time, large numbers of Turks had joined the Iranic population against the Arabs. The seriousness of the rebellion prompted the caliphate to dispatch a fresh Arab force led by Junaid bin Abdul Rahman al-Murri to assist Al-Sulami. Appointed as the new governor of Khorasan, al-Murri's mission was to combine his forces with Al-Sulami fighting in Central Asia. The combined Arab force engaged in very heavy combat for several months, managing to capture Samarqand by the spring of 730 CE. Junaid then returned to Khorasan in northeast Iran, a region whose indigenous population was also ripe for rebellion.

Fighting against the Arabs continued to intensify into 736–737 CE. A major battle occurred in 737 CE at the left bank of the Amu-Darya river between a Turk-Iranic (mostly Soghdian) military coalition led by the Turkic leader Sulu and the Arab forces of Asad bin Abdullah. The latter prevailed but the Arabs had to continue combat into 748 CE before being able to re-impose their occupation. The new governor of Khorasan, Nasr bin Sayyar attempted to win over the local populace by granting concessions to local elites, but these measures failed to stem the prevailing anti-Arab discontent in the population, sentiments echoed in northern Persia.

The Rise of the Abbasids and the Exploits of Abu-Muslim Khorasani (747–755 CE)

The Arabs of Khorasan had also grown weary of Ummayad rule, with the Abbasids soon exploiting local Iranian sentiments against the caliphate. By 747–748 CE, Abu Muslim Khorasani (an Iranian leader allied to the Abbasids) succeeded in rallying the Iranian population of Khorasan and Transoxiana against the Ummayads in favour of the Abbasids. Khorasani and the rebels defeated Sayyar and cleared the Ummayads from Merv and then all of Khorasan. With these military successes, Abu Muslim reached all the way to Damascus, the centre of the Ummayad Caliphate, by 750 CE. Thanks in large part to Iranian military assistance, the Ummayads had been overthrown in favour of the new Arab caliphs, the Abbasids.

After their brief initial sojourn in Kufa, the Abbasids had established their permanent caliphate in Baghdad (750–1258 CE). The Abbasids showed little interest in addressing the national aspirations and prevailing discontent of their Iranian regions. It was in eastern Iran (especially Khorasan) where antipathy against the Abbasid caliphate became exceptionally marked. In practice, very little had changed for the Iranian population as the Abbasids were just as determined to retain Arab dominance, just as their Ummayad predecessors had done.

Despite his loyalty to the Abbasids, the latter ordered the execution of Abu Muslim Khorasani in 755 CE. The Abbasids had cynically exploited Abu Muslim and the Khorasanis in the battle to overthrow the Umayyads.[8] Having used the Iranians to reach their objective of seizing the caliphate, the Abbasids betrayed their former comrades' national ambitions. With their political and military power secure in Baghdad, the recently installed Abbasid Caliphate now perceived Abu Muslim and his Iranian followers as expendable. As with the Ummayads, the Iranians were again oppressed. Abu Muslim Khorasani was evidently viewed as a dangerous liability for the caliphate as he retained the potential for leading the Iranian population in a dangerous anti-Abbasid revolt.

Khorasan and Central Asia: The Sindbad and Muqanna Anti-Abbasid Rebellions

The murder of Abu Muslim Khorasani in 755 CE led to the outbreak of a major revolt in Nishabur that same year by a leader known as Sindbad. Declaring himself a follower of the late Khorasani, Sindbad's rebellion quickly spread to all of Khorasan and Tabaristan in northern Iran. The rebels viewed the late Abu Muslim Khorasani as a hero of the common folk who had played a major role in the overthrow of the oppressive Ummayads. The Abbasids succeeded in crushing Sindbad's rebellion and re-imposing Arab rule in Khorasan, but northern Persia remained defiant (see below).

The crushing of Sindbad's rebellion did little to stem Iranian discontent. One of the late Abu Muslim Khorasani's commanders, a leader from Merv known as Hisham bin Hakim or al-Muqanna, succeeded in sparking a serious new anti-Arab rebellion in Transoxiana by 776. The success of Muqanna in attracting support for his cause is seen in one remarkable example where over sixty villages declared their collective allegiance for the new rebellion.[9] Bukhara soon fell to the Muqanna rebels, known as 'the people in white clothes' (as these wore white clothes and carried white banners), in contrast to the Abbasids whose banners and clothing were black.

The Caliph al-Mahdi (r. 775–785 CE) in Baghdad dispatched a powerful Abbasid force led by Jibrail bin Yahya to crush Muqanna and the rebels. Yahya first deployed to Narshakh (in the Bukhara region) and captured this after a bitter four-month siege. The two local rebel leaders, Khashvi and Hakim bin Ahmad, were killed by Yahya but this action failed to dissuade remaining local rebels from continuing the struggle. A second battle ensued in the environs of Narshakh with Yahya's forces again prevailing in this engagement.[10] Despite Yahya's successes, Muqanna's rebellion continued unabated, reaching the height of its power by 777 CE. By this time the rebels had swept the Arabs out of the Kashka Darya valley, the Derafshan valley,[11] and areas further southward to Termez. Meanwhile Yahya's capture of Narshakh had simply shifted the base of the rebellion into Soghdia.

Muqunna's forces now joined with Turkish warriors, engaged in a series of battles against the Arab forces of Yahya in the Samarqand region in 777 CE, and inflicted several defeats upon them. In response, fresh Arab forces were dispatched into Central Asia in 778 CE by Muaz bin Muslim, now the governor of Khorasan. This deployment proved successful as the Arabs regained Samarqand. The rebels then took refuge in the fortress of Sanam (in the Kish region), where Muqanna was located. More battles ensued with the Arabs finally capturing the Sanam fortress by the summer of 780 CE. The Arab victors now proceeded to punish the survivors of Sanam fortress by putting them all to death; Muqanna refused to surrender to the Arabs and committed suicide.[12]

Despite having crushed Sindbad and Muqanna yet another rebellion broke out in Central Asia in 806. Led by Rafi bin Laith from Soghdia, the movement was defeated by the Arabs four years later in 810.[13] It was only the establishment of an indigenous Iranian dynasty (the Samanids) in the Central Asian region that led to the waning of anti-caliphate resistance. Nevertheless, anti-Arab sentiments remained especially strong in the Iranian interior. One example is the serious revolt by a local Mazdakite during the reign of Caliph Harun al-Rashid (r. 786–809 CE) in Iran's interior (esp. Isfahan) northwest (esp. Hamedan) and Rayy towards the north. The caliph's delegates, Abu Dolaf Elji and Abdullah bin Malek, suppressed this revolt with great brutality.[14] While the caliphate was able to suppress Iranian military resistance in the Iranian interior, northern Iran and Azerbaijan would prove more difficult to subdue.

Military Legacy of the Sassanian Spah: Battles in Northern Persia (650s–early 800s CE)

The Arabs failed to subdue the north of Iran during their conquests. The region of Tabaristan roughly corresponded with modern-day Gilan, Mazandaran, parts of Talysh and Gorgan. Even as Arab authority was established a century after the conquest of Iran, many of the local north Iranian post-Sassanian princes remained defiant. Just one century after the Arab conquests of Sassanian Iran, a neo-Mazdakite rebellion had broken out in Gorgan in 778–779 CE. This led to bitter battles against Amr bin Ala, the Caliph Muhammad ibn Mansur al-Mahdi's (744 or 745–785 CE) delegate in Tabaristan. The Gorgan rebels had fought alongside the followers of a pre-Islamic cult known as the Bateni who were distinguished by their red banners.[15]

As noted by Overlaet, 'Daylaman remained unconquered ... until at least the eighth century AD ... early Dailamite rulers even exhibited extreme anti-Muslim attitudes and sought the restoration of the Persian Empire and of the ancient religions'.[16] Of special note are the types of Dailamite military gear uncovered in northern Iran which (as discussed in previous chapters) is of the late-Sassanian type. Islamic sources make clear that northern Iran was one of those territories deemed as the 'enemy of Islam'.[17] This raises questions as to why the Arabs were unable to militarily prevail in northern Iran. There are at least two general reasons why this was the case: climate and the close-quarters combat skills of the northern Iranian population. While this may surprise Western or European readers, northern and much of northwest Iran feature so-called 'European' type temperate climates with forested regions and snow-capped mountain ranges. One hypothesis is that the Arabs had difficulty coping with the local terrain and weather, which differs from Middle East climates, especially during the winter. Nevertheless this explanation may be challenged as the Arabs certainly conquered Spain and did even make it into ancient Gaul (approx. modern France) until the checking of their advance at the battle of Tours in 732 CE (barely one century after the conquest of Sassanian Iran). The fact remained that the Arabs were (and remain) tough and resilient fighters, capable of quickly adapting to different battle environments.

The second factor may have to do with the martial abilities of the northern Iranians at the time. As noted in Chapter 7, the Dailamites of northern Persia proved to be among the Sassanian spah's best infantry, being especially adept at close-quarter combat. It would also appear that the Dailamites had retained elements of the former spah's appellations and battle tactics during their battles against the caliphate, as will be seen below.

Vendidad-Hormuz. Northern Iranian warriors fought a number of bitter battles against the caliphate, these continuing well into the late 700s CE. The case of Vendidad-Hormuz of northern Persia is of interest as much information has been provided by Ibn Isfandyar's *History of Tabaristan*. One of these pertains to a major battle between Vendidad-Hormuz and the forces of Caliph al-Mahdi (r. 775–785 CE) numbering 10,000 troops.[18] Ibn Isfandyar has provided the following description of the battle:[19]

> [W]hen the Arabs reached Tabaristan, the people, altogether 4,000 in total, hid in the high mountain tops and the local forests with 400 horns, 400 drums and Tabar [axe] and Dahra [local type of very sharp north Iranian scythe] ... Vendidad with 100 Savar [as in Savaran cavalry] appeared in front of the Arabs and engaged in attack and pursuit [tactics] drawing them to areas already designated [where the 4,000 fighters were ensconced]. Then all of a sudden 4,000 Tabaristanis engaged in the percussion of large drums and 400 horns which made the Arabs think that the dawn of judgment was at hand ... then 4,000 cut-down trees were cast upon their heads [the Arabs]. Then they [Tabaristani or Dailamites] drew out their swords and from the outset massacred 2,000 of the Arabs ... Ferasha [the Arab commander] was apprehended and beheaded ... the remaining Arabs were released.

The above description depicts the Dailamites as deploying axes, scythes and swords in their close-quarter fighting against the Arabs. Note the use of ambuscade-type tactics (drawing the enemy to pre-designated areas to drop lumber upon them) and savaran-style attack-feigned retreat tactics. Perhaps Vendidad may have had some knowledge of Sassanian military doctrine, possibly in part through Pahlavi-language military manuals that may have still existed in the region. Vendidad soon joined forces with Sherwin Ispadbodh (lit. 'Spah Commander') against the caliphate. Ibn Isfandyar avers that Sherwin 'would not allow the Muslims [caliphate troops] to be buried in the soil of ... Tabaristan'.[20]

Weapons and tactics used against the caliphate. Ibn Isfandiyar has provided detailed descriptions of the weapons and tactics utilized by the Dailamites against the caliphate.[21] Standard weapons of north Iranian warriors at this time were virtually the same as seen among Dailamite units of the spah: mail and plate armour, sword, mace, dagger, axe, and the Dailamite-Gilani two-pronged zhupin javelin. North Iranian savaran warriors are described as having bargostvan horse armour for their steeds. It is not clear if the bargostvan armour of the Dailamites of this time was of the 'frontal only' type as seen at Taghe Bostan, or whether it provided more comprehensive coverage of the steed. It would appear that, in northern Persia, various aspects of the former Sassanian spah were still being maintained. This is further suggested by the descriptions of Ibn Isfandiyar of the various counter-siege and siege weaponry utilized by the northern Iranians in their battles against the caliphate.[22] Examples include their use of mangonels and specialized catapult-type weapons, the use of Sassanian-style khandaq ditches, and siege towers. Reports are also given of the construction of towers and the rolling of large boulders down mountain sides against caliphate troop columns. Of special interest are reports of permanent barracks for the housing of professional combat troops (mainly Dailamite and Gil). There was also great reliance on a rapid message system in which spies quickly reported on the actions of caliphate troops.[23]

Babak Khorramdin in Azerbaijan (816–837 CE): The Caliphate's Greatest Challenge

According to Tabari both Vendidad and Sherwin later accepted the caliphate's authority after a massive counterattack by the latter captured a number of fortresses by the early 800s CE;[24,25] but in practice northern Persia remained one of the least Islamicized regions of the caliphate. In addition, the caliphate had yet to destroy the military potential of northern Persia. This is evidenced by the rise of the Buyid Dailamite dynasty in the 930s CE which seized control over much of Iran until the arrival of the Seljuk Oghuz Turks in the 11th century CE. Especially significant was the support of northern Iran to Babak Khorramdin in Azerbaijan against the caliphate by the 830s CE. Note that the Republic of Azerbaijan was known as Arran at the time and did not share the name of historical Iranian Azerbaijan until 1918. Turkic languages were not yet prevalent in Azerbaijan with Babak having been identified as a Persian by both Armenian and Islamic sources.[26]

Babak Khorramdin's movement (816–837 CE) was the most dangerous military threat posed by an Iranian rebellion against the caliphate.[27] This movement came closest to ejecting the caliphate from not only Azerbaijan but from all Iranian realms. Babak was the leader of the *Khorram-dinan* (Persian *Xorramdinan*: 'Those Who Follow the Joyful Religion) sect which was an Iranian movement based on the teachings of the pre-Islamic religion of Mazdakism.[28] The Khorram-dinan was initially a mystical sect whose followers shunned violence, but with Babak's determination to liberate Iran from the caliphate, the movement's pacifism gave way to a warrior ethos.

Babak's Bazz castle in Azerbaijan. Babak's base of operations against the caliphate was the Bazz castle in Azerbaijan. Bazz remains a formidable site, with many of its structures surviving to the present. The castle was originally built in the Parthian era (250 BCE–224 CE) with its main structure strengthened and defences improved by the succeeding Sassanian dynasty (224–651 CE). Bazz was built on an elevation of approximately 2,500m and surrounded by deep and narrow crevices (approximately 500m in depth).[29] These crevices were flanked by rocky walls which made attacks against the castle extremely difficult. This prevented the caliphate from bringing its numerical advantage to bear as the narrow defiles severely limited the number of troops that could be deployed against Bazz. Infantry in the initial stages of attacking would be channeled into the narrow rocky passes and be highly vulnerable to the ambushes and counterattacks of

Babak's fighters. Attackers approaching Bazz had to cross a single narrow and meandering defile to then traverse a very narrow corridor, just one person wide. As a result, attacking caliphate forces at Bazz could be easily staved off with modest numbers of fighters. These same crevices, narrow passes and steep climbs negated any advantages posed by caliphate cavalry and also made the deployment of siege engines exceedingly difficult. The caliphate also could not attack in winter due to the region's very heavy snowfalls and dense rains.

Babak was always able to retreat and find succour at Bazz in case his battles against the caliphate's armies went awry. This ensured that Babak's rebellion would endure for a long time, as his forces could always sortie and attack at times and places of their choosing. Set-piece battles could also be engaged in whenever circumstances became favourable. Nevertheless, Bazz was not Babak's sole fortress as sources do mention a number of other fortifications used by the Khorram-dinan.[30]

Babak defeats the armies of the caliphate (813–833 CE). Babak's rebellion began in 813 CE. The first to rally to Babak's banner were mainly the local Azerbaijani farming population.[31] The farmers were exhorted by Babak to fight against the caliphate as warriors[32] and to kill their Arab opponents in battle.[33] By 818–819 CE, Babak and his warriors had cleared Azerbaijan's castles, strategic passes and strongholds of Arab/caliphate troops.[34] The caliph opposing Babak at this time was Abu Jaafar Abdollah al-Mamoun ibn Harun (r. 813–833 CE), referred to as Mamoun.

Babak proved to be an exceptional military leader who gained the steadfast loyalty of his followers throughout his three-decade campaign.[35] As word went out of Babak's successes against the caliphate, volunteer fighters streamed into Azerbaijan from all across the Iranian realms.[36] Large numbers of anti-caliphate fighters came from the north (Rayy, Karaj, Qom, Tabaristan), northwest (i.e. Hamedan), Central Asia (esp. Balkh), the interior (i.e. Isfahan and Kashan), Khorasan in the northeast, the west (Luristan and many Kurds) and even from Basra (in modern southern Iraq).[37] Armenia, already ripe for rebellion,[38] was also home to members of the Khorramdin.[39] Babak's followers in Armenia would also launch a number of attacks against local caliphate garrisons during the three-decade rebellion.[40]

Mamoun's first serious military actions against Babak occurred in 819–820 CE when General Yahya bin Moad was appointed to crush Babak and the new Iranian independence movement. Babak defeated Moad in a series of battles in 820 CE. Mamoun responded by dispatching fresh forces led by General Isa Mohammad bin Abu Khaled into Azerbaijan in 821 CE. Isa and his forces were also crushed when they fell into a deadly trap in a defile in Azerbaijan: the rebels virtually wiped out Isa and the entire caliphate force.[41] Three years later, the caliphate dispatched a third force led by Ahmad bin Jonayd Eskafi into Azerbaijan. Babak and his fighters clashed with Ahmad in a hard-fought battle in 825 CE, resulting in yet another comprehensive defeat for the caliphate.[42] Mamoun then dispatched a fourth force led by Ibrahim bin Layt bin Fazl, but this force also failed to prevail against the Iranian rebels. Mamoun dispatched a fifth army led by Mohammad bin Himayd Tusi in 827–828 CE. Tusi's advance achieved initial successes in a series of battles against Babak over six months.[43] Nevertheless, Babak's main forces and his Bazz castle remained intact, allowing the rebels to organize their counterstrikes. Tusi's forces were then annihilated in a major close-quarter battle by Babak's forces in 829 CE.[44] Mamoun died four years later in 833 CE, with Babak and his forces still at large in Azerbaijan, greatly endangering the caliphate's authority in Iran. Babak's victories against five major caliphate armies in 816–833 CE had shattered the myth of Arab military superiority and finally given rise to hopes that Iran would finally be liberated. News of Babak's victories continued to galvanize fighters from across Iran to join the anti-caliphate rebellion in Azerbaijan.[45]

Caliph al-Motassem and the Battle of Hamedan (833–836 CE). Concerns over the Iranian rebellion are evidenced in Mamoun's last will and testament to his successor, al-Motassem (r. 833–842 CE), imploring him to use whatever means necessary to crush Babak.[46] By the time of Motassem's ascension, Babak had seized control of a vast swathe of territory ranging from Ardabil and Marand in the west and on the Caspian Sea to the east as well as Moghan and Jolfa in the north; even Shirvan and Shamakhi to the north of the Araxes River in the Caucasus were now under Babak's sway.[47] With Azerbaijan and portions of the Caucasus already broken away, Motassem now faced the possibility of other parts of Iran seceding from the caliphate. As noted previously, the caliphate had been facing serious challenges to its authority in northern Persia. Just as Motassem had assumed leadership of the caliphate in Baghdad in August 833 CE, a large Iranian contingent arrived from Isfahan, Jebal and Hamedan to assemble at Hamedan and await Babak's arrival there.

Motassem appointed Eshaq bin Ibrahim bin Moshab as the commander of a powerful army assigned to crush the pro-Babak fighters in Hamedan. Moshab engaged in a great battle in early 834 CE in which the caliphate won its first crushing victory over the Iranian rebels, reputedly slaying more than 60,000 of Babak's troops. The survivors of the Hamedan debacle escaped to Byzantium to then return to Iran and re-join Babak's growing forces.[48] The Hamedan defeat did not deter large numbers of volunteers from joining Babak's cause. The scale of support for Babak from across the Iranian realms resulted in the rebel forces growing to 100,000[49] and possibly even 200,000[50] fighters by 836 CE. In response Motassem moved his capital from Baghdad to Samara in 836 CE where he made careful military preparations with his professional Turkish troops.[51]

Declaration of alliance between Maziyar and Babak. By the ninth century CE the Dailamite region (or Tabaristan) had witnessed the rise of Maziyar, an Iranian prince of the House of Karen.[52] Maziyar had been confirmed as governor of northern Persia by al-Mamoun just before his death in 833 CE.[53] Maziyar is believed to have had a personal guard of 1,200 Dailamite warriors commanded by his brother Shahriyar.[54] Like Babak, Maziyar endeavoured to revive the culture, customs and religion of pre-Islamic Iran.[55] Maziyar who was in communication with Babak in Azerbaijan further west, had also forged an official alliance with him by 837 CE.[56] Their aim was to eject the Arabs not just from Azerbaijan and the Iranian north but from the entire Iranian realm and to revive the former Sassanian Empire and the Zoroastrian religion.[57] Ibn Isfandyar has noted that Maziyar proclaimed, 'I [Maziyar], Afshin Kheydar son of Kavus and Babak made a pact and alliance to take back the government from the Arabs and give it back to the Kasraviyan [Sassanians].'[58,59]

Despite these ambitions, the Maziyar-Babak alliance achieved little. Babak's anti-caliphate rebellion was crushed in 837 CE (see below) with Maziyar having little capability to militarily support his ally. Maziyar was then betrayed by his brother Kuhyar, who surrendered him over to the caliphate. The northern Iranian rebel was bought to Baghdad for execution where he died in 839 CE. It is unclear however, if Maziyar took his own life to avoid humiliation at Arab hands while awaiting execution or if he actually was executed.

Interestingly, Ibn Isfandyar's quote of Maziyar also makes reference to Afshin son of Kavus who was in fact Haydar bin Kavus Afshin.[60,61] Motassem appointed Afshin as governor of Azerbaijan and the chief general to lead the caliphate's final military campaigns against Babak and the Iranian rebels in August 835 CE.[62] Afshin is an infamous figure in Iranian history; he is known as the Iranian general who betrayed Iran's last hope for independence from the caliphate.

While Afshin was a loyal soldier of the caliphate,[63] he never completely abandoned his Iranian identity.[64] Zarrinkoub has noted that numbers of Iranian princes did serve the caliphate for personal and/or material interests.[65] Afshin was certainly given great financial favour by Motassem, especially in the provision of generous payments for the general and his officers.[66] When Afshin achieved military successes against Babak in 836–837 CE Motassem granted greater gifts such as the daily dispatch of robes of honour and horses, jewels, a crown, etc.[67] Much favour was also lavished by the caliph on the Turkish troops assisting Afshin.[68] Despite these factors, Afshin's role (and loyalties) are difficult to ascertain. While true that Afshin was instrumental in crushing Babak's rebellion in 836–837 CE, he is also cited by Ibn Isfandyar as being the ally of Babak and Maziyar in restoring Iran's political and cultural independence from the caliphate.[69] Afshin appears to have entertained secret communications with both Babak and Maziyar, one of many facts that later surfaced and led to his fall from grace with the caliphate.[70] Afshin was put on trial in 841 CE and accused by his enemies of having 'pro-Iranian' sympathies especially with respect to ancient Iranian culture and theology.[71]

The caliphate strikes back (835–836 CE). Before sending Afshin and his army to Azerbaijan, al-Motassem implemented a massive military build-up programme (i.e. rebuilding fortresses in Azerbaijan,[72] recruiting spies,[73] reconnaissance,[74] extracting information from prisoners[75]) and replaced his Arab contingents with the more militarily effective professional Turkish troops.[76] Mamoun had already begun the practice of regularly dropping Arabs from the caliphate's military registry to replace these with Turkish (mainly) slave troops.[77] Motassem fully inducted the Turks into the caliphate's armies at the expense of the Arabs.[78] The Turks were to play a critical role in destroying Babak's rebellion in 836–837 CE.[79]

Babak suffered his first critical defeat at the hands of a vanguard caliphate force moving ahead of Afshin's main forces.[80] Afshin then struck into Azerbaijan by first advancing to Barzand and carefully progressing along the Barzand-Ardabil route.[81] Babak suffered his second major defeat and very heavy losses when Afshin struck his forces at Arshaq. One of Babak's commanders (Adin) had managed to score a victory against the caliphate's forces at Hashtadsar in 836 CE.[82] Babak remained defiant,[83] but the Iranian cause was ultimately doomed as Afshin's methodical military campaign began to slowly bear fruit.[84] Afshin had implemented highly effective cavalry patrols against the rebels, forcing Babak to launch desperate attacks. These continuous clashes wore down Babak's military strength, allowing Afshin to draw closer to Bazz castle. Afshin's strategy succeeded in bottling up Babak and the last of the rebels at Bazz.

Bazz falls to Caliphate's Turkish troops (837 CE). It was in August 837 CE when Afshin unleashed his final assault at Bazz. Siege engines and naphtha throwers unleashed their deadly barrages against Bazz's defenders, entrance gates and defence structures. The caliphate's professional Turkish troops succeeded in scaling Bazz's walls to engage in fierce hand to hand combat against Babak's surviving defenders. The mainly Turkish troops captured Bazz and hoisted the caliphate's banners on 15 August 837 CE.[85] Afshin then freed 7,600 Arab prisoners who had been held captive in the castle.[86] Caliphate troops then looted and destroyed Bazz on Afshin's orders.[87] Babak and his rebellion had been extinguished. He was captured in Armenia in September 837 CE and executed in Samara (in modern Iraq) in January 838 CE.

Babak's Enduring Legacy: Rise of Shah Ismail and the Safavids

Had Babak's decades-long rebellion succeeded, Iran could well have broken out of the caliphate's grasp towards independence and revived its ancient pre-Islamic religions. Nevertheless, the caliphate failed to destroy Iran's distinct (non-Arab) identity and culture. The Khorramdin movement in particular was not destroyed with many of its survivors becoming gradually absorbed into various Islamic sects.[88] Other survivors of Babak's movement fled westwards, towards Byzantium, where 'Byzantine sources talk of Persian warriors seeking refuge in the 830s from the caliph's armies by taking service under the Byzantine emperor Theophilos.'[89]

It would again be in Azerbaijan where the bid to restore Iranian independence would resurface in the person of Shah Ismail and the Safavids. The Khorramdinan sect and its Mazdakite/Zoroastrian ideas would in fact endure well into the 1500s when Shah Ismail and the Safavids took over Iran and restored her full independence as an Iranian state.[90] It is notable that Sheikh Safi (1252–1334 CE), founder of the Safavids and Shah Ismail's ancestor, had organized resistance against the Mongol invaders in Azerbaijan for over three decades (1300–

1334 CE).[91] The sheikh had gained many followers in his native city of Ardabil (known as Abadan Piruz or Shahram Piruz in Sassanian times) as well as northern Iran.[92] When Shah Ismail came to power in the sixteenth century he finally restored independence to the entirety of the Iranian realms, roughly corresponding to the frontiers of the ancient Sassanian Empire. In this endeavour, Shah Ismail won the military and political support of the entire Iranian populace.

Turkish historian and scholar Abdulbaki Golpinarli concurs that the Qizilbash warriors who bought Shah Ismail to power in Iran in 1501 CE were the spiritual descendants of Babak Khorramdin and the Khorram-dinan who had risen in Azerbaijan to fight for Iran's independence six centuries before. Despite having been a devote Shiite Muslim, Shah Ismail in fact had strong ties to Iran's *Yazdani* (lit. Cult of Angels) which is essentially the descendant of ancient Iranian cults such as Mithraism, Zorvanism, and Mazdakism.[93]

Chapter 19

Legacy

The Sassanian spah was to leave a powerful and enduring legacy centuries after the downfall of the Sassanian Empire. This chapter provides a brief overview of the spah's legacy in the military systems of the Romano-Byzantines, Caliphates and the Turkic realms.

Savaran in Roman Service

A topic that has increasingly engaged the interest of both Iranian and Western military historians is the role of savaran warriors recruited into Roman service. The discussion in this section will examine the role Sassanian units played in the militaries of the Romano-Byzantines.

There were three principal ways in which Rome was able to recruit savaran units into Roman military service. The first was political infighting within the Sassanian royal house (see Hormuzd, below). The second was through savaran prisoners of war who were recruited into Roman service, as discussed below. The third method was through economic enticements. The Romans apparently paid well to recruit mercenaries into their military. This would not be the first time Iranian warriors would be serving in enemy armies due to economic enticements. After the Battle of Qadissiyah in 637 CE, for example, Dailamite and savaran warriors of the spah were recruited into invading Arabo-Islamic armies and received double the pay of regular Arab troops (Chapter 17). So high was the proportion of non-Romans in Roman armoured cavalry units that Mitterauer and Chapple have concluded that 'clibanarii under the late Roman emperors were all mercenaries, which cannot be said of ... the Sassanid armoured cavalry'.[1]

Brief overview of non-Sassanian Iranian cavalry in Roman service. The recruitment of Iranian cavalry into Roman service was of course nothing new; for example, the emperor Marcus Aurelius (121–180 CE), after defeating the Ia-zyges Alans in Pannonia (modern Hungary), sent a 5,000-man contingent of North Iranic cavalry to Britain in 175 CE.[2] Alan cavalry in France led by their king Sang-i-ban (lit. Guardian of the Rock/Menhir), were reported as fighting with Visigoth and Roman armies against the Huns in 341 CE.[3] Other examples include citations of Parthian cavalry serving with Roman forces in Europe (i.e. the *notitia dignatatum*'s report of *equites sagittarri parthi seniores* and *equites sagittarri parthi iuniores* serving troops under the *magister equitum praesentalis*). The recruitment of Iranian and Iranian-type cavalry was to become prominent in the post-Parthian era, notably the Sassanian savaran and the Armenian naxarars.

Previous scholarship on 'barbarians' serving with the Roman armies often emphasized the Germanic element, with modern scholarship now acknowledging the role of 'eastern' professional cavalry in the Roman/Western world. The 'eastern' cavalry are mainly of the Iranian-Armenian as well as Turkic-Hun types. The personal retinue of the great Romano-Byzantine generals such as Belisarius and Narses included a high proportion of Iranians, Armenians (and other Caucasians), as well as Turks and Huns. It is notable that Germanic warriors are not mentioned as having been among those elites. This is mainly because 'eastern' warriors such as the later savaran knights were equally adept with lance, sword and archery, whereas mounted Germanic warriors fought mainly with sword and lance.[4] As noted in Chapter 9, Rome's greatest 'eastern' military opponent was the Sassanian spah and its elite savaran cavalry. The *Strategikon* perhaps best summarizes what distinguished the Germanic warriors from their savaran counterparts by stating that the 'Blond Peoples [Germanic]' preferred fighting on foot rather than on horseback.[5]

The first Roman savaran units. Cedrenus provides us with an interesting insight into the development of cavalry units in the Roman army in the aftermath of Valerian's disastrous war against Shapur I: 'Valerian made war against Shapur of the Persians and was captured ... Gallienus [son of Emperor Valerian] established the first cavalry cohorts for the majority of the Roman soldiers till then were infantry.'[6]

Cavalry was of course nothing new in the Roman armies, but Cedrenus' reference of Rome's 'first cavalry cohorts' in the aftermath of his father Valerian's defeat and capture would suggest the possibility that these were formed (at least in part) in response to the threats of the savaran-led forces of the spah. Peterson, for example, has noted that Roman armies adopted various types of Sassanian equipment for the cavalry (esp. helmets) by the 300s CE,[7] but the use of the term *persae* in connection to Roman cavalry had yet to manifest. In the overall sense, it may be suggested that the defeats suffered in battles with Sassanian forces had prompted the Roman political and military leadership to adopt and/or develop cavalry along the lines of their opponents.

The first definite mention of Sassanian savaran units in Roman service is made by the *notitia dignitatum* which cite the *equites persae clibanarii* which was a *vexillatio palatina* commanded by Constantinople's *magister equitum praesentalis*.[8] Cosentino attributes the origins of this particular unit to the savaran of Hormuzd, brother of King Shapur II (r. 309–379 CE) who had defected to the Romans at the time of Constantine I (r. 324–337 CE). Interestingly, Constantine I's successor Constantius II (337–361 CE) is the first Roman emperor believed to have introduced savaran-style cavalry to Europe. By the late 350s CE, there are reports of a *scola scutariorum clibanariorum* in Rome attended by 'men ... of Persian origin ... their equipment shows ... Persian origins'.[9] The *equites persae clibanarii* and *scola scutariorum clibanariorum* were made up of savaran armoured knights (warrior and horse) which were now in Roman service. It is here where a detailed description by Julian depicts the 'Persian' nature of the military equipment of the new Roman cavalry contingents of Constantius II:

[T]heir limbs were fitted with armour that followed closely the outline of the human form. It covers the arms from wrist to elbow and thence to the shoulder, while a coat of mail protects the shoulders, back and breast. The head and face are covered by a metal mask which makes its wearer look like a glittering statue, for not even the thighs and legs and the very ends of the feet lack this armour. It is attached to the cuirass by fine chain-armour like a web, so that no part of the body is visible and uncovered, for this woven covering protects the hands as well, and is so flexible that the wearers can bend their fingers.[10]

The above description of 'Roman' armoured cavalry is virtually identical with that of Ammianus Marcellinus cited in Chapter 6: 'All the [Sassanian] troops were clothed in steel, in such a way that their bodies were covered with strong plates, so that the hard joints of the armour fitted every limb of their bodies.'[11]

Iranians with Roman military offices. Yet more examples of Roman military men of Iranian origins are cited by Cosentino,[12] who has noted that 'Persian cavalry was appreciated by Roman generals and its introduction into the Roman army would have been important in case of a clash on an open and flat ground.'[13] One example is a certain Barzimeres, a *scutatiorum tribunus* who was sent by Emperor Valens (r. 364–368, co-emperor 375–378) in 374–377 CE to capture Babak, the king of Armenia. By the 380s CE the name *Narses* (who may be Iranian or Armenian) appears as a *comes* in the western regions (Hispania, Gaul, or Brittania) of the Roman Empire. There is also the citation of a Varanes in 408, son of a famous Persian who may have been one of those elite savaran warriors who had defected with Hormuzd from Shapur II to the Romans. Varanes then reached the high level position of consul in the Pars Orientis in 410 CE in Constantinople. Yet another Iranian in Constantinople in 409 CE was Arsacius, who held the office of *magister militum*. By the mid-450s CE there are reports of a Chosroes (*comes et dux thebaides* in Romano-Byzantine ruled Egypt) and Artacius (cited in the *Vita Auxenti*).

The numerus persoiustiniani. This 'Perso' or Sassanian unit was most likely formed from a number of Sassanian units that had surrendered to the Romano-Byzantines in 530–531 CE and 540–561 CE. It is possible that at least some of these were savaran warriors who had surrendered to Belisarius after his capture of the fortress of Sisauranon in 541 CE.[14] According to Procopius these troops were:[15] '800 horsemen, the best of the Persians, who were keeping guard under command of a man of note, Bleschames by name … the Persians he sent with Bleschames to Byzantium, and razed the fortification wall of the fortress to the ground. And the emperor not long afterwards *sent these Persians and Bleschames to Italy to fight against the Goths*' (emphasis added).

Procopius' report makes clear that captured savaran warriors were soon dispatched to Europe to fight the Goths. Boss has provided an overview of the types of equipment that these ex-Sassanian savaran warriors were most likely employing during their military sojourn in Europe. These are proposed to have had two-piece helmets of the Dura-Europos type (although they may have had helmets of the Spangenhelm type), a mail face protection (suspended from the frontal rim of the helmet), a shirt of mail possibly worn over a plate thorax or lamellar, a small shield worn at the arm, and a 'Persian' bow case (or kamandan) and a 3.5m lance.[16] The uniform or *brahmag e artesharih* (lit. uniform of warriors; see Chapter 15) of these 'European savaran' are characterized as tight trousers of the Persian form of the type seen in the depiction of the three wise men at Ravenna along with shoulder epaulettes described in the *Strategikon* (Chapter 15).

Procopius has specifically mentioned the names of savaran officers such as Bleschames and Artabazes in the Italian campaigns,[17] which is yet another indication that the *numerus persoiustiniani* may indeed have been first formed in 541 CE. These certainly did not return to the east, as indicated by the sixth century CE Italian inscription of the Church of St. Eufemia in Grado. This inscription, dated circa 579 CE, cites the *numerus persoiustiniani* as having remained stationed in Italy even after the conclusion of the Gothic wars.[18] By this time the unit's ranks had probably swelled with non-Iranian recruits as the soldier commemorated by the Italian inscription is cited as a certain Iohannes, which is a Latin name.

The *numerus felicum persoarmeniorum*. A papyrus from Ravenna has cited the military unit known as the *numerus felicum persoarmeniorum* in c. 591 CE.[19] As noted previously, knights from Persoarmenia were much like savaran knights. The Romano-Byzantines were especially appreciative of Armenian warriors with those from an Armeno-Iranian military tradition being especially respected.[20] Mention is made, for example, of the brothers Narses, Isaakes and Aratios, who were possibly linked to the famous Kamsarakan noble clan; these had deserted to Romano-Byzantine forces.[21] It is also notable that a number of these Perso-Armenian warriors attained the rank of *militum*.

Haldon has noted of Sassanian influences on the Romano-Byzantines such as bow cases and the pendant aventail attached to the helmet.[22] Interestingly, much of Byzantine dress was to show a distinct Sassanian influence, especially in colour displays and design patterns. It is possible that the Sassanian style of gem-studded dress may have been introduced as early as the time of Diocletian (r. 284–305 CE).[23] According to Kondakov, the Byzantines borrowed much of their system of uniforms from the Sassanians.[24] It would appear that this process of borrowing Sassanian military fashions continued even during the Sassanian-Byzantine wars of 602–622 CE. Haldon also highlights the importance of Romano-Byzantine experience against large numbers of lance-bearing mail-clad cavalry, and Byzantium's role in transmitting 'eastern' types of cavalry armour systems, especially of the combined type (mail, and other types of armour) to the western Europeans, notably from the time of Nikephorus Phocas (963–969) until the eleventh to twelfth centuries.[25]

Western reference to training of Iranian-type knights. Western scholarship now acknowledges the importance of the influence of Iranian knights and their training methods upon the Roman military. As noted by Cosentino:

As it is well known, the Sasanians were particularly appreciated by the Romans because of their heavy armoured cavalry. In a recent article I tried to pay attention to the special qualities necessary for fighting as a clibanarius. First of all a special kind of extremely resistant horse was required, which had to be able to carry the weight of the horseman's armour and that of his own protection. *Then, a strong military training for the rider was also necessary, as he had to be able to violently charge the enemy without losing his stability.* (emphasis added) Such a thing was extremely difficult, especially because until the end of the sixth century the horsemen did not use stirrups. Therefore, it is likely that Hormuzd and his retinue were employed as clibanarii. What is certain is that both Hormuzd and his homonymous son served in Roman cavalry.[26]

Cosentino points out the importance of training the heavy armoured knight to achieve stability at high speeds, even as he charges towards a hostile target with his lance aimed for impact. The rider would have to retain his stability even as he impacted the target with what is essentially the velocity and force of a slow-moving modern automobile. To achieve this without stirrups required rigorous and long-term training as well as above-average physical strength.

Sassanian legacy in polo. Perhaps one of the most enduring legacies bequeathed to Europeans by the savaran cavalry is in the game of polo. The Persian term *chaugan*, which roughly translates as 'special stick with a curved point', has cognates in European languages such as *chicane* (French), *choca* (Portugal), *Schaggun* (German), and *chekan* (Russian).[27] It would appear that Romano-Byzantine contacts provided an avenue for the transmission of polo to the West. Al-Jahiz, writing in the *Kitab al-Mahasin*, describes interactions between Khosrow II and his Byzantine counterpart, Maurice. Below are excerpts of those exchanges; note especially the references to the game of polo:[28]

> An unheard of gift was presented by Abarwiz [Khosrow II Parveez] to the king of Rum [Maurice] on account of the struggle against Bahram Chubin ... On the day of Niruz [Nowruz Iranian new year] the next year, the king of Rum repaid Abarwiz by a horseman made of gold riding a silver horse ... in his hand the horseman held a silver Sauljan [Arabic for Chaugan polo stick] and alongside him was a silver Maydan [hippodrome] in the middle of which was placed a ball.

It would appear that Maurice had meant to honour Khosrow II by the dispatch of a gift signalling respect for one of ancient Iran's most revered cavalry traditions. Given the Romano-Byzantine appreciation for Iranian-style cavalry, it is apparent that Iranian-style cavalry sports and exercises were also known. The Arabs also adopted the game of polo, as well as much of the Sassanians' military legacies, as seen later in this chapter.

Palmyra: An Overview of the Iranian Military Legacy

As noted in Chapter 9, the only major setbacks suffered by the armies of Shapur I (r. 240–270 CE) during his successful campaigns against the Roman armies occurred during military confrontations with Palmyra. The Palmyran aristocracy and military (notably cavalry) already had a distinct Iranian influence before the rise of the Sassanians. Seyriq's very thorough analysis of Palmyran costumes and weapons notes a strong Parthian influence. Examples include trousers, which, like those of the Parthians, were part of the Palmyran military uniform (especially cavalry),[29] as were tunics.[30] According to Boss the Palymran costume was the Iranian (Parthian-Persian) type of embroidered long-sleeved tunic and embroidered trousers which was 'adopted by the Roman army'[31] as well as east Germanic warriors. Seyriq's examination also discusses the Palmyran method of carrying swords, which is similar to the depictions in Parthian reliefs.[32] There is also evidence of the use of the Iranian two-handed sword by the Palmyrans.[33]

The Lance Joust and the Duel

One of Iran's most deeply rooted military traditions was the man-to-man duel, which could take the form of a mounted lance joust or close-quarter combat on foot (Chapter 15). As noted previously in Chapter 15, the Firuzabad panel near Ardashir's palace depicts a lance joust between the early Sassanians and the late Parthians: there are three Sassanian horsemen (Ardashir I, prince Shapur I, and an unidentified Sassanian knight) locked in combat with their 'equal ranking' Parthian adversaries (Ardavan V, Darbandan, and an unidentified Parthian).[34,35] It is possible that Iranian-Armenian and Turkic-Hun type duel traditions may have influenced the Roman and European military traditions.

Mard o Mard: championship duels. Sassanian pahlavans often challenged the best of Rome's warriors by shouting 'mard o mard' (man-to-man), thereby inviting their adversaries to engage them in duels before the onset of full-scale combat between their respective armies.

The Roman soldier-historian Procopius, in his account of the Sassanian attack on Dara (530 CE), described a duel that started when 'one Persian, a young man and riding very close to the Roman army, began to challenge all of them'.[36] The Romans responded by sending a Germanic wrestler and bath attendant named Andreas to fight the Sassanian champion. Procopius writes that 'both rushed madly upon each other with their spears, and the weapons driven against their corselets were turned aside with mighty force'.[37]

It is notable that the outcome of the joust-duel was expected to be honoured even if the Sassanian pahlavan was killed by his opponent. A remarkable example of this occurs when Bahram Gur (r. 420–438 CE) yielded the battlefield to the Romans in 421 CE when his champion from the elite Immortal guards, Ardazan, was defeated and killed by his Gothic opponent in the Roman army, Areobindus.

Mard o mard duels were not a part of the Roman military tradition at first, but this changed, possibly due to Roman military contacts with the Iranians. The *Bellum Gothicum*, for example, provides an account of the Iranian commander Artabazes of the *numerus persoiustiniani* serving in Europe accepting the challenge of the Goth warlord Wallaris as the two opposing armies were assembling near Faenza, Italy, in 542 CE.[38] Non-Romans influenced by the Iranian military tradition of fighting duels with lances fought for the Roman side. As noted previously in Chapter 6, Armenian naxarar knights were equipped and fought like their Iranian counterparts. Procopius reports on an Armenian knight in Belisarius' service named Anzalas who fought a duel against Coccas, a Roman traitor who was serving in the Gothic ranks. Anzalas was victorious when he overcame Coccas' lance charge by shifting his horse to the side to then be 'placed on his enemy's flank and ... thrust his spear ... Coccas fell from his horse ... a dead man'.[39]

The tradition of Sassanian warrior-kings engaging in the duel is depicted in rock reliefs, notably in a relief at Nagshe Rustam that shows, in two panels, King Bahram II duelling his enemies. The upper panel portrays Bahram unseating Roman Emperor Carus (r. 282–283 CE) with his lance and the lower panel depicts Bahram employing his lance to defeat a Sassanian rival.[40] As noted previously in Chapter 6, the Sassanian lance joust was itself a part of a wider and older Iranian martial tradition (i.e. Saka of Chorasmia, Scythians, etc.).[41,42]

The Arabo-Islamic Caliphates (661–1258)

The legacy of the Sassanian military machine was to strongly resonate in the succeeding caliphates. As noted by Inostransev, 'The more closely the early history of Islam is investigated, the more exactly we are able to establish the strong Persian influence on the evolution of Islamic ideas and institutions.'[43] This is not altogether surprising as the overall Sassanian legacy on the Islamic caliphates with respect to arts, architecture, etc. is well established.

Transmission of Sassanian military theory to the Arabs. The first example of the transmission of military ideas to the Arabs was noted in previous chapters when the Iranian convert to Islam, Salman Farsi, taught the Arabs to dig a defensive trench for use by their foot archers. But apart from this well-known case in the early days of Islam in Arabia, how were Sassanian military ideas passed on to the Arabs during and after the Arab conquests? Hamblin notes that such transmission first occurred over the course of the Arab conquest of Iran (637–651 CE),[44] when many Sassanian veterans, notably savaran warriors and Dailamite infantry and archers, joined the Arab armies. These veterans were of two types, converts to Islam and paid mercenaries. The latter were paid double the salary of Arab troops, a testimony to the respect the Arabs had for professional Iranian warriors. Hamblin also observes that transmission occurred through the gradual adoption of Sassanian weaponry, a process that began in the early days of the caliphates. An example of this is the case of an Arab commander who obtained permission to distribute Sassanian weapons from local Iranian armouries to equip Muslim warriors campaigning in Transoxiana. The adoption of Sassanian-type weapons is notable as by the time of the Abbasid rebellion in Khorasan against the Ummayads, numbers of local Arab troops were equipped with weapons and equipment similar to that of their Iranian counterparts. A third means of transmission was the adoption of Sassanian military theory and organization. This was concomitant in part with the translation of Pahlavi language military literature into Arabic. In all of these endeavours, the role of the savaran and dehkans was seminal (see below).

The Azadan and military literature: translations into Arabic. Professional Sassanian warriors had already settled in Yemen in the time of Khosrow I. Specifically, Khosrow I had dispatched 800 warriors led by a commander named Vahriz to secure the region in the late 570s–late 590s CE against the Abyssinian(s) who were friendly with the Byzantines (Chapter 8). As noted by Matofi, the Vahriz soldiers remained in Yemen, marrying local Yemeni women and thus giving rise to the Abna clan.[45] By the time of the advent of Islam, the Abna had negotiated with prophet Mohammed, converting to Islam and joining the prophet's army. Full-fledged Sassanian military influence upon the Arabs, however, would begin in earnest during and after the Muslim conquests of the Sassanian Empire.

After the fall of Sassanian Persia, many of the Sassanian cavalry elites had remained settled in Iraq and even Syria. These cavalry elites had often been assigned to frontier posts and fortified settlements along the Romano-Byzantine frontiers. As a result of the Heraclius-Khosrow II wars in 628, the Sassanian Empire was forced to cede its territorial conquests in Syria to the Byzantines, who in turn lost these to the Arabo-Islamic armies by the early 640s CE. By the time of the Arab conquests, these Sassanian troops, along with local citizens who were employed by them, were still present in the (former) Sassanian-ruled regions of Syria. Khorasan and the eastern realms of the former Sassanian Empire still retained a significant presence of the cavalry elites of the dehkans. These all played an important role in the transmission of Sassanian military ideas to the Arabs.

One of the most remarkable aspects of the Arab conquest of Sassanian Persia is how Iran retained its distinct culture and identity. This is all the more remarkable as ancient peoples such as the Babylonians, Syrians and Egyptians essentially abandoned their historical identities in favour of Arab culture. The question has often been raised as to how and why Iran did not become a culturally Arab country, despite having adopted Islam. One of the answers may lie in the military legacy of the Sassanians and the translations of their military literature into Arabic.

As noted by Zakeri, the savaran knights known now as the *Asbaran* constituted the militant front of the Azadan nobility which had converted to Islam.[46] As clients of the Arabs they resented their second-class status and played a major role in helping the Abbasids eject the Ummayads from power in 750 CE. Once in power the Abbasids placed many of these Iranians in important administrative positions (i.e. as government officials, administrators, secretaries, etc.). It was these officials of mainly Iranian background who undertook the translation of Pahlavi (Middle Persian) texts, much of which contained military knowledge. A key figure in this important process of translating Pahlavi texts into Arabic was an Iranian convert to Islam known as Roozbeh son of Dadveh son of Jushnasp (Gushnasp), otherwise known as Ibn-Muqaffa (c. 756 CE). He translated a large number of Pahlavi books into Arabic, notably books on the ancient kings of Iran. In this respect, these literary developments took two distinct forms. The first was the 'heroic' martial epic type with the other being more of the 'technical' type with direct (Pahlavi to Arabic) translations of Sassanian military literature.

The first category of the heroic martial epic is identified by Stern as pre-Islamic Iran's heroic tales of warriors and their military exploits.[47] Zakeri notes that this process of keeping alive the pre-Islamic (military) traditions of Iran over the generations had two distinct impacts.[48] The first was to retain the martial spirit of ancient Iran, which in turn preserved Iranian national identity. In this endeavour, the *Shahname* epic also became a valuable source of information on pre-Islamic Iran's military tactics, martial and heroic traditions and weaponry. The transmissions of Iranian heroic literature also left a profound impact upon non-Iranian Muslims, as much pre-Islamic literature became available in Arabic. Nevertheless this latter case was also very much oral and soon passed on down the generations to become a significant part of the lore of Arabicized countries throughout the caliphate.

The second 'technical' category of Pahlavi works translated into Arabic comprised Sassanian books and treatises on military sciences, tactics, weapons, etc., much of which has already been discussed in the introduction and previous chapters (i.e. *Oyoon ol-Akhbar*, etc.). What is of interest is how direct the parallels are between the later Arabic literature of military treatises and their older Sassanian-based counterparts. One example is a comparison of the *Kitab ol-Ayin* and the fourteenth-century Arabic text, the *Nihayat al S'ul* (Table 7). There are at least six direct parallels between the two documents, as well as direct parallels between the *Kitab ol-Ayin* and the Byzantine *Strategikon* manual written possibly sometime in the later sixth century CE (see Table 4, Chapter 9). The citations of the *Strategikon* in Table 4 pertain to that document's descriptions of Sassanian fighting methods from the Romano-Byzantine point of view.

Hamblin has drawn two conclusions with respect to comparisons between the *Kitab ol-Ayin* and *Nihayat al S'ul*.[49] The first pertains to descriptions of Sassanian military tactics and their appearance in the *Strategikon*. Hamblin notes that this suggests that Sassanian military manuals provided information that was not simply 'theoretical' but also applied on the battlefield. The parallels between the *Kitab ol-Ayin* and the *Nihayat al S'ul* are also strongly indicative that the Sassanians put their theories to use on the battlefield. Hamblin's second conclusion pertains to the direct influence of Sassanian military literature on later Arab language treatises, thus indicating a strong pre-Islamic Iranian influence on the armies of the caliphates.

The Shuubiya movement, the futuwwa and the faris. One of the important outcomes of this virtual explosion of translation of non-Arab works into Arabic by the Azadan was the emergence of the Shuubiya movement. While the actual ideological Arab-Persian cultural interactions of this movement are outside the scope of our discussion, of interest is the impact of this movement upon the Sassanian-to-Arab military transmission.

One of the outcomes of the Shuubiya movement was the *futuwwa*, a term broadly synonymous with 'Islamic chivalry' which Western scholars have noted

Table 7. Comparisons between the *Kitab ol Ayin* and *Nihayat al S'ul*.
(adapted from Hamblin, 1986)

	Kitab ol Ayin	*Nihayat al S'ul*
Courage	'The men selected should be courageous, bold, alert, and stern'. (p. 113, 1.18)	[soldiers] '... should be courageous and bold' (1.8)
Discipline of the Senses	[select soldiers] '... who do not wail, cough or sneeze (p. 113, 1.19)	[soldiers must] '... not be noisy or suffering from coughing or excessive sneezing' (1.8)
Horses	[select] '... mounts for them which don't whine or neigh' (p. 113, 1.19)	[the commander] 'should select ... quiet mounts that are not inclined to whining or neighing' (1.4)
Ambushes and Wild Beasts	'... ambushers should not frighten wild animals or birds ...' (p. 114 1.2)	[soldiers] 'should not startle/frighten wild animals or birds' (1.32)
Ambushes and Booty	'... If the ambushers wish to take booty it is best to have more than one ambush' (p. 114, 1.3)	'... now it is better that the ambush party be divided into two groups ...' (1.39)
Water Supplies	'... the place of their ambush should be ... near water which they can drink if they are forced to stay a long time' (p. 113, 1.2 to p. 114, 1.10)	[select] 'a position close to water so that, should the operation be delayed, they will not be afflicted by thirst ...' (1.21)

as having influenced European chivalry, but with roots in pre-Islamic Iran's martial tradition. Zakeri has discussed the connections between the Azadan and the futuwwa movement in considerable detail;[50] these will be briefly summarized in two points here. First, much of the original literature of the movement was of Iranian origin. Iranian terms certainly entered Arabian usage, one example being horsemanship. Second, the originators of the movement were the *Asawira* (*Asbaran* or savaran knights) who were descended from the House of Sassan in Khorasan, Balkh and eastern Iran in general.[51] In addition, the Arabic literature pertaining to the futuwwa originated in Balkh. Nevertheless, the rise of the futuwwa is invariably much more complex than the overview provided here. Other possible influences have been ascribed to former Sassanian urban elites who formed artisan guilds and evoked Salman Farsi as their master. Recall that Salman was the Iranian convert to Islam who hailed from the savaran dehkan class (Chapter 17). In general, Salman appears as one of the original founders of the futuwwa, especially due to his close ties to the prophet Mohammad and his significant military service to the Muslims. By the tenth–eleventh centuries CE, the futuwwa were evident in Khorasan, being composed of groups of men known as *javan* (Persian: youth). The Abbasid Caliph al-Nasser (1158–1225 CE) organized a formal futuwwa class from local princes and other nobles with the caliph as the master of the order. These futuwwa were mounted knights, essentially an echo of the savaran knights of the Sassanians. Like the savaran knights, these futuwwa knights were fully expected to follow strict rules of proper conduct, notably generosity, patience, protection of the helpless and weak, etc., virtues nearly identical to the pahlavan martial culture of the Sassanians. It is notable that in modern day Arab cultures, the term futuwwa often denotes characteristics of generosity, chivalrous qualities and other standards of high virtue.

The term *faris* means 'knight' in Arabic, which is indeed of interest as the Arab term for Persian is also *Farsi*, or *Fors*. Al-Masoudi's Muruj defines the faris as thus:[52] 'A true cavalier ... who does not count on living long ... he never returns from battle before the day is done ... when [ordinary] soldiers, fearing their lives, look for encouragement to go on – [the faris/cavaliers] storm the ranks with drawn swords'.

The above description is essentially little different from that of the savaran knights, whose military role as elites was essential to the field army, especially during battle when the regular troops were under extreme duress. Again, it is here where one may find information of the importance of Sassanian military influence upon the Arabs in the *shuubiya* movements. Of special interest are the comments of al-Jahiz, who despite being pro-Arab in these debates is quick to highlight the importance of the Persian cavalry of old and their mighty influences upon the Arabs. As noted by al-Jahiz in *Bayan*:[53]

> You did not use to fight in the night, did not know of raids and ambush, or of right, left, centre, or flank of the army, neither of the vanguard or rearguard; nor of reconnaissance patrol or [darraja]. You had not known of war equipments such as wheeled convoy [rattla], small mangonels [arrada], mangonels [majaniqh], armoured vehicles [dabbaba], or ditches or spike horns, or coats of mail [aqbiya] or trousers [sarawwil], or the hanging of swords, or of drums or banners, or protective armour, or coats of mail [jawshan], or helmets [khud], or arm-guards, or bells, or lassos, or Banjikan [apparent reference to Panjagan which fired five arrows simultaneously] or hurling of oil and fire ... Your [the Arabs'] javelins were made of elastic wood, and your spears were made of cow horns, and you used to ride horses unsaddled, whereas the Persians had saddles.

There are two important observations that may be made here. The first is pointed out by Zakeri, who notes that 'several of the weapons listed [by al-Jahiz] played a pivotal role in the institution of the Futuwwa'.[54] Zakeri then goes on to describe the initiation ceremonies of the futuwwa in which the items are used, etc., again demonstrating parallels with Sassanian military culture.

The second observation that may be made from al-Jahiz's description is the Arab adoption of Sassanian military organization and weaponry, as alluded to earlier with Hamblin.[55] Put simply, the description highlights the direct influence upon the Arabs of a wide spectrum of military ideas and equipment. The first is in the arena of military organization and tactics. As noted in Chapter 9, Sassanian armies had a well-defined rationale for having a left, centre, right, rearguards, etc., which were passed on to the Arabs, a major factor in enabling the caliphates to create powerful and professional standing armies. What is interesting to investigate is whether Iranian military personnel of the post-Sassanian type were brought by the Arabs to help prosecute their successful conquest of

Spain in 711–718 CE. As noted in Chapter 17, the early Muslims in Arabia had had significant experience with rapid raids, but the addition of formal military tactics such as reconnaissance would have granted the caliphate's armies significantly better (battlefield) situational awareness. It would also appear that a significant array of siege warfare equipment had also been adopted by the Arabs or caliphates, notably Sassanian-type mangonels and the use of flammable substances. The system of ditches had of course been passed on very early to the Arabs, as discussed with respect to Salman Farsi. The knowledge of spikes and deadly iron traps were certainly encountered early by the Arabs, as their warriors did have to contend with these at the Battle of Nahavand (Chapter 17). As per the Arabian faris knights, al-Jahiz is providing descriptions of the late Sassanian composite knights who wore armour and mail, helmets, etc. Interestingly, it would appear that Sassanian equestrian technology had deeply influenced the Arabs as well. This is significant as the Arabs were superb horsemen in their own right. Last but not least is al-Jahiz's mention of the *banjikan*, which is apparently identical to the panjagan which could fire five arrows simultaneously (Chapter 5). This would again suggest that the Arab borrowing of Iranian military technology had been comprehensive. The powerful legacy of the Sassanian military in the Abbasid Caliphate has led Agoston and Masters to conclude that 'the Abbasid Caliphate (750–1250) borrowed heavily from the Sassanids in terms of military organization, logistics, tactics, provincial and imperial administration, court culture and manners'.[56]

The Turkic world, the Ottoman Empire and the Turco-Iranian Legacy

The role of the Sassanians in the military developments of the Turkic and Hsiang-Nou peoples has been acknowledged by Western historiography. Newark for example, states that 'Sasanid Persian weaponry and armour influenced steppe warriors such as the Huns and Turks, and later influenced the Arabs.'[57] Nevertheless, the notion of 'influence' with respect to the Iranian and Turkic worlds is a complex process as the two peoples have been strongly intermixed since pre-Islamic times due to wars, economic activity and migrations. What has occurred, especially with respect to military technology and doctrine, is a complex process of mutual influence in which Iranians have influenced Turks and related Hsiang-Nou peoples and vice versa. This process of mutual military influence between Central Asia and the Iranian plateau was one that pre-dated the Turkic and Hsiang-Nou arrivals, and can be possibly traced back to the early spread of Indo-European peoples and their arrivals onto the Iranian plateau, Afghanistan and northern India. The Iranian branch of the Indo-Europeans established hegemony over Iran and Afghanistan, forming ruling aristocracies that would often be faced with military challenges from their Iranic kinsmen in Central Asia. Cyrus the Great was killed while campaigning against the Massagetae, who were subjugated by Darius the Great. Chapter 6 has already outlined the important influence of the Iranic peoples of Central Asia upon the Achaemenids and the Parthians, followed by the mighty influence of the Turk and Hsiang-Nou peoples upon the

Sassanians. Meanwhile Iranian influences continued to manifest among the Turks, especially the Seljuk Turks and their Ottoman successors in Anatolia.

The military systems of the Iranians and the Turks were already influencing each other by the late Sassanian era, a process that was to continue well into the Islamic era, resulting in what may be termed as the Turco-Iranian military tradition. This is a topic which merits its own analytical study. Suffice it to say that the Turks significantly influenced the armies of the caliphates, with many Turkic warriors serving the Abbasids, who greatly appreciated their military skills even over those of the Arabs.

This was clearly demonstrated in the three-decade long anti-Caliphate rebellion (816–837 CE) of Babak Khorramdin in Azerbaijan. In that rebellion, the caliphate's armies were repeatedly defeated by Babak and his warriors up to the early 830s CE. News of Babak's victories galvanized warriors throughout Iran and motivated them to join the rebellion against the caliphate.[58] The tide finally turned against Babak when the caliphate employed a predominantly Turkish army led by an Iranian general named Afshin in 836–837 CE. Pipes has noted the critical role Turkish troops played in the destruction of Babak's revolt.[59] Numbers of Turkish warriors had joined the caliphate's armies as early as 674 CE, shortly after the fall of the Sassanian Empire in 651 CE. These were both captured slaves from Central Asia pressed into military service and early converts to Islam. Early Turkish warriors were highly effective cavalrymen, having gained much experience in mounted warfare in their military encounters with the Sassanians. Caliph al-Motassem (933–CE), who presided over Babak's defeat, is also recognized as having fully incorporated Turkish warriors into the caliphate's armies at the expense of the Arabs.[60] Bugha al-Kabir, for example, who was an important caliphate general in the war against Babak, was a Turk.[61]

Latham and Paterson have noted the importance of the Turkish-Iranian military legacy of the Middle East, one key domain being archery.[62] The mutual military influences of the Iranians and the Turks can be seen in their respective military lexicons. The Turkish terms for *tufenk* and *zahtaneh* (musket, gun) for example, are Persian in origin.[63] The *Yeni-Cheri* or Janissaries of the Ottoman armies wore costumes of Persian inspiration[64] with the Ottoman *mehertane* military music also having roots in the Iranian martial tradition.[65] Ottoman Turks used a number of weapons bearing names of Persian origin. Examples include the *acemi kilic* (a slender sabre of Persian origin), and the *qaddara* or *gaddara* (a type of Persian knife).[66] Turkish maces bear Persian names as well, such as *gurz*, and the *shesh-par* (six feathered/faceted mace). The Turkish influence on the Iranians was equally vast, one example being the prevalence of Turco-Mongolian military terminology as late as the late eighteenth century. The military of the Zands (1750–1794) used Turkic terminology and systems of organization such as *ghazi* (regular trooper), *oon bashi* (leader of 10 ghazi), *elli-bashi* (leader of 50 troops), *yooz bashi* (leader of 100 troops or 10 oon bashi), *besh-yooz bashi* (leader of 500 troops), *meen bashi* (commanding 1,000 men or 10 yooz-bashi) and *iki meen bashi* (commander of 2,000 troops).[67]

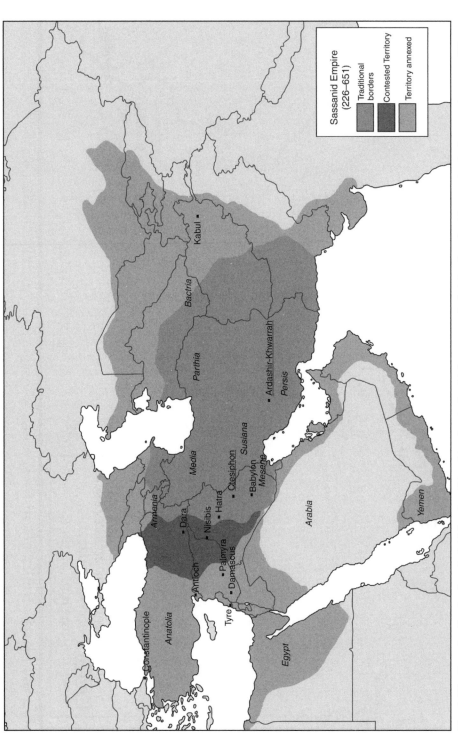

Map 1. The Sassanian Empire from its initial and traditional borders in the third century to its height of territorial expansion in the seventh century CE. (Source: Ancient History Encyclopedia Website, original source/creator of map by Wikipedia user Dcoetzee)

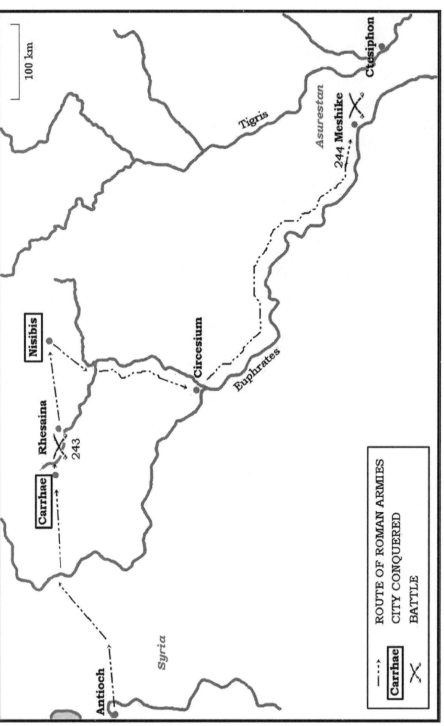

Map 2. Military Operations of Gordian III in 242–244 CE. (Courtesy: Katazyna Maksymiuk, Geography of Roman-Iranian Wars: Military Operations of Rome and Sassanian Iran, Siedlce, 2015, p. 32)

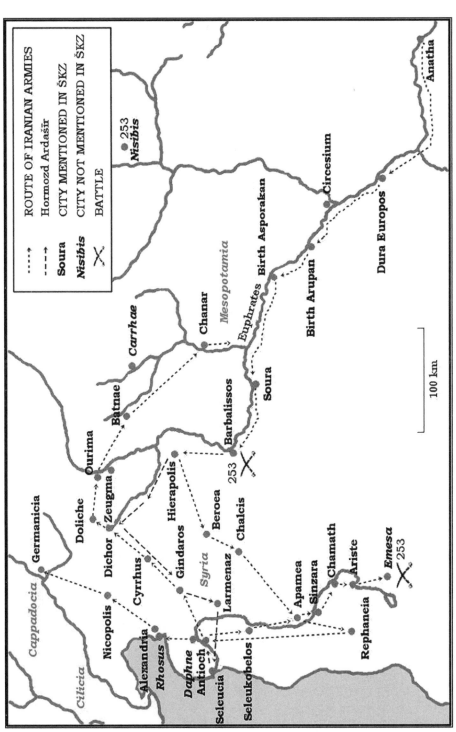

Map 3. Military operations of Shapur I in 253–256 CE according to the ŠKZ. (Courtesy: Katazyna Maksymiuk, Geography of Roman-Iranian Wars: Military Operations of Rome and Sassanian Iran, Siedlce, 2015, p. 35)

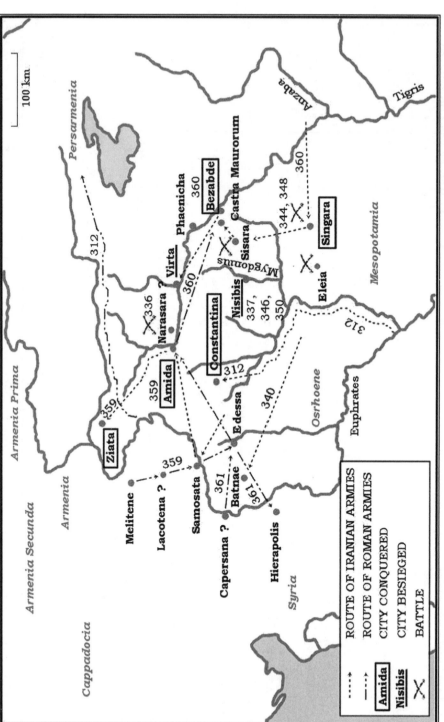

Map 4. Military Operations of Shapur II against the Romans in 312–360 CE. (Courtesy: Katazyna Maksymiuk, Geography of Roman-Iranian Wars: Military Operations of Rome and Sassanian Iran, Siedlce, 2015, p. 50)

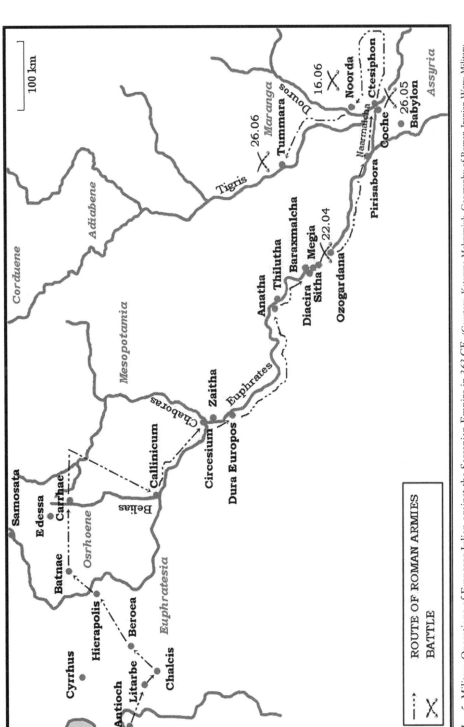

Map 5. Military Operations of Emperor Julian against the Sassanian Empire in 363 CE. (Courtesy: Katarzyna Maksymiuk, Geography of Roman-Iranian Wars: Military Operations of Rome and Sassanian Iran, Siedlce, 2015, p. 55)

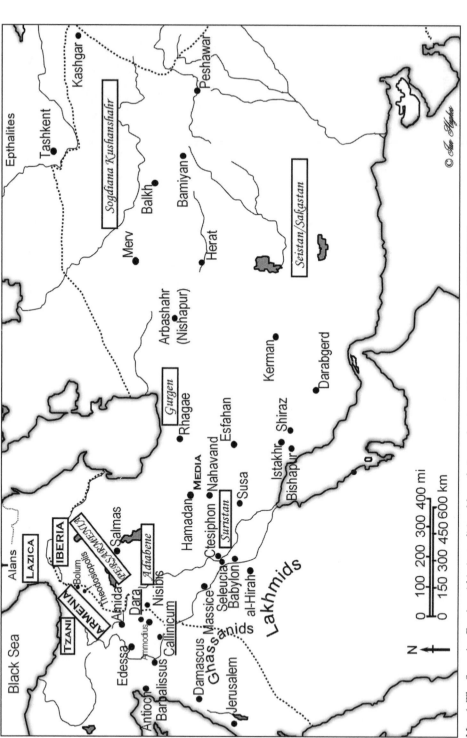

Map 6. The Sassanian Empire within its traditional boundaries at the time of Emperor Justinian (r. 527–565 CE). (Source: Ian Hughes, 2009)

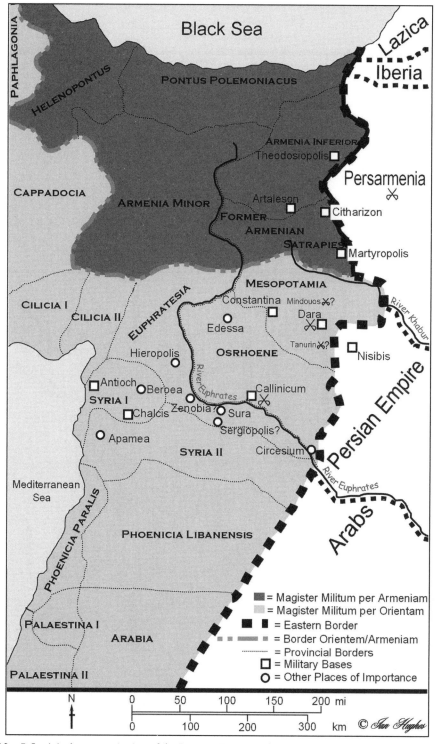

Map 7. Justinian's re-organization of the Romano-Byzantine frontier during sixth century CE.
(Source: Ian Hughes, 2009)

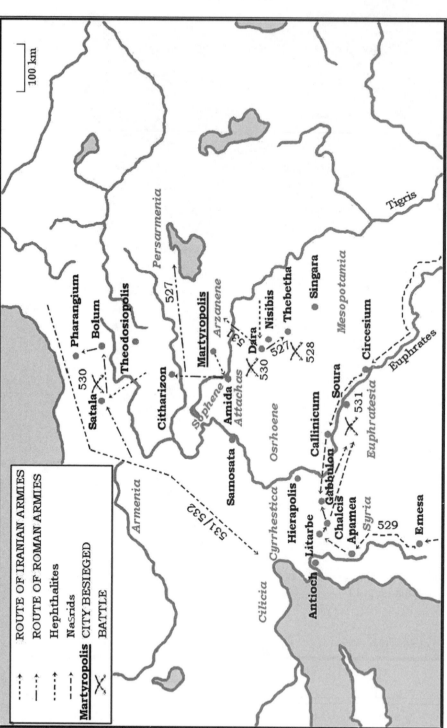

Map 8. Operations in 527–531 CE of the Roman and Sassanian armies. (Courtesy: Katazyna Maksymiuk, Geography of Roman-Iranian Wars: Military Operations of Rome and Sassanian Iran, Siedlce, 2015, p. 65)

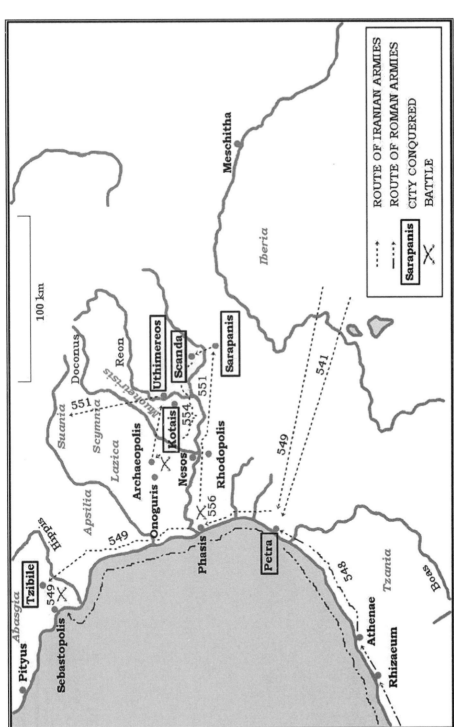

Map 9. Battles between Roman and Iranian armies in Lazica in 541–556. (Courtesy: Katazyna Maksymiuk, Geography of Roman-Iranian Wars: Military Operations of Rome and Sassanian Iran, Siedlce, 2015, p. 72)

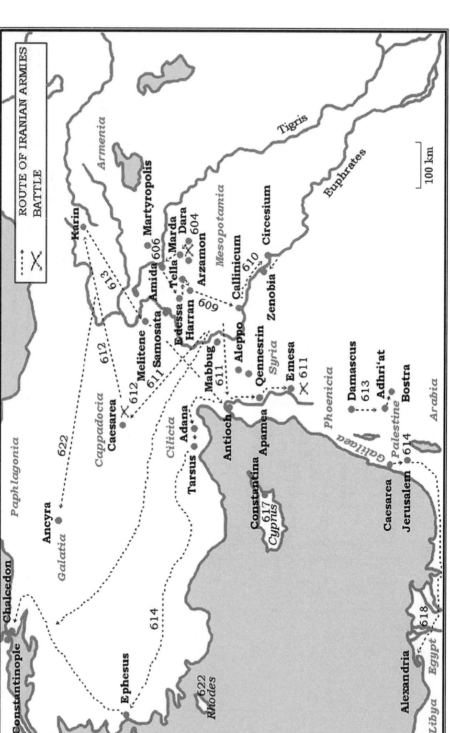

Map 10. Operations of the Spah against the Romano-Byzantine Empire in 603–622, during the reign of Khosrow II. (Courtesy: Katazyna Maksymiuk, Geography of Roman-Iranian Wars: Military Operations of Rome and Sassanian Iran, Siedlce, 2015, p. 86)

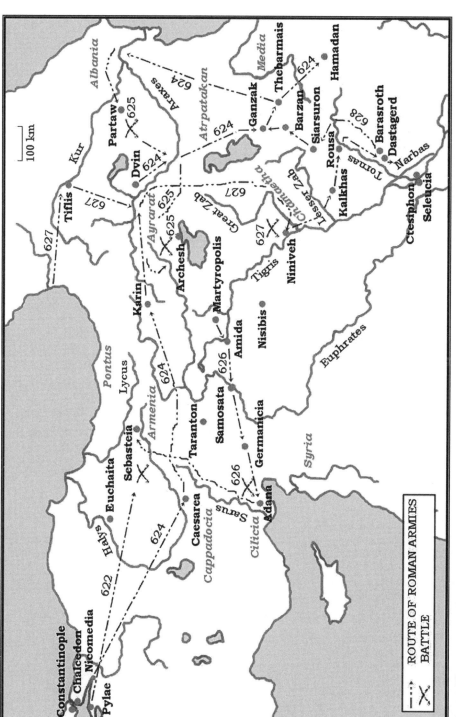

Map 11. The operations of Heraclius against the Sassanian Empire in 622–628 CE. (Courtesy: Katazyna Maksymiuk, Geography of Roman-Iranian Wars: Military Operations of Rome and Sassanian Iran, Siedlce, 2015, p. 92)

Notes

Introduction

1. Lukonin, 1983, p. 234.
2. Howard–Johnston, 1995, pp. 162, 165.
3. Farzin, 1387/2008, p. 10.
4. Consult Inostrancev 1926 and 1969 in references.
5. Inostrancev, 1969, p. 32.
6. Al-Masoudi (tr. Payandeh, 2002), pp. 97–98.
7. Of Iranian origin, Persian or Kurdish.
8. See discussion in Imam-Shoushtari, 1971, p. 195.
9. Inostrancev, 1926, p. 10.
10. See references for full citation of Rubin (1995); see especially pp. 227, 234–239. Readers are cautioned, however, that Rubin's article deals primarily with tax affairs and only tangentially with military affairs, which are the focus of this book.
11. Matofi, 1999, p. 196.
12. Shahbazi, 1986, pp. 489–499.
13. Jalali, 1383/2004, pp. 12–25.
14. Herodian, VI, 2.2–5.
15. *Ammianus Marcellinus*, XVII, V, 3–8.
16. Dio, LXXX, 4.1.
17. Nafisi, 1952, p. 22.
18. Pirnia, 1929, p. 244.
19. Greatrex, 1998, p. 11.
20. Potter, 1990, pp. 370–380.
21. Blockley, 1992, pp. 103–104.
22. Nöldeke, (1973, original print 1879), p. 3.
23. Mommsen (1996, original print 1885), Vol. II, p. 3.
24. Yarshater, 1971, pp. 517–532.
25. Daryaee, 2006, p. 495.
26. Daryaee, 2006, pp. 502–503.
27. Daryaee, 2006, p. 501.
28. Shahbazi, 2001, p. 61.
29. Daryaee, 2006, p. 501.
30. Charles, 2011, pp. 291–309.
31. Potter, 1990, pp. 370–380.
32. Dio, LV, 10. 7.
33. Rubin, 2008, p. 101.
34. Ewald & Norena, 2011, p. 242.
35. Fowden, 1993, pp. 27–31.
36. Farzin, 1387/2008, pp. 97–112.
37. Jalali, 1382/2003, p. 13.
38. Whitby, 1994, pp. 234–235.
39. Brown, 1971, p. 160, 163; Frye, 1984, p. 293.
40. Whitby, 1994, p. 235.

41. The fifth unfinished tomb possibly belongs to Artaxerxes III or Darius III, the last Achaemenid king. The case of Nagshe Rustam appears to be indicative of some type of Sassanian cognizance of a more ancient Achaemenid legacy.
42. Sarkhosh-Curtis, 1993, p. 57.
43. Amanat, 2012, p. 42.
44. Rose, 2011, p. 63.
45. Daryaee, 2009, p. 79.
46. Whitby, 1994, p. 235.
47. Goldman, 1993, p. 203–204.
48. Sefat–Gol, 1382/2003, p. 16.
49. Potter, 1990, pp. 370–380.
50. Keegan, 1993, p. 286.
51. Tafazolli, 2000, p. 14.
52. Karantabias, 2005, p. 30.
53. See detailed discussion by Jalali, 1383/2004, pp. 58–59.
54. Zaehner, 1955, p. 10.
55. See Safa (1384/2006) in references.
56. See Ansari (1383/2004) in references.
57. Farzin, 1387/2008, pp. 11–12.
58. Inostrancev, 1926, p. 18.
59. See text by Yaghmai (1367/1989) in references.
60. Alizadeh, Pahlavani & Sadrnia, 2004, p. 102.
61. Axworthy, 2010, p. 86.
62. Newman, 2006, p. 13.
63. Savory, 1994, p. 252. This copy of the *Shahname* was completed after Ismail's death.

Chapter 1: Martial Ardour, Origins and Missions of the Spah

1. Greatrex, 1998, p. 44.
2. Ibid.
3. Jalali, 1382/2003, p. 13.
4. *Ammianus Marcellinus*, XX, XI, 83.
5. As cited by Dodgeon & Lieu, 1991, p. 221.
6. Libanius, *Orationes* (tr. Norman, 1987), XVIII, 205–211.
7. *Ammianus Marcellinus*, XXII, XII, 1.
8. Howard-Johnston, 1995, p. 165.
9. Shahbazi, 1986, pp. 489–499
10. Jalali, 1383/2004, pp. 12–15.
11. Jalali, 1382/2003, p. 13.
12. McDonough, 2011, p. 293.
13. Bavzani, 1359/1980, p. 61.
14. The inscription records a dialogue in Parthian Pahlavi between two youths named Mihrban and Gerdazad who remark, '*Ardashir Xwadaw pad Xar Ayesid pad Xar ce Aneyos/sh*'; ['Lord Ardashir comes/rides upon a donkey which is mad/insane'] (Livshits, 2002, p. 34). Note that *xar* (donkey) remains a derogatory term in Iran and the Caucasus.
15. Jalali, 1382/2003, p. 13.
16. As cited from Nöldeke by Dodgeon & Lieu, 1991, p. 277, Appendix I.
17. Zarrin'kub, 1381/2002, p. 185.
18. Masia, 2000, p. 185.
19. McDonough, 2011, p. 295.
20. Jalali, 1382/2003, pp. 13–14.
21. Lukonin, 1372/1993 (tr. to Persian by Reza), p. 58.
22. Tashkari, 1356/1977, p. 23.
23. Mashkoor, 1366/1987, p. 87.

24. Tajbaksh, 1355/1976, p. 314.
25. Jalali, 1382/2003, p. 14.
26. Azghandi, 1374/1995, p. 18.
27. McDonough, 2011, p. 295.
28. Bayani, 1350/1971, p. 33.
29. As cited from Rawlinson, 1885, *History of the Sassanian or New Persian Empire* (1882), Chapter VI, pp. 124.
30. McDonough, 2011, p. 291.
31. McDonough, 2011, p. 293.
32. The term *Aryan* denotes "nobleman" and/or "freeman" in Old Iranian languages with cognates in Old Irish or Gaelic. The semantics of the term *Aryan* is completely distinct from the racialist ideology of Nordic supremacy. Such Eurocentric writings were first formulated in the nineteenth century by racialist philosophers such as Chamberlain. Mallory makes clear that 'as an ethnic designation, the word [Aryan] is most properly limited to the Indo-Iranians, and most justly to the latter where it still gives its name to the country Iran ... the great Persian king Darius described himself as Aryan' (1989, pp. 125–126).
33. Garsoian, 1976, pp. 194–196.
34. McDonough, 2011, p. 294.

Chapter 2: Organization: Military Titles and Recruitment

1. *Letter of Tansar* (ed. Minovi, 1911), pp. 50, 19–20.
2. *Dinkard* (ed. Madan, 1932), p. 4.
3. As cited by Grignasci, 1966, p. 42.
4. *Karnamag*, Chapter 4.19.
5. Tafazzoli, 2000, p. 6.
6. Tafazolli, 2000, pp. 16–17.
7. *Wast* in Parthian-Pahlavi.
8. Jalali, 1383/2004, p. 93.
9. Ibid.
10. Christensen, 1944, p. 210.
11. Consult Firdowsi's *Shahname* (VIII, pp. 343). The *Shahname* may be accessed on-line at: http://www.kavehfarrokh.com/iranica/firdowsi-2/.
12. Tafazzoli, 2000, pp. 4–5.
13. Jalali, 1383/2004, p. 113.
14. Tafazzoli, 2000, p. 10.
15. Ibid.
16. Baladuri, *Futuh al-Buldan* (ed. De Goeje, 1866 & 1969), p. 343, section 708.
17. *Tabari* (ed. De Goeje), I, 6, p. 3249.
18. Ibid.
19. Nöldeke, 1973, p. 284.
20. Pourdavood, 1336/1957, p. 244–245.
21. Jalali, 1383/2004, p. 111.
22. Farzin, 1387/2008, p. 102. Marek J. Olbrycht (Manpower resources and army organization on the Arsakid Empire. *Ancient Society*, 46, pp. 291–338, 2016) notes that total number of troops (elite and supporting levies/contingents) could have been 120,000 when the empire fully mobilized across all provinces and allied regions. However our discussion here pertains to elite professional troops capable of equitably challenging Roman and Turkic-Hun warriors.
23. Lucian, *Quomodo Hist.* (tr. Kilburn, 1959), p. 29.
24. Debevoise, 1968, p. 83; Widengrem, 1976, pp. 261–283.
25. See translation of SKZ (Shapur Kaba Zartusht) in Frye, 1984, Appendix 4.
26. Farzin, 1387/2008, p. 104.
27. Dinawari, Abu Hanifa, *Akhbar ol Tawwal* (tr. Damghani, 1368/1989), p. 121.
28. Ibid.
29. Lukonin, 1372/1993 (tr. to Persian by Reza), pp. 106–107.

30. Consult excerpt by Dodegeon & Lieu, 1991, p. 31
31. See discussion by Charles, 2007, pp. 305–308.
32. Consult Tabari, as translated by Nöldeke, p. 271.
33. Pigulevskaya, 1354/1975 (tr. to Persian by Keshavarz), p. 110. This is based on *Tabari*'s (ed. De Goeje, I, p. 869) analysis of the three offices.
34. Nöldeke 1973 (tr. to Persian by Zaryab), pp. 55–56.
35. See discussion by Wiesehofer, 1996, p. 188.
36. Tafazzoli, 2000, p. 9.
37. Zarrin'kub, 1381/2002, p. 184.
38. Nafisi, 1331/1952, p. 257.
39. Osheidari, 1371/1992, p. 97.
40. Wiesehofer, 1996, p. 188.
41. Ibid.
42. Tafazzoli, 2000, p. 10.
43. Consult also Vullers, 1962, Volume I, p. 76.
44. For a full discussion on the etymology of *Arteshtar* and its origins refer to W. Sundermann in the *Encyclopedia Iranica*, 'ARTĒŠTĀR'.
45. The Avestan/Sanskrit root term *Raθa/Ratha* (lit. rotate/rotation on an axis) is consistent with the earlier Indo-Aryan arrivals into the Near East, the Iranian plateau and the Indian subcontinent where warriors would be riding battle chariots (See overview of Indo-European, specifically Indo-Aryan and proto-Iranian arrivals in Mallory, 1989, pp. 35–56). Archeological expeditions demonstrate that the chariot was used in the proto-Iranian realms since the third millennium BCE (see for example, Ghirshman, 1977, p. 15.). The *Yasht* hymns also make reference to 'charioteers' described as *Raθaēštā* (Yasht 10.112).
46. Consult Mayrhofer's *Onomastica Persepolitana: Das altiranische Namengut der Persepolis*, 1973, item no. 8.1423.
47. *Yasht*, 13.88–89.
48. The term linguistically evolved into *Ratēštār* and then to *Artēštār*, most likely by the Parthian era.
49. Consult W. Sundermann in the *Encyclopedia Iranica*, 'ARTĒŠTĀR'.
50. Nöldeke, 1973, p. 173.
51. *Tabari* (ed. De Goeje), I, p. 869.
52. Christensen, 1944, p. 122, 140, 394.
53. Foss, 2002, p. 160–171.
54. Tafazzoli, 2000, p. 12.
55. As cited by Jalali, 1383/2004, p. 108.
56. Ibid.
57. Procopius, *Persian Wars*, I.6, 11.
58. Tafazzoli, 2000, p. 10.
59. Ibid.
60. Tafazzoli, 2000, p. 7.
61. *Karnamag*, Chapter 15, 9.
62. Jalali, 1383/2004, p. 87.
63. Zarrin'kub, 1381/2002, p. 190.
64. Hekmat, 1342/1964, p. 1089.
65. Jalali, 1383/2004, p. 109.
66. Ibid.
67. Ibid.
68. Christensen, 1944, p. 421.
69. Reza, 1374/1995, p. 16.
70. Lukonin, 1985, p. 703.
71. Ibid.
72. Lukonin, 1985, pp. 702–706.
73. Mahamedi, 2003, p. 154.
74. *Tarikh Yagoubi* (tr. to Persian by M.I. Ayti), Volume I, p. 219.

75. Nafisi, 1331/1952, p. 249.
76. Jalali, 1383/2004, p. 112.
77. Note that the reference is to historical Azarbaijan or Azerbaijan south of the Araxes in Iran; the south Caucasian region known today as the Republic of Azerbaijan was not known as *Azerbaijan* until 27 May 1918; this territory was generally known as *Albania* and *Arran* during the pre-Islamic and Islamic eras (for example, see historical maps compiled by Galichian in 2010, 2012).
78. The term *kanarang* may have an East Iranic origin. For further discussion see Diakonov (1967, p. 421) who notes that the kanarang was responsible for facing the Hephthalites and Kushans.
79. For a detailed overview of all these titles, consult Osheidari, 1371/1992, pp. 69, 187 and 431.
80. Sami, 1342/1964, Volume II, p. 50.
81. Wiesehofer, 1996, p. 198.
82. *Tarikh Yagoubi* (tr. to Persian by M.I. Ayti, 1342/1963), Volume I, p. 219.
83. Jalali, 1383/2004, p. 110.
84. Adontz, 1970, pp. 168–169.
85. Christensen, 1944, p. 368.
86. Tafazolli, 2000, p. 13.
87. *Tarikh Yagoubi* (tr. to Persian by M.I. Ayti, 1342/1963), Volume I, p. 219.
88. Jalali, 1383/2004, p. 112.
89. Mashkoor, 1345/1966, p. 162.
90. MohammadiMalayeri, 1372/1993, p. 321.
91. As cited by Jalali, 1382/2003, p. 19.
92. Imam-Shushtari, 1350/1971, p. 60.
93. Jalali, 1383/2004, p. 60.
94. Imam-Shushtari, 1350/1971, p. 60.
95. Tafazolli, 2000, p. 21.
96. Aljahshiyari's *Kitab ol al-Vozara va al-Kitab* (tr. by Tabatabai, 1348/1970), p. 29.
97. Ibid.
98. Ibid.
99. Tafazzoli, 2000, p. 27.
100. Dinawari, Abu Hanifa, *Akhbar ol Tawwal* (ed. Guirgass, 1888), p. 57.
101. Tafazzoli, 2000, p. 27.
102. See for example *Tabari* (ed. De Goeje, 1879–1901), I, p. 962.
103. Browne, 1900, p. 231.
104. Tafazzoli, 2000, p. 23.
105. *Theophylact*, 4.1.
106. Critical to this coup were Khosrow II's maternal uncles, Bindoe and Bestam. It is not clear if the murder of Hormuzd II was directly instigated by Khosrow II himself (thereby being guilty of patricide) or done independently at the initiative of Khosrow II's uncles.
107. Dinawari, Abu Hanifa, *Akhbar ol Tawwal* (tr. Damghani, 1368/1989), p. 116.
108. See discussion by Daryaee, 2009, pp. 127–129.
109. Ghirshman, 1962, p. 176. Interestingly, Anahita's hairstyle is reminiscent of the Mediterranean goddess Kore.
110. See author's photographs in Farrokh, 2005, pp. 7 and 54. Note that the Nagshe Rajab site also shows knights standing with suspended broadswords behind the mounted monarch. It is possible that the Mobad represented is Kartir.
111. Consult Ghirshman, 1962, pp. 169–172.
112. Frye, 1984, p. 128.
113. Other titles included *Ohrmzad Mobad* (High priest of Ohrmazd or Ahura-Mazda), *Kartir e Bokht-Rawan-Wahram e Ohrmazd Mobad* (Kartir the Mobad of the Blessed Wahram and Ohrmazd) and *Ewenbed* (Master of Ceremony).
114. Daryaee, 2009, p. 128.
115. Abbas & Imam-Shushtari, 1347/1968, p. 23.
116. Ivanov, 1980, p. 171.
117. See detailed discussion by Jalali, 1383/2004, pp. 59–58.

118. Nizam ol Molk Tusi, *Siyasat Nameh* (ed. Ghazvini & Modaressi–Chahardahi, 1343/1964), p. 119.
119. *Raftarnamye Anoushirvan* (tr. Imam-Shushtari, 1348/1970), pp. 248–249.
120. Mohammadi, 1340–1341/1961–1962, pp. 31–34.
121. Mohammadi, 1340–1341/1961–1962, p. 32.
122. *Agathias*, III, XVII, 6–9.
123. Moghtader, 1315/1936, p. 167.
124. See for example Adontz, 1970, pp. 8–24, 165–182.
125. As noted by Professor Mark Whittow of Oxford University: 'The oldest outside influence in Trans-Caucasia is that of Persia (p. 203) ... many of its populations, including Armenians and Georgians, as well as Persians and Kurds, the Transcaucasus had much closer ties with the former Sassanian world to its south and east than with the world to the west' (p. 204) (Whittow, 1996, pp. 203–204).
126. See for example discussion by Adontz, 1970, Chapter IX.
127. Kolesnikoff, 2535/1976, p. 245.
128. Sami, 1342/1964, p. 60.
129. Moses of Dasxuranci, *History of the Albanians* (tr. Dowsett, 1961), pp. 110–113.
130. As cited by Mostashari, 2006, p. 17.
131. *Sebeos* (tr. Thompson, 1999), 11, 14, 16–19.
132. Zarrin'kub, 1381/2002, p. 196.
133. Pigulevskaya, 1372/1994, p. 203.
134. Whitby, 1994, p. 255.
135. Jalali, 1383/2004, p. 62.
136. Sami, 1342/1964, p. 60.
137. Chegini & Nikitin, 1996, p. 42.
138. Zarrin'kub, 1381/2002, p. 205.
139. Jalali, 1383/2004, p. 67.
140. Nafisi, 1331/1952, pp. 2–3.
141. Jalali, 1383/2004, p. 67.
142. Daryaee, 2009, p. 40.
143. Daryaee, 2009, p. 41.
144. Sami, 1342/1964, p. 60.
145. *Ammianus Marcellinus*, XIX, II, 3.
146. Reza, 1374/1995, p. 88.

Chapter 3: Military Reforms of the Sixth Century CE

1. Lit. 'He of the Immortal Spirit'.
2. Daryaee, 2009, pp. 26–30, 88.
3. Rubin, 1995, p. 229.
4. Daryaee, 2009, p. 27.
5. Litvinskij, 1999, p. 140.
6. Daryaee, 2009, p. 28.
7. Pigulevskaya, 1354/1975, p. 125.
8. Christensen, 1944, p. 370.
9. *Tabari*, I, p. 489.
10. Tafazzoli, 2000, p. 8.
11. Frye, 1985, p. 154.
12. Tafazolli (2000, p. 8) explains this as being due to religious reasons as the northern marches were also seen as the gate to hell according to Zoroastrian theology.
13. Markwart, 1901, p. 125.
14. Christensen, 1944, p. 375.
15. As cited from Tafazzoli, 2000, p. 8.
16. *Firdowsi* (ed. Foroughi, 1364/1985), p. 501.
17. *Firdowsi* (ed. Mohl, 1995), pp. 2195–2186.

18. Christensen, 1944, p. 371.
19. Adontz, 1970, pp. 168–169.
20. Greatrex, 1998, p. 45.
21. See entire discussion by Rubin (1995).
22. Schindel, 2003, pp. 675–690.
23. Howard-Johnston, 2010, pp. 50–51.
24. Howard-Johnston, 2010, p. 53.
25. Reza, 1374/1995, pp. 96–97.
26. HowardJohnston, 2010, p. 54.
27. Reza, 1374/1995, p. 97.
28. Howard-Johnston, 2010, p. 53.
29. Reza, 1374/1995, p. 97.
30. Howard-Johnston, 2010, p. 55.
31. Reza, 1374/1995, p. 97.
32. Ibid.
33. *Sirat Anoushirvan* (ed. Mohammadi, 1349/1970, pp. 31–34) pp. 371–372.
34. *Sirat Anoushirvan* (ed. Mohammadi, 1349/1970, pp. 31–34) p. 372.
35. Dinawari, *Akhbar ol Tawwal* (ed. Guirgass, 1888), p. 74.
36. Matofi, 1378/1999, p. 209.
37. *Tarikh-e Gozide* (ed. Navai, 1363/1984), p. 110.
38. Zoka, Shushtari, & Ghaem-Maghami, 1349/1970, pp. 21–30.
39. Matofi, 1387/1999, p. 209.
40. Dinawari, *Akhbar ol Tawwal* (ed. Guirgass, 1888), p. 79.
41. Tafazzoli, 2000, p. 14.
42. Dinawari, *Akhbar ol Tawwal* (tr. Arabic to Persian, Damghani, 1368/1989), p. 101.
43. Imam-Shushtari, 1350/1971, p. 103.
44. Ibid.
45. Ibid.
46. Matofi, 1378/1999, p. 210.
47. Whitby, 1994, p. 247.
48. These are cited from the compendium made by Matofi, 1378/1999, pp. 210–211.
49. Turnbull, 2004, p. 25.
50. See for example of Khosrow Anoushirvan's visit to the empire's Caucasian marches in Ganja, Derbent and regions facing the Turkic Khazars in the *Sirat Anoushirvan* (ed. Mohammadi, 1349/1970), pp. 355–356.
51. Jalali, 1383/2004, p. 103.
52. *Theophylact*, III, 18.7–9.
53. Lukonin, 1985, p. 700.
54. Ibid.
55. Procopius, *Wars*, I, XXIII, 14.
56. Whitby, 1994, p. 258.
57. Christensen, 1944, p. 444.
58. Whitby, 1994, p. 250.
59. As cited from Whitby, 1994, pp. 249–250.
60. Whitby, 1994, p. 250.
61. Rubin, 1995, p. 228.
62. See discussion by Mielczarek, 1993, p. 57.
63. Masoudi, *Muruj al Dhahab* (ed. Lunde & Stone, 1989), p. 210.
64. Rubin, 1995, p. 259.

Chapter 4: Military Training, Polo, the Hunt, and Military Music

1. Shaabani, 1373/1994, pp. 102–103.
2. Jalali, 1383/2004, p. 127.
3. Matofi, 1378/1999, p. 197.

4. *Strabo*, XIV, III, 18.
5. *Ammianus Marcellinus*, XIX, VI, 7.
6. As cited by Dodgeon & Lieu, 1991, pp. 156, 158.
7. *Libanius*, LIX, 64.
8. *Ammianus Marcellinus*, XXIII, VI, 83.
9. *Libanius*, Or. (Tr. Norman, 1987), LIX, 99–120.
10. Pigulevskaya, 1354/1975, pp. 127–128.
11. Hekmat, 1342/1964, p. 1087.
12. *Nameye Tansar be Goshnasp* [Letter of Tansar to Goshnasp] (Edited and compiled by M. Minovi, 1932), pp. 15–16.
13. The *Akhbar ol Tawwal* as cited by Imam-Shustari, 1350/1971, p. 102.
14. *Ammianus Marcellinus*, XXV, I, 13.
15. *Strategikon*, XI, I.
16. Daryaee, 2010, pp. 5.
17. Daryaee, 2002, p. 284.
18. Daryaee, 2002, pp. 282–283.
19. Consult article by Yektai (1349/1970) in references.
20. As cited by Daryaee, 2002, p. 287.
21. See studies for example by Grabner, Stern, and Neubauer (2007) in references.
22. *Shahname* (ed. Mohl, 1995), p. 1539.
23. Jalali, 1383/2004, p. 128.
24. *Shahname* (ed. Mohl, 1995), p. 1539.
25. Ibid.
26. Pigulevskaya, 1354/1975, p. 128.
27. As cited by Inostransev, 1926, pp. 41–42.
28. As cited by Dodgeon & Lieu, 1991, p. 224.
29. *Libanius*, LIX, 70.
30. Hanaway, 1971, pp. 22–27.
31. Hanaway, 1971, p. 26.
32. *Divan-e Farrokhi-Sistani* (ed. Dabirsiaqi, 1335/1957), p. 77.
33. *Divan-e Farrokhi-Sistani* (ed. Dabirsiaqi, 1335/1957), p. 79.
34. *Divan-e Farrokhi-Sistani* (ed. Dabirsiaqi, 1335/1957), p. 152.
35. Saad-Salman, *Divan* (ed. Yasemi, 1339/1961), p. 193.
36. Saad-Salman, *Divan* (ed. Yasemi, 1339/1961), p. 223.
37. Moezzi, *Divan-e Ash'ar* (ed. Eqbal, 1318/1940), p. 222.
38. Hanaway, 1971, p. 27.
39. Hanaway, 1971, p. 30.
40. Hanaway, 1971, p. 33.
41. See for example Firdowsi, *Shahname* (ed. Minavi, 1313/1934), Volume II, pp. 417–418.
42. Asadi-Tusi's *Garshasp-Name* (French translation, Huart in 1926 and Masse in 1951), pp. 122–123; Persian version (ed. Yaghmai, 1317/1938), pp. 270–271.
43. Reference to metal plate discovered in Afghanistan (end of the fourth-early fifth centuries) housed in the private collecton of Leon Levy and Shelby White, New York.
44. Metal plate housed at Hermitage Museum, St. Petersburg (Inv. S-42). On the reverse side of the plate is a Soghdian inscription (circa fifth century CE). This was discovered in the village of Klimova in the Perm region.
45. Hermitage Museum, Saint-Petersburg (Inv. S-216). This was discovered in the city of Tcherdyne in the Perm region.
46. Inostransev, 1926, p. 14.
47. Khaleqi-Motlagh, 1390/2011, pp. 219, 226.
48. Beizai-Kashani, 1382/2003, p. 21.
49. Khorasani, 2006, pp. 347–349.
50. Consult Abbasi's 2-volume *Tarikh e Koshti Iran* [History of Wrestling in Iran] (1374/1995) in references.

51. Consult the ancient *Denkard* (Book 8, Chapter 26) from the Sassanian era.
52. See also Abbasi, 1335/1956, Volume III, pp. 179–184.
53. Abbasi, 1374/1995, Vol. II, p. 133.
54. Ibid.
55. Chart for steel balls and their respective weights is now available on-line at the *Technicon Engineering* website (http://steelmedia.com/steel-balls-data.htm).
56. Heliodorus, *Aethiopica*, IX, 14, 3–15.1.
57. Mohammad-Jahani, 1377/1988, p. 6.
58. Agathias, *Historiae*, 3.17.
59. Khorasani, 2006, p. 351.
60. As cited by Khorasani, 2006, p. 345.
61. Sims, Marshak & Grube, 2002, p. 100.
62. *Ammianus Marcellinus*, XIX, II, 11,13; XX, VI, 7.
63. Plate dated to fourth century CE is discovered in Anatolia and is currently housed in the British Museum, London. Inv. B.M.124091.
64. Abbasi, 1335/1956, Volume III, pp. 179–184.
65. There are reports of Pahlavans wielding sticks weighing up to 9kg (Kazemini, 1343/1964, pp. 78–81).
66. See account of a challenge between a Pahlevan named *Darvish Mofred* and a hooligan in Kazemini (1343/1964, pp. 78–81).
67. Consult discussion by Khorasani, 2006, pp. 333–344.
68. Matofi, 1378/1999, p. 648.
69. As cited by Matthee, 1991, p. 394.
70. Nikororov, 2000, p. 71.
71. As cited by Farmer,1939, pp. 2785.
72. Sekunda, 1992, p. 4.
73. Xenophon, *Cyropedia* (ed. Miller, 1914, V, III, 52.
74. *Callisthenes* (tr. Wallis Budge, 1889), p. 96.
75. Farmer, 1939, pp. 27–30; Farmer, 1931, pp. 120–138.
76. *Strabo*, XV, II, 18.
77. Plutarch, *Crassus*, XXIII, 10.
78. *Justin*, XLI, 2, 8.
79. Nikonorov, 2000, p. 74.
80. *Herodian*, IV, 11, 3.
81. Plutarch, *Crassus*, XXIII, 8–9.
82. Nikororov, 2000, p. 71.
83. Dzhumaev, 1992, p. 48.
84. Humble, 1989, pp. 102, 104.
85. Nikonorov, 2000, p. 73.
86. See reconstruction of this type of drummer in Mongolian armies in Turnbull, 2004, Plate D, pp. 37–38.
87. Belyaev, 1933, p. 12.
88. Boeheim, 1983, pp. 211–212, 514–515.
89. Vyzgo, 1980, pp. 152, 155.
90. Nikonorov, 2000, p. 74.
91. Plutarch, *Crassus* (ed. Warner, 1972), XXVI, 4.
92. Farmer, 1939, p. 2788.
93. Hermitage Museum, St. Petersburg, Inv. S233 B.
94. Jalali, 1383/2004, p. 78.
95. Wiesehofer, 1996, p. 198.
96. Jalali, 1383/2004, p. 78.
97. Nikonorov, 2000, p. 73.
98. Nikonorov, 2000, p. 75.
99. Leo Diaconus, *History*, III, 1; VI, 13; VIII, 4; IX, 9.

100. Agathias, *Historiae*, III, 25.
101. Farmer, 1939, p. 2787.
102. *Strabo*, XV, I, 52. Note that Strabo identifies Chandragupta Maurya as 'Sandrocottus'.
103. *Strabo*, XV, I, 8.
104. *Shahname* (ed. & tr. to French by Mohl, 1831–1868), Vol. I, pp. 137, 178–179, 228–229, 278–279, 334–335, 404, 418, 420, 444, 468, 470, 488; Vol. II, pp. 4, 16; Vol. III, pp. 292, 317; Vol. IV, p. 98; Vol. V, p. 668; VII, p. 314.
105. As cited by Farmer, 1939, p. 2786.
106. Dodgeon & Lieu (1991, p. 297) in their description of the *Shahname* in reference to these events.
107. *Shahname* (ed. Mohl, 1985), p. 1807.
108. Gorgani, *Vis o Ramin* (tr. Lipkin, 1963), pp. 73–75, 79.
109. Tapper, 1997, p. 39.
110. *Tarikh-e Rozat ol Safa* (1851, Reprinted 1960–1961), Volume VIII, pp. 836.

Chapter 5: Archery

1. *Tir-Yasht*, VIII, 6.
2. *Menog-e Xrad*, XLIII, 1–12.
3. As cited by Modi, 1969, p. 186.
4. Inostransev, 1926, pp. 36, Footnote 2.
5. *Herodotus*, I, 136.
6. *Strabo*, XV, III, 18.
7. Procopius, *Wars*, I, 18.
8. *Ammianus Marcellinus*, XXV, I, 13.
9. Paterson, 1966, p. 69.
10. Modi, 1969, p. 178.
11. Matofi, 1378/1999, p. 293.
12. See for example descriptions of Abbasi (1335/1956, Volume III, pp. 179–184) with respect to post-Islamic Safavid archery training.
13. Strabo, XIV, III, 18; Matofi, 1378/1999, p. 197.
14. Tafazzolli, 1993, p. 193.
15. Pigulevskaya, 1354/1975, p. 128.
16. As cited by Inostransev, 1926, p. 36.
17. *Herodian* VI 5, 1–6, 6.
18. As cited by Inostransev, 1926, p. 35.
19. Inostransev, 1926, p. 38–39.
20. Zutterman, 2003, p. 120.
21. Paterson, 1966, p. 70.
22. As cited by Bivar, 1972, p. 276.
23. Tafazzoli, 1993, p. 193.
24. Ibid.
25. Coulston, 1985, pp. 220–366.
26. Khorasani, 2006, p. 291.
27. Matofi, 1378/1999, pp. 443–447.
28. Khorasani, 2006, p. 293.
29. Matofi, 1378/1999, p. 219.
30. Khorasani, 2006, p. 293.
31. Karpowicz, 2004, pp. 100–103.
32. Overlaet, 1998, pp. 290–297.
33. *Mehr Yasht*, X, 129.
34. Tafazzoli, 1993, p. 193.
35. *Libanius*, LIX, 69.
36. Hermitage, St. Petersburg, Inv. S-252 (dated 7th century CE).
37. Modi, 1969, p. 180.
38. Miller, McEwan and Bergman, 1986, p. 191.

39. Ibid.
40. *Vendidad*, XIV, 9.
41. Inostransev, 1926, p. 51.
42. *Tabari* (de Goeje, 1879–1901), Volume I, 955.
43. Al-Jahiz, *Bayan* (ed. Harun, 1960), Volume III, 18.
44. Al-Maqdasi, *Kitab al-bad* (ed. Huart, 1903), Volume III, 193.
45. Ibid.
46. *Tabari* (de Goeje, 1879–1901), Volume II, 454.
47. Tafazzoli, 1993, p. 191.
48. Nicolle, 1996, p. 24.
49. Overlaet, 1998, p. 295.
50. Matofi, 1378/1999, p. 443.
51. *Ammianus Marcellinus*, XIX, V, 1; XXIII, VI, 83; XXIV, VI, 18.
52. Inostransev, 1926, p. 25.
53. Zakeri, 1995, p. 51.
54. Inostransev, 1926, p. 25, Footnote 3.
55. Hekmat, 1342/1964, p. 1088.
56. Jandora, 2010, p. 107.
57. Michalak, 1987, p. 81.
58. Coulston, 1986, p. 62.
59. Procopius, *Wars*, I, 14.35.
60. Heath, 1980, p. 44.
61. Miller, McEwan and Bergman, 1986, p. 188.
62. *Ammianus Marcellinus*, XXV, I, 13; Procopius, *Wars*, I, 18.
63. Houtum-Schindler, 1888, p. 587.
64. Miller, McEwen & Bergman, 1986, p. 179.
65. Miller, McEwen & Bergman, 1986, p. 189.
66. Karasulas, 2004, pp. 18–27, 48–55.
67. Wise, 1987, p. 38.
68. Note for example depiction of the Parthian shot on cover page of Mallory (1989) text.
69. Procopius, *Wars*, I, 14.
70. Matofi, 1378/1999, p. 152.
71. Maurice, *Strategikon*, XI, I.
72. Hermitage Museum, St. Petersburg, Inv. S-247.
73. Maurice, *Strategikon*, XI.I.
74. *Ammianus Marcellinus*, XIX, V, 5.
75. Ibid.
76. *Ammianus Marcellinus*, XIX, V, 1.
77. Procopius, *Wars*, I, XVIII.
78. Personal Communication, 12 May 2003.
79. Maurice, *Strategikon*, XI.I.
80. Greatrex & Lieu, 2002, p. 116.
81. Stein, 1949, p. 500.
82. Procopius, *Wars*, II, XXV, 1–35.

Chapter 6: The Savaran

1. Jalali, 1383/2004, p. 48.
2. Son-in-law of Emperor Diocletian (r. 284–305 CE).
3. *Taj* (ed. Nowbakht, 1329/1950), p. 30.
4. Jalali, 1383/2004, pp. 34.
5. Bivar, 1972, p. 279.
6. *Ammianus Marcellinus*, XXVI, X, 8.
7. Rostovtzeff, 1933, pp. 217–218.
8. Speidel, 1984, pp. 151–156.

9. Coulston, 1986, p. 63.
10. Grotowski & Brzezinski, 2010, p. 126.
11. Frye, 1963, p. 270.
12. Grotowski & Brzezinski, 2010, p. 126.
13. Bivar, 1972, p. 278, Footnote 24.
14. Zakeri, 1995, p. 49.
15. Mehreen (Shushtari), 1349/1971, p. 76; Jalali, 1383/2004, p. 35.
16. Rundgren as cited from Bivar, 1972, p. 278, Footnote 24.
17. Sekunda, 1992, p. 29.
18. Michalak, 1987, p. 74.
19. Readers are referred to the excellent overview provided by Cernenko (1989) in the references.
20. Litvinskij & Piyankov, 1966, p. 44.
21. Dandamaev & Lukonin, 1989, p. 234.
22. Head, 1992, p. 31.
23. Sekunda, 1992, p. 29.
24. Head, 1992, p. 31, Figure 21a on p. 34.
25. Head, 1992, p. 31.
26. Head, 1992, p. 69.
27. As cited by Wiesehofer, 1996, p. 90.
28. Xenophon, *Anabasis*, I.VIII.
29. Xenophon, *Cyropedia*, VII.I.
30. Head, 1992, p. 37.
31. Arrian, *Anabasis*, I.15.
32. Diodorus, 17.53.1.
33. Head, 1992, p. 34.
34. Badian, 1965, pp. 160–161.
35. Head, 1992, p. 67.
36. Olbrycht, 2011, p. 82.
37. Mielczarek, 1993, p. 52.
38. Head, 1992, p. 39.
39. As cited by Mielczarek, 1993, p. 68.
40. Mielczarek, 1993, p. 53.
41. Michalak, 1987, p. 73.
42. Cassius Dio, 40, 14, 2.
43. Sallust, *Histories*, 16–17.
44. Justin, *Epitome*, 41, 2, 10.
45. Mielczarek, 1993, p. 58.
46. Bivar, 1972, p. 274.
47. Plutarch, *Crassus*, XXVII.
48. Coulston, 1986, p. 68.
49. Herrmann, 1989, p. 757.
50. Michalak, 1987, p. 74.
51. Mielczarek, 1993, p. 55.
52. Wilcox, 1999, pp. 10, 55.
53. National Museum of Iran, Catalogue: 295–299.
54. Khorasani, 2006, p. 246.
55. Wilcox, 1999, pp. 10, 55.
56. Coulston, 1986, p. 65. See also photographs in Ghirshman, 1962, Pl. 122 and Bivar, 1972, Pl. 1a.
57. Berg & Lampe, 2002, p. 32.
58. Bivar, 1972, p. 279.
59. Recent findings (just prior to this book being in press) of a new rock relief depicting a Parthian or early Sassanian lancer will be discussed by the author and Gholamreza Karamian, in Siedlce University's (Poland) HISTORIA I ŚWIAT journal and the upcoming text by author on the Parthian army.

60. Consult the *Liber de Caesaribus* as cited by Dodgeon & Lieu, 1994, p. 113.
61. Moses Khorenatsi, *History of the Armenians* (tr. Thompson, 1978), II, 79.
62. The triple pointing crown or helmet of the king cannot be ascertained; for more on this consult Bivar, 1972, p. 281 and Figure 19.
63. Bivar, 1972, p. 281.
64. Bivar, 1972, p. 275.
65. Coulston, 1986, p. 63.
66. Bivar, 1972, p. 275.
67. Shahbazi, 1986, p. 496.
68. Peterson, 1992, p. 35.
69. See discussion by Ghirshman, 1962, pp. 119–202.
70. See Tsetskhladze (2001) and Soudavar-Farmanfarmain (2009) in references.
71. Herrmann, 1989, p. 758.
72. Coulston, 1986, p. 66.
73. Robinson, 1967, Fig. 81.
74. Paterson, 1966, p. 84.
75. Heliodorus, *Aethiopica*, IX, 14, 3–15.1 & 14.5.
76. As cited by Dodgeon & Lieu, 1991, pp. 157–158.
77. *Ammianus Marcellinus*, XXV, I, 12.
78. As cited by Dodgeon & Lieu, 1991, pp. 157–158.
79. Tafazzoli, 1993, p. 193.
80. Heliodorus, *Aethiopica*, IX, 14, 3–15.2–3.
81. Heliodorus, *Aethiopica*, IX, 14, 3–15.1.
82. *Ammianus Marcellinus*, XXV, I, 12.
83. Reference to metal plate discovered in Afghanistan (end of the fourth–early fifth centuries) housed in the private collection of Leon levy and Shelby White, New York.
84. Ghirshman, 1962, p. 85.
85. Head, 1992, p. 28, 32, 46, 61 (note that page 61, Figure 46a depicts and describes a Thracian warrior with the Akenakes); Sekunda, 1992, pp. 20, 56.
86. Cernenko, 1989, pp. 14, 16.
87. Khorasani, 2006, p. 87.
88. Masia, 2000, p. 205.
89. Brzezinski, & Mielzcarek, 2002, p. 47, Plate H.
90. National Museum of Iran, Inventory number: 1574/7999.
91. Khorasani, 2006, pp. 97–98.
92. Khorasani, 2006, p. 98.
93. Bivar, 1972, p. 284.
94. Ghirshman, 1977, pp. 1–5.
95. Herrmann, 1989, p. 760.
96. Herrmann, 1989, p. 761.
97. Jalali, 1383/2004, p. 52.
98. Healy, 1992, p. 58.
99. *Ammianus Marcellinus*, XXV, I, 18.
100. Michalak, 1987, p. 83.
101. Reza, 1374/1995, p. 16.
102. Michalak, 1987, p. 83.
103. Khorasani, 2006, p. 94.
104. Khorasani, 2006, p. 95.
105. Balint, 1978, pp. 180–184, Figures 6 & 7.
106. Procopius, *Wars*, I, 12.
107. Coulston, 1986, p. 63.
108. Michalak, 1987, p. 63.
109. As presented by author, Gholmareza Karamian and Adam Kubic at the 3rd Colloquia Baltica-Iranica conference (Siedlice University, Poland, Nov 25–26 2016), different varieties of seg-

mented helmets with unique decorated motifs had appeared in Western-Northern Iran, Southern-Iran/Persian Gulf region and Central Asia by the late Sassanian era (proceedings to be published in 2017).

110. Coulston, 1986, p. 67.
111. Gorelik, 1979, pp. 46–48, Figure 44.
112. Khorasani, 2010, pp. 167–172.
113. Khorasani, 2006, pp. 251–261.
114. Khorasani, 2006, p. 252.
115. Pour-Davood, 1347/1968, p. 45.
116. As cited by Allan & Gilmour, 2000, p. 189.
117. Kobylinksy, 2000, p. 66.
118. Allan & Gilmour, 2000, p. 189.
119. Khorasani, 2006, p. 252.
120. As cited from Harper (1985, p. 247).
121. Khorasani, 2006, p. 260.
122. Khorasani, 2006, p. 258.
123. *Shahname* (ed. Mohl, 1995), p. 1739.
124. Zakeri, 1995, p. 252.
125. Khorasani, 2006, p. 252.
126. Zoka, 1350a/1971a, p. 66; Sekunda, 1992, pp. 45–46, 48, 60–61, Plates C, F, H & L; Head, 1992, pp. 26, 29, 46–47, Plates 2 & 3.
127. Pour-Davood, 1347/1968, p. 42.
128. Khorasani, 2006, p. 262.
129. As cited by Khorasani, 2006, p. 262.
130. Al-Sarraff, 2002, p. 162.
131. Al-Sarraff, 2002, p. 162.
132. Khorasani, 2006, p. 264 (item: National Museum of Tehran, Catalogue: 349).
133. Matofi, 1378/1999, p. 431.
134. As cited by Khorasani, 2006, pp. 262–263.
135. Al-Sarraff, 2002, p. 163.
136. Michalak, 1987, p. 82.
137. Römisches Germanisches Museum, Mainz, Germany, Inv. 037985 and Inv. 037986.
138. Michalak, 1987, p. 83.
139. Herrmann, 1989, p. 762.
140. *Shahname* (ed. Mohl, 1995), pp. 200, 300, 993.
141. *Shahname* (ed. Mohl, 1995), pp. 191, 300, 314, 357, 495, 619, 857.
142. Belnitsky, 1946, p. 190.
143. Reza, 1374/1995, p. 116.
144. Sami, 1342/1964, p. 62.
145. Herodotus, VII, 85.
146. Jalali, 1383/2004, p. 49.
147. As cited by Dodgeon & Lieu, 1991, p. 298, Appendix I.
148. As cited by Sinor, 1981, p. 142.
149. *Shahname* (ed. Mohl, 1995), II, pp. 546–551.
150. Khorasani, Shafeian & Singh (in Press).
151. Ibid.
152. Farzin, 1387/2008, p. 103.
153. Farzin, 1387/2008, p. 103.
154. *Karnamg-e Ardashir* (tr. Mashkoor, n.d.), pp. 38, 40.
155. *Karnamg-e Ardashir* (tr. Hedayat, 1963), p. 200.
156. Christensen, 1944, p. 208.
157. Jalali, 1383/2004, p. 38.
158. Mehreen (Shushtari), 1349/1971, p. 77.
159. Nyberg, 1974, p. 163.

160. Foss, 2002, p. 170.
161. Farzin, 1387/2008, p. 104.
162. Tafazzoli, 2000, p. 12.
163. Matofi, 1378/1999, p. 203.
164. Ibid.
165. *Ammianus Marcellinus*, XIX, I, 5.
166. According to the Bundahishn 'in the reign of Shapur son of Hormuzd, the Arabs came and siezed the banks of the River Karun [Ulay] and remained there for many years pillaging and attacking' (Bundahishn, XXXIII, 16).
167. As cited by Dodgeon & Lieu, 1991, p. 291, Appendix I.
168. Ibid.
169. Osheidari, 1371/1992, p. 231.
170. *Menog-e Xrad* (tr. Tafazzoli, 1975), Part I, line 64.
171. *Karnamag-e Ardashir* (tr. Faravashi, 1354/1975), Part VI, line 16, p. 61; Part VIII, line 7, p. 81; Part IX, line 19, p. 87.
172. Jalali, 1383/2004, p. 39.
173. As discussed by Farzin (1387/2008, p. 107).
174. Nafisi, 1331/1952, p. 22.
175. Pirnia, 1308/1929, p. 244.
176. Farzin, 1387/2008, p. 107.
177. Cosentino, 2004, p. 253.
178. Ayvazyan, 2012, p. 53.
179. Ayvazyan, 2012, pp. 79–80.
180. Jalali, 1383/2004, p. 63.
181. Daryaee, 2009, p. 16.
182. Whittow, 1996, p. 204.
183. Pasdermajian, 1369/1990, p. 159.
184. Jalali, 1383/2004, p. 63.
185. Pasdermajian, 1369/1990, p. 140.
186. Pigulevskaya, 1354/1975, p. 101.
187. Jalali, 1383/2004, p. 63.
188. Pasdermajian, 1369/1990, p. 159.
189. Jalali, 1383/2004, p. 64.
190. Christensen, 1944, p. 210.
191. *Sebeos* (tr. Thompson, 1999), Chapter 28, p. 50.
192. Whittow, 1996, p. 204.
193. Greatrex, 2005, p. 498.
194. Nicolle, 1996, p. 58.
195. Greatrex, 2005, p. 499.
196. Matofi, 1378/1999, p. 172.
197. Frye, 1984, p. 319.
198. Nicolle, 1996, pp. 58, 60.
199. Reza, 1374/1995, p. 17.
200. Chavannes, 1903, pp. 137, 313.
201. Reza, 1374/1995, pp. 17–18.
202. Raspopova, 2006, pp. 70–80.
203. Raspopova, 2006, p. 82.
204. Hermitage Museum, St. Petersburg (Inv. S-247).
205. Babaie, 1384/2005, pp. 42–43.

Chapter 7: Infantry, Auxiliary Contingents and Naval Forces

1. Kolesnikoff, 2535/1976, p. 122.
2. Jalali, 1382/2003, p. 15.
3. Howard-Johnston, 1995, p. 75.

4. Foss, 2002, p. 170.
5. Tafazolli, 2000, p. 13.
6. Penrose, 2008, p. 258.
7. Jalali, 1383/2004, p. 113.
8. Sami, 1342/1964, p. 70; Christensen, 1944, p. 170.
9. Foss, 2002, p. 170.
10. Daryaee, 2009, p. 46.
11. Jalali, 1382/2003, p. 15.
12. Jalali, 1382/2003, p. 15.
13. Sami, 1342/1964, p. 62.
14. Consult *Agathias* 3.17, especially in his description of Dailamite skill and resilience in close quarter face to face combat (notably with sword and dagger).
15. Tafazolli, 2000, p. 13.
16. Howard-Johnston, 1995, p. 219.
17. Sami, 1342/1964, p. 62.
18. Jalali, 1383/2004, p. 37.
19. Penrose, 2008, p. 258.
20. Notably in reference to the fallen Sassanian trooper at Dura Europus.
21. Wilcox, 1999, p. 34.
22. Zoka, 1350a/1971a, p. 140.
23. Hekmat, 1342/1964, p. 1089.
24. Jalali, 1383/2004, p. 50.
25. Lee, 2009, p. 4.
26. Ziapour, 1349/1970, p. 286.
27. Ammianus Marcellinus, XXIII, VI, 83.
28. Nafisi, 1331/1952, p. 277.
29. See comprehensive overview of late Dailamite military equipment by Overlaet (1988, pp. 267–297).
30. Mobbayen, 1386/2007, pp. 109–110.
31. *Agathias* 3.17.
32. Overlaet, 1998, p. 268.
33. Mobbayen, 1386/2007, p. 115.
34. Jalali, 1383/2004, p. 62.
35. Matofi, 1378/1999, p. 439.
36. Overlaet, 1998, pp. 278–285, 287–289.
37. Overlaet, 1998, pp. 286–287.
38. Overlaet, 1998, pp. 290–297.
39. Overlaet, 1998, pp. 268–277.
40. Mobbayen, 1386/2007, pp. 110–112.
41. Mobbayen, 1386/2007, pp. 119–120.
42. Mobbayen, 1386/2007, p. 112.
43. Jalali, 1382/2003, p. 15.
44. Penrose, 2008, p. 258.
45. Ibid.
46. Wilcox, 1999, p. 47.
47. Jalali, 1382/2003, p. 15.
48. Wilcox, 1999, p. 33, 46, Figure G1.
49. Procopius, *Wars*, II, XIV.
50. Penrose, 2008, p. 258.
51. Ward, 2009, p. 31.
52. As cited by Khorasani, 2006, p. 263.
53. Sidnell, 2006, p. 73.
54. Pigulevskaya, 1377/1998, p. 447.
55. As cited from Dodegeon & Lieu, 1991, p. 31.

56. Jalali, 1383/2004, pp. 40–51; Mashkoor, 1366/1987, Vol. II, p. 1140.
57. Mashkoor, 1366/1987, Vol. II, p. 1140.
58. See discussion of chariots in the (proto) Indo-European context by Mallory (1989, pp. 38–42, 45, 53, 55, 69, 136–137, 228).
59. Rankin, 1996, p. 11.
60. Jalali, 1383/2004, p. 64.
61. Pasdermajian, 1369/1990, p. 64.
62. Jalali, 1383/2004, pp. 64–65.
63. Pigulevskaya, 1372/1993, p. 253.
64. Jalali, 1383/2004, p. 65.
65. Pigulevskaya, 1372/1993, p. 372.
66. Jalali, 1383/2004, p. 62.
67. Jalali, 1383/2004, p. 36.
68. Jalali, 1383/2004, p. 36.
69. Matofi, 1378/1999, p. 221.
70. Middle Persian; new Persian term is *Falaxon*.
71. Khorasani, 2010, p. 158.
72. Matofi, 1378/1999, p. 221.
73. Libanius, *Or.* LIX, p. 103.
74. Bamban, 1998, p. 117.
75. Penrose, 2008, p. 258.
76. Wilcox, 1999, p. 46.
77. Khorasani, 2010, p. 158.
78. *Ammianus Marcellinus*, XIX, V, 1.
79. Khorasani, 2010, p. 158.
80. Tafazzolli, 1993, p. 191.
81. Khorasani, 2010, p. 158.
82. A summary of this report entitled 'Bones suggest women went to war in ancient Iran' was also provided by the Pakistan-based *Daily Times* news outlet (date: 13/12/2004).
83. Cernenko, 1983, p. 37, Plate F3.
84. Brzezinski & Mielczarek, pp. 43–44, Plate A3.
85. Pokorny (1959) provides a comprehensive overview of the Indo-Germanic lexicon.
86. Mayrhofer, 1969, pp. 661–666.
87. Sekunda, 1992, p. 22.
88. Ward, 2009, p. 31.
89. Dodgeon & Lieu, 1991, p. 352, Footnote 17.
90. *Zonaras*, XII, 23, 595, 7–596, 9.
91. Dodgeon & Lieu, 1991, p. 181.
92. Libanius, *Orationes* (ed. Norman, 1987), LIX, 114.
93. Hekmat, 1342/1964, p. 1089.
94. Nafisi, 1331/1952, p. 22.
95. Jalali, 1382/2003, p. 17.
96. Nafisi, 1331/1952, p. 22.
97. Jalali, 1383/2004, p. 39.
98. Zoka, 1350a/1971a, p. 144.
99. Ibid.
100. Jalali, 1382/2003, p. 17.
101. As cited by Azari, 1351/1972, pp. 128, 131.
102. Charles, 2007, p. 303.
103. *Arrian*, 3.14.4, 3.14.6.
104. *Curtius Rufus*, 5.2.10.
105. Hekmat, 1342/1964, p. 1082.
106. Charles, 2007, pp. 305–306.
107. Scullard, 1974, pp. 201–202.

108. *Gordian*, 26.3–27.1.
109. *Gordian*, 33.1.
110. As cited by Dodgeon & Lieu, 1991, p. 285, Appendix I.
111. Charles, 2007, p. 306.
112. See for example *Chronicon Anonymum* (354, 27–28).
113. *Eumenius* 5(9), 21, 1–3.
114. Reigned alone from 284–286 CE, reigned as Augustus of the eastern regions of the Roman Empire from 286–305 CE with Maximian as Augustus of the western regions of the empire.
115. *History of the Armenians* (translated by Thompson), as cited by Charles, 2007, p. 312. Charles does not regard this as a reliable source as the text was written probably in the fifth century and may have been influenced by contemporary events.
116. Azari, 1351/1972, p. 132.
117. *Tarikh al-Rusol wa ol Moluk*, translated by Bosworth (1999). Charles however, notes that 'it seems best to view this fragment with considerable caution' (2007, p. 311).
118. Firdowsi (ed. Foroughi, 1985), p. 358.
119. *Orationes*, 59.65.
120. *Historia Religiosa*, 1.11.
121. Ibid. The *Historia Religiosa* reports that the Bishop Jacob, who is said to have played a leading role in the city's defence, was responsible for this stratagem.
122. Julian, *Orat.* (2.63b).
123. Julian, *Orat.* (2.64b).
124. Julian, *Orat.* (2.65b–2.65c).
125. See for example, *Chronicum Paschale* (ed. Dindorf & Niebuhr, 1832), 537, line 13.
126. *Amminaus Marcellinus*, XIX, 2, 3.
127. Azari, 1351/1972, p. 133.
128. *Amminaus Marcellinus*, XXIV, 6, 12.
129. *Amminaus Marcellinus* (XXIV, 6, 15) reports 2,500 Sassanian and 70 Roman dead with *Zosimus* (3.25.7) reporting 75 Roman dead.
130. See Charles, 2007, p. 322.
131. *Amminaus Marcellinus*, XXV, 1, 14.
132. *Amminaus Marcellinus*, XXV, 3, 2.
133. *Amminaus Marcellinus*, XXV, 3, 4.
134. *Amminaus Marcellinus*, XXV, 3, 5 & 11.
135. *Amminaus Marcellinus*, XXV, 6, 2.
136. Moghtader, 1315/1936, pp. 168–169. Note that Moghtader was ranked as Colonel in the Iranian Army when he wrote this work.
137. Nafisi, 1331/1952, p. 293.
138. Nersessian, 2001, p. 172.
139. *Tabari* (Persian translation by Belami), pp. 945–947.
140. Litvinskij (1998b), 1996, p. 139.
141. Azari, 1351/1972, p. 134.
142. Matofi, 1378/1999, p. 184.
143. *Tabari* (Persian translation by Belami), pp. 1032–1033.
144. Greatrex & Lieu, 2002, p. 113.
145. Procopius, *Wars*, VIII, 14.1–44.
146. Greatrex & Lieu, 2002, p. 184.
147. Azari, 1351/1972, p. 136.
148. Masoudi's *Movaraj ol Zahab*, Volume I, p. 665.
149. Ahmad bin Yahya Baladuri's *Futuh ol Boldan* (translated to Persian by Azartash, 1346/1967), pp. 49–50.
150. Donner, 1981, p. 192.
151. *Tabari*, XII, 2267.
152. As cited in Matofi, 1378/1999, p. 188.
153. Masoudi's *Muruj al Dhahab*, Volume I, p. 665.

154. *Al-Muqaddimah* (original Arabic version), Volume I, p. 541.
155. Benjamin, 1888, p. 275.
156. Azari, 1351/1972, p. 140.
157. *Al-Muqaddimah* (original Arabic version), Volume I, p. 541.
158. Nafisi, 1331/1952, p. 215.
159. Azari, 1351/1972, p. 141.
160. Masoudi, *Muruj al Dhahab*, p. 273.
161. Gardizi, *Zein ol Akhbar* (ed. & an. Habibi, 1347/1968), p. 36.
162. Azari, 1351/1972, p. 136.
163. *Chronicle of Seert* (ed. & tr. Scher, 1908), ii.87.
164. Charles, 2007, pp. 315–316.
165. Nader Shah had frightened the Moghul elephants with camels mounted with jars that had been stuffed with brushes set on fire (Matofi, 1378/1999, p. 822; Hanway, 1753, p. 369).
166. *Amminaus Marcellinus*, XXV, 1, 15.
167. Whitehouse & Williamson, 1973, p. 31.
168. Whitehouse & Williamson, 1973, p. 32. Ardashir I also subjugated the Arabs of Oman.
169. Jalali, 1382/2003, p. 18.
170. Curatola & Scarcia, 2007, p. 93.
171. *Bundahishn*, XXXIII, 16.
172. Nöldeke, 1973, p. 54.
173. Tashkari, 1356/1977, p. 35.
174. According to the Bundahishn 'Shapur became of age and drove away those Arabs and took the land from them. He killed many rulers of the Arabs and scattered many of them', XXXIII, 16).
175. *Ammianus Marcellinus*, XXII, VI, 11.
176. Quaritch Wales 1965, p. 41.
177. Raeen, 1350/1972, p. 287.
178. The Yemenite Arabs led by Sayf Bin Ze'yazan had risen in revolt against the Abyssinian occupation. The Yemenites had first appealed in vain to the Byzantine Empire for assistance. The latter were reluctant to support the Yemenites as the Abyssinian occupation force was allied to Byzantium. Sayf Bin Ze'yazan then dispatched his emissaries to Khosrow I in a direct appeal for Sassanian military intervention against the Abyssinians.
179. Jalali, 1382/2003, p. 18.
180. Sami, 1342/1964, p. 199.
181. Greatrex & Lieu, 2002, p. 197.
182. Potter, 2008, pp. 126–148.
183. For a comprehensive list of such terms consult Hourani (1995, p. 65) and Mojtahed-Zadeh (1999, p. 62).
184. Numbers of these terms are Arabicized amongst the Arabs such as *Nakhuda/Nakhudha* and *Nawakhid* in Arabic plural (Persian: Nav-Khoda), and *Sanbuq* (Persian: Sanbuk). Note the Indo-European origin of the Persian term *Nav-* that is analogous to the European use of the term 'navy'.

Chapter 8: Preparations for War

1. Hekmat, 1342/1964, p. 1090.
2. Jalali, 1383/2004, p. 73.
3. Sami, 1342/1964, Volume II, p. 55.
4. *Strategikon*, XI, I, 6–8.
5. *Theophylakti Simocattae Historiae*, pp. 93–94.
6. Matofi, 1378/1999, p. 182.
7. The Abyssinians, who had adopted Monophysite Christianity, had been encouraged by the Romano-Byzantines to invade. The Abyssinians crossed the Red Sea into the Arabian Peninsula and landed there by 522 CE. They then clashed with the Himyarites of southern Arabia, but the latter defeated and expelled the invaders by 525 CE. The Romano-Byzantines then assisted

the Abyssinians with supplies and vessels, allowing them to again cross the Red Sea, and this time they overpowered the Himyarites and killed the Himyarite king, Dhu Nuwas.

8. Jalali, 1383/2004, p. 74.
9. Sami, 1342/1964, II, pp. 68–69.
10. In such a scenario, many of the ships and crews would have been lost at sea en-route to Yemen.
11. Jalali, 1383/2004, p. 77.
12. *Shahname* (ed. Foroughi, 1985), p. 419, *Shahname* (ed. Mohl, 1995), p. 1807.
13. Jalali, 1383/2004, p. 76.
14. Jalali, 1383/2004, p. 71.
15. Dinawari, Muslim ibn Qutaybah, *Uyun al-Akhbar* (Dar ol Kotoab al-Elmiya, 1986), p. 193.
16. Inostransev, 1926, p. 14.
17. Dinawari, Muslim ibn Qutaybah, *Uyun al-Akhbar* (Dar ol Kotoab al-Elmiya, 1986), p. 193.
18. Inostransev, 1926, p. 14.
19. Ibid.
20. Dinawari, Muslim ibn Qutaybah, *Uyun al-Akhbar* (Dar ol Kotoab al-Elmiya, 1986), p. 195.
21. Inostransev, 1926, p. 16.
22. Maurice, *Strategikon*, XI, I.
23. Dinawari, Muslim ibn Qutaybah, *Uyun al-Akhbar* (Dar ol Kotoab al-Elmiya, 1986), p. 193.
24. Maurice, *Strategikon*, VIII, II.
25. Maurice, *Strategikon*, XI, I.
26. Dinawari, Muslim ibn Qutaybah, *Uyun al-Akhbar* (Dar ol Kotoab al-Elmiya, 1986), p. 192.
27. Inostransev, 1926, p. 14.
28. Ibid.
29. Ibid.
30. Ibid.
31. *Ammianus Marcellinus*, XVIII, VI, 8–16.
32. Dodgeon & Lieu, 1991, p. 389, footnote 12.
33. Dodgeon & Lieu (1991, p. 297) in their description of the *Shahname* in reference to these events.
34. Lee, 1986, p. 455.
35. Jalali, 1383/2004, p. 90.
36. *Toqi'ate Kasra Anoushirvan* (ed. Zavari, 2009), p. 79.
37. *Chronicon Anonymum* (ed. & tr. by Chabot, 1937), XLI, 4.
38. *Toqi'ate Kasra Anoushirvan* (ed. Zavari, 2009), p. 69.
39. Al-Jahiz, *Taj* (tr. Arabic to Persian, H. Nowbakht, 1950), pp. 217–218.
40. Dinawari, Muslim ibn Qutaybah, *Uyun al-Akhbar* (Dar ol Kotoab al-Elmiya, 1986), p. 193.
41. Inostransev, 1926, p. 14.
42. Procopius, *Wars*, II, 18.
43. Maurice, *Strategikon*, I, IX.

Chapter 9: Tactics and Strategies along the Roman and Caucasian Frontiers
1. Moghtader, 1318–1319/1940–1941, p. 91.
2. Christensen 1989, pp. 223–224.
3. Inostransev, 1969, p. 42.
4. *Shahname* (ed. Khaleghi-Motlagh, 1385/2006), Volume IV, pp. 147–158, 179–180.
5. *Shahname* (ed. Khaleghi-Motlagh, 1385/2006), Volume IV, pp. 147–158.
6. Shahbazi, 1986, p. 497.
7. Dinawari, Muslim ibn Qutaybah, *Uyun ol-Akhbar* (Cairo, 1948), pp. 112–115.
8. *Herodian* VI, 5.5–10.
9. Jalali, 1383/2004, p. 80.
10. Ibid.
11. Turnbull, 2004, p. 25.
12. *Ammianus Marcellinus*, XXIII, 5, 17.
13. Jordanes, *Historia Romana*, 282, p. 36 (27–31).
14. Festus, *Brevarium*, 22, p. 64 (2–7)

15. *Ammianus Marcellinus*, XXIII, 5, 17.
16. See for example Millar (1993), Greatrex (1998), Greatrex & Lieu (2002), Dignas & Winter (2007), and Dodgeon & Lieu (1991) in References.
17. *Oracula Sibyllina*, XIII, 13–20.
18. *Zosimus*, III, 32.4.
19. Shapur inscription (Parthian Pahlavi), SKZ, lines 6–7.
20. Dignas & Winter, 2007, p. 79.
21. Dodgeon & Lieu, 1991, p. 35; Ghirshman, 1962, p. 159.
22. *Cedrenus* (ed. Bekker, 1838–1839), i, p. 450.
23. SKZ (Shapur Kaba Zartusht), Greek lines 9–10.
24. Loriot, 1975, p. 773.
25. Shapur inscription (Parthian Pahlavi), SKZ, line 6.
26. Bivar, 1972, p. 279.
27. Shapur inscription (Parthian Pahlavi), SKZ, line 6.
28. Boss, 1993, pp. 56, 66; Boss, 1994, pp. 20–25.
29. Bivar, 1972, p. 279.
30. Boss, 1994, p. 25.
31. Boss, 1994, p. 24.
32. Masia, 2000, pp. 191–192.
33. Khorasani, 2006, p. 85.
34. Boss, 1994, p. 25.
35. Bivar, 1972, p. 286.
36. Ghirshman, 1962, p. 118.
37. Matheson, 2001, Plate 43.
38. Malalas, *Synopsis Sathas* (cf. Stauffenberg, 1939), p. 62.
39. *Zonaras* (ed. Dindorf, 1870), XII, 17, pp. 580.
40. *Zonaras*, XII, 19, p. 583, 1–5.
41. *Zosimus*, III, 32(4).
42. *Zonaras*, XII, 19, p. 583, 5–9.
43. Shapur inscription (Parthian Pahlavi), SKZ, line 6 and (Greek), SKZ, line 10.
44. Dignas & Winter, 2007, p. 80.
45. Frye, 1985, p. 125.
46. *Zosimus*, I, 27.2
47. Dignas & Winter, 2007, p. 80.
48. Shapur inscription (Parthian Pahlavi), SKZ, lines 18–22.
49. As cited from Nöldeke by Dodgeon & Lieu, 1991, p. 298, Appendix I.
50. Ferrill, 1986, pp. 14, 52.
51. Matheson, 2001, Plate 39.
52. Ferrill, 1986, Plate 8; Ghirshman, 1962, pp. 153–156.
53. *Oracula Sibyllina* XIII, 89–102.
54. Rostovtzeff et al., 1953, Fig. C.
55. Consult overview of the savaran by Heliodorus, *Aethiopica*, IX, 14, 3–15.
56. *Cedrenus*, i, p. 454, 3–6.
57. Dodgeon & Lieu, 1991, p. 367, Footnote 46.
58. As cited from Nöldeke by Dodgeon & Lieu, 1991, p. 298, Appendix I.
59. *Petrus Patricius*, 10, p. 187.
60. Barker, 1981, pp. 130–132.
61. Ghirshman, 1962, p. 76, Figure 87 (a).
62. Ghirshman, 1962, p. 7, Figure 10. See reconstruction of this weapon by Peterson (1992, pp. 23–25).
63. Ghirshman, 1962, p. 3, Figure 4.
64. Barker, 1981, p. 130.
65. Barker, 1981, p. 131.
66. Barker, 1981, p. 130.

67. Barker, 1981, p. 131.
68. Ibid.
69. SHA *Gallieni*, 10, 7–8.
70. Southern, 2001, p. 149; Potter, 2004, pp. 651–652.
71. Odahl, 2004, p. 59.
72. Note that just two years after 284 CE, Diolectian was 'co-ruler' with Maximian from 286 CE to 305 CE; Diolectian was 'Augustus of the East'with Maximian as 'Augustus of the West'.
73. Barnes, 1981, p. 17.
74. Dodgeon & Lieu, 1991, p. 125.
75. Potter, 2004, p. 293.
76. Festus, *Breviarum*, 25, p. 65.
77. Wiesehofer, 1996, p. 198.
78. Jalali, 1383/2004, p. 79.
79. Consult *Ammianus Marcellinus* (tr. Hamilton, 1986; Rolfe, 1939) and *Julian (Julianus) Apostata, Orationes* (ed. Bidez, 1932) in references.
80. *Julian* (ed. Bidez, 1932) III, 11–13.30, pp. 132–138.
81. *Chronicon Anonymum* (ed. & tr. by Chabot, 1937), XXXVI.
82. Khorasani, 2010, p. 234.
83. Ibid.
84. Khorasani, 2010, p. 295.
85. Dinawari, Muslim ibn Qutaybah, *Uyun al-Akhbar* (Beirut, 1986), pp. 191–192.
86. Maurice, *Strategikon*, XI, I.
87. Dignas & Winter, 2007, p. 66.
88. Pigulevskaya, 1354/1975, p. 127.
89. Matofi, 1378/1999, p. 216.
90. Bivar, 1972, p. 289.
91. Dinawari, Muslim ibn Qutaybah, *Uyun ol-Akhbar* (Cairo, 1948), p. 112.
92. *Shahname* (ed. Mohl, 1995), pp. 1538–1539.
93. *Shahname* (ed. Khaleghi-Motlagh, 1385/2006), Vol. II, p. 85.
94. Ibid.
95. Maurice, *Strategikon*, XI, I.
96. Ibid.
97. Inostransev, 1926, p. 13.
98. *Shahname* (ed. Khaleghi-Motlagh, 1385/2006), Vol. II, p. 219.
99. Inostransev, 1926, p. 13.
100. *Ammianus Marcellinus*, XXIV, 6, 12.
101. Matofi, 1378/1999, p. 172.
102. See discussion by Wiesehofer, 1996, p. 199.
103. Christensen, 1944, p. 212.
104. Inostransev, 1926, p. 29.
105. Mohammadi, 1340–1341/1961–1962, pp. 31–34.
106. Inostransev, 1926, p. 14, 29.
107. Procopius, *Wars*, I, 14; II, 18.
108. *Chronicon Anonymum* (ed. & tr. by Chabot, 1937), XXII.
109. *Ammianus Marcellinus*, XXV, 3, 4.
110. Inostransev, 1969, pp. 42–43; Inostransev, 1926, p. 13.
111. Inostransev, 1926, p. 25.
112. Khorasani, 2010, p. 311.
113. Farzin, 1387/2008, p. 21.
114. Khorasani, Shafeian and Singh (in Press).
115. *Shahname* (ed. Mohl, 1995), Vol. XII, p. 12.
116. Khorasani, Shafeian and Singh (in Press).
117. *Shahname* (ed. Warner, 1905–1925), Vol. XII, p. 12.
118. Khorasani, Shafeian and Singh (in Press).

119. Ibid.
120. Sidnell, 2006, p. 20.
121. Khorasani, Shafeian and Singh (in Press).
122. For a full overview of the historical background to this war, consult Greatrex (1998, pp. 5–42).
123. Hughes, 2010, p. 55.
124. Greatrex, 1998, p. 170.
125. For a full description of the battle formations and tactics at Dara consult Greatrex (1998, pp. 169–185) and Hughes (2010, pp. 53–59).
126. Greatrex, 1998, p. 171.
127. Greatrex, 1998, pp. 173, 175.
128. Hughes, 2010, p. 56.
129. Greatrex, 1998, p. 170.
130. Hughes, 2010, p. 57.
131. Procopius, *Wars*, I, XIII.
132. Procopius, *Wars*, I, XIII.
133. Hughes, 2010, p. 57.
134. Procopius, *Wars*, I, XIII.
135. Ibid.
136. Hughes, 2010, p. 53.
137. Hughes, 2010, p. 63.
138. Hughes, 2010, p. 59.
139. Greatrex, 1999, p. 202.
140. Greatrex, 1999, p. 204.
141. Procopius, *Wars*, I, XVIII.
142. Greatrex, 1999, p. 204.
143. Hughes, 2010, p. 62–63.
144. Greatrex, 1999, p. 204.
145. Hughes, 2010, p. 63.
146. Hughes, 2010, p. 63–64.
147. Zachariah, *Historia*, IX.4, 95.4–95.26.
148. *Chronicle of John Malalas* (tr. Jeffreys, Jeffreys, & Scott, 1986), 464.
149. Hughes, 2010, p. 64.
150. Greatrex, 2010, pp. 205–206.
151. Procopius, *Wars*, II, 8.
152. Procopius, *Wars*, I, 14, 18.
153. Local lore of the south Caucasus is replete with expressions that emphasize the virtues of courage under difficult circumstances.
154. *Shahname* (ed. Mohl, 1995), p. 1539.
155. Procopius, *Wars*, I, 4.
156. Inostransev, 1926, p. 14.
157. Inostransev, 1926, p. 15.
158. Inostransev, 1926, p. 16.
159. Dinawari, Muslim ibn Qutaybah, *Uyun al-Akhbar* (Beirut, 1986), p. 193.
160. Inostransev, 1926, p. 16.
161. Ibid.
162. Abbasi, 1335/1956, Volume II, p. 419. Note that Abbasi's descriptions of these battles (and those of Matofi, 1378/1999, pp. 647) vary from Western historiography, notably Savory (1980, pp. 85–86), who makes no mention of an advance guard or 'commandos' silencing Ottoman sentries; nor does Savory mention the arrival of 500 other 'commandos' masquerading as businessmen.
163. These 'merchants' had tricked the Ottoman authorities by claiming that they were waiting for a few days for their goods to arrive in Tabriz.
164. Clodfelter, 2002, p. 61; Dupuy & Dupuy, 1977, p. 586.
165. Matofi, 1378/1999, p. 647.

166. Karantabias, 2005, p. 35.
167. Inostransev, 1926, p. 14.
168. Jalali, 1383/2004, p. 85.
169. Pigulevskaya, 1354/1975, p. 424.
170. Zachariah, *Historia*, IX.2 (92.25–93.27).
171. *Tabari*, XIII, 2459–2460.
172. Jalali, 1383/2004, p. 51.
173. Ibid.
174. Ibid.
175. Sami, 1342/1964, Volume II, p. 62.
176. Inostransev, 1926, p. 14.
177. Dinawari, Muslim ibn Qutaybah, *Uyun al-Akhbar* (Beirut, 1986), p. 193.
178. Dodgeon & Lieu, 1991, pp. 357, Footnote 20.
179. Jalali, 1383/2004, p. 82.
180. Ibid.
181. *Ammianus Marcellinus*, XXIV, III, 10–11.
182. Dodgeon & Lieu, 1991, p. 231.
183. *Ammianus Marcellinus*, XXIV, I, 11.
184. Dodgeon & Lieu, 1991, p. 232.
185. Ferrill, 1988, p. 53.
186. Jalali, 1383/2004, p. 81.
187. Consentino, 2004, p. 250.
188. *Ammianus Marcellinus*, XXIV, II, 4–5.
189. Dodgeon & Lieu, 1991, p. 391, Footnote 15.
190. *Ammianus Marcellinus*, XXIV, VI, 15.
191. As cited by Dodgeon & Lieu, 1991, pp. 269–270.
192. As cited by Dodgeon & Lieu, 1991, p. 293, Appendix I.
193. *Ammianus Marcellinus*, XXV, 1.18.
194. Mahamedi, 2003, p. 157.
195. Jalali, 1383/2004, p. 81.
196. Ibid.
197. *Ammianus Marcellinus*, XXV.7.5.
198. Festus, *Breviarium*, 29.
199. Augustine, *De Civitate Dei*, IV.29.
200. *Zonaras*, XIII, 13, 15.
201. As cited by Dodgeon & Lieu, 1991, pp. 251–252.
202. As cited by Dodgeon & Lieu, 1991, p. 292, Appendix I.
203. Consult Izady, 1992, p. 102.
204. Clodfelter, 2002, p. 60.
205. Jalali, 1383/2004, p. 86.
206. Frye, 1977, p. 15.
207. Sami, 1342/1964, Vol II, p. 72.
208. Jalali, 1383/2004, p. 86.
209. Sami, 1342/1964, Vol II, p. 72.
210. Ravandi, 1352/1973, p. 63.
211. Jalali, 1383/2004, p. 89.
212. Imam-Shushtari, 1350/1971, p. 60.
213. *Tabari* (Persian translation by Payandeh, 1989), Volume II, p. 724.
214. *Toqi'ate Kasra Anoushirvan* (ed. Zavari, 2009), p. 70.

Chapter 10: Logistics and Support

1. Ghozanlu, 1315/1936, p. 214; Mashkoor, 1366/1987, p. 1140.
2. *Dinkard* VIII. 26. 12.
3. *Dinkard* VIII. 26. 10. 12.

4. Marks, 2010, p. 415.
5. This was part of the author's research for the text of *Iran at War: 1500–1988* (2011), during which he interviewed numerous veterans of the Iran-Iraq war including '*Farzin*', who was interviewed on 20 January 2009. There is also a famous photograph of an Iranian soldier in the early days of the Iran-Iraq war eating rice which he carries in his pockets; this picture is posted on Iranian.com: http://www.iranian.com/Revolution/photos.html.
6. Marks, 2010, p. 415.
7. Kistler & Lair, 2007, p. 174.
8. Dodgeon & Lieu, 1991, p. 357, Footnote 20.
9. Christensen, 1944, p. 213.
10. Mohammadi-Malayeri, 1372/1993, p. 251.
11. *Dinkard* VIII. 26. 27.
12. Jalali, 1383/2004, p. 114.
13. Jalali, 1383/2004, p. 87.
14. Jalali, 1383/2004, p. 57.
15. Mohammadi-Malayeri, 1372/1993, pp. 250–251.
16. Pour-Davood, 1347/1968, p. 19.
17. Lukonin, 1985, p. 711.
18. Jalali, 1383/2004, p. 114.
19. Tafazzoli, 1993, p. 193.
20. Jalali, 1382/2003, p. 117.
21. Jalali, 1382/2003, p. 18.
22. Imam-Shushtari, 1350/1971, p. 230.
23. Elgood, 2008, pp. 28–34, 44, 46, 65, 69–71, 202.
24. Matofi, 1378/1999, p. 207.
25. Imam-Shushtari, 1350/1971, p. 230.
26. Matofi, 1378/1999, p. 207.
27. Matofi, 1378/1999, p. 208.
28. Imam-Shushtari, 1350/1971, p. 230.
29. *Dinkard* VIII. 26. 11.
30. As noted by Shahbazi, 'the backbone of the army was its cavalry ... had a high official as Stor-Bizishk (*Asb* in pre-Islamic Iran, *Encyclopedia Iranica*, p. 728).
31. Hekmat, 1342/1964, p. 1087.
32. *Dinkard* VIII. 26. 11.
33. Jalali, 1382/2003, p. 18.
34. Matofi, 1378/1999, p. 208.

Chapter 11: Post-Battle Scenarious and War Diplomacy

1. Jalali, 1383/2004, p. 93.
2. Procopius, *Wars*, I, XVIII.
3. *Herodotus* IV.81.
4. Procopius, *Wars*, I, XVII.
5. Tashkari, 1356/1977, p. 151.
6. *Shahname* (ed. Foroughi, 1985), p. 358.
7. Whitby, 1994, p. 241.
8. Sami, 1342/1964, p. 69.
9. Malalas, *Chronographia* (ed. Dindorf, 1831), 441, 14–19.
10. Whitby, 1994, p. 240.
11. Pigulevskaya,1377/1998, p. 448.
12. Jalali, 1383/2004, p. 128.
13. Moghtader, 1315/1936, p. 171; Osheidari, 1371/1992, p. 317.
14. Jalali, 1383/2004, p. 117.
15. More specifically, Wiesehofer (1996, p. 188) refers to this as the 'castle of oblivion'; note that Wiesehofer does not cite the Persian term 'Faramoushkhaneh' in his text.

16. Tashkari, 1356/1977, p. 151.
17. *Shahname* (ed. Mohl, 1374/1995), p. 1553.
18. Jalali, 1383/2004, p. 92.
19. SKZ, Sassanian Pahlavi, lines 20–21; Parthian Pahlavi, lines 15–16; Greek, lines 34–35.
20. *Chronicle of Seert* (ed. & tr. by Scher, 1908), p. 221.
21. Jalali, 1383/2004, p. 92.
22. Mahamedi, 2003, p. 157.
23. *Ammianus Marcellinus*, XXV, 7, 11.
24. Kettenhofen, 'Deportations', *Encyclopedia Iranica*, p. 302.
25. *Chronicle of Joshua the Stylite* (ed. & tr. Wright, 1882), pp. 40–41.
26. Crone, 1991, p. 30; see also Procopius, *Wars*, II, 11.31–11.35, 14.1–14.4.
27. Kettenhofen, 'Deportations', *Encyclopedia Iranica*, p. 302.
28. Foss, 2003, p. 153.
29. *Toqi'ate Kasra Anoushirvan* (ed. Zavari, 2009), p. 62.
30. Mashkoor, 1366/1987, p. 863.
31. Howard-Johnston, 1995, p. 201.
32. *Tabari*, I, p. 827.
33. As cited from Nöldeke by Dodgeon & Lieu, 1991, p. 298, Appendix I.
34. See for example report by Whitehouse & Williamson, 1973, pp. 33–35.
35. Bullough, 1963, p. 57.
36. Bullough, 1963, p. 55.
37. *Shahname* (ed. Mohl, 1995), pp. 1537–1538.
38. Jalali, 1383/2004, p. 74.
39. Lee, 1986, p. 456.
40. Libanius, *Or.*, XVIII, 164.
41. Jalali, 1383/2004, p. 74.
42. Ayvazyan, 2010, p. 42–43.
43. Consult Ghirshman, 1962, p. 222. The buckle is housed in the Wiesbaden Museum in Germany.
44. Brogan, 1936, p. 202.
45. Frye, 1984, p. 326.
46. Lee, 1986, p. 456.
47. Procopius, *Wars*, 11.4.14–26.
48. As cited by Lee, 1986, p. 457.

Chapter 12: The Spah in Central Asia: Warfare, Military Developments and Tactics

1. Frye, 1996, p. 175.
2. Sinor, 1981, p. 133.
3. *Ammianus Marcellinus*, XXXI, II, 9.
4. As cited by Sinor, 1981, p. 134.
5. Maurice, *Strategikon*, XI, II, 2.
6. *Tarikh-e Jahangoshay-e Juvaini* (tr. Boyle, 1958), p. 30.
7. Sinor, 1981, pp. 135.
8. As cited by Hanaway, 1971, p. 29.
9. As cited by Sinor, 1981, p. 135.
10. Brunel, 1958, pp. 42–43.
11. As cited by Sinor, 1981, p. 137.
12. Nikonorov, 2000, p. 74.
13. *Ammianus Marcellinus*, XXX1, II, 6.
14. Sinor, 1981, p. 137.
15. Coulston, 1986, p. 70.
16. Sinor, 1981, p. 137.
17. Bivar, 1972, p. 287.
18. Dien, 1986, p. 35
19. Dien, 1986, p. 33.

20. Dien, 1986, p. 34.
21. Ibid.
22. Dien, 1986, pp. 37–38.
23. Coulston, 1986, p. 70.
24. Bivar, 1972, p. 289.
25. As cited by Sinor, 1981, p. 139.
26. *Pangeyric on Anthemius* (ed. & tr. Anderson, 1936), I, pp. 30–31.
27. Maurice, *Strategikon*, XI, 2,8.
28. *Ammianus Marcellinus*, XXXI, II, 9.
29. Sinor, 1981, p. 140.
30. *Ammianus Marcellinus*, XXXI, II, 9.
31. Raspopova, 2006, p. 79.
32. Dien, 1986, p. 39.
33. Bivar, 1972, p. 283.
34. Dien, 1986, p. 41.
35. Nikonorov, 2000, p. 74.
36. Turnbull, 2004, Plate D, pp. 37–38.
37. Nikonorov, 2000, p. 75.
38. Nikonorov, 2000, p. 76.
39. Coulston, 1986, p. 70.
40. Sinor, 1981, p. 142.
41. Yu, 1967, p. 109.
42. Zarrin'kub, 1381/2002, p. 668.
43. *Tarikh-e Alam Araye Abbasi* (ed. Torkaman, 2003), Volume I, pp. 54–65.
44. Matthee, 1991, p. 392.
45. Vamberry, 1884, pp. 165; Marvin, 1886, pp. 13–14.
46. Sinor, 1981, p. 143.
47. Bivar, 1972, p. 287.
48. As cited by Sinor, 1981, p. 137.
49. Maurice, *Strategikon*, XI, II, 19.
50. Theodoret, I, 11–12.
51. See article 'Chionites' in the *Encyclopedia Iranica* by W. Felix.
52. Sims-Williams, 2008, p. 92.
53. Frye, 1985, p. 137.
54. *Ammianus Marcellinus*, XVII, V, 1.
55. Sims-Williams, 2008, p. 92.
56. *Ammianus Marcellinus*, XVIII, VI, 20; XIX, I, 7–11.
57. Docherty, 2008, p. 104.
58. Dinawari, Abu Hanifa, *Akhbar ol Tawwal*, pp. 84–85.
59. Ibid.
60. Daniel, 2001, p. 63.
61. Frye, 1996, p. 176.
62. Frye, 1984, p. 352.
63. Zarrin'kub, 1381/2002, p. 215.
64. Matofi, 1378/1999, p. 173.
65. Frye, 1996, p. 176.
66. Frye, 1988, p. 38.
67. Matofi, 1378/1999, p. 173.
68. Greatrex, 1998, p. 45.
69. Sims-Williams, 2008, p. 93.
70. Greatrex, 1998, p. 46.
71. Greatrex, 1998, p. 46. Kurbanov disagrees with this date and states this as 468 CE (2010, pp. 164).
72. Kurbanov, 2010, p. 104.
73. Greatrex, 1998, p. 45.

74. Litvinskij 1998, p. 100.
75. Kurbanov, 2010, p. 164.
76. Harmatta 1969, p. 394.
77. Kurbanov, 2010, p. 165.
78. Procopius, *Wars*, I, 3.
79. Procopius, *Wars*, I, 3.
80. The battle most likely took place in the Kopetdag mountains.
81. As cited by Kurbanov, 2010, p. 166.
82. Procopius, *Wars*, I, 3.
83. Kurbanov, 2010, p. 104.
84. *Joshua the Stylite* (ed. & tr. Wright, 1882), 10.
85. Kurbanov, 2010, p. 166–167.
86. Procopius, *Wars*, I, 4.
87. Procopius, *Wars*, I, 4.
88. Matofi, 1378/1999, p. 184
89. Kurbanov, 2010, p. 170.
90. Greatrex, 1998, p. 47.
91. Schindel, 2005, p. 296.
92. *Tabari*, vol.2, pp. 631–634; Dinawari, Abu Hanifa, *Akhbar Al-Tawwal*, p. 29; Procopius, *Wars*, I, 4.
93. *Tabari*, vol. 2, pp. 631–634; also *Tabari*, Iran during the Sassanians, pp. 359–397; *History of Persia before Islam*, pp. 464.
94. Matofi, 1378/1999, p. 175.
95. Ibid.
96. Procopius, *Wars*, I, 4.
97. Dien, 1986, pp. 37–38.
98. Sims-Williams, 2008, p. 94.
99. Schindel, 2003, pp. 675–690.
100. *Tabari*, II, pp. 631–634.
101. *Shahname* (ed. A. Warner & E. Warner, 1905–1925), VI, p. 1271.
102. Howard-Johnston, 1995, p. 195 (citation also from p. 195).
103. Consult Frye, 2007, p. 108, note 28.
104. Il-Arslan was the son of Kara-Churin (Tardu?) and grandson of the historical Ishtemi-Khan, one of the legendary founders of the first Turkish kingdoms.
105. Reza, 1374/1995, p. 110.
106. Reza, 1374/1995, p. 110.
107. *Tabari* (tr. Payande, 1974), p. 726.
108. Matofi, 1378/1999, p. 182.
109. Firdowsi as cited by Reza, 1374/1995, p. 112, Footnote 35.
110. *Tabari* (tr. Bosworth, 1999), p. 301.
111. Reza, 1374/1995, p. 111.
112. *Tabari* (tr. Bosworth, 1999), p. 301.
113. *Theophylactos Simocatta*, 3.18.10.
114. Reza, 1374/1995, p. 111.
115. As cited by Reza, 1374/1995, p. 111.
116. Dinawari, Abu Hanifa, *Akhbar ol Tawwal* (tr. Neshat, 1346/1967), pp. 84–85.
117. Matofi, 1378/1999, p. 182.
118. Safa, 1369/1990, p. 14.
119. Shahbazi, 1986, p. 522.
120. Zarrin'kub, 1381/2002, p. 240. Note that Tiberius had been actually ruling the empire in 574 CE when the official emperor, Justin II had descended into madness. When Justin II passed away in 578 CE, Tiberius II was then officially declared emperor of the Romano-Byzantine Empire.
121. Safa, 1369/1990, p. 14; Jalali, 1383/2004, p. 75.
122. Reza, 1374/1995, p. 114.
123. Kolesnikoff, 1355/1976, p. 124.

124. Matofi, 1378/1999, p. 183.
125. As cited by Matofi, 1378/1999, p. 183.
126. Reza, 1374/1995, pp. 113–114.
127. Ibid.
128. Safa, 1369/1990, p. 16.
129. Matofi, 1998, pp. 182–183.
130. Dinawari, Abu Hanifa, *Akhbar ol Tawwal* (tr. Neshat, 1967), pp. 54–86.
131. Safa, 1369/1990, p. 16.
132. Reza, 1374/1995, p. 119.
133. Safa, 1369/1990, p. 16.
134. Czegledy, 1958, p. 22.
135. *Tabari* (tr. Bosworth, 1999), p. 302.
136. Safa, 1369/1990, p. 17.
137. *Tabari* (tr. Payande, 1974), p. 726.
138. Reza, 1374/1995, p. 120.
139. Dinawari, Abu Hanifa, *Akhbar ol Tawwal* (tr. Neshat, 1967), p. 86.
140. *Tabari* (tr. Bosworth, 1999), pp. 302–303.
141. Safa, 1369/1990, pp. 16–20.
142. Dinawari, Abu Hanifa, *Akhbar ol Tawwal* (tr. Neshat, 1967), pp. 86–87.
143. Reza, 1374/1995, p. 122.
144. *Tha'alibi* (tr, Zotenberg, 1900), p. 651.
145. Reza, 1374/1995, p. 122.
146. *Tabari* (tr. Payande, 1974), p. 772.
147. Czegledy, 1958, p. 23.
148. Howard-Johnston, 2010, p. 62.
149. Reza, 1374/1995, pp. 140–142.
150. *Sebeos* (tr. Thompson, 1999), Chapter 28, p. 50.
151. Ibid.
152. Howard-Johnston, 2010, p. 63.
153. *Sebeos* (tr. Thompson, 1999), Chapter 28, p. 52.
154. *Sebeos* (tr. Thompson, 1999), Chapter 28, p. 52, Footnote 323.
155. *Sebeos* (tr. Thompson, 1999), Chapter 28, p. 52.
156. Reza, 1374/1995, p. 130.
157. Reza, 1374/1995, p. 143.
158. Ibid.
159. Sims-Williams, 2008, p. 97.
160. Ibid.
161. Reza, 1374/1995, p. 154.

Chapter 13: Military Architecture

1. Kramers, 1936, p. 618.
2. Matofi, 1378/1999, p. 240.
3. Curatola & Scarcia, 2007, p. 92.
4. Curatola & Scarcia, 2007, p. 93.
5. Sarre & Herzfeld, 1920, p. 76.
6. Curatola & Scarcia, 2007, p. 93.
7. Sarfaraz, 1348/1969, p. 27.
8. Negroponzi & Cavallero, 1967, p. 41.
9. Sarre & Herzfeld, 1920, p. 76.
10. See for example the full report by Whitehouse & Williamson, 1973, pp. 33–35.
11. Ibid.
12. Ghirshman 1964, p. 35.
13. Parsa Ghasemi's research study entitled *Tal-e Khandagh ('Moated Mounds') – Military Structures in Ancient Fars* has been submitted for review at the time of writing.

14. Matofi, 1378/1999, p. 240.
15. Matheson, 2001, p. 138.
16. Curatola & Scarcia, 2007, p. 92.
17. Huff, 2008, p. 45.
18. Matheson, 2001, p. 138.
19. Huff, 2008, p. 49.
20. *Ibn-Balkhi* (tr. De Strange, 1912), p. 45.
21. Huff, 2008, p. 44.
22. Boucharlat, 1977, p. 329.
23. Siroux, 1965, p. 39.
24. See discussion by Kambaksh-Fard, 1345/1966, pp. 2–6.
25. *Babak* (from Ardashir e Babakan); *Khorramdin* (Persian: he/those of the joyous religion).
26. See Madelung (2009, pp. 53–65), Najmi (1368/1989) and Nafisi (1382/2003) in their examination of events and primary sources narrating the Babak rebellion and the role of the castle of Bazz.
27. Gregory Nazianzenus, *Oriationes* (ed. Bernardi, 2004), V, 10.
28. Den Boeft, Drijvers & Den Hengst, 2002, p. 102.
29. *Ammianus Marcellinus*, XXIV, V, 6.
30. *Ammianus Marcellinus*, XXIII, VI, 23.
31. Libanius, *Orationes* (ed. Norman, 1987), I, 132–134.
32. Howard-Johnston, 1995, p. 167.
33. Howard-Johnston, 1995, p. 185.
34. Dignas & Winter, 2007, p. 14.
35. Frye, 1977, p. 7.
36. Xenophon, *Anabasis*, I, 7, 15.
37. Mahamedi, 2003, p. 145.
38. Dignas & Winter, 2001, p. 142.
39. Frye, 1977, p. 8.
40. Whitby, 1986, pp. 717–735.
41. Minorsky (1943–6, pp. 243–265) has noted of Emperor Heraclius' reluctance to storm Ctesiphon on account of its formidable defences.
42. Consult Procopius, *Wars*, I, X, 1–19.
43. Dignas & Winter, 2001, p. 38.
44. Christensen, 1944, p. 213.
45. Note that this 'Albania' in the Caucasus is different from its Southeastern European counterpart.
46. As noted previously, the term 'Azerbaijan' or '*Azarbaijan*' historically refers to the province of that name in Iran south of the Araxes River; the modern-day Caucasian Republic of that name was first named 'Azerbaijan' on 27 May 1918 and was not referred to as Azerbaijan prior to that date.
47. Zarrin'kub, 1381/2002, p. 223.
48. Kramers, 1936, p. 613.
49. Barkhudaryan, 1969, pp. 125–147; *Matthew of Odessa's Chronicle* (translated by Hrach Bartikyan, 1973), pp. 151–152, 332 (see esp. note 132a).
50. See for example, *Ibn al Fakih* (as cited by Kramers, 1936, p. 616) who reports that the garrisons were entirely Persian.
51. Kramers, 1936, p. 613.
52. See report by Eric A. Powell, 'The Shah's Great Wall' in the *Archaelogy Journal* (Volume 61, No. 4, July–August, 2008).
53. In Baladuri's *Kitab Futuh al-Buldan* ('Book of the Conquests of the Lands'), first European translation edited by M.J. de Goeje in *Liber expugnationis regionum* (Leiden, 1870; Cairo, 1901).
54. Consult study by Han-Magomedov (1979) in references.
55. Trever, 1959, p. 268.
56. Howard-Johnston, 1996, p. 192.
57. Consult *Moses Khorenats'i* (II 50, 85) regarding events in Armenia and Albania during the Alan invasions.
58. Frye, 1977, p. 11.

59. Kramers, 1936, p. 613.
60. Dignas & Winter, 2001, p. 38.
61. Greatrex, 1998, p. 14
62. See for example, Mohammadi (1340–1341/1961–1962), Al-Darasat al-Adibiyya, Nos 3–4, pp. 237–378 in references.
63. See for example Mohammadi-Malayeri (1372/1993; 1374/1996) in references.
64. Howard-Johnston, 1995, p. 191.
65. Chegini & Nikitin, 1996, pp. 44–45.
66. Mahamedi, 2003, p. 146.
67. Frye, 1977, p. 14.
68. Chegini & Nikitin, 1996, pp. 44–45.
69. Mahamedi, 2003, p. 146.
70. Frye, 1977, p. 14.
71. The definition of 'farsang' has varied through history as farsang was 6.23km in the ninteenth century with the modern definition of farsang being the equivalent of 10km at present. The term itself is derived of Old Iranian *parasang*, for which no precise measurement can be ascertained.
72. As cited by Mahamedi, 2003, p. 147.
73. Chegini & Nikitin, 1996, pp. 44–56.
74. Bivar & Fehrevari, 1966, p. 30.
75. *Tabari*, III, p. 1275.
76. Bivar & Fehrevari, 1966, p. 39.
77. The term Gorgan is derived from Old Iranian *Varkana* (Land of the Wolf) and linguistically corresponds to modern Persian *Gorg-an* (The Wolves). The original inhabitants of the region are believed to have been the Hyrcanians.
78. Known also colloquially as *Sadd-e Anoushirvan* (Dam of Anouhirvan), *Sadd-e Firuz* (Dam of Firuz), *Sadd-e Iskander* (Dam of Alexander), and *Qizil-Yilan* (Turkic: 'Red Snake').
79. The team composed of Nokandeh, Sauer, Rekavandi, Wilkinson, Abbasi, Schwenninger, Mahmoudi, Parker, Fattahi, Usher-Wilson, Ershadi, Ratcliffe, & Gale, reported their findings in the *Iran* journal in 2006 (see references). The British specialists hailed from the Universities of Edinburgh and Durham. The studies of the British-Iranian team continued until early 2008.
80. *Science Daily News* (Feb, 18, 2008), 'Excavations In Iran Unravel Mystery Of "Red Snake"'.
81. Christensen, 1944, p. 287.
82. Frye, 1977, p. 13.
83. Weight cited from Frye, 1977, p. 13 discussing report by Najib Bakran, a thirteenth century Persian author.
84. Arne, 1945, p. 9.
85. Nokandeh et al. reported thirty-six in 2006 (p. 121) with the 2008 excavations having unearthed another four.
86. It is possible that more castles and structures could be uncovered in possible future excavations.
87. Jalali, 1383/2004, p. 87.
88. Howard-Johnston, 1995, p. 193.
89. Parsa Ghasemi's research study entitled *Tal-e Khandagh ('Moated Mounds') – Military Structures in Ancient Fars* has been submitted for review at the time of writing.
90. Dehkhoda, 1377/1998, p. 9983.
91. Pazoki, 1373/1994, p. 24.
92. Parsa Ghasemi's research study entitled *Tal-e Khandagh ('Moated Mounds') – Military Structures in Ancient Fars* has been submitted for review at the time of writing.
93. *Bundahishn*, XXXIII, 16.
94. Ibid.
95. Mahamedi, 2003, p. 145.
96. Ibid.
97. The term 'Sabur, the lord of the shoulders' is in reference to Shapur II, who allegedly pierced the shoulders of his vanquished Arab foes, lined them up, and passed a rope through their pierced shoulders to then force-march his captives in the desert.

98. Al-Hamavi, *Mu'jam al-Buldan* (ed. Wüstenfeld, 1870), II, p. 65.
99. Frye (1977, p. 11) also disagrees that 'war' in this context would mean 'sea'.
100. Mahamedi, 2003, p. 145.
101. Pliny as cited by Wilson, 2011, p. 50.
102. Al-Bakri, *Kitab al-Mu'djam Masta'djam* (ed. Wüstenfeld, 1877), p. 641.
103. Al-Hamavi, *Mu'jam al-Buldan* (ed. Wüstenfeld, 1870), II, p. 476.
104. Frye, 1977, p. 10.
105. Jalali, 1383/2004, p. 86.
106. Mohammadi-Malayeri, 1372/1993, pp. 243–255.
107. Baladuri, *Futuh al-Buldan* (ed. De Goeje, 1866 & 1969), p. 298.
108. Pigulevskaya, 1975, p. 410.
109. Mahamedi, 2003, p. 157.
110. Frye, 1977, p. 10.
111. Jalali, 1383/2004, p. 88.
112. Kramers, 1936, p. 616.
113. Mashkoor, 1366/1987 (volume II), p. 836.
114. Amid, 1377/1998, p. 1210.
115. Amid, 1377/1998, p. 1029.
116. Mashkoor, 1366/1987 (volume II), p. 836.
117. Wiesehofer, 1996, p. 198.
118. *Tabari* (tr. Neshat, 1973), p. 126.
119. Ibid.

Chapter 14: Siege Operations

1. Maurice, *Strategikon*, XI.1.
2. Inostrancev, 1926, p. 16.
3. Pazoki, 1374/1995, pp. 42–55.
4. Pazoki, 1374/1995, p. 43.
5. Lukonin, 1372/1993, p. 94.
6. Lukonin, 1372/1993, p. 94.
7. See for example Jalali, 1382/2003, p. 83.
8. Diakonov, 1346/1967, p. 424.
9. Oates & Oates, 1959, p. 208.
10. Procopius, *Wars*, I.17, II.17, 26, 27.
11. *Ammianus Marcellinus*, XIX, XX, XXIII, XXIV.
12. Inostransev, 1926, p. 16.
13. Pazoki, 1374/1995, p. 50.
14. Jalali, 1383/2004, pp. 51, 85.
15. Matofi, 1378/1999, p. 221.
16. Khorasani, 2010, p. 137.
17. *Ammianus Marcellinus*, XIX, V, 6.
18. Matofi, 1378/1999, p. 221.
19. Ibid.
20. *A Chinese Biographical Dictionary* (London: Arthur Probsthain, 1898).
21. Bradbury, 1998, pp. 255–256.
22. Matofi, 1378/1999, p. 444.
23. Jalali, 225, p. 51.
24. *Ammianus Marcellinus*, XIX, VII, 7.
25. Matofi, 1378/1999, p. 215.
26. Khorasani, 2010, p. 225.
27. Matofi, 1378/1999, p. 215.
28. Khorasani, 2010, p. 101.
29. Matofi, 1378/1999, p. 215.
30. As cited by Matofi, 1378/1999, p. 215.

31. Inostrancev, 1926, p. 50.
32. *Ammianus Marcellinus*, XIX, VI, 4–5, 7–9, 11.
33. Saket &Yahaqhi, 1389/2010, p. 26.
34. Inostrancev, 1926, pp. 16.
35. Jalali, 1383/2004, p. 83.
36. Greatrex & Lieu, 2002, p. 106.
37. Procopius, *Wars*, II, 13.
38. Howard-Johnston, 2010, p. 54.
39. Imam-Shushtari, 1350/1971, p. 87.
40. Ibid.
41. Moghtader, 1347/1968, p. 35.
42. Greatrex & Lieu, 2002, p. 113.
43. Jalali, 1383/2004, p. 84.
44. Imam-Shushtari, 1350/1971, p. 87.
45. *Ammianus Marcellinus*, XIX, VII, 2; XX, V, 1.
46. Jalali, 1383/2004, p. 83.
47. *Ammianus Marcellinus*, XIX, VII, 5.
48. *Ammianus Marcellinus*, XIX, VII, 7.
49. *Ammianus Marcellinus*, XX, VII, 13.
50. *Ammianus Marcellinus*, XX, VII, 12.
51. *Ammianus Marcellinus*, XX, XI, 15.
52. *Ammianus Marcellinus*, XX, XI, 12.
53. Inostransev, 1926, p. 16.
54. Procopius, *Wars*, I, 17; II, 17, 26, 27.
55. Procopius, *Wars*, I, 7.
56. Pazoki, 1374/1995, p. 44.
57. Pazoki, 1374/1995, pp. 44–47.
58. *Theodoret* (ed. & tr. Canivet & Leroy-Molinghen), I, 11–12.
59. Dodgeon & Lieu, 1991, p. 384, Footnote 6.
60. Jonathan Watts, '"Foreigner" helped build Terracotta Army', *Guardian Newspaper*, 28 June 2006.
61. Julian, *Or.* II (ed. Bidez, 1932), 11–13.30.
62. Ibid.
63. *Ammianus Marcellinus*, XIX, V, 6.
64. Inostransev, 1926, p. 50.
65. *Ammianus Marcellinus*, XX, VII, 6.
66. Raspopova, 2006, p. 84.
67. Jalali, 1383/2004, p. 83.
68. Safa, 1369/1990, p. 16.
69. *Ammianus Marcellinus*, XXIII, VI, 83.
70. Inostrancev, 1969, p. 89.
71. Jalali, 1383/2004, pp. 83–84.
72. Ibid.
73. Ibid.
74. Zoka, 1350a/1971a, p. 144.
75. Theophanes, *Chronographia*as cited by Dodegeon & Lieu, 1991, p. 205.
76. Jalali, 1383/2004, p. 84.
77. Julian, *Or.* II (ed. Bidez, 1932), 13.
78. Whitby, 1844, p. 240.
79. Dinawari, Muslim ibn Qutaybah, *Uyun ol-Akhbar*, p. 194.
80. Ibid.
81. Pazoki, 1374/1995, p. 48.
82. Ibid.
83. Whitby, 1994, p. 239.
84. *Ammianus Marcellinus*, XIX, I, 4.

85. Menander (ed. & tr. Blockley, 1985), 18.6.
86. Pazoki, 1374/1995, p. 50.
87. University of Leicester, news release, 'University of Leicester archaeologist uncovers evidence of ancient chemical warfare, CSI-style arguments suggest Persians routed Romans with poison gas', 14 January 2009.
88. Tanya Syed, 'Ancient Persians gassed the Persians', BBC News, 9 January 2009.
89. 'Sasanian Chemical Warfare? A Scientific Re-Assessment', Payvand News of Iran, 4 February 2009.
90. Ali Asghar Ramezanpour, 'Ekhtelaf-e nazar darbaraye tavasole Sassanian be selah-e shimiyayi' [Differences of opinion regarding the usage of chemical weapons by the Sassanians], BBC Persian, 20 January 2009.
91. Charles, 2007, p. 314.
92. See Theodoret, *Historia Religiosa* I (tr. Price, 1985), 11–12.
93. Julian, *Orat.* (2.64b).
94. See for example, *Chronicum Paschale*, 537, line 13 (consult Dindorf & Niebuhr, 1832).
95. Julian, *Orat.* (2.65b–2.65c).
96. Ibid.
97. Charles, 2007, p. 316.
98. *Ammianus Marcellinus*, XVIII, X.
99. Shapur II is described in *Ammianus Marcellinus* as 'wearing in place of a diadem a golden image of a ram's head set with precious stones, distinguished too by a great retinue of men of the highest rank and of various nations' (XIX, I).
100. *Ammianus Marcellinus*, XIX, II, III.
101. *Ammianus Marcellinus*, XIX, I.
102. *Heliodorus*, IX, 15, 3.
103. As noted in *Ammianus Marcellinus* (XIX, Chapter 1), 'a skilful observer [fighter at Amida] caught sight of him [Grumbates' son] as soon as he chanced to come within range of his weapon, and *discharging a ballista, pierced both cuirass and breast*' [emphasis added].
104. *Ammianus Marcellinus*, XIX, 7, 6–7.
105. *Ammianus Marcellinus* (XIX, Chapter 2) reports that 'on the morning of the third day *gleaming bands of horsemen* filled all places which the eye could reach, and the ranks, advancing at a quiet pace, *took the places assigned them by lot*. The Persians beset the whole circuit of the walls. The part which faced the *east* fell to the lot of the *Chionitae*, the place where the youth so fatal to us was slain, whose shade was destined to be appeased by the destruction of the city. The *Gelani* [from Hyrcania, i.e. northern Persia] were assigned to the *southern* side, the *Albani* guarded the quarter to the *north*, and to the *western* gate were opposed by the *Segestani* [the Seistan-Baluchistan Saka], the bravest warriors of all'.
106. See discussion of these these infantry tactics by Matofi, 1378/1999, pp. 170–171.
107. Matofi, 1378/1999, p. 171. The situation at Amida had deteriorated to such an extent that a plague began to infect the city, however oncoming rains washed this away.
108. As noted in *Ammianus Marcellinus* (XIX, Chapter 7) the garrison fired 'round stones ... by the iron arms of ... scorpions shattered the joints of the towers' which caused the Sassanian ballistic towers to collapse'.
109. These attacks were fraught with danger as the Amidans were able to target Shapur II with their missiles. Many of the elite savaran of the royal guards were killed in the endeavor to protect their king during these assaults.
110. Matofi, 1378/1999, p. 172.
111. Dodgeon and Lieu (1991, p. 190); note that this date is not certain.
112. *Ammianus Marcellinus* XX, VI, 2–7.
113. The use of this term in *Ammianus Marcellinus* (XX, VI, 6) is not clear. Perhaps this may be in reference to some type of propelled projectile, but its shape (rounded or missile-like) and composition (wood or stone) cannot be determined.
114. *Ammianus Marcellinus* (XX, VI, 6).
115. *Ammianus Marcellinus* (XX, VI, 7, 8).

116. Procopius, *Wars*, II, XII, 4–6.
117. Downey, 1953, p. 343, Footnote 8.
118. Procopius, *Wars*, II, V.7.
119. Procopius, *Wars*, II, V.28–33.
120. Procopius, *Wars*, II, VII, 16–18. During Megas' 10-day absence from Antioch, Emperor Justinian had dispatched the ambassadors John (son of Rufinius) and Julian (a *secretis*) which, as noted by Downey, was a bid for direct and higher level negotiations with Khosrow (Downey, 1953, p. 342).
121. Procopius, *Wars*, II, VII, 19.
122. Germanus was either a nephew or cousin of Justinian.
123. Procopius, *Wars*, II, VI, 11.
124. Procopius, *Wars*, II, VI, 14.
125. Procopius, *Wars*, II, VIII, 2.
126. Procopius, *Wars*, II, VIII, 4.
127. Paulus, an interpreter who had approached the city's walls to encourage the populace to pay the ransom, had also been nearly killed by arrows shot from Antioch's walls.
128. Procopius, *Wars*, II, VIII, 13.
129. Ibid.
130. Ibid.
131. Procopius, *Wars*, II, VIII, 30.
132. *Theophanes* (De Boor, 1883–1885), 292, 6–25.
133. Greatrex & Lieu, 2002, p. 184.
134. *Sebeos* 115–116, 69.
135. Avni, 2010, p. 41.
136. Jewish pro-Persian sympathies were not overcome by the Romans (Radin, 1915, p. 370). The Parthians were also supported by the Pharisees who, as Craven noted, 'seemed to feel that they received a greater measure of understanding from the Parthian than the Roman, and consequently became loyal adherents of the pro-Parthian party' (Craven, 1920, p. 53).
137. As cited by Conybeare (1910, pp. 507, 508). Note that the original account in Greek has been lost; see, for example, preservation of Strategius in Georgian and Arabic sources (Garitte, 1960, 1973–1974).
138. Avni, 2010, p. 41.
139. Avni, 2010, pp. 40, 42–44.
140. Cited from Avni, 2010, p. 42.
141. Levine, 2002, pp. 406–411.
142. Wightman, Hennessy, & Bennett, 1989, pp. 12–15.
143. Ben-Ami & Tchekhanovets, 2008, pp. 38–39.
144. Avni, 2010, p. 42.
145. Avni, 2010, p. 36–40.
146. See study by Nagar (2002).
147. Avni, 2010, p. 44.
148. Howard-Johnston, 2010, p. 65.
149. Jalali, 1383/2004, pp. 84–85.
150. Jalali, 1383/2004, p. 84.
151. *Ammianus Marcellinus*, XX, XI, 8.
152. *Ammianus Marcellinus*, XX, XI, 9–10.
153. *Ammianus Marcellinus*, XX, XI, 12.
154. *Ammianus Marcellinus*, XX, XI, 13.
155. *Ammianus Marcellinus*, XX, XI, 15.
156. *Ammianus Marcellinus*, XX, XI, 16.
157. *Ammianus Marcellinus*, XX, VII, 16; XX, XI, 7.
158. *Ammianus Marcellinus*, XX, XI, 18.
159. *Ammianus Marcellinus*, XX, XI, 20–21.
160. *Ammianus Marcellinus*, XX, XI, 22.

161. *Ammianus Marcellinus*, XX, XI, 23.

162. *Ammianus Marcellinus*, XX, XI, 32.

163. Khosrow's arrival in Lazica had been made possible by the king of Lazica who had declared the allegiance of his throne and kingdom to Ctesiphon. This action was due to the excesses of Romano-Byzantine officials who had alienated the Lazicans (Consult Procopius, *Wars*, II, 15.1–30).

164. Procopius, *Wars*, II, 17.1–28.

165. Belisarius had captured Sisauranon (near Nisibis, which he had failed to capture) with the Al-Harith Arabs raiding into modern-day Iraqi Kurdistan.

166. Procopius, *Wars*, II, 19.47–9.

167. It is possible that Khworian and his savaran forces had been outmatched with respect to cavalry warfare by their opponents.

168. Mehreen (Shushtari), 1349/1971, pp. 194–195.

Chapter 15: Sassanian Military Culture
1. Jalali, 1383/2004, p. 73.

2. *Taj* (tr. to Persian by Nowbakht, 1329/1950), pp. 217–218.

3. Imam-Shoushtari, 1350/1971, p. 228.

4. Jalali, 1383/2004, p. 97.

5. Ibid.

6. Jalali, 1383/2004, p. 76.

7. For these rules of conduct for opening the battle, consult the *Dinkard*, Book VIII, Chapter XXVI.

8. Maurice, *Strategikon*, VIII, I.

9. Jalali, 1383/2004, p. 103.

10. Jalali, 1383/2004, p. 129.

11. Mashkoor, 1345/1966, p. 162.

12. Wiesehofer, 1996, p. 199.

13. See thorough discussion of this by Bayani, Malekzadeh and Rezvani, 1349/1970, p. 38.

14. Khorasani, Shafeian and Singh, in Press.

15. Consult Mode (2006) in references.

16. Karan is the son of Kaveh Ahangar (Ironsmith), an especially powerful mythological motif in West Iranian folklore, especially among the Kurds and Lurs.

17. *Shahname* (ed. Warner, 1905–1925), Vol. II, 12.

18. Jalali, 1383/2004, p. 64.

19. *Sebeos* (tr. Thompson, 1999), Chapter 28, p. 52.

20. Whitby, 1994, p. 236.

21. Michalak, 1987, p. 74.

22. Brzezinski & Mielzcarek, 2002, pp. 9, 14–15.

23. For a full description see Ghirshman, 1962, pp. 125–130.

24. Bryant, 1989, pp. 57–58, see also reconstruction of battle between Japanese warriors and Mongol invaders in Plates D and E.

25. *Dinkard* (ed. De Menasce, 1973), p. 200.

26. *Quintus Curtius Rufus* (tr. Rolfe, 1985), 3.3.10.

27. *Bundahishn* (ed. Anklesaria, 1908), p. 31.

28. Sekunda, 1992, p. 9.

29. *Julian* (ed. Bidez, 1932), III, 11–13.30.

30. Potter, 1990, pp. 370–380; See also discussion by Greatrex, 1998, p. 11.

31. Widengren, 1976, Figure 22, p. 258.

32. Goldman, 1993, pp. 202–205.

33. Jalali, 1383/2004, p. 55.

34. see Xenophon, Cyropaedia, I, III 2.

35. Goldman, 1993, pp. 227, 229, 231–232.

36. Holmes-Peck, 1964, pp. 110–112.

37. Holmes-Peck, 1964, p. 117.
38. See also article '*Afrasiab: wall paintings*' in *Encyclopedia Iranica* by Matteo Compareti.
39. Goldman, 1993, p. 226.
40. Hermitage, Inv. S-216 & Inv. S-250.
41. Goldman, 1993, p. 211.
42. Widengren, 1976, pp. 273–274.
43. *Theoph. A.M.* 6115, 308.27–312.8.
44. Khaleqi-Motlagh, 1390/2011, p. 228.
45. Overlaet, 1998, p. 275 (see especially Figure 158).
46. Jalali, 1383/2004, p. 56.
47. Ibid.
48. Ibid.
49. Christensen, 1944, p. 211.
50. Tajbakhsh, 1355/1976, p. 315.
51. *Ammianus Marcellinus*, XX.VI.3.
52. An interesting example of this is the fourth century CE Sassanian shield boss bearing the *Shir Eiran* (Lion of Iran/Persia) displayed at the British Museum in London.
53. Mehreen (Shushtari), 1349/1971, p. 85.
54. Jalali, 1383/2004, p. 101.
55. Hekmat, 1342/1964, p. 1090.
56. Sami, 1342/1964, p. 72.
57. Consult Khaleghi-Motlagh, 'Drafsh e Kaviani' in *Encyclopedia Iranica*.
58. Jalali, 1383/2004, p. 100.
59. Boss, 1993, p. 66.
60. Holmes-Peck, 1964, p. 116.
61. Goldman, 1993, p. 218.
62. *Sebeos* (tr. Thompson, 1999), Chapter 28, pp. 49–50.
63. *Sebeos* (tr. Thompson, 1999), Chapter 28, p. 49.
64. *Sebeos* (tr. Thompson, 1999), Chapter 28–29, pp. 53–54.
65. *Letter of Tansar* (ed. Minovi, 1932), 11; see also discussion by Jalali, 1383/2004, p. 122.
66. Tafazolli, 2000, p. 3.
67. *Menog e Xrad* (ed. Anklesaria, 1913), Q 30.9–10.
68. As cited by Tafazolli, 2000, p. 4.
69. Tafazzoli, 2000, p. 3.
70. Khaleqi-Motlagh, 1390/2011, p. 226.
71. Khaleqi-Motlagh, 1390/2011, pp. 219, 226.
72. Khaleqi-Motlagh, 1390/2011, p. 226.
73. Daryaee, 2009, p. 43.
74. The descendants of the Sassanian Dehkan knights, known as the 'Dehqan' class in Islamic times, played a major role in preserving the culture and history of pre-Islamic Iran as discussed by Tafazzoli (2000 pp. 33–57).
75. Khaleqi-Motlagh, 1390/2011, p. 218.
76. Consult for example Zenkowsky (1960, pp. 94, 297) and Swietochowski (1995, pp. 29, 94–95) regarding the Russian role in eliminating Persian language and culture in the Caucasus following their victories over Iran in 1828.
77. Mehdiyeva notes of how 'Soviet authorities falsified documents and re-wrote history books' (2003, p. 280) to further undermine the cultural and historical links between Iran and the South Caucasus during the post-Tsarist Soviet era.
78. Rawlinson, 1885, Volume III, pp. 305.
79. *Ammianus Marcellinus*, XVII, V, 3, 10.
80. Consult detailed discussion on Byzantine-Sassanian relations by Garsoian (1993, pp. 568–592) in references.
81. *Ammianus Marcellinus*, XIX, I, 5.
82. *Ammianus Marcellinus*, XIX, VII, 8.

83. *Ammianus Marcellinus*, XIX, I, 2–3.
84. Whitby, 1994, p. 239.
85. *Nikephoros* (ed. & tr. by Mango, 1990), 15.
86. Whitby, 1994, pp. 240–241.
87. See for example *Theophylact*, III, XII, 12.
88. Jalali, 1383/2004, p. 50.
89. Pour-Davood, 1347/1968, p. 64.
90. *Menog-e Xrad* (ed. Anklesaria, 1913), Q 30.9–10.
91. *Andarz-e Oshnar-e Danag* (tr. Nazer, 1373/1994), pp. 22–23.
92. As cited and described by Khaleqi-Motlagh, 1390/2011, p. 219.
93. Daryaee, 2009, p. 43–50.
94. Jalali, 1383/2004, p. 121.
95. Sami, 1342/1964, Vol. II, p. 80.
96. Ibid.
97. Khaleqi-Motlagh, 1390/2011, p. 229.
98. As cited and described by Khaleqi-Motlagh, 1390/2011, p. 228.
99. Khaleqi-Motlaqh, 1377a/1998a, p. 401.
100. Khaleqi-Motlaqh, 1377a/1998a, p. 404.
101. Khaleqi-Motlaqh, 1377a/1998a, p. 402.
102. Ibn Balkhi as cited by Farzin, 1387/2008, p. 107.
103. Bivar, 1972, p. 281.
104. Hanaway, 1971, p. 27.
105. *Theophanes*, 322.11–14.
106. Whitby, 1994, p. 237.
107. Ghirshman, 1962, pp. 218–219.
108. Xenophon, *Cyropedia*, CIII, 8.
109. Chardin, 1983, pp. 268, 290.
110. Adontz, (1970), Chapter X, 27–31, XI, 46–64.
111. As cited and described by Hanaway, 1971, p. 32.
112. Hanaway, 1971, p. 31.
113. Wilcox, 1999, pp. 16, 23.
114. Jalali, 1383/2004, p. 103.
115. *Tabari*, XIII (tr. Y. Friedman, 1999), p. 2247.
116. Jalali, 1383/2004, p. 116.
117. Matofi, 1378/1999, p. 203.
118. As cited and described by Lukonin, 1985, pp. 710–711.
119. Foss, 2002, p. 171.
120. Lerner, 2002, p. 102.
121. Overlaet, 1998, p. 87.
122. Nigosian, 1993, p. 81.
123. Nigosian, 1993, p. 18.
124. *Yasht*, 10, 6.
125. Haug, 1878, p. 205.
126. Hinnells, 1988, p. 76.
127. Nigosian, 1993, p. 18.
128. Taraporewala, 1980, p. 151.
129. Taraporewala, 1980, p. 151; Nigosian, 1993, p. 18.
130. Hinnells, 1988, p. 76.
131. Taraporewala, 1980, p. 151.
132. Nigosian, 1993, p. 19.
133. Hinnells, 1988, p. 76.
134. Quintius Rufus, *History of Alexander*, IV, 13, 2.
135. Daryaee, 2009, p. 20.
136. Consult detailed discussion of this topic in Hinnells, 1988, pp. 74–91.

137. Shah,1987, p. 261.
138. Daryaee, 2009, pp. 3, 72.
139. Duchesne-Guillemin, 1993, p. 867.
140. Shah, 1987, p. 261.
141. Daryaee, 2009, p. 3.
142. Taraporewala, 1980, p. 52.
143. For a thorough analysis of Mithraism, consult Yamauchi, 1990, pp. 493–521.
144. Nigosian, 1993, p. 26.
145. Daryaee, 2009, p. 34.
146. Taraporewala, 1980, pp. 151–152.
147. Daryaee, 2009, p. 3.
148. Hinnells, 1988, p. 27.
149. *Yasna*, 65, 1.

Chapter 16: Military Weaknesses of the Spah

1. Wilcox, 1999, p. 42.
2. Yarshater, 1993, pp. 1005, 1008. Mazdak was the prophet of a reformist Zoroastrian movement that based its theology on Zoroaster's egalitarian teachings.
3. See especially discussion regarding the political history of Sassanian-Parthian realations during the Sassanian era by Pourshariati (2008, pp. 31–155).
4. *Ammianus Marcellinus*, XX, XI, 83.
5. Matofi, 1378/1999, pp. 896–897.
6. Consult Rau (2008, p. 16) and Bournoutian's 'Ebrauhem Kalel Khan Javaunsher' in *Encyclopedia Iranica*.
7. Jalali, 1383/2004, pp. 93–94.
8. Ibid.
9. Whitby, 1994, p. 232.
10. *Theophylact* (ed. De Boor & De Wirth, 1972), 9.5–10.1.
11. *Chronicle of Seert* (ed. & tr. Scher, 1908), II, 65.
12. Mielczarek, 1993, p. 53.
13. Plutarch, *Crassus*, 1993, 19.1.
14. Plutarch, *Crassus*, 1993, 21.
15. Mielczarek, 1993, p. 53.
16. Mehreen (Shushtari), 1349/1971, p. 77.
17. Howard-Johnston, 1995, p. 167.
18. Howard-Johnston, 1995, p. 168.
19. Howard-Johnston, 1995, pp. 168–169.
20. Frye, 1993, p. 154.
21. The sources cited provide an excellent and comprehensive examination of the events discussed.
22. *Theophanes*, 6102, 609–610.
23. Greatrex & Lieu, 2002, p. 190.
24. *Sebeos*, 115–116, 69.
25. Howard-Johnston, 2010, p. 63.
26. Hardy, 1929, pp. 186–187.
27. *Sebeos* (tr. Thompson, 1999), Chapter 28, p. 54.
28. Howard-Johnston, 2010, p. 58.
29. *Theophanes*, A.M. 6113, 304.13–18.
30. Howard-Johnston, 1999, p. 16.
31. *Moses of Dasxuranci*, II.10 (132.21–133.11).
32. *Sebeos* 125–126, 81–83.
33. Benjamin, 1888, p. 264. See also *Theophanes*, A.M. 6117, 315.2–26.
34. Reza, 1374/1995, p. 160.
35. Reza, 1374/1995, pp. 161–162.
36. *Moses of Dasxuranci*, II.11, 135.5–140.14.

37. Ibid.
38. Whitby, 1994, pp. 232, 253.
39. Consult article by Karantabias (2005) in references.
40. Khorasani, 2006, p. 291.
41. Karantabias, 2005, p. 30.
42. Consult article on this topic by Lerner (2002) in references.
43. Consult Herrmann's detailed examination of Parthian and Sassanian equestrian technology (1989) in references.
44. Nicolle, 2005, p. 21.
45. Karantabias, 2005, pp. 31–34.
46. Karantabias, 2005, p. 33.
47. Karantabias, 2005, pp. 36–37.
48. Theophanes, *Chronographia* (ed. De Boor, 1883–1885), A.M. 6117.
49. Mackey, 1998, p. 46.
50. Gabriel & Boose, 1994, p. 645.
51. As cited by Matofi, 1378/1999, p. 187.
52. Matofi, 1378/1999, p. 187.
53. Frye, 1984, p. 337.
54. Nicolle, 1996, p. 61.

Chapter 17: Fall of the Spah and the Empire

1. Donner, 1995, p. 359.
2. Landau-Tasseron, 1995, p. 320.
3. Landau-Tasseron, 1995, pp. 303–316.
4. Zakeri, 1995, p. 306.
5. Jandora, 2010, p. 98.
6. Ibid.
7. Jandora, 2010, p. 105.
8. Jandora, 2010, p. 104.
9. As cited by Jandora, 2010, p. 101.
10. Ibid.
11. *Tabari* (ed. De Goeje, 1879–1901), I, p. 2224.
12. Jandora, 2010, p. 104.
13. Nicolle, 1996, p. 24.
14. As cited by Nicolle, 1996, p. 24.
15. Jandora, 2010, p. 104.
16. Landau-Tasseron, 1995, p. 332.
17. Donner, 1995, p. 337–360.
18. Another account states that Abu Ubeidah was drowned as he and his men attempted to swim across the Euphrates.
19. Donner, 1981, p. 192.
20. Jandora, 2010, p. 110.
21. Daniel, 2001, p. 66.
22. Ibid.
23. Donner, 1981, p. 205; Matofi, 1378/1999, p. 188. The Arab army was composed of a group from Medina (Waqqas' core army), a second group from Medina recently arrived on Omar's orders, tribesmen from Najd, troops of commanders Al-Muthanna and Al-Jarir, and reinforcements from southern Iraq and from Syria.
24. Donner, 1981, p. 204.
25. *Tabari*, XII (ed. De Goeje, 1879–1901). *Tabari* also reports that 60,000 troops (or half of Rustam's army) arrived with their servants. Ibn Is-Haqh also cites the proportional difference as one Arab against ten Sassanian troops (6,000 Arabs versus 60,000 Sassanians).
26. *Tabari*, XI (ed. De Goeje, 1879–1901). As noted by Masoudi 'upon each elephant was seated twenty of their warriors with armor and horned helmets [Khorasan Savaran cavalry?] ... around

each elephant stood infantry [Dailamites?], cavalry, and warriors' (as cited in Matofi, p. 188). These elephants were most likely deployed as a strike package, with an emphasis on close-quarter combat by the escorting infantry. During combat, the elephant's crew could discharge missiles from the cab.

27. For a comprehensive analysis of this topic and the factors contributing to the Arab success in conquering Iran, consult Towfiqhi & Hanifi (2009) in the references.
28. Composition of Waqqas' forces as discussed in endnote 23.
29. Jandora, 1990, p. 28. Donner, 1981, p. 205; Matofi, 1378/1999, p. 188.
30. Jandora, 2010, p. 109.
31. Known by the Arabs as 'The Day of Concussion'.
32. Known by the Arabs as 'The Day of Succors'.
33. See *Moses of Dasxuranci* (tr. Dowsett, 1961), pp. 110–113 and *Sebeos* (Macler, 1904), pp. 98–99.
34. Daniel, 2001, p. 66.
35. As cited in Matofi, 1378/1999, p. 188.
36. As noted by Iraqi historian Makiya: 'historians are agreed that the Arabs won because Iranians abandoned their army in droves to join the Islamic advance' (1998, p. 264).
37. Frye, 1988, p. 61.
38. Matofi, 1378/1999, p. 189.
39. Nicolle, 1993, p. 14. Many of these ex-Sassanian troops were to be settled in Kufa.
40. Matofi, 1378/1999, p. 189.
41. With the death of Shahyar, there was no Sassanian force left to oppose the Arab advance to Ctesiphon.
42. It is possible that the shock of the defeat at Qadissiyah along with the loss of the Kaveh national standard had so shaken the Sassanian leadership that sound tactical reasoning had been compromised.
43. Benjamin, 1888, p. 278.
44. *Tabari*, XIII (ed. De Goeje, 1879–1901), 2247.
45. Ibid.
46. Newark, 1994, p. 91.
47. *Tabari*, XIII (ed. De Goeje, 1879–1901), 2452.
48. *Tabari*, XIII (ed. De Goeje, 1879–1901), 2454.
49. Newark, 1994, p. 50. According to Newark: 'Dogs were fed off gold platters and aromatic substances were mistaken for food spices and tipped into soups' (1994, p. 91).
51. Benjamin, 1888, p. 278.
52. The Arabs had issued an edict that declared: 'If the books herein are in accord with Islam, then we don't need them. If the books herein are not in accord with Islam, then they are Kafir [infidel]' (as cited by Mackey, 1998, pp. 46).
53. As noted by Mackey (1998, p. 47), one of the actions of the Arabs in 648–648 CE was to destroy the crown and beards of the colossal bulls at Persepolis.
54. Litvinskij, Jalilov & Kolesnikov, 1996, p. 464.
55. Matofi, 1378/1999, p. 190.
56. *Tabari*, XIII (ed. De Goeje, 1879–1901), 2459–2460.
57. *Tabari*, XIII (ed. De Goeje, 1879–1901), 2460.
58. *Tabari*, XIII (ed. De Goeje, 1879–1901), 2464.
59. Ibid.
60. Matofi, 1378/1999, p. 189.
61. *Tabari*, XIII (ed. De Goeje, 1879–1901), 2473.
62. Matofi, 1378/1999, p. 190.
63. Donner, 1981, p. 215.
64. *Tabari*, XIII (ed. De Goeje, 1879–1901), 2534–2545.
65. *Tabari*, XIII (ed. De Goeje, 1879–1901), 2546.
66. *Tabari*, XIII (ed. De Goeje, 1879–1901), 2546–2547.
67. *Tabari*, XIII (ed. De Goeje, 1879–1901), 2549–2561.
68. Donner, 1981, p. 215.

69. Donner, 1981, p. 215–216.
70. Matofi, 1378/1999, p. 191.
71. *Tabari* XIII (ed. De Goeje, 1879–1901), 2601.
72. As cited in Matofi, 1378/1999, p. 191.
73. Ibid.
74. As discussed in Chapter 13, the spah was very proficient in the construction of defensive positions. Farrokh, 2007, p. 272.
75. As cited in Matofi, 1378/1999, p. 191.
76. Matofi, 1378/1999, p. 191.
77. The Arabs had yet to develop a sophisticated logistics system like the Byzantines and Sassanians.
78. Numan's troops are reputed to have chanted 'Allah Akbar' (God is Great) as they charged towards the Sassanians.
79. The Arabs kept Numan's death a secret until the conclusion of the battle (*Tabari*, XIII, 2598).
80. The ex-Sassanian professional troops now serving the caliphate would have most likely imparted their knowledge and tactics to the Arabs by this time.
81. Frye, 1988, p. 60.

Chapter 18: Post-Sassanian Resistance and Rebellion against the Caliphate
1. As noted by Ettinghausen, Iran had 'lost its independence, though not its cultural identity' (1972, p. 1).
2. Mackey, 1998, p. 51.
3. Clawson, 2005, p. 17.
4. As cited by Mackey (1998, p. 63).
5. Details of Pirouz's arrival and sojourn in China are chronicled in the *Old Book of Tang* and the *New Book of Tang*.
6. It is important to note that the term 'Zoroastrianism' cannot be used in a blanket sense when referring to the practitioners of Iranic cults in Central Asia. Recent scholarship now suggests that when discussing Zoroastrianism in Central Asia, one must also account for the various local variants of Indo-Iranian cults and religions which would have possibly incorporated and/or synthesized the beliefs systems and practices of the Zoroastrian state religion of the Sassanian Empire, especially from the fourth-fifth centuries CE; for an introduction to this topic consult Foltz (1998) in references.
7. *Tabari*, II, pp. 1445–1446.
8. For details consult Frye, 1988, p. 156.
9. *Tabari*, II, pp. 1879–1889.
10. Another important rebel, Hakim Bagha, was also killed during the Second Battle of Narshakh.
11. Situated above the oasis of Bukhara.
12. Litvinskij, Jalilov & Kolesnikov, 1998, p. 464.
13. Bosworth, 1997, pp. 385–386.
14. Nizam ol Molk Tusi, *Siyasat Nameh* (ed. Sh'er, 1371/1992) pp. 359–60; Fasih Khafi, *Mojmal-e Fasihi* (ed. M. Farrokh, 1341/1962); Amoretti, 1975, pp. 504–505; Madelung, 2009, p. 64.
15. Hence the Bateni desgination as the Sorkh-Alaman or 'red-banner ones'.
16. Overlaet, 1998, p. 268.
17. Imam Zain al-Abidin, *Al-Sahifah Al-Sajjadiyyah* (tr. S.A. Muhani, 1987), p. 251.
18. Matofi, 1378/1999, p. 303.
19. Ibn Isfandyar, *Tarikh Tabaristan* (tr. Eqbal, 1366/1987), p. 185.
20. Ibn Isfandyar, *Tarikh Tabaristan* (tr. Eqbal, 1366/1987), p. 196.
21. Ibn Isfandyar, *Tarikh Tabaristan* (tr. Eqbal, 1366/1987), pp. 59, 64, 108–109, 18, 185, 205, 234, 274.
22. Ibn Isfandyar, *Tarikh Tabaristan* (tr. Eqbal, 1366/1987), pp. 44, 60, 210–211, 232, 234–237.
23. Matofi, 1378/1999, p. 304.
24. *Tabari* (tr. SUNY, 2007), Vol. XXX, pp. 253–255.
25. Ibid.

26. *Vardan Areweltsi* (tr. & ed. Muyldermans, 1927), p. 119; Ibn al-Nadim, *Kitab Al-Fehrest* (ed. Flügel, 1871), pp. 406–407.
27. Lewis, 2002, pp. 109–110.
28. Madelung, 2009, pp. 63–65; Goldschmidt & Davidson, 2005, p. 81; Whittow, 1996, pp. 195, 203, 215.
29. Kambaksh-Fard, 1345/1966, pp. 2–6.
30. Nafisi, 1382/2003, pp. 69–71.
31. Ibn al-Nadim, *Kitab Al-Fehrest* (ed. Flügel, 1871), p. 406.
32. *Abu ol-Maali*, (ed. Daneshpajuh, 1962), Chapter 5.
33. Zarrin'kub, 1381/2002, p. 237.
34. Babak and his fighters were lightly armed at first, many of these reportedly only employing slings (*Tabari*, II, 1379–1389).
35. Consult Sadighi (1938, pp. 268–272) for a full analysis of Babak's temperament and character.
36. Frye, 1988, p. 115.
37. Nafisi, 1382/2003, pp. 32–33.
38. The local governor of Armenia, Hatam bin Harthama, had written to Babak about his disaffection against the caliphate. This was due to the caliphate having killed his father (Harthama bin Ayan) despite the latter's years of loyal service to Baghdad (*Tabari*, II, pp. 1026). Hatam bin Harthama, however, died shortly after writing his letter to Babak, but this had already further encouraged Babak in his rebellion (Sadighi, 1938, p. 238).
39. Nafisi, 1382/2003, pp. 32–33.
40. Consult Nafisi (1382/2003, pp. 138–141) regarding Babak's operations in Armenia.
41. Isa either managed to escape or was intercepted and killed by Babak (*Tabari*, III, pp. 1072).
42. The caliphate also suffered the humiliation of witnessing Babak making Ahmad his prisoner.
43. It is possible that Tusi's successes were at least partly due to the employment of Turkish horse-archers and heavy cavalry.
44. Tusi had marched his forces into a mountain pass in which Babak's forces lay in ambush. Babak and the rebels rushed down from the mountains upon Tusi's troops and engaged them in a ferocious hand-to-hand battle. Babak's forces gained the upper hand, killing many of the caliphate's troops and forcing the rest to flee from Azerbaijan. Tusi and a number of his surviving troops were surrounded and killed by Babak's forces.
45. For a succinct overview of Babak's rebellion from the perspective of contemporary Byzantine sources consult Whittow (1996, pp. 195, 203, 215).
46. *Tabari*, III, pp. 1138.
47. Masoudi, *Al-Tanbih wa al-Ashraf* (ed. de Goeje, 1893), p. 322; Ibn al-Nadim, *Kitab Al-Fehrest* (ed. Flügel, 1871), pp. 406; see also Nafisi, 1382/2003, p. 36 and map on that page showing territories controlled by Babak.
48. Nizam ol Molk Tusi, *Siyasat Nameh* (ed. J. She'ar, 1969), pp. 362–363; *Tabari*, III, p. 1165.
49. *Abu ol-Maali*, (ed. Daneshpajuh, 1962), Chapter 5.
50. Masoudi, *Al-Tanbih wa al-Ashraf* (ed. de Goeje, 1893), p. 323.
51. Pipes, 1981, p. 151.
52. The Karen clan is traced to the Partho-Sassanian eras.
53. Rekaya, 1973, p. 155.
54. Ibid.
55. Sadighi, 1938, p. 218.
56. Rekaya, 1973, p. 157.
57. Consult Sadighi, 1938, pp. 287–305.
58. Ibn Isfandyar as cited by Nafisi, 1382/2003, p. 57.
59. There are some scholars who primarily interpret Babak's rebellion in religious-political terms (see Sadighi, 1938 and Von Grunebaum, 1961 in references).
60. The term 'Afshin' was the royal princely title of the rulers of Osrushana in Central Asia (situated to the south of the bend of the Syr Darya river, with its territory stretching from Kojand to Samarqand) at the time of the Arab conquests.

61. As noted by *Tabari* (III, pp. 1065–66) the region was forced to submit to the caliphate in 794–795 CE, during the reign of Harun al-Rashid (r. 786–809 CE). Haydar bin Kavus did not become 'Afshin' of Osrushana until the death of his father Kavus (possibly mid-820s). Haydar had been forced to flee to Baghdad (c. 820 CE) due to Osrushana's dynastic rivalries. He returned with a caliphate army to subdue Osrushana and his father Kavus (the kingdom's contemporary Afshin). Haydar then assisted a caliphate army led by Ahmad bin abu-Khalid into Osrushana, forcing his father to submit to the Abbasids. Kavus then fled briefly into the Central Asian steppes. With this success, Haydar (now the Afshin of Osrushana) returned to Baghdad and adopted Islam.
62. Frye, 1988, pp. 115, 130.
63. After his return to Baghdad, Afshin had entered regular military service with the caliphate, serving as commander of the royal bodyguard of al-Mamoun's brother, Abu Eshaq Mohammad (future Caliph al-Motassem), who was governor of Egypt at the time. Afshin organized one of Abu Eshaq's bodyguard units (the Maghreba) composed of Egypt's native Arab settlers. As one of the caliphate's military leaders, Afshin played a critical role in subduing Egypt's Christian Copts and its rebellious Arabs in the 830s CE.
64. Nafisi, 1382/2003, p. 46. Interestingly, Afshin had worked to forge alliances with prominent Baghdad citizens of Iranian descent who were opposed to the Taherids in Central Asia.
65. Zarrin'kub, 1381/2002, p. 232. Material enticements had swayed numbers of prominent Iranian knights and professional military men to support the Arabs against their country during the invasion of Iran two centuries before in 637–651 CE. The caliphate was capable of creating disunity among the Iranians by catering to those elements most vulnerable to material inducements.
66. Afshin, for example, received 10,000 dirhams/day on horseback and 5,000 dirhams/day not on horseback.
67. For a full description consult *Tabari*, III, pp. 1230, 1232, 1233.
68. One example is Motassems's patronage of a bountiful wedding party between Hassan (Afshin's son) and Otroja, daughter of Ashnas (an important Turkish military officer); for more information, consult Masoudi in the *Muruj al-Dhahab* (see edition with Pellat, 1968–1979, in section 2815).
69. These complex issues are analyzed in detail by Rekaya (1973, pp. 159–176) with respect to the chronology and complexity of the Babak-Maziyar-Afshin alliances and the nature of the correspondences between the three.
70. While true that Afshin was having secret communications with Maziyar and Babak, he was still beholden to the caliph in his campaign against Babak. The psychological reasons for Afshin's contradictory stance remain a matter of conjecture. Perhaps Afshin may have taken issue with the Mazdak-based egalitarian philosophies of Babak and the Khorram-dinan. At the same time, Afshin apparently had pro-Iranian sympathies as well (albeit in secret correspondence with Babak and Maziyar).
71. Afshin's accusers presented 'evidence' of his Iranian or 'anti-Islamic' tendencies by presenting ancient Iranian symbols and texts that had allegedly been discovered in his house. Afshin was first imprisoned in Samara, where he was starved to death by May 841 CE.
72. Motassem had sent Abu Said Mohammad to rebuild destroyed caliphate forts and to station sentries along critical roads to ensure the safe arrival of Afshin's armies. When Afshin deployed into Azerbaijan, he also built fortresses along his path of advance.
73. Afshin successfully recruited numbers of Babak's spies, mainly as a result of his lenient policy of pardoning captured spies and offering them double the pay that Babak could provide.
74. Afshin was to engage in a very intense reconnaissance campaign, especially in his careful study of the topography of the Ardabil region.
75. One of Babak's captains named Eshma was captured in 835 CE and sent to Baghdad. Motassem extracted critical military information from his prisoner. Under torture, Eshma yielded information with respect to (1) Babak's military tactics (2) Azerbaijan's geography and (3) main routes used by the Iranian rebels (*Tabari*, III, p. 1172).
76. Motassem viewed Arab troops as less reliable than Turkish troops (Pipes, 1981, p. 152).
77. Pipes, 1981, p. 150. Al-Bili (2001, p. 12) also notes that Turkish military ascendancy had already been under way during the reign of al-Mamoun. Pipes (1981, p. 150) also avers that these slave

troops or Gholams rose to great prominence by Motassem's time by becoming the main element in the elite royal palace guards, police forces, governorships, etc. The promotion of the Turks led to a 'Praetorian Guard effect' resulting in the significant rise of Turkish power within the caliphate after Motassem's death. Motassem also dressed his Turkish troops in the finest attire to distinguish them from his non-Turkish troops. Note that restricted numbers of Turkish troops were already in service with the Abbasid army during the period of Mansur (Qaedan, 2003/1343, p. 124). Numbers of Turkish warriors had been in the service of the caliphate's armies as early as 674 CE, shortly after the fall of the Sassanian Empire in 651 CE. These Turks were (1) captured slaves from Central Asia who had been pressed into military service and (2) early converts to Islam.

78. A prominent caliphate general, Bugha al-Kabir for example, was a Turk. Nafisi (1382/2003, p. 46) describes Bugha as a Khazar Turk from the Caspian region.
79. See full discussion by Pipes (1981, pp. 144–157) regarding the history of deployment of Turkish troops and the primacy of their military role during the reign of Motassem.
80. *Tabari* (III, p. 1171) records this as Babak's first defeat during his long war of independence against the caliphate.
81. Kennedy (2006, Chapter XII, pp. 21) notes that Afshin's military leadership was 'careful and competent, shrewd and thoughtful'.
82. Interestingly by this time, the caliphate forces also included Afshin's brother, Fazl bin Kavus. The latter had entered the caliphate's service and embraced Islam.
83. Babak's overconfidence is demonstrated in a letter sent to Byzantine emperor Theophilos (r. 829–842 CE), declaring that 'Motassem has nobody else left, thus he sent his tailor and cook to fight me' (Sadighi, 1938, p. 257).
84. Nafisi, 1382/2003, pp. 97–117.
85. Consult G.H. Yusofi's article 'Babak Korrami' in the *Encyclopedia Iranica*, available on-line: http://www.iranicaonline.org/articles/babak-korrami.
86. Yaghoubi, *Tarikh* (tr. Ayti, 1342/1963), II, p. 579.
87. *Tabari*, III, pp. 1233–1234.
88. Yarshater, 1985, p. 1005.
89. Whittow, 1996, p. 195.
90. Consult Lenczowski, 1978, p. 79; Sperl, Shackle, & Awde, 1996, p. 193; Halm, 2004, p. 80.
91. Van der Leeuw, 2000, p. 198.
92. Consult Frye, 1988, p. 114, regarding Abadan Pirouz.
93. Izady, 1992, p. 144. Shah Ismail is known for his strong sentiments in favour of this movement, as acknowledged by modern-day Alevis in eastern Turkey. To this day, the Alevis of Turkey regard Shah Ismail as an *avatar* and refer to him as the *Saheb e Zaman* (lit. Master of Time), a concept derived from the ancient Zoroastrian-related cult, Zorvanism (Hinnels, 1988, pp. 71–73).

Chapter 19: Legacy

1. Mitterauer & Chapple, 2010, p. 108.
2. These were settled at Chester, Ribchester and Hadrian's Wall, initially under the command of Roman general Artorius Bastus. For a detailed analysis of the movements and arrivals of Iranian peoples to Britain, consult Littleton & Malcor (2000, pp. 18–26), Sulimirski (1970, pp. 173–174) and the entire article by Shadrake & Shadrake (1994/1995) in the references.
3. Newark, 1994, p. 24; Caratini, 1968, p. 65. The Visigoths and Romans had placed the Alans and Sang-i-ban in the center, suspecting he was about to defect to Attila and the Huns. As a result, when Attila struck, the Alans absorbed the main thrust of the Hun attack, allowing the Visigoths to then outflank the Huns.
4. Cosentino, 2004, p. 254.
5. Maurice, *Strategikon*, XI, 4, 11–12.
6. *Cedrenus*, (ed. Bekker, 1838–1839), i, p. 454.
7. Peterson, 1992, pp. 34–35.
8. Consult *Notitia Dignitatum* (ed. Seeck, 1876) in references.
9. Macdowall, 1995, p. 19.

10. Julian, Or. (ed. Bidez, 1932), I, 37C–38A.
11. *Ammianus Marcellinus*, XXV, I, 12.
12. Cosentino, 2004, pp. 251–252.
13. Cosentino, 2004, p. 251.
14. Cosentino, 2004, p. 252.
15. Procopius, *Wars*, II, XIX.
16. Boss, 1993, p. 66, Plate 3B.
17. Procopius, *Wars*, II, III, XIX. Note that Artabanes was an Armenian of Iranian, or more speci-fically Parthian descent; or, as Procopius would state, 'Artabanus, son of John of the Arsacidae'.
18. Cosentino, 2004, pp. 252–253.
19. Cosentino, 2004, p. 253.
20. Cosentino, 2004, pp. 253–254.
21. Cosentino, 2004, p. 254.
22. Haldon, 1975, pp. 21, 29.
23. Arberry, 1953, p. 44.
24. Kondakov, 1924, p. 11.
25. Haldon, 1975, p. 29.
26. Consult Cosentino, 'Some examples of social assimilation between Sasanians and Romans (fourth–sixth century)' (2003) in references.
27. Inostrancev, 1926, p. 43.
28. Al-Jahiz, *Kitab al-Mahasin* (ed. Van Bloten, 1898), 369–4, 371–3.
29. Seyrig, 1937, p. 7.
30. Seyrig, 1937, p. 10.
31. Boss, 1993, p. 56, Figure 60.
32. Seyrig, 1937, p. 27.
33. Seyrig, 1937, p. 28.
34. For a full description see Ghirshman, 1962, pp. 125–130.
35. The rules of ranked combat were suspended at times of national crisis when the empire was being invaded. In such a scenario the savaran, infantry and other auxiliary units (i.e. battle elephants) would fight collectively as comrades-in-arms against the enemy troops (see Chapter 9). There are parallels to this in the Japanese martial tradition (see Bryant, 1989, pp. 57–58; Plates D and E).
36. Procopius, *Wars*, I, XIII 29.
37. Procopius, *Wars*, I, XIII 36. The lances failed to kill either opponent; Andreas drew his sword first, with which he then killed his adversary.
38. Cosentino 2004, p. 253.
39. Procopius, *Wars*, VIII, XXXI 11–16.
40. Whitby, 1994, p. 236.
41. Michalak, 1987, p. 74.
42. Brzezinski & Mielzcarek, 2002, pp. 9, 14–15.
43. Inostransev, 1926, p. 11.
44. See full article by Hamblin (1986) in references.
45. Matofi, 1378/1999, p. 181.
46. Zakeri, 1995, p. 291.
47. As cited by Zakeri, 1995, p. 292.
48. Zakeri, 1995, p. 292.
49. Hamblin, 1986, p. 104.
50. Zakeri, 1995, pp. 302–303.
51. Ibid.
52. Al-Masoudi, *Muruj al Dhahab wa Ma'adin al-Jawahir* (tr. & ed. Lunde & Stone, 1989), 3, p. 237.
53. Al-Jahiz, *Bayan* (ed. Harun, 1960; Beirut publication, 1968), 3, 16–18.
54. Zakeri, 1995, p. 308 (for full discussion see pp. 308–310).
55. Hamblin, 1986, p. 99.
56. Agoston & Masters, 2009, p. 279.
57. Newark, 1994, p. 87.

58. For a succinct overview of Babak's rebellion (especially from the perspective of contemporary Byzantine sources) consult Whittow, 1996, pp. 195, 203 & 215.
59. Pipes, 1981, pp. 144–157.
60. Pipes, 1981, p. 150.
61. Nafisi, 1382/2003, p. 46.
62. Latham & Paterson, 1970, xxiii.
63. Nicolle, 1995, p. 22.
64. Nicolle, 1995, p. 20.
65. Nicolle, 1995, p. 32.
66. Nicolle, 1995, p. 21.
67. Matofi, 1378/1999, p. 859.

References

Primary Sources

Abu ol-Maali Mohammad bin Obaydollah, Bayan-e Adyan, edited by M.T. Daneshpajuh, Tehran: FIZ 10, 1962.

Agathangelos, History of the Armenians, (I), translated by R.W. Thomson, State University of New York Press (Albany), 1976.

Agathias, Historiae, translation by J.D. Frendo, Berlin-New York: Walter de Gruyter, 1975.

Al-Bakri, Kitab al-Mu'djam Masta'djam, edited and translated to German by F. Wüstenfeld, Göttingen-Paris, 1877.

Al-Jahiz Abu Osman amr ibn Bahr

   Al-Jahiz, Abu Osman amr ibn Bahr, Al Bayan *wa Tabyeen*. Beirut: Dar al Mashriq, 1968.

   Al-Jahiz, Abu Osman amr ibn Bahr, Al Bayan *wa Tabyeen*, edited by A.M. Harun, Cairo, 1960.

   Al-Jahiz, Abu Osman amr ibn Bahr, Kitab al Mahasin *wa al Addad*, edited by G. Van Bloten, Leiden, 1898.

   Al-Jahiz Abu Osman amr ibn Bahr, Taj, translated from Arabic to Persian H. Nowbakht, Tehran: Entesharate Komissione Moaref, 1329/1950.

Aljahshiyari's Kitab ol al-Vozara va al-Kitab, translated from Arabic to Persian by Abulfazl Tabatabai, 1348/1970, Tehran: Taban.

Ammianus Marcellinus: The Later Roman Empire, translated by W. Hamilton, Penguin Books (London, England), 1986. See also J.C. Rolfe, Harvard University Press (Cambridge, Massachusetts), 1939.

Andarz-e Oshnar-e Dana [The Advice/Counsel of Oshnar the Wise], edited I.M. Nazer, Tehran: Hirmand, 1373/1994.

Arrian, Anabasis of Alexander, translation by E.J. Chinnock, Hodder & Stoughton, 1884.

Augustine

   Augustine, De Civitate Dei (City of God), translated by R.W. Dyson, New York: Cambridge University Press, 1998.

   Augustine, De Civitatae Dei, edited by B. Dombart & A. Kalb, Turnhout, 1955.

Baladuri

   Baladuri, Ahmad bin Yahya, Futuh al Buldan, edited by M.J. de Goeje, Leiden: 1866 (republished 1969).

   Baladuri, Ahmad bin Yahya, Futuh al Buldan, translated to Persian by A. Azartash, Tehran: Bonyad-e Farhang-e Iran, 1346/1967.

Balkhi, Description of the Province of Fars in Persia at the beginning of the 14th century AD, translated by G. Le Strange (from manuscript of Ibn al-Balkhi in British Museum), London: British Museum, 1912.

Callisthenes, The History of Alexander the Great (Syriac verison of the Pseudo-Callisthenes), translated by W. Budge, Cambridge: Cambridge University Press, 1889.

Cassius Dio, Roman History, translated by E. Carey, London: William Heinemann, 1914.

Cedrenus, Compendium Historiarum, Edited by I. Bekker (Bonn), 1838–1839.

Chronicle of Seert, edited and translated by A. Scher, Patrologia Orientalia 1908.

Chronicle of Joshua the Stylite, edited and translated by W.C. Wright, Cambridge, 1882.

Chronicum Paschale, edited by L. Dindorf & B. Niebuhr (Bonn), 1832.

Dinawari, Abu Hanifa

   Dinawari, Abu Hanifa, Akhbar al Tawwal. edited by V. de Guirgass, Leiden: 1888.

Dinawari, Abu Hanifa, Akhbar al Tawwal, translated from Arabic to Persian by S. Neshat, Tehran: Entesharate Bonyade Farhange Iran, 1346/1967.

Dinawari, Abu Hanifa, Akhbar al Tawwal, translated from Arabic to Persian by M.M. Damghani, Tehran: Nashre Ney, 1368/1989.

Dinawari, Muslim ibn Qutaybah, Uyun al Akhbar

Dinawari, Muslim ibn Qutaybah, Uyun al-Akhbar, Beirut, Lebanon: Dar ol Kotoab al-Elmiya, 1986.

Dinawari, Muslim ibn Qutaybah, Uyun al-Akhbar, Cairo: Bina, 1948 (reprinted 1964 in Cairo).

Note: This four-volume work contains a subsection '*Kitab al-Harb*' which in turn contains an Arabic translation of portions of the Pahlavi work, the '*Kitab al-Ayin*', Cairo, 1964.

Diodorus Siculus, translated by C.H. Oldfather, Cambridge, MA.: Harvard University Press, 1935.

Eumenius in E. Galletier (Editor), *Panegyrici Latini*, Volume IX, 21, 1–3, Paris: Budé, 1949–1955.

Eutropius, Translated by J.S. Watson, London: George Bell and Sons, 1886.

Farrokhi-Sistani, Hakim, Divan-e Farrokhi-Sistani, edited by M. Dabirsiaqi, Tehran: Eqbal: 1335/1957.

Fasih Khafi, Mojmal-e Fasihi, edited by M. Farrokh, Mashad: Ketabforoushiye Bastan, 1341/1962.

Festus, Breviarium, translated by M.P. Arnaud-Linder, Paris: Les Belles Lettres, 1994.

Garshasp-Name

Asadi-Tusi, Abu Mansur Ali Ibn Ahmad, *Garshasp-Name*, translated into French by Cl. Huart (translation up to line 2543), Paris: Librarie Orientaliste, 1926; edited by H. Massé, following from Huart's translation, Paris: Librarie Orientaliste, 1951.

Asadi-Tusi, Abu Mansur Ali Ibn Ahmad, *Garshasp-Name*, edited by H. Yaghmai, Tehran: Berokhim, 1317/1938.

Gorgani, Fakhrredin Asad, Vis o Ramin, translated by D. Davis, Washington DC: Mage, 2008; translated to Russian by S.I. Lipkin, Moscow: Khudozhestvennaia Literatura, 1963.

Gregory Nazianzenus (Saint Grégoire de Nazianze), Oriationes, translated to French and edited by J. Bernardi, Paris: Les Belles Lettres, 2004.

Hamavi, Mu'jam al-Buldan, edited by F. Wüstenfeld, Leipzig: Brockhaus, 1870.

Heliodorus, Aethiopica, edited by R.M. Rattenbury & T.W. Lumb, Paris: Les Belles Lettres, 1960.

Herodian, History of the Empire. Translated by C.R. Whittaker, Cambridge, MA: Harvard University Press, 1970.

Herodotus, The Histories, translated by A. Selincourt, London: Penguin Books, 1972.

Ibn Khaldun

Ibn Khaldun, Adbul Rahman, The Muqaddimah: An Introduction to History, translated from Arabic to English by F. Rosenthal, Princeton University Press, 1967.

Ibn Khaldun, Muqaddimah, Beirut: Maktabat Lubnan, 1992.

Ibn al-Nadim, Kitab Al-Fehrest, edited by G. Flügel, Leipzig: Vogel, 1871.

Ibn Isfandyar Kateb, Baha-eddin Mohammad ibn Hassan, Tarikh-e Tabaristan, edited and translated from Arabic into Persian by A. Eqbal, Tehran: Entesharat-e Padideh, 1366/1987.

Imam Zain al-Abidin, Al-Sahifah Al-Sajjadiyyah, translated by S.A. Muhani, edited by L. Bakhtiar & Z. Sa'adi, Tom's River, N.J.: Imam Sahe-Bu-Zaman Association, 1987.

John of Ephesos, Historiae Ecclesiasticae Pars Tertia, edited and translated by E.W. Brooks, Louvain: L. Durbecq, 1952.

Jordanes, Historia Romana, edited by Th. Mommsen, Berlin: MGH, 1882.

Julian (Julianus) Apostata, Oriationes, edited by J. Bidez, Paris: Les Belles Lettres, 1932.

Justin, Epitome of the Philippic History of Pompeius Trogus, translated by J.S. Watson, London: Henry G. Bohn, 1853.

Juvaini, Tarikh-e Jahangoshay-e Juvaini [The History of the World Conqueror], translated from Persian to English by J.A., Boyle, Manchester University Press, 1958.

Karnamag e Ardashir

Karnamag e Ardashir, translated from Pahlavi to Modern Persian by B. Faravashi, Tehran University, 1354/1975.

Karnamag e Ardashir, translated from Pahlavi to Modern Persian by M.J. Mashkoor, Tehran: Bita, n.d.

Karnamag e Ardashir, translated from Pahlavi to Modern Persian by S. Hedayat, Tehran: Amir Kabir, 1342/1963.

Kitab al-Taj Fi al Sirat Anoushirvan, translated from Arabic to Persian by M. Mohammadi, (1340–1341/1961–1962), Al-Darasat al-Adibiyya, Nos 3–4, pp. 237–378.

Lebor Gabala Erenn [Book of the Takings of Ireland]. Original text edited and translated by R A Stewart Macalister & D. Litt, Educational Company of Ireland Ltd, 1938.

Leo Dioconus (Leo the Deacon), The History of Leo the Deacon, translated and edited by A.M. Talbot & D.F. Sullivan, Washington D.C.: Dumbarton Oaks, 2007.

Letter of Tansar

    Nameye Tansar be Goshnasp [Letter of Tansar to Goshnasp], edited and compiled by Mojtaba Minovi, Tehran: Matba-e Majlis, 1932.

    Letter of Tansar, translated to English by M. Boyce, Rome, 1968.

Le Troisieme Livre de Denkart: Traduit du Pehlevi, translated to French by J.P. de Menasce, Paris, 1973.

Libanius, Orationes, translated by A.F. Norman, New York: Cambridge University Press, 1987.

Lucian, Quomodo Historia Conscribenda Sit, translated by K. Kilburn, London: W. Heinemann, 1959.

Malalas

    Malalas, Chronographia, edited by L. Dindorf, Bonn: *Corpus Scriptorum Historiae Byzantinae*, 1831.

    The Chronicle of John Malalas: A Translation, translated by E. Jeffreys & R. Scott, Mebourne: Australian Association for Byzantine Studies, 1986.

    Malalas, Synopsis Sathas, edited by A.S. von Stauffenberg, Stuttgart: W. Kohlhammer, 1931.

Maqdisi, Abu Mohammad, Kitib al-Bad wa al-Tarikh, edited and translated into French by C. Huart, Paris: Emest Leroux, 1903.

Masoudi, Abu al Hassan

    Masoudi, Abu al Hassan, Al-Tanbih wa al-Ashraf, translated from Arabic to Persian by A. Payandeh, Tehran: Elmi va Farhangi, 2002.

    Masoudi, Abu al Hassan, Al-Tanbih wa al-Ashraf, edited and translated to French by M. de Goeje, Leiden, 1893.

    Masoudi, Abu al Hassan, Muruj al Dhahab wa ma'adin al-Jawahir, translated and edited by P. Lunde and C. Stone, London: Kegan Paul International, 1989.

    Masoudi, Abu al Hassan, Muruj al Dhahab wa ma'adin al-Jawahir, translated to French and edited by B. de Meynard, Paris, 1861–1877 (revised and edited by C. Pellat, 1968–1979).

Maurice's Strategikon, translated by G.T. Dennis, University of Pennsylvania Press, Pennsylvania, 1984.

Matthew of Odessa, translated by H. Bartikyan, Yerevan: Hayastan Publishing, 1973.

Menander (The History of Menander the Guardsman), edited and translated by R.C. Blockley 1985, Liverpool: Francis Cairns.

Menog-e Xrad

    Menog-e Xrad, Danak-u Mainyo Xard, Pahlavi, Pazand, and Sanskrit. Edited T.D. Anklesaria, Bombay, 1913.

    Menog-e Xrad, translated from Pahlavi to Modern Persian by A. Tafazzoli, Tehran: Bonyad-e Farhang e Iran, 1975.

Moezzi, Amir Abdollah Mohammad, Divan-e Ash'ar, edited by A. Eqbal, Tehran: Entesharate Islamiyeh, 1318/1940.

Molaghab, Mohammad bin Mansour bin Saeed, translated from Arabic to Persian by Ahmad Soheili Khonsari, Adab al Haadab va Al-Shoja'a, Tehran: Entesharate Eghbal, 1346/1968.

Monshi, I.B., *Tarikh-e Alam Araye Abbasi*, edited by I.B. Torkaman, Tehran: Amir Kabir, 2003.

Moses of Dasxuranci, History of the Albanians, translated by C.J.F. Dowsett, London, 1961.

Moses Khorenats'i, History of the Armenians, translated by R.W. Thompson, Cambridge, MA: Harvard University Press, 1978.

Mostowfi, Hamdollah, Tarikh-e Gozide, edited by A. Navai, Tehran: Amir Kabir Publications, 1339/1960 (second print 1363/1984).

Nikephoros, Patriarch of Constantinople, a Short History, edited and translated by C. Mango, Washington: Dumbarton Oaks, 1990.

Notitia Dignitatum: Accedunt Notitia urbis Constantinopolitanae et Laterculi Provinciarum, edited by O. Seeck, Berolini: Weidmann, 1876.

Nizam ol Molk

Nizam ol Molk Tusi, Abu Ali Hassan, Siyasat Nameh, edited by A. Ghazvini & M. Modaressi-Chahardahi, Tehran: Entesharate Ketabforoushiye Zavar, 1343/1964.

Nizam-al-Molk Tusi, Abu Ali Hassan, Siyasat Nameh, edited by J. She-ar, Tehran: Amir Kabir, 1371/1992.

Oracula Sibyllina, Translated into German by J. Geffcken, Leipzig: Hinrichs, 1902.

Petrus Patricius in C. Müller (editor), *Fragmenta Historieorum Graecorum*, Volume IV, pp. 181–91, Paris: Firmin Didot, 1841–1870; consult also citations of *Petrus Pratricus* in Dodgeon & Lieu (1991), pp. 53, 54, 58, 59, 115, 116, 199, 312–313 (Footnote 46 for Chapter 3).

Plutarch, Fall of the Roman Republic, translated by R. Warner, Penguin Books, London, 1972.

Procopius of Caesarea I: History of the Wars Books I & II, translated by H.B. Dewing, Harvard University Press, Cambridge, 1914.

Quintus Curtius Rufus, History of Alexander, translated to English J.C. Rolfe, Cambridge, Massachusetts: Harvard University Press, 1985.

Raftarnamye Anoushirvan be Khameye Khod-e Ou, translated by S.M.A Imam-Shushtari, published in the Persian Language journal *Majaleye Baresihaye Tarikhi*, 4th year, Nos 5 & 6, 1348/1970.

Res Gestae Divi Augusti, edited by P.A. Brunt & J.M. Moore, Oxford: Oxford University Press, 1970.

Saad-Salman, Masoud, Divan-e Saad-Salman, edited by R. Yasemi, Tehran: Pirouzi, 1339/1961.

Sallust, Histories, translated by P. McGushin, Oxford: Oxford University Press, 1992.

Scriptores Historia Augusta (SHA) (Volumes I–III), translated by D. Magie, Cambridge, MA: Harvard University Press, 1924; for history of Gordian III, *Volume II (The Three Gordians)*.

Sebeos

Sebeos, The Armenian History Attributed to Sebeos, translated by R.W. Thomson, Liverpool University Press, Liverpool, 1999.

Sebeos, The Armenian History Attributed to Sebeos, translated by Macler, Paris: Imprimerie Nationale, 1904.

Shahname

Shahname, Firdowsi, edited and compiled by J. Khaleghi-Motlagh, Tehran: Markaze Dayeratolmaaref-e Bozorg-e Islami, 1385/2006.

Shahname, Firdowsi, edited, compiled and translated into English by R. Davis, Penguin, 2006.

Shahname, Firdowsi, edited, compiled and translated into French by J. Mohl (Le Livre de Rois, Paris: 1831–1868), Persian version (including Mohl's version of French edits translated into Persian) published in Tehran: Entesharate Sokhan, 1374/1995.

Shahname, Firdowsi, edited, compiled by M.A. Foroughi, Tehran: Entesharate Javidan, 1364/1985.

Shahname, Firdowsi, edited and translated into English by A. Warner & E. Warner, London: 1905–1925.

Shahname, Firdowsi, edited and translated into Russian by M.N.O. Osmanov, Moscow: Institute of Oriental Studies of the Academy of Sciences of the USSR, 1960–71. Translated into Persian (Tehran: Entesharate Alam, 2005).

Shahname, Firdowsi, edited by M. Minavi, Tehran: Ketabforoushiye Berukhim, Tehran: 1313/1934.

Sidonius Apollinaris, Panegyric on Anthemius, edited and translated by W.B. Anderson, Loeb, 1936.

Strabo, Geography, translated by H.L. Jones (ed.), Perseus project, Tufts University, 2000.

Tabari

Tabari, Abu Jaafar Mohammad bin Jarir, Tarikh al-Rusul wa al-Molook, edited by M.J. De Goeje (15 volumes), Leiden: E.J. Brill, 1879–1901.

Tabari, Abu Jaafar Mohammad bin Jarir, The History of al-Tabari, Volume V: The Sasanids, The Byzantines, The Lakhmids and Yemen, translated by C.E. Bosworth, New York: State University of New York (SUNY) Press, 1999. This is part of entire volume of translations of all of Tabari's volumes (re-printed by SUNY, 2007).

Tabari, Abu Jaafar Mohammad bin Jarir, Tarikh al-Rusul wa al-Molook, translated to Persian by A. Payandeh, Tehran: Entesharate Asatir, 1368/1989; reprinted Tehran: Entesharate Bonyade Farhange Iran, 1352/1974.

Tabari, Abu Jaafar Mohammad bin Jarir, Tarikh al-Rusul wa al-Molook, translated to Persian by S. Neshat [section pertaining to Iran from 651 CE], Tehran: Bongahe Tarjome va Nashre Ketab, 1351/1973.

Tarikh-e Rozat ol Safa, Mir Khand, (Volumes I–VII) & Reza Gholi Hedayat, (Volumes VIII–X), Tehran: Entesharat-e Ketabfoorooshiye Khayyam, Markazi va Pirooz, 1339–1340/1960–1961.

Tha'alibi, Ghurar Siyar ol-Molook, translated from Arabic to French by H. Zotenberg in *Histoires des Rois des Perses*, Paris: Imprimerie Nationale, 1900.

Theodoret

    Theodoret, Historia Religiosa I, partly translated by R.M. Price, Cistercian Studies Series 88, Kalamazoo, Michigan: Cistercian Publications, 1985.

    Theodoret, Historia Religiosa I, edited and translated to French by P. Canivet and A. Leroy-Molinghen, Paris: Editions de Cerf, 1977–1979.

Theophanes the Confessor, Chronographia, edited by C. De Boor, Leipzig: Teubner, 1883–1885.

Theophanes (Chronicle of), Anni Mundi 6095–6305 (A.D. 602–813), edited & translated by H. Turtle-dove, Philadelphia: University of Pennsylvania Press, 1982.

Theophanes von Mytilene [Theophanes of Mytilene], in (ed. F. Jacoby) 'Die Fragmente der Griechischen Historiker Part I–III', Leiden: E.J. Brill, 1943.

Theophylakti Simocattae Historiae, edited by C. De Boor, re-edited by P. Wirth, Stuttgart: Teubner, 1972.

Toqi'ate Kasra Anoushirvan, edited by M.J.T., Zavari, Tehran: Entesharate Shafie, 2009.

Vardan Areweltsi, The Arab Domination of Armenia, Extracts from the Universal History of Vardan, translated to French by J. Muyldermans, Paris: Louvain, 1927.

Xenophon

    Xenophon, Cyropedia, edited by W. Miller, London & Cambridge, MA: William Heinemann Ltd. & Harvard University Press, 1914.

    Xenophon, Anabasis, translated by C. Anthon, New York: Harper & Brothers Publishers, 1914.

Yaghoubi Ibn Ahmad Ibn abi-Yaghoub: Tarikh Yaghoubi [History of Yaghoubi], translated to Persian by M.I. Ayti, Tehran: Bongah, 1342/1963.

Zachariah, Historia Ecclesiastica Rhetori Vulgo Adscripa, edited by E.W. Brooks, Louvain: Peeters Publishers, 1924.

Zonaras, Epitome Historiarum, edited by L. Dindorf, Leipzig: Teubner, 1870.

Zoroastrian Texts

    Bundahishn, edited by T.D. Anklesaria & B.T. Anklesaria, Bombay: British India Press, 1908.

    Khordeh Avesta comprising Ashem, Yatha, the Five Nyaeshes, the Five Gehs, Vispa Humata, Namsetaeshne, patet-Avesa, patet Pashemanee, all the Nirangs, Bajs and namaskars, fifteen Yashts, the Afringans, the Afrins, and the Ashirvad. Edited by Navroji Pestonji Kavasji Kanga, Bombay, 1936.

    The Yasna, Visparad, Afrinagan, Gahs and Miscellaneous Fragments, translated by L.H. Mills (1887), edited in M. Muller (1898), *Sacred Books of the East*, Volume 31, Oxford: Oxford University Press.

    Vendidad: The Zoroastrian Book of the Law, edited by C.F. Home, Whitefish, Montana: Kessinger Publishing, 2010.

    Dinkard, Complete text of, edited by D.M. Madan, Bombay: The Society for the Promotion of Researches into the Zoroastrian Religion, 1911.

    Le troisieme Livre de Denkart-Traduit de Pehlevi, edited by J.P. de Menasce, Paris: Klincksieck, 1973.

    Numbers of texts (Vendidad, Yasna, Tir-Yasht, etc.) available on-line at www.avesta.org.

Zosimus, Historia Nova, translated by J.J. Buchanan & H.T. Davis, San Antonio: Trinity University Press, 1967.

Anonymous Primary Sources

Chronicon Anonymum, edited and translated by J.B. Chabot, Louvain, 1937.

Nehaye al-Arb fi al-Akhbar al-Faris wa Al-Arab [History of the Persians and the Arabs], (Medieval Persian translator unknown) edited and compiled by R. Alzabi-Nejad & Y. Kalantari, Mashad: Entesharate Daneshgahe Firdowsi, 1994.

Secondary Sources

Abbas, E. & Imam-Shushtari, S.M.A. (1347/1968). *Ahd-e Ardashir* [the Era of Ardashir]. Tehran: Selseley-e Entesharat-e Anjoman-e Asar-e Melli.

Abbasi, M. (1374/1995). *Tarikh e Koshti Iran* [History of Wrestling in Iran] 2 Volumes. Tehran: Entesharate Firdows.

Abbasi, M. (1335/1956). *Sayah Nameye Chardin* [The Travelogues of Chardin] (10 volumes). Tehran: Amir Kabir.

Adontz, N. (1970, tr. N.G. Garsoian). *Armenia in the Period of Justinian: the Political Conditions Based on the Naxarar System*. Lisbon: Calouste Gulbenikian Foundation.

Agoston, G., & Masters, B. (2009). *Encyclopedia of the Ottoman Empire*. New York: Facts on File.

Al-Bili, O.S.A.I. (2001). *Prelude to the Generals: A Study of Some Aspects of the Reign of the Eighth Abbasid Caliph Al-Mu'tasim bi-Allah*. New York: Ithica Press.

Alizadeh, S., Pahlavani, A., & Sadrnia, A. (2004). *Iran: A Chronological History*. Herts, England: Melisende.

Allan, J.W., & Gilmour, B. (2000). *Persian Steel: The Tanavoli Collection*. Oxford: Oxford University Press.

Allan, J.W. (1986). Armour. *Encyclopedia Iranica*, 2, pp. 489–499.

Amanat, A. (2012). *Imagining the End: Visions of Apocalypse from the Ancient Middle East to Modern America*. I.B. Tauris.

Amid, H. (1377/1998). *Farhange Farsiye Amid* [The Amid Persian Lexicon]. Tehran: Amir Kabir.

Amoretti, B.A. (1985, reprint 1993). Sects and Heresies, in R.N. Frye (ed.), *Cambridge History of Iran: Vol. 4 The Period from the Arab Invasion to the Saljuqs*, New York: Cambridge University Press, pp. 481–519.

Ansari, A. (1383/2004). *Rustam dar Ravayate Soghdi* [Rustam in the Soghdian tradition]. Tehran: Firdows.

Arberry, A.J. (1953). *The Legacy of Persia*. Oxford: Clarendon Press.

Arne, J. (1945). *Excavations at Shah Tepe, Iran*. Stockholm: Sino-Swedish Expedition.

Avni. G. (2010). The Persian Conquest of Jerusalem (614 C.E.)-An Archaeological Assessment. *Bulletin of the American Schools of Oriental Research*, 357, pp. 35–48.

Axworthy, M. (2010). *Empire of the Mind: A History of Iran*. Jackson, TN: Basic Books.

Ayvazyan, A. (2012). *The Armenian Military in the Byzantine Empire: Conflict and Alliance under Justinian and Maurice*. Paris & Yerevan: Institut Tchobanian.

Azari, A. (1351/1972). Nagshe Fil dar Janghaye Iran Bastan [The role of battle elephants in Ancient Iran]. *Baresihaye Tarikhi*, 1, pp. 127–142.

Azghandi, A. (1374/1995). *Artesh va Siyasat* [The Army and Politics]. Tehran: Nashre Ghoomes.

Babaie, A. (1384/2005). *Tarikh e Artesh e Iran* [The History of the Iranian Army]. Tehran: Iman Publications.

Badian, E. (1965). Orientals in Alexander's Army. *The Journal of Hellenic Studies*, 85, pp. 160–161.

Balint, C. (1978). Vestiges archaelogiques de l'epoche tardives des Sassanides et leurs relations avec les people de steppes. *Acta Archaeologica Hungarica*, 30, pp. 173–212.

Bamban, R. (1998). *The Military History of the Parsiks*. Woodland Hills, CA: Institute of Historical Studies.

Barker, P. (1981). *The Armies and Enemies of Imperial Rome*. Worthing, England: Flexiprint Ltd.

Barkhudaryan, S. (1969). Vermendi harbanakan zaka bolukfune [The Armenian-Caucasian Albanian Kingdom of Derbend]. *Patma-Bansirakan Handes*, 3, pp. 125–147.

Barnes, T.D. (1981). *Constantine and Eusebius*. Cambridge: Harvard University Press.

Bavzani, A. (1359/1980). *Iranian: Tarikh e Iran ba Tekye bar Oza Eghtesadi va Ejtemai* [The Iranians: The History of Iran with an Emphasis on Economic and Social Conditions]. Tehran: Entesharate Roozbahan.

Bayani, Sh. (1355/1976). *Shamgah-e Ashkanian va Bamdad-e Sassanian* [The Dusk of the Parthians and the Dawn of the Sassanians]. Tehran: Entesharate Daneshgah Tehran (Tehran University Press).

Bayani, Sh. (1350/1971). *Iran e Javidan* [Immortal Iran]. Tehran: Entesharate Shoraye Markaziye Jashne Shahanshahiye Iran.

Bayani (Malekzadeh), M., & Rezvani, M.I. (1349/1970). *Simaye Shahan va Nam Avaran e Iran e Bastan* [The Profile of the Kings and Notable men of Ancient Iran]. Tehran: Entesharat e Shoraye Markaziye Jashn e Shahanshahiye Iran.

Beizai-Kashani, H.P. (1382/2003). *Tarikh-e Varzesh-e Bastani-ye Iran: Zoorkhaneh* [The History of the Ancient Sports of Iran: the Zoorkhaneh]. Tehran: Entesharat-e Savvar.

Belnitsky, A.M. (1946). Istoricheskaya Topographia Gerata VI Veka [The historical topography of Herat 6th century]. Moscow & Leningrad (modern St. Petersburg): Alisher Navoi, Sbornik Satei.

Belyaev, V.M. (1933). *Muzikalnye Instrumenty Uzbekistana* [Musical Instruments of Uzbekistan]. Moscow: Muzgiz.

Ben-Ami D., & Tchekhanovets, Y. (2008). A hoard of golden coins from the Givati Parking Lot and its importance to the Study of the History of Jerusalem in the late Byzantine Period, in E. Meyron (ed.), *City of David: Studies of Ancient Jerusalem, the 10th Annual Conference*, Jerusalem: Megalim, pp. 35–44.

Benjamin, S.G.W. (1888). *Persia*. London: T. Fisher Unwin.

Berg, E.M. & Lampe, R.L. (2002). Modeling the Joust. Thesis Project No.: 48-JLS-0013, Worcester Polytechnic Institute, 71 pp.

Bivar, A.D.H. (1972). Cavalry equipment and tactics on the Euphrates frontier. *Dumberton Oak Papers*, 26, pp. 273–291.

Bivar, A.D.H., & Fehrevari, G. (1966). The walls of Tammisha. *Iran*, IV, pp. 35–50.

Blockley, R.C. (1992). *East Roman Foreign Policy:* Formation and Conduct from Diocletian to Anastasius. Leeds: Francis Cairns.

Boeheim, W. (1983, original print 1890). *Handbuch der Waffenkunde* [Handbook/Journal of Weapon Customer]. Leipzig: Verlag von E.A. Seeman.

Boss, R. (1994). The Sarmatians and the development of early German mounted warfare. *Ancient Warrior*, I, pp. 18–25.

Boss, R. (1993). *Justinian's Wars: Belisarius, Narses and the Reconquest of the West*. England: Montvert Publications.

Bosworth, C.E. (1997). *The Encyclopedia of Islam, New Edition, Volume VIII*, Leiden & New York: Brill.

Boucharlat, R. (1977). La forteresse Sassanide de Tureng-Tepe, in J. Deshayes (ed.), *Le plateau Iranien et l'Asie Centrale des origines a la conquête Islamique*, Paris: Colloques Internationaux du C.N.R.S. No. 567, pp. 329–342.

Bullough, V.L. (1963). The Roman Empire vs. Persia, 363–502: A Study of Successful Deterrence. *The Journal of Conflict Resolution*, Vol. 7, No. 1, pp. 55–68.

Bradbury, J. (1998). *The Medieval Siege*. Suffolk, England: Boydell and Brewer Press.

Brogan, O. (1936). Trade between the Roman Empire and the Free Germans. *The Journal of Roman Studies*, 26 (Part 2), pp. 195–222.

Brown, F.E. (1936). *Arms and Armour: Excavations at Dura-Europos*. Yale University Press.

Brown, P. (1971). *The World of Late Antiquity from Marcus Aurelius to Muhammad*. London: Thames and Hudson.

Browne, E.G. (1900). Some accounts of the Arabic work entitled 'Nihayatu'l l-irab fi akhbari'l-Furs wa'l-Arab'. *Journal of the Royal Asiatic Society of Great Britain and Ireland*, April, pp. 195–259.

Brunel, C. (1958). David d'Ashby auteur reconnu des Faits des Tartares [David d'Ashby renowned author of the Facts of the Tartars]. *Romania*, 79, pp. 39–46.

Bryant, A.J. (1989). *The Samurai*. London: Osprey Publishing.

Brzezinski, R. & Mielzcarek, N. (2002). *The Sarmatians 600 BC–450 AD*. Oxford: Osprey Publishing.

Campbell, B. (2004). *Greek and Roman Military Writers*. New York: Routledge.

Caratini, R (ed.) (1968), 'Les Alains', in *Bordas Encyclopedie: 93 Histoire Ancienne*, Georges Lang, Paris, p. 65.

Cernenko, (1989). *The Scythians 700–300 BC*. London: Osprey Publishing.

Chardin, J. (1983). *Voyage de Paris à Ispahan I: De Paris à Tiflis*. Paris: François Maspero, éditions La Découverte.

Charles, M.B. (2011). The Sassanian 'Immortals'. *Iranica Antiqua*, XLVI, pp. 289–313.

Charles, M.B. (2007). The rise of the Sassanian Elephant Corps: Elephants and the later Roman Empire. *Iranica Antiqua*, XLII, pp. 301–346.

Chavannes, E. (1903). *Documents sur le Tou-Kiue (Turks) Occidenteux* [Documents on the Tou-Liue (Turks)]. Paris: Librairie d'Amérique et d'Orient Adrien Maisonneuve.

Chegini, N.N. & Nikitin, A.V. (1996). Sassanian Iran- economy, society, arts and crafts, in Litvinskij, B.A., Guand-Da, Z. & Samghabadi, R.S. (Eds), *History of Civilizations of Central Asia: The Crossroads of Civilization AD 250 – 750*, pp. 39–80, Paris: UNESCO.

Christensen, A. (1944). *L'Iran Sous Les Sassanides* [Iran under the Sassanians]. Copenhagen: Levine & Munksgaard. Translated to Persian by Gh. R. Yasmi, 1989), *Iran dar Zaman e Sassanian* [Iran during the Sassanian Era/Iran under the Sassanians], Tehran: Amir Kabir.

Clawson, P. (2005). *Eternal Iran*. London: Palgrave Macmillan.

Clodfelter, M. (2002). *Warfare and Armed Conflicts: A Statistical Reference to Casualty and Other Figures, 1500-2000*. Jefferson NC: McFarland & Company.

Conybeare, F.C. (1910). Antiochus Strategos' account of the sack of Jerusalem in A.D. 614. *The English Historical Review*, 25, pp. 502–517.

Cosentino, S. (2004). Iranian contingents in Byzantine Army. In *Convengo Inter-nazionale La Persia e Bisanzio (Roma: 14–18 ottobre 2002), Attidei Convengi Lincei 201*, Rome: Accademia Nazionale dei Lincei, pp. 245–261.

Cosentino, S. (2003). Some examples of social assimilation between Sasanians and Romans (4th–6th century), *Proceedings of the 5th conference of the Societas Iranologica Europaea*, held October 2003, published 2006, pp. 379–386.

Coulston, J.C. (1986). Roman, Parthian and Sassanid tactical developments, In P. Freeman and D. Kennedy (eds), *The Defense of the Roman and Byzantine East*, B.A.R. Series, pp. 59–75.

Coulston, J.C. (1985). Roman Archery Equipment, in M.C. Bishop (ed.), The Production and Distribution of Roman Military Equipment, *Proceedings of the Second Roman Military Equipment Seminar, BAR International Series 275*, Oxford, pp. 220–366.

Cowan, R. (2003). *Imperial Roman Legionary AD 161–284*. Botley, England: Osprey Publishing.

Craven, L. (1920). *Antony's Oriental Policy until the Defeat of the Parthian Expedition*. Columbia, Missouri: University of Missouri.

Crone, P. (1991). Kavad's heresy and Mazdak's revolt. *Iran*, Vol. 29, pp. 21–42.

Curatola, G., & Scarcia, G. (Translated by M. Shore, 2007). *The Art and Architecture of Persia*. New York: Abbeville Press.

Czegledy, K. (1958). Bahram Chobin and the Persian apocalyptic literature. *Acta Orientalia*, VIII, pp. 21–43.

Dandamaev, & Lukonin (1989). *The Culture and Social Institutions of Ancient Iran*. New York: Cambridge University Press.

Daniel, E.L. (2001). *The History of Iran*. London: Greenwood Press.

Daryaee, T. (2010). *On the Explanation of Chess and Backgammon*. University of California, Irvine: Persian Text Series of Late Antiquity No. 1, Dr. Samuel M. Jordan Center for Persian Studies & Culture.

Daryaee, T. (2009). *Sassanian Persia: the Rise and Fall of an Empire*. I.B. Tauris.

Daryaee, T. (2006). The construction of the past in late antique Persia. *Historia*, 55, pp. pp. 493–503.

Daryaee, T. (2002). Mind, body and the cosmos: chess and backgammon in ancient Persia. *Iranian Studies*, 35, 4, pp. 281–312.

Debevoise, N.C. (1968). *The Political History of Parthia*. New York: Greenwood Press.

Dehkhoda, A. (1377/1998). *The Dehkhoda Encyclopedic Persian Dictionary, supervised by Dr. Mohammad Moïn & Dr. Jafar Shahidi, Volume 7*. Tehran: Loghatnameh Dehkhoda Institute.

Den Boeft, J., Drijvers, J.W., & Den Hengst, D. (2002). *Philological and Historical Commentary on Ammianus Marcellinus XXIV*. Leiden: Brill.

Diakonov, M.M. (1377/1999). *Tarikhe Maad* [History of the Medes]. Tehran: Entesharate Elmi va Farhangi.

Diakonov, M.M. (1346/1967). *Tarikhe Iran Bastan* [History of Ancient Iran]. Tehran: Bongahe Tarjome va Nashre Ketab.

Dien, A.E. (1986). The Stirrup and Its Effect on Chinese Military History. *Ars Orientalis*, 16, pp. 33–36.

Dignas, B., & Winter, E. (2007). *Rome and Persia in Late Antiquity: Neighbours and Rivals*. New York: Cambridge University Press.

Docherty, P. (2008). *The Khyber Pass: A History of Empire and Invasion*. Union Square Press.

Dodgeon, M.H. & Lieu, S.N.C. (1991). *The Roman Eastern Frontier and the Persian Wars (AD 226–363)*. London & New York: Routledge.

Donner, F.M. (1981). *The Early Islamic Conquests*. Princeton: Princeton University Press.

Downey, G. (1953). The Persian campaign in Syria in AD 540. *Speculum*, 28, pp. 340–348.

Duchesne-Guillemin, J. (1985, reprint 1993). Zoroastrian religion, in E. Yarshater (ed.), *Cambridge History of Iran: Vol. 3 (2) The Seleucid, Parthian and Sasanid Periods*, New York, Cambridge University Press, pp. 866–908.

Dupuy, R.E., Dupuy, T.N. (1977, reprinted 1986). *The Harper Encyclopedia of Military History: From 3500 B.C. to the Present*. New York: Harper & Row.

Dzhumaev, A.B. (1992). Pravila i traditsii voennoi muzyki v Srednei Azii v drevnosti i srednevekove [Rules and traditions of military music in Central Asia in ancient times and the Middle Ages], in E.V. Rtveladze (ed.), International Conference 'Srednaya Aziya I Mirovaya Tsivilizatsiya' [Central Asia and Word Civilization], Tashkent, Uzbekistan, pp. 47–49.

Elgood, C.L. (translated to Persian by B. Forqani, 1387/2008). *Tarikhe Pezeshkiye Iran va Sarzamine Khelafate Sharqi* [The Medical history of Persia and the lands of the Eastern Caliphate]. Tehran: Amir Kabir.

Ettinghausen, R. (1972). *From Byzantium to Sasanian Iran and the Islamic world: Three Modes of Artistic Influence*. Leiden: Brill.

Ewald, B.C., & Norena, C.F. (2011). *The Emperor and Rome: Space, Representation and Ritual*. New York: Cambridge University Press.

Farmer, H.G. (1939). An outline history of music and musical theory, in A.U. Pope & E. Ackerman (eds.), *A Survey of Persian Art*, London & New York: Oxford University Press, pp. 2783–2804.

Farmer, H.G. (1939). *Studies in Oriental Musical Instruments*. Glasgow: The Civic Press.

Farmer, H.G. (1931). *The Organ of the Ancients: From Eastern Sources (Hebrew, Syriac, Arabic)*. London: W. Reeves.

Farrokh, K. (2005). *Elite Sassanian Cavalry*. Oxford: Osprey Publishing.

Farrokh, K. (2011). *Iran at war 1500–1988*. Oxford: Osprey Publishing.

Farzin, A.A. (1387/2008). Jyanavspar dar Shahname [Jyanavspar in the Shahname]. *Majaleyye Daneshkadeye Adabiyyat va Oloom e Ensaniye Daneshgahe Tehran*, Summer, 186, pp. 97–112.

Ferrill, A. (1986). *The Fall of the Roman Empire*. London: Thames & Hudson.

Foltz, R. (1998). When was Central Asia Zoroastrian? Mankind Quarterly, Vol. 38, No. 3, pp. 189–200.

Foss, C. (2003). The Persians in the Roman near East (602–630 AD). *Journal of the Royal Asiatic Society (Third Series)*, 13, 2, pp. 149–170.

Foss, C. (2002). The Sellarioi and other officers of Persian Egypt. *Zeitschrift fur Papyrologie und Epigrafik*, 137, pp. 169–172.

Fowden, G. (1993). *Empire to Commonwealth: Consequences of Monotheism in Late Antiquity*. Princeton: Princeton University Press.

Freeman, & D. Kennedy (eds) (1986). *The Defense of the Roman and Byzantine East*. Oxford: B.A.R.

Frye, R.N. (2007). *The History of Bukhara*. Princeton, New Jersey: Markus Wiener Publishers.

Frye, R.N. (1988). *The Golden Age of Persia: Arabs in the East*. London: Weidenfeld and Nicolson.

Frye, R.N. (1985, reprint 1993). The political history of Iran under the Sassanians. In E. Yarshater (Ed.), *Cambridge History of Iran: Vol. 3 (1) The Seleucid, Parthian and Sasanid Periods*, New York, Cambridge University Press, pp. 116–177.

Frye, R.N. (1984). *The History of Ancient Iran*. Munich, Germany: C.H. Becksche Verlagsbuchhanndlung.

Frye, R.N. (1977). The Sassanian system of walls for defence. In M. Rosen-Ayalon (ed.), *Studies in Memory of Gaston Wiet, Jerusalem: The Hebrew University of Jerusalem - Institute of Asian and African Studies*, pp. 7–15.

Frye, R.N. (1963). *The Heritage of Persia*. Cleveland, Ohio: World Publishing company.

Gabriel, R.A. & Boose, D.W. (1994). *The Great Battles of Antiquity*. London: Greenwood Press.

Galichian, R. (2012). *Clash of Histories in the South Caucasus: redrawing the map of Azerbaijan, Armenia and Iran*. London: Bennet & Bloom.

Galichian, R. (2010). *The Invention of History: Azerbaijan, Armenia and the Showcasing of Imagination*. London: Gomitas Institute & Yerevan, Armenia: PrintInfo Art Books.

Garitte, G. (1973–1974). Expugnationis Hierosoliymae A.D. 615 [The capture of Hierosoliymae in 615 CE] Sciptores Arabici. Louvain: Secrétariat du Corpus SCO.

Garitte, G. (1960). *La prise de Jerusalem par les Perses en 614* [The Capture of Jerusalem by the Persians in 614] (*Corpus Scriptorum Christianorum Orientalium*). Louvain: Peeters Publishers.

Garsoian, N. (1985, reprint 1993). Byzantium and the Sassanians. In E. Yarshater (Ed.), *Cambridge History of Iran: Vol. 3 (1) The Seleucid, Parthian and Sasanid Periods*, New York, Cambridge University Press, pp. 568–592.

Garsoian, N. (1976). Prolegomena to a study of the Iranian element in Arsacid Armenia. *Hamdes Amsorea*, 90, pp. 177–234.

Ghasemi, P. (under review). *Tal-e Khandagh ('Moated Mounds')*.

Ghirshman, R. (1977). *L'Iran et la migration des Indo-Aryens et des Iraniens*. Leiden: E.J. Brill.

Ghirshman, R. (1971). *Persia: the Immortal Kingdom*. London: Orient Commerce Establishment.

Ghirshman, R. (1964). *The Art of Ancient Iran (Volume I)*. New York: Golden Press.

Ghirshman, R. (1962). *Iran, Parthians and Sassanians*. London: Thames & Hudson.

Ghozanlu, J. (1315/1936). *Tarikhe Nezamiye Iran* [The Military History of Iran]. Tehran: Chapkhaneye Markazi.

Goldman, B. (1993). Later pre-Islamic riding costume. *Iranica Antiqua*, XXVIII, pp. 201–246.

Goldschmidt, A., & Davidson, L. (2005). *A Concise History of the Middle East* (8th Edition). Boulder, Colorado: Westview Press.

Gorelik, M. (1979). Oriental Armour of the Near and Middle East from the 8th to the 15th centuries AD as shown in works of art. In R. Elgood (ed.), *Islamic Arms and Armour*, London: Scolar Press, pp. 30–63.

Grabner, R.H., Stern, E., & Neubauer, A.C. (2007). Individual differences in chess expertise: a psychometric investigation. *Acta Psychologica*, 124, 3, pp. 398–420.

Granscay, S.V. (1949). A barbarian chieftain's helmet. *The Metropolitan Musuem of Art Bulletin*, VII (10), pp. 272–281.

Greatrex, G. (2005). Byzantium and the East in the 6th Century, in (Michael Maas (ed.), *The Cambridge Companion to the Age of Justinian*, Chapter 19, pp. 477–509, New York: Cambridge University Press.

Greatrex, G. (1998). *Rome and Persia at War: 502–532*. Leeds: Francis Cairns Publications.

Greatrex, G., & Lieu, S.N.C. (2002). *The Roman Eastern Frontier and the Persian Wars Part II (AD 363–630)*. London & New York: Routledge.

Grignasci, M. (1966). Quelques specimens de la Literature Sassanide conserves dans les Biliotheques d'Istanbul, *Journal Asiatique*, 254, pp. 1–142.

Grotowski, P.L., & Brzezinski, R. (2010). *Arms and Armor of the Warrior Saints*. Leiden: Brill Academic Publishers.

Haldon, J.F. (1975). Some aspects of Byzantine military technology from the sixth to the tenth centuries. *Byzantine and Modern Greek Studies*, 1, pp. 11–47.

Halm, H. (translated by J. Watson & M. Hill, 2004). *Shi'ism*. Columbia University Press.

Hamblin, W. (1986). Sassanian military science and its transmission to the Arabs. *BRISMES Proceedings of the 1986 International Conference on Middle Eastern Studies*, pp. 99–106.

Han-Magomedov, S.O. (1979). *Derbent*. Moscow: Arts.

Hanaway Jr., W.L. (1971). The concept of the hunt in Persian literature. *Boston Museum Bulletin*, Vol. 69, No. 355/356, Persian Carpet Symposium, pp. 21–69.

Hanway, J. (1753). *An historical account of the British trade over the Caspian Sea : with a journal of travels from London through Russia into Persia ; and back again through Russia, Germany and Holland. To which are added, the revolutions of Persia during the present century, with the particular history of the great usurper Nadir Kouli* (4 Volumes). London: Dodsley.

Hardy, E.R. (1929). New light on the Persian occupation of Egypt. *Journal of the Society of Oriental Research*, 13, pp. 185–189.

Harmatta, J. (1969). Late Bactrian Inscriptions. *Acta Antiqua Academiae Scientarium Hungarica*, 17, 1969, pp. 297–432.

Harper, (1985). The ox-headed mace in pre-Islamic Iran. *Acta Iranica*, 24, 2ieme serie, Vol. X, Papers in Honour of Mary Bryce, pp. 247–259.

Haug, M. (1878, reprinted 2004 by Kessinger Publishing). *Essays on the Sacred Language, Writings and Religion of the Parsees*. Boston: Houghton, Osgood & Company.

Head, D. (1992). *The Achaemenid Persian Army*. Stockport, England: Montvert Publications.

Healy, M. (1993). *Battle of Kursk*. London: Osprey Publishing.

Hekmat, A.A. (1342/1964). *Iranshahr-Jeld e Dovom* [The Iranian Realm – Volume II]. Tehran: 22nd Publication of the National UNESCO Commission of Iran.

Herrmann, G. (1989). Parthian and Sassanian saddlery: New Light from the Roman West. In L. De Meyer and E. Haerinck (eds), *Atchaeologia Iranica et Orientalis: Miscellania in Honorem Louis Vanden Berge*, Gent: Peeters Publishers, pp. 757–809.

Hinnells, J.R. (1988). *Persian Mythology*. London, England & Yugoslavia: Hamlyn.

Holmes-Peck, E. (1964). The Representation of Costumes in the Reliefs of Tag-i-Bostan. *Arbitus Asiae*, XXXI, pp. 101–124.

Hourani, G. (1995). *Arab Seafaring: Expanded Edition*. New Jersey: Princeton University Press.

Houtum-Schindler, A. (1888). On the Length of the Persian Farsakh. *Proceedings of the Royal Geographical Society and Monthly Record of Geography, New Monthly Series* 10 (9), pp. 584–588.

Howard-Johnston, J. (2010). The Sassanian strategic dilemma. In Börm, H., & Wiesehöfer, J. (eds), *Commutatio et contentio. Studies in the Late Roman, Sasanian, and Early Islamic Near East*, pp. 37–70, Düsseldorf: Wellem Verlag.

Howard-Johnston, J. (1999). Heraclius' Persian campaigns and the revival of the East Roman Empire 622–630. *War in History*, 6, pp. 1–44.

Howard-Johnston, J. (1995). The two great powers in late antiquity: a comparison. *The Byzantine and Early Islamic Near East III: States, Resources and Armies*, Princeton: The Darwin Press Inc., pp. 157–226.

Huff, D. (2008). Formation and ideology of the Sassanian state in the context of the archaeological evidence, in V. Sarkhosh-Curtis & S. Stewart (eds), *The Sassanian Era-The Idea of Iran – Volume III*, London: I.B. Tauris, pp. 31–59.

Hughes, I. (2010). *Belisarius: The Last Roman General*. Barnsley: England: Pen & Sword Military.

Humble, R. (1989). *Warfare in the Middle Ages*. Leicester: Magna Books.

Ibrahimzadeh, S. (1350/1971). *Shahane Sassani va Eghtesade Farhange Iran* [Sassanian Kings and Economy of Iranian Civilization]. Kerman, Iran: Komiteye Jashne Shahanshahiye Madreseye Aliye Modiriyat.

Imam-Shushtari, S.M.A. (1350/1971). *Tarikhe Shahryari dar Shahanshahiye Iran* [History of Imperial Monarchy/kingship in Imperial/Monarchial Iran]. Tehran: Vezarate Farhang va Honar.

Inostrancev, C.A. (1926). (Translated by L. Bogdanov). The Sassanian military theory. *The Journal of the CAMA Oriental Institute*, 7, pp. 7–52.

Inostrancev, C.A. (1348/1969, Translated from Russian to Persian by K. Kazemzadeh). *Motaleati Darbaraye Sassanian* [Studies regarding the Sassanians]. Tehran: Bongahe Tarjome va Nashre Ketab.

Ivanov, M.S. (translated from Russian into Persian, 1359/1980). *Tarikhe Iran Bastan* [History of Ancient Iran]. Tehran: Entesharate Donya.

Izady, M. (1992). *The Kurds: A Concise History and Fact Book*. Washington: Taylor & Francis.

Jalali, I. (1383/2004). *Arteshe Iran dar Asre Sassanian* [The Army of Iran in the Sassanian Era]. Kerman, Iran: Entesharate Vadiat.

Jalali, I. (1382/2003). Artesh, Tashkeelat va Vahedhaye an dar Asr e Sassanian [The Army, Composition and Units in the Sassanian Era]. *Reshteye Amoozesh e Tarikh*, Fall and Winter, No. 13, pp. 12–20.

Jandora, J.W. (2010). Archers of Islam: A Search for 'Lost' History. *The Medieval History Journal*, 13, pp. 97–114.

Jandora, J.W. (1990). *The March from Medina: A Revisionist History of the Army Conquests*. Clifton, New Jersey: Kingston Press.

Kambaksh-Fard, S. (1345/1966). Qal'a-ye Jomhur yā Dezh-a Bazz [castle of Jomhur or the Fortress of Bazz]. *Honar o Mardom*, 50, November–December, pp. 2–6.

Karantabias, M.A. (2005). The crucial development of heavy cavalry under Herakleios and his usage of steppe nomad tactics. *Hirundo: The McGill Journal of Classical Studies*, IV, pp. 28–41.

Karasulas, A. (2003). Personal Communication.

Karasulas, A. (2002). *Mounted Archers of the Eurasian Steppe: The Essence of Central Asian Warfare.* Unpublished Honours Thesis. The University of New England, Australia.

Kazemini, K. (1343/1964). *Naqsh-e- Pahlevani va Nehzat-e Ayyari dar Tarikh-e Ejtemai va Hayat Siyasi-e Mellat-e Iran* [The Role of Pahlevani and the Movement of Ayyan in the Social History and Political Settings of the People of Iran]. Tehran: Chapkhaneye Bank-e Melli-e Iran.

Keegan, J. (1993). *A History of Warfare.* New York: Vintage Books.

Kennedy, H.N. (2006). *The Byzantine and Early Islamic Near East.* Ashgate Publishing.

Khaleqi-Motlaqh, J. (1390/2011). Ferdowsi wa Shahnama-Sarai, in E. Sa'adat (ed.), *The Encyclopedia of Persian Language and Literature*, Tehran: The Academy of Persian Language & Literature, pp. 208–229.

Khaleqi-Motlaqh, J. (1377a/1998a). Bar va Ayyin dar Iran Bastan [Time and Ritual/custom in Iran] (1). *Oloom-e Ensani-Iran Nameh*, 19, pp. 392–438.

Khaleqi-Motlaqh, J. (1377b/1998b). Bar va Ayyin dar Iran Bastan [Time and Ritual/custom in Iran] (2). *Oloom-e Ensani-Iran Nameh*, 21, pp. 34–75.

Khorasani, M.M. (2010). *Lexicon of Arms and Armor from Iran:* A Study of Symbols and Terminology. Legat Verlag: Tübingen, Germany.

Khorasani, M.M. (2006). *Arms and Armor from Iran:* The Bronze Age to the End of the Qajar Period. Legat Verlag: Tübingen, Germany.

Khorasani, M.M., Shafeian, H., & Singh, A. (in Press). Tactics, Weapons and Techniques of Persian Warriors in the Book of Kings. *Katsujinken.*

Kistler, J.M., & Lair, R. (2007). *War Elephants.* Lincoln, Nebraska: University of Nebraska Press.

Kobylinsky, L. (2000). Persian and Indo-Persian Arms, in A.R. Chodynski (ed.), *Persian and Indo-Persian Arms and Armor of 16th–19th Century from Polish Collections*, Malbrock: Muzeum Zamkoye w Malborku, pp. 57–74.

Kolesnikoff, A. (translated from Russian into Persian by Mohammad-Rafiq Yahyai, 1355/1976). *Iran dar astaneye Yooreshe Tazian* [Iran at the eve of the Arab Invasion]. Tehran: Entesharate Agah.

Kondakov, N.P. (1924). Les costumes orientaux a la cour Byzantine. *Byzantion*, 1, pp. 7–49.

Kramers, J.H. (1936). The military colonization of the Caucasus and Armenia under the Sassanids. *Bulletin of the School of Oriental Studies*, Vol. 8 (2/3), pp. 613–618.

Kurbanov, A. (2010). *The Hephthalites: Archaeological and Historical Analysis.* PhD Thesis, Department of History and Cultural Studies of the Free University, Berlin.

Landau-Tasseron, E. (1995). Features of the pre-conquest Muslim army in the time of Muhammad, in A. Cameron (ed.). *The Byzantine and early Islamic Near East*, pp. 299–336. Princeton: Darwin Press.

Latham, J.D., & Paterson, W.F. (1970). *Saracen Archery.* Holland Press.

Lee, A.D. (2009). *War in Late Antiquity: A Social History.* Hoboken, NJ: Wiley Blackwell Publishing.

Lee, A.D. (1986). Embassies as evidence for the movement of military intelligence between the Roman and Sassanian Empires, In P. Freeman & D. Kennedy (eds), *The Defense of the Roman and Byzantine East*, Oxford: B.A.R. Series, pp. 455–461.

Lenczowski, G. (1978). *Iran under the Pahlavis.* Hoover Institution Press.

Lerner, J.A. (2002). Sword in its scabbard, in A.L. Juliano & J.A. Lerner (eds), Monks and Merchants: Silk Road Treasures from Northwest China (Gansu and Ningxia 4th-7th Century), pp. 102–103.

Levina, L.M. & Nikitin, A.B. (1991). Ob odnoj gruppe iranskikh reznykh kamnej iz Vostochnovo Priaralja [On a group of Iranian carved stones from Eastern Aral region]. *Vestnik Drevnej Istorii*, 199, 53–65.

Levine, L.I. (2002). *Jerusalem: Portrait of the City in the Second Temple period (586 B.C.E.–70 C.E.).* Philadelphia: Jewish Publication Society.

Lewis, B. (2002). *The Arabs in History.* Oxford: Oxford University Press.

Littleton, C.S. & Malcor, L.A. (2000). *From Scythia to Camelot.* London: Garland Publishing.

Litvinskij, B.A. (1998a). La civilisation de l'Asie centrale antique [The civilization of Central Asia], in Deutsches Archäologisches Institut, Eurasien-Abteilung, Außenstelle Teheran (ed.), *Archäologie in Iran und Turan 3*, Rahden: Verlag Marie Leidorf.

Litvinskij, B.A. (1998b). The Hephthalite Empire, in Litvinskij, B.A., Guand-Da, Z., & Samghabadi, R.S. (eds), *History of Civilizations of Central Asia: The Crossroads of Civilization AD 250 – 750*, Paris: UNESCO, pp. 135–162.

Litvinskij, B.A., Jalilov, A.H., & Kolesnikov, A.I. (1998). The Arab conquest, in Litvinskij, B.A., Guand-Da, Z., & Samghabadi, R.S. (Eds), *History of Civilizations of Central Asia: The Crossroads of Civilization AD 250 – 750*, Paris: UNESCO, pp. 449–472.

Litvinskij, B.A. & Piyankov, I.V. (1966). Voennoe delo u narodov Srednej Azii [Warfare among the peoples of Central Asia]. *Vestnik Drevnej Istorii*, 3, pp. 36–52.

Livshits, V.A. (2002). Parthians joking? *Manuscripta Orietalia: International Journal for Oriental Manuscript Research*, 8, pp. 27–35.

Loriot, X. (1975). Les premieres annees de la grande crise du III siecle: De l'avenement de Maximin le Thrace (235) a la mort de Gordien III (244) [The early years of the Great Crisis of the third century: From the advent of Maximin the Thracian (235) to the death of Gordian III (244)], in H. Temporini (ed.), *Aufstieg und Niedergang der Romischen Welt II* [The Rise and Fall of the Roman World II], Berlin: Walter de Gruyter, pp. 657–787.

Lukonin, V.G. (1372/1993, translated into Persian by E. Reza). *Tamadone Iran-e Sassani* [Iranian Sassanian Civilization]. Tehran: Entesharate Elmi va Farhangi.

Lukonin, V.G. (1985, reprint 1993). Political, Social and Administrative Institutions: Taxes and Trade. In E. Yarshater (Ed.), *Cambridge History of Iran: Vol. 3 (2) The Seleucid, Parthian and Sasanid Periods*, New York, Cambridge University Press, pp. 681–746.

Macdowall, S. (1995). *Late Roman Cavalryman AD 236–565*. London: Osprey Publishing.

Mackey, S. (1998). *The Iranians: Persia, Islam and the Soul of a Nation*. New York: The Penguin Group.

Madelung, W. (2009). Khurrammiya, in P. Bearman, Th. Bianquis, C.E. Bosworth, E. van Donzel & W.P. Heinrichs (eds), *Encyclopaedia of Islam*, Leiden: Brill, pp. 53–65.

Mahamedi, H. (2003). Wall as a system of frontier defense, in T. Daryaee (ed.), *The Spirit of Wisdom: Menog I Xrad: Essays in Memory of Ahmad Tafazzoli*, Costa Mesa, California: Mazda Publishers, pp. 145–160.

Makiya, K. (formerly Al-Khalil, S). (1998). *Republic of Fear: The Inside Story of Saddam's Iraq*. Los Angeles, California: Pantheon Books.

Mallory, P.J. (1989). *In Search of the Indo-Europeans: Language, Archaelogy and Myth*. London: Thames & Hudson.

Marks, G. (2010). *Encyclopedia of Jewish Food*. New Jersey: John Wiley & Sons Inc.

Markwart, J. (1901). *Eran: Eransahr nach der Geographie des Ps. Moses Xorenaci* [Eran: Eranshahr according to/after the Geography of Ps. Moses Xorenaci]. Berlin: Weidmannsche Buchhandlung.

Marvin, C.T. (1886). *Reconnoitring Central Asia*. London: Swan, Sonnenschein, Le Bas & Lowrey.

Mashkoor, M.J. (1366/1987). *Tarikhe Siyasiye Sassanian* [The Political History of the Sassanians]. Tehran: Donyaye Ketab.

Mashkoor, M.J. (1345/1966). Tabaghat-e Mardon dar Iran-e Ghadim [Social stratification in ancient Iran]. *Baresiyahye Tarikhi*, 3, pp. 155–166.

Mashkoor, M.J. (1343/1964). *Iran dar Ahd-e Bastan* [The Iran in Ancient Times]. Tehran: Entesharate Sazman-e Tarbiat-e Moalem va Tahghighat-e Tarbiati.

Masia, K. (2000). The evolution of swords and daggers in the Sassanian Empire. *Iranica Antiqua*, XXXV, pp. 185–288.

Matheson, S.A. (2001). *Persia: An Archaeological Guide*. Tehran: Yassavoli Publications.

Matini, J. (1992). Nazaree be naghshe-ha-ye ghadeeme-ye Iran [An examination of the ancient maps of Iran]. *Iranshenasi: A Journal of Iranian Studies*, IV(2), pp. 269–302.

Matofi, A. (1378/1999). *Tarikh-e-Chahar Hezar Sal-e Artesh-e Iran: Az Tamadon-e Elam ta 1320 Khorsheedi, Jang-e- Iran va Araqh* [The 4000 Year History of the Army of Iran: From the Elamite Civilization to 1941, the Iran-Iraq War]. Tehran: Entesharat-e Iman.

Matthee, R.P. (1991). *The Politics of Trade in Safavid Iran*. Cambridge: Cambridge University Press.

Mayrhofer, M. (1973). *Onomastica Persepolitana: Das altiranische Namengut der Persepolis* [Onomastica Persepolitana: The ancient Iranian Nomenclature/terminology of Persepolis]. Vienna: Osterreichische Akademie der Wissenschaften.

Mayrhofer, M. (1969). Das angebliche Iranische Etyman des Amazonen-Namens [The alleged etymology of the Amazons names], in V. Pisani (ed.), *Studi linguistici in onore di Vittore Pisani II*, Brescia: Paideia, pp. 661–666.

McDonough, S. (2011). The legs of the throne, in J.P. Arnason & K.A. Raaflaub (eds), *The Roman Empire in Context: Historical and Comparative perspectives*, Hoboken, NJ: John Wiley & Sons Ltd., pp. 290–321.

McDowall, D. (1999). *A Modern History of the Kurds*. London: I.B. Tauris.

McDowall, S. (1995). *Late Roman Cavalryman 236–565 AD*. Great Britain: Osprey Publishing Warrior Series 15.

Mehdiyeva, N. (2003). Azerbaijan and its foreign policy dilemma. *Asian Affairs*, 34, pp. 271–285.

Mehreen (Shushtari), A. (1349/1971). *Keshvardari va Jame-eye Iran dar Zamane Sassanian* [Governance and Society duting the Sassanian Era]. Tehran: Vhap-e Ashna.

Metzger, S. (2002). Tragic Byzantine Commander. *MHQ: Quarterly Journal of Military History*, 15, pp. 42–29.

Michalak, M. (1987). The origins and development of Sassanian heavy cavalry. *Folia Orientalia*, 24, pp. 73–86.

Mielczarek, M. (1993). *Cataphracti and Clibanarii: Studies on the Heavy Armoured Cavalry of the Ancient World*. Lodz, Poland: Oficyna Naukowa.

Millar, F. (1993). *The Roman Near East 31 BC–AD 337*. Cambridge, Ma: Harvard University Press.

Miller, R., McEwen, E., Bergman, C. (1986). Experimental Approaches to Ancient near Eastern Archery. *World Archaeology*, 18 (2), *Weaponry and Warfare*, pp. 178–195.

Minorsky, V. (1943–1946). Roman and Byzantine campaigns in Atropatene. *Bulletin of the School of Oriental and African Studies*, 11, pp. 243–265.

Mitterauer, M., & Chapple, G. (2010). *Why Europe? The Medieval origins of its Special Path*. Chicago: University of Chicago Press.

Mobbayen, A. (1386/2007). Hozur-e Daylamian dar Tashkilat-e Nizamiye Hokumathaye Motegharen [The presence of the Dailamites in successive governments]. *Pazhoheshnamey Tarikh*, Year Two, Number 7, pp. 109–122.

Mode, M. (2006). Heroic Fights and Dying Heroes: The Orlat Battle Plaque and the Roots of Sogdian Art, in M. Compareti, P. Raffetta, G. Scarcia, L.E. Cafoscarina (eds), *Ērān ud Anērān: Studies Presented to Boris Il'ič Maršak on the Occasion of his 70th Birthday*, Venice: Libreria Editrice Cafoscarina, pp. 419–54.

Modi, J.J. (1969). Archery in ancient Persia: a few extraordinary feats. *Bombay Branch of the Royal Asiatic Society Journal*, XXV, pp. 175–186.

Moghtader, Gh. (1347/1968). *Pasdaran Shahanshahiye Iran dar Advare Mokhtalefe Tarikh* [The Guardians of Imperial Iran in Different Historical Cycles/Epochs]. Tabriz, Iran: Shomareye 13 Shoraye Markaziye Shahanshahiye Azarbaijan.

Moghtader, Gh. (1318–1319/1940–1941). *Tarikh e Nezamiye Iran* [The Military History of Iran]. Tehran: Bina.

Moghtader, Gh. (1315/1936). *Janghaye Haft-sad Saleye Iran va Rom* [The 700 year Wars of Iran and Rome]. Tehran: Shojaie-Golestaneh.

Mohammad-Jahani, A. (1377/1988). *Koshtiye Kordi ba Chukheh* [Kurdish wrestling with Chukheh]. Tehran: Nashre Beh Afarin.

Mohammadi-Malayeri, M. (1374/1996). *Farhange Iran pish az Islam va Asar aan dar Tamadone Islami va Adabiyate Arabi* [The Culture of Iran before Islam and its Influence on Islamic Civilization and Arabic Literature]. Tehran: Entesharate Toos.

Mohammadi-Malayeri, M. (1372/1993). *Tarikh va Farhange Iran dar Dowrane Enteghal az Asre Sassani be Asre Islami* [The History and Culture of Iran during the Transition Period from the Sassanian Era to the Islamic Era]. Tehran: Entesharate Yazdan.

Mojtahed-Zadeh, P. (1999). *Security and Territoriality in the Persian Gulf*. London: Curzon Press.

Mommsen, Th. (1996, original print 1885). *The Provinces of the Roman Empire*. New York: Barnes & Noble.

Mostashari, F. (2006). *On the Religious Frontier: Tsarist Russia and Islam in the Caucasus*. I.B.Tauris.

Nafisi, S. (first printed in 1334/1955 by Tabesh Publishers, reprinted 1382/2003). *Babak Xorramdin Delavar-e-Azarbaijan* [Babak Khorramdin, the Brave heart of Azarbaijan]. Tehran: Entesharate Asatir.

Nafisi, S. (1331/1952). *Tarikhe Tamadon e Sassani* [The History of Sassanian Civilization]. Tehran: Entesharate Daneshgahe Tehran.

Nagar, Y. (2002). Human skeletal remains from the Mamilla Cave, Jerusalem. *Atiqot*, 43, pp. 141–148.

Najmi, S. (1368/1989). *Nehzat e Sorkh Alamhaye Mazandaran* [The Revolution of the red-bannered ones of Mazandaran]. Tehran: Entesharate Adib.

Negroponzi, M.N., & Cavallero, M.C. (1967). The Excavations at Choche. *Mesopotamia*, 2, pp. 41–56.

Nersessian, V. (2001). *Treasures from the Ark: 1700 years of Armenian Christian Art*. London: The British Library.

Newark, T. (1994). *Medieval Warlords*. Hong Kong: Colorcraft Ltd.

Newman, A.J. (2006). *Safavid Iran: Rebirth of a Persian Empire*. London: I.B. Tauris.

Nicolle, D. (2005). *Rome's Enemies: The Desert Frontier*. Oxford: Osprey Publishing Men at Arms Series.

Nicolle D. (1996). *Sassanian Armies: The Iranian Empire early 3rd to mid-7th centuries AD*. Stockport, UK: Montvert Publications.

Nicolle, D. (1995). *The Janissaries*. London: Osprey Publishing Elite Series.

Nicolle, D. (1993). *Armies of the Muslim Conquest*. Oxford: Osprey Publishing.

Nigosian, S.A. (1993). *The Zoroastrian Faith: Tradition and Modern Research*. Montreal: McGill University Press.

Nikonorov, V.P. (2000). The use of musical percussion instruments in ancient Near Eastern warfare: the Parthian and Middle Asian evidence, in (eds) E. Hickmann, I. Laufs & R. Eichmann, *Studien zur Muzikarchaologie II* [Studies in Music Archaeology], *Muzikarchaologie Fruher Metallzeiten* [Music Archaeology of Early Metal Ages], Papers from the First Symposium of the International Study Group on Music Archaeology at Monastery Michaelstein, May 16–24, 1998, pp. 71–81.

Nokandeh, J., Sauer, E.W., Rekavandi, H.O., Wilkinson, T., Abbasi, G.A., Schwenninger, J.L., Mahmoudi, M., Parker, D., Fattahi, M., Usher-Wilson, L.S., Ershadi, M., Ratcliffe, J., & Gale, R. (2006). Linear Barriers of Northern Iran: The Great Wall of Gorgan and the Wall of Tammishe. *Iran*, Vol. 44, pp. 121–173.

Nöldeke, T. (1973, original print 1879). *Geschichte der Perser und Araber zur Zeit der Sassaniden* [History of the Persians and the Arabs in Sassanian Times]. Leiden: Nachdruck. Persian translation by Abbas Zaryab, *Tarikhe Iranian va Arabha dar Roozegar-e Sassanian* [History of the Persians and the Arabs in Sassanian Times], Tehran: Entesharate Asar e Melli.

Norwich, J.J. (1997). *A Short History of Byzantium*. New York: Alfred A. Knoff.

Nyberg, H.S. (1974). *A Manual of Pahlavi Part II: Glossary*. Wiesbaden: Otto Harrassawotiz.

Oates, D., & Oates, J. (1959). Ain Sinu: A Roman Frontier Post in Northern Iraq. *Iraq*, Vol. 21, No. 2, pp. 207–242.

Odahl C.M. (2004). *Constantine and the Christian Empire*. New York: Routledge.

Olbrycht, M.J. (2011). First Iranian military units in the army of Alexander the Great. *Anabasis: Studia Classica et Orientalia*, 2, pp. 67–84.

Osheidari, J. (1371/1992). *Daneshnameye Mazdisna* [Compendium/Tome of the Mazdisna]. Tehran: Nashr-e Markaz.

Overlaet, B.J. (1998). Regalia of the ruling classes in late Sassanian times: the Riggisberg strap mountings, swords and archer's fingercaps. In K. Ovtavsky (ed.), *Fruhmittelalterliche Kunst Zwischen Persien und China in der Abegg-Stiftung*, Riggisberg: Abegg-Stiftung, pp. 267–297.

Overlaet, B.J. (1982). Contribution to Sassanian armament in connection with a decorated helmet. *Iranica Antiqua*, XVII, pp. 189–206.

Pasdermajian, H. (Translated into Persian from French by M. Ghazi, 1369/1990). *Tarikhe Armanistan* [The History of Armenia]. Tehran: Entesharate Zarrin.

Paterson, W.F. (1966). The Archers of Islam. Journal of the Economic and Social History of the Orient, 9, nos 1–2, pp. 69–87.

Pazoki, N. (1374/1995). Shivehaye Qale-giri dar Nabardhaye Iranian [Methods for capturing fortresses in the battles of Iranians]. *Oloom e Siyasi*, 9, pp. 42–55.

Pazoki, N. (1373/1994). *Estehkamat-e Defai dar Iran-e Doreye Eslami* [Defensive Fortifications in Iran of the Islamic Period)]. Tehran: ICHTO Publications.

Penrose, J. (2008). *Rome and her Enemies: An Empire Created and Destroyed by War*. Oxford: Osprey Publishing.

Peterson, D. (1992). *The Roman Legions Recreated in Color Photographs*. London: Windrow and Greene.

Pigulevskaya, N. (Translated into Persian by E. Reza in 1377/1998). *Shahrhaye Iran dar Roozegare Partian va Sassanian* [The Cities of Iran during the Parthian and Sassanian Eras]. Tehran: Tehran: Entesharat-e Elmi va Farhangi.

Pigulevskaya, N. (Translated into Persian by E. Reza in 1372/1993). *Aarab dar Hodod-e Marzhaye Rum-e Sharqi va Iran dar Sadehaye Chaharom va Sheshom-e Miladi* [The Arabs near the Borders of Eastenr Rome and Iran in the 4th to Sixth centuries CE]. Tehran: Moaseseye Motaleat va Tahqiqat-e Farhangi.

Pigulevskaya, N. (Translated into Persian by K. Keshavarz in 1354/1975). *Tarikh-e Iran az Doran Bastan ta Payan-e Sadeh-e Hezhdahom-e Miladi* [The History of Iran from Ancient Times to the end of the Eighteenth Century CE]. Tehran: Entesharat-e Payam.

Pipes, D. (1981). *Slave Soldiers and Islam: the Genesis of a Military System*. Yale University Press.

Pirnia, H. (1369/1990). *Tarikhe Iran Bastan* [The History of Ancient Iran Volumes I, II & III]. Tehran: Donyae Ketab.

Pirnia, H. (1308/1929). *Irane Ghadeem ya Tarikhe Mokhtasare Iran ta Engheraze Sassanian* [Ancient Iran or a Brief History of Iran until the Decline of the Sassanians]. Tehran: Matbae'e Majlis.

Pokorny, J. (1959). *Indogermanisches Etymologisches Wörterbuch* [Indo-Germanic/Indo-European Etymological Dictionary]. Bern: Francke.

Potter, D.S. (2004). *The Roman Empire at Bay: AD 180–395*. New York: Routledge.

Potter, D.S. (1990). *Prophecy and History in the Crisis of the Roman Empire, a Historical Commentary on the Thirteenth Sibyline Oracle*. Oxford: Clarendon Press.

Potter, L.G. (2008). The consolidation of Iran's frontier on the Persian Gulf in the nineteenth century. In R. Farmanfarmaian (ed.), *War and Peace in Qajar Persia: Implications Past and Present*, London: Routlidge, pp. 126–148.

Pour-Davood, I. (1347/1968). *Zin Abzar* [armaments]. Tehran: Chapkhaneye Arteshe Shahanshahi.

Pour-Davood, I. (1336/1957). *Yad-dashthaye Gathaha* [Notes on the Gathas]. Tehran: Entesharate Anjomane Iranshenasi.

Pourshariati, P. (2008). *Decline and Fall of the Sassanian Empire: The Sasanian-Parthian Confederacy and the Arab Conquest of Iran*. London: I.B. Tauris.

Qaedan, A. (2003/1382). *Sazmandehi-y Nezami va Sazman-e Razm va Tahavolat An dar Tarix-e Eslam* [*Military Organization and Battle Formation and their Development in the History of Islam*]. Tehran: Moassese-ye Chap va Entesharat-e Daneshgah-e Emam Hosseyn.

Quaritch Wales, H.G. (1965). *Angkor and Rome; a Historical Comparison*. London: Bernard Quaritch, Ltd.

Radin, M. (1915). *Jews among the Greeks and Romans*. Philadelphia: Jewish Publication Company of America.

Raeen, I, (1350/1972). *Daryanavardiye Iranian* [Iranian Seafaring]. Tehran: Chapkhaney Sekkeh.

Rance, P. (2004). Drungus, δρουγγος, and δρουγγιστί: A Gallicism and Continuity in late Roman Cavalry Tactics. *Phoenix*, Vol. 58, No. 1/2, pp. 96–130.

Rankin, D. (1996). *Celts and the Classical World*. London & New York: Routledge.

Raspopova, V.I. (2006). Soghdian arms and armour in the period of the great migrations. In M. Mode & J. Tubach (eds), *Arms and Armour as Indicators of Cultural Transfer: The Steppes and the Ancient World from Hellenistic Times to the early Middle Ages*, Wiesbaden: Dr. Ludwig Reichert Verlag, pp. 79–85.

Rau, J. (2008). *The Nagorno-Karabakh conflict between Armenia and Azerbaijan: A brief historical outline*. Berlin: Verlag-Koester.

Ravandi, M. (1352/1973). *Tarikh Ejtemaie Iran* [Social History of Iran] (8 Volumes). Tehran: Gilan Press.

Rawlinson, G. (1885). *The Seven Great Monarchies of the Eastern World or the History, Geography, and Antiquities of Chaldaea, Assyria, Babylon, Media, Persia, Parthia, and Sassanian, or New Persian Empire.* New York: John B. Alden.

Rekaya, M. (1973). Maziyar: resistance ou integration d'une province Iranienne au monde Musulman au milieu de IX siècle AP.JC [maziyar: resistence or integration of an Iranian province in the Muslim world in the 9th century CE]. *Studia Iranica*, 2, pp. 143–191.

Reza, E. (1374/1995). *Iran va Torkan dar Roozegare Sassanian* [Iranians and Turks in Sassanian Times]. Tehran: Entesharate Elmi va Farhangi.

Robinson, H.R. (1967). *Oriental Armor*. London: Herbert Jenkins.

Rose, J. (2011). *Zorastrianism: an Introduction*. London: I.B. Tauris.

Rostovtzeff, M.I. (1933). *The Excavations at Dura-Europos: Preliminary Report of the Fourth Season of Work*. New Haven: Yale University Press.

Rubin, B.B. (2008). *(Re)presenting Empire: The Roman Imperial Cult in Asia Minor*. Unpublished PhD thesis, University of Michigan, Ann Arbor.

Rubin, Z. (1995). Reforms of Khusro Anushirwan. In A. Cameron (ed.), *The Byzantine and Early Islamic Near East III: States, Resources and Armies*, Princeton: The Darwin Press Inc., pp. 227–297.

Sadighi, G. (1938). *Les Mouvements Religieux Iraniens au IIe et au IIIe Siècle de l'Hégire* [Iranian Religious movements in the Second and Third Centuries Hejira]. Paris: Les Presses Modernes.

Safa, Z. (1384/2006). *Hamase-sarai dar Iran* [Epic Storytelling in Iran]. Tehran: Firdows.

Safa, Z. (1369/1990). *Bahram Chobin az Tarjomeye Tabari* [Bahram Chobin from Tabari's Translations]. Tehran: Amir Kabir.

Safa, Z. (1356/1977). *Kholaseye Tarikh-e Sisyasi va Ejtemaie va Farhangiye-Iran az Aghaz ta Payan-e Asr-e Safavi* [A summary of the political, social and cultural history from the beginning to the end of the Safavid era]. Tehran: Amir Kabir.

Saket, S., & Yahaghi, M.J. (1389/2010). Arayeshe Sepah va Fonoon e Razmi dar Doreye Sassani va baztabe aan dar Shahnameye Firdowsi [Organization of the army and military tactics/techniques in the sassanian era and the examination/overview of this in the Shahname of Firdowsi]. *Faslnameye Elmi va Pazhoheshi Kavioshname*, 20, pp. 9–32.

Sami, A. (1342/1964). *Tamadon e Sassani* [Sassanian Civilization – 2 volumes]. Shiraz: Chapkhaneye Mousavi.

Sarfaraz, A.A. (1348/1969). Bishapur, the Great City of the Sasanians [in Persian]. *Bastanshenasi va Honar e Iran*, 1 (2), pp. 69–74.

Sarkhosh-Curtis, V. (1993). *Persian Myths*. London: British Museum Press.

Sarre, F., & Herzfeld, E. (1920). *Archäologische Reise im Euphrat-and Tigris-Gebiet II*. Berlin: Verlag von Dietrich Reimer/Ernst Vohsen.

Savory, R.M. (1994). Land of the Lion and the Sun, in Lewis, B. (ed.), *The World of Islam: Faith, People and Culture*, London: Thames & Hudson, pp. 245–271.

Savory, R.M. (1980). *Iran under the Safavids*. Cambridge University Press.

Schindel, N. (2005). Sassanian mint abbreviations: the evidence of style. *Numismatic Chronicle*, 165, pp. 287–299.

Schindel, N. (2003). The Sasanians Eastern Wars in the 5th century: The Numismatic Evidence, in A. P. Anaino & A. Piras (eds), *Proceedings of the 5th Conference of the Societas Iranologica Europaea, October 6–11, Volume I: Ancient and Middle Iranian Studies I*, Milano: Mimesis, pp. 675–690.

Scullard, H.H. (1974). *The Elephant in the Greek and Roman World*. Ithaca, New York, Cornell University Press.

Sefat-Gol, N. (1382/2003). Gozaresh be Zabane Hollandi Darbareye Iran-e Asr-e Safavi [Report in Dutch regarding Iran in the Safavid Era]. *Ketab-e Mah-e Tarikh va Joghrafiya*, pp. 14–19.

Sekunda, N. (1992). *The Persian Army: 560–330 BC*. London: Osprey Publishing Elite Series.

Seyrig, H.A. (1937). Armes et costumes iraniens de Palmyre [Iranian costumes and arms of Palmyra. *Syria*, 18, pp. 4–31.

Shaabani, R. (1373/1994). *Mabaniye Tarikhiye Ejtema-e Iran* [Historical Foundations of the Society of Iran]. Tehran: Nashre Ghomes.

Shadrake, S. & Shadrake, T. (1994–1995). Britannia and Arthur. *Ancient Warrior*, Volume I, Winter, pp. 26–33.

Shah, U.P. (1987). *Jaina-Rūpa-Maṇḍana, Volume 1*. New Delhi: Abhinav Publications.

Shahbazi, Sh. (2001). Early Sasanians' Claim to Achaemenid Heritage. *Name-ye Iran-e Bastan: The International Journal of Ancient Iranian Studies*, 1 (no.1), pp. 61–73.

Shahbazi, Sh. (1989). Bahram VI Chobin. *Encyclopedia Iranica*, 2, pp. 519–522.

Shahbazi, Sh. (1987). ASB. *Encyclopedia Iranica*, 2, pp. 724–731.

Shahbazi, Sh. (1986). Army, pre-Islamic Iran. *Encyclopedia Iranica*, 2, pp. 489–499.

Sidnell, P. (2006). *Warhorse: Cavalry in Ancient Warfare*. London: Hambledon Continuum.

Sims, E., Marshak, B., & Grube, E. (2002). *Peerless Images: Persian Painting and its Sources*. New Haven: Yale University Press.

Sims-Williams, N. (2008). Sassanians in the East: A Bactrian archive from Northern Afghanistan, in V. Sarkhosh-Curtis & S. Stewart (eds), *The Sassanian Era-The Idea of Iran – Volume III*, London: I.B. Tauris, pp. 88–97.

Sinor, D. (1981). The Inner Asian warriors. *Journal of the American Oriental Society*, 101 (2), pp. 133–144.

Siroux, M. (1965). Atesh-gah pres d' Ispahan. *Iranica Antigua*, V, pp. 39–82.

Soudavar-Farmanfarmaian, F. (2009). Georgia and Iran: Three Millennia of Cultural Relations: An overview. *Journal of Persianate Studies*, 2, 1–43.

Southern, P. (2001). *The Roman Empire from Severus to Constantine*. New York: Routledge.

Spatari, N. (2002). *L'enigma delle Arti Asittite* [The enigma of Assitite Arts]. Musaba: Santa Barbera Foundation.

Speidel, M.P. (1984). Catafractii Clibanarii and the rise of the later Roman mailed cavalry: a gravestone from Claudiopolis in Bithynia. *Epigraphica Anatolica*, 4, pp. 151–156.

Sperl, S., Shackle, C., Awde, N. (1996). *Qasida Poetry in Islamic Asia and Africa*. Brill Academic Publications.

Stein, E. (1949). *Histoire du Bas-Empire* [History of the lower empire]. Paris, Brussels, Amsterdam: Desclee de Brouter.

Sulimirski, T (1970), *The Sarmatians*. Thames & Hudson, London.

Sundermann, W. (1996). Origin and the rise of the Chionites/Xyon/Huns, In J. Herrmann & E. Zurcher (eds), *History of Humanity Volume III: From the Seventh Century B.C. to the Seventh Century A.D.*, New York: UNESCO, pp. 473–474.

Swietochowski, T. (1995). *Russia and Azerbaijan: A Borderland in Transition*. New York: Columbia University Press.

Tafazzoli, A. (2000). *Sassanian Society: I. Warriors II. Scribes III Dehqans*. New York: Bibliotheca Persica Press.

Tafazzoli, A. (1993). A list of terms for weapons and armour in Western Middle Iranian. *Silk Road Art and Archeology*, 3, pp. 187–198.

Tajbaksh, A. (1355/1976). *Tarikhe Mokhtasare Tamadon va Farhang e Iran ghabl az Islam* [The Brief History of the Civiliztion and Culture of Iran before Islam]. Tehran: Entesharate Daneshgahe Melli e Iran.

Tapper, R. (1997). *The Frontier Nomads of Iran: A Political and Social History of the Shahsevan*. Cambridge University Press.

Taraporewala, I.J.S. (1980). *The Religion of Zarathustra*. Tehran: Sazman e Faravahar.

Tashkari, A. (1356/1977). *Iran be Ravayate Chin e Bastan* [Iran as narrated in Ancient China]. Tehran: The Center for International Relations department of the Minstry of Foreign Relations.

Tor, D.G. (2007). *Violent Order: Religious War, Chivalry, and the 'Ayyar Phenomenon in the Medieval Islamic World*. Würzburg: Ergon.

Towfighi, P.S., & Hanifi, S.M. (2009). *From Persian Empire to Islamic Iran: A History of Nationalism in the Middle East*. New York: Edwin Mellen Press.

Trever, K.V. (1959). *Ocherki po istorii i Kultur kavkazkoi Albanii* [Essays on the History and Culture of Caucasian Albania]. Moscow: USSR Academy of Sciences Publishing House.

Trousdale, W. (1975). *The Long Sword and Scabbard Slide in Asia*. Washington: Smithsonian Institution Press.

Tsetskhladze, G.E. (2001). Georgia iii. Iranian Elements in Georgian Art and Archeology. *Encyclopedia Iranica*, X, pp. 470–480.

Turnbull, S. (1987, reprint 2004). *The Mongols.* Oxford: Osprey Publishing.

Ulansey, D. (1989). *The Origins of Mithraic Mysteries.* Oxford: Oxford University Press.

Vamberry, A. (1884). *Arminius Vamberry: His Life and Adventures.* London: T. Fisher Unwin.

Van der Leeuw, C. (2000). *Azerbaijan: A Quest for Identity.* Palgrave Macmillan.

Von Grunebaum, G.E. (1961). *Medieval Islam.* Chicago: University of Chicago Press.

Vullers, J.A. (1864 reproduced 1962). *Lexicon Persico-Latinum: Etymologicum (3 volumes).* Graz, Austria: Akademische Druck.

Vyzgo, T.S. (1980). *Muzkalnye instrumenty Srednei Azii: Istoriicheskie Ocherki* [Musical instruments of Central Asia: Historical Essays]. Moscow: Muzika.

Ward, S.R. (2009). *Immortal: A Military History of Iran and its Armed Forces.* Washington, DC: Georgetown University Press.

Whitby, M. (2002). *Rome at War 293–696 AD.* Oxford: Osprey Essential Histories Series.

Whitby, M. (1994). The Persian king at War, in *The Roman and Byzantine Army in the East,* ed. E. Dabrowa Proceedings of a Colloquium held at the Jagiellonian University, September, 1992, Krakow, pp. 227–263.

Whitby, M. (1986). Procopius and the development of defences in Upper Mesopotamia. In P. Freeman and D. Kennedy (eds), *The Defense of the Roman and Byzantine East,* B.A.R. Series, pp. 717–35.

Whitehouse, D., & Williamson, A. (1973). Sasanian maritme trade. *Iran,* Vol. 11, pp. 29–49.

Whittow, N. (1996). *The Making of Byzantium: 600–1025.* Berkley: University of California Press.

Widengren, G. (1976). Iran, der grosse Gegner Roms: Konigsgewalt, Feudalismus, Militarwesen [Iran, the great enemy of Rome: Monarchial Power, feudalism, Military nature/charateristic], in H. Temporini and W. Haase (eds), *Aufstieg und Niedergang der Romischen Welt II* [The Rise and Fall of the Roman World II], Berlin: Walter de Gruyter, pp. 219–306.

Wiesehofer, J. (Translated from German to English by Azizeh Azodi, 1996). *Ancient Persia: From 550 BC to 650 AD.* London: I.B. Tauris Publishers.

Wightman, G.J., Hennessy, J.B., & Bennett, C.M. (1989). *The Damascus Gate, Jerusalem: excavations by C.M. Bennett and J.B. Hennessy at the Damascus Gate, Jerusalem, 1964–66.* Oxford: B.A.R. International Series, 519.

Wilcox, P. (1999). *Rome's Enemies (3): Parthians and Sasanid Persians.* Oxford: Osprey Publishing.

Wilson, A.T. (2011). *The Persian Gulf.* New York: Routledge.

Winter, E., & Dignas, B. (2001). *Rom und das Perserreich* [Rome and the Persian Empire]. Berlin, Germany: Akademie Verlag.

Wise, T. (1987). *Ancient Armies of the Middle East.* London: Osprey Publishing.

Yaghmai, E. (1367/1989). *Ze Goftar-e Dehqan: Shahname Firdowsi be Nazm va Nasr* [From the Speech/Word/Sermon of the Dehkan: The Shahname of Firdowsi in Poetry and Prose]. Tehran: Toos.

Yamauchi, E. (1990). *Persia and the Bible.* Grand Rapids: Baker Book House.

Yarshater, E. (1985, reprint 1993). Mazdakism, in E. Yarshater (ed.), *Cambridge History of Iran: Vol. 3 (2) The Seleucid, Parthian and Sasanid Periods,* New York: Cambridge University Press, pp. 991–1024.

Yarshater, E. (1971). Were the Sasanians Heirs to the Achaemenids? *La Persia nel Medioevo* (Accademia Nazionale dei Lincei, Rome), Quaderno No. 160, pp. 517–31.

Yektai, M. (1349/1970). Pishineye Tarikh-e Shatrang [The historical background of chess]. *Baresihaye Tarikhi,* 23–24, pp. 55–76.

Yu, Y. (1967). *Trade and Expansion in Han China.* University of California Press.

Zaehner, R.C. (1955). *Zurvan: a Zoroastrian Dilemma.* New York: Biblio & Tannen.

Zakeri, M. (1995). *Sasanid Soldiers in Early Muslim Society: The Origins of Ayyārān and Futuwwa.* Otto Harrassowitz Verlag.

Zarrin'kub, A. h. (1381/2002). *Ruzgaran:Tarikh-e Iran az Agahz ta Soqoot-e Saltanat-e Pahlavi* [The Events of the History of Iran from the Beginnings until the Fall of the Pahlavi Dynasty]. Tehran: Sokhan.

Zenkowsky, S.A. (1960). *Pan-Turkism and Islam in Russia.* Cambridge: Harvard University Press.

Ziapour, J. (1349/1970). *Poushak-e Iranian az 14 Gharn Peesh ta Emrooz* [The Clothing of Iranians from 14 Centuries Ago Until the Present]. Tehran: Ministry of Culture.

Zoka, Y. (1350a/1971a). *Arteshe Shahanshahi e Iran az Khourosh ta Pahlavi* [The Imperial Army Iran from Cyrus to Pahlavi]. Tehran: Chapkhaneye Vezarate Farhang va Honar.

Zoka, Y. (1350b/1971b). *Pishineye San va Rezhe dar Iran* [The History of Marches/Reviews/Processions and Parades in Iran]. Tehran: Chapkhaneye Vezarate Farhang va Honar.

Zoka, Y., Shushtari, M.A.E., & Ghaem-Maghami, J. (1349/1970). *Pishineye San va Rezhe dar Iran* [The History of Marches/Reviews/Processions and Parades in Iran]. Tehran: Entesharate Vezarate Farhang va Honar.

Zutterman, C. (2003). The bow in the ancient Near East, a re-evaluation of archery from the late 2nd millennium to the end of the Achaemenid Empire. *Iranica Antiqua*, XXXVIII, pp. 119–165.

Index

Abargar castle, 333
Abaxtar-Spahbod, 24
Abbasid(s), 334–5, 350–1, 356
Abbasid caliphate, 317, 320, 322, 334, 355
   see also caliphate(s), Ummayad caliphate
Abdast, 90
   see also Tabar, Tabarzin, Tabarz/e/n,
     Chakosh, Warz/Wazr, Warz-wazig,
     gauntlet, hatchet, axe, mace, Gurz
Abivard, 237
Abkhaz, 181
Abna, 143, 351
Abrus, 172
Abu Bakr, 320
Abu Ubeidah Taghti, 134–5, 321–2
Abu Moussa, 329
Abyssinian(s), 134, 139, 142–3, 351
Academy of Athens, 7
Achaemenid(s), xvii–xxi, 2–3, 12, 21–2, 25, 35,
   37, 46, 51, 57, 61, 64, 74–7, 85, 87–8, 94,
   110, 111–12, 120, 128–30, 166, 194, 237,
   251, 266–7, 278–9, 284, 292, 296, 327, 355
Achaemenid Empire, xvii, xx, 106, 278, 302,
   306
   see also Persian Empire
Aden, 139, 143
Adiabene, 5, 203, 204
Adurbaygan, 24
   see also Media Atropatene, Aturpatekan,
     Azerbaijan, Azarbaijan
Adrianople (battle of, 378 CE), 192
Aegean, 139
Aethiopica, 48, 91
see also Heliodorus
Afa-sar, 283
see also Mah-sar, Sar, Shalvar, Mok, Mocak,
    Kafshak, Kurtak, Kustik, Kamar,
    Kamar-band, Kapah, Pargoo, Kulah
Afghanistan, 87, 200–201, 207, 209, 213,
   220–1, 235, 332, 355
Afraban, 287
Afrasiyab (of the Shahname epic), 150
Afrasiyab (in Central Asia), 281
Africa, 142
Afshin, 117

see also Savaran, Asbaran, Akhshid, Dehkan(s),
    Chakeran, Framandar-savaran, Aswaran,
    Aswaran-sardar, Savar-e Nezam Sangin
    Aslahe, Javidan, Var-thragh niyagan
    khodai, Akhshid, Afshin, Chakeran,
    Savaran-e shamshir-zan-e dah-hezar,
    Pushtighban, Pushtiban, Pusht-aspan,
    Pushtighban-salar, Pushtighban-sardar,
    Hazarbod, Gund Shahanshah,
    Ham-harzan, Ham-harz, Hm-hrz,
    Jan-separan, jyanavspar, Janvespar, Jalinus,
    Pishmarg/Peshmarg, Savaran-e Khorasan,
    Sarhangan, Pirouzetai, Khosrowgetai,
    Granikan-Salar
Afshin (general of Caliphate), 341–2, 356
Agathias, 49, 54
Aghrab(s), 246–7, 251, 253, 269
see also Scorpion(s), Scorpio, Hasak, Xasak,
    Rutaila, Siege engine(s), Naft-andazan,
    Naffata, Charx, Kashkanjir, Khaar-kaman,
    Mangonel(s), Manjeniq, Aradeh, Arrada,
    Ballistae, Catapult(s), Battering ram(s),
    Mobile tower(s), Darraga, Dabbabat,
    Xarak/Kharak, Testudo
Ahmad bin Jonayd Eskafi, 339
Ahvaz/Ahwaz, 148, 215, 325, 329
Ahura-Mazda, 17, 89, 273–4, 294–6
Aigan, 170
Alkus (of the Shahname epic), 275
Akenakes, 87, 94
see also Tour, Dagger(s), Dasnag, Celan, Kard,
    Nran
Akhshid, 117
see also Savaran, Asbaran, Afshin, Dehkan(s),
    Chakeran, Framandar-savaran, Aswaran,
    Aswaran-sardar, Savar-e Nezam Sangin
    Aslahe, Javidan, Var-thragh niyagan
    khodai, Akhshid, Afshin, Chakeran,
    Savaran-e shamshir-zan-e dah-hezar,
    Pushtighban, Pushtiban, Pusht-aspan,
    Pushtighban-salar, Pushtighban-sardar,
    Hazarbod, Gund Shahanshah,
    Ham-harzan, Ham-harz, Hm-hrz,
    Jan-separan, jyanavspar, Janvespar, Jalinus,
    Pishmarg/Peshmarg, Savaran-e Khorasan,

Sarhangan, Pirouzetai, Khosrowgetai, Granikan-Salar
Akhorbad, 11, 185
   see also Akhoramar
Akhormar, 185
   see also Akhorbad
Al-Bakri, 340
Al-Baladuri, 233, 241
Al-Faqih, 207
Al-Hamavi, 235, 239–40
Al-Jahez, 273
Al-Ma'moun, 107
Al-Masoudi, 134–6, 290, 319, 325, 353
Al-Mundhir, 116, 171, 1723
Al-Na'uman, 116–17
Al-Raqqah, 159
Al-Tabari, 9, 27, 56, 59, 62, 100, 107–108, 113, 130–1, 134–5, 143, 156–7, 178, 181–2, 191, 209, 214, 216, 218–19, 236, 241–2, 263, 280, 319, 322, 328, 338
Alan(s), xxiii, 21, 25, 110, 181, 192, 233, 272, 344
   see also Sarmatian(s), Scythians, Saka, Saka Paradraya, Saka Haumaverga, Yueh-Chi, Kushan(s)
Alan Pass, 233
Alania, 25
Alao-wa-ding, 246
Albania, 3–4, 20–1, 28–9, 139, 206, 232–3, 260, 307, 309, 325
   see also Republic of Azerbaijan, Arran
Albanian(s), 20–1, 26, 28, 127, 232, 261, 309, 325
Alexander (of Macedon), xix, 35, 51, 76–7, 106, 130, 166
Alexander Severus, xvii, 10, 57, 126, 130–1, 150–1
Alexandria, 306
Algan, 168
Amaj, 66
Amankuh, 216
Amazon(s), 128
   see also Gordafarid, Apranik, Azadeh Dailam, Negan, Banu (Khorramdin)
Ambaragh 184, 231, 238
   see also Eiran-ambaraghbad, Zynpt, Ganz
Ammianus Marcellinus, xi, xvii, 1, 22, 38–9, 56, 91–3, 95, 99, 113, 120, 122, 132, 138, 146, 149, 152, 161–3, 165, 178–80, 195–6, 198, 228, 245, 247, 249–50, 254, 260, 262, 269, 288, 298, 346
Amida, 21–2, 124, 260
   see also Diyarbakr

Amida (siege of, 359 CE), 69, 113, 127, 131–2, 164, 194, 201–202, 245, 247, 249, 254, 256, 260–1, 288
Amida (siege of, 502–503 CE), 189, 250, 289
Amlash, 282
Amu Darya, 334
Amud, 108
   see also Gurz, Amud-e Ahanin
Amudarya, 207
Amud-e Ahanin, 108
   see also Gurz, Amud
Anahita, xiv, 17, 294–6
   see also Temple of Anahita,
Anahita (Temple of), 295
   see also Anahita
Anastasius (Emperor), 230–1
Anastasius of Dara, 193
Anatolia, 4, 139, 145, 149, 156, 181, 183, 215, 234, 260, 265–6, 268–9, 301–302, 304–307, 315, 355
Anatolian, 25
Anbar (definition), 185
Anbar (in Central Asia), 184
Anbar (in Iraq), 152, 184
Andarz-e Oshnar-e Danag, 289
Andarzbad aspwaregan, 38–9, 41
Andemankaran-salar, 12
Andreas, 169
An-Eirean, 10, 18
Angion, 78
Anglon (Battle of, 541 CE), 70–1
Angust-ban, 90
Anoushzad, 125, 189
Antigonus, 78
Antioch, 152, 155–7, 178, 190, 192, 250, 254, 270–1, 304
Antioch (siege of, 540 CE), 262–7
Antiochus III, 78
Antiochus IV, 78
Antiochus Strategius, 267–8
Antonine Wall, 236
Apamea, 190, 304
Apranik, 129
   see also Gordafarid (of the Shahname epic), Azadeh Dailam, Negan, Banu (Khorramdin), Amazon(s)
Arab(s), 4–5, 19, 23–5, 29–30, 43, 50, 61, 63, 72–3, 113, 116–17, 123, 126–7, 129, 134–9, 149, 171–2, 177–9, 181, 184, 190, 194, 223, 225, 230, 238–41, 267, 272, 280, 285, 294, 297–8, 304, 306, 308, 312–37, 339–42, 344, 348, 350–2, 354–6
Arabeh, 126
   see also Arabehaye jangi, Chariot(s)

Arabehaye jangi, 126
see also Arabeh, Chariot(s)
Arabo-Islamic, 3, 116, 134, 162, 164, 299, 301,
303, 314, 318, 321, 323, 332–3, 344, 351
Arabia, 24, 30, 126, 143, 241, 313–14, 317–18,
320, 327, 350, 355
Arabia Felix, 139
Arabian, 129, 137–8, 212, 224, 238, 253, 306,
313, 315, 318, 321, 353
Arabian peninsula, 126
Arabic, xi, 195, 233, 253, 332, 348, 351–3
Arabization, 332
Arachosia, 77
Arachosian(s), 77
Ardabil, 340, 342–3
Aradeh, 247, 251, 253
see also Arrada, Scorpion(s), Scorpio, Hasak,
Xasak, Siege engine(s), Naft-andazan,
Naffata, Charx, Kashkanjir, Khaar-kaman,
Mangonel(s), Manjeniq, Aghrab(s), Rutaila,
Ballistae, Catapult(s), Battering ram(s),
Mobile tower(s), Darraga, Dabbabat,
Xarak/Kharak, Testudo
Aramaic, 186
Arash, 56
Araxes River, 20, 28, 232, 234, 274, 307, 340
Arbayastan, 5
Arch of Galerius, 160
Archery, xv–xvi, xxii, 32, 38–9, 41, 43–5, 48,
53–9, 61–3, 65–71, 73, 75–6, 78–9, 82–4,
89–91, 95–6, 100, 102–103, 108, 110–11,
113, 117, 123, 125, 127–8, 132, 136, 146,
149–50, 154, 156–60, 165–6, 168, 170,
172–3, 179, 187, 195–8, 201, 203–204,
206, 210–11, 213, 217–19, 221, 227, 244,
246, 248, 252, 255, 264, 266, 272, 289,
310, 315, 318–19, 322–3, 330, 345, 356
see also Tir-wazig, Tir/Tigr, Tirbad, Horse
archery, Horse archer(s), Kaman, Kamam,
Kamandan, Qaba, Tirdan, Kantir/Kantigr,
Zeh/Zih, Zeh e yadaki, Watarain, Gorytos,
Nawak, Shivatir-e zrehbaran, Shiva-tir
Ardashir I Babakan, xi, xiii, xvii, xix, xxi, 3–4,
11, 13, 15, 17, 20–2, 36, 53, 57, 82, 84, 89,
91, 97, 103, 112–13, 126, 130–1, 137,
150–2, 156, 163, 182, 188–9, 191, 239,
277, 280, 288, 295, 299, 302, 349
Ardashir II, 295
Ardashir Khurra, 226
Ardavan (Artabanus) V, 3, 61, 82, 89, 125, 277,
295, 349
Ardig, 9
see also Karezar, Jang, Pad-razm, Nibard,
Zambag, Paykar

Argbad, 10–11
Aristotle, 35
Armenia, 3–4, 14, 20, 24–5, 70, 72, 114–16,
139, 149, 155, 158–9, 178, 180, 190, 206,
215, 232–3, 256, 280, 292, 304, 306–307,
309, 339, 342, 346
see also Perso-Armenia
Armenian(s), 7–9, 12, 20–1, 26, 28, 72, 77, 94,
98, 110, 115–16, 131, 133–4, 158–60, 177,
181, 220–1, 232, 238, 240, 276, 280,
285–6, 299–300, 303–304, 307, 325, 338,
344–5, 347, 349–50
Arrada, 253, 354
see also Aradeh, Scorpion(s), Scorpio, Hasak,
Xasak, Siege engine(s), Naft-andazan,
Naffata, Charx, Kashkanjir, Khaar-kaman,
Mangonel(s), Manjeniq, Aghrab(s), Rutaila,
Ballistae, Catapult(s), Battering ram(s),
Mobile tower(s), Darraga, Dabbabat,
Xarak/Kharak, Testudo
Arran, 368
see also Albania, Republic of Azerbaijan,
Arrian, 77, 130
Arsacids 13
see also Parthia, Parthian(s), Parthian dynasty,
Parthian Empire, Ashkan
Arshak, 177
Asad bin Abdullah, 334
Ashkan, 168
see also Arsacids, Parthia, Parthian dynasty,
Parthian Empire, Parthian(s)
Ardazan (Ardazanes), 169, 349
Arsht, 79, 80
see also Kontos, Fras, Astr, Rumh, Nezak,
Neyze, Neyze-daran, Javeliner(s),
Javelin(s), Zhupin
Arta, 291
Artabazes, 347, 349
Artavazdes II, 300
Artaxerxes I, xix
Artaxerxes II, 76, 295
Arteshtar, 11
Arteshtaran, 286, 289–90
Arteshtaran-salar, 10–12
Arxamus/Arxamoun (battle of, 603 CE), 266
Aryan(s), 6–7, 20, 75, 153, 289–90, 300
Asabar Nipek, 34
see also Matigan e Hazar Datastan
Asawira, 353
see also Asbaran, Savaran
Asb, 109
see also Raksh, Tagavar, Zin, Zin-e Khadang,
Fetrak, Setam, Zarrin Setam, Enan, Naal,
Taziyane

Asbaran, 73, 111, 351, 353
  see also Savaran, Dehkan(s), Akhshid, Afshin,
    Chakeran, Framandar-savaran, Aswaran,
    Aswaran-sardar, Savar-e Nezam Sangin
    Aslahe, Javidan, Var-thragh niyagan
    khodai, Akhshid, Afshin, Chakeran,
    Savaran-e shamshir-zan-e dah-hezar,
    Pushtighban, Pushtiban, Pusht-aspan,
    Pushtighban-salar, Pushtighban-sardar,
    Hazarbod, Gund Shahanshah, Ham-
    harzan, Ham-harz, Hm-hrz, Jan-separan,
    jyanavspar, Janvespar, Jalinus, Pishmarg/
    Peshmarg, Savaran-e Khorasan, Sarhangan,
    Pirouzetai, Khosrowgetai, Granikan-Salar
Ascan, 168, 170, 172
Ashuristan, 153, 190
Asp-astar, 90
  see also Astar (whip), Astar-e-asp, Asp-son
Asp-son, 90
  see also Astar (whip), Astar-e-asp, Asp-astar
Asronan, 290
  see also Mobadan Mobad, Mobad(s), Magi,
    Herbadan, Dasturan, Dadwaran, Radan
Astar, 90
  see also Astar-e-asp, Asp-son, Asp-Astar
Astarabadh, 138
  see also Zadrakarta
Astar-e-asp, 90
  see also Astar, Asp-son, Asp-Astar
Assyrian, 40, 68, 87
Astr, 90
  see also Arsht, Kontos, Fras, Rumh, Nezak,
    Neyze, Neyze-daran, Javeliner(s),
    Javelin(s), Zhupin
Aswar, 15
Aswaran, 15, 73
  see also Savaran, Dehkan(s), Akhshid, Afshin,
    Chakeran, Framandar-savaran, Asbaran,
    Aswaran-sardar, Savar-e Nezam Sangin
    Aslahe, Javidan, Var-thragh niyagan
    khodai, Akhshid, Afshin, Chakeran,
    Savaran-e shamshir-zan-e dah-hezar,
    Pushtighban, Pushtiban, Pusht-aspan,
    Pushtighban-salar, Pushtighban-sardar,
    Hazarbod, Gund Shahanshah,
    Ham-harzan, Ham-harz, Hm-hrz,
    Jan-separan, jyanavspar, Janvespar, Jalinus,
    Pishmarg/Peshmarg, Savaran-e Khorasan,
    Sarhangan, Pirouzetai, Khosrowgetai,
    Granikan-Salar
Aswaran-sardar 10, 15, 273
  see also Savaran, Dehkan(s), Akhshid, Afshin,
    Chakeran, Framandar-savaran, Asbaran,
    Aswaran, Savar-e Nezam Sangin Aslahe,

Javidan, Var-thragh niyagan khodai,
    Akhshid, Afshin, Chakeran, Savaran-e
    shamshir-zan-e dah-hezar, Pushtighban,
    Pushtiban, Pusht-aspan, Pushtighban-salar,
    Pushtighban-sardar, Hazarbod, Gund
    Shahanshah, Ham-harzan, Ham-harz,
    Hm-hrz, Jan-separan, jyanavspar,
    Janvespar, Jalinus, Pishmarg/Peshmarg,
    Savaran-e Khorasan, Sarhangan,
    Pirouzetai, Khosrowgetai, Granikan-Salar
Atashgah, 227
Atik canal, 323–4
Atravan, 186
  see also Jundi-Shapur
Atropatene, 28, 30
  see also Media Atropatene, Adurbaygan,
    Aturpatekan, Azerbaijan, Azarbaijan
Aturpatekan, 3, 309
  see also Adurbaygan, Azerbaijan, Azarbaijan,
    Atropatene, Media Atropatene
Augustus, xix, 293
Augustine, 180
Avar(s), 59, 70, 101, 149, 195, 197, 211, 268–9,
    307
  see also Turkic-Avar(s), Turk(s), Turkish, Gok
    Turk(s), Turkic, Ottoman(s), Tatar,
    Turkic-Hun, Hun(s), Khazar(s), Hunnic,
    Uighur(s), Hsiang-Nou, Seljuk(s), Oghuz
Avaryr (Battle of, 451 CE; also Battle of
    Vartanantz), 20, 115, 133–4
Avaze, 220
Avesta, xviii, 12, 56, 61, 105, 106, 187, 286
Avestan, 8–9, 11, 45
Awestarag, 90
  see also Shamsher, Safser, Sword(s),
    Shamsher-wazig, Fencing, Italian grip,
    Baldric hanging, Tex, Dar, Kamar,
    Kamar-band, Niyam, Sousser, Saif,
    Mintaqa, Goti, Scabbard (slide suspension),
    Lappet suspension system, P-mount
    (system), Shap-sheraz/Shamshirdar
Axe(s), 90, 218, 337
  see also Abdast, Tabar, Tabarzin, Tabarz/e/n,
    Chakosh, Warz/Wazr, Warz-wazig,
    gauntlet, hatchet, mace, Gurz
Ayadgar e Zareran, 55
Ayvan-e Karkheh, 225, 229
Ayyaran, 128
Azadan, 13, 351–3
Azadeh Dailam, 129
  see also Gordafarid (of the Shahname epic),
    Apranik, Negan, Banu (Khorramdin),
    Amazon(s)
Azargoshnasp, 274, 293

Azarmahan, 190

Azata, 75

Azarethes, 70, 117, 171–4, 188

Azerbaijan (in northwest Iran), 3, 20, 24–5, 28, 129, 181, 203, 215, 227, 232–4, 274, 289, 293, 300, 304, 307, 309, 326, 330, 336, 338–41

also Azarbaijan, 14, 110, 205, 341–2, 343, 356

see also Adurbaygan, Aturpatekan, Atropatene, Media Atropatene

Babak (father of Ardashir I), 295

Babak Khorramdin, 227, 236, 332, 338–43, 356

Babylon, 230, 325–6

Babylonian(s), 76, 326, 351

Bactria, 205, 212–13, 333

Bactrian(s), 77, 212

Badqeis, 214

Badkobeh, 253

see also Baku

Badr (battle of, 624 CE), 317–18

Baghdad, 334–5, 340–1

Baghdad Museum, xv

Bagrewand, 30

Bahrain, 137, 329

Bahram (General, Battle of the Bridges, 634 CE), 134–5, 321–2

Bahram (of the Shahname epic), 275

Bahram I, 17

Bahram II, xiii, xv, 17, 45, 82–3, 277, 291, 350

Bahram V Gur, xv–xvi, 31, 53, 60–1, 116–17, 125, 134, 202–205, 207, 211, 235, 241, 293, 299, 327, 349

Bahram Chobin, 4, 10, 13, 16, 56, 109, 114, 142, 201, 212–20, 222, 238, 253, 265–6, 274, 293, 298–303, 313

Bakhtiaris, 50

Baku, 21, 253

see also Badkobeh

Balaam, 206

Bal'ami, 108

Balanj, 138

see also Kashtig/Kashti, Navbad, Bandar, Bar, Daftar, Dunij, Didban, Rah-nameh, Nav-khoda

Balash, 209

Baldric hanging, 31, 117

see also Italian grip, Shamsher, Safser, Sword(s), Broadsword(s), Two-handed sword(s), Shamsher-wazig, Fencing, Awestarag, Tex, Dar, Kamar, Kamar-band, Niyam, Sousser, Saif, Mintaqa, Goti, Scabbard (slide suspension), Lappet

suspension system, P-mount (system), Shap-sheraz/Shamshirdar

Balkan/Balkans, 156, 307

Balkh, 184, 207, 216, 219, 222, 339, 353

Ballistae, 217, 220, 228, 245, 246, 249, 251, 255, 257, 261, 269, 271

see also Siege engine(s), Battering ram(s), Catapult(s), Mobile tower(s), Darraga, Dabbabat, Xarak/Kharak, Testudo, Naft-andazan, Naffata, Charx, Kashkanjir, Khaar-kaman, Mangonel(s), Manjeniq, Aradeh, Arrada, Aghrab(s), Rutaila, Scorpion(s), Scorpio, Hasak, Xasak

Baluchi, 279

Bandar, 138

see also Kashtig/Kashti, Navbad, Balanj, Bar, Daftar, Dunij, Didban, Rah-nameh, Nav-khoda

Bani Hanifah 314

see also Bani Sheiban, Arab(s), Bedouin(s), Lakhmid(s), Wada'i, Ghassanid(s), Yemenite Arab(s)

Bani Sheiban 313

see also, Bani Hanifah, Arab(s), Bedouin(s), Lakhmid(s), Wada'i, Ghassanid(s), Yemenite Arab(s)

Banu (Khorramdin), 129

see also Gordafarid (of the Shahname epic), Apranik, Azadeh Dailam, Negan, Amazon(s)

Bar, 138

see also Kashtig/Kashti, Navbad, Balanj, Bandar, Daftar, Dunij, Didban, Rah-nameh, Nav-khoda

Bararan (Pass), 216, 219

Barbalissos (battle of, *c.*253 CE), 54, 155–6, 159

Bargostvan, xiv, 33, 88–9, 108–109, 337

see also Tighfaf

Barsham (Barsamenes), 169–71

Barsom, 295

Barvan/Parvan, 123

Barzand, 342

Bashlyk, 93, 105

Basra, 339

Battering ram(s), 249–250, 251, 252, 253, 262, 269, 270

see also Scorpion(s), Scorpio, Hasak, Xasak, Siege engine(s), Naft-andazan, Naffata, Charx, Kashkanjir, Khaar-kaman, Mangonel(s), Aradeh, Arrada, Manjeniq, Aghrab(s), Rutaila, Ballistae, Catapult(s), Mobile tower(s), Darraga, Dabbabat, Xarak/Kharak, Testudo

Bazanush, 110
  see also see also Valerian
Bazu-band, xiv, 32, 42
Bazz (fortress/castle), 129, 227–8, 338–40, 342
Bedakhsh, 11, 14
Bedouin(s), 238, 315, 317, 319, 324
  see also Ghassanid(s), Arab(s), Lakhmid(s),
  Wada'i, Bani Sheiban, Bani Hanifah,
  Yemenite Arab(s)
Belisarius, 68, 70, 148–9, 156, 168–74, 176,
  192, 272, 345–6, 349
Benjamin of Tiberias, 267
Bezabde, (siege of, 360 CE), 249–50, 269–71
Bibliotheque Nationale de Paris, xv, xvi
Bishapur, xiv, 18, 85–7, 98, 153–4, 156, 225–7,
  279, 290, 293
Bizhan (of the Shahname epic), 46, 105
Black Sea, 5, 139, 234, 271, 302, 307
Bleschames, 346
Bondar, 33
Borea, 263
Bosphorus, 268–9
Bouzes, 168–70, 263
Brahmag e Artesharih, xiv, 114, 277–83, 285,
  347
Bridges (Battle of the, 644 CE), 134, 321
Britain, 344
British Empire, 22
British Museum (London), xv, 101, 106, 291
Broadsword(s), xiv–xvii, xxii, 18, 37, 87, 95,
  103, 154, 282, 290–4, 310, 337
  see also Sword(s), Two-handed sword(s),
  Shamsher, Fencing, Italian grip, Baldric
  hanging, Shamsher-wazig, Safser,
  Awestarag, Dar, Tex, Kamar, Kamar-band,
  Niyam, Sousser, Saif, Mintaqa, Goti,
  Scabbard (slide suspension), Lappet
  suspension system, P-mount (system),
  Shap-sheraz/Shamshirdar
Buddhist, 333
Bukhara, 52, 204–205, 220, 333, 335
Bulgar(s), 268–9
Bundahishn, 25, 138, 238–9, 278
Buyid(s), 338
Buzurgan, 3, 13, 291
  see also Vuzurgan
Buzurgmehr, 291
Byzantine(s), 4, 28–9, 54, 70, 116, 134–5, 139,
  142–3, 162, 172, 182, 214, 223, 263,
  265–9, 272, 293, 300–301, 304, 306–11,
  313, 315–17, 320–1, 324, 330, 342, 347–8,
  351–2

  see also Byzantium, Byzantine Empire, Rome,
  Roman(s), Roman empire, Romano-
  Byzantine(s)
Byzantine Empire, 168, 265, 304, 306–307,
  313–14
Byzantium, 25, 134–5, 139, 265, 297–8,
  303–306, 312–15, 320, 327, 340, 342,
  346–7
  see also Byzantine(s), Byzantine Empire,
  Rome, Roman(s), Roman empire,
  Romano-Byzantine(s)

Cabinet des Medailles, xv
Caesar, 155
Caesarea (Mazaka), 30, 311
Caliph(s), 224, 303
Caliphate(s), 50, 129, 223, 228, 314, 317,
  320–1, 325, 329–34, 336–42, 344, 350,
  352, 354–6
  see also Abbasid caliphate, Ummayad caliphate
Callinicum, 178
Callinicum (Battle of, 531 CE), 70, 117, 159,
  168, 171–4, 187–8, 310
Caltrops, 177, 324
Camel cataphract(s), 130
Camel Corps, 125
Cappadocia, 4, 30, 156, 190, 304, 307
Cappadocian(s), 77
Carpat, 126
  see also Arabeh, Arabehaye jangi, Chariot(s)
Carrhae, 152, 155–7, 159
Carrhae, (battle of, 53 BCE), 9, 13, 51, 99, 103,
  151, 300
Caspian Sea, 128, 191, 203, 207, 220, 233–6,
  340
Cassius Dio, 78
Cataphractus, 73
  see also Cataphractii, Clibanarius, Clibanarii,
  klibanion, klibanarios, Griv, Pan,
  Gardaan-ban, Grivpan, Griv-ban/
  Griw-ban, Tanur, Tanurig, Tanvar
Cataphractii, 73
  see also Cataphractus, Clibanarius, Clibanarii,
  klibanion, klibanarios, Griv, Pan,
  Gardaan-ban, Grivpan, Griv-ban/
  Griw-ban, Tanur, Tanurig, Tanvar
Catapult(s), 247, 251, 253, 255, 270, 338
  see also Scorpion(s), Scorpio, Hasak, Xasak,
  Siege engine(s), Battering ram(s), Mobile
  tower(s), Darraga, Dabbabat, Xarak/
  Kharak, Testudo, Naft-andazan, Naffata,
  Charx, Kashkanjir, Khaar-kaman,
  Mangonel(s), Manjeniq, Aradeh, Arrada,
  Ballistae, Aghrab(s), Rutaila

Caucasus, xx, xxii, 3–5, 18, 20, 22, 25–9, 31, 65, 87, 123, 127, 133–4, 139, 158–9, 174, 181, 183–4, 189, 194, 198, 206, 212, 215, 224, 230, 232–4, 240–1, 271–2, 281–2, 287, 292, 299, 301–302, 304, 306–309, 312, 314, 330, 340
   see also Transcaucasus, Circassia
Caucasian(s), 6, 20–1, 23–5, 28–31, 35, 72, 139, 141, 149, 159, 206, 220, 229, 232–3, 256, 281, 345
Cedrenus, 153–4, 155, 157, 345
Celan, 90
   see also Dasnag, Akenakes, Tour, Dagger(s), Kard, Nran
Celtic, 101, 282
Celt(s), 84
Central Asia, xi, xxii–xxiii, 4–5, 14, 16, 18–19, 21, 24–7, 48–9, 52, 64–5, 72, 74–6, 87, 94, 99, 101, 107, 110, 114, 116, 127, 131, 134, 142–3, 149–51, 174, 182–4, 191, 194–7, 199–201, 204, 206–207, 212, 216, 219–21, 223, 229–30, 232, 235–8, 240–1, 260, 278, 281–2, 285–6, 302–303, 308, 312, 314, 321, 332–3, 335, 339, 355–6
Central Asian(s), 6, 18, 21, 23, 27, 28, 31, 37, 51, 61–2, 67–8, 72, 77, 110, 118, 141–2, 144, 151–2, 179, 184, 190, 194–202, 205–206, 210–12, 215, 219–20, 222, 231, 235, 260, 276–7, 280–2, 285, 299–300, 302–305, 313, 335
Chakeran, 117
   see also Savaran, Afshin, Dehkan(s), Chakeran, Framandar-savaran, Aswaran, Aswaran-sardar, Savar-e Nezam Sangin Aslahe, Javidan, Var-thragh niyagan khodai, Akhshid, Afshin, Akhshid, Savaran-e shamshir-zan-e dah-hezar, Pushtighban, Pushtiban, Pusht-aspan, Pushtighban-salar, Pushtighban-sardar, Hazarbod, Gund Shahanshah, Ham-harzan, Ham-harz, Hm-hrz, Jan-separan, jyanavspar, Janvespar, Jalinus, Pishmarg/Peshmarg, Savaran-e Khorasan, Sarhangan, Pirouzetai, Khosrowgetai, Granikan-Salar
Chakosh, 106
   see also Abdast, Tabar, Tabarzin, Gauntlet, Tabarz/e/n, Warz/Wazr, Warz-wazig, Axe, hatchet, mace, Gurz
Chaldiran (battle of, 1514), 55, 288
Charax, 138
Chariot(s), 126, 129
   see also Arabeh, Arabehaye jangi, Carpat
Charkh (Varzesh-e bastani exercise), 48–9

Charx, (a type of siege equiptment) 245, 248, 251, 253
   see also Siege engine(s), Naft-andazan, Naffata, Ballistae, Catapult(s), Battering ram(s), Mobile tower(s), Darraga, Dabbabat, Xarak/Kharak, Testudo, Kashkanjir, Khaar-kaman, Mangonel(s), Manjeniq, Aradeh, Arrada, Aghrab(s), Rutaila, Scorpion(s), Scorpio, Hasak, Xasak
Chatrang 38
   see also Chess
Chaugan, 42–3, 348
Chaugan-wazig, 42
   see also Chaugan, Polo
Chehr Abad, 281
Chekan, 43
   see also Chaugan, Choka, Chicane, Schaggun, Polo
Chertomlyk, 88
Chess, 38
   see also Chatrang
Chicane, 43
   see also Chaugan, Chekan, Choka, Schaggun, Polo
Chin Shih Huang-Ti, 251
China, 21, 25, 107, 137, 197, 199–200, 212, 251, 291, 308, 332–3
China (Great Wall of), 236
Chinese, 195–8, 200, 210–11, 213, 220, 223, 245, 251, 268, 281, 291, 308, 332–3
Chionite(s), 4, 21, 194, 201–202, 235, 259–61, 302
Choka, 43
   see also Chaugan, Chekan, Chicane, Schaggun, Polo
Chol(s), 20, 237
Chorasmia, 74–5, 277, 350
Chorasmian, 74–5
Christian(s), 7, 20, 26, 28, 116, 182, 190, 268, 322
Christianity, 6, 20, 115
Chronicle of Seert, 136, 190
Chronicon Anonymum, 159, 161–2
Chul(s), 191, 205
Cilicia, 145
Cilician Gates, 305
Cincinnati Art Museum, xv, 280
Circassia, 139
   see also Transcaucasus, Circassia
Circesium, 29
Claudiopolis (Bithynia), 73
Cleveland Museum of Art, 98
Clibanarius, 15, 73, 348

see also Clibanarii, Cataphractus, Cataphractii,
    klibanion, klibanarios, Griv, Pan,
    Griv-ban/Griw-ban, Gardaan-ban,
    Grivpan, Tanur, Tanurig, Tanvar
Clibanarii, 73, 344, 348
    see also Clibanarius, Cataphractus,
    Cataphractii, klibanion, klibanarios, Griv,
    Pan, Gardaan-ban, Griv-ban/Griw-ban,
    Grivpan, Tanur, Tanurig, Tanvar
Coche, 132, 228
    see also Veh-Ardashir
Colchis, 234
    see also Georgia, Iberia, Lazica
Commagene, 171
Composite bow, 59, 65, 67, 103, 157, 195, 210
    see also Composite bow
Compound bow, 59, 91, 198, 310
    see also Composite bow
Constantia (Salamis), 139
Constantine I the Great, 131, 178, 345
Constantinople, 34, 139, 192–3, 206, 230, 234,
    264, 306–308, 313, 317, 346
Constantinople (siege of, 626 CE), 265, 268–9
Constantius II, xvii, 91, 131, 269, 271, 287, 345
Ctesiphon, 3–6, 16–17, 21, 34–6, 41, 83,
    115–17, 122, 132, 148, 151–2, 158, 177–9,
    184, 192, 194, 201, 203, 205, 209, 215–16,
    220, 225, 231, 266, 289, 293–4, 299–300,
    308–309, 313, 317, 324, 325, 327
Ctesiphon (battle of, 233 CE), 89, 91, 126,
    150–2, 156, 159
Ctesiphon (defenses, 363 CE), 228–30
Ctesiphon (siege of, 638 CE), 325–7
Cunaxa (Battle of, 401 BCE), 76
Cyropedia, 76, 292
Cyrus (the Great), xx, 75, 129, 194, 237, 355
Cyrus the Younger, 76

Dabbabat, 252–3
    see also Aghrab(s), Rutaila, Scorpion(s),
    Scorpio, Hasak, Xasak, Siege engine(s),
    Naft-andazan, Naffata, Charx, Kashkanjir,
    Khaar-kaman, Mangonel(s), Manjeniq,
    Aradeh, Arrada, Ballistae, Catapult(s),
    Battering ram(s), Mobile tower(s), Darraga,
    Xarak/Kharak, Xarak/Kharak, Testudo
Dabestan, 287
    see also Frahang, Honar, Honarmand,
    Farhang
Dabir(s), 15–16, 20, 32, 177, 187–8, 191–2,
    212, 255
Dabirbod, 35
Dabirestan, 16
Dacia, 156

Dadwaran, 290
    see also Mobadan Mobad, Mobad(s), Magi,
    Asronan, Dasturan, Herbadan, Radan
Daftar, 138
    see also Kashtig/Kashti, Navbad, Balanj,
    Bandar, Bar, Dunij, Didban, Rah-nameh,
    Nav-khoda
Dagestan, 230, 232
Dagger(s), 49, 74, 86–7, 90, 94, 110–11, 117,
    121, 123–4, 210, 218, 261, 275, 337
    see also Akenakes, Tour, Dasnag, Celan, Kard,
    Nran
Dagisthaeus, 272
Dahigan, 290
Dailam, 36
Dailamite(s), 20, 23, 36, 38, 47, 49, 101, 103,
    120, 122–4, 129, 135, 137, 149, 155, 201,
    215–18, 229, 254, 266, 272, 282, 297, 312,
    322, 324–5, 327–8, 330–1, 336–8, 340,
    344, 350
    see also Gels, Jastan
Damascus, 305, 334
Daphne, 78
Dar, 90
    see also Awestarag, Shamsher, Safser,
    Sword(s), Broadsword(s), Two-handed
    sword(s), Shamsher-wazig, Fencing, Italian
    grip, Baldric hanging, Tex, Kamar,
    Kamar-band, Niyam, Sousser, Saif,
    Mintaqa, Goti, Scabbard (slide suspension),
    Lappet suspension system, P-mount
    (system), Shap-sheraz/Shamshirdar
Dara, 29, 134, 142, 231, 245
Dara (battle of, 530 CE), 66, 68, 112, 124, 146,
    156, 165, 168–73, 188, 275, 349
Dara (siege of, 540 CE), 248
Dara (siege of, 573 CE), 124, 193, 215, 248,
    255, 262
Dara (siege of, 603–604 CE), 265–6, 299, 304
Darabgerd, 11, 97
Daray hindi, 54
Darb-e Mehr, 274
Darbandan, 61, 82, 89, 277, 349
Darraga, 252–3
    see also Aghrab(s), Rutaila, Scorpion(s),
    Scorpio, Hasak, Xasak, Siege engine(s),
    Naft-andazan, Naffata, Charx, Kashkanjir,
    Khaar-kaman, Mangonel(s), Manjeniq,
    Aradeh, Arrada, Ballistae, Catapult(s),
    Battering ram(s), Mobile tower(s),
    Dabbabat, Xarak/Kharak, Testudo
Darigbedum, 142
Darius I (the Great), xix, xxi, 75, 129, 194, 237,
    268, 355

Darius II, xix
Darius III, 130, 278
Daskylion (Battle of, 396 BCE)
Dasnag, 90
  see also Celan, Akenakes, Tour, Dagger(s),
    Kard, Nran
Dastegerd, 121, 225, 229, 285, 291
Dasturan 290
  see also Mobadan Mobad, Mobad(s), Magi,
    Asronan, Dadwaran, Herbadan, Radan
Datoyean, 221
David of Ashby, 196
Dehsalar, 12
Dehkan(s), xiii, 9, 18, 23–4, 35–6, 73, 100, 117,
    298, 300, 318, 351, 353
  see also Savaran, Asbaran, Akhshid, Afshin,
    Chakeran, Framandar-savaran, Aswaran,
    Aswaran-sardar, Savar-e Nezam Sangin
    Aslahe, Javidan, Var-thragh niyagan
    khodai, Akhshid, Afshin, Chakeran,
    Savaran-e shamshir-zan-e dah-hezar,
    Pushtighban, Pushtiban, Pusht-aspan,
    Pushtighban-salar, Pushtighban-sardar,
    Hazarbod, Gund Shahanshah,
    Ham-harzan, Ham-harz, Hm-hrz,
    Jan-separan, jyanavspar, Janvespar, Jalinus,
    Pishmarg/Peshmarg, Savaran-e Khorasan,
    Sarhangan, Pirouzetai, Khosrowgetai,
    Granikan-Salar
Derbent Pass, 26, 233
Derbent (wall of), 181, 224, 230–5, 241
Dezh-e Bahman, 110
Dezh-e Shapur Khwast, 227
Dezhban, 15–16, 182, 188
Dhu Qar, (battle of, 602 CE) 25, 313
Dhu Yazan, 142
  see also Ma'adi Karab, Sayf Bin Dhu Yazan
Didban, 138
  see also Kashtig/Kashti, Navbad, Balanj,
    Bandar, Bar, Daftar, Dunij, Rah-nameh,
    Nav-khoda
Dinawari, 10, 17, 32, 108, 144–6, 148, 150,
    162, 175, 177, 207, 215, 217, 219, 255
Dinkard, xix, 8, 39, 277–8
Diocletian, 131, 159, 229, 347
Dir, 108
  see also Mail, Lamellar, Scale armour, Pos/
    Posh, Zreh, Zereh, Gurdih, Saqain,
    Jowshan, Gowshan
Divan, 33, 41, 185
Divan Iran Dorost-bad, 185
Divan-spah, 32
  see also Diwan al-jund
Divashtich, 333

Diwan al-Jund, 32
  see also Divan-spah
Dizbed, 11
Don River, 277
Donbak, 55
  see also Tombag, Tablak
Drachma(s), 208, 212
Draconis Persicus, 284
  see also Drafsh, Drafsh (e) Kaviani, Tamga(s)
Drafsh, 9, 41, 126, 282–5
  see also Drafsh (e) Kaviani, Tamga(s),
    Draconis Persicus,
Drafsh (e) Kaviani, (Standard of Kaveh) 21, 36,
    64, 115, 164, 284–5, 322, 325, 327
  see also Drafsh (e) Kaviani, Tamga(s),
    Draconis Persicus
Draxt-i-Asurig, 59
Dron, 69
  see also Sanwar, Panjagan
Dura Europos, 16, 79, 84–5, 88–9, 121–2, 125,
    162, 211, 250, 346
Dura Europos (siege of, c.256 CE), 156, 254,
    256–9
Dunij, 138
  see also Kashtig/Kashti, Navbad, Balanj,
    Bandar, Bar, Daftar, Didban, Rah-nameh,
    Nav-khoda
Dustar 58
  see also Siyah, Kaman-saz
Dvin, 28, 307

Eastern Europe/East Europe, 19, 82, 87, 101,
    128, 188, 196, 234, 278, 284
Eastern European, 199
Edessa, 30, 155–7, 265–6
Edessa (siege of, 543 CE), 134, 249, 255
Edessa-Carrhae (battle of, c.260), 155–7, 159
Egypt, 12, 67, 130, 220, 302, 305–307, 315,
    320–1, 332, 346
Egyptian(s), 305, 320, 351
Eire-an, 10, 18, 190
  see also Eiran-shahr, Sassanian Empire
Eiran-ambaraghbad, 8, 11, 184, 185, 222, 231
  see also Ambaragh, Ganz, Zynpt
Eiran-dabirbod, 15, 16, 141, 273
Eiran-Shahr, 3–5, 7, 72, 286
  see also Eire-an, Sassanian Empire
Eiran-spahbod, 11–13, 25, 141, 178
Elamite, 224
Elephant(s), 65, 122, 126, 129–37, 150, 164,
    179–80, 185, 215–18, 243, 254–5, 259–61,
    266, 277, 307, 312, 322–4
  see also Pil-savaran, Pil, Fil
Emesa, 304

Enan, 109
  see also Asb, Raksh, Tagavar, Zin, Zin-e
    Khadang, Setam, Zarrin Setam, Fetrak,
    Naal, Taziyane
Epaulettes, 285, 347
  see also Rang
Equites Persae clibanarii, 345
  see also Notitia Dignitatum, Magister equitum
    praesentalis, Magister militum per
    orientem, Equites sagittarri parthi iuniores,
    Equites sagittarri parthi seniores, Scola
    scutariorum clibanariorum, Numerus
    persoiustiniani, Numerus felicum
    persoarmeniorum, Vexillatio palatina
Equites sagittarri parthi iuniores, 344
  see also Notitia Dignitatum, Magister equitum
    praesentalis, Magister militum per
    orientem, Equites sagittarri parthi seniores,
    Equites Persae clibanarii, Scola
    scutariorum clibanariorum, Numerus
    persoiustiniani, Numerus felicum
    persoarmeniorum, Vexillatio palatina
Equites sagittarri parthi seniores, 344
  see also Notitia Dignitatum, Magister equitum
    praesentalis, Magister militum per
    orientem, Equites sagittarri parthi iuniores,
    Equites Persae clibanarii, Scola
    scutariorum clibanariorum, Numerus
    persoiustiniani, Numerus felicum
    persoarmeniorum, Vexillatio palatina
Erekhsha, 56
Erzurum, 181
Ethiopia, 130
Ethiopian, 31
Euphrates River, 5, 29–30, 83, 114, 134–5, 152,
  171–3, 177–8, 229, 263, 321–2, 325
Eurasian, 197
Europe, 50, 159, 171, 192, 284, 344, 346, 349
European(s), 34, 50, 195, 268–9, 277, 307, 336,
  347, 353

Faramoushkhaneh, 189
  see also Gelkard, Zendanigh
Farhad (Phraates) V, xix
Farhang 40
  see also Frahang, Honar, Honarmand,
    Dabestan
Faris, 352–3, 355
Farr, xx, 164, 292–4
Fathali Shah, xx, xxi
Faustus of Byzantium, 293
Fencing, 90, 118
  see also Italian grip, Baldric hanging,
    Shamsher, Sword(s), Broadsword(s),

Two-handed sword(s), Shamsher-wazig,
    Safser, Awestarag, Dar, Tex, Kamar,
    Kamarband, Niyam, Sousser, Saif,
    Mintaqa, Goti, Scabbard (slide suspension),
    Lappet suspension system, P-mount
    (system), Shap-sheraz/Shamshirdar
Fereydoun (of the Shahname epic), 105–106
Ferghana, 220
Festus, 152, 180
Fetrak, 109
  see also Asb, Raksh, Tagavar, Zin, Zin-e
    Khadang, Setam, Zarrin Setam, Enan,
    Naal, Taziyane
Fil, 137
  see also Pil-savaran, Pil, Shatranj, Elephant(s)
Firdowsi, xxii–xxiii, 15, 41, 150, 162–3, 174,
  188–9, 214–16, 247, 276, 332
  see also Shahname, Xvatay-namak
Firoozan, 176, 325–6, 330–1
Firouz, 124, 168–73, 188
Firouz Khosrow, 234
First Flavian Legion, 262
First Parthian Legion, 262
Firuzabad, xiii, 94, 97, 101, 110, 151–3, 156,
  279–80, 349
Firuzabad (palace of Ardashir I), 226–7
Firuzabad (Battle of, 224 CE), 61, 72, 79–80,
  82–5, 89, 109, 118, 150, 175, 277–8
Foulkon, 172
Frahang, 40, 46, 287
  see also Farhang, Honar, Honarmand,
    Dabestan
Frahangestan, 40
Framandar-savaran, 10, 15, 122, 273
  see also Savaran, Dehkan(s), Akhshid, Afshin,
    Chakeran, Asbaran, Aswaran-sardar,
    Savar-e Nezam Sangin Aslahe, Javidan,
    Aswaran, Var-thragh niyagan khodai,
    Savaran-e shamshir-zan-e dah-hezar,
    Pushtighban, Pushtiban, Pusht-aspan,
    Pushtighban-salar, Pushtighban-sardar,
    Hazarbod, Gund Shahanshah,
    Ham-harzan, Ham-harz, Hm-hrz,
    Jan-separan, jyanavspar, Janvespar, Jalinus,
    Pishmarg/Peshmarg, Savaran-e Khorasan,
    Sarhangan, Pirouzetai, Khosrowgetai,
    Granikan-Salar
France, 344
Fras, 90
  see also Kontos, Arsht, Astr, Rumh, Nezak,
    Neyze, Neyze-daran, Javeliner(s),
    Javelin(s), Zhupin
Futuwwa, 352–4

Galilee, 267

Gallic, 247, 261

Gallienus, 345

Ganz, 184, 231, 238
  see also Eiran-ambaraghbad, Ambaragh, Zynpt

Ganzak, 307

Gaozong, 332

Gardaan-ban, 74

Gaugamela (Battle of, 331 BCE), 77, 130

Gaul, 99, 336

Gaius Avidius Cassius, 5

Galerius, 6, 72, 131, 158–60, 180, 287

Garshasp, 44–6

Garshaspname, 44–5

Gauntlet, 90
  see also Abdast, Tabar, Tabarzin, Tabarz/e/n,
    Chakosh, Warz/Wazr, Warz-wazig, Axe,
    hatchet, mace, Gurz

Gelai, 261
  see also Gilan

Gelkard, 189
  see also Faramoushkhaneh, Zendanigh

Gels, 123
  see also Dailamite(s), Jastan

Genghis Khan, 152

Georgia, 4–5, 14, 20, 28, 123, 139, 234, 271,
  292, 309
  see also Colchis, Iberia, Lazica

Georgian, 307, 309

Gepid(s), 268–9

German(s), 98–9, 153
  see also Germanic, Goth(s), Gothic,
    Germania, Germany, Ostrogoth(s),
    Visigoth(s)

Germania, 156
  see also Gothic, Goth(s), German(s),
    Germany, Germanic, Ostrogoth(s),
    Visigoth(s)

Germanic 153–4, 156, 344–5, 349
  see also Gothic, Goth(s), German(s),
    Germany, Germania, Ostrogoth(s),
    Visigoth(s)

Germanus (nephew or cousin of Justinian I),
  263–4

Germanus (Romano-Byzantine general during
  reign of Khosrow II), 265

Ghagha bin Amr, 135

Ghassanid(s), 29–30, 110, 172–3, 241, 314
  see also Arab(s), Bedouin(s), Lakhmid(s),
    Wada'i, Bani Sheiban, Bani Hanifah,
    Yemenite Arab(s)

Ghateef, 138

Gilan, 20, 49, 127, 203, 261, 336, 337
  see also Gelai

Gil(s), 20, 338

Gladius, 157

Gok Turk(s), 5, 200, 202, 212–13, 220, 223
  see also Turkic, Turk(s), Avar(s), Turkic-
    Avar(s), Turkish, Ottoman(s), Tatar,
    Turkic-Hun, Hun(s), Hunnic, Khazar(s),
    Uighur(s), Hsiang-Nou, Seljuk(s), Oghuz

Golgosp, 33

Gordafarid (of the Shahname epic), 129
  see also Apranik, Azadeh Dailam, Negan,
    Banu (Khorramdin), Amazon(s)

Gordian III, xiv, 130, 151–5, 279

Gorgan, 20, 191, 203, 206, 235–8, 336

Gorgan (Wall of), 27, 206, 229–1, 235–7
  see also Tammisha (Wall of)

Gorytos, xiv, 58, 61, 128
  see also Tir/Tigr, Tir-wazig, Tirbad, Archery,
    Horse archery, Horse archer(s), Kaman,
    Kamam, Kamandan, Qaba, Tirdan, Kantir/
    Kantigr, Zeh/Zih, Zeh e yadaki, Nawak,
    Watarain, Shivatir-e zrehbaran, Shiva-tir

Gotarzes relief, 79

Goti, 94
  see also Kamar-band, Kamar, Dar, Awestarag,
    Shamsher, Safser, Sword(s), Broadsword(s),
    Two-handed sword(s), Shamsher-wazig,
    Fencing, Italian grip, Baldric hanging, Tex,
    Niyam, Sousser, Saif, Mintaqa, Scabbard
    (slide suspension), Lappet suspension
    system, P-mount (system), Shap-sheraz/
    Shamshirdar

Gothic, 153–4, 156, 192, 347, 349–50
  see also Goth(s), Germania, Germanic,
    German(s), Germany, Ostrogoth(s),
    Visigoth(s),

Goth(s), 171, 192, 346, 349
  see also Gothic, Germania, Germanic,
    German(s), Germany, Ostrogoth(s),
    Visigoth(s)

Gowshan, 108
  see also Jowshan, Mail, Lamellar, Scale
    armour, Gurdih, Zreh, Zereh, Dir, Pos/
    Posh, Saqain

Granikan-Salar, 307
  see also Savaran, Asbaran, Dehkan(s), Akhshid,
    Afshin, Chakeran, Framandar-savaran,
    Savar-e Nezam Sangin Aslahe, Aswaran,
    Aswaran-sardar, Javidan, Var-thragh
    niyagan khodai, Savaran-e shamshir-zan-e
    dah-hezar, Pusht-aspan, Pushtighban,
    Pushtiban, Pushtighban-salar,
    Pushtighban-sardar, Hazarbod, Gund
    Shahanshah, Ham-harzan, Ham-harz,
    Hm-hrz, Jan-separan, jyanavspar,

Janvespar, Jalinus, Pishmarg/Peshmarg, Savaran-e Khorasan, Sarhangan, Pirouzetai, Khosrowgetai

Granicus River (Battle of, 334 BCE), 77

Greco-Persian wars, 106

Greece, 76, 130

Greek(s), xv, 38, 76, 128, 162, 186, 266, 269, 278, 306

Gregory Nazianzenus, 228–9

Griv, 74
see also Pan, Grivpan, Griv-ban/Griw-ban, Gardaan-ban, Clibanarii, Clibanarius, Cataphractus, Cataphractii, klibanion, klibanarios, Tanur, Tanurig, Tanvar

Grivpan, 74
see also Pan, Griv, Griv-ban/Griw-ban, Gardaan-ban, Clibanarii, Clibanarius, Cataphractus, Cataphractii, klibanion, klibanarios, Tanur, Tanurig, Tanvar

Grumbates, 202

Gubarzes, 272

Gudarz (of the Shahname epic), 163

Guiw/Guiv (of the Shahname epic), 163, 275

Gumbrates, 21, 260

Gund, 9, 15–16

Gund-Dabir, 16

Gund-salar, 9

Gund Shahanshah, 9, 113, 172, 203, 215
see also Savaran, Dehkan(s), Akhshid, Afshin, Chakeran, Asbaran, Framandar-savaran, Aswaran, Aswaran-sardar, Javidan, Var-thragh niyagan khodai, Savar-e Nezam Sangin Aslahe, Savaran-e shamshir-zan-e dah-hezar, Pushtighban, Pushtiban, Pusht-aspan, Pushtighban-salar, Pushtighban-sardar, Hazarbod, Ham-harzan, Ham-harz, Hm-hrz, Jan-separan, jyanavspar, Janvespar, Jalinus, Pishmarg/Peshmarg, Savaran-e Khorasan, Sarhangan, Pirouzetai, Khosrowgetai, Granikan-Salar

Gur, 138

Gurdih, 90
see also Mail, Lamellar, Scale armour, Pos/Posh, Zreh, Zereh, Dir, Saqain, Jowshan, Gowshan

Gurz, 32, 41, 105–108, 110, 117, 284, 294, 356
see also Amud, Amud-e Ahanin

Haena, 8
see also Hen

Hadrian's Wall, 236

Hafez, 196

Hamedan, 186, 234, 336, 339–40

Hamedan (battle of, 734 CE), 340

Ham-harz, 12, 112
see also Savaran, Dehkan(s), Akhshid, Afshin, Chakeran, Asbaran, Framandar-savaran, Aswaran, Aswaran-sardar, Javidan, Var-thragh niyagan khodai, Savar-e Nezam Sangin Aslahe, Savaran-e shamshir-zan-e dah-hezar, Pushtighban, Pushtiban, Pusht-aspan, Pushtighban-salar, Pushtighban-sardar, Hazarbod, Ham-harzan, Hm-hrz, Gund Shahanshah, Jan-separan, jyanavspar, Janvespar, Jalinus, Pishmarg/Peshmarg, Savaran-e Khorasan, Sarhangan, Pirouzetai, Khosrowgetai, Granikan-Salar

Ham-harzan, 112
see also Savaran, Dehkan(s), Akhshid, Afshin, Chakeran, Asbaran, Framandar-savaran, Aswaran, Aswaran-sardar, Javidan, Var-thragh niyagan khodai, Savar-e Nezam Sangin Aslahe, Savaran-e shamshir-zan-e dah-hezar, Pushtighban, Pushtiban, Pusht-aspan, Pushtighban-salar, Pushtighban-sardar, Hazarbod, Ham-harz, Hm-hrz, Gund Shahanshah, Jan-separan, jyanavspar, Janvespar, Jalinus, Pishmarg/Peshmarg, Savaran-e Khorasan, Sarhangan, Pirouzetai, Khosrowgetai, Granikan-Salar

Hamrazm, 288

Harashi (al-), 333

Harirud River, 216

Harran, 152

Harun al-Rashid, 336

Hasak, 253
see also Xasak, Scorpion(s), Scorpio, Aghrab(s), Rutaila, Siege engine(s), Naft-andazan, Naffata, Charx, Kashkanjir, Khaar-kaman, Mangonel(s), Manjeniq, Aradeh, Arrada, Ballistae, Catapult(s), Battering ram(s), Mobile tower(s), Darraga, Dabbabat, Xarak/Kharak, Testudo

Hashem (al-), 327–8

Hashtpay, 40

Hatchet, 90
see also Abdast, Tabar, Tabarzin, Tabarz/e/n, Chakosh, Warz/Wazr, Warz-wazig, Axe, Gauntlet, Mace, Gurz

Hatra, 131

Hazar, 9–10

Hazarbod, 17, 112

Hazarmard, 9–10

Hazaruft, 10

Hebarbodan-hebarbodh, 141

Heliodorus, 48, 91–4, 98–9, 113, 156, 260
  see also Aethiopica
Hen, 8
  see also Haena
Hephthalite(s), 4, 21, 23–6, 29, 31, 36, 55, 64,
    99–101, 107, 127, 134, 141–4, 147, 174,
    184, 194–5, 201–14, 220, 222, 235, 237
  see also Hephthalite-Hun(s), Turco-
    Hephthalite(s)
Hephthalite-Hun(s), 73, 196, 199, 230, 302
  see also Hephthalite(s), Turco-Hephthalite(s)
Heraclius, xi, 19, 134, 136, 139, 223, 267–9,
    289, 293, 300, 302, 304, 306–309, 311–14,
    322, 324, 327, 351
Herat, 213–17
Herat (battle of, April 588 CE), 216
Herbadan, 290
  see also Mobadan Mobad, Mobad(s), Magi,
    Asronan, Dasturan, Dadwaran, Radan
Hermitage Museum (St. Petersburg), xiii,
    xv–xvii, 53, 94, 125, 280–2, 291–3, 310
Hermogenes, 68, 168
Herodian, 51, 57, 131, 151
Herodotus, 56, 76
Herul(s), 169
Herulian, 170
Hira, 116–17, 241
Historia Ecclesiastica, 178
Historia Augusta, 10, 130–1
Hm-hrz, 112
  see also Savaran, Dehkan(s), Akhshid, Afshin,
    Chakeran, Asbaran, Framandar-savaran,
    Aswaran, Aswaran-sardar, Javidan,
    Var-thragh niyagan khodai, Savar-e Nezam
    Sangin Aslahe, Savaran-e shamshir-zan-e
    dah-hezar, Pushtighban, Pushtiban,
    Pusht-aspan, Pushtighban-salar,
    Pushtighban-sardar, Hazarbod, Ham-harz,
    Ham-harzan, Gund Shahanshah,
    Jan-separan, jyanavspar, Janvespar, Jalinus,
    Pishmarg/Peshmarg, Savaran-e Khorasan,
    Sarhangan, Pirouzetai, Khosrowgetai,
    Granikan-Salar
Holwan, 327–8
Honar, 113, 286
  see also Honarmand, Frahang, Farhang,
    Dabestan
Honarmand, 113
  see also Honar, Frahang, Farhang, Dabestan
Hormuzan, 280, 329
Hormuzd (prince, brother of Shapur II), 178,
    298, 344–6
Hormuzd (general at Battle of Qadissiyah), 325
Hormuzd (prince, brother of Pirouz), 206, 344

Hormuzd I, 17
Hormuzd II, xiv, 83, 154
Hormuzd IV, 6, 15–17, 182, 213–14, 220,
    298–9, 305
Hormuzd Kushanshah, 83
Horse archer(s), 10, 52, 57, 65–6, 68, 76, 78–9,
    89–91, 100, 103, 127, 150–2, 154, 156–7,
    159, 161, 166–7, 169, 179–80, 197–8,
    209–11, 246
  see also Tir/Tigr, Tir-wazig, Tirbad, Archery,
    Horse archery, Kaman, Kamam,
    Kamandan, Qaba, Tirdan, Kantir/Kantigr,
    Zeh/Zih, Zeh e yadaki, Watarain, Gorytos,
    Nawak, Shivatir-e zrehbaran, Shiva-tir
Horse archery, xvi, 57, 66, 69, 75, 78–9, 82, 89,
    103, 109, 149, 151, 160, 197, 204, 217,
    310–11
  see also Tir/Tigr, Tir-wazig, Tirbad, Archery,
    Kaman, Kamam, Kamandan, Qaba,
    Tirdan, Kantir/Kantigr, Zeh/Zih, Zeh e
    yadaki, Watarain, Gorytos, Nawak, Horse
    archer(s), Shivatir-e zrehbaran, Shiva-tir
Hsiang-Nou, 21, 195, 200, 355
  see also Turkic-Avar(s), Avar(s), Turk(s),
    Turkish, Gok Turk(s), Ottoman(s), Turkic,
    Tatar, Turkic-Hun, Hunnic, Khazar(s),
    Uighur(s), Hun(s), Seljuk(s), Oghuz
Hun(s), 26, 59, 64, 70, 101, 149, 169, 172,
    194–5, 198, 201, 206, 208, 234, 276, 281,
    310, 313, 344–5, 355
  see also Turkic-Avar(s), Avar(s), Turk(s),
    Turkish, Gok Turk(s), Ottoman(s), Turkic,
    Tatar, Turkic-Hun, Hunnic, Khazar(s),
    Uighur(s), Hsiang-Nou, Seljuk(s), Oghuz
Hunnic, 101, 103, 310
  see also Turkic-Avar(s), Avar(s), Turk(s),
    Turkish, Gok Turk(s), Ottoman(s), Turkic,
    Tatar, Turkic-Hun, Hun, Khazar(s),
    Seljuk(s), Oghuz
Hydro-engineering, 251–2

Iberia, 4, 20, 234, 256
  see also Colchis, Georgia, Lazica
Iberian(s), 5, 28
Ibn Balkhi, 291
Ibn Isfandyar, 337, 341
Ibn Khaldun, 135–6
Ibn Muqaffa (Roozbeh son of Dadveh son of
    Jushnasp [Gushnasp]), 351
Ibrahim bin Layt bin Fazl, 339
Il-Arslan, 213, 219–20
  see also Shaban
India, 21, 77, 130–1, 133–4, 143, 202, 205, 355
Indian, 54, 77, 130, 136–7, 186

Indian Ocean, 138
Indo-European, 7, 22, 56–7, 64, 126, 291, 355
Infantry, 20
Irafa, 319–20
Iran, xxi, 2–4, 12–13, 17, 20–2, 24–5, 27–8,
    46–7, 49–52, 56, 64–5, 73, 79, 93, 100,
    105–106, 117–18, 122–4, 126, 128, 130,
    134, 136, 138–9, 143, 155, 160, 177, 179,
    181–3, 186, 189–90, 194, 196, 200–201,
    203, 205, 214, 217, 223–5, 230, 232–6,
    238–9, 241–2, 245, 257–8, 261, 268, 272,
    279–81, 287, 289, 292, 294, 297–300,
    302–303, 306–309, 312–15, 318–22,
    325–31, 333–6, 338–43, 348, 350–3, 355
Iran-Iraq war, 183
Iranian(s), xii, xvii–xix, xxii–xxiii, 2–7, 15, 18,
    20–2, 24–7, 35–6, 40, 46–7, 49–51, 56, 59,
    65–6, 68, 72, 75–7, 80, 87, 93–4, 96, 106,
    110, 114–15, 117–18, 128–30, 132, 136,
    139, 147–50, 153, 155, 158–9, 164, 166,
    168, 181–4, 186–7, 192, 194–6, 200–203,
    205–206, 209, 211, 217, 219–20, 222, 228,
    233–4, 238–9, 241, 244, 246, 251, 256–7,
    270, 273–5, 277–81, 283–4, 286–8,
    291–300, 303, 305, 310, 321, 327–30, 332,
    334–56
Iranian plateau, xii, 21–2, 27, 56, 64, 224, 232,
    236, 328, 355
Iranic, 7, 12, 15, 20–2, 63, 82, 85, 93, 128, 151,
    153, 164, 267, 274, 280, 283, 333–4, 344,
    355
Iraq, 126, 152, 190, 322, 339, 342, 351
Iraqi, 321, 327
Isfahan, 14, 221, 227, 305, 336, 339–40
Isfahani, Hamza, 290–1
Ishtemi Khan 26–7
    see also Sizabul
Iskandarname, xix
    see also Nizami Ganjavi
Islamic, 8, 22, 24–5, 56–7, 64, 73, 150, 186,
    195, 200, 202–203, 232–4, 236, 239–40,
    246, 252, 267, 273, 275, 287, 292, 319,
    336, 338, 342, 350, 352–3, 355–6
Issus (Battle of, 333 BCE), 77
Istakhr, 295, 329
Italian grip, 50, 98, 218
    see also Baldric hanging, Shamsher, Safser,
    Sword(s), Broadsword(s), Two-handed
    sword(s), Shamsher-wazig, Fencing,
    Awestarag, Dar, Tex, Kamar, Kamar-band,
    Niyam, Sousser, Saif, Mintaqa, Goti,
    Scabbard (slide suspension), Lappet
    suspension system, P-mount (system),
    Shap-sheraz/Shamshirdar

Iwan, 44, 54, 125
Izad-Gushnasp, 216

Jahiz, 62, 148, 348, 354–5
Jalinus, 114
    see also Savaran, Dehkan(s), Akhshid, Afshin,
    Chakeran, Framandar-savaran, Asbaran,
    Aswaran, Aswaran-sardar, Savar-e Nezam
    Sangin Aslahe, Javidan, Var-thragh niyagan
    khodai, Savaran-e shamshir-zan-e
    dah-hezar, Pushtighban, Pushtiban,
    Pusht-aspan, Pushtighban-salar,
    Pushtighban-sardar, Hazarbod, Gund
    Shahanshah, Ham-harzan, Ham-harz,
    Hm-hrz, Jan-separan, jyanavspar,
    Janvespar, Pishmarg/Peshmarg, Savaran-e
    Khorasan, Sarhangan, Pirouzetai,
    Khosrowgetai, Granikan-Salar
Jalula (battle of, 651 CE), 176, 325, 327–9
Jamasp, 21, 23–4
    also Zamasp, 23–4
Jang, 9
    see also Ardig, Karezar, Pad-razm, Nibard,
    Zambag, Paykar
Jan-separan, xvii, xix, 113–14, 203
    see also Savaran, Dehkan(s), Akhshid, Afshin,
    Chakeran, Framandar-savaran, Asbaran,
    Aswaran, Aswaran-sardar, Savar-e Nezam
    Sangin Aslahe, Javidan, Var-thragh niyagan
    khodai, Savaran-e shamshir-zan-e
    dah-hezar, Pushtighban, Pushtiban,
    Pusht-aspan, Pushtighban-salar,
    Pushtighban-sardar, Hazarbod, Gund
    Shahanshah, Ham-harzan, Ham-harz,
    Hm-hrz, Jan-separan, jyanavspar,
    Janvespar, Jalinus, Pishmarg/Peshmarg,
    Savaran-e Khorasan, Sarhangan,
    Pirouzetai, Khosrowgetai, Granikan-Salar
Janvespar, xvii, xix, 114, 172
    see also Savaran, Dehkan(s), Akhshid, Afshin,
    Chakeran, Framandar-savaran, Asbaran,
    Aswaran, Aswaran-sardar, Savar-e Nezam
    Sangin Aslahe, Javidan, Var-thragh niyagan
    khodai, Savaran-e shamshir-zan-e
    dah-hezar, Pushtighban, Pushtiban,
    Pusht-aspan, Pushtighban-salar,
    Pushtighban-sardar, Hazarbod, Gund
    Shahanshah, Ham-harzan, Ham-harz,
    Hm-hrz, Jan-separan, Jyanavspar, Jalinus,
    Pishmarg/Peshmarg, Savaran-e Khorasan,
    Sarhangan, Pirouzetai, Khosrowgetai,
    Granikan-Salar
Japan, 197, 277
Japanese, 50

Jastan, 123
see also Dailamite(s), Gels
Javanmardi, 182
Javanshir, 325
Javelin(s), 123–4, 128, 218, 324, 354
see also Zhupin
Javeliner(s), 124
see also Arsht, Kontos, Fras, Astr, Neyze-
daran, Neyze, Rumh, Nezak, Javelin(s),
Zhupin
Javidan, vxiii, 15, 66, 112–13, 133, 165, 169–70,
203, 286, 300
see also Savaran, Dehkan(s), Akhshid, Afshin,
Chakeran, Asbaran, Framandar-savaran,
Aswaran, Aswaran-sardar, Var-thragh
niyagan khodai, Savar-e Nezam Sangin
Aslahe, Savaran-e shamshir-zan-e
dah-hezar, Pushtighban, Pushtiban,
Pusht-aspan, Pushtighban-salar,
Pushtighban-sardar, Hazarbod, Gund
Shahanshah, Ham-harzan, Ham-harz,
Hm-hrz, Jan-separan, jyanavspar,
Janvespar, Jalinus, Pishmarg/Peshmarg,
Savaran-e Khorasan, Sarhangan,
Pirouzetai, Khosrowgetai, Granikan-Salar
Jericho, 266, 305
Jerusalem, 182, 190, 265, 304–305
Jerusalem (siege of, 614 CE), 266–8
Jew(s), xvii, xx, 182, 267
Jewish, 7, 110, 182, 266–8, 283, 317
John Lydus de Mensibus, 181
Jordanes, 152, 198
Josephus Flavius, 110
Jovian, 132–3, 180, 190
Jowshan, 108
see also Gowshan, Mail, Lamellar, Scale
armour, Gurdih, Zreh, Zereh, Dir, Pos/
Posh, Saqain
Juan-Juan, 197, 200
Julian, (the Apostate) 1, 39, 91–3, 96, 99, 122,
125, 131–2, 137, 150, 160–1, 165, 177–81,
184, 190, 192, 228–30, 239, 251–2, 255,
278, 298, 345
Jundi-Shapur, 186
see also Atravan
Justin (Philippic History), 51, 78
Justin II, 26–30, 193
Justinian I, 7, 143, 174, 192–3, 230, 263–4,
272, 310
Jyanavspar, xvii, xix, 113
see also Savaran, Dehkan(s), Akhshid, Afshin,
Chakeran, Framandar-savaran, Asbaran,
Aswaran, Aswaran-sardar, Savar-e Nezam
Sangin Aslahe, Javidan, Var-thragh niyagan

khodai, Savaran-e shamshir-zan-e
dah-hezar, Pushtighban, Pushtiban,
Pusht-aspan, Pushtighban-salar,
Pushtighban-sardar, Hazarbod, Gund
Shahanshah, Ham-harzan, Ham-harz,
Hm-hrz, Jan-separan, Janvespar, Jalinus,
Pishmarg/Peshmarg, Savaran-e Khorasan,
Sarhangan, Pirouzetai, Khosrowgetai,
Granikan-Salar

Kaaba Zartusht, 293
Kabade, 48
Kabul, 29
Kabul Museum, xv
Kafshak, 283
see also Afa-sar, Mah-sar, Sar, Shalvar, Mok,
Mocak, Kurtak, Kustik, Kamar,
Kamar-band, Kapah, Pargoo, Kulah
Kaftan(s), 280–1
Karnamag-e Ardaxsir (Ardashir)-e Papakan,
xxiii, 112–13, 137
Kanarang, 14
Kaman, 58
see also Tir/Tigr, Tir-wazig, Tirbad, Archery,
Kamam, Kamandan, Qaba, Tirdan, Kantir/
Kantigr, Zeh/Zih, Zeh e yadaki, Watarain,
Gorytos, Nawak, Horse archer(s), Horse
archery, Shivatir-e zrehbaran, Shiva-tir
Kamand, 90, 108, 110
Kamam, 69
see also Tir/Tigr, Tir-wazig, Tirbad, Archery,
Kamandan, Qaba, Tirdan, Kantir/Kantigr,
Zeh/Zih, Zeh e yadaki, Watarain, Gorytos,
Nawak, Horse archer(s), Horse archery,
Kaman, Shivatir-e zrehbaran, Shiva-tir
Kamandan, 58, 61–2, 347
see also Tir/Tigr, Tir-wazig, Tirbad, Archery,
Tirdan, Kantir/Kantigr, Zeh/Zih, Zeh e
yadaki, Watarain, Gorytos, Nawak, Horse
archer(s), Horse archery, Kaman, Qaba,
Kamam, Shivatir-e zrehbaran, Shiva-tir
Kaman-saz, 58
see also Dustar, Siyah
Kamar, 90, 282–3
see also Kamar-band, Kustik, Kurtak, Afa-sar,
Mah-sar, Sar, Shalvar, Mok, Mocak,
Kafshak, Kapah, Pargoo, Kulah, Dar,
Awestarag, Shamsher, Safser, Sword(s),
Broadsword(s), Two-handed sword(s),
Shamsher-wazig, Fencing, Italian grip,
Baldric hanging, Tex, Niyam, Sousser,
Saif, Mintaqa, Goti, Scabbard (slide
suspension), Lappet suspension system,

P-mount (system), Shap-sheraz/
Shamshirdar
Kamar-band, 42, 90
  see also Kamar, Kustik, Kurtak, Afa-sar,
  Mah-sar, Sar, Shalvar, Mok, Mocak,
  Kafshak, Kapah, Pargoo, Kulah, Dar,
  Awestarag, Shamsher, Safser, Sword(s),
  Broadsword(s), Two-handed sword(s),
  Shamsher-wazig, Fencing, Italian grip,
  Baldric hanging, Tex, Niyam, Sousser,
  Saif, Mintaqa, Goti, Scabbard (slide
  suspension), Lappet suspension system,
  P-mount (system), Shap-sheraz/
  Shamshirdar
Kamsarakan, 347
Kanishka (the Great), 87
Kantir/Kantigr, 69
  see also Tir/Tigr, Tir-wazig, Tirbad, Archery,
  Tirdan, Zeh/Zih, Zeh e yadaki, Watarain,
  Gorytos, Nawak, Horse archer(s), Horse
  archery, Kaman, Kamam, Kamandan,
  Qaba, Shivatir-e zrehbaran, Shiva-tir
Kapah, 283
  see also Kustik, Kamar, Kamar-band, Afa-sar,
  Mah-sar, Sar, Shalvar, Mok, Mocak,
  Kafshak, Kurtak, Pargoo, Kulah
Kara, 8
Karaj, 339
Karan the Bold, (of the Shahname epic), 166,
  276
Karanay, 54
Karawan, 8
Kard, 90
  see also Celan, Akenakes, Tour, Dagger(s),
  Dasnag, Nran
Kardar, 16
Karen (house of), 13, 209, 340
Karezar, 9
  see also Ardig, Jang, Pad-razm, Nibard,
  Zambag, Paykar
Karframandar, 293
Kartir, xiii, 17–18, 291
Karun River, 138, 189, 238
Kashan, 339
Kashkanjir, 245–6, 253
  see also Siege engine(s), Naft-andazan,
  Naffata, Ballistae, Catapult(s), Battering
  ram(s), Mobile tower(s), Darraga,
  Dabbabat, Xarak/Kharak, Testudo, Charx,
  Khaar-kaman, Mangonel(s), Manjeniq,
  Aradeh, Arrada, Aghrab(s), Rutaila,
  Scorpion(s), Scorpio, Hasak, Xasak

Kashtig/Kashti, 138
  see also Navbad, Balanj, Bandar, Bar, Daftar,
  Dunij, Didban, Rah-nameh, Nav-khoda
Kavad I, xvi, 12, 21–4, 26, 37, 73, 115, 124,
  168, 174, 188–90, 208, 211–12, 232, 235,
  250, 280, 289, 291, 293, 299, 302, 327
Kaveh Ahsengar/Ahangar, 284
Kay-Khosrow (of the Shahname epic), 110, 150
Kerch, 94
Kereshaspa (of the Shahname epic), 45
  see also Saam
Kerman, 22, 182, 190
Kermanshah, 100, 105, 294
Khaar-kaman, 246, 253
  see also Siege engine(s), Naft-andazan,
  Naffata, Ballistae, Catapult(s), Battering
  ram(s), Mobile tower(s), Darraga,
  Dabbabat, Xarak/Kharak, Testudo, Charx,
  Kashkanjir, Mangonel(s), Manjeniq,
  Aradeh, Arrada, Aghrab(s), Rutaila,
  Scorpion(s), Scorpio, Hasak, Xasak
Khabur River, 29
Khagan, 26, 212–23, 242, 293, 303
Khanate(s), 26, 308
Khandaq, 176, 224, 238–41, 314, 318, 338
Khandaq-e Shapur, 230, 238–41, 313, 321
  see also War-e Tazigan
Khaneqin, 328
Khazar(s), 4, 19, 21, 23, 28, 31, 127, 139, 179,
  181, 199, 212, 223, 230–5, 291, 302, 304,
  306–309, 311–12, 314
  see also Turkic-Khazar(s), Turkic-Avar(s),
  Avar(s), Turkish, Gok Turk(s), Turkic,
  Ottoman(s), Tatar, Turkic-Hun, Hun(s),
  Turk(s), Hunnic, Uighur(s), Hsiang-Nou,
  Seljuk(s), Oghuz
Khvan-salar, 12
Khwarezm, 131, 205
Khwarezmian(s), 155
Khojand, 333
Khorad-Barzin, 215–17
Khorasan, 2–3, 14, 25–6, 94, 107, 117–19, 131,
  182, 191, 200–201, 203, 205–206, 209,
  212–13, 215–16, 219–20, 222, 235–7,
  332–5, 339, 350–1, 353
Khorasani, Abu Muslim, 334–5
Khorrazad, Farrokhzad, 326
Khorenatsi, Moses (Movses), 83, 131
Khorramabad, 227
Khosrow I Anoushirvan xiii, 4, 6, 12, 18–19,
  21–33, 35–7, 40, 73, 100, 106, 121, 123–5,
  134, 138–9, 141–4, 147–8, 164, 181–2,
  186, 188, 190–3, 207, 211–13, 230–1,
  233–7, 240–1, 248–9, 255–6, 262–5,

271–2, 280–1, 288, 290–1, 293, 299–300, 302, 304–305, 351

Khosrow II, xi, xiv, xvii, xxi, 9–10, 16–17, 25, 44–5, 54, 80, 86, 100, 103, 105, 107, 114, 118, 125, 133–4, 136, 139, 220–1, 241, 265–6, 280, 282, 285, 289, 291, 293–5, 298–300, 302, 304–306, 308–309, 311–14, 322, 324–5, 327, 348, 351

Khosrowgetai, 307

    see also Savaran, Asbaran, Dehkan(s), Akhshid, Afshin, Chakeran, Framandar-savaran, Savar-e Nezam Sangin Aslahe, Aswaran, Aswaran-sardar, Javidan, Var-thragh niyagan khodai, Savaran-e shamshir-zan-e dah-hezar, Pusht-aspan, Pushtighban, Pushtiban, Pushtighban-salar, Pushtighban-sardar, Hazarbod, Gund Shahanshah, Ham-harzan, Ham-harz, Hm-hrz, Jan-separan, jyanavspar, Janvespar, Jalinus, Pishmarg/Peshmarg, Savaran-e Khorasan, Sarhangan, Pirouzetai, Granikan-Salar

Khosrowshonum, 328

Khuzestan, 5, 137–8, 189–91, 215, 326, 328–9

Khud/Khod, 108

    see also Khwod, Miqfar, Spangenhelm(s), Ridge Helmet, Sarwar, Targ, Selsele aviz

Khwod, 90

    see also Khud/Khod, Miqfar, Spangenhelm(s), Ridge Helmet, Sarwar, Targ, Selsele aviz

Khworian, 272

Kidarite(s), 26, 194, 205–207, 212

Kitab ol Ayin, 167, 352–3

Klibanarios 74

    see also Klibanion, Cataphractus, Cataphractii, Clibanarius, Clibanarii, Griv, Pan, Gardaan-ban, Grivpan, Griv-ban/ Griw-ban, Tanur, Tanurig, Tanvar

Klibanion, 74

    see also Klibanarios, Cataphractus, Cataphractii, Clibanarius, Clibanarii, Griv, Pan, Gardaan-ban, Grivpan, Griv-ban/ Griw-ban, Tanur, Tanurig, Tanvar

Koi-Krylgan-Kala, 74

Kontos, 74, 79

    see also Fras, Arsht, Astr, Rumh, Nezak, Neyze, Neyze-daran, Javeliner(s), Javelin(s), Zhupin

Koos, 54–5

Kopis, 75–6

Koshti, 49

Kublai Khan, 246

Kufa, 240, 322, 334

Kuh-e Khwaja, 106

Kulagysh, 94, 117–18

Kulah, 279, 283

    see also Kustik, Kamar, Kamar-band, Afa-sar, Mah-sar, Sar, Shalvar, Mok, Mocak, Kafshak, Kapah, Pargoo, Kurtak

Kurd(s), 3, 22, 55, 181–2, 203, 204, 279, 339

Kurdish, 3, 22, 40, 55, 112, 114, 241

Kurdistan, 13, 203, 326, 328, 330

Kushan(s), 4, 21, 86–7, 154–5, 158, 194, 197, 202, 221–2, 280–1

    see also Saka Paradraya, Saka Haumaverga, Scythian(s), Saka(s), Alan(s), Sarmatian(s), Yueh-Chi

Kurtak, 283

    see also Kustik, Kamar, Kamar-band, Afa-sar, Mah-sar, Sar, Shalvar, Mok, Mocak, Kafshak, Kapah, Pargoo, Kulah

Kustik, 49, 282

    see also Kamar, Kamar-band, Kurtak, Afa-sar, Mah-sar, Sar, Shalvar, Mok, Mocak, Kafshak, Kapah, Pargoo, Kulah

Kushnavaz, 55, 134, 208–10, 212

Kut-Ilkhan, 308

Lakhmid(s), 30, 72, 116–17, 171–2, 241, 313–14, 321

    see also Wada'i, Arab(s), Bedouin(s), Ghassanid(s), Bani Sheiban, Bani Hanifah, Yemenite Arab(s)

Lamellar, 84, 109, 118, 122, 211, 347

    see also Mail, Scale armour, Gurdih, Pos/ Posh, Zreh, Zereh, Dir, Saqain, Jowshan, Gowshan

Lappet suspension system, xvii, 37, 59, 61–2, 102, 117–18, 123, 198, 210, 293–4, 310

    see also Shamsher, Safser, Tex, Sword(s), Broadsword(s), Two-handed sword(s), Shamsher-wazig, Fencing, Italian grip, Baldric hanging, Awestarag, Dar, Kamar, Kamar-band, Niyam, Sousser, Saif, Mintaqa, Goti, Scabbard (slide suspension), P-mount (system), Shap-sheraz/ Shamshirdar

Lashgare Ghalb, 163

Lashkar, 8, 163

    see also Spada, Spah, Sepah, Zor

Lazica, 5, 20, 123, 134, 271–2, 307

    see also Georgia, Iberia, Colchis

Leo I, 206

Leo Diaconus, 54

Letter of Tansar, 8, 35, 39, 286

Li-Shi-Min, 223

Libanius, 1, 38–9, 42–3, 60, 91–2, 127, 129, 131, 229

Liber de Caesaribus, 83
Limes, 229, 241
Louvre Museum (Paris), xv, 97, 101–102, 191
Lur(s), 50, 279
Luristan, 106, 227, 330, 339
Lycaonian(s), 172

Ma'adi Karab, 143
  see also Dhu Yazan, Sayf Bin Dhu Yazan
Mace(s), 32–3, 41, 47, 56, 68, 90, 105, 108–10,
  111, 117, 119, 122, 158, 166, 185, 204,
  275, 284, 291, 294, 328, 337, 356
  see also Gurz, Abdast, Tabar, Tabarzin,
  Tabarz/e/n, Chakosh, Warz/Wazr,
  Warz-wazig, Axe, Gauntlet, Hatchet
Macedonian, 77, 166
Macrinus, 125
Magi, xiii–xiv, 11, 17, 106, 164, 186, 189,
  273–4, 278–9, 286, 290–1, 294
  see also Mobadan Mobad, Mobad(s), Asronan,
  Herbadan, Dasturan, Dadwaran, Radan
Magind, 90
  see also Spar, Spar-wazig
Maginot (line/wall), 176, 230–2
Magister equitum praesentalis, 344–5
  see also Notitia Dignitatum, Equites sagittarri
  parthi iuniores, Equites sagittarri parthi
  seniores, Equites Persae clibanarii, Scola
  scutariorum clibanariorum, Numerus
  persoiustiniani, Numerus felicum
  persoarmeniorum, Magister militum per
  orientem, Vexillatio palatina
Magister militum per orientem, 174
  see also Notitia Dignitatum, Equites sagittarri
  parthi iuniores, Equites sagittarri parthi
  seniores, Equites Persae clibanarii, Scola
  scutariorum clibanariorum, Numerus
  persoiustiniani, Numerus felicum
  persoarmeniorum, Magister equitum
  praesentalis, Vexillatio palatina
Magnesia (Battle of, 190 BCE), 78
Mahdi (al-, Muhammad ibn Mansur), 335–7
Mah-sar, 283
  see also Afa-sar, Sar, Shalvar, Mok, Mocak,
  Kafshak, Kurtak, Kustik, Kamar,
  Kamar-band, Kapah, Pargoo, Kulah
Mahrod, 328
Mail, 83–4, 105, 118, 122, 211, 337, 347, 354–5
  see also Scale armour, Lamellar, Gurdih, Pos/
  Posh, Zreh, Zereh, Dir, Saqain, Jowshan,
  Gowshan
Malalas, 154, 155, 173
Malatzes, 264–5
Malayer, 330

Mamoun (Abu Jaafar Abdollah al-Mamoun ibn
  Harun), 339–40
Mangonel(s), 246, 257, 261, 337, 354–5
  see also Siege engine(s), Naft-andazan,
  Naffata, Ballistae, Catapult(s), Battering
  ram(s), Mobile tower(s), Darraga,
  Dabbabat, Xarak/Kharak, Testudo, Charx,
  Khaar-kaman, Kashkanjir, Manjeniq,
  Aradeh, Arrada, Aghrab(s), Rutaila,
  Scorpion(s), Scorpio, Hasak, Xasak
Manichean, 8
Manjeniq (*also* Manjaniq), 247–8, 251, 253
  see also Scorpion(s), Scorpio, Hasak, Xasak,
  Siege engine(s), Battering ram(s), Mobile
  tower(s), Darraga, Dabbabat, Xarak/
  Kharak, Testudo, Naft-andazan, Naffata,
  Charx, Kashkanjir, Khaar-kaman,
  Mangonel(s), Aradeh, Arrada, Aghrab(s),
  Rutaila, Ballistae, Catapult(s)
Manzar, 61
Maranga (Battle of, 22 June 363), 161, 179–80,
  184
Marathon (Battle of), xviii
Marco Polo, 52
Mard o Mard, 82, 274–7, 349–50
Marcus Aurelius Carus, 83, 277, 344, 350
Marcus Lucinius Crassus, 13, 52, 66, 151, 157,
  292
Mardin, 29
Marlik, 105, 107, 311
Marzban(s), 9, 14, 20, 25, 30, 114, 143, 168,
  215, 291, 318, 331
Masjed-e-Suleiman, 98
Massagetae, 75, 194, 237, 355
Massagatean, 74
Matigan e Hazar Datastan, 34
  see also Asabar Nipek
Maurice, 10, 39, 141, 162–3, 195, 215, 243,
  265–6, 269, 300, 348
Mazandaran, 60, 203, 236, 336
Mazdak, 23–4, 297
Mazdakism, 338, 343
Mazdakite, 23–4, 336, 342
Maziyar, 236, 340–1
Mecca, 317
Meccan, 316, 318
Mede(s), 3, 40, 57, 68, 78, 123, 127, 155, 194,
  204, 224, 230, 278–9
  see also Persian(s), Sagarthian(s)
Media, 2, 13, 77, 151
Media Atropatene, 3, 233, 300, 307
  see also Atropatene, Adurbaygan, Aturpatekan,
  Azerbaijan, Azarbaijan
Median, 224, 295

Medina, 113, 138, 317–18, 327
Mediterranean, 138, 266
Medo-Persian, 87, 94, 106, 274
Meel, 47
Mehertane, 356
Mehran (house of), 209
Mehran (general during Arabo-Islamic
    conquests), 325–8
Mehr-Mihroe, 271–2
Mehr-Narseh, 10, 117
Mehr-Yasht, 60
Mehregan, 21, 34, 293
    see also Mithra
Menandor Protector, 193
Menog-e Xrad, 56, 113, 286, 289
Merv, 3–4, 9, 27, 64, 203, 208, 235, 334–5
Mesopotamia, xvii, 4–5, 24, 28, 30, 93, 134,
    137, 142, 155, 190, 203, 238–9, 266,
    301–302, 309, 314, 321–2, 325, 329, 332
Mesopotamian, 24–5, 27, 29, 73, 141, 178, 184,
    215
Metropolitan Museum of Art, xv–xvi, 98
Meymane-ye sepah, 162
    see also Meysare-ye sepah, Qalb-e sepah
Meysare-ye sepah, 162
    see also Meymane-ye sepah, Qalb-e sepah
Middle East, 26, 184, 266, 336, 356
    see also Near East
Middle Persian, xxii–xxiii, 12, 15–16, 22, 46,
    62, 69, 89–90, 186, 192, 241, 245, 286, 351
    see also Pahlavi, Parthian Pahlavi, Sassanian
    Pahlavi, New Persian
Mintaqa, 108
    see also Shamsher, Safser, Sword(s),
    Broadsword(s), Two-handed sword(s),
    Shamsher-wazig, Fencing, Italian grip,
    Baldric hanging, Awestarag, Dar, Kamar,
    Kamar-band, Niyam, Sousser, Saif, Tex,
    Goti, Scabbard (slide suspension), Lappet
    suspension system, P-mount (system),
    Shap-sheraz/Shamshirdar
Miqfar, 108
    see also Khwod, Khud/Khod, Spangenhelm(s),
    Ridge Helmet, Sarwar, Targ, Selsele aviz
Mirmillos, 122, 254
    see also Paighan, Paighan-salar, Payik
Mithra, 21, 34, 106, 273–4, 283, 293–6
    see also Mehregan
Mithradates I, 294
Mithradates III, 294
Mithraism, 343
Misiche (Battle of, 244 CE), 152–6, 159
    see also Peroz Shapur
Moad, Yahya bin, 339

Mobad(s), 17–18, 25–6, 147, 164, 188, 212,
    273–4, 284, 294–5
    see also Mobadan mobad, Magi, Asronan,
    Herbadan, Dasturan, Dadwaran, Radan
Mobadan mobad, 15, 17, 273, 291
    see also Mobad(s), Magi, Asronan, Herbadan,
    Dasturan, Dadwaran, Radan
Mobile tower(s), 249–50
    see also Darraga, Dabbabat, Xarak/Kharak,
    Testudo, Aghrab(s), Rutaila, Siege
    engine(s), Naft-andazan, Naffata, Charx,
    Kashkanjir, Khaar-kaman, Mangonel(s),
    Manjeniq, Aradeh, Arrada, Ballistae,
    Catapult(s), Battering ram(s), Scorpio,
    Scorpion(s), Hasak, Xasak
Mocak, 283
    see also Afa-sar, Mah-sar, Sar, Shalvar, Mok,
    Kafshak, Kurtak, Kustik, Kamar,
    Kamar-band, Kapah, Pargoo, Kulah
Mohammad (prophet), 317–20, 351, 353
Mok, 283
    see also Afa-sar, Mah-sar, Sar, Shalvar, Mocak,
    Kafshak, Kurtak, Kustik, Kamar,
    Kamar-band, Kapah, Pargoo, Kulah
Mongol(s), 33, 52, 152, 195–6, 198–9, 277, 342
Mongolian, 195, 356
Mongolian draw, 64, 118, 195, 310
Motassem (al-), 340, 356
Mug castle *see* Abargar castle
Muqanna, (Hisham bin Hakim), 332, 335
Museum für Islamische Kunst (Museum for
    Islamic Art), xv–xvi, 292
Muslim(s), 317–18, 320–1, 336–7, 343, 350–3,
    355
Mygdonius River, 251, 259–60

Naal, 109
    see also Asb, Raksh, Tagavar, Zin, Zin-e
    Khadang, Setam, Zarrin Setam, Fetrak,
    Enan, Taziyane
Naan, 183
    see also Nagara
Naan-e-sangak
    see also Naan, Nagara
Nackchevan, 307
Nabed (Nabades), 70–1
Nader Shah, 22, 119, 137
Naffata, 253
    see also Naft-andazan , Siege engine(s),
    Kashkanjir, Ballistae, Catapult(s), Battering
    ram(s), Mobile tower(s), Darraga,
    Dabbabat, Xarak/Kharak, Testudo,
    Khaar-kaman, Charx, Mangonel(s),

Manjeniq, Aradeh, Arrada, Aghrab(s),
    Rutaila, Scorpion(s), Scorpio, Hasak, Xasak
Naft-andazan, (sing. Naft-andaz), 217, 253
    see also Naffata, Siege engine(s), Kashkanjir,
    Ballistae, Catapult(s), Battering ram(s),
    Mobile tower(s), Darraga, Dabbabat,
    Xarak/Kharak, Testudo, Khaar-kaman,
    Charx, Mangonel(s), Manjeniq, Aradeh,
    Arrada, Aghrab(s), Rutaila, Scorpion(s),
    Scorpio, Hasak, Xasak
Nagara, (ancient Persian bread), 183
    see also Naan, Naan-e-sangak
Nagara, (Mongol battle drum) 199
    see also Nakar, Naqareh
Nagshe Rajab, xv, 17–18, 87, 279
Nagshe Rustam, xiii–xiv, xix, 17, 82–3, 85–6,
    89, 101, 153–4, 156, 158, 277, 279, 350
Nahavand (Battle of, 651 CE), 312, 325,
    329–31, 355
Nahrewan canal, 299
Nakar, 52, 199
    see also Nagara, Naqareh
Nakhirzan, 325–6
Narde-Gushnasp, 216
Narseh (Narses), xiv, 6, 17, 158–9, 287, 295
Narses (brother of Bahram V Gur), 203
Narses (Romano-Byzantine general during
    reign of Khosrow I), 192, 345
Narses (Romano-Byzantine general during
    reign of Khosrow II), 265
National Museum of Iran, xv–xvi, 60, 79, 95,
    101, 107, 291, 274
Navbad, 138
    see also Kashtig/Kashti, Balanj, Bandar, Bar,
    Daftar, Dunij, Didban, Rah-nameh,
    Nav-khoda
Nav-khoda, 138
    see also Kashtig/Kashti, Navbad, Balanj,
    Bandar, Bar, Daftar, Didban, Dunij,
    Rah-nameh
Nawak, 62, 319
    see also Tir/Tigr, Tir-wazig, Tirbad, Archery,
    Horse archery, Horse archer(s), Kaman,
    Kamam, Kamandan, Qaba, Tirdan, Kantir/
    Kantigr, Zeh/Zih, Zeh e yadaki, Gorytos,
    Watarain, Shivatir-e zrehbaran, Shiva-tir
Nawreseda-jawanan, 38, 41–2
Naxarar(s) 7, 72, 114–16, 134, 220–2, 238, 276,
    280, 286, 306, 309, 344, 350
Nazareth, 267
Near East, 59, 61, 79, 121, 155, 157, 183, 233,
    245, 265, 304, 307, 321
    see also Middle East
Near Eastern, 66, 84, 230, 296

Negan, 129
    see also Gordafarid (of the Shahname epic),
    Apranik, Azadeh Dailam, Banu
    (Khorramdin), Amazon(s)
Nehemiah ben Hushiel, 266–7
Nemruz-spahbod, 24
Neshan, xxi, 282
Neshastegan, 241
Nev-Shapur, 191, 206, 216, 238
    see also Nishabur
New-ardaxshir, 40
New Persian, 106
    see also Middle Persian, Pahlavi, Parthian
    Pahlavi, Sassanian Pahlavi,
Ney, 54
Neyze-daran 79–80, 120–1, 123–4, 297
    see also Arsht, Kontos, Fras, Astr, Nezak,
    Neyze, Rumh, Javeliner(s), Javelin(s),
    Zhupin
Neyze, 80, 108
    see also Arsht, Kontos, Fras, Astr, Nezak,
    Neyze-daran, Rumh, Javeliner(s), Javelin(s),
    Zhupin
Nezak, 79–80
    see also Arsht, Kontos, Fras, Astr,
    Neyze-daran, Neyze, Rumh, Javeliner(s),
    Javelin(s), Zhupin
Nibard, 9
    see also Ardig, Karezar, Jang, Pad-razm,
    Zambag, Paykar
Nicetas, 304
Nihavand, 101
Nikephorus Phocas, 347
Nineveh, 309, 311
Nisean, 159
Nishabur, 27, 206, 335
    see also Nev-Shapur
Nisibis, 4, 28–9, 124, 146, 152, 157, 190,
    230–1, 245, 247–8, 263, 300
Nisibis (Battle of, 217 CE), 125
Nisibis (siege of, c.337 or 338 CE), 131, 201,
    251, 259, 302
Nisibis (siege of, 350 CE), 122, 131–2, 136–7,
    247, 251–2, 254–5, 259–60
Nihayat al S'ul, 352–3
Nizami Ganjavi, xix
    see also Iskandarname
North Africa, 192, 332
Notitia Dignitatum, 73, 344
    see also Equites sagittarri parthi seniores,
    Equites sagittarri parthi iuniores, Equites
    Persae clibanarii, Scola scutariorum
    clibanariorum, Numerus persoiustiniani,
    Numerus felicum persoarmeniorum,

Magister equitum praesentalis, Magister militum per orientem, Vexillatio palatina
Nowruz, 21, 34, 293, 348
Nran, 94
   see also Celan, Akenakes, Tour, Dagger(s), Dasnag, Kard
Numan, 177, 330–1
Nu'man III, 313
Numerus felicum persoarmeniorum, 116
   see also Notitia Dignitatum, Magister equitum praesentalis, Magister militum per orientem, Equites sagittarri parthi seniores, Equites sagittarri parthi iuniores, Equites Persae clibanarii, Numerus persoiustiniani, Scola scutariorum clibanariorum, Vexillatio palatina
Numerus persoiustiniani, 346–7, 349
   see also Notitia Dignitatum, Magister equitum praesentalis, Magister militum per orientem, Equites sagittarri parthi seniores, Equites sagittarri parthi iuniores, Equites Persae clibanarii, Numerus felicum persoarmeniorum, Scola scutariorum clibanariorum, Vexillatio palatina
Nysa, 203

Odenathus, 151, 157–8
Oman, 318
Omar, bin al-Khattab al-Faruq, 303, 313, 320–2, 327, 331
Oracula Sibyllina, 152, 156
Orontes River, 264
Ossetian, 283
Ostrogoth(s), 192
   see also Visigoth(s), Gothic, Goth(s), Germania, Germanic, German(s), Germany
Ottoman(s), 49–50, 52–3, 55, 176, 181, 203, 288, 355–6
Ottoman empire, 22, 181, 355
Oxus River, 74, 204–205, 220

P-mount (system), 101–103, 117, 210, 212, 293–4, 310
   see also Shamsher, Safser, Tex, Sword(s), Broadsword(s), Two-handed sword(s), Shamsher-wazig, Fencing, Italian grip, Baldric hanging, Awestarag, Dar, Kamar, Kamar-band, Niyam, Sousser, Saif, Mintaqa, Goti, Scabbard (slide suspension), Lappet suspension system, Shap-sheraz/Shamshirdar
Pa zadan, 48
Pacific Ocean, 138

Pad-razm, 9
   see also Ardig, Karezar, Jang, Nibard, Zambag, Paykar
Pahlavan(s), xxiii, 12, 41, 46–50, 169, 182, 205, 216–19, 274–5, 286–90, 349, 353–4
   see also Yalan-yalbod
Pahlavi xii, 8–9, 12, 15, 46, 111, 113, 128, 140, 162, 167, 186, 192, 240–1, 337, 350–2
   see also Middle Persian, Parthian Pahlavi, Sassanian Pahlavi, New Persian
Paighan, xxii, 120–4, 144, 210, 254, 262, 297
   see also Paighan-salar, Payik, Mirmillos
Paighan-salar, xxii, 15, 120–2
   see also Paighan, Payik, Mirmillos
Pakistan, 138
Palestine, 266–7, 304–306, 315
Palestinian, 266
Palmyra, 151, 157, 348–9
Palmyran(s), 94, 157–8, 349
Pamir (mountains), 332
Panjagan, 62, 354–5
   see also Sanwar, Dron
Panjikent, 109, 117–18, 285, 333
Pannonia, 156, 344
Pargoo, 283
   see also Kustik, Kamar, Kamar-band, Afa-sar, Mah-sar, Sar, Shalvar, Mok, Mocak, Kafshak, Kurtak, Kapah, Kulah
Parthia, 2, 77, 190
Parthian(s) xi–xiii, xvii, 3–7, 9, 13, 16, 22, 26, 34, 38, 51–4, 57, 59, 61, 66, 68, 72, 74, 76–89, 95–6, 99, 103, 106, 115, 120, 125, 127, 129–30, 145, 149–52, 154, 156–7, 160–1, 168, 194, 197, 229, 233, 236, 238, 243, 255–6, 267, 274, 277–9, 281, 284–5, 292, 294, 298, 300, 338, 344, 349, 355
   see also Arsacids, Parthia, Parthian dynasty, Parthian Empire, Ashkan
Parthian dynasty, 3, 5, 20, 72, 295
   see also Arsacids, Parthia, Parthian(s), Parthian Empire, Ashkan
Parthian Empire, xix, 294
   see also Arsacid(s), Parthia, Parthian(s), Parthian dynasty, Ashkan
Parthian Pahlavi, xv, 3, 7
   see also Middle Persian, Pahlavi, Sassanian Pahlavi, New Persian
Parthian shot, 65, 68–9, 79, 118, 160
Pax Perpetuum, 192
Pazyryk, 88
Pazyryk carpet, 281
Paygospan, 14, 25
Payik, 121
   see also Paighan, Mirmillos, Paighan-salar

Paykar, 9
 see also Ardig, Karezar, Jang, Pad-razm,
   Nibard, Zambag
Pedan, 90
Peroz Shapur, 153
 see also Misiche (battle of, 244 CE)
Persepolis, xx, xxi, 87, 97, 186, 279, 327
 see also Persepolis graffiti
Persepolis, graffiti, 97, 279
 see also Persepolis
Persia, 6, 15, 20–1, 26, 36, 40, 43, 48–9, 56,
   74–5, 91, 93, 96, 98–9, 107, 123, 125, 129,
   132, 135, 143, 151, 161, 178, 180, 184,
   186, 192, 199, 201, 223, 228–9, 238, 267,
   279, 282, 287, 295, 313, 316, 323, 327,
   329–31, 333, 335–8, 340, 351
Persian(s), xii–xiii, xix, xxi–xxii, 2–3, 20–1, 26,
   38, 43–5, 51, 55, 58, 66, 68–9, 70–1, 73,
   76, 91, 110, 113, 115–16, 128–9, 131,
   137–8, 146, 151, 154–7, 160, 168, 173–4,
   178, 180, 183, 186, 192, 195, 209, 213,
   232, 234, 237, 240–1, 246, 250, 264, 267,
   270, 275, 278, 281, 283, 285–7, 292, 295,
   298, 305, 310–11, 321–3, 326, 330, 332,
   338, 342, 345–50, 352–4, 356
 see also Mede(s), Sagarthian(s)
Persian Empire, xix, 2, 14, 24, 336
 see also Achaemenid Empire
Persian Gulf, 5, 24, 30–1, 113, 120, 123, 126,
   137–43, 149, 212, 225, 238, 240, 329
Persis, 3, 13, 84, 113, 151, 190, 285, 295, 328–9
Perso-Armenia, 27–30, 114, 347
 see also Armenia
Peter (body guard of Justinian), 172–3
Peteyak, 169–70
Petra, 139, 234, 247
Petra (siege of, 541 CE), 255, 271
Petra (siege of, 551 CE), 269, 271–2
Phalanx, 77, 162–3
Pharas, 169–70
Phocas, 265–6
Pil, 137
 see also Pil-savaran, Fil, Shatranj, Elephant(s)
Pil-savaran, 129
 see also Pil, Fil, Elephant(s)
Pishmarg/Peshmarg, 114, 241
 see also Savaran, Dehkan(s), Akhshid, Afshin,
   Chakeran, Framandar-savaran, Asbaran,
   Aswaran, Aswaran-sardar, Savar-e Nezam
   Sangin Aslahe, Javidan, Var-thragh niyagan
   khodai, Savaran-e shamshir-zan-e
   dah-hezar, Pushtighban, Pushtiban,
   Pusht-aspan, Pushtighban-salar,
   Pushtighban-sardar, Hazarbod, Gund

Shahanshah, Ham-harzan, Ham-harz,
   Hm-hrz, Jan-separan, Jyanavspar,
   Janvespar, Jalinus, Savaran-e Khorasan,
   Sarhangan, Pirouzetai, Khosrowgetai,
   Granikan-Salar
Pilaxan, 127–8
 see also Slinger(s), Sling
Pirouz, xvi, 31, 45, 55, 72, 85, 134, 174, 201,
   205–12, 220, 222, 235, 237, 280–1, 291,
   299
Pirouz III, 332–3
Pirouz-dokht, 209
Pirouzetai, 307
 see also Savaran, Asbaran, Dehkan(s), Akhshid,
   Afshin, Chakeran, Framandar-savaran,
   Savar-e Nezam Sangin Aslahe, Aswaran,
   Aswaran-sardar, Javidan, Var-thragh
   niyagan khodai, Savaran-e shamshir-zan-e
   dah-hezar, Pusht-aspan, Pushtighban,
   Pushtiban, Pushtighban-salar,
   Pushtighban-sardar, Hazarbod, Gund
   Shahanshah, Ham-harzan, Ham-harz,
   Hm-hrz, Jan-separan, jyanavspar,
   Janvespar, Jalinus, Pishmarg/Peshmarg,
   Savaran-e Khorasan, Sarhangan,
   Khosrowgetai, Granikan-Salar
Pirouz Shapur, 153
Plutarch, 51
Podosaces, 178
Pole(s), 52
Polo, 38, 40, 42–3, 348
 see also Chaugan-wazig
Polybius, 78
Pontus, 4
Pos/Posh, 90
 see also Mail, Lamellar, Scale armour, Gurdih,
   Zreh, Zereh, Dir, Saqain, Jowshan,
   Gowshan
Praetorian Guard, 190
Praetorian prefect, 152, 156
Przewalski Horse, 196
Procopius, 56, 66, 68, 70–1, 103, 121, 124–5,
   143, 148, 162, 164, 168–70, 172–4, 178,
   187–8, 208–209, 245, 250, 263–4, 346–7,
   349–50
Publius Crassus, 53
Punjab, 131
Pur-e Vahman, xvi–xvii, 64, 68, 118–19, 282,
   292, 310
Pusht-aspan, 112
 see also Savaran, Asbaran, Dehkan(s), Akhshid,
   Afshin, Chakeran, Framandar-savaran,
   Aswaran, Aswaran-sardar, Javidan,
   Var-thragh niyagan khodai, Savar-e Nezam

Sangin Aslahe, Savaran-e shamshir-zan-e
dah-hezar, Pushtighban, Pushtiban,
Pushtighban-salar, Pushtighban-sardar,
Hazarbod, Gund Shahanshah,
Ham-harzan, Ham-harz, Hm-hrz,
Jan-separan, jyanavspar, Janvespar, Jalinus,
Pishmarg/Peshmarg, Savaran-e Khorasan,
Sarhangan, Pirouzetai, Khosrowgetai,
Granikan-Salar
Pushtiban, 112
see also Savaran, Asbaran, Dehkan(s), Akhshid,
Afshin, Chakeran, Framandar-savaran,
Aswaran, Aswaran-sardar, Javidan,
Var-thragh niyagan khodai, Savar-e Nezam
Sangin Aslahe, Savaran-e shamshir-zan-e
dah-hezar, Pushtighban, Pusht-aspan,
Pushtighban-salar, Pushtighban-sardar,
Hazarbod, Gund Shahanshah,
Ham-harzan, Ham-harz, Hm-hrz,
Jan-separan, jyanavspar, Janvespar, Jalinus,
Pishmarg/Peshmarg, Savaran-e Khorasan,
Sarhangan, Pirouzetai, Khosrowgetai,
Granikan-Salar
Pushtighban, 15, 112–13, 203, 288
see also Savaran, Asbaran, Framandar-savaran,
Aswaran, Aswaran-sardar, Javidan,
Var-thragh niyagan khodai, Dehkan(s),
Akhshid, Afshin, Chakeran, Savar-e Nezam
Sangin Aslahe, Savaran-e shamshir-zan-e
dah-hezar, Pushtiban, Pusht-aspan,
Pushtighban-salar, Pushtighban-sardar,
Hazarbod, Gund Shahanshah,
Ham-harzan, Ham-harz, Hm-hrz,
Jan-separan, jyanavspar, Janvespar, Jalinus,
Pishmarg/Peshmarg, Savaran-e Khorasan,
Sarhangan, Pirouzetai, Khosrowgetai,
Granikan-Salar
Pushtighban-salar, 112
see also Savaran, Asbaran, Dehkan(s), Akhshid,
Afshin, Chakeran, Framandar-savaran,
Aswaran, Aswaran-sardar, Javidan,
Var-thragh niyagan khodai, Savar-e Nezam
Sangin Aslahe, Savaran-e shamshir-zan-e
dah-hezar, Pushtighban, Pushtiban,
Pusht-aspan, Pushtighban-sardar,
Hazarbod, Gund Shahanshah,
Ham-harzan, Ham-harz, Hm-hrz,
Jan-separan, jyanavspar, Janvespar, Jalinus,
Pishmarg/Peshmarg, Savaran-e Khorasan,
Sarhangan, Pirouzetai, Khosrowgetai,
Granikan-Salar
Pushtighban-sardar, 112
see also Savaran, Asbaran, Dehkan(s), Akhshid,
Afshin, Chakeran, Framandar-savaran,

Aswaran, Aswaran-sardar, Javidan,
Var-thragh niyagan khodai, Savar-e Nezam
Sangin Aslahe, Savaran-e shamshir-zan-e
dah-hezar, Pushtighban, Pushtiban,
Pusht-aspan, Pushtighban-salar, Hazarbod,
Gund Shahanshah, Ham-harzan,
Ham-harz, Hm-hrz, Jan-separan,
jyanavspar, Janvespar, Jalinus, Pishmarg/
Peshmarg, Savaran-e Khorasan, Sarhangan,
Pirouzetai, Khosrowgetai, Granikan-Salar
Pyro-techniques, 253, 256

Qadissiyah (Battle of, 637 CE), 21, 63, 116,
135–6, 146, 164, 177, 285, 318–20, 322–6,
344
Qajar(s), xx–xxi, 140, 299
Qalb-e sepah, 162
see also Meymane-ye sepah, Meysare-ye sepah
Qasr-e Shirin, 225
Qizil, 281
Qizilbash, 181, 288, 343
Qodum, 51
Qom, 339
Qudays (fort of), 323
Quintus Curtius Rufus, 130, 278, 295
Quraysh, 317

Radan, 290
see also Mobadan Mobad, Mobad(s), Magi,
Asronan, Dadwaran, Herbadan, Dasturan
Rafi bin Laith, 335
Raftarnameye Anoushirvan, 19
Rah-nameh, 138
see also Kashtig/Kashti, Navbad, Balanj,
Bandar, Bar, Daftar, Didban, Dunij,
Nav-khoda
Rajjala-rumah, 319
Raksh 109
see also Asb, Tagavar, Zin, Zin-e Khadang,
Fetrak, Setam, Zarrin Setam, Enan, Naal,
Taziyane
Ran-ban, 90
Rang, 285
see also Epaulettes
Rasmiozan, 299
Ravenna, 278–9, 347
Rayy, 13, 16, 186, 214, 221, 305, 328, 331, 336,
339
see also Tehran
Razutis, 126, 309
Rema, 260
Republic of Azerbaijan, 3–4, 20, 28, 139, 232,
253, 260, 309, 368
see also Albania, Arran

Resaina, 130
Rev Ardashir, 138
Reza Abbasi Museum, xv
Rhesaina, 153
Rhodes (siege of, 1522), 67–8
Rhodos (Rhodes), 139
Ridge Helmet, 84, 121
  see also Spangenhelm(s), Khwod, Khud/Khod,
    Miqfar, Sarwar, Targ, Selsele aviz
Romano-Byzantine(s), xviii, 4–6, 10, 16–19,
    23–4, 26, 28–31, 34, 36, 39–40, 43–4, 48,
    54, 60, 63–5, 68–72, 89, 100, 114–15,
    123–4, 126, 139, 141–50, 156, 164–5,
    168–74, 176, 184, 188, 190, 192–3, 195,
    197–9, 201, 206, 211–16, 220, 222–3,
    229–31, 234, 237, 241, 243, 246, 248–9,
    256–7, 263–4, 265–6, 268, 271–3, 286,
    288–9, 298–300, 302–309, 311–13, 315,
    318–20, 322, 344–8, 352
  see also Rome, Roman(s), Roman Empire,
    Byzantine(s), Byzantine Empire, Byzantium
Rome, xix, 2, 4–5, 15, 18, 25, 42, 79, 130–1,
    149–50, 154–5, 158–60, 164, 168, 184,
    202, 291, 298, 344–5
  see also Roman(s), Roman Empire, Romano-
    Byzantine(s), Byzantine(s), Byzantine
    Empire, Byzantium
Roman(s), xi, xvii–xviii, xxi, 1–6, 13–15, 20–1,
    28, 30, 38–9, 42, 50, 52–3, 57, 59, 64–6,
    69–71, 73, 78–9, 81, 83–4, 90–2, 95, 98–9,
    103, 110, 116, 121–7, 129–33, 139, 142,
    145–7, 149–62, 165, 168–9, 173, 177–81,
    183–4, 186, 190, 192, 194–5, 201, 211,
    224, 226, 229–30, 232, 234, 237, 239,
    243–5, 247–52, 254–62, 267–71, 274, 277,
    279, 284, 287, 289, 291, 295, 298,
    300–303, 310–11, 314, 344–50
  see also Rome, Roman Empire, Romano-
    Byzantine(s), Byzantine(s), Byzantine
    Empire, Byzantium
Roman Empire, xxi, 5, 14, 155, 161, 259, 346
  see also Rome, Roman(s), Romano-
    Byzantine(s), Byzantine(s), Byzantine
    Empire, Byzantium
Romance of Ardashir, 43, 57
Romisch-Germanisches Zentral Museum, xv,
    107, 311
Roozbeh (son of Marzban) see Salman Farsi (the
    Persian)
Royal banquet, 291–2
Royal hunt, 125, 291–2
Royal Museums of Art and History-Iranian
    Collection, xv
Rozyaneh, 33

Rumania, 156
Rumh, 108
  see also Arsht, Kontos, Fras, Astr,
    Neyze-daran, Neyze, Nezak, Javeliner(s),
    Javelin(s), Zhupin
Russia, 180, 233, 287, 299
Russian(s), xx, 3, 20–1, 24, 28, 287, 299
Rustam (of the Shahname epic), 44, 46–7, 109,
    163, 166–7, 175
Rustam Farrokhzad, 9, 135–6, 164, 322–6
Rutaila, 253
  see also Scorpion(s), Scorpio, Hasak, Xasak,
    Aghrab(s), Siege engine(s), Naft-andazan,
    Naffata, Charx, Kashkanjir, Khaar-kaman,
    Mangonel(s), Manjeniq, Aradeh, Arrada,
    Ballistae, Catapult(s), Battering ram(s),
    Mobile tower(s), Darraga, Dabbabat,
    Xarak/Kharak, Testudo
Ruyeen-ney, 54

Saad, 325
Saam (of the Shahname epic), 45, 56
  see also Kereshaspa
Sabdiz, xiv
Sabir(s), 21, 272
Safavid(s), 46, 49–50, 52, 55, 57, 176, 181–2,
    200, 203, 288, 342
Safavid dynasty, 22
Safser, 90
  see also Shamsher, Sword(s), Broadsword(s),
    Two-handed sword(s), Shamsher-wazig,
    Fencing, Italian grip, Baldric hanging,
    Awestarag, Dar, Tex, Kamar, Kamar-band,
    Niyam, Sousser, Saif, Mintaqa, Goti,
    Scabbard (slide suspension), Lappet
    suspension system, P-mount (system),
    Shap-sheraz/Shamshirdar
Sagarthian(s), 46, 110
  see also Mede(s), Persian(s)
Sage-ye sepah, 165
Saif, 108
  see also Shamsher, Sword(s), Broadsword(s),
    Two-handed sword(s), Fencing, Italian
    grip, Baldric hanging, Shamsher-wazig,
    Safser, Awestarag, Dar, Tex, Kamar,
    Kamar-band, Niyam, Sousser, Mintaqa,
    Goti, Scabbard (slide suspension), Lappet
    suspension system, P-mount (system),
    Shap-sheraz/Shamshirdar
Saka(s), 22, 75–7, 88, 94, 110, 194, 260–1, 277,
    350
  see also Saka Paradraya, Saka Haumaverga,
    Scythian(s), Alan(s), Sarmatian(s),
    Yueh-Chi, Kushan(s)

Saka Haumaverga, 76
  see also Saka Paradraya, Saka(s), Scythian(s),
    Alan(s), Sarmatian(s), Yueh-Chi, Kushan(s)
Saka Paradraya, 68, 75, 87, 94
  see also Saka(s), Saka Haumaverga,
    Scythian(s), Alan(s), Sarmatian(s),
    Yueh-Chi, Kushan(s)
Saka-istan, 2, 13
  see also Seistan, Seistan-Baluchistan
Saka-istani(s), 127
Salamis (Battle of), xix
Salar, 12
Sallust, 78
Salman Farsi (the Persian), 318, 350, 353, 355
Salmas, 279
Samanid dynasty, xxiii, 335
Samara, 340, 342
Samarqand, 52, 109, 117–18, 220, 334–5
Samos, 139
Samostasa, 177
Sanaa, 143
Sanam fortress, 335
Sang, 47
Sang-i-ban, 344
Sanwar, 69
  see also Dron, Panjagan
Saqain, 108
  see also Mail, Lamellar, Scale armour, Gurdih,
    Zreh, Zereh, Dir, Pos/Posh, Jowshan,
    Gowshan
Sar, 283
  see also Afa-sar, Mah-sar, Shalvar, Mok,
    Mocak, Kafshak, Kurtak, Kustik, Kamar,
    Kamar-band, Kapah, Pargoo, Kulah
Sarcophagus of Helena, 83
Sar Mashad, xv, 45, 291
Sarkhastan, 236
Sarpol-e Zahab, 79, 88
Sarcophagus of Klazomenai, 76
Sari, 60, 291
Sarmatian(s), xxiii, 81–2, 84–7, 94, 128, 153–4,
    188, 277–8
  see also Alan(s), Scythians, Saka, Saka
    Paradraya, Saka Haumaverga, Yueh-Chi,
    Kushan(s)
Sardar(s), 19, 40, 70, 235
Sardasht, 40
Sarhang, 9
Sarhangan, 32, 313
  see also Asbaran, Dehkan(s), Akhshid, Afshin,
    Chakeran, Framandar-savaran, Savar-e
    Nezam Sangin Aslahe, Aswaran,
    Aswaran-sardar, Javidan, Var-thragh
    niyagan khodai, Savaran-e shamshir-zan-e

dah-hezar, Pusht-aspan, Pushtighban,
    Pushtiban, Pushtighban-salar,
    Pushtighban-sardar, Hazarbod, Gund
Shahanshah, Ham-harzan, Ham-harz,
    Hm-hrz, Jan-separan, jyanavspar,
    Janvespar, Jalinus, Pishmarg/Peshmarg,
    Savaran-e Khorasan, Savaran, Pirouzetai,
    Khosrowgetai, Granikan-Salar
Sari, 235
Sarlashkaran, 32
Sarwar, 90
  see also Spangenhelm(s), Ridge Helmet,
    Khwod, Khud/Khod, Miqfar, Targ, Selsele
    aviz
Sassan (grandfather of Ardashir I), 295
Sassanian(s), xi–xxiii, 1–30, 32–5, 37–50,
    52–74, 76–7, 79–87, 89–95, 97–8, 100–18,
    120–48, 150–64, 166–218, 220–333,
    336–8, 341, 343–56
Sassanian dynasty, xvii–xviii, 2–4, 10, 15–16,
    43, 87, 112, 123, 139, 188, 237, 278,
    297–8, 332, 338
Sassanian Empire, 1–7, 9–10, 17, 19, 23, 25,
    27–30, 33, 35, 39, 72, 92, 114, 116, 126,
    129, 143, 147, 150, 152, 177–8, 182, 184,
    186, 190, 193, 195, 200–201, 209, 212–14,
    221–4, 230, 233–4, 238–41, 246, 259,
    265–8, 270, 272, 280, 282, 288–9, 297–8,
    302–305, 307–308, 312, 314–16, 318,
    320–2, 328, 332, 341, 343–4, 351, 356
  see also Eire-an, Eiran-Shahr
Sassanian Pahlavi, xv, xxii, 7, 49, 55, 74, 80, 283
  see also Middle Persian, Pahlavi, Parthian
    Pahlavi, New Persian
Satala (Battle of, 298 CE), 159
Savaran, 9, 15, 17–18, 21, 24–5, 39–41, 47–8,
    53, 57, 59, 65, 68, 70, 72, 74, 77, 80, 89,
    91, 96, 98–100, 105, 108–14, 116–19,
    121–7, 131–5, 137, 144–7, 149–51,
    153–64, 166, 168–73, 178–80, 185, 191,
    194, 196–9, 201–204, 206, 209–12,
    215–18, 220–2, 229, 237–9, 243–4, 248,
    250, 254–5, 259–63, 265–6, 269, 271–2,
    274, 277, 283, 286, 288, 298, 300–301,
    303, 306–307, 309, 311–14, 318, 322–5,
    327–8, 330–1, 337, 344–8, 350–1, 353–4
  see also Asbaran, Dehkan(s), Akhshid, Afshin,
    Chakeran, Framandar-savaran, Savar-e
    Nezam Sangin Aslahe, Aswaran,
    Aswaran-sardar, Javidan, Var-thragh
    niyagan khodai, Savaran-e shamshir-zan-e
    dah-hezar, Pusht-aspan, Pushtighban,
    Pushtiban, Pushtighban-salar,
    Pushtighban-sardar, Hazarbod, Gund

Shahanshah, Ham-harzan, Ham-harz,
    Hm-hrz, Jan-separan, jyanavspar,
    Janvespar, Jalinus, Pishmarg/Peshmarg,
    Savaran-e Khorasan, Sarhangan,
    Pirouzetai, Khosrowgetai, Granikan-Salar
Savaran-e Khorasan, 117, 119, 219
    see also Savaran, Asbaran, Dehkan(s), Akhshid,
    Afshin, Chakeran, Framandar-savaran,
    Aswaran, Aswaran-sardar, Javidan,
    Var-thragh niyagan khodai, Savaran-e
    shamshir-zan-e dah-hezar, Pusht-aspan,
    Pushtighban, Pushtiban, Pushtighban-salar,
    Pushtighban-sardar, Hazarbod, Gund
    Shahanshah, Ham-harzan, Ham-harz,
    Hm-hrz, Jan-separan, jyanavspar,
    Janvespar, Jalinus, Pishmarg/Peshmarg,
    Savar-e Nezam Sangin Aslahe, Sarhangan,
    Pirouzetai, Khosrowgetai, Granikan-Salar
Savar-e Nezam Sangin Aslahe, 72
    see also Savaran, Asbaran, Dehkan(s), Akhshid,
    Afshin, Chakeran, Framandar-savaran,
    Aswaran, Aswaran-sardar, Javidan,
    Var-thragh niyagan khodai, Savaran-e
    shamshir-zan-e dah-hezar, Pusht-aspan,
    Pushtighban, Pushtiban, Pushtighban-salar,
    Pushtighban-sardar, Hazarbod, Gund
    Shahanshah, Ham-harzan, Ham-harz,
    Hm-hrz, Jan-separan, jyanavspar,
    Janvespar, Jalinus, Pishmarg/Peshmarg,
    Savaran-e Khorasan, Sarhangan,
    Pirouzetai, Khosrowgetai, Granikan-Salar
Sayf Bin Dhu Yazan, 139, 142–3
    see also Dhu Yazan, Ma'adi Karab
Sayyar, Nasr bin, 334
Scabbard (slide suspension), xvii, 37, 85–7, 94,
    101, 117, 123, 157, 210, 279, 282, 293–4,
    310
    see also Shamsher, Safser, Tex, Sword(s),
    Broadsword(s), Two-handed sword(s),
    Shamsher-wazig, Fencing, Italian grip,
    Baldric hanging, Awestarag, Dar, Kamar,
    Kamar-band, Niyam, Sousser, Saif,
    Mintaqa, Goti, Lappet suspension system,
    P-mount (system), Shap-sheraz/
    Shamshirdar
Scale armour, 76
    see also Mail, Lamellar, Gurdih, Pos/Posh,
    Zreh, Zereh, Dir, Saqain, Jowshan,
    Gowshan
Schaggun, 43
    see also Chaugan, Chekan, Choka, Chicane,
    Polo
Schlieffen Plan, 28–9, 305

Scorpio, 247
    see also Scorpion(s), Hasak, Xasak, Aghrab(s),
    Rutaila, Siege engine(s), Naft-andazan,
    Naffata, Charx, Kashkanjir, Khaar-kaman,
    Mangonel(s), Manjeniq, Aradeh, Arrada,
    Ballistae, Catapult(s), Battering ram(s),
    Mobile tower(s) Darraga, Dabbabat,
    Xarak/Kharak, Testudo
Scorpion(s), 246–7, 251, 256, 260
    see also Scorpio, Hasak, Xasak, Aghrab(s),
    Rutaila, Siege engine(s), Naft-andazan,
    Naffata, Charx, Kashkanjir, Khaar-kaman,
    Mangonel(s), Manjeniq, Aradeh, Arrada,
    Ballistae, Catapult(s), Battering ram(s),
    Mobile tower(s) Darraga, Dabbabat,
    Testudo, Xarak/Kharak
Scythian(s), xxiii, 63, 68, 74–6, 84, 87, 94, 128,
    166, 169, 172, 188, 194, 211, 233, 277–8,
    350
    see also Saka(s), Saka Paradraya, Saka
    Haumaverga, Alan(s), Sarmatian(s),
    Yueh-Chi, Kushan(s)
Scola scutariorum clibanariorum, 345
    see also Notitia Dignitatum, Magister equitum
    praesentalis, Magister militum per
    orientem, Equites sagittarri parthi seniores,
    Equites sagittarri parthi iuniores, Equites
    Persae clibanarii, Numerus persoiustiniani,
    Numerus felicum persoarmeniorum,
    Vexillatio palatina
Sebasteia, 30
Sebeos, 116, 221–2, 276, 285–6, 306, 325
Sebochthes, 193
Seleucia, 228
Seleucid(s), 22, 77–8, 194
Seistan, 22, 106
    see also Saka-istan, Seistan-Baluchistan
Seistan-Baluchistan, 260
    see also Saka-istan, Seistan
Seistani, 22
Seistan and Baluchistan, 22
Seljuk Turk(s), 356
Senmurv, 93, 281
    see also Simurgh
Sepah, 8
    see also Spada, Spah, Zor, Lashkar
Separ, 47, 108
    see also Turs
Setam, 109
    see also Asb, Raksh, Tagavar, Zin, Zin-e
    Khadang, Naal, Zarrin Setam, Fetrak,
    Enan, Taziyane
Shaat al Arab/Arvand Rud, 138

Shaban, 214, 218
see also Il-Arslan
Shah Abbas I, 176, 181–2, 292
Shah Ismail I, xxiii, 22, 55, 200, 288, 342–3
Shah Ram Pirouz, 191
Shah Tahmasp, 181
Shahab, 14
Shahen, 299, 304, 307, 309
Shahanshah (king of kings), 1, 19–20, 31, 33–4,
    57, 112–13, 115–17, 142, 164, 167, 191,
    205, 207–209, 221–2, 234–5, 255–6, 264,
    273–4, 282, 285–91, 295, 298–9, 316
Shahname, xi, xix, xxii–xxiii, 15, 25, 33, 41,
    44–7, 49, 51, 54–6, 64, 106, 109–10, 112,
    114, 125, 129, 131, 144, 147, 150, 162,
    163, 166–7, 174, 182, 188, 190–1, 212,
    219, 243, 247, 275–6, 284, 286–7, 289,
    290, 332, 352
see also Firdowsi, Xvatay-name
Shahram Pirouz, 237
Shahraplakan, 299, 307, 309
Shahrak, 329
Shahrbaraz, Farrokhan, 10, 182, 190, 220,
    266–9, 282, 299–300, 304–308
Shahrestan, 224
Shahrestan-e Vuzurg, 206
Shahyar, 326
Shalvar, 279, 283
see also Afa-sar, Mah-sar, Sar, Mok, Mocak,
    Kafshak, Kurtak, Kustik, Kamar,
    Kamar-band, Kapah, Pargoo, Kulah
Shamakhi, 340
Shamaras, (of the Shahname epic), 276
Shamsher, 90, 108
see also Sword(s), Broadsword(s), Two-handed
    sword(s), Fencing, Italian grip, Baldric
    hanging, Shamsher-wazig, Safser,
    Awestarag, Dar, Tex, Kamar, Kamar-band,
    Niyam, Sousser, Saif, Mintaqa, Goti,
    Scabbard (slide suspension), Lappet
    suspension system, P-mount (system),
    Shap-sheraz/Shamshirdar
Shamsher-wazig, 41, 50, 90
see also Sword(s), Broadsword(s), Two-handed
    sword(s), Fencing, Italian grip, Baldric
    hanging, Shamsher, Safser, Awestarag, Dar,
    Tex, Kamar, Kamar-band, Niyam, Sousser,
    Saif, Mintaqa, Goti, Scabbard (slide
    suspension), Lappet suspension system,
    P-mount (system), Shap-sheraz/
    Shamshirdar
Shap-sheraz/Shamshirdar, 11
see also Baldric hanging, Shamsher, Safser,
    Sword(s), Broadsword(s), Two-handed

sword(s), Shamsher-wazig, Fencing,
    Awestarag, Dar, Tex, Kamar, Kamar-band,
    Niyam, Sousser, Saif, Mintaqa, Goti,
    Italian grip, Scabbard (slide suspension),
    Lappet suspension system, P-mount
    (system)
Shapur-Razi, 209
Shapur I, xiii–xv, xxi, 4, 17, 20, 32, 50, 54, 82,
    85–6, 89, 96, 98, 121, 130, 131, 147,
    151–7, 159, 190–1, 254, 256–7, 277, 283,
    299, 302, 345, 348–9
Shapur II, xiv, xvii, 21–2, 42, 72, 91–4, 113,
    122, 131–3, 138, 149, 160–1, 164, 178–80,
    184, 190–2, 194, 201–202, 225, 235,
    238–42, 245, 247, 249–51, 255–6, 259–62,
    269, 271, 278–9, 287–91, 293, 298–9, 302,
    345–6
Shapur III, xvi, 94
Shapurdukhtat, xiv, 291
Shast, 58
Shatranj, 137
see also Pil, Fil
Shaypoor, 54
Sheikh Safi, 342–3
Sherwin Ispadbodh, 337–8
Shiraz, xx
Shirvan, 340
Shivatir-e zrehbaran, 98, 197
see also Shiva-tir, Tir/Tigr, Tir-wazig,
    Tirbad, Archery, Kamam, Kaman,
    Kamandan, Qaba, Tirdan, Kantir/Kantigr,
    Zeh/Zih, Zeh e yadaki, Watarain, Gorytos,
    Nawak, Horse archer(s), Horse archery
Shiz, (Takhte Suleiman) 205, 229, 233, 307
Shushtar (siege of, 637 or 638 CE) 191, 329
Shuubiya movement, 352, 354
Sidonius Apollinaris, 198
Siege engine(s), 215, 257, 260–2, 342
see also Ballistae, Catapult(s), Battering ram(s),
    Mobile tower(s), Darraga, Dabbabat,
    Xarak/Kharak, Testudo, Naft-andazan,
    Naffata, Charx, Kashkanjir, Khaar-kaman,
    Mangonel(s), Manjeniq, Aradeh, Arrada,
    Aghrab(s), Rutaila, Scorpion(s), Scorpio,
    Hasak, Xasak
Silk Route, 5, 26, 200, 222, 308
Simmas, 169–70, 172, 173
Simurgh, 93, 281
see also Senmurv
Sindbad, 332, 335
Singara, 177, 190–1, 226, 245
Singara (siege of, *c.*337 or 338 CE), 201, 259
Singara (battle of, 343 or 344 CE), 127, 129
Singara (battle of, 350 CE), 161

Singara (siege of, 360 CE), 261–2

Sinj, 54

Siraf, 191, 225–6

Sirat Anoushirvan, xiii, 19, 31, 164, 234

Sisauranon fortress, 346

Siyah 58

  see also Dustar, Kaman-saz

Siyasat-Nameh, 18

Sizabul, 26

  see also Ishtemi Khan

Sling, 127

  see also Slinger(s), Pilaxan

Slinger(s), 127

  see also Sling, Pilaxan

Smbat Bagratuni, 4, 21, 116, 220–2, 238, 276, 285–6, 302–303, 305–306, 313

Sneh/Sneih, 90

  see also Zay-abzar, Zen-abzar

Soghdia, 29, 117, 201, 276, 335

  see also Soghdian

Soghdian(s), xxiii, 77, 94, 108, 117–18, 202, 220, 222, 281, 333–4

Sohrab (of the Shahname epic), 129, 175

Solokha, 277

Song dynasty (Chinese dynasty, China), 246

Sophene, 190

Sousser, 94

  see also Shamsher, Sword(s), Broadsword(s), Two-handed sword(s), Fencing, Italian grip, Baldric hanging, Shamsher-wazig, Safser, Awestarag, Dar, Tex, Kamar, Kamar-band, Niyam, Saif, Mintaqa, Goti, Scabbard (slide suspension), Lappet suspension system, P-mount (system), Shap-sheraz/Shamshirdar

Sozomen, 178

Spada, 8, 75–7

  see also Spah, Sepah, Zor, Lashkar

Spah, xvii, xxi, 1–6, 8, 10–13, 15–16, 18–20, 22–32, 34, 36, 38–9, 46–8, 53, 56, 59, 64, 66, 68, 70–2, 83, 92, 96, 99–100, 107, 112–13, 115–16, 120–1, 123, 125–7, 129, 131–2, 134–9, 141–52, 155, 157–64, 171, 174, 177–96, 198, 201–202, 206–209, 212–24, 228–32, 234–5, 237–9, 241–5, 247–51, 253–4, 256, 259–60, 263–4, 266, 268–71, 273, 276–7, 279–80, 282–3, 285–6, 288, 290, 292–3, 297–306, 308–10, 312–15, 318, 322–3, 327–8, 336–7, 344–5

  see also Sepah, Spada, Zor, Lashkar

Spah-dabir, 16

Spah-dadvar, 11, 189

Spahbod, 10, 12, 14–15, 21, 24–5, 30, 32, 115, 141, 194, 220, 224, 301–304, 308, 312–13, 315

  see also Sparapet

Spahbod-adurbaygan, 24

Spahbodan-spahbod, 12, 25

Spahsalar, 25

Spain, 50, 156, 330, 332, 336, 355

Spangenhelm(s), 85, 93–4, 123, 154, 160, 347

  see also Ridge Helmet, Khwod, Khud/Khod, Miqfar, Sarwar, Targ, Selsele aviz

Spar, 90

  see also Spar-wazig, Magind

Sparapet, 12, 21, 115, 325

  see also Spahbod

Spar-wazig, 90

  see also Spar, Magind

Spies, 255–6

Ssu-ma Ch'ien, 195–6

Stabodh, 141

Staikin Verkh, 75–6

Stirrups, 59, 87, 107–108, 118–19, 197, 210–12, 310–11, 348

Stor-bizishk, 11, 185–6

Strabo, 38, 51, 54, 56

Strategikon, xi, 39–40, 68–70, 145, 148, 162–3, 167, 172, 195, 198, 201, 243, 269, 274, 285, 345, 347, 352

Strvoshbad, 141

Sukhra, 56

Suleiman the Magnificent, 181

Sunicas, 168, 170, 172–3

Sunitae, 21

Sura, 263

Suren, 13, 178, 280

  see also Suren-Pahlav

Suren-Pahlav, 178, 279, 284

  see also Suren

Surena, (general in Battle of Carrhae 53 BCE), 9, 51–2, 66, 78–9, 292

Surp Nshan Basilica, 280

Susa, 130, 189

Svant(s), 21

Sword(s), xiv, xvi–xvii, xxii, 21, 31, 35, 39, 41, 43–5, 48–50, 61–2, 68, 75–9, 85–7, 89–91, 94–5, 100–106, 108–13, 117–18, 121–3, 125, 128, 134–5, 148, 150, 154, 157–8, 160, 166, 185, 195, 198–9, 201, 204, 207, 210–11, 218, 261, 271, 273, 275–6, 279, 281–4, 289, 291, 293–5, 310, 319–20, 327–8, 337, 345, 349, 354

  see also Broadsword(s), Two-handed sword(s), Shamsher, Fencing, Italian grip, Baldric hanging, Shamsher-wazig, Safser,

Awestarag, Dar, Tex, Kamar, Kamar-band, Niyam, Sousser, Saif, Mintaqa, Goti, Scabbard (slide suspension), Lappet suspension system, P-mount (system), Shap-sheraz/Shamshirdar

Syria, xvii, 59, 135, 156, 158, 190, 215, 229, 262–3, 266, 271, 301–302, 304–306, 315, 322, 332, 351

Syrian, 215, 263, 321, 351

Tabar, 90, 106–107
  see also Abdast, Tabarzin, Tabarz/e/n, Chakosh, Warz/Wazr, Warz-wazig, gauntlet, hatchet, axe, mace, Gurz

Tabira, 54

Tabaristan, 235–6, 335–7, 339–40

Tabarzin, 90, 106–107, 117, 123, 125
  see also Abdast, Tabar, Tabarz/e/n, Chakosh, Warz/Wazr, Warz-wazig, gauntlet, hatchet, axe, mace, Gurz

Tablak, 55
  see also Tombag, Donbak

Tabriz, 128, 176, 181

Tagavar, 109
  see also Asb, Raksh, Zin, Zin-e Khadang, Fetrak, Setam, Zarrin Setam, Enan, Naal, Taziyane

Taghe Bostan, xiv, xx, 17, 44, 54, 62–3, 86, 94, 100–102, 105, 107, 109, 117–18, 136, 211, 280–1, 282, 285, 291, 294–6, 311, 337

Tahmasp I, xxiii

Taj, 73, 273, 290

Tajikestan, 83, 332

Takhte Suleiman *see* Shiz

Takhteh Shena, 48

Taleghan, 208

Talmud, xx, 7, 283

Talysh, 203, 336

Tamga(s), xiv, 284
  see also Drafsh, Drafsh (e) Kaviani, Draconis Persicus

Tammisha (Wall of), 27, 206, 230–2, 235–7
  see also Gorgan (Wall of)

Tanais, 277

Tang (Chinese dynasty, China), 223, 308, 332–3

Tang-e-Sarvak, xv, 79

Tangestanis, 22

Tanur, 74
  see also Tanurig, Tanvar, Griv, Pan, Gardaan-ban, Grivpan, Griv-ban/Griw-ban, Clibanarii, Clibanarius, Cataphractus, Cataphractii, klibanion, klibanarios

Tanurig, 74

  see also Tanur, Tanvar, Griv, Pan, Gardaan-ban, Grivpan, Griv-ban/Griw-ban, Clibanarii, Clibanarius, Cataphractus, Cataphractii, klibanion, klibanarios

Tanvar, 74
  see also Tanur, Tanurig, Griv, Pan, Gardaan-ban, Grivpan, Griv-ban/Griw-ban, Clibanarii, Clibanarius, Cataphractus, Cataphractii, klibanion, klibanarios

Targ, 90
  see also Spangenhelm(s), Ridge Helmet, Khwod, Khud/Khod, Miqfar, Sarwar, Selsele aviz

Tarikhe-e Gozide, 32

Tarim Basin, 281

Tarsus (Mountains), 145, 156

Tasanud, 316

Taziyane, 109
  see also Asb, Raksh, Tagavar, Zin, Zin-e Khadang, Naal, Zarrin Setam, Fetrak, Enan, Setam

Tbilisi, 309

Tehran, 25, 186, 221, 299, 305, 328, 331
  see also Rayy

Tehran Museum, xvi, 60, 291
  see also National Museum of Iran

Testudo, 172, 252
  see also Scorpion(s), Scorpio, Hasak, Xasak, Aghrab(s), Rutaila, Siege engine(s), Naft-andazan, Naffata, Charx, Kashkanjir, Khaar-kaman, Mangonel(s), Manjeniq, Aradeh, Arrada, Ballistae, Catapult(s), Battering ram(s), Mobile tower(s), Darraga, Dabbabat, Xarak/Kharak

Tex, 90
  see also Shamsher, Safser, Sword(s), Broadsword(s), Two-handed sword(s), Shamsher-wazig, Fencing, Italian grip, Baldric hanging, Awestarag, Dar, Kamar, Kamar-band, Niyam, Sousser, Saif, Mintaqa, Goti, Scabbard (slide suspension), Lappet suspension system, P-mount (system), Shap-sheraz/Shamshirdar

Thalpan Bridge, 109

Thannuris desert, 176

Theoctistus, 264–5

Theodore, 304, 307

Theodoret, 131, 251

Theodosiopolis, 30

Theodosiopolis (siege of, 576 CE), 256

Theophanes, 254, 266, 291, 311

Theophilos, 342

Theophylactos Simokattes, 196
Thessaloniki, 160
Thracian, 166
Tiberias, 267
Tiberius II Constantine, 215
Tieji, 197
Tighfaf, 108
    see also, Bargostvan
Tigran, 300
Tigranocerta (battle of, 69 BCE), 300
Tigris River, 5, 54, 177, 228–9, 259, 261, 326,
    328
Timesitheus, 152
Tir/Tigr 14, 58, 60, 69
    see also Tir-wazig, Tirbad, Archery, Horse
    archery, Horse archer(s), Kaman, Kamam,
    Kamandan, Qaba, Tirdan, Kantir/Kantigr,
    Zeh/Zih, Zeh e yadaki, Watarain, Gorytos,
    Nawak, Shivatir-e zrehbaran, Shiva-tir
Tirbad, 14–15
    see also Tir/Tigr, Tirdan, Archery, Horse
    archery, Horse archer(s), Kaman, Kamam,
    Kamandan, Qaba, Tirdan, Kantir/Kantigr,
    Zeh/Zih, Zeh e yadaki, Watarain, Gorytos,
    Nawak, Shivatir-e zrehbaran, Shiva-tir
Tirdan, xiv, 58, 61–2, 66, 85, 89, 108, 152, 154
    see also Archery, Horse archery, Horse
    archer(s), Tir/Tigr, Tir-wazig, Tirbad,
    Kaman, Kamam, Kamandan, Qaba, Kantir/
    Kantigr, Zeh/Zih, Zeh e yadaki, Watarain,
    Gorytos, Nawak, Shivatir-e zrehbaran,
    Shiva-tir
Tirdat, 110, 130, 158
Tir-Wazig, 57, 69
    see also Tir/Tigr, Tirbad, Archery, Horse
    archery, Horse archer(s), Kaman, Kamam,
    Kamandan, Qaba, Tirdan, Kantir/Kantigr,
    Zeh/Zih, Zeh e yadaki, Watarain, Gorytos,
    Nawak, Shivatir-e zrehbaran, Shiva-tir
Tir-Yasht, 56
Tocharian, 281
Tocharistan, 29, 207, 333
Tombag, 55
    see also Tablak, Donbak
Tong Shou, 211
Toqi'ate Anoushirvan, 147–8, 182, 190
Tour 94
    see also Akenakes, Dagger(s), Dasnag, Celan,
    Kard, Nran
Tours (battle of, 732 CE), 336
Transcaucasus, 20, 234
    see also Caucasus, Circassia
Transoxiana, 207, 321, 333–5, 350

Trajan, 5, 229
Turan, 131
Turanian, 163
Turco-Hephthalite(s), 13, 25, 31, 109, 114, 116,
    142, 202, 213–23, 235, 238, 253, 274, 276,
    285, 293, 298, 301–306
    see also Hephthalite(s), Hephtalite-Hun(s),
    Hephtalite(s), Hun(s)
Turco-Iranian (military tradition) 44, 67, 118,
    202, 355, 356
Turkmenistan, 3–4, 207
Turk(s), 19, 26–9, 50, 52, 144, 184, 194–6, 200,
    212–14, 216–17, 219–20, 223, 235–6, 302,
    306, 308, 311, 313, 321, 333–4, 342, 345,
    355–6
    see also Turkic-Avar(s), Avar(s), Turkish, Gok
    Turk(s), Turkic, Ottoman(s), Tatar,
    Turkic-Hun, Hun(s), Khazar(s), Hunnic,
    Uighur(s), Hsiang-Nou, Seljuk(s), Oghuz
Turkey, 139, 145, 152, 171, 200
Turkic, 4, 19, 21, 52, 101, 127, 179, 194–202,
    223, 230–1, 234–5, 276, 281–2, 308,
    311–12, 314, 319, 334, 338, 344, 355, 356
    see also Turkic-Avar(s), Avar(s), Turk(s),
    Turkish, Gok Turk(s), Tatar, Ottoman(s),
    Turkic-Hun, Hun(s), Khazar(s), Hunnic,
    Uighur(s), Hsiang-Nou, Seljuk(s), Oghuz
Turkic-Avar(s), 101, 308
    see also Turkic, Turk(s), Gok Turk(s), Avar(s),
    Turkish, Ottoman(s), Tatar, Turkic-Hun,
    Hun(s), Khazar(s), Hunnic, Uighur(s),
    Hsiang-Nou, Seljuk(s), Oghuz
Turkic-Hun, 44, 48, 59, 73, 101, 281, 309–10,
    345, 349
    see also Turkic-Avar(s), Avar(s), Turk(s),
    Turkish, Gok Turk(s), Tatar, Ottoman(s),
    Turkic, Hun(s), Khazar(s), Hunnic,
    Uighur(s), Hsiang-Nou, Seljuk(s), Oghuz
Turkic-Khazar(s), 309, 311
Turkish, 26–7, 29–30, 53, 67, 129, 176, 196,
    213–14, 216–17, 219–20, 222–3, 235, 242,
    281, 303, 306, 308, 311, 335, 340–3, 356
    see also Avar(s), Turkic-Avar(s), Turk(s),
    Turkic, Gok Turk(s), Tatar, Ottoman(s),
    Turkic-Hun, Hun(s), Khazar(s), Hunnic,
    Uighur(s), Hsiang-Nou, Seljuk(s), Oghuz
Turs, 108
    see also Separ
Tus, 221
Tusi, Mohammad bin Himayd, 339

Uhud, 317
Uighur, 196

see also Avar(s), Turkic-Avar(s), Turk(s),
  Turkic, Turkish, Gok Turk(s), Tatar,
  Ottoman(s), Turkic-Hun, Hun(s),
  Khazar(s), Hunnic, Uighur(s),
  Hsiang-Nou, Seljuk(s), Oghuz
Ukraine, 75–6, 87, 94
Ummayad(s), 333–5, 350–1
Ummayad caliphate, 320, 332–4
  see also Caliphate(s), Abbasid caliphate
Un-Eirean, 18
  see also An-Eirean
Ursicinus, 147, 260
Uzbek, 52, 182, 200

Vahriz, 30, 56, 134, 139, 143–4, 351
Valens, 192
Valerian, xiii–xiv, 54, 110, 151, 155–9, 190–1,
  279, 345
  see also Bazanush
Var-thragh niyagan khodai, vxiii, 15, 66, 112
  see also Savaran, Dehkan(s), Akhshid, Afshin,
  Chakeran, Framandar-savaran, Asbaran,
  Aswaran, Aswaran-sardar, Savar-e Nezam
  Sangin Aslahe, Javidan, Savaran-e
  shamshir-zan-e dah-hezar, Pushtighban,
  Pushtiban, Pusht-aspan, Pushtighban-salar,
  Pushtighban-sardar, Hazarbod, Gund
  Shahanshah, Ham-harzan, Ham-harz,
  Hm-hrz, Jan-separan, jyanavspar,
  Janvespar, Jalinus, Pishmarg/Peshmarg,
  Savaran-e Khorasan, Sarhangan,
  Pirouzetai, Khosrowgetai, Granikan-Salar
Varanga, 85, 93
Vardan Mamikonian, 28
Vartanantz (Battle of, 451 CE) *see* Avaryr (Battle
  of, 451 CE)
Varzesh-e bastani, 46
  see also Zoorkhaneh
Vasht, 9
Vasht-salar, 9
Vastryoshan-salar, 12
Veh-Ardashir, 190, 228, 326
  see also Coche
Vendidad-Hormuz, 337–8
Ventidus, 145
Vespasian, 229
Vexillatio palatina, 345
  see also Notitia Dignitatum, Magister equitum
  praesentalis, Magister militum per
  orientem, Equites sagittarri parthi iuniores,
  Equites sagittarri parthi seniores, Equites
  Persae clibanarii, Scola scutariorum
  clibanariorum, Numerus persoiustiniani,
  Numerus felicum persoarmeniorum

Vis o Ramin, 55
Visigoth(s), 344
  see also Goth(s), Gothic, Germania, Germanic,
  German(s), Germany, Ostrogoth(s)
Vuzurg-framandar, 12, 141
Vuzurgan, 3, 13
  see also Buzurgan

Wada'i, 117
  see also Lakhmid(s), Ghassanid(s), Arab(s),
  Bedouin(s), Bani Sheiban, Bani Hanifah,
  Yemenite Arab(s)
Walters Art Gallery, xv, 292
Waqqas, Saad Bin Ebi, 135, 318, 322–5
War, 240
War-e Tazigan, 239–40
  see also Khandaq-e Shapur,
Warz-wazig, 90
  see also Abdast, Tabar, Tabarzin, Tabarz/e/n,
  Chakosh, Warz/Wazr, Axe, Gauntlet,
  Hatchet, Mace, Gurz
Warz/Wazr, 90
  see also Abdast, Tabar, Tabarzin, Tabarz/e/n,
  Chakosh, Warz-wazig, Axe, Gauntlet,
  Hatchet, Mace, Gurz
Wastaryosan, 290
Weh Antioch Khosrow, 190
West Asian, 66
Witiges, 192
Wizarishn-e Chatrang ud Nishishn-e New
  Ardaxshir, 41
Wolfsheim, 192
Wuzurg-Mehr, 41

Xarak/Kharak, 253
  see also Hasak, Xasak, Scorpion(s), Scorpio,
  Aghrab(s), Rutaila, Siege engine(s),
  Naft-andazan, Naffata,, Charx, Kashkanjir,
  Khaar-kaman, Mangonel(s), Manjeniq,
  Aradeh, Arrada, Ballistae, Catapult(s),
  Battering ram(s), Mobile tower(s), Darraga,
  Dabbabat, Testudo
Xasak, 253
  see also Hasak, Scorpion(s), Scorpio,
  Aghrab(s), Rutaila, Siege engine(s),
  Naft-andazan, Naffata, Charx, Kashkanjir,
  Khaar-kaman, Mangonel(s), Manjeniq,
  Aradeh, Arrada, Ballistae, Catapult(s),
  Battering ram(s), Mobile tower(s), Darraga,
  Dabbabat, Xarak/Kharak, Testudo
Xenophon, 51, 76–7, 230, 292
Xerxes I, xix, xxi, 75–6, 130, 268, 278
Xiaotangshan, 210
Xvatay-namak, xxii

see also Firdowsi, Shahname
Xwararan-Spahbod, 24
Xwarasan-Spahbod, 24

Yahya, Jibrail bin, 335
Yalan-bad, 11
Yalan-yalbod, 274,
    see also Pahlavan(s)
Yamama, 138
Yarmuk (battle of, 636 CE), 322
Yasht, 294
Yazdani, 343
Yazdegird I, 10, 16, 190
Yazdegird II, 13, 20–1, 26, 133, 194, 205–206,
    232, 237
Yazdegird III, 223, 325–7, 328–30, 332
Yemen, 30–1, 116, 123, 134, 139, 142–4, 318,
    351
Yemenite, 139, 142–3
Yemenite Arab(s), 142
    see also Wada'i, Ghassanid(s), Lakhmid(s),
    Bedouin(s), Bani Sheiban, Bani Hanifah,
    Arab(s)
Yerevan, 50
Yil-Tegin, 219–20
Youwuwei Jianggium, 333
    see also Zuoweiwei Jiangjun
Yueh-Chi, 87

Zab River, 260
Zachariah, 173
Zadrakarta, 237
    see also Astarabad
Zahak (of the Shahname epic), 106, 284
Zambag, 9
    see also Ardig, Karezar, Jang, Pad-razm,
    Nibard, Paykar
Zand dynasty, 140, 356
Zang, 54
Zanjirgah, 216
Zarrin Setam, 109
    see also Asb, Raksh, Tagavar, Zin, Zin-e
    Khadang, Naal, Taziyane, Fetrak, Enan,
    Setam
Zavareh (of the Shahname epic), 275
Zay-bazar 90
    see also Zen-abzar, Sneh/Sneih
Zeh, 59
Zih, 69
    see also Zeh e yadaki, Watarain, Tir-wazig,
    Tir/Tigr, Tirbad, Horse archery, Horse
    archer(s), Kaman, Kamam, Kamandan,
    Qaba, Tirdan, Kantir/Kantigr, Gorytos,
    Nawak, Shivatir-e zrehbaran, Shiva-tir,

Zeh e yadaki, 33
    see also Zeh/Zih, Watarain, Tir-wazig, Tir/
    Tigr, Tirbad, Horse archery, Horse
    archer(s), Kaman, Kamam, Kamandan,
    Qaba, Tirdan, Kantir/Kantigr, Gorytos,
    Nawak, Shivatir-e zrehbaran, Shiva-tir
Zemarchus, 26
Zen-abzar, 90
    see also Zay-abzar, Sneh/Sneih
Zenbed, 185
Zendanigh, 11, 189
    see also Gelkard, Faramoushkhaneh
Zeno, 207
Zenobia, 263
Zereh, 108
    see also Zreh, Mail, Lamellar, Scale armour,
    Gurdih, Pos/Posh, Dir, Saqain, Jowshan,
    Gowshan
Zharovka, 84
Zhupin, 123, 337
    see also Javelin(s)
Zin, 109
    see also Asb, Raksh, Zin-e Khadang, Fetrak,
    Setam, Zarrin Setam, Enan, Naal,
    Taziyane, Tagavar
Zin-e Khadang, 109
    see also Asb, Raksh, Zin, Fetrak, Setam, Zarrin
    Setam, Enan, Naal, Taziyane, Tagavar
Ziyad Ibn Abihi, 106
Zonaras, 129, 131, 154–5
Zoor, 8
    see also Zor
Zoorkhaneh, 38, 41, 46–7
    see also Varzesh-e bastani
Zor, 8
    see also Zoor
Zor-Mehr 'Sokhra', 209
Zoroaster, 273, 283
Zoroastrian(s), 17, 20, 46, 49, 80, 89, 106, 133,
    136, 164, 189, 206, 268, 273–4, 282–3,
    292, 294, 341–2
Zoroastrianism, 26, 333
Zornay, 51
Zorvanism, 343
Zosimus, 152, 154–5, 201
Zreh, 90
    see also Zereh, Mail, Lamellar, Scale armour,
    Gurdih, Pos/Posh, Dir, Saqain, Jowshan,
    Gowshan
Zuoweiwei Jiangjun, 333
    see also Youwuwei Jianggium
Zynpt, 184–5
    see also Eiran-ambaraghbad, Ambaragh, Ganz